D1483369

Comparative Political Economy

Comparative Political Economy
A Retrospective

Charles P. Kindleberger

The MIT Press
Cambridge, Massachusetts
London, England

This book was set in Palatino by Asco Typesetters, Hong Kong.

Printed and bound in the United States of America.

Library of Congress Cataloging-in-Publication Data

Kindleberger, Charles Poor, 1910–
  Comparative political economy : a retrospective / Charles P.
  Kindleberger.
      p.   cm.
  Includes bibliographical references and index.
  ISBN 0-262-11246-9 (hc : alk. paper)
  1. Finance—Case studies. 2. Foreign exchange—Case studies.
3. International trade—Case studies. 4. Economic policy—Case
studies. I. Title.
HG101.K56   2000
330—dc21   99-39610
                                                       CIP

In Memory of S. M. K.
Who Tolerated These Interests

Contents

1   Introduction

Painters who are mature, and even on occasion dead, have retrospective shows of work that has been exhibited before, assembled to demonstrate something—perhaps a change in styles, perhaps the gradual evolution of his or her interests. If the artist is extant and participating in the selection, the collection may represent simply favorites of the artist, rather than those of a curator or gallery viewers. The essays assembled in these pages have been exhibited (published) before, most twice and a few anthologized. They also reflect in a broad way a shift in interests from foreign exchange to international trade, economic growth, economic history, and, especially, financial history. In addition, they contain an element that was unintentional, or at least subconscious: the admixture with economics (and history) of dollops of sociology and especially political science. These "foreign" elements produce misgivings. My self-image is economist, economic historian, or, best, historical economist, who tests economic propositions against the historical record in more than one setting. To have attracted the attention of political scientists, as has happened to an extent, makes me uneasy, as if I were in danger of being expelled from my club. "Political economy" in the book's title is chosen to sooth such concerns.

Seventeen of the twenty-one papers originally appeared in a variety of outlets, scholarly journals, pamphlets, public lectures, and *Festschriften*, and then were reprised in one of the eleven volumes of collected papers that publishers have been generous or weak enough to take on in the past. I have selected nothing from the first of these collections—*Europe and the Dollar* (1966)—because the thoughts in two papers that strike me today as interesting are better treated in later work that I have chosen. The argument against flexible exchange rates, written in 1960 for the Commission on Money and Credit, is trumped by chapter 3 below, which appeared in 1969. Similarly, chapter 9, also 1969, extends the argument of the 1965 "Balance-of-Payments Equilibrium and the International Market for Liquidity" in *Europe and the Dollar*, and uses simple equations for exposition rather than substantives ranged "above" and "below the line," the form favored by Fritz Machlup when he was editor of the Princeton Institute of International Finance publications.

Except for "Competitive Exchange Depreciation ...," chapter 2, the first paper I published some 64 years ago, I am not especially interested in whether a paper is earlier or later. But chapter 2 of 1934 was a term paper in a course taught by Benjamin Beckhardt in my first semester of graduate work at Columbia, and therefore a ground-breaker (for me). It can readily be seen from the illustrations that I should have taken the seasonals out of the trade data in Danish and New Zealand exports of butter to Britain, but my course in statistics had not been finished. If pressed, I might argue that competitive exchange depreciation has relevance today to the financial troubles in the Far East with the Thai baht, the Malaysian ringgit, the South Korean won, and the Indonesian rupiah all depreciating and the Hong Kong and Chinese currencies under pressure. The comparison should not be carried too far, however, since the Danish and New Zealand depreciations were intentional acts of policy, to gain trade advantages, whereas the Eastern troubles came from mismanaged domestic policies, reckless foreign lending, and overvalued currencies offering opportunities to foreign speculators.

(Parenthetically, the three other collections of papers not represented here are) *Multinational Excursions* [1984], on the multinational corporation, a subject in which I have lost research interest; *Marshall Plan Days* [1987], with excessive autobiographical content; and *Essays in History: Financial, Economic, and Personal* [1999], which had gone to press elsewhere before this project was launched.)

The reader should not make much of the division of the twenty-one papers into five unbalanced sections of ostensible changing interest: foreign exchange, international trade, economic growth, finance, and political economy. Each paper, or at any rate most, ranges broadly over topics other than the one under which it is categorized. Most are strong on comparison (within Western Europe for the most part, or on relations between Europe and the United States), on economic or financial history, and on social science beyond the confines of economics. Chapter 4, on "Group Behavior in International Trade," published next in time in this collection, leaves a gap of seventeen years. The delay was caused by three years of graduate study, ten of work in banking, the military, and government service before starting teaching in 1948. On arriving at MIT I wrote a book to justify U.S. aid to Europe and developing countries, rashly entitled *The Dollar Shortage* (1950). When dollars became abundant in the 1960s I suffered as seminar chairmen would twit me about the title. If I had called it "Persistent Disequilibrium in Balances of Payments" I would have been better protected, since history reveals that balances of payments do not always automatically correct themselves.

The exchange-rate theme surfaces in later chapters as well. My 1969 paper, given at a conference and making the case for fixed rates, drew in comment a formidable debater, Milton Friedman. He started his remarks by telling the audience that they were lucky to hear only the mistakes I emitted orally, as there were many more in the written version given him in advance. With my peaceable nature, I seem to invite this egregious form of scholarly discourse. In a seminar in Princeton in 1948, I defended the Marshall Plan and drew from Professor Frank D. Graham the first question, or rather comment: "I cannot recall having heard so much nonsense in such a short space of time." Looking back from the 1990s, I believe that the cases for fixed exchange rates and the Marshall plan have not been wholly invalidated.

"Group Behavior..." came about as I took on a moonlighting assignment to teach a year-long course on the economy of Europe at Columbia University, two hours a week in term time. I would go to New York Tuesday night in a sleeper train called "The Owl," teach Wednesday morning from 10 to 12, and return to Boston either on the "Yankee Clipper" at 1 o'clock or, if I had something to do in New York, on the "Merchant" at 5. Having lived in England for a year and a half in the war (plus a year in France, Belgium, and Germany), and worked on the German and French economies during the war, and on the German economy and the Marshall plan from 1945 to 1948, I was fairly well equipped to teach the second term of the course on modern times, but needed to make up gaps in European economic history for the first. In the course of intensive reading, much on the train from New York to Boston, I discovered that a number of European countries had not reacted to the sharp fall in the world price of wheat in the 1880s, as economic theory would predict, and found myself starting down the tracks of comparison, history, and drawing other social sciences into economic analysis. Chapter 5, on "The Rise of Free Trade in Western Europe, 1820–1875," was a much later complement to "Group Behavior...."

There is another long delay in the Table of Contents after the 1951 paper until 1965 when chapter 8, written with Emile Despres and Walter Salant, appeared in the *Economist*. A number of papers were written, including those in *Europe and the Dollar*, plus two textbooks, *International*

Economics (1st ed. 1953, 5th 1973), and *Economic Development* (1st ed. 1958, 2nd 1965). In addition there was a series of monographs dealing with the terms of trade, trade in relation to the national economy, and economic growth. An attempt at another textbook, explicitly directed to political economy—*Power and Money: The Politics of International Economics and the Economics of International Politics*—came later, in 1970. It failed, falling intellectually between two stools, and written for courses that did not exist.

Interest in economic growth had begun with France, and participation in a seminar at the Harvard Center for International Affairs, which produced a symposium, *In Search of France* by Stanley Hoffmann et al. (1963). I was one of the *alii* with a paper on "The Postwar Resurgence of the French Economy," which was a strong but unsuccessful contender for inclusion here. I also wrote a book, *Economic Growth in France and Britain, 1851–1950* (1964). A term at the stimulating Institute for World Economy in Kiel, West Germany, led to a two-part article, here telescoped into one, "Germany Overtaking England, 1806–1914" (chapter 6). The exercise developed an interest as to which country at a given time is the leading economic power (with responsibilities for stabilizing the world economy) which finally culminated in a monograph, *World Economic Primacy, 1500– 1990* (1996). An epistomologist might be interested in noting that my work in history started in the nineteenth century, as chapters 4, 5, and 6 demonstrated, and then went back in time a century per decade. A paper on financial innovation in the sixteenth century is included in *Essays in History* (1999) and hence excluded from this compilation. The temporal retrogression has not been linear, to be sure; interest in the twentieth century, now coming to a close, has not been abandoned.

Chapter 7, on "The Aging Economy," was a Harms lecture, again at the Institute of World Economy in Kiel. I cannot now recall when I first developed an interest in economic decline. I once thought of learning Spanish and studying that country, which declined from the seventeenth century to the twentieth but has lately been rejuvenated. The monograph on *World Economic Primacy* tries to combine growth and decline into something akin to the human life-cycle, but without death and with allowance for second births. "The Aging Economy" was written as I thought the United States, like Britain before it, was slowing down, although I made allowance for, and now recognize, its acceleration in the late 1990s.

"Standards as Public, Collective, and Private Goods" (chapter 8) is perhaps misplaced under Economic Growth and belongs in Political Economy. If I am allowed, however, with so many papers in the last section, and few in this, I choose a place that more nearly balances the proportions. The paper was originally given in a seminar at the University of Stockholm when I spent a term there in the fall of 1982. From a local economist it received a comment that amused and somewhat irritated me: "An interesting paper but you should mathematize it." Perhaps I should have warned readers earlier, if they are not familiar with the fact, that I don't do mathematical models, and feel little need for them.

Finance is next. One evening on a Public Broadcasting television panel, chaired by Professor Milton Katz of the Harvard Law School, I had an epiphany. We were discussing the United States balance of payments, its "disequilibrium" and its "deficit," about which the country had been moaning in the last years of the Eisenhower Administration and the first of Kennedy's. It came over me suddenly that the world was applying the wrong model to the U.S. payments. It was treating the United States as if it were an industrial firm, rather than a bank. Industrial firms are in trouble when their liabilities grow, banks are not when their assets grow with deposits. Two colleagues and close friends, Emile Despres and Walter Salant, and I published "The Dollar: A Minority View" (chapter 9). In our view the United States, acting like a bank, provided liquidity to the world in the form of dollar deposits. The current account was in surplus, but the world used some of the aid and capital furnished by Washington and New York to build liquidity in international money, the dollar. Just as banks are not in trouble when assets and deposits go up together, so the United States was not. In the longer run we were wrong, since the dissuasive definition of balance-of-payments equilibrium encouraged foreign central banks after a time to take additions to liquidity in gold, rather than dollars.

I cannot recall the origin of the interest in financial centers that led to the long Princeton Institute of International Finance *Study*, as opposed to *Essays*, such as chapters 10 and 17. It was written after I had finished the first edition of *The World in Depression, 1929–1939* (chapter 19), first published in German in 1971 and in the original English in 1973. That book developed the notion that world finance is organized in a pyramid, with a hierarchical leader at the peak with certain duties to keep the system stable. Within countries, as between countries, there were smaller pyramids, and the process of building them could be studied in the history of financial centers. Comparison led to a riddle: what do the Crédit lyonnais, the Dresdner Bank, the Midlands Bank, the Bank of Nova Scotia, and the First Boston Corporation have in common? Answer: Each later had its head office in a city other than the eponymous one, to wit, Paris, Berlin,

London, Toronto, and New York, respectively, proving that banks gravitate in Darwinian fashion to form centers that bring savers and spenders together. At a recent (1997) conference of the European Association of Banking History in Madrid, I asked an economist of the Bank of Santander where the bank's head office was, hoping for another point for my scatter diagram, Madrid. Unhappily, he said Santander. But the topic of financial centers remains salient. As I write, the *Economist* of May 9, 1998, has a thirty-six-page insert (many of the pages advertising, to be sure) entitled "Capitals of Capital: A Survey of Financial Centres." Competition for top financial dog arises especially as the European Monetary Union and the euro take their places: London? Frankfurt? Paris? or still New York?

There is, however, a countermovement thought to be under way. Raleigh in North Carolina lacks the qualities of historic financial centers, but two banks there are expanding rapidly by acquiring substantial institutions in St. Louis, Detroit, and Florida. Frances Cairncross, an editor of the *Economist*, has written a book, *The End of Geography*, holding that electronic communication will allow business to be done from home and without travel. Office buildings will empty out, and air travel will shrink to college students, honeymooners, and tourists. I remain sceptical. Branch banks will continue to be needed for small business where the banker wants to look the borrower in the eye; and big business—mergers and acquisitions, initial public offerings, friendly and hostile takeovers—will need to gather groups of investment bankers, lawyers, and accountants in one place to look closely at one another's expressions and body language. It cannot be done by telephone conference calls. Face-to-face won't go away.

Equally or even more timely is the subject of financial crises, brought forward by the troubles in East Asia. After writing on the stock-market crash of 1929 and the ensuing depression, it seemed useful to pursue financial crises backward in history. This resulted in a monograph, *Manias, Panics, and Crashes: A Study of Financial Crises*, which came out in 1978. I wanted to call it "Manias, Bubbles, Panics, and Crashes," but the late Martin Kessler, then an editor at Basic Books, ruled that three substantives in a title were enough. The 1987 stock-market crash in New York led to a second edition (1989), that in Tokyo in January 1990 to a third. In each case more historical matter was added along with the proximate stimulus, such as the Tulip Bubble in Amsterdam in 1636, mentioned in the first two editions, but filled out in the third. Chapter 2 of the book, outlining the model of a financial crisis in words, not algebra, and called by Lawrence Summers in a National Bureau conference "canonical," is included here as chapter 12.

Gresham's Law (chapter 19) is one of four "laws" discussed in the Mattioli lectures that were given in 1980 at Bocconi University in Milan. The subject belongs to the history of thought as well as to economic history or historical economics. The law, developed especially for two precious metals or two currencies, is extended in the lecture to two financial assets that are not fixed ineluctably in price as are, for example, the $5 bill and the $10 bill. There was considerable discussion in each of these lectures, not all like that of Milton Friedman on chapter 3 above, in complete discord. The interested reader is referred to the book, which came out with considerable delay in 1989 and in paperback in 1997, *Economic Laws and Economic History*. For the curious, the other "laws" treated were Engel's law on consumption, the Iron Law of Wages, and the Law of One Price.

Chapter 14, comparing British Financial Reconstruction after the Napoleonic wars with that after World War I, was published in a *Festschrift* for my old and close friend, Walt W. Rostow. In retirement at 65 years of age, I was hired at MIT half time for five years, equivalent to full time for one term of two, and available for jaunts in the off term. One such was to the University of Texas in Austin, the inspiration for which came not, as it happened, from Rostow, but from a former MIT student, Professor Hussain Askari. I did, however, attend the Rostow seminar. At one point we got entangled in a discussion of Britain's return to gold after 1815, which inspired the research. This was abetted by the fact that Texas oil money had equipped the university library with treasures not available at MIT or Harvard College, this oil money not being allowed to be spent on faculty salaries.

Going back a century of financial history per decade of mine, I got to the eighteenth century and the South Sea and Mississippi bubbles of 1720 in the first edition of *Manias, Panics, and Crashes* (1978). The seventeenth century focused on a spreading debasement of gold and silver coins primarily in the Holy Roman Empire, called in German the *Kipper- und Wipperzeit*, which peaked in 1619–1623. The name was doubtless chosen for its rhyming quality, but also because the words describe how venal money changers would jiggle their scales as they weighed debased coins to confound the peasants and small shopkeepers whom they were swindling. This paper is another also-ran, out-of-the-money candidate for inclusion here as is that dealing with the distribution of Spanish American silver arriving from "Peru" (now Bolivia) and Mexico in the sixteenth and seventeenth centuries. Some, perhaps a third, stayed in Europe; much moved either directly to the Far East in the Manila galleon, or eastward in ships of the East India Company or its Dutch counterpart, the Vereinige Oostindische Compagnie, around the Cape of Good Hope, or in other ships by means of the ancient path to the eastern Mediterranean and thence by caravan and dhow to India, or via Amsterdam through the Baltic to Russia and beyond.

The final item under finance (chapter 15) is on a modern topic— intermediation, and its unravelling when two parties who initially needed an intermediary to deal, acquire enough information to eliminate the market-maker and deal with one another directly. In modern guise the process goes forward in banking, with treasurers of large corporations acquiring skilled staffs and knowledge enough to go straight to institutions with savings to invest—or the institutions to them—rather than borrowing from banks where the institutions have deposited their funds. Industrial corporations issue certificates of deposit (CDs) for short-term monies, and bonds for long; insurance companies and pensions funds buy them. Loans by commercial banks dry up. Borrowers and lenders may need investment bankers as advisers, along with lawyers and accountants, but the function of banking undergoes change. The same process occurred earlier in trade to save the cost of sending goods to Amsterdam or London, and then hauling them away again. Financial intermediation outlasted that in goods because the costs of handling money are less than those of commodities.

Wile the papers under Political Economy are listed in chronological order, I prefer to start this discussion with chapter 18, the conclusion to the monograph *The World in Depression, 1929–1939* (1973). This was written for a Deutsche Taschenbuch Verlag (German pocketbook press) series on decades of world history in the twentieth century. Its theme was that world economic stability needed one major country as a stabilizer, and that in the 1930s, the British, weakened by World War I and the return to gold at an overvalued exchange rate, could no longer serve in that capacity, and the isolationist United States would not. Initially I postulated three functions for the stabilizer: keeping its markets open, maintaining the system of exchange rates and international payments, and in a crisis, acting as a lender of last resort. (In a later work I added two more functions of the hierarchical leader of the world economy [see p. 408 below]). I called the overall function one of leadership; political scientists called it hegemony, and developed a literature of their own about it. It happened, moreover, that I borrowed the notion of leadership from a paper by a pair of political scientists. Leadership has some negative overtones if one thinks of *Der Führer* and *Il Duce*, but the semantics have some importance and hegemony seems to me closer to using force.

Chapter 19, on "Economic Responsibility," was a memorial lecture for Fred Hirsch of Warwick University, England, which develops the theme of leadership further. The same theme is recurred to in chapter 20, "International Public Goods without International Government," the presidential address to the American Economic Association, given in the last days of 1985 and published in March 1986. It is in fact an argument for government in general, in contrast to the school of "Public Choice," which abhors or at least decries government regulation and especially government production. The problem again is who is in charge. In ordinary quiet times on trend, nobody in charge may be good enough, and there is little need for leadership except possibly leadership by example. In crisis, however, or stressful times, more is needed. I have dealt with this theme in a slight book entitled *Centralization vs Pluralism* (1996), adding that when crises arise in a federal or pluralistic state, it may be very difficult, approaching impossibility, to shift gears to more centralized authority, as the history of the Dutch Republic classically demonstrates.

Chapter 20, on "Rules vs Men," written for a *Festschrift* for Professor Kurt Borchardt of the University of Munich, and, as in the case of Rostow, disagreeing to some extent with his position, extends the theme of quiet times and crises, and the difficulty of changing political behavior when one succeeds the other. The question arises in much of economic history, but perhaps most notably in the Weimar Republic, when Heinrich Brüning, the German chancellor, regarded his options as extremely limited, hemmed in as he was by the Versailles treaty on reparations and the Dawes plan of 1924 with its commitments to the gold standard. Even before Britain went off gold in September 1931, some economists in Germany, in government and out, thought that Brüning should break away and declare that *force majeur* required flouting the commitments that limited action. Borchardt felt Brüning had no alternative options; Carl-Ludwig Holtfrerich thought he did. To a great extent Brüning was trapped by his own political commitment to demonstrate to the world that Germany could not pay reparations, a recipe like that of Charles Lamb for roast pig that called for bringing the pig into the parlor and burning the house down. To be sure it is inconvenient to break rules or commitments openly, since once broken, new precedents are created and the old rules are hard to reinstate.

Two papers, chapters 16 and 17, have been stranded by the present tactic of starting Political Economy with chapter 18 on leadership (or hegemony). Chapter 18 deals with two episodes in which France undertook noncooperative action in international finance, first ignoring the impact of its action on other countries, initially Britain and then the United States, and second challenging the policy of the world leader at the time, the United States. In each case, foreign exchange was converted into gold; neither action achieved lasting success. The theme is that while large strong countries have responsibilities for world economic and financial stability, and small countries do not, middle powers are in a position to create trouble, but lack the power to overcome it. Some "small countries" like Canada and Sweden may lead by example, but in serious disturbances that may not help greatly. And it should be noted that if a group of small countries behave in identical fashion—as Belgium, Holland, and Switzerland did in converting dollars into gold after Britain abandoned the gold standard in September 1931—they can damage the system as can a near-great power.

Chapter 16 on the analogy between money and language—each is a medium of exchange—is a show of bravura. The gold standard can be viewed as Latin, synthetic monies like the Special Drawing Right (and the euro?) are Esperanto, and flexible exchange rates require everyone to read and speak in his or her own language and to read or listen to writers and speakers of other tongues through translations. The paper was written in 1969, and teases the French a bit. In the fall of 1997 in Switzerland I learned that the German (or Schwyzer-deitch) cantons of the country talk to their francophone fellow citizens in English, or perhaps more accurately American. The same was true, I understand of Giscard d'Estaing and Helmut Schmidt, president of France and chancellor of the Federal Republic of Germany, respectively. I have been told further that the one-time president of the Bundesbank, Otto Emminger, spoke American to his central-bank colleagues with a Southern accent, after spending some time as a prisoner of war in Texas. It is an absorbing question today how the dollar and the euro will get along—the Gresham's law issue—and if the dollar is the equivalent of English as a medium of exchange, what other language, if any, will parallel the euro.

A few remarks may be noted in closing. My interests, insofar as they can be judged from this small and skewed sample, have bounced around over a considerable period. This is not the recipe for great success, but it helps to avoid diminishing returns. Second, lectures and seminars have been given in Sweden, Italy, and Singapore, but the papers deal mainly with Western Europe and especially Great Britain, France, and Germany, with some limited attention to the United States. Third, no attempt has been made to eliminate repetition. In assembling the papers, I see I have used a quotation from Sir Robert Peel more than once; there are doubtless other examples. With old men, I am told, repetition happens. I regard the harm done as exiguous and not worth the cost of the surgery needed to eliminate it.

Yale Professor William Parker has reminded us somewhere of the Roman mother, Cornelia, saying about her sons, the Gracchi, "These are my jewels." (The words, Parker said, were carved into the pedestal of a statute of Cornelia in his home town around which the town hobos used to gather.) These jewels may not shine very brightly, but they may be worth collecting from their dispersion over six decades.

Foreign Exchange

2

Competitive Currency Depreciation between Denmark and New Zealand

Competitive currency debasement, especially if intended to furnish an advantage for a particular export in a particular foreign market, should provide a better case study for the isolation of the effects of exchange depreciation than can be secured from a general analysis of the foreign trade of any one country undergoing depreciation. If the light of investigation is focused upon the consequences of depreciation in one commodity only, the determination of its effects on prices, value and volume is more definite, because the forces of the other factors involved, tariffs, quotas, and the like, may be more closely computed and set aside.

Butter Market—Motive for Rivalry

An instance of this sort is afforded by Denmark and New Zealand, which, from 1930 to 1933, competed with one another in depreciating their respective exchanges in order to gain advantages in the export of butter to England. An examination of the courses of their exchanges on London, the prices of butter there, and the value and volume of butter shipped, after the non-monetary factors have been reviewed and their importance weighed, should enable us to reach rather more definite conclusions concerning the effects of depreciation on exports than the general classical theory, with its all-important qualification, "other things equal," is able to give.

While the whole cause of the competitive currency depreciation of Denmark and New Zealand is not to be found in the London butter market, as the full burden of its effects cannot be shown there, yet it is possible to demonstrate, by relating data drawn from the pages of the *Board of Trade Journal*, that this commodity has played an important rôle in the depreciation drama. In 1931 Denmark and New Zealand led their

From *Harvard Business Review* 12, no. 4 (July 1934).

rival producing countries as "Countries of Origin" of butter imported into the United Kingdom by a wide margin, the former furnishing 2,466,838 hundredweight, the latter 1,935,033 out of a total of 8,060,068.[1] In the same year butter comprised slightly more than 30% (by value) of the total exports of New Zealand, amounting to £10,659,527 out of a total of £35,153,028. The year previous, butter had constituted £11,854,056 of a total of £44,940,692, or approximately 28%.[2] In 1931, too, the United Kingdom had purchased 88% of New Zealand's entire export,[3] which amounted to 4.4% of the United Kingdoms's total import. Denmark in the same year supplied 5.4% of all British imports.[4] Butter can thus be seen to be an important export, and is, in fact, the principal export of each country. Further than that, it is the only one of importance in which they compete, for the second export commodity of Denmark is bacon, which is distinctly a minor export of New Zealand, and Denmark does not export wool which is second on the New Zealand list. Thus, in so far as the depreciations of Denmark and New Zealand were competitive, a question on which the chronological sequence of depreciation will throw some light, the butter market in London furnished the motive for rivalry.

Theoretical Analysis

If we apply the general classical theory of currency depreciation to a competitive case, it follows *a priori* that the country which depreciates the more gains in the given foreign market, *i.e.*, increases sales because of lower prices,[5] at the expense of the less devalued currency, provided always costs do not rise *pari passu* with the depreciation. But in pursuing this line of reasoning, it must be recognized that there is a point beyond which a currency cannot be devalued to a nation's advantage, this point being soon reached if the depreciating country has a relatively inelastic demand for those goods it is accustomed to import. The point is approached when succeeding amounts of depreciation bring a slightly higher monetary return in the local currency from a greater increase of volume of exports, which return is counterbalanced by the even greater amount the country must pay for necessary imports on account of their higher prices. Depreciation for export advantage beyond this point, determinable separately in each instance, must tend toward a situation in which the depreciating country will gain complete control of the foreign market by devaluing its currency to zero if prices and costs have not risen to infinity at home. Here it would undoubtedly find that it had achieved a highly "favorable" balance of trade in goods, if it were interested in so

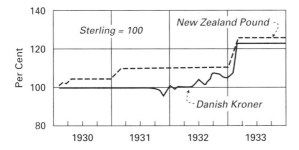

Figure 2.1
New Zealand pound and Danish kroner as percentage of their par ratios with British pound sterling

doing, since it would give away exports in enormous amounts and be entirely unable to import.

Rates of Exchange

Returning from this theoretical excursion to the problem for analysis, it is necessary to ascertain what determined the rates of exchange of the countries under consideration and enabled them to depreciate in competition with one another. It will be seen that the courses of Danish and New Zealand exchange on London—and the rate of depreciation from gold does not interest us here—have been set, since 1931 in the case of the former, since 1930 for the latter, largely by governmental control. Denmark, by virtue of the fact that the Government had vested sole rights to buy and sell foreign bills of exchange in the National Bank (Act of January 30, 1932), could change the external value of the kroner in any degree it wished simply by refusing to buy or sell exchange except at its own price. New Zealand has not had a freely competitive exchange market since the World War, taking its rate on the other currencies of the world from the British pound sterling. Since 1929, however, it has assumed the right independently to fix the percentage ratio at which the New Zealand pound will exchange for the pound sterling; that is to say, it may now decree that £100 equal 100, 105, 125, or 200 pounds New Zealand. The ratio of the two currencies is set and from time to time varied by the Dominion Government. Thus, it will be seen that the governments of both Denmark and New Zealand were prepared for the competitive depreciation vis-a-vis one another, being equipped with manipulative control over their respective currencies.

The rates on London, expressed in the case of Denmark both in kroner to the pound and as a percentage of the kroner-pound sterling parity, and for New Zealand as the official percentage of the pound sterling at which the New Zealand pound stood, are presented herewith in monthly averages since 1930.

Denmark followed England off the gold standard in September, 1931, and for a year kept the kroner depreciated at approximately the same percentage from gold as the pound sterling. Such deviations as existed in 1931 are of a minor sort and can probably be explained on the ground of technical difficulties experienced by the foreign exchange market in maintaining the parity of sterling without the foreign exchange control granted to the National Bank in January, 1932. This explanation holds especially true for the October and November, 1931, fluctuations, for up to the 18th of the latter month, when certain restrictions were placed upon exchange dealing, there was no foreign exchange regulation whatsoever.

In this depreciation Denmark was pursuing about the same course as the other Scandinavian countries, with minor changes due to differences in technique and in fundamental elements in her foreign trade position. New Zealand, however, had not been on the gold standard since the World War, and had been pegging her foreign exchange rate to sterling. In 1930, in order to foster the export trades, she moved the ratio between the New Zealand pound and the pound sterling from 100, fixing a 5% depreciation for the greater part of that year, and a 10% depreciation for 11 months of 1931 (relative to sterling, not gold). New Zealand, therefore, had had a competitive advantage for the export of butter, as well as other products, over Denmark at the beginning of 1932.

The Danish Government, in order to relieve the plight of the considerable dairy and agricultural interests of the country, sought to offset the New Zealand advantage (which will be shown below, when the tariff question is considered, to have been even greater than the exchange differential), by depreciating the kroner from the pound sterling parity. New Zealand in its turn was not content to rest idly by as Denmark closed the gap between the rates and nullified her competitive advantage. In January, 1933, she reduced her rate on London by another 15%. Denmark retaliated the following month with a 17% further depreciation from sterling. The race came to a halt, in a manner of speaking, as negotiations for the Anglo-Danish Trade Agreement, initialed April 24 and ratified in June, were interpreted as establishing in definitive terms the portion of the import trade of the United Kingdom to be allotted to Denmark.

Table 2.1
Rate on Copenhagen*—Monthly Averages (Par: 18.159 kroner to the pound sterling)

	1930	1931	1932	1933
January	18.205	18.165	18.125	19.3125
February	18.1912	18.1675	18.1875	22.375
March	18.165	18.1625	18.15	22.4375
April	18.1675	18.1675	18.1875	22.4375
May	18.1625	18.165	18.25	22.4375
June	18.1625	18.165	18.7812	22.4375
July	18.16	18.165	18.375	22.4375
August	18.1625	18.1675	18.565	22.375
September	18.1625	18.18	19.375	22.40
October	18.1575	17.87	19.2812	22.40
November	18.16	17.375	19.2187	22.40
December	18.1562	18.25	19.2187	22.40

Danish kroner as a percentage of Pound Sterling parity (derived from above)

	1930	1931	1932	1933
January	100.25	100.03	99.81	106.35
February	100.17	100.04	100.13	123.21
March	100.03	100.03	99.98	123.56
April	100.04	100.04	100.13	123.56
May	100.03	100.03	100.50	123.56
June	100.03	100.03	103.41	123.56
July	100.00	100.03	101.18	123.56
August	100.03	100.04	102.23	123.21
September	100.03	100.12	106.69	123.35
October	99.99	98.40	106.17	123.35
November	100.00	95.68	105.83	123.35
December	99.99	100.50	105.83	123.35

Tariff Enactments of Great Britain

Before turning to the study of butter prices in London in order there to see the effects of depreciation, it may be well to recount the provisions of the tariff enactments of Great Britain which directly affected Danish and New Zealand exports of butter. At the time of the abandonment of the gold standard, Great Britain announced that she would depart from the free trade policy she had maintained since the middle of the previous century. A tariff was proposed by the National Government, was passed, and

Table 2.1 (continued)

New Zealand pound as a percentage of the pound sterling†			
	1930	1931	1932	1933
January	101.06	106.35	109.5	115.2
February	102.04	109.5	109.5	124.75
March	102.59	109.5	109.5	124.75
April	104.36 (103.91)‡	109.5	109.5	124.75
May	104.5	109.5	109.5	124.75
June	104.5	109.5	109.5	124.75
July	104.5	109.5	109.5	124.75
August	104.5	109.5	109.5	(124.75) §
September	104.5	(109.5) §	109.5	(124.75) §
October	104.5	(109.5) §	109.5	124.75
November	104.5	(109.5) §	109.5	124.75
December	104.5	109.5	109.5	124.75

* From the *London Economist*.

† From the "Gold Exchange Index" published (usually) in the first issue of the month of *The Statist*.

‡ In May, 1930, issue. Later issues give 104.36.

§ The table "Gold Exchange Index" is not included in issues covering these months. The trends, however, permit the filling in of the missing data with figures identical with the series for the months preceding and following the omissions.

took effect on March 1, 1932, levying a general 10% *ad valorem* duty on all imports except those from the Dominions and Crown Colonies of the Empire. Certain exceptions were made, but butter was not among them. Thus, butter from Denmark, but not that from New Zealand, was taxed 10% of declared value upon its importation into the United Kingdom after February, 1932.

The Ottawa agreements of 1932, initialed at Ottawa on August 20, ratified, and put into effect on November 15, guaranteed free entry of butter into the United Kingdom from New Zealand for a period of at least three years, and in addition contained the promise of England to seek the substitution of a specific duty of 15s. per hundredweight for the 10% *ad valorem* rate on all butter coming into the United Kingdom from sources other than the component parts of the Empire. This rate was in fact applied to Danish butter in the Anglo-Danish Trade Agreement of April which halted the depreciation race. The provision which bore directly on butter is to be found in Article 4, Section 2, in which it is stipulated that England would purchase not less than 2,300,000 hundredweight of butter

Table 2.2
First butter in London—Inclusive of duty (in shillings per hundredweight)

	1930		1931		1932		1933	
	Denmark	New Zealand	Denmark	New Zealand	Denmark	New Zealand	Denmark	New Zealand
January			140.5	121.5	130.0	106.3	115.5	88.5
February	177.5	157.0	151.5	125.0	139.5	111.3	114.0	85.5
March	166.0	146.5	145.5	126.5	131.6	116.4	106.0	83.2
April	146.8	135.2	128.0	116.6	122.0	114.5	95.5	75.0
May	136.5	137.5	121.5	114.3	111.0	104.5	98.8	83.8
June	138.3	136.3	122.0	117.5	107.2	104.0	95.8	86.8
July	151.2	142.4	121.8	118.8	113.5	119.3	98.0	84.8
August	152.0	142.0	126.5	119.3	118.8	114.2	107.4	93.8
September	153.5	133.0	132.8	119.8	126.3	120.3	116.8	107.0
October	152.8	126.4	137.8	127.8	123.8	119.5	114.3	108.3
November	147.5	118.3	135.5	122.5	126.2	104.8	119.6	94.4
December	140.0	115.3	137.2	111.8	126.3	92.8	91.6	75.3

Source: *Board of Trade Journal.*

annually from Denmark, that if the total import were above, 8,100,000 hundredweight, Denmark would be allotted her share of the increase, presumably 23/81, and that if for any reason some other country should not provide the quota expected of it, Denmark would divide the amount to be made up with the other producers on an equitable basis. Denmark, it might be said in passing, had granted Great Britain certain dispensations regarding her annual import of coal, in exchange for this and other preferences, primarily of an agricultural nature.

Prices of First Butter in London

The prices of "First Danish" and "First New Zealand" butter, inclusive of duty and expressed in shillings per hundredweight, are presented in table 2.2.

Related to these prices we have the quantities of butter imported by months into England from Denmark and New Zealand, and the value amounts in pounds sterling over the same period.

Danish and New Zealand butter prices in London (see figure 2.2) have shown for the period under consideration a marked trend downward, and this despite the fact that for more than half of the period, *i.e.*, since

Figure 2.2
Prices of first butter in London

September, 1931, England was off the gold standard, which might have
been expected to increase the prices of her imports. The chart, however,
must be studied with some qualification because the relationship of these
prices and the exchange rates is obscured to some extent by the definite
and wide seasonal variation. The price of butter is high in winter, low in
summer, probably because of changes in the output of the English dairies
and in the import from the other producing countries. The price seasonal
cannot be attributed to the supply imported from Denmark or New Zealand, because seasonals in these quantities (see figure 2.3) tend to offset
one another. Imports from Denmark are large in summer and small in
winter; from New Zealand, where climatic conditions in the southern
hemisphere are exactly the opposite, small in summer and large in winter.
It is impossible, unfortunately, in a study covering such a short period to
eliminate the seasonal variations satisfactorily.

In our interpretations of these graphs, too, we must assume British
demand as a constant, both for the seasons of the year, and from year to
year. This assumption is more valid in the case of a staple product of
almost universal consumption such as butter, than it would be, say, for
limousines. But, in any event, there is no possible way of measuring
changes in the demand for butter that might result from changes in the
standard of living as employment, real wages, *etc.*, rose or fell, or as oleo-

margarine companies conducted strenuous advertising campaigns. This constant demand, too, can be judged from the totals in table 2.3 to be relatively elastic since larger amounts of the commodity have been imported as the price has fallen.

Returning to a consideration of figure 2.2, it will be observed that there is a definite relationship between the two price trends, and it can further be demonstrated, in our view, that this relationship has been altered by the comparative rates of depreciation from sterling that the two countries maintained. Where the dotted line representing New Zealand in figure 2.1 rises, the dotted line in figure 2.2 falls, due allowance being made for the seasonal fluctuation. When the line of depreciation for the Danish kroner goes up, the price of Danish butter descends inordinately, no correction being necessary here for the tariff, since the "inclusive of duty" price indicates, by the March, 1932, drop in price, that the whole tariff was absorbed by the exporter in Denmark. These movements are not precise or infallible, of course, because in addition to the seasonal variations and the comparatively unreal assumption of constant demand, there are other and varying sources of supply. The depreciation affects only the "supply price" which may or may not correspond to the market price. But the correlation is strong enough to maintain and fortify the assumption made previously (in note 5) that the full benefit of depreciation was used to lower the price in the foreign market, in so far as costs remained relatively stable in the depreciating countries.

Quantity of Butter Imported to England

Figure 2.3 shows the amounts of butter in hundredweight that New Zealand and Denmark furnished the London market during the years 1930–1932 and for eleven months of 1933. Denmark maintained about the same volume in 1931 as in 1930, reaching a low for the period in March, 1932, when the tariff went into effect. This low was due to the fact that previous to the tariff greater than seasonal amounts had been shipped to escape the duty. But when the adjustment to the impost had been made, and when Denmark had actively begun to depreciate the kroner relative to sterling, in June, 1932, the high point in volume was reached. The year 1932 ended with a higher total volume than the two previous years. During the first four months of 1933, again, when the depreciation race was even more intense, volume was distinctly more than seasonally high. When the conditions of the export were settled by the Trade Agreement, volume decreased below the 1932 comparable monthly figures.

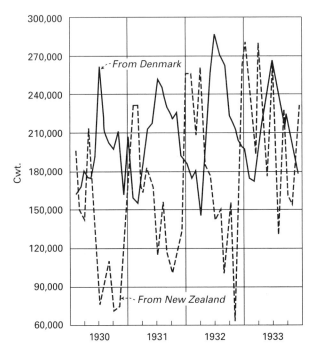

Figure 2.3
Butter imports into England—cwt.

New Zealand has a definite volume trend upward for all four years, over all of which time New Zealand was progressively depreciating her pound from sterling. The annual highs march successively upward, and the lows, with the single unexplainable exception of October, 1932, pursue the same course. The totals for the three years, given in table 2.3, reveal this more strikingly, the increase of 1931 over 1930 being 24%, while the increase of 1932, during which year the depreciation from sterling remained constant at 10%, was 14%, due in part to the tariff imposts against competitors outside the Empire. For 11 months of 1933, volume totalled 2,263,736 hundredweight, as against 1,916,010 hundredweight during the corresponding period of 1932, an increase of 18%.

Value of Butter Export from Denmark and New Zealand

The amounts paid, for butter, to Denmark[6] and to New Zealand are set forth for the same years in figure 2.4 and show an opposite result, showing, of course, the part played by the declining price. The value of the

1931 export of butter from Denmark was below that of 1930, reflecting the downward course of world gold prices during the depression, as volume remained relatively stable. New Zealand during the same year received about the same payment in England for a much larger volume than she had exported the previous year. At the same rate of depreciation during 1932 she received a slightly higher value for her 14% increase in volume, while Denmark, beginning to depreciate in the summer months and burdened with the tariff, received £2,200,000 less for exporting 120,000 hundredweight more than the preceding year. In 1933 New Zealand received a 7% smaller return in sterling from an 18% increase in volume, while Denmark sold her approximately equal volume for 27% less return, both computations being on the 11-month basis. These figures, it is necessary to emphasize, relate to the amounts paid in London, and must be transposed at the current exchange rate into the domestic currencies of Denmark and New Zealand in order to see the effect from the point of view of the exporter and the producer for export. These data, however, suffice to reveal how depreciation affects the amount of foreign purchasing power that exports produce.

Volume and Value of Butter of Each Country Compared

The effects of the depreciation of each currency can be more clearly set forth when the volume and value of the butter export of each country are compared directly. Figure 2.5, on which both series are drawn to scale so that they may be compared, contains volume and value figures for Denmark. Upon examination, it is seen that value was above volume in 1930 and slightly below it in 1931, due to the fall in world prices. But when Denmark undertook to depreciate the kroner in relation to sterling, value sank far below quantity, the 1932 disparity widening further when the additional 17% depreciation of 1933 took effect. In short, as the kroner was depreciated in terms of sterling, Denmark was paid a great deal less in British pounds for a larger volume of product. The effect on the exporter can be estimated by subtracting the costs of shipping, insurance, packing, *etc.*, and converting the sum into kroner. But for the country as a whole the foreign purchasing power arising from the export trade was reduced.

Figure 2.6 reveals value slightly above quantity for New Zealand's account, until the last part of 1930 when New Zealand depreciated her currency 5%. This gap was further widened in January, 1932, and again in

Table 2.3
Butter—from Denmark

	Quantity				Value			
	1930	1931	1932	1933	1930	1931	1932	1933
	(In hundredweight)				(In thousands of pounds)			
January	162,272	158,341	173,866	173,272	1,390	1,062	1,077	805
February	166,254	153,896	179,268	171,527	1,429	1,100	1,100	784
March	180,850	181,440	145,505	200,675	1,469	1,267	864	819
April	174,932	213,779	182,738	224,525	1,232	1,323	952	838
May	186,633	216,145	255,794	238,786	1,247	1,302	1,195	905
June	260,158	251,957	286,274	265,789	1,727	1,485	1,251	963
July	212,663	243,948	267,608	243,936	1,552	1,427	1,275	939
August	199,390	228,671	260,055	215,145	1,506	1,356	1,266	917
September	196,821	219,001	220,355	224,128	1,445	1,374	1,181	1,071
October	221,541	224,536	213,871	193,728	1,563	1,476	1,101	905
November	162,620	189,500	201,792	178,336	1,174	1,238	1,064	882
December	204,391	184,824	196,538	188,994	1,370	1,231	1,008	866
Year total	2,318,525	2,466,070	2,583,664	2,519,119	17,103	15,640	13,425	10,696

Butter—from New Zealand

	Quantity				Value			
	1930	1931	1932	1933	1930	1931	1932	1933
	(In hundredweight)				(In thousands of pounds)			
January	196,654	230,610	255,528	253,295	1,618	1,303	1,274	1,025
February	148,241	230,408	207,416	190,733	1,175	1,348	1,077	741
March	141,444	162,547	258,739	277,336	1,035	978	1,421	1,020
April	214,679	181,654	186,301	220,239	1,373	1,009	1,018	737
May	133,025	170,459	173,831	173,223	877	912	843	860
June	76,016	114,097	141,457	256,819	504	633	695	1,014
July	90,094	156,108	149,276	127,247	632	856	761	502
August	110,304	115,233	101,717	225,772	778	638	545	986
September	71,077	98,196	154,585	158,019	481	533	817	758
October	74,289	88,476	61,364	151,846	489	512	331	771
November	133,124	131,213	225,796	229,207	847	730	1,130	1,029
December	181,149	256,032	274,328	249,457	1,006	1,375	1,241	939
Year total	1,564,436	1,925,611	2,190,338	2,512,447	10,786	10,774	11,151	10,195
Butter from all exporting countries								
Year	6,821,620	8,060,068	8,449,108		46,870	46,298	41,481	

Source: "Accounts Relating to Trade and Navigation," published monthly by the Board of Trade.

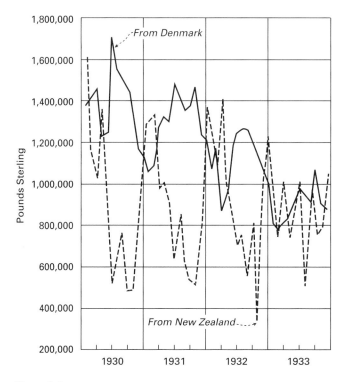

Figure 2.4
Butter imports into England—pounds sterling

1933 when the pound was moved still more from its sterling parity. In depreciating her currency slightly more than 5% from 1930 to 1932, New Zealand received 3.4% more pounds *in England* for 40.02% more butter. In 1933 (eleven months) she received 7% fewer pounds in England for an 18% additional increase in the volume of exported butter.

Summary

Throughout this paper we have been discussing the butter export of Denmark and New Zealand under competitive depreciation in terms of prices, volume and value in London, rather than in the exporting countries. These comparisons have not indicated the benefits from the depreciation received directly by the exporters, but suffice to make clear the competitive aspects of the case and the effects of the currency war upon the national foreign trade of Denmark and New Zealand.

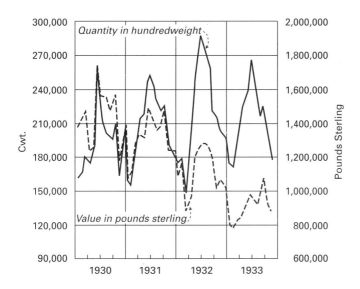

Figure 2.5
Butter imports to England from Denmark

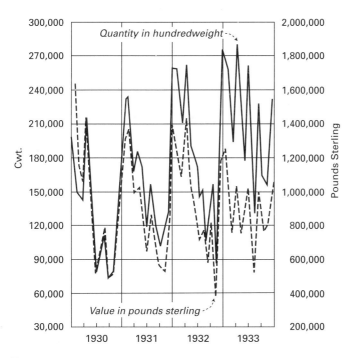

Figure 2.6
Butter imports to England from New Zealand

The attempt has been made from this viewpoint to show that currency depreciation, undertaken for an advantage in a highly competitive foreign market, which is of first importance to other countries, will breed other depreciation, and that the competition in the debasement of currencies will secure absolute advantages to neither contestant. In foreign trade it is impossible to cut prices, drive a competitor to bankruptcy and gain a wider share of the market, because of the necessity placed upon the governments of competitor countries of using every means to maintain foreign markets for their citizen producers for export. The exchange depreciation of New Zealand in 1930 and 1931 broke the price of butter in London and forced Denmark to retaliate in order to maintain her share of the market. Having enjoyed an export advantage, New Zealand could not, in its own opinion, see that advantage wiped out, and hence depreciated further. This time Denmark responded more promptly. The competitive currency depreciation was halted in June, 1933, and prices rose after June of that year, when the United Kingdom specified to Denmark what share of the butter market she might claim from year to year.

New Zealand had, previous to the whole-hearted retaliation by Denmark in 1933, succeeded in selling a great deal more butter in the London market for a slightly higher return. She had a small gain of a questionable value to her national economy to show for distinct losses to Denmark and the other competitors in the London market. Beginning in 1933, however, even that small value increase evaporated as still larger amounts of butter were sent to London. England, paying less in pounds for a larger total import of butter, has been the only gainer.

Notes

1. *Board of Trade Journal*, Vol. 128, January–June, 1932, p. 153.

2. *Ibid.*, Vol. 129, July–December, 1932, p. 488.

3. *Ibid.*, Vol. 128, January–June, 1932, p. 524.

4. *Ibid.*, Vol. 128, January–June, 1932, p. 222.

5. It is assumed here and throughout this paper that the currency depreciation lowers the foreign price of the export rather than raises its domestic price in terms of the depreciated money. The depreciation cannot both lower the price abroad and raise it at home by the full extent of the debasement, and it seems reasonable to suppose that when the depreciation is undertaken, in order to gain an export advantage, the differential will be applied to the price abroad. Especially would this be the case in a highly competitive commodity. The reality of this assumption is attested by retail butter prices in London and in Wellington, New Zealand, published in the *New Zealand Official Year Book for 1933*, p. 570:

International Retail Price Comparisons (in local monies)

		Butter per pound	
		London	Wellington
1930	February	21d.	$18\frac{1}{2}$d.
	May	18	$15\frac{1}{4}$
	August	19	17
	November	17	$13\frac{1}{2}$
1931	February	17	15
	May	16	14
	August	16	15
	November	16	$14\frac{1}{2}$
1932	February	15	$12\frac{1}{4}$
	May	14	$12\frac{1}{4}$
	August	15	12

From the *trends* of these data, it is clear that the price of butter has not been raised in New Zealand by the depreciation of her currency from sterling. The retail prices do not bear the same relationship to one another as do the wholesale, so that it is in the trends and not the direct comparison that we are interested. The wholesale price is higher in New Zealand than in London on account of the depreciation (98s. 6d. per hundredweight in England, 106s. 8d. in New Zealand in June, 1932, when the New Zealand pound stood at 109.5% of sterling— *ibid.*, p. 578), but the trend of the retail prices indicates that this was reached by lowering the English price rather than by raising the New Zealand price. Unfortunately wholesale prices are not available to prove the point more conclusively.

6. "The value of imports represents the costs of the goods (including packing) to the consignee, plus insurance and freight to the place of importation, and is exclusive of any duty payable in the United Kingdom."—From Introduction to "Accounts Relating to Trade and Navigation."

3

The Case for Fixed
Exchange Rates, 1969

Students of current Federal Reserve literature may recognize that I have borrowed the title of the chapter—with one important change—from an article by Harry G. Johnson in the June issue of the Chicago review of the Federal Reserve system, published by the Federal Reserve Bank of St Louis.[1] I do not propose to argue with the Johnson paper point by point, although its author is kind enough to make the case for fixed exchange rates before knocking it down. I may be permitted, however, to quote three sentences from it, to agree with one and a portion of another, and to express what I hope is reasoned dissent from most of two:[2]

(1) ... the case for fixed rates is part of a more general argument for national economic policies conducive to international economic integration (p. 14). [I agree with this.]

(2) The fundamental argument for flexible exchange rates is that they would allow countries autonomy with respect to their use of monetary, fiscal and other policy instruments ... by automatically ensuring the preservation of external equilibrium (p. 12).

(3) A flexible exchange rate is not a panacea [agreed, CPK]; it simply provides an extra degree of freedom, by removing the balance of payments constraint in policy formation (p. 23).[3]

International economic integration is presumably regarded as a benefit, but loss of autonomy under fixed rates is a cost which outweighs it. Or under flexible rates, the benefit of an additional degree of freedom for domestic macroeconomic policy is greater than the loss from suboptimal world resource allocation resulting from the separation of national markets

Reprinted from *The International Adjustment Mechanism*, Conference Series no. 2, Proceedings of a Conference Held in October 1969, Boston, Mass., Federal Reserve Bank of Boston, March 1970, pp. 93–108.

for goods and factors. This sets the terms of the debate in which I propose to show that the extra degree of freedom sought by Johnson is illusory. But note that the case is often made, for example by such an advocate as Sohmen, that the fixed-exchange-rate system breaks up world markets because national policies cannot be sufficiently harmonized to operate it without controls, whereas flexible exchange rates, plus forward markets, produce world economic integration. There is a hint of this position in the Johnson paper when he expatiates on the propensity of the market mechanism to produce exactly the kind of forward trading to eliminate exchange risk in a world of flexible rates, and this must be dealt with. The question is whether flexible exchange rates are a second-best solution in a world of frail men blown about by political winds to an extent that the first-best solution of a single world money is unattainable, or whether they constitute a first-best solution in their own right.

A Universal versus Qualified Flexible-Exchange-Rate System

Johnson's paper fails to make a distinction between a universal flexible-exchange-rate system and the adoption of flexible exchange rates by one or more individual countries in a world where at least one major currency is fixed or passive. Nor was this distinction originally made by Milton Friedman in his famous *Essay in Positive Economics*[4] which Johnson cites in glowing terms, an omission which, as Professor Friedman now magnanimously concedes, has been productive of much confusion.[5] With his present understanding of the point, Friedman has modified his original advocacy of a system of flexible exchange rates in favor of flexibility for any country that wants it, but specifically not for the USA and presumably not for small ones. (Banana republics are also exempted by Johnson on the ground that they do not have the illusion that the price of bananas in local money is a major determinant of the cost of living, as contrasted with the price of imported goods.)

Friedman's change of view, overlooked by Johnson, led to the curious result last May in a television debate between Friedman and Samuelson, which I had the honor of chairing, that I agreed with Friedman on flexible exchange rates, Samuelson agreed with Friedman, and Samuelson disagreed with me. The resolution of this inequality, of course, was that, integrated over time, Friedman had two positions, and Samuelson and I each only one.

The extra degree of freedom which a country obtains by adopting a flexible exchange rate does not come full-blown like Athena from the brow of Zeus. It is not created by an economist-alchemist in his study or laboratory. There is no free lunch, and we are still some distance from perpetual motion. Either the country itself refrains from interfering in exchange market, or its trading partners—or some major trading partners—abstain from interference while the country itself intervenes, or exchange rates are agreed internationally. In the last instance, of course, there is no extra degree of freedom for anyone, and wrong rates may persist unaltered because of failure to co-operate in changing them, as in the French-German confrontations of November 1968 and March 1969. Where a country itself forebears from affecting its exchange rate, using rules instead of management, as Professor Friedman would say, or locking the door and throwing the key away, as it appears to me, the gain in autonomy for monetary and fiscal policy is an illusion. Along with one more variable, there is one more target—the exchange rate. Where a large country agrees to let the country with a floating rate set whatever rate it wants, the freedom for one comes from a loss of freedom for the other.

Freely Fluctuating Rates

Let me dwell for a minute on the case of an exchange rate which is freely fluctuating with no official intervention. It is implicit in the case for floating rates that the "external equilibrium," which comes from allowing the supply to equal the demand for foreign exchange in a free market, is equilibrium not only for the balance of payments but also for other macroeconomic parameters—prices, wages, employment, interest rate, etc. There is no justification for this view. A foreign-exchange rate may clear the market for foreign exchange but exert pressure upward or downward on prices, employment, and so on.

In Canada, the floating exchange rate was abandoned because an overvalued rate exerted great deflationary pressure on the Canadian economy. Adherents of the flexible exchange rate system, Canadian and foreign, dismiss this case contemptuously as the result of the monetary foibles of one central banker whose monetary policy was mistaken. This will not do. The case demonstrates that a fluctuating exchange rate may not give monetary autonomy but provides another parameter to be controlled in managing the domestic economy. Mundell has said somewhere that floating exchange rates require more careful attention to monetary policy, rather than provide autonomy, because if capital continues to move across a floating rate, in response to changes in interest rates—as was true in the Canadian instance—low interest rates will depress the exchange rate, and high ones raise it. There may be possibilities of fine tuning here, but there is surely not autonomy.

But suppose capital moves not in response to domestic interest rate changes but autonomously—because capitalists do not like government policy in the nationalization of electricity (Italy, 1963), or because of student–worker riots (France, May–June 1968). The list is endless and includes most recently a loss of one-third of the Danish reserves in five days in May 1969, or a Belgian loss of $300 million (15 per cent of its reserves) in two weeks at the time of French devaluation in August 1969. The balance of payments would be cleared by depreciation, but the new and lower rate would be likely to undervalue the currency and stimulate possible irreversible rises in wages and prices. It is of some interest that a well-known advocate of a floating rate for the UK, Samuel Brittan, notes that it is important to float a currency at the right time, "with very careful internal preparation."[6] Where is the gain in autonomy?

Where the country retains control over its exchange rate and can intervene to prevent short-run movements which might work at cross purposes with domestic policy, it obtains its extra degree of freedom—if it in fact acquires it—at the expense of some other country. This is the well-known $N-1$ problem which makes it evident that a system of N flexible exchange rates for N countries is overdetermined. If one (major) country gives up its control of the rate, the extra degree of freedom of the others is produced, not from thin air, but by transfer. Johnson may be urging other countries, and especially Britain, to move to a flexible-exchange-rate system and leave the USA stuck with whatever rate the reciprocal of the $N-1$ countries produces. If so, he should stop worrying about the "deficit" in the US balance of payments, on which he has written so fully, since having lost an instrumental variable, the USA must also give up a target. And he should be aware that he is condemning certain import-competing industries to rather more rapid extinction than they otherwise attend, since it is likely that other countries will continue to embrace slightly undervalued exchange rates, export surpluses, and gains in reserves. I gather that the "new" Professor Friedman is willing to accept the logic of this position, and so am I.

If Johnson wants flexible exchange rates with co-ordinated intervention by various countries, it is hard to see how different this is from the present position where we try, but fail, to get disequilibrium rates changed by mutual agreement. This is a bargaining or game-theoretic problem with a nonzero solution.[7] It is good that the French finally did devalue in August, and unhappy that the Germans did not seize the occasion to revalue the Deutsche mark upward. The French had had a problem (de Gaulle) which had made it difficult for them to devalue, and the Germans continue to have strong political forces opposed to revaluation. It is difficult to speak on these matters on which we have little experience, but my intuition tells me that fixed rates with discontinuous changes in parities which are out of line (admittedly not yet a workable system) are as easy or easier to operate than continuous co-operation on continuously moving rates.

Partial and General Equilibrium

Economists frequently confuse partial and general equilibrium. In partial equilibrium everything else is unchanged. Demand and supply clear the market for a commodity without effects on other demands, supplies national income, prices, wages, etc., or with effects so small that they can be safely ignored. The theoretical argument for flexible exchange rates comes from the application of partial-equilibrium analysis in which *ceteris* are *paribus*; or from an analysis which is converted from partial to general equilibrium by one or more heuristic devices which may be legitimate in teaching but can be applied to the real world only at great risk.

Such a device, for example, in a two-country, two-commodity world is to fix exports in physical terms in each country so that one unit of exports costs one unit of the domestic currency, both before and after changes in the exchange rate. This builds money illusion and exchange illusion into the system. Or the exchange-rate change is made to produce an alteration in the balance of payments by means of assumed appropriate changes in spending in the system, working in the background to change incomes in the direction needed. Or depreciation raises real interest rates which cuts spending.

In all these formulations, it appears that the balance of payments is being maintained by changes in the exchange rate, but other real variables must be manipulated in the background in the right direction and amount to achieve the final result. The extra degree of autonomy is again illusory, resulting from the addition of a variable, the exchange rate, as if it were independent of other parameters in the system, and there were no feedbacks. It must be recognized that the exchange rate in most countries, and especially those where foreign-traded goods, whether exports or imports, enter significantly into the cost of living, is such a pervasive parameter, linked to prices, wages, credit conditions, taxes, etc., that it cannot be treated like the price of potatoes.

In the third quotation above, Johnson goes on to say: "... a flexible exchange rate does not and cannot remove the constraint on policy imposed by a limitation of total available national resources and the consequent necessity of choice among available alternatives; ..." How true. Disequilibrium in the balance of payments of an ordinary country—I do not speak of the special problem of a financial center—is the result of one or more of the following: excess spending, excess money creation, too low a rate of interest, too high prices, too high wages, distrust of the currency.

The first-best policy is to correct the cause of the disequilibrium. Exchange depreciation eliminates a deficit in the balance of payments only as it works to produce a change in the real value of one or more of the parameters, that is as it works to cut the real value of money, wages, spending, etc. It assumes that actors in the economy are responsive to money values, but unaware of what is taking place in real terms.

In the 'banana republics,' this is not the case, so that flexible exchange rates lead to a perpetual chase between inflation and depreciation, with most participants in the drama hedged against any cut in real income by one or another protective device which is triggered off when the exchange rate falls. On this account, Johnson recommends fixed exchange rate and a loss of autonomy for these countries. France succeeds in a devaluation, however, only as President de Gaulle (as in 1958) or President Pompidou (as he hoped in 1969 and 1970) succeeds in enforcing a cut in real wages. The British cannot improve their balance of payments unless they do likewise.

Most economists hesitate to put reliance on money illusion but are ready, even eager, to embrace exchange illusion. In the modern world where the citizens of large countries are as intelligent as those of banana republics, this is unwise. The flexible exchange rate does not operate on the real forces in the system. It is sometimes argued that it provides a cover under which changes in real values can be brought about which cannot be handled under fixed rates. This is the moot but unresolvable question as to whether fixed or floating rates instill more discipline in central bankers and trade unions. But where is the autonomy?

The Case against Flexible Exchange Rates

The main case against flexible exchange rates is that they break up the world market. There is no one money which serves as a medium of exchange, unit of account, store of value, and standard of deferred payment. Imagine trying to conduct interstate trade in the USA if there were fifty different state monies, no one of which was dominant. This is akin to a system of barter, the inefficiency of which is explained time and again by textbooks. Under a system of freely fluctuating exchange rates, the world market for goods and capital would be divided. Resource allocation would be vastly suboptimal. In fact, such a system clearly would not last long.

What would happen in such circumstance is what happens in every case where there is no money: a money evolves. In prisoner-of-war camps, such money evolved from cigarettes. In the USA, there seems little doubt that New York money would take over. Each state would reckon its money in terms of New York units. New York money would become the intervention or vehicle currency in which all states reckoned, calculated cross rates, and undertook transactions. Montana would pay for imports from Texas initially by converting Montana units into New York money which would be exchanged for Texas money. After a time, it would probably pay New York units directly to Texas and have them accepted directly. New York units would become the *numéraire* in which other currencies were quoted. The price of any other state currency would be expressed in terms of the New York unit, but the price of the New York unit would be impossible to express, since it would be the reciprocal of the price of all other units, appropriately weighted, which is the way "money" is priced.

This is the system followed by the world, with sterling serving as the *numéraire* prior to 1913, and the dollar from 1919 to 1933 and again after 1934. Individual countries could add to their sterling or dollar holdings by developing an export surplus or borrowing. Leaving aside gold production, which is basically irrelevant, world money outside the leading financial center could be increased only as the center had an import surplus or loaned abroad beyond its export surplus. If such borrowing went so far as to tighten interest rates, say in New York, and after the link to gold had been loosened, dollar creation offset it. In this way, dollar creation regulated the money supply of the world through the modality of the US balance of payments on current account and foreign lending.

Under any system of flexible exchange rates, the drive to establish an international money is virtually inevitable. Even if central banks could be persuaded to give up the practice of intervening in the foreign exchanges —which I doubt—individual traders among those brave enough to continue in business under the uncertainty would hold foreign exchange from time to time to limit risks, and would almost certainly converge on a single currency to hold as a vehicle currency or *numéraire*. Under present circumstances it would be the dollar. Gradually with time the traders would exert pressure on their governments to maintain the stability of their foreign holdings in terms of domestic currency. The stable exchange rate system, in my judgment, is inherent in the evolutionary processes by which barter moves to become efficient trading through use of a single money.

The process is not unopposed, nor unbeset by other pressures. The natural tendency of the human species to want to have its cake and eat it too, frequently leads to loose monetary policies, especially in time of war or crisis. One hundred per cent of the populace, including government, demanding shares of national income summing up to 110 per cent or more of the total, each backing its demand with market or political power, produces structural inflation.

Professor Friedman believes that there is no such phenomenon as structural inflation, as he blames central bankers for yielding to the demands on them for more credit when wages are pushed up. This is one way to look at it, though not a very fruitful one. Sometimes central bank and treasury officials initiate inflationary spending or increases in money; at other times, which are worth differentiating from the first, they are helpless victims of irresistible political pressures elsewhere in the economy. If they were to try to resist, they would be replaced. The counsel of perfection which advises potential central bankers to refuse to take the job unless they are granted political independence to resist any and all forces pushing for expansion in the economy is intellectually interesting but not helpful.

In the 'banana republics,' to use Johnson's phrase, fixed exchange rates are desirable but impossible. The consequence is a race between internal inflation and external depreciation in which all but the weakest forces in the society learn to protect themselves, but money is unable to perform its functions as a store of value and standard of deferred payment. Contracts are written in commodities or foreign exchange; riches are stored in goods, luxury apartments, numbered accounts in Zug. Monetary conditions are pathological, and the choice between fixed and flexible exchange rates is not open.

Where there is monetary discipline, the issue is whether to let the local money supply be determined independently, and in line with local needs, habits, predilections, idiosyncrasies, at the cost of some shrinkage of the efficiency of the world's capital and goods markets, and the functioning of the international corporation, or to work to try to reshape local money requirements in the light of the larger system. There is a public good/ private good problem here. If the Phillips curves of Britain and Germany differ sharply, with Britain having such a strong need for full employment that it is willing to tolerate considerable inflation, and Germany so fearful of inflation that it is willing to tolerate substantial unemployment, particularly that of Mediterraneans, resolution is a serious problem.

It may be necessary after time—if these attitudes are unyielding—to adjust exchange rates. Admitted. In a rational world, however, it would seem unfortunate to break up the world market for goods and capital even temporarily—until a new basis of fixed rates could be evolved—because of such attitudes which should be capable of compromise and agreement on a world wide rate of inflation. Making such an agreed rate stick in the short run creates serious problems. Again admitted. There is no escape from inflation control through exchange depreciation which only worsens it. Where national differences in tradeoffs between full employment and inflation are held with paranoid intensity and cannot be compromised, there may be no choice but to break up the world market.

Rejoinders and Rebuttals

Friedman, Johnson, and especially Sohmen, all believe that the disintegration of the world market can be minimized or, in Sohmen's view, eliminated by encouraging the development of forward markets. I do not want to go into this topic at great length partly because of the difficulty in its lucid exposition, and partly because I have been arguing the case with Professor Sohmen for about ten years now without making any dent on his position (nor he on mine). Let me give one side of the case, however, which seems to me irrefutable.

The flexible-exchange-rate scholars suggest that a system of floating rates would not be particularly damaging to trade, capital movements, or the activities of international corporations because forward markets would grow up—covering risks for as far ahead as years—to allow all exchange risks to be hedged. With forward markets, uncertainty as to exchange rates would be eliminated. Hence flexible exchange rates would not be seriously adverse to world economic integration.

I find four holes in this argument. First, and a technical one, forward markets add nothing essential to the capacity for hedging which can also be undertaken by borrowing in one market and lending in the other, earning or paying the interest-rate differential. This assumes perfect capital markets, to be sure, but these are virtually available to large international corporations. The convenience of forward markets for smaller firms, and the reduction in transactions costs—both of which may be granted—

produce no change in the theoretical capacity to hedge exchange risks without forward markets.[8]

Secondly, hedging does not eliminate exchange risk. Under a system of flexible exchange rates, a trader faces two risks, one on the price he pays or receives for foreign exchange, the other the possibility that his competitors may get a more favorable rate. It is possible to hedge against the first risk, not against the second. Accordingly, forward markets or hedging through spot transactions by borrowing/lending does not remove all risk.

Thirdly, as Anthony Lanyi states in a judicious treatment of the costs and benefits of flexible exchange rates, which, however, comes out in favour of flexibility, hedging is needed not for particular transactions, but for activities.[9] Business will not undertake investment in exporting, importing, producing abroad, foreign-security underwriting, etc., secure only in the knowledge that it can hedge the foreign-exchange risk in individual transactions. It must have a sense of where comparative advantage lies over a longer period. Granted, there are risks of foreign-exchange controls under fixed rates. This is the *tu quoque* argument used by small boys (which makes it advantageous to attack first). The issue here is only whether a system of flexible exchange rates inhibits world integration, as Johnson asserts, or not.

Fourthly, and the issue which Sohmen and I have the most difficulty in seeking to resolve, forward markets or spot markets with hedging through borrowing/lending cannot guarantee a businessman the existing exchange rate before he enters the market since his entry may produce a change in the rate. Johnson, for example, states (op. cit., p. 20):

Under a flexible exchange rate system, where the spot rate is also free to move, arbitrage between spot and forward markets, as well as speculation, would ensure that the expectation of depreciation was reflected in depreciation of the spot as well as the forward rate, and hence tend to keep the cost of cover within reasonable bounds.

This is protecting a trader against a change in the rate by producing that change, the logic of which escapes me. Johnson and many like him have confused the spread between the spot and forward rates, which is equal to the interest differential, with the cost of hedging, which is the difference between the rate at which an individual calculates a deal will be profitable, and the rate he pays for his exchange. If his calculations were made on the basis of a given spot rate, and he is able to cover through the spot market with borrowing/lending, or through the forward market at the interest differential, his cost of cover is equal to the interest differential, plus or minus. But if the exchange rate moves because of his transaction—and those of like-minded people responding to the same phenomena—the interest-differential fails to measure his cost. He is able to hedge only by moving the rate to such an extent that a change occurs in the current account—imports being cut off by depreciation, for example, or exports stimulated, or by a capital movement—in the present instance a speculative capital inflow.

Any unbalanced movement in trade or one-way movement of capital will change the rate, regardless of the existence of battalions of forward-exchange traders and arbitrageurs, and must change it sufficiently to induce an opposite movement in trade or capital. If there are large amounts of capital eager to undertake stabilizing speculation, the rate will not move far. If not, it may have to move far. Arbitrage cannot accommodate a purchase of forward exchange without an effect on the spot rate. The two forward transactions may cancel out but the spot rate must move far enough to induce an opposite flow of funds, or surplus of current payments, to match the spot transactions of the arbitrageurs.

In Sohmen's system, the spot rate stays fairly steady, but changes in the forward rate induced by direct forward transactions or by the forward half of arbitrage transactions can be offset by trader contracts for future imports and exports, stretching forward perhaps for two or more years. But this requires forward markets for goods of equal length; if not, the traders have exchanged a speculative position in foreign exchange for one in commodities.

In short, forward exchange is one of those complex topics which is reassuring to the lazy analyst, at least on my showing. For all its complexity, it changes nothing and can be ignored.

"Best" and "Best Available" Solutions

Let me turn from digging away at the opposition to something more positive, and start with the best and worst of international monetary systems. The first-best, in my judgment, is a world money with a world monetary authority. The authorities should be charged with regulating the world money supply so as to maintain its value stable, or perhaps declining very slightly each year to stimulate employment. This would be an economically integrated world, with a common set of prices and interest rates, adjusted in all cases for the total or partial separation of some markets for some goods, services, and kinds of investment money—

including distance from major markets. The distribution of money and credit among regions or countries would respond to trade and capital flows unhindered by governmental obstacles. It is the system worked out in the USA, and sought—but not yet achieved—in the EEC. It is probable that some redistributive mechanism is necessary to relieve those hardships which the market may inflict on certain regions and industries in this system, perhaps automatically through the tax system, with its different distributions of benefits and costs, perhaps in part through subsidies, subventions, foreign aid, and the like to marginal participants in the market process.

This is an economic first-best in my judgment. Most economists will agree that it is politically unattainable. When economists move from the first best to more feasible if less efficient solutions, however, note that they are undertaking implicit political theorizing in rejecting this or that solution as politically unworkable. There is no rigor, no science, no experimentation, some historical observations, and much intuition in these judgments. But economists cannot dodge the necessity for political theorizing since no one else is available to do it.

Almost identical with the first-best solution is the fixed-exchange-rate system with co-ordinated policies. According to a theorem of Hicks, two or more goods which have a fixed price can be regarded as a single good. By analogy, two monies which are freely convertible into one another at a fixed rate of exchange can be regarded as a single money. Regulation of the money supply so as to keep the monies freely convertible into one another at a fixed price requires co-ordination of money creation and extinction, along the lines of the distribution of money under the system of a single money used throughout the world. The gold standard was regarded as such a system for co-ordinating and harmonizing policies in this fashion, with countries gaining gold though trade surpluses or capital inflows expanding their money supply in some appropriate multiple of the gain, while those which lost gold contracted in the same degree. The gold standard, or a system of credit money with fixed rates, assumes that prices, wages, interest rates, etc., throughout the system will be adjusted to one another, and to the world money supply, by economic forces and not to serve political ends.

Most economists insist that this system has been tried and found wanting, since separate countries do not order their monetary, fiscal, price, wage, etc., policies as called for by the system, but rather respond to local pressures, generally resisting deflation, accepting inflation, operating along Phillips curves, etc., at different rates, and in response to different historical experience and with different mental blocks, so as to make the system inoperable. Most of them focus on the different price experience of different countries, and with the aid of an explicit or implicit theory of purchasing-power parity, call for adjustment of exchange rates, usually on a continuous basis.

Economists, moreover, have little difficulty in agreeing on the worst system. Nth best in a system of 1st, 2nd, 3rd ... nth best, is fixed exchange rates maintained by interferences with movements of trade, capital, and persons (such as tourists). This system confuses the container with the thing contained. Some economists have no difficulty in accepting control over capital movements, so long as tourists and goods are free, on the ground that capital movements are not always dictated by efficiency considerations so much as capital flight from situations which people cannot escape, especially normal taxation.

If the best is unattainable and the worst must be avoided, what is second-best and still feasible? In particular, how much economic efficiency should be traded off against alleged political feasibility in a world where hard political data or even firm opinions on the behavior of political figures in relation to monetary phenomena are impossible to obtain?

Take such an issue as centralization. Most of us amateur, implicit, political theorizers agree that decentralization and local participation are good, but that for some problems, such as regulation of the money supply, central control is inescapable. In the world monetary system, national sovereignty makes operation of an international credit standard impossible, or does it? I have recently read a plea for raising the price of gold by a distinguished economist who bases his argument on the explicit political ground that while gold was wasteful compared to credit money (an economic argument), it was useful (politically) in making the money supply of individual countries independent of the actions of other countries. This strikes me as both wrong and misguided: wrong because the deep-seated forces of the world will be searching for a single convenient money as a medium of exchange, unit of account, etc., under any monetary system, whether flexible exchange rate or based on national monetary policies relying on national gold reserves; misguided because an economist has little business making sweeping economic pronouncements based on political judgments. The shoemaker should stick to his last. The economist who finds largely political rather than economic reasons for his recommendations has either run out of ideas to support his prejudices or is in the wrong business.

Options and Choices

If we rule out a world currency with a world money supply established internationally, and a fixed-exchange-rate system in which each country has responsibility for establishing its money supply in accordance with agreed rules, such as under the gold-standard "game," the choice of a real second-best comes down in the minds of most economists to a national currency standard, or to flexible exchange rates. Of late, freely flexible exchange rates have been abandoned in favor of either a wide hand, that is rate fluctuation constrained within fairly wide limits; or a crawling, sliding, creeping peg.

Each of these recognizes that speculation may drive the rate way up or way down and impose burdens on domestic policy, and possible irreversible movements in prices and wages which should be avoided. The sliding peg, much better that the band proposal, recognizes that there are likely to be many occasions when short-run exchange movements should be constrained but not the long run (the band constrains long-run movements but not short). The question for investigation is whether it is second-best to relax the discipline of a fixed-exchange-rate system and give up the attempt to harmonize national macroeconomic policies into a converging world position, at some cost in efficient resource allocation, or to undertake the harder political task for higher economic reward.

There is a choice which Despres, Salant and I have long advocated, and to which Professor Friedman has come around. Professor Friedman regards it as a variant of the flexible-exchange-rate system; in my judgment, it belongs in the fixed-rate stable. I refer to the standard referred to by Professor Edmund Phelps in a recent conference as "How to Stop Worrying and Get to Love the Dollar." It requires the USA to stop worrying about its balance of payments (other than the current account, which is currently in a poor position) and to remove its restrictions on capital movements. Other countries can adopt whatever exchange rate they choose. Professor Friedman would recommend that Britain, Germany and France follow policies of freely floating rates. I would leave it up to them but, as a betting man, be prepared to make a small wager that they would continue, as in the past, to keep their currencies fixed in terms of dollars, even after the withdrawal of such inducements as the German-US military offset agreement. If I proved to be wrong in the short run, moreover, I would be prepared to bet that in the long run the convenience of maintaining reserves in the dollar, the world's *numéraire*, a money's money, would be so compelling that they would again stabilize.

To achieve the integration I seek and to limit risks, it would be advisable for countries to indicate to the world whether or not they intend to stabilize their currencies. With those which did so seek, I have recommended elsewhere that the USA seek to work out common monetary policies, so as to defuse the dollar standard from the political dynamite of an imposed dollar standard. The details lie outside the scope of this paper.

In short, I regard as third best, with a chance of its achievement, a dollar standard managed internationally since I judge unattainable the first-best world money and world central bank; and the second-best fixed-exchange-rate system with independently operated national monies. Fourth best is the crawling peg. The flexible-exchange-rate system is well down the list.

Notes

1. See Harry G. Johnson, "The case for flexible exchange rates, 1969," Federal Reserve Bank of St Louis, *Review*, vol. 51, no. 6 (June 1969), pp. 12–24. (Also published by the Institute of Economic Affairs, along with a paper by John E. Nash, under the title "UK and floating exchanges," *Hobart Papers*, no. 46, London, May 1969). Note that Johnson borrowed his title from Milton Friedman, whose paper is noted in note 4 below.

2. I choose not to cavil at what I consider as small imperfections in the paper, e.g. the contradiction between the suggestion on p. 18 that sterling should belong to a fixed-rate bloc—either the dollar or some continental currency run by the EEC—and the conclusion on p. 24 that the pound should float, or the disingenuous suggestion, in the light of the history of moral suasion by Federal Reserve authorities, that if the authorities know something that the speculators do not know, they can calm speculative fears by making that knowledge public.

3. See Egon Sohmen, *Flexible Exchange Rates*, 2nd edn (Chicago, Ill: University of Chicago Press, 1969).

4. Milton Friedman, "The case for flexible exchange rates," in Milton Friedman, *Essays in Positive Economics* (Chicago, Ill.: University of Chicago Press, 1953), pp. 157–203, abridged in R. E. Caves and H. G. Johnson (eds), *Readings in International Economics* (Homewood, Ill.: Richard D. Irwin for the American Economic Association, 1968), ch. 25.

5. See his discussion in F. Machlup, chairman, "Round table on exchange rate policy," *American Economic Review, Papers and Proceedings*, vol. 59, no. 2 (May 1969), pp. 265 ff.

6. See his "U.K. external economic policy," in International Economic Association, *North American and Western European Economic Policies* (London: Macmillan, 1971), p. 95:

The great fear about a floating pound is that in the transitional period, while the current balance is deteriorating, the rate would be entirely dependent on stabilizing speculation. If the market took a pessimistic view and import prices rose severely at a time when inflationary expectations were very high, there would be, it is feared, a risk of a cumulative cycle inflation and exchange depreciation on almost a Latin American scale. To offset such cost-inflationary forces by financial policy might require very severe unemployment if it were manageable at all.

7. Note that circumstances are more important than principle in these matters. In 1932 sterling was flexible and the dollar fixed; Britain opposed currency stabilization and the USA favored it. After the abandonment of the old gold price in March 1933, British official opinion saw the need for currency stabilization, and the USA moved into opposition.

8. I made this argument to Paul Einzig, who countered that my view of the matter is static, as opposed to his which is dynamic (*A Dynamic Theory of Forward Exchange*, 2nd edn, London: Macmillan, 1967, p. xv). Apart from frictions which may reduce the capacity of forward markets to provide facilities for hedging, I am unable to see what a "dynamic theory" of forward exchange may mean.

9. Anthony Lanyi, "The case for floating exchange rates reconsidered," *Essays in International Finance*, no. 72 (Princeton, NJ: Princeton University Press, February 1969), p. 5.

International Trade

4   **Group Behavior and**
                                         International Trade

The primary tool of analysis in economics is the market. But Walker has expressed the opinion that an economics adequate for prediction and policy must include a theory of extramarket behavior.[1] Polanyi, further, has attempted to demonstrate that the emphasis on the market is likely to be misleading and that a rounded theory of social behavior would include economic drives as only one strand in a broad web of social motivation.[2] The present chapter is designed to suggest that, in certain situations in international trade, a useful tool of analysis may be found in a theory of group behavior at the national level. Unhappily, no theory adequate for the task appears to have been developed. I shall offer a few suggestions about the types of variables with which such a theory should deal.

My method is to take the world decline in the price of wheat after 1870 and to indicate the responses to it in Great Britain, Germany, France, Italy, and Denmark. If a theory of market behavior were sufficient for prediction, it might be expected that the reduction in the price of wheat would lead to increased imports in Europe. Foreign sources of supply would be substituted for domestic. Resources engaged in the production of wheat would shift to other occupations. Some increase in wheat consumption would take place at the expense of other grains, to the extent that wheat would fall in price more than rye, oats, and barley would. Some of these changes did, in fact, occur, but the results were not uniformly of this character.

After I have established the differences in response I shall turn to a series of explanations dependent on nonmarket factors. None of these is completely satisfactory. What appears to be needed is a comprehensive theory of group behavior to deal with groups as large as nations—in particular, a theory that systematically makes allowances for variation in the relation among the subgroups that make up the larger entity.

I am conscious of the amateurish character of the economic history and sociology in what follows, and I am not inclined to apologize for this inevitable shortcoming. Interdisciplinary cooperation must begin with the utilization, however crude, of the products of other social sciences by practitioners in separate fields. I have greatly benefited from the assistance of experts in other fields,[3] but I have been obliged to restrict my use of their techniques, lest my special focus of interest be lost among a host of fine points.

The main facts concerning the world decline in the price of wheat after the American Civil War and its causes are generally understood and accepted. The rapid spread of the American rail network in the 1870s and 1880s made it possible to transport wheat to tidewater more cheaply and in far greater quantities than the canal system had been able to handle. A parallel development occurred in railroad construction from the Ukrainian wheat fields to the Crimean ports. The technological shift from wooden to iron ships—another indirect effect of the Civil War—reduced transatlantic freight rates and those to western Europe from the Crimea. The availability of demobilized manpower, untilled land, and wartime accumulations of money capital, coupled with the development of farm machinery for extensive cultivation, resulted in an expansion of the American supply, which passed the economies of production and distribution on to the consumer in Europe as cheaper wheat. In addition, the weather in the United States was favorable during the 1880s, and yields were high. The European peasant and landowner met increased competition in grain production from overseas.[4]

The difficulties of European wheatgrowers were not caused solely by overseas competition. A series of bad seasons reduced yields and brought about a deterioration in quality. A Royal Commission of Inquiry, sitting from 1879 to 1882, reached the conclusion that the loss of British farm income was primarily caused by untoward weather and only secondarily by foreign competition. The effects of the two causes were not unrelated. In a closed economy, a short crop is at least partially compensated for—so far as farm income is concerned—by an increase in price. In an international, bihemispheric economy, an increase in the local price produced by a series of short crops is likely to be forestalled by imports from overseas.[5]

The view exists, however, that what hurt European agriculture was not overseas competition or any other factor peculiar to agriculture but overall depression, lasting from 1873 to 1896. It is recognized that the price of wheat fell somewhat more than prices in general and this is ascribed to the growth of production in the United States. This relative decline, given by one writer as only 10 percent, is regarded as much less significant for the agricultural depression than was the general fall in prices.[6] The reasoning, however, is not persuasive in the light of price developments on, say, the Copenhagen market, which was unaffected by tariffs. Between 1873 and 1896 wheat fell in price by 53 percent and rye by 48 percent, as compared with a decline of 36 percent in the *Statist's* index of wholesale prices. And after 1873 American wheat appeared in European markets that had never before seen it, including some cities, such as Trieste, known as export centers for European supplies.[7]

The combination of weather and overseas competition, then, produced potential economic distress for the farming community in the form of short crops and low prices. The remainder of this analysis, for convenience, treats the matter as a question solely of prices. In this connection, some importance attaches to the question of timing. The price of wheat fell from $1.70 to $0.66 a bushel in England from 1873 to 1894, and the sharpest decline was probably that from $1.31 in 1882 to $0.90 in 1886.[8] Action to meet the collapse in the price of wheat was taken, if at all, primarily in response to this pressure. But the nature of the response and the timing differed from country to country.

No action was taken in Britain. The issue had already been settled some years before, in 1846, with the repeal of the Corn Laws. The decline in the world price of wheat produced an improvement in the terms of trade for the rising industrial classes and a basis for lowering, or withholding increases in, the wages of the industrial labor force. The latter, in turn, received a new batch of recruits in the form of agricultural workers displaced from the farm by the unprofitability of wheat growing.

The 1846 repeal of the Corn Laws, fourteen years after the political settlement between the landed gentry and industry and commerce in the Reform Bill, had no immediate economic effect. The period of high farming in Britain continued uninterrupted. British agriculture in general was efficient and profitable from 1837, when the long period of distress after the Napoleonic wars came to end, until 1873. The American Civil War and the Crimean War had helped to postpone the effects of cheap wheat imports, but even in the 1850s there had been no significant effects of the repeal. Land under the plow in Britain reached a peak in 1872 never again attained, even in World War II.[9]

The bad summers from 1875 to 1879, the rinderpest attack of 1877, and the widespread loss of sheep to liver rot in 1879 may have convinced the farmers that their difficulties resulted from the vindictiveness of nature rather than a change in their position in the community. Landowners remained the richest class in the country for several years after the disaster of 1879. By 1886 their relative position had begun to slip.[10] No action was taken to halt the decline in farm prices or to assist the farming community.[11] The dominant group in the society—the rising industrial class—was content to have cheaper food and cheaper labor. Rents fell, young men left the farm for the town, land planted to crops shrank rapidly. The response to the decline in the world price of wheat was to complete the liquidation of agriculture as the most powerful economic force in Britain.

In Germany, France, and Italy the farmer was protected by the imposition of tariffs. In Germany the tariff on grain was enacted first in 1879, after fourteen years of free trade. Duties under this law were almost purely nominal, but rates were raised sharply in 1885 and again in 1887. The timing of tariff enactments in France and Italy was broadly similar, with the exception of the first step and with a significant difference insofar as Italy was concerned. Major increases in grain tariffs took place in Germany and France in 1885 and 1887. In Italy the first step was delayed until 1887, although the second followed quickly in 1888.

The German situation is more properly analyzed in terms of the tariff on rye, which in the period to 1890 was identical to that on wheat. Gerschenkron makes clear that Bismarck's alliance ran not between industry and agriculture as such, but between two powerful components of each, iron and rye.[12] Within industry the interests of the expanding steel industry were opposed to those of the fabricators of metal, who wanted cheap supplies. In this capital-intensive industry, moreover, the level of wages was relatively unimportant. In agriculture the large farms of the Junkers in eastern Germany produced rye as a cash crop for shipment to western Germany and for export. Their interest in high prices should have been opposed by the peasants of northern and western Germany, who bought grain for animal feed and had an interest in low prices. Despite this interest, however, the peasants of Germany politically followed the leadership of the landed nobility and supported tariffs on grain. Gerschenkron claims that they were deluged with propaganda and deluded by the concurrent imposition of tariffs on pigs and other animals—which, however, afforded a much lower level of protection.[13] Even within the ranks of labor there were groups who appeared not to oppose the tariffs.

The enactment of the tariff on wheat in France required the repeal of the Le Chapelier Law of 1791, which forbade associations based upon economic interest. A modification of this law in 1865 had made it possible to establish associations for the improvement of agricultural techniques. Its final repeal in 1884 paved the way for agricultural syndicates, which began by acting as producer cooperatives in the buying of fertilizer and agricultural machinery and in establishing credit unions. Very shortly these groups began to agitate for higher tariffs. The owners of large farms, marketing a higher proportion of their crop for cash than did the owners of small farms, had a greater interest in the price of wheat; but all farmers were affected by it. In only ten of eighty-seven departments of France did grain occupy less than half the tillable land in 1882, and only in one, Corsica, did the percentage fall below 40.[14] There is some evidence that the leadership in the political drive for protection was taken by the cattle interests of Normandy and Brittany. But all parts of the country, from the northern wheat districts to the southern wine areas (suffering from the depredations of *phylloxera*), were united in their zeal to raise the relative level of French farm prices.

The success of efforts to obtain protection for agriculture was aided by a compromise with industrial interests. Agriculture and industry had not always readily adjusted their conflicts of interest. In the time of Napoleon, French commercial policy had favored industrial exports at the same time that it forbade the export of wheat or of agricultural products used by industry. Agricultural interests thereafter tried on several occasions to secure protection on such industrial supplies as hides, wool, oil seeds, and silk. In 1881 the farm interests hoped that commerce and industry would agree to a tariff of 10 percent on foodstuffs in exchange for the concession of freedom to import agricultural raw materials. The compromise of 5 percent, which did not apply to wheat, produced little satisfaction. After the final repeal of the Le Chapelier Law in 1884 and more effective organization, the markedly higher rates of 1885 and 1887 on grain and animals were won with the assistance of threats of retaliation against industry.

Italian tariff policy in the 1870s and 1880s favored industry over agriculture. In 1864 wheat had been subjected to a duty of 0.5 lira per quintal to raise revenue. This was increased to 0.75 lira in 1866 to meet the costs of the war. The tariff revision of 1878, undertaken primarily to regularize the duties of the newly formed kingdom, increased the rate on wheat to 1.40 lire per quintal. These rates were low. In other directions there was no protection for agriculture. Imports of rice and barley, for example, were free of duty. Yet industry enjoyed a considerable measure of protection.

The question of taxes on food was widely discussed. An excise tax of 2 lire per quintal of wheat had been imposed internally in 1869 to improve governmental finances; although vigorously opposed by urban and industrial interests, it continued in effect for fourteen years. The experience with this tax appears to have given the Italian government pause when rising imports of grain from overseas, encouraged by the appreciation of the lire, began in 1884. Three years later, in 1887, the tariff was raised to 3 lire, a full two years after similar action was taken in France and Germany. The rate was increased again to 5 lire in 1888, after the tariff war with France led to the loss of the French market for the wines of southern Italy, to compound the distress of the region.[15] But by this time it was too late. The Italian peasant had already begun to emigrate. Gross emigration across the Atlantic, primarily from agricultural regions of Italy, increased from an average of 25,000 annually in the period 1876 to 1880 to 73,000 in 1885; 83,000 in 1886; 130,000 in 1887; and 205,000 in 1888.[16] The 1888 figure , which is presumed to reflect the period of nominal tariff rates before April 1887, with a time lag, was to remain the peak for thirteen years. Recovery of wheat prices under the impact of the tariffs and other factors slowed the pace of emigration somewhat. Once started, however, the flow became cumulative and self-perpetuating. Early emigrants encouraged first their families and then their relatives and neighbors to follow.

The response of Germany, France, and Italy to the decline in the world price of wheat was to impose tariffs in an attempt to maintain the relative price of wheat and to protect grain producers. In Germany, the movement was led by Bismarck as a step toward a new political alignment of Junkers and steelmakers, but it had the consent of many of those whose interests were adversely affected. In France, agriculture—more or less as a whole—negotiated through the tariff in reaching a settlement with industry. The reluctance of Italian industry to agree to increased tariffs and the delay in imposing them meant that the Italian response to the decline in prices was to quit Europe.[17]

Denmark—like Britain, the Netherlands, and Belgium—did not impose a tariff on wheat. Instead, it gave up the attempt to compete in the world export market for wheat and became a wheat importer. This shift was incidental, however, to a revolution in Danish agriculture, which was converted from the growing of grain to animal husbandry. Denmark was assisted in responding thus by its proximity to the rapidly industrializing markets of England and Germany, with their expanding national incomes, and by the high income elasticity of demand for butter and bacon. Given the demand, however, there are certain remarkable features of the response of supply that merit investigation. Of particular importance are the middle-sized farm, which predominated in Danish agriculture, the agricultural school system, and the cooperative movement. The second of these at least, and perhaps the whole response to the decline in wheat prices, was deeply affected by the German defeat of Denmark in 1864 and the loss of the province of Schleswig.

Of all the countries of Europe, only in Denmark has the size of the productive unit been stabilized at the medium-sized farm—around fifty acres.[18] In other countries, over considerable periods of time, farm size had increased or decreased. Periodic reversals occur under the influence of such discontinuous events as land reform—primarily the redistribution of church or noble lands and parcellation of peasant strips (or enclosures) when these became too numerous and too narrow to work (that is, extensive farming became more profitable than intensive). Aside from these turning points, however, farm size appears to have a tendency to increase, as in Hungary, East Prussia, and England up to World War I, or to decrease, as in France, Switzerland, and western Germany. In some countries, like Italy and Poland, the two processes take place side by side. Land purchases by the wealthy, primogeniture, high income taxes, poaching laws, veneration of blood sports in the culture, and the like, tend to increase farm size. Equal inheritance and rapid population growth tend to reduce the size of the farm unit.[19]

In Denmark a variety of factors appears to have established and maintained the middle-sized farm. The principle of equal inheritance has been offset by small family size, by a frontier of the sea to which extra sons could escape, and by easy credit, which enabled farmer-brothers to buy out their share of the patrimony. High land taxes made the maintenance of unproductive estates expensive. But the state intervened from an early date, and continuously (1682, 1725, 1769, 1819), to prevent the aristocracy from adding peasant land to their holdings and to prevent undue subdivision as well. A policy of dividing large holdings into small, but not minuscule, units prevailed for several centuries and was reaffirmed in legislation providing for small holdings in 1899 and 1909. The institution of the middle-sized farm, which happens to be inefficient for grain production but is well suited to certain types of animal output, goes deep into Danish agricultural life.

The Folk School, or agricultural high school, was originated in 1844 by a remarkable man, Bishop N. F. S. Grundtvig, for the purpose of educating the rural population not in scientific agriculture but in "the Danish language and history and … its constitution and economic life." Classes are held in the five winter months for men and for three months in the summer for women, normally in some part of the country other than that in which the student lives. The schools attempt to provide the agricultural segment of the population with a unity of background and an awareness of the life of the urban population of the country.

The first Folk School was founded in Schleswig. After the loss of the province to Germany, this school was moved to Danish territory. Thereafter the movement spread rapidly.[20] By 1870, before the collapse of wheat prices, there were sixty or seventy such schools in the country.

The cooperative movements in Sweden and Denmark have been widely studied. For present purposes, therefore, it is sufficient to make a limited series of points. To sell butter in international trade required bringing the "peasant" butter of uneven taste and texture up to "manor" quality. This meant a standardized product. After the invention of the cream separator, the manufacture of butter could take place on a large scale, even though the labor-intensive production of milk still required the medium-sized farm. Economies of scale in marketing were available not only in butter but in eggs and bacon as well. In this situation the spread of the producers' cooperative movement in Danish agriculture was rapid after the establishment of the first cooperative dairy in Jutland in 1882.[21]

Denmark's response to the decline in world wheat prices, then, was to revolutionize her agriculture and to change herself from an exporter of grains to an importer. It may be observed that the acreage devoted to cereal production in Denmark increased rather than declined after animal industry had developed.

These differences in European responses to the decline in the world price of wheat in the 1870s and 1880s may be summarized as follows. In Britain, agriculture was permitted to be liquidated. In Germany, large-scale agriculture sought and obtained protection for itself. In France, where the demography, pattern of resources, and small scale of industrial enterprise favored farming, agriculture as a whole successfully defended its position with tariffs. In Italy, the response was emigration. In Denmark, grain production was converted to animal husbandry. What factors outside the market account for these national differences? A number of attempts have been made to explain at least some of the various responses. The present section undertakes to review and comment upon these efforts.

The most familiar contrast, perhaps, is between the free-trade ideas developed in Britain by Smith, Ricardo, and Mill and the theory of national economy propounded in Germany, especially by Friederich List. A variant of the List doctrine can be found in the "nationalist economics" of Paul-Louis Cauwès in France,[22] although it is difficult to make the case that Cauwès' ideas were more than an aberration in an intellectual atmosphere that was much more sympathetic to the doctrines of the Manchester School. The place of Smith and List in Denmark appears to have been taken by Bishop Grundtvig, whose métier was poetry and national mysticism rather than economics; and no particular figure rationalized the action taken in Italy. It might be fair to say that the economists of Britain and the national economists of Germany provided the rationale for the action taken rather than its impetus.[23] And the relative unimportance of this function may be indicated by the actions of France and Italy, taken in the absence of any distinctive rationale.

In its vulgar version the foregoing explanation is reduced to the single word "nationalism." Britain adhered to the international system; Germany and France were nationalistic in their responses. But this reasoning has evident weaknesses. Italy's solution was essentially international, or one possible only in an international world, although the attempt was made to apply the "nationalist" solution of tariffs. It could be said that the Italian solution was more international than the British, where the displaced agricultural workers shifted into industry within their own country. The international solution, that is, may involve a shift in international trade or an international movement in factors. The explanation breaks down, further, on the side of nationalism. If we set aside for the moment the subtle differences between the French and the German behavior, the Danish solution, like the French and the German, was a highly nationalistic one—taken without tariffs, to be sure, but in an atmosphere of nationalist emotion. Nationalism and internationalism in this context are compound variables of great complexity. They require, rather than furnish, explanation.

A more elaborate analysis, which fits the present case to a degree, though it makes no mention of it, is that developed by the Danish economist, Carl Major Wright.[24] Wright observes that a country can respond to an adverse change in world market conditions by intervention to correct the world situation, by isolation from it, or by adaptation to it. His book contains a message for small countries like his own. These, he believes, are too weak to intervene in the world market and will not be allowed by the great powers to isolate themselves from it. In consequence, they have to adapt themselves to it. Toward this end he advocates increasing mobility of factors and competition among producers.

The contrast of intervention, isolation, and adaptation is suggestive as far as it goes, but it fails to canvass the alternatives fully or to explain the factors affecting choice among them. France and Germany isolated themselves from the world market, to the extent of the tariff. No country intervened to raise the world price of wheat, though this has been undertaken through international cooperation in the present century. England, Italy, and Denmark all adapted to the change, but in a variety of ways. Since a series of alternative adaptations was available and since adaptation was undertaken by large countries as well as by small, Wright's analysis fails to explain the differences in behavior that did occur. His emphasis on the necessity of small countries to adapt, however, suggests that larger countries are unable to adapt in the same way that is open to small countries. In Britain, for example, some substitution of cattle for sheep occurred, and over a longer period animal husbandry expanded to fill part of the gap left by a decline in croplands.[25] But, on the whole, Britain was content to import its wheat and its high-value protein foods as well. British agriculture lacked the energy, the resources, and the ability to devise the institutions that would have been necessary for large-scale conversion from arable cropping to animal husbandry.

Several Continental writers have provided an illuminating framework of analysis against which to contrast the behavior of Italy (and southeastern Europe from Hungary to the Volga) with that of the other countries. For example, F. Delaisi[26] distinguishes between Europe A, lying within a circle drawn through Stockholm, Vienna, Barcelona, Bilbao, and Glasgow, and Europe B, outside the circle. Europe A includes northern Italy, upper Austria, and Bohemia and Moravia, but leaves out Ireland, northern Scotland, and most of Spain. In Europe A, industrialization was possible because of the rise of the bourgeois and their insistence on the spread of education; even in agriculture there was established a basis for rural democracy as peasants acquired land. In Europe B, however, constitutions and parliaments had no roots, illiteracy prevailed, and the bourgeois class was small and timid, working with the aristocracy against the peasant and urban laborer rather than challenging the power of the feudal nobility.

When technological advance made industrialization possible, Europe A adopted it; Europe B gradually collapsed. After 1880 emigration rose sharply from Europe B, comprising particularly Italy, Austria-Hungary, Spain, Portugal, and Finland, as far as Delaisi's statistics went, but including also Russia, Yugoslavia, and Greece. For the countries covered by Delaisi, emigration overseas in the decade 1881 to 1890 amounted to 180,000 annually. In successive decades the annual average climbed to 265,000, 629,000, and 907,000 by 1901 to 1913.[27] In Europe *A*, on the other hand, emigration to overseas areas declined, after hitting new peaks in 1881 to 1885. This was because of the opportunities afforded by the expansion in industry.

This explanation by no means covers the situation in its entirety. Britain was much further along in the urbanization process than was Germany or France. This may help to a degree to explain why industry was ready to permit the liquidation of agriculture and why emigrants from agriculture found their way into cities rather than abroad. After industrialization has started, however, and has reached a point where the process is self-generating and cumulative, the rate of growth should be more important than the existing level of industry. And this pace after 1870 was faster in Germany than in Britain. Nor was industrialization meaningless in France: "While France accepted the new techniques and institutions of industry, and even played a significant role in developing them, she did not permit agriculture to be eclipsed, or to suffer revolutionary change."[28]

As between Italy and Denmark, the quality of agriculture was evidently more important than the proportions of population engaged in rural pursuits (which were of the same order of magnitude after adjustment for definitions of urban life). Delaisi's division of Europe into two, and his discussion of the extent to which the collapsing feudal structure was replaced by modern industrial and national institutions, are interesting. The fact of industrialization and the explanation of its concentration in northwestern Europe, however, fail to account for the differences among the responses of the several countries to the decline in the price of wheat.[29]

None of the foregoing explanations completely accounts for the differences in response to the market; and perhaps the differences should be approached from the standpoint of a theory of group behavior. To be adequate, such a theory must include not only criteria for differentiating the responses of national groups as a unit but also a system of analysis for interrelations among the subgroups within the larger unit. The existing theory of group behavior appears not to have coped adequately with this sort of question. In the main, social psychologists, sociologists, anthropologists, and so on, have concentrated their attention on the relation of the individual to the group, to the relative neglect of the structure of the very large group (the nation) and of functional groups within it.[30] Where intergroup relations have attracted attention, it had been focused on the problems posed by cultural minorities and the relations between groups differentiated by age, sex, and similar factors, rather than on large functional groups. Without a foundation in scientific literature, the following notions on group behavior are general and tentative.

A group must exist in space and time. To be effective, a group must have a system of communication and a set of common values. The existence of the national group in *space* hardly merits discussion. It is an elementary principle of geography that mountain ridges make the best national boundaries—though they are disliked by the military interests charged with protecting the group—since they are the national barriers of language, culture, and commerce. Rivers provide a system of intercommunication rather than a barrier to it, and a country lying in a great plain, like Poland, has uncertain limits. Water in larger amounts is helpful in demarcating the national space. The existence of Britons as a homogeneous group has been assisted by their insular position, while subgroups are demarcated by highlands. Changes in the national space have an important reaction on national cohesion. The Danish "groupiness," or group consciousness, was enhanced by the loss of Schleswig; the French, by that of Alsace-Lorraine. Italy and Germany, at the same time, gained group solidarity from unification in space.

The existence of a group in *time* is connected with its *set of values*. This must be sufficiently attractive or forceful in the spiritual or emotional life of the group for its members to express their loyalty to the group by remaining a part of it through time and bringing their children up as members. The existence of the group in time suggests a difference between material things and social institutions. Matter can wear out evenly over time; when a functional group recognizes that it is doomed to extinction, however, it is difficult to let it decline slowly at the normal rate of depreciation by refusal to maintain it. When faith in the continuity of the organization or group is lost, the group is likely to disintegrate.

The importance of *communication* to the group is increasingly emphasized by social psychologists working with small functional groups, such as the personnel of factories or unions. It is equally important in larger groups. Switzerland, where four languages are spoken, is cited as an illustration of its unimportance in certain situations. In this case space and a powerful set of values are sufficient to hold the group together. The subgroup of agriculture is typically weaker in cohesion than urban groups because of its dispersal in space and the resultant difficulty of communication among its members. The Folk Schools in Denmark and the formation of agricultural syndicates in France were requirements for the maintenance of the agricultural group in the face of the threat from reduced wheat prices.

An existence in space and a system of communication are not enough to constitute a functional group. The parts of the group must share a sense of identification and emotional involvement and a feeling of participation and purpose before the separate subgroups can be considered to make up a group. This sense of unity and purpose may be enhanced by the existence of an antithetical "out-group." If the sense if not very strong to begin with, however, the development of an out-group may lead to the disintegration of the "in-group."

The major contrast is between Denmark and Italy. In the former, national feeling was intense, as a result of territorial loss, and social cohesion was high. The rural population felt itself a unit and identified itself with the larger national unit. In Italy, despite the recent unification of 1860, the peasant's sense of belonging to the national group was feeble. A blow to his means of livelihood led to the disintegration of the national group, as far as he was concerned. He withdrew—the type of reaction which the classical economists thought was difficult because of cultural barriers and which, indeed, is today barred by the xenophobia of other national groups. Similar responses took place in the Balkans, the Iberian Peninsula, and throughout the rest of feudalistic Europe.

The weakness of the national group in Europe B, to use Delaisi's designation, was a result of the failure of national unity to replace the disintegrated feudal group structure. National groups lacked intercommunication and common values. Illiteracy, for example, ran from 10 percent in the Po Valley in Italy to 30 percent in Florence and Rome, 50 percent in Naples, and 70 percent in Calabria.[31] No new emotional attachment replaced the feudal ties that had bound the peasant to the latifundium. Group cohesion was too weak to meet the challenge and the group, under pressure, collapsed.

The importance of the out-group to the cohesion and efficiency of the national group is illustrated effectively by the role played by German aggression and the loss of Schleswig in the Danish response to the decline in wheat prices. Other examples are not lacking in economic history. The French payment of the five-billion-mark indemnity in 1871 was an act of national dedication—and even immolation. To generalize from this experience to the behavior of exports, imports, prices, and the banking system in similar situations where the group stimulus is absent is a familiar practice of economists,[32] but it is highly questionable.

The contrasting behavior of Britain, Germany, and France requires an understanding of more than the degree of group cohesion at the national level. Attention must be given to the relations among the separate subgroups. These, to be sure, have a bearing on the overall cohesiveness of the nation: a country in which the subgroups are not sharply differentiated and where a degree of social mobility between them exists is likely to have greater cohesion. For the moment, however, our attention is restricted to the relations among the economic subgroups.[33]

Walker asks, "When do men accept the verdict of the market, and when do they attempt to alter it?"[34] A parallel question can be put for group behavior: When does an ascendant subgroup liquidate another subgroup within the large group, and when does it make adjustment to it? Under what circumstances do relationships among subgroups tend to stay in continuous equilibrium, and when do divergences of interest lead in cumulative fashion (as Marx predicted) to schism and clash? Why did industry allow the liquidation of agriculture in Britain, but not in Germany or France? The question appears not to be a simple one of relative strengths or even of more complex strategies of coalition, such as those suggested in *The Theory of Games.* There was no reason for German steel manufacturing to accept coalition with an essentially backward[35] group of agriculturists or for French industry to make concessions to the prescientific peasant. The answer may be found in areas outside the normal province of the economic theorist or the economic historian. The decisive factors do not appear to lie in the field of economics at all, but in that of sociology.

One clue to intergroup behavior may be found in the notion that not all group relations are competitive. Bateson, the anthropologist, has listed a series of stable interdependent subgroup relationships, which, to be sure, primarily apply to subgroups based on age and sex. These include bipolar relations, such as spectator-exhibitionist, dominance-submission, succoring-dependence, aggression-passivity, and the like, but may extend to more complex arrangements. Among the latter Bateson distinguishes what he calls the "ternary relationship," which contains serial elements but includes face-to-face contact between the first and third elements. The function of the middle member in his illustrations—parent-nurse-child and officer-n.c.o.-enlisted man—is to discipline the third member in the forms of behavior that he should adopt toward the first.[36] The relations of the middle class to the wealthy and to the working classes may partake of this character in some political and social respects.[37]

This clue, by no means unambiguous, may assist in explaining what took place in Germany. Gerschenkron expresses the view that the Junkers deceived the peasants of western Germany, whose interest lay in cheaper grain prices, by provision for a tariff on animals and by other means. The reaction, however, may contain elements of submission of the peasant groups before the will of the Junker with higher status. Residual traces of the feudal relationship existed; probably more important were the battles won for the glory of the national group in 1864, 1866, and 1870. A portion of labor and even the steel barons were content to maintain the economic position of the Junkers, in the face of opportunity to liquidate them, because of the element of status, which for labor outweighed class interest. The leadership and dominance exhibited by the Junker class probably explain the major part of its success in maintaining its position through the Caprivi tariff, World War I, the inflation, and the Nazi regime.

Another clue may lie in that most complex conception, the basic personality type of a culture or subculture. This notion, developed by the social psychologist with the help of anthropological data, denies that human nature is a constant in time or space, but holds that the basic personality type of a culture will condition responses to external stimuli and in turn be altered by them. Of particular importance, it is held, is the way in which a society rears its children.[38]

This matter is far too complex and elusive to pursue here beyond the rough generalization that the basic personality type differs among England, France, and Germany in putting primary emphasis in the culture (below the level of the national group) on, respectively, the individual, the family, and the class. If we accept this, it may assist in explaining why Britain was willing to liquidate agriculture, while France and Germany were not.

Economic and political liberalism, born in Britain, required social mobility to give importance to the individual at the level next below the national group. Mobility in space was provided for Britain, as for Scandinavia and the Netherlands, by the sea, which served as a frontier.[39] At home, despite the class structure, social mobility upward derived from the willingness of the aristocracy to admit successful commercial and industrial interests to the ownership of land and their sons to the public schools. Downward mobility was provided by primogeniture, which drew off the increase in the aristocracy into the middle class. Whatever the facts, the concept of class as a functional subgroup was not recognized in the culture. A blow to a broad economic interest was regarded as affecting not a class but a loose aggregation of individuals.[40] This may account for the passivity of the nation in watching unmoved the liquidation of agriculture in the thirty years after 1879.[41]

The opposition of industry and agriculture in France was more apparent than real; both were concerned not with economic interest as such but with economic interest in a context of the dominant social institution of the family. This has been studied in industry, where the conclusion has been reached that the size of firm which could be kept in the family from generation to generation limited the growth of industry.[42] The unwillingness of the French to emigrate is further evidence. And the continuity of the French farm in the family group from generation to generation is a commonplace.

In Germany the major subgroup, at least at the extremes, was the class. To the extent that the nobility was a farming group in occupation, group solidarity and economic interest were unified in the Junker portion of agriculture, while they were opposed among the peasants. Such conflict of group and economic interest in not, however, unusual: Walker has expressed surprise that the farmers of Australia supported a program of land settlement contrary to their economic interest.[43] But these farmers gained more through the growth in numbers of their group than they lost through the increase of supply. The question was one of class and, within the total class structure, of dominance.

The Danish response to the decline in the world price of wheat was by far the most satisfactory, whether in social and economic terms or in economic terms alone. It raised the level of real income for the producer group at the same time as it preserved the gain of cheaper bread for the consumer. Social upheaval was avoided. Was the whole episode an accident? Was this sort of solution possible for the other countries? To what extent is it possible to capitalize disaster in this fashion on a general scale?

The mind of the economist is likely to try to find a parallel in certain situations that occur when wage increases lead to expansion rather than to contraction of output because they provide the incentive to a recombination of factors in more efficient fashion. The classic example is the elimination of the sweatshop through the efforts of union leaders, which increased incomes for both laborers and enterprisers and also reduced the cost of clothing. This was brought about by requiring firms in the garment industry to employ their newly expensive labor efficiently. The market opportunity for combining capital and labor in more efficient fashion had existed before the success of the union drive. Until the system was pushed off dead center, however, the path of least resistance was opposition to the demands of the union.

The parallel is not exact. Dairying to replace grain cultivation had been initiated in the 1860s before the decline in the price of wheat—primarily, however, on large estates.[44] The motive was only partly economic. In part it was observed that the soil was being impoverished by grain crops. There was still another difference. Although a market opportunity offered by the relative prices of grain and butter already existed, it was considerably increased by the decline in the price of wheat in the 1870s and 1880s and the rise in the demand for butter in the growing urban centers of England. A real impetus to the conversion came from the price decline. Particularly remarkable was the capacity of the Danish economy, or polity, to develop the institutions necessary to complete the conversion on a large scale to take maximum advantage of the economic opportunity.

It may be contended that there was a marked degree of accident in the existence of the middle-sized farm, which was inefficient for wheat, and in the development of the agricultural high school, in response to the loss of Schleswig. The explanation for the prevalence of the middle-sized farm would appear to lie deep in the Danish basic personality type, which emphasizes stability rather than growth.[45] The development of the Folk School was perhaps partly an accident, but the Danish peasant had always shown a communicating tendency,[46] and this fact may be more important than the particular form of institution devised at the particular time.

The development of the cooperative in response to a technological need raises more fundamental problems. What factors govern the capacity of a society to develop institutions required to enable it to take advantage of economic, political, and social opportunities? Are these adaptations always accidental? Under certain conditions are they made automatically, or can they be contrived through direction after conscious decision?

Most commentators on the cooperative believe that this development was the product of the prevalence of the freehold in Danish land tenure, together with the high degree of education in Danish farmers. "Tenant farmers will not co-operate because, co-operative accounts being open to inspection, they fear their landlords might raise the rents if it were found that they were prospering."[47] But the emphasis given to the form of land tenure goes deeper than this. The point is that cooperation in Denmark flourished because of the social cohesion that enabled the farmers to create the necessary institutions, when the occasion demanded economies of scale in marketing along with labor-intensive production. The prevalence of freeholds bespeaks equality of status, which makes communication freer in all directions. Education increases the quantity and quality of communication. Together with a high degree of communication, a closely held set of values, and internal social mobility—all of which are interrelated—Denmark had social cohesion. It was this factor that enabled her to create the institutions needed to take advantage of an economic opportunity. In the absence of the economic opportunity, however, the institutions would not have been devised.

In general, then, the flexibility of a society in devising institutions to accomplish its purposes under changing conditions is a function of its social cohesion, which in turn depends upon its internal social mobility, system of communications, and set of values. If social cohesion is high, it may be possible to find a response to external change that will bring about a new identification of the interests of the subgroups with those of the total group at an improved level of satisfaction for all. If the system of communication is sufficiently effective, moreover, it may be impossible to isolate the decision-making process, so that the response of the society appears to be automatic.

What I have said can be reduced to some fairly elementary propositions. The response that will be made to an economic stimulus in international trade cannot always be predicted from the nature and extent of the stimulus. It may require a knowledge of the group situation within the separate countries affected. The response may be the disintegration of the group, leading to emigration if that is possible, or, if no such outlet is available, to pathological political behavior. The effect, on the other hand, may range from the liquidation of a particular subgroup in the society for the benefit of others, as in Britain; to the protection of the affected group at the general expense, as in France and Germany; to an inspired act of re-adjustment undertaken by the group as a whole. Which of these actions will be taken lies deep in the structure of the society. For accurate prediction and policy formation, an adequate theory of the behavior of large groups and their components is needed as an adjunct to the analytical tools of the market.

Notes

1. *From Economic Theory to Policy,* passim.

2. *The Great Transformation,* passim.

3. Especially helpful have been Duncan Ballantine, John Blum, K. W. Deutsch, A. Gerschenkron, Bert F. Hoselitz, G. K. Krulee, E. E. Morison, W. W. Rostow, and J. E. Sawyer.

4. See Nourse, *American Agriculture,* appendix A. An earlier and entirely orthodox account is furnished by Veblen in "Price of Wheat since 1867."

5. See Ensor, *England, 1870–1914*, p. 116; and Ernle, *English Farming*, pp. 379–381.

6. See Jensen, *Danish Agriculture*, pp. 192 ff., esp. p. 212.

7. Ibid., statistical appendix. For a series of interesting contemporary European views see the Report of the U.S. Commissioner of Agriculture (1883), pp. 326–351 (quoted by Nourse, *American Agriculture*, pp. 271 ff.).

8. Slight differences in range and timing existed in separate markets because of differing transfer costs and the accessibility of different sources of supply. In Sweden, for example, which is not covered here, the comparable decline went from $1.34 per bushel in 1881 to $0.78 in 1887. See table II of the appendix to the useful "Decline and Recovery of Wheat Prices" (Food Research Institute, p. 347), which gives annual figures for a large number of countries.

9. Lewis and Maude, *English Middle Classes*, p. 171.

10. See Ensor, *England, 1870–1914*, p. 117.

11. This statement should perhaps be qualified by reference to the fair-trade agitation of the 1880s and the rise of protectionist sentiment in the 1890s under Joseph Chamberlain. Both these movements, however, were industrial in origin and sought to enlist rural support as an afterthought.
    Some weight should perhaps also be given to the roles of bad weather and pestilence, which delayed recognition of the importance of overseas competition. It is not certain that the reaction would have been equally passive had the country as a whole clearly understood the deep-seated nature of agriculture's troubles.

12. See Gerschenkron, *Bread and Democracy*, p. 45.

13. Ibid., pp. 26–29 and 57–58.

14. Golob, *The Méline Tariff*, pp. 81–82. I rely heavily on Golob's treatment.

15. International Institute of Agriculture, *World Trade*, pp. 794–798.

16. Hourwich, *Immigration and Labor*, p. 201, notes for a somewhat later period that more than 70 percent of Italian immigrants to the United States came from agricultural regions. Gross emigration rates differ from net, it may be observed, by rather sizable amounts because of the practice of transatlantic migration on a seasonal basis for harvesting, particularly to Argentina, by so-called *golondrinos* ("swallows").

17. For lack of readily available secondary material I have not investigated the course of events in Austria-Hungary, Sweden, Spain, and Portugal—which took action against new wheat imports—or in the Netherlands, Belgium, or Switzerland—which did not. A cursory examination of the tariff schedules (see Food Research Institute, "Decline and Recovery of Wheat Prices, table 7, p. 350) and of annual figures for gross emigration overseas (*Annuaire statistique de France*, 1914–15, pt. 3, p. 164) suggests that Austria-Hungary and Sweden were equally tardy in protecting agriculture and equally affected by emigration. Gerschenkron (*Bread and Democracy*, pp. 40–41) gives an interpretation of the Swiss experience.

18. See Jensen, *Danish Agriculture*, p. 133.

19. A more complete statement might attach importance to types of soil.

20. Jensen, *Danish Agriculture*, p. 101: "After the defeat in the war of 1864, the work which was already begun was taken up by able and enthusiastic men." See also Westergaard, *Economic Developments*, p. 13: "For the economic life of Denmark [the War of 1864] was of still

greater importance in that it gave industry a strong impetus for attacking and solving the many problems which pressed upon it within the country's narrowed boundaries."

21. For an account of forerunners see Faber, *Co-operation in Danish Agriculture*, pp. 25–30.

22. See Golob, *The Méline Tariff*, pp. 145 ff.

23. I have discussed elsewhere the antithesis between the views of Keynes, who asserted that the world is ruled by little else than the theories of economists and political philosophers, and those of Arnold, who classes the economist with the lawyer and the scholar as performing a purely ceremonial role (see Arnold, *Folklore of Capitalism*, esp. chap. 4; and Keynes, *General Theory of Employment*, p. 383).

24. See his *Economic Adaptation to a Changing World Market*.

25. Ensor, *England, 1870–1914*, p. 117. It may be observed that some protection was afforded to British cattle interests by the sanitary regulations, passed in the 1890s, that forbade the import of live animals from the Continent and overseas. The principal competition for home-grown meat, even at this time, however, was in meat imported from the Southern Hemisphere, a trade that developed with the innovation of refrigerated ships in the 1880s. Beef grazing, however, is far less labor intensive than dairying and would have been, from the point of view of employment, a much less satisfactory adaptation.

26. In *Les Deux Europes*.

27. Delaisi, *Les Deux Europes*, p. 207. These sources are called "new," in contrast with Germany, Ireland, and Britain, in Jerome, *Migration and Business Cycles*. It may be noted that emigration from Ireland fluctuated parallel to that of Europe *A*, even though it lies in Europe *B* in Delaisi's scheme.

28. Golob, *the Méline Tariff*, p. 8.

29. Roepke (*Social Crisis of Our Times*) finds the clue to the development of agriculture in the various countries of Europe in the existence or absence of a sturdy peasant body. Its absence accounts for the injury to British agriculture; its presence for the Danish success (pp. 245–246). The peasantry of Italy and "southeast Europe lacked soundness" (p. 204). Wheat protection favors large estates and is detrimental to peasant agriculture (p. 247). But this analysis fails to cover the French case, where peasants gained from protection; and Roepke himself fatally damages the consistency of his position in the statement, "Admittedly, agriculture is that part of the national economic system to which the principles of a free market economy could only be applied with broad reservations" (p. 205).

30. This statement is perhaps unfair to Talcott Parsons and Robert K. Merton and their structural-functional approach to sociology, with which I am inadequately acquainted. For an attempt to apply this to the French economy see Sawyer, "Strains in Modern France."

31. Delaisi, *Les Deux Europes*, pp. 46–47.

32. See, for example, Machlup, "Three Concepts of Balance of Payments," p. 59n.

33. An individual in the society, of course, will belong to a variety of subgroups based on his occupation, class, religion, avocations, age, sex, race, and so on.

34. *From Economic Theory to Policy*, p. 109.

35. This characterization is objected to as unfair to the Junkers, who—whatever their disagreeable attributes—were men of responsibility who energetically farmed their own land in

the face of natural difficulties rather than live off the unearned increment in absentia. Yet they were backward in the sense that they clung to traditional crops farmed with traditional techniques. Perhaps a more appropriate adjective is "static."

36. Bateson, "Morale and National Character."

37. See, for example, Lewis and Maude, *English Middle Classes*, passim.

38. See Benedict, *Patterns of Culture*; Kardiner, *Psychological Frontiers of Society*; Kluckhohn, *Mirror for Man*. Given the emphasis on anthropological data, primary attention has been devoted to the personality types of culture rather than subcultures, and Kardiner, for example, regards Western man as a homogeneous type. This notion is in process of correction at the hands of Bateson, Gorer, Meade, and others.

39. See Innis, *Political Science in the Modern State*, p. 87.

40. A number of writers have referred to the alleged inability of the British farmer to cooperate because of his individualism. See, for instance, Russell, who states in his foreword to Faber's *Co-operation in Danish Agriculture*, pp. vii–viii: "The British method, in short, proved less capable of adaptation to new and adverse conditions than the Danish. Critics may argue … that the British farmer is so confirmed an individualist and so imbued with the idea of running his own farm in his own way that he cannot co-operate with his neighbor. It may or may not be so." See also Haggard, *Rural Denmark*, p. 273: "The Danes look upon their land as a principal means of livelihood … —in short, as a business proposition in which the Nation is most vitally concerned. In the main, although we [British] may not acknowledge it, we look upon our land, or much of it, as a pleasure proposition in which the individual only is concerned." Haggard also cites (pp. 192–193) the sad case of a Norfolk honorable secretary of a rat and sparrow club who was unable to enlist any cooperation from potential benefactees.

41. See note 11 above.

42. Landes, "French Entrepreneurship."

43. *From Economic Theory to Policy*, pp. 123 and 222–223. Another case is probably that of the American Medical Association, which is unified in opposing expenditures on health by governmental bodies, which would increase the incomes of the vast majority of its members.

44. Faber, *Co-operation in Danish Agriculture*, pp. 31–32.

45. See Benedict, *Patterns of Culture*, pp. 53–56, and chap. 4 for a discussion of the Spenglerian contrast between Apollonian and Faustian cultures and the description of a self-balancing society. Bateson has described another such primitive society in *Naven*. Oppenheimer mentions other instances of the prevalence of small and medium-sized landholdings in Utah, Iowa, and New Zealand in "The Tendency of Development," in Calverton, *Making of Society*, pp. 40–42. Cf. Haggard's literary description of the Danes as "tolerant-minded" (*Rural Denmark*, p. 212).

46. See Faber, *Co-operation in Danish Agriculture*, p. 7.

47. Haggard, *Rural Denmark*, p. 190.

References

Arnold, Thurman W. *The Folklore of Capitalism*. New Haven, CT: Yale University Press, 1937.

Bateson, Gregory. "Morale and National Character." In G. Watson, ed., *Civilian Morale.* Cambridge: Cambridge University Press, 1942, pp. 71–81.

Benedict, Ruth. *Patterns of Culture.* Cambridge Mass.: Houghton Mifflin, 1934.

Delaisi, F. *Les deux Europes.* Paris: Payot, 1929.

Ensor, R. C. K. *England, 1870–1914.* Oxford: Oxford University Press, 1936.

Faber, Harald. *Co-operation in Danish Agriculture.* 2nd ed. London: Longmans Green, 1931.

Food Research Institute. "Decline and Recovery in Wheat Prices in the Nineties." *Wheat Studies* 10 (1934).

Gerschenkron, Alexander. *Bread and Democracy in Germany.* Berkeley: University of California Press, 1942.

Golob, E. O. *The Méline Tariff: French Agriculture and National Economic Policy.* New York: Columbia University Press, 1944.

Haggard, H. Rider. *Rural Denmark and Its Lessons.* London: Longmans, Green, 1911.

Hourwich, I. A. *Immigration and Labor.* New York: Hubesch, 1922.

International Institute of Agriculture. *World Trade in Agricultural Products.* Rome: IIA, 1940.

Jenson, Einar. *Danish Agriculture: Its Economic Development.* Copenhagen: Munksgaard, 1937.

Jerome, H. *Migration and Business Cycles.* New York: National Bureau of Economic Research, 1926.

Keynes, John Maynard. *The General Theory of Employment, Interest, and Money.* New York: Harcourt, Brace, 1936.

Kluckhorn, Clyde. *Mirror for Man.* New York: Whittlesey House, 1949.

Landes, David S. "French Entrepreneurship and Industrial Growth in the Nineteenth Century," *Journal of Economic History* 9 (1949): 45–61.

Lewis, Roy, and Angus Maude. *The English Middle Classes.* London: Phoenix House, 1949.

Nourse, E. G. *American Agriculture and the European Market.* New York: McGraw-Hill, 1924.

Oppenheimer, Franz. "The Tendency of the Development of the States." In V. F. Calverton, ed., *The Making of Society.* New York: Random House, 1937.

Polanyi, Karl. *The Great Transformation.* New York: Farrar and Rinehart, 1944.

Roepke, Wilhelm. *The Social Crisis of Our Times.* Chicago: Chicago University Press, 1950.

Sawyer, John E. "Strains in the Social Structure of Modern France." In E. M. Earle, ed., *Modern France.* Princeton, N. J.: Princeton University Press, 1951.

Walker, E. Ronald. *From Economic Theory to Policy.* Chicago: University of Chicago Press, 1943.

Wright, Carl Major. *Economic Adaptation to a Changing World Market.* Copenhagen: Munksgaard, 1939.

5

The Rise of Free Trade in Western Europe, 1820 to 1875

The textbook theory of tariffs and their converse, the movement to freer trade, has more elements than we need for the nineteenth century, but also lacks some. In the usual comparative statistics a tariff may be said to have ten effects: on price, trade, production (the protective effect), consumption, revenue, terms of trade, internal income distribution, monopoly, employment, and the balance of payments.

For present purposes we can dispense with the employment effect. The terms-of-trade effect arises only in connection with export taxes; and the monopoly effect must be converted to dynamic form, that increased imports stimulate growth by forcing competition and responsive innovation.

We may illustrate the bulk of the needed effects with the simplest of partial-equilibrium diagrams of a familiar sort. In figure 5.1, an import tariff, t, raises the domestic price, P_t, above the world price, P_w (assumed to be unaffected by the tariff), reduces trade from MM to $M'M'$, expands production by MM', and reduces consumption by $M'M$. An increase in rent to producers consists in the quadrilateral a; revenue accruing to the government is represented by b. Removal of the tariff reverses all movements. An export tax as in figure 5.2 reduces price and trade, cuts down on producers' rent, increases consumption, reduces production, and earns governmental revenue. Conversely, removal of an export tax raises price, production, and producers' rent, enlarges trade, reduces domestic consumption, loses revenue. In the nineteenth century, when direct taxation was limited, the revenue effect could not be disregarded as it is today. Prohibition of exports or imports had in varying degree all other effects on price, trade, production, consumption, redistribution, monopoly, but wiped out revenue (and the terms of trade). This assumed that the prohibition or prohibitive tax was not undermined by smuggling.

Static theory needs two further elements. The first is a theory of incidence. With more than two factors, are rents retained by the initial recipient

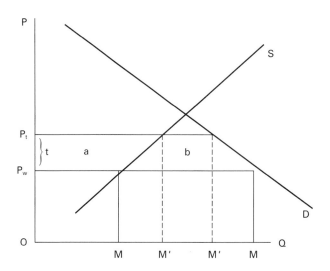

Figure 5.1
Import tax in partial equilibrium

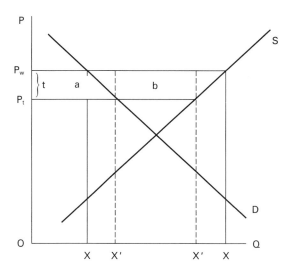

Figure 5.2
Export tax in partial equilibrium

or are they competed away in bidding for still more scarce resources? The second is another factor, or institutional interest, beyond the normal agriculture and manufacturing, that is, the merchant, with whom may be included shipping. The merchant is interested in maximizing trade not for its impact on production or consumption, but to increase turnover, on which—provided national merchants and ships are used—he earns a return. For trade any goods will do, including those of foreigners which have no impact on domestic production or consumption of the goods in question. (Shipping interests of course insist on the use of national-flag vessels.)

Such is the economic model. Political and sociological elements will be added as required and will include: the view (for example, of Cobden) that free trade leads to peace; trade treaties as foreign treaties in general, desired for reasons of foreign policy, balance of power, and the like; ideology; bandwagon effects; and the need of most men to be consistent. It is especially necessary to indicate the relationships between economic interest and political power.

In his interesting study of the formation of the United States tariff of 1824, Jonathan Pincus asserts that tariff making can be explained by the success or failure of various interests in obtaining rents, the quadrilateral a in figure 5.1. In his view the tariff is a collective good, passage of which requires limited numbers of concentrated producers: if the interested parties are diffuse, the fallacy of composition takes over as each element seeks to become a "free rider," leaving the transaction costs of engineering the tariff change to others. This is a theory applicable to representative democracies and leaves little room for executive leadership.[1] Nor does it make allowance for intermediate goods.

That diffuse interests are less well served than concentrated ones in the legislative process is widely accepted in the theory of tariff formation by comparing producers and final consumers. Households count for little in tariff making, since the interest of any one is too small to stir it to the political effort and financial cost necessary to achieve results. With intermediate goods, however, the consumption effect cannot be disregarded; industries that rely on a given import, or on a product exported by another industry, may be as effectively concentrated as producers of final goods.

In the Pincus theory, the movement toward free trade in western Europe would have to be based on the dominance of the interests of consumers of intermediate imports over those of their producers, and of producers of exports over consumers of exported intermediates. A variety of other general explanations has been offered.

In Bastiat's view, the rise of free trade was the result of the spread of democracy.[2] Free trade has also been regarded as the interest of the bourgeois class in England and of the landed aristocracy on the Continent, while protection has been sought by the aristocracy in England and by the bourgeois manufacturing classes on the Continent.[3]

Somewhat more dynamically, Johnson asserts that countries whose competitiveness in world markets is improving tend to move in the free-trade direction, while countries whose competitiveness is deteriorating tend to move to increasing protection. A footnote states, "Outstanding examples are the adoption of free trade by Britain in the 19th century ... the espousal of freer trade by the United States and Canada in the period after the Second World War."[4]

In what follows we shall find these views insufficiently detailed.

The beginnings of free trade internationally go back to the eighteenth century. French Physiocratic theory enunciated the slogan *laissez faire, laissez passer* to reduce export prohibitions on agricultural products. Pride of place in practice, however, goes to Tuscany, which permitted free export of the corn of the Sienese Maremma in 1737, after the Grand Duke Francis had read Sallustio Bandini's *Economical Discourse*.[5] Beset by famine in 1764, Tuscany gradually opened its market to imported grain well before the Vergennes Treaty of 1786 between France and Britain put French Physiocratic doctrine into practice. Grain exports in Tuscany had been restricted under the "policy of supply," or "provisioning," or "abundance," under which the city-states of Italy limited exports from the surrounding countryside in order to assure food to the urban populace. Bandini and Pompeo Neri pointed out the ill effects this had on investment and productivity in agriculture.

The policy of supply was not limited to food. In the eighteenth and early nineteenth centuries there were restrictions on exports in, for instance, wool and coal (Britain), ashes, rags, sand for glass, and firewood (Germany), ship timbers (Austria), rose madder (the Netherlands), and silk cocoons (Italy). The restrictions on exports of ashes and timber from Germany had conservation overtones. The industrial revolution in Britain led further to prohibitions on export of machinery and on emigration of artisans, partly to increase the supply for local use, but also to prevent the diffusion of technology on the Continent. We return to this below.

What was left in the policy of supply after the Napoleonic wars quickly ran down. Prohibition of export of raw silk was withdrawn in Piedmont, Lombardy, and Venetia in the 1830s, and freedom to export coal from

Britain was enacted in the 1840s. Details of the relaxation of restrictions are recorded for Baden[6] as part of the movement to occupational freedom. The guild system gradually collapsed under the weight of increasing complexity of regulation by firms seeking exceptions for themselves and objecting to exceptions for others. A number of prohibitions and export taxes lasted to the 1850s—as industrial consumers held out against producers, or in some cases, like rags, against collectors of waste products. Reduction of the export tax on rags in Piedmont in 1851 produced a long, drawn-out struggle between Cavour and the industry, which had to close up thirteen plants when the tax was reduced.[7] To Cavour salvation of the industry lay in machinery and in substitution of other materials, not in restricting export through Leghorn and Messina to Britain and North America.

Elimination of export taxes and prohibitions in nineteenth-century Europe raises doubt about the universal validity of the theory of the tariff as a collective good, imposed by a concentrated interest at the expense of the diffuse. The interests of groups producing inputs for other industries are normally more deeply affected than those of the consuming industries, but it is hardly possible that the consuming is always less concentrated than the producing industry.

The question of export duties sought by domestic manufacturers on their raw materials, and of import duties on outputs demanded by producers for the domestic market was settled in the Netherlands in the eighteenth century in favor of mercantile interests.[8] These were divided into the First Hand—merchants, shipowners, and bankers; the Second Hand—which carried on the work of sorting and packing in staple markets and of wholesaling on the Continent; and the Third Hand—concerned with distribution in the hinterland. Dutch staple trade was based partly on mercantile skills and partly on the pivotal location of Amsterdam, Rotterdam, and other towns dedicated to trade in particular commodities, largely perishable, nonstandardized, and best suited to short voyages. The First Hand dominated Dutch social and political life and opposed all tariffs on export or import goods, above a minimum for revenue, in order to maximize trade and minimize formalities. From 1815 to 1830, when Holland and Belgium were united as the Low Countries, the clash between the Dutch First Hand and Belgian producers in search of import protection from British manufacturers was continuous and heated.

The First Hand objected to taxes for revenue on coffee, tea, tobacco, rice, sugar, and so on, and urged their replacement by excises on flour, meat, horses, and servants.[9] They urged that tariffs for revenue be held down to prevent smuggling and to sustain turnover. The safe maximum was given variously as 3 percent,[10] 5 percent,[11] and on transit even as 0.5 percent. Transit in bond and transit with duty-cum-drawback were thought too cumbersome. The Dutch made a mistake in failing to emulate London, which in 1803 adopted a convenient entrepot dock with bonding.[12] Loss of colonies and of overseas connections in the Napoleonic wars made it impossible from early in the period for Holland to compete with Britain in trade. Equally threatening was Hamburg, which supplied British and colonial goods to Central Europe in transit for 0.5 percent revenue duty maximum,[13] many products free, and all so after 1839.[14] More serious, however, was the rise of direct selling as transport efficiency increased. Early signs of direct selling can be detected at the end of the seventeenth century when Venice and Genoa lost their role as intermediaries in traffic between Italy and the West.[15] By the first half of the nineteenth century such signs were abundant. "By the improved intercourse of our time [1840], the seller is brought more immediately into contact with the producer."[16] Twenty years earlier the Belgian members of a Dutch-Belgian fiscal commission argued that "there was no hope of restoring Holland's general trade. Owing to the spread of civilization, all European countries could now provide for themselves in direct trading."[17]

It is a mistake to think of merchants as all alike. As indicated, the First, Second, and Third Hands of the Netherlands had different functions, status, and power. In Germany republican merchants of Hamburg differed sharply from those of the imperial city, Frankfurt, and held out fifty years longer against the Zollverein.[18] Within Frankfurt there were two groups, the English-goods party associated with the bankers, and the majority, which triumphed in 1836, interested in transit, forwarding, and retail and domestic trade within the Zollverein. In Britain a brilliant picture had been drawn of a pragmatic free trader, John Gladstone, father of William, opposed to timber preferences for Canada, enemy of the East India Company monopoly on trade with China and India, but supportive of imperial preference in cotton and sugar and approving of the Corn Laws on the ground of support for the aristocracy he hoped his children could enter via politics.[19] The doctrinaire free traders of Britain were the cotton manufacturers like Gladstone's friend, Kirman Finlay, who regarded shipowners and corn growers as the two great sets of monopolists.

The doctrinaire free trade of the Dutch merchants led to economic sclerosis[20] or economic sickness.[21] Hamburg stayed in trade and finance and did not move into industry. In Britain merchants were ignorant of industry, but were saved by the coming of the railroad and by limited liability, which provided an outlet for their surplus as direct trading squeezed profits from stapling. The economic point is simple: free trade may stimulate, but it may also fossilize.

The movement toward freer trade in Britain began gross in the eighteenth century, net only after the Napoleonic wars. In the initial stages there was little problem for a man like Wedgwood to advocate free trade for exports of manufactures under the Treaty of Vergennes with France, and at the same time to advocate prohibitions on the export of machinery and emigration of artisans.[22] Even in the 1820s and 1830s a number of the political economists—Torrens, Baring, Peel, Nassau Senior—favored repeal of the Corn Laws but opposed export of machinery.[23] The nineteenth century is seen by Brebner not as a steady march to laissez-faire but as a counterpoint between Smithian laissez-faire in trade matters and, after the Reform Bill, Benthamic intervention of 1832, which produced the Factory, Mines, Ten Hours, and similar acts from 1833 to 1847.[24]

First came the revenue aspect, which was critical of the movement to freer trade under Huskisson in the 1820s, Peel in the 1840s, and Gladstone in the 1850s. Huskisson and Gladstone used the argument that the bulk of revenue was produced by taxes on a few items—largely colonial products such as tea, coffee, sugar, tobacco, and wine and spirits—and that others produced too little revenue to be worth the trouble. Many were redundant (for example, import duties on products that Britain exported). Others were so high as to be prohibitory or encouraged smuggling and reduced revenue. When Peel was converted to free trade, it was necessary to reintroduce the income tax before he could proceed between 1841 and 1846 with repeal of 605 duties and reductions in 1,035 others. The title of Sir Henry Parnell's treatise on freer trade (1830) was *Financial Reform*.

But Huskisson was a free trader, if a cautious one. He spoke of benefits to be derived from the removal of "vexatious restraints and meddling interference in the concerns of internal industry and foreign commerce."[25] Especially he thought that imports stimulated efficiency in import-competing industry. In 1824 the prohibition on silk imports had been converted to a duty of 30 percent, regarded as the upper limit of discouragement to smuggling. In a speech on March 24, 1826, said by Canning to be the finest he had heard in the House of Commons, Huskisson observed that Macclesfield and Spitalfield had reorganized the industry under the spur of enlarged imports and expanded the scale of output.[26]

Both Michel Chevalier[27] and Count Cavour[28] referred to this positive and dynamic response to increased imports in England.

Restrictions on export of machinery and emigration of artisans went back, as indicated, to the industrial revolution. Prohibition of export of stocking frames was enacted as early as 1696. Beginning in 1774 there was a succession of restrictions on tools and utensils for the cotton and linen trades and on the emigration of skilled artisans. The basis was partly the policy of supply, partly naked maintenance of monopoly. Freedom had been granted for the emigration of workmen in 1824. After the depression of the late 1830s, pressure for removal of the prohibition came from all machinery manufacturers. Following further investigation by a Select Committee of Parliament, the export prohibition was withdrawn.

The main arguments against prohibition of the export of machinery and emigration of artisans were three: they were ineffective, they were unnecessary, they were harmful. Ineffectuality was attested to by much detail in the Select Committee reports on the efficiency of smuggling. Machinery for which licenses could not be obtained could be dispatched illegally in a number of ways—by another port, hidden in cotton bales, in baggage, or mixed with permitted machinery—and in a matter of hours. Guaranteed and insured shipments could be arranged in London or Paris for premiums up to 30 percent.

That prohibition was unnecessary was justified first by the inability of foreigners, even with English machinery and English workmen, to rival English manufacturers. Britain had minerals, railways, canals, rivers, better division of labor, "trained workmen habituated to all industrious employments."[29] "Even when the Belgians employed English machines and skilled workers, they failed to import the English spirit of enterprise and secured only disappointing results."[30] In 1825 the Select Committee concluded it was safe to export machinery, since seven-year-old machinery in Manchester was already obsolete.[31]

In the third place prohibition was dangerous. Restriction on emigration of artisans failed to prevent their departure, but did inhibit their return.[32] Restriction of machinery, moreover, raised the price abroad through the cost of smuggling and stimulated production on the Continent. Improvement in the terms of trade through restriction of exports (but failure to cut them off altogether) was deleterious because of its protective effect abroad.

Greater cohesion of the Manchester cotton spinners than of the machinery makers spread over Manchester, Birmingham, and London may account for the delay from 1825 to 1841 in freeing up machinery and support Pincus' theory on the need of concentrated interests. But the argument of consistency was telling. In 1800 the Manchester manufacturers of cloth had demanded a law forbidding export of yarn, but did not obtain it.[33] The 1841 Second Report concluded that machinery making should be put on the same footing as other departments of British industry.[34] It is noted that Nottingham manufacturers approved free trade, but claimed an exception in regard to machinery used in their own manufacture.[35] Babbage observed that machinery makers are more intelligent than their users, to whose imagined benefits their interests are sacrificed, and referred to the "impolicy of interfering between two classes."[36] In the end, the Manchester Chamber of Commerce became troubled and divided by the inconsistency; the issue of prohibition of machinery was subsumed into the general attack on the Corn Laws.[37] In the 1840s, moreover, the sentiment spread that Britain should become the workshop of the world, which implied the production of heavy goods as well as cotton cloth and yarn.[38]

Rivers of ink have been spilled on the repeal of the Corn Laws, and the present chapter can do little but summarize the issues and indicate a position. The questions relate to the Stolper-Samuelson distribution argument, combined with the Reform Bill of 1832 and the shift of political power from the landed aristocracy to the bourgeois; incidence of the Corn Laws and of their repeal, within both farming and manufacturing sectors; the potential for a dynamic response of farming to lower prices from competition; and the relation of repeal to economic development on the Continent, especially whether industrialization could be halted by expanded and assured outlets for agricultural produce, a point of view characterized by Gallagher and Robinson as "free-trade imperialism."[39] A number of lesser issues may be touched upon incidentally: interaction between the Corn Laws and the Zollverein, and the tariff changes in the 1840s; the question of whether repeal of the Corn Laws and of the Navigation Acts would have been very long delayed had it not been for potato famine in Ireland and on the Continent; and the question of whether the term "free-trade imperialism" is better reserved for Joseph Chamberlain's empire preference of fifty years later.

In the usual view the Reform Bill of 1832 shifted power from land and country to factory and city, from the aristocratic class to the bourgeois, and inexorably led to changes in trade policies that had favored farming and hurt manufacturing. One can argue that repeal of the Corn Laws represented something less than that, and that the Reform Bill was not critical. The movement to free trade had begun earlier in the Huskisson reforms; speeches in Parliament were broadly the same in 1825, when it was dominated by landed aristocrats, as in the 1830s and 1840s. Numbers had changed with continued manufacturing expansion, but not much more. Or one can reject the class explanation, as Polanyi does, and see something much more ideological. "Not until the 1830s did economic liberalism burst forth as a crusading passion." The liberal creed involved faith in man's secular salvation through a self-regulating market, a faith that was held with fanaticism and evangelical fervor.[40] French Physiocrats were trying to correct only one inequity, to break out of the policy of supply and permit export of grain. British political economists of the 1830s and 1840s, who won over Tories like Sir Robert Peel and Lord Russell and ended up in 1846 with many landlords agreeable to repeal of the Corn Laws, represented an ideology.[41] "Mere class interests cannot offer a satisfactory explanation for any long-run social process."[42]

Under a two-sector model free trade comes when the abundant factor acquires political power and moves to eliminate restrictions imposed in the interest of the scarce factor, which has lost power. In reality factors of production are not monolithic. Some confusion in the debate attached to the incidence of the tax on imported corn within both farming and manufacturing. The Anti-Corn Law League of Cobden and Bright regarded it as a tax on food, which took as much as 20 percent of the earnings of a hand-loom weaver. Cobden denied the "fallacy" that wages rose and fell with the price of bread.[43] Benefits, moreover, went to the landlord and not the farmer or farm laborer, as rents on the short leases in practice rose with the price of corn.[44] There are passages in Cobden which suggest that the brunt of the Corn Laws fell on the manufacturing and commercial classes rather than labor,[45] but the speeches run mainly in terms of a higher standard of living for the laborer who would spend his "surplus of earnings on meat, vegetables, butter, milk and cheese," rather than on wheaten loaves.[46] The Chartists were interested not in repeal, but in other amenities for the workers. Peel's conversion came with his conclusion that wages did not vary with the price of provision, and that repeal would benefit the wage earner rather than line the pockets of the manufacturer.[47]

In any event, with Gladstone's reductions in duties on meat, eggs, and dairy products, with High Farming (that is, improved farming techniques), and with end to the movement off the farm and out of handwork into the factory, real wages did rise in the 1850s, but so did profits on manufacturing. As so often happens in economic debates over outcomes, history blurred the experiment. Theory suggested that repeal of the Corn Laws would benefit either wages in manufacturing or manufacturers' profits. It benefited both. Nor did repeal bring a reduction in incomes to landlords—at least not for thirty years; the farm response to repeal, and to high prices of food produced by the potato famine, was more High Farming.

Cobden may have been only scoring debating points rather than speaking from conviction when on a number of occasions he argued that the repeal would stimulate landlords "to employ their capital and their intelligence as other classes are forced to do in other pursuits" rather than "in sluggish indolence," and to double the quantity of grain, or butter, or cheese, that the land is capable of providing,[48] with "longer leases, draining, extending the length of fields, knocking down hedgerows, clearing away trees which now shield the corn,"[49] and to provide more agricultural employment by activity to "grub up hedges, grub up thorns, drain, ditch."[50] Sir James Caird insisted that High Farming was the answer to the repeal of the Corn Laws,[51] and many shared his view.[52] The fact is, moreover, that the 1850s were the golden age of British farming, with rapid technical progress through the decade, though it slowed thereafter. Repeal of the Corn Laws may not have stimulated increased efficiency in agriculture, but it did not set it back immediately, and only after the 1870s did increases in productivity run down.

The political economists in the Board of Trade—Bowring, Jacob, MacGregor—sought free trade as a means of slowing down the development of manufacturing on the Continent. They regarded the Zollverein as a reply to the imposition of the Corn Laws and thought that with its repeal Europe, especially the Zollverein under the leadership of Prussia, could be diverted to invest more heavily in agriculture and to retard the march to manufacturing. There were inconsistencies between this position and other facts they adduced: Bowring recognized that Germany had advantages over Great Britain for the development of manufacturing, and that Swiss spinning had made progress without protection.[53] The 1818 Prussian tariff which formed the basis for that of the Zollverein was the lowest in Europe when it was enacted—although the levying of tariffs on cloth and yarn by weight gave high effective rates of protection despite low nominal duties to the cheaper constructions and counts. Jacob noted that the export supply elasticity of Prussian grain must be low, given poor transport.[54] "To export machinery, we must import corn";[55] but imports of corn were intended to prevent the development of manufacturers abroad, whereas the export of machinery assisted it. The rise and progress of German manufacturing were attributed to restrictions imposed by France and England on the admission of German agricultural products and wood, but also to "the natural advantages of the several states for manufacturing industry, the genius and laborious character and the necessities of the German people, and ... especially the unexampled duration of peace, and internal tranquility which all Germany enjoyed."[56]

The clearest statements are those of John Bowring. In a letter of August 28, 1839, to Lord Palmerston he asserted that the manufacturing interest in the Zollverein "is greatly strengthened and will become stronger from year to year unless counteracted by a system of concessions, conditional upon the gradual lowering of tariffs. The present state of things will not be tenable. The tariffs will be elevated under the growing demands and increasing power of the manufacturing states, or they will be lowered by calling into action, and bringing over to an alliance, the agricultural and commercial interests."[57] In his testimony before the Select Committee on Import Duties in 1840 he went further: "I believe we have created an unnecessary rivalry by our vicious legislation; that many of these countries never would have been dreamed of being manufactures."[58]

From this viewpoint, repeal of the Corn Laws was motivated by "free-trade imperialism," the desire to gain a monopoly of trade with the world in manufactured goods. The Zollverein in the 1830s merely indicated the need for haste.[59] Torrens and James Deacon Hume, among others, had been pushing for importing corn to expand exports in the 1820s, before the Zollverein was a threat.

Reciprocity had been a part of British commercial policy in the Treaty of Vergennes in 1786 and in treaties reducing the impact of the Navigation Laws in the 1820s and 1830s. The French were suspicious, fearing that they had been outtraded in 1786. They evaded Huskisson's negotiations in 1828. But reciprocity was unnecessary, given David Hume's Law. Unilateral reduction of import duties increased exports.[60] Restored to the British diplomatic armory in 1860, reciprocity later became heresy in the eyes of political economists, and of the manufacturing interests as well.

The view that ascribes repeal of the Corn Laws to free-trade imperialism, however, fails adequately to take account of the ideology of the political economists, who believed in buying in the cheapest market and selling in the highest, or of the short-run nature of the interests of the Manchester merchants themselves. It was evident after the 1840s that industrialization on the Continent could not be stopped, and likely that it could not be slowed down. The Navigation Acts were too complex; they needed to be eliminated.[61] The Corn Laws were doomed, even before the Irish potato famine (though that hastened the end of both Corn Laws and Navigation Acts), along with its demonstration of the limitation of market solutions under some circumstances.[62]

As Mill said, "A good cause seldom triumphs unless someone's interest is bound up with it."[63] Free trade is the hypocrisy of the export interest, the clever device of the climber who kicks the ladder away when he has attained the summit of greatness.[64] But in the English case it was more a view of the world at peace, with cosmopolitan interests served as well as national.

It is difficult in this to find clearcut support for any of the theories of tariff formation set forth earlier. Free trade as an export-interest collective good, sought in a representative democracy by concentrated interests to escape the free rider, would seem to require a simple and direct connection between the removal of the tariff and the increase in rents. In the repeal of the Corn Laws, and the earlier tariff reductions of Huskisson and Peel, the connection was roundabout—through Hume's law, which meant that increased imports would lead to increased prices or quantities exported (or both) on the one hand, and/or through reduced wages, or higher real incomes from lower food prices, on the other. Each chain of reasoning had several links.

Johnson's view that free trade is adopted by countries with improving competitiveness is contradictory to the free-trade-imperialism explanation, that free trade is adopted in an effort to undermine foreign gains in manufacturing when competitiveness has begun to decline. The former might better account in timing for Adam Smith's advocacy of free trade seventy years earlier—though that had large elements of French Physiocratic thought—or apply to the 1820s when British productivity was still improving, before the Continent had started to catch up. Actually, free-trade imperialism is a better explanation for the 1830s than for the end of the 1840s, since by 1846 it was already too late to slow, much less to halt, the advance of manufacturing on the Continent.

Vested interests competing for rents in a representative democracy, thrusting manufacturers seeking to expand markets, or faltering innovators trying as a last resort to force exports on shrinking markets—rather like the stage of foreign direct investment in Vernon's product cycle when diffusion of technology has been accomplished—none of these explanations seems free of difficulties when compared with an ideological explanation based on the intellectual triumph of the political economists, their doctrines modified to incorporate consistency. The argument took many forms: static, dynamic, with implicit reliance on one incidence or another, direct or indirect in its use of Hume's law. But the Manchester school, based on the political economists, represented a rapidly rising ideology of freedom for industry to buy in the cheapest and sell in the dearest market.

It overwhelmed the Tories when it did not convert them. Britain in the nineteenth century, and only to a slightly lesser extent the Continent, were characterized by a "strong, widely-shared conviction that the teachings of contemporary orthodox economists, including Free Traders, were scientifically exact, universally applicable, and demanded assent."[65] In the implicit debate between Thurman Arnold, who regarded economic theorists (and lawyers) as high priests who rationalize and sprinkle holy water on contemporary practice, and Keynes, who thought of practical men as responding unconsciously to the preaching of dead theorists, the British movement to free-trade was a vote, aided by the potato famine, for the view of Keynes.

France after 1815 was a high-tariff country that conformed to the Pincus model of a representative democracy with tariffs for various interests, except that (a) there were tariffs for all, and (b) it was not a democracy. The Physiocratic doctrine of laissez-faire for agricultural exports had been discredited in its reciprocal form by the disaster wreaked by imports up to 1789 under the Treaty of Vergennes. The Continental system, moreover, provided strong protection to hothouse industries, which was continued in the tariff of 1816 and elaborated in 1820 and 1822. To the principles of Turgot, that there should be freedom of grain trade inside France but no imports except in period of drought, were added two more: protection of the consumer by regulating the right of export of wheat—a step back from Physiocratic doctrine—and protecting the rights of producers by import tariffs.[66] In introducing the tariff of 1822 for manufactures, Saint-Cricq defended prohibitions and attacked the view that an industry that could not survive with a duty of 20 percent should perish, saying that the government intended to protect all branches together: "agriculture, industry, internal commerce, colonial production, navigation, foreign commerce finally, both of land and of sea."[67]

It was not long, however, before pressures for lower duties manifested themselves. Industries complained of the burden of the tariff on their purchases of inputs, and especially of the excess protection accorded to iron. It was calculated that protection against English iron cost industrial consumers fifty million francs a year and had increased the price of wood— used for charcoal, and owned by the many noble *maîtres de forges*—by 30 percent on the average and in some places 50 percent.[68] Commissions of inquiry in 1828 and 1834 recommended modifications in duties, especially to enlarge supplies that local industry was not in a position to provide and to convert prohibitions into tariffs. A tumult of conflict broke out in the

Chamber of Deputies among the export interests of the ports, the textile interests of Alsace and Normandy, the maîtres de forges, and the consumers of iron, with no regard, says the protectionist Gouraud, for the national interest. The chambers were then dissolved by the cabinet and tariffs adjusted downward—in coal, iron, copper, nitrates, machinery, horses. Reductions of the 1830s were followed in the peaks of business by similar pressure for reductions in prosperous phases of the cycle of the 1840s and 1850s.[69]

A troubling question that involved conflicting interests in this period was presented by sugar, for which it was impossible to find a solution agreeable at the same time to colonial planters, shipowners, port refiners, consumers, and the treasury. Colonial supply was high in cost, and a duty of 55 francs per 100 kilograms on foreign supplies was needed to appease the sugar ports. This, however, made it economical to expand beet-sugar production, begun during the Continental blockade, and the sugar ports turned to taxing this domestic production, less heavily at first, but with full equality in 1843. By this time it was too late, and with the freeing of the slaves in 1848, French colonial sugar production no longer counted.

The free-trade movement in France had its support in Bordeaux, the wine-exporting region; Lyons, interested in silk; and Paris, producer of so-called Paris articles for sale abroad (cabinetwork, perfumes, imitation jewelry, toys, and so on). Later Norman agricultural interests in the export to London of butter and eggs teamed up with Bordeaux wine interests to resist the attempts by textile interests to enlist agriculture in favor of higher tariffs.[70]

Intellectual support of free trade led by Bastiat from Bordeaux, and with Michel Chevalier as its most prestigious member, is dismissed by Lévy-Leboyer as unimportant.[71] Nonetheless, Chevalier had an important part in negotiation of the Anglo-French Treaty of Commerce of 1860, and in persuading Napoleon III to impose it on France in the face of the united opposition of the Chamber of Deputies. Some attention to his thought is required.

The prime interest of the Société d'économie politique and of Chevalier was growth.[72] His two-year visit to the United States in 1833 to 1835 impressed him with the contribution of transport to economic growth and contributed to his 1838 major work on *The Material Interests of France in Roads, Canals and Railroads.* American protectionist doctrine of Henry Carey seems not to have affected him. Polytechnician and graduate of the Ecole des mines, Chevalier's first interest in freer trade came from a project to establish woolen production in the Midi, and to obtain cheaper wool.[73]

Much of his later reasoning was in terms of the penalty to industry from expensive materials: charging thirty-five francs for a quintal of iron worth twenty imposes on industry "the labor of Sisyphus and the work of Penelope."[74] His major argument, at the Collège de France and in his Examen du système commercial, cited the success of Spitalfield and Macclesfield when Huskisson permitted competition of imports, as well as the experience of the manufacturers of cotton and woolen textiles in Saxony who were worried by the enactment of Zollverein but sufficiently stimulated by import competition so that in two or three years their industry was flourishing.[75] The letter of Napoleon III to Fould[76] talks in specifics of the need to abolish all duties on raw materials essential to industry to encourage production, and to reduce by stages the duties on goods that are consumed on a large scale. In the more general introduction the letter states that "lack of competition causes industry to stagnate," an echo of the Chevalier view. Chevalier himself was one of the judges of the Universal Exposition of 1855 in Paris and noted that France received so many prizes that no one dared confess to being a protectionist.[77]

There were economic purposes behind the Anglo-French treaty that exchanged reductions in French duties on manufactures for British removal of discrimination against French and in favor of Portuguese wines and brandy, as evidenced by the proposal in France in 1851 for tariffs of 20 percent, 10 percent, and duty free on wholly manufactured goods, semifinished manufactures, and raw materials;[78] by actual reductions in duties on coal, iron, and steel in 1852 as the railroad boom picked up; and by the legislative proposal designed by Napoleon III in 1855, but not put forward until after the Crimean War, to admit 241 items duty free, reduce tariffs on 19 others, remove all prohibitions, and set a top limit of 30 percent. This last was turned down by the chamber, and Napoleon promised not to submit a new tariff proposal before 1861.

Economic interests were involved, and the theories of great men like Cobden and Chevalier. However, there was more: Napoleon III was starting to engage on foreign adventure. He wanted to rid Italy of Austrian rule by use of arms. The British opposed his military measures, despite their recent use of force in Crimea. The treaty was used to hold British neutrality, as much as or more than to stimulate growth in France. Moreover, it did not need to be submitted to the chamber. Under the constitution of 1851, the emperor had the sole power to make treaties, and such treaties encompassed those dealing with trade.

The move was successful both politically and economically. With the help of the French armies, Italy was unified under the leadership of Piedmont, and French growth never faltered under the impetus of increased imports. French industries met competition successfully and checked the growth of imports after two years.[79] While the effects of the treaty are intermingled with those of the spread of the French railroad network, it "helped to bring about the full development of the industrial revolution in France."[80]

Further, it added impetus to the free-trade movement in Europe. This was under way in the early 1850s, following repeal of the Corn Laws. The Swiss constitution of 1848 had called for a tariff for revenue only, and protective duties were reduced progressively from 1851 to 1885. The Netherlands removed a tariff on ship imports and a prohibition against nationalization of foreign ships. Belgium plugged gap after gap in its protective system in the early 1850s, only to turn around at the end of the decade and adopt free trade down the line. Piedmont, as we shall see, and Spain, Portugal, Norway, and Sweden (after 1857) undertook to dismantle their protective and prohibitive restrictions.[81] With the Anglo-French treaty the trickle became a flood. France, Germany, Italy, and Britain engaged in negotiating reciprocal trade treaties with the most-favored nation clause.[82]

Following the French defeat at Sedan in 1870 and the abdication of Louis Napoleon, the Third Republic brought in the protectionist Thiers. The Cobden treaty was denounced in 1872. Reversal of policy waited upon repeal of the Le Chapelier law of 1791, taken in the heat of the French revolution against associations, which forbade economic interests to organize. Dunham claims that a country with leadership would have accepted a moderate tariff in 1875, but that the free traders had neither organization nor conviction, that is, they had too many free riders.[83]

The French movement to free trade was taken against the opposition of the separate interests,[84] in the absence of strong export interests, with an admixture of economic theory of a dynamic kind, and imposed from above. The motivation of that imposition was partly economic, partly— perhaps even mainly—political. Moreover, it had a bandwagon effect in spreading freer trade.

In the French case, the leadership overwhelmed the concentrated economic interests. That leadership earned its surplus, to use Frohlich, Oppenheimer, and Young's expression, in a coin different than economic, that is, in freedom to maneuver in foreign policy. It may be possible to subsume increases in leadership surplus in this form into an "economic theory of national decision-making" with costs to vested interests accepted in exchange for political benefits to a national leader, ruling by an imposed constitution, the legitimacy of which is not questioned. The effort seems tortured.

As mentioned earlier, the Prussian tariff of 1818 was regarded when it was enacted as the lowest in Europe.[85] But the duties on coarse yarns and textiles were effectively high, since the tariff was levied by weight. Jacob in 1819 noted that the "system of the Prussian government has always been of manufacturing at home everything consumed within the Kingdom; of buying from others, nothing that can be dispensed with," adding, "As scarcely any competition exists, but with their own countrymen, there is little inducement to adopt the inventions of other countries, or to exercise their facilities in perfecting their fabrics; none of these have kept pace."[86] Baden, on joining the Zollverein, which adopted the Prussian tariff for the totality, believed itself to be raising its tariff level when it joined.[87] What Baden did, however, was to acquire enforcement: its long border previously had been effectively open.

The Prussian tariff dominated that of the Zollverein, organized in the years from 1828 to 1833, primarily because Prussia took a very liberal view of tariff revenues. Most goods by sea entered the German states via Prussia, directly or by way of the Netherlands, but the text of the Zollverein treaty of 1833 provided that the revenues from the duties after deduction of expenses would be divided among the contracting states according to population.[88] Prussia thus received 55 percent, Bavaria 17 percent, Saxony 6.36 percent, Württemberg 5.5 percent, and so on; Prussia was said in 1848 to have sacrificed about two million thalers a year, exclusive of the fiscal loss sustained by smuggling along the Rhine and Lake Constance.[89] This can be regarded as a side payment made by the beneficiary of income distribution under Pareto-optimal conditions to gain its policy, or as the disproportionate share of overhead costs of the collective good saddled on the party that most wanted it.[90]

Despite adjustments made in Prussian customs duties between 1819 and 1833, the tariff remained low by British standards. Junker grain growers were hopeful of importing British manufactures in order to sell Britain more grain. Junker bureaucrats, brought up on Adam Smith and free trade by instinct, were fearful that highly protective rates would reduce the revenue yield.[91]

Outside of Prussia plus Hamburg, Frankfurt, and the other grain-growing states of Mecklenburg, Pomerania, and so on, there was interest in higher tariffs; but apart from the Rhineland, there was little in the way of organized interests. Von Delbrück comments that Prussia and Pomerania had free-trade interests and shipping interests, but that outside the Rhineland, which had organized chambers of commerce under the French occupation, there were few bureaucrats or organs with views on questions of trade and industry. Nor did the Prussian government see a need to develop them.[92]

Saxony was sufficiently protected by its interior location so as not to feel threatened by low tariffs—which, as mentioned, were not really low on coarse cloths. On joining the Zollverein, Baden was concerned over raising its tariff and worried lest it be cut off from its traditional trading areas of Switzerland and Alsace. It fought with the Zollverein authorities over exemptions for imported capital equipment, but gradually with Bavaria and Württemberg, evolved into a source of pressure for higher tariffs on cotton yarns and iron. Fischer points out that the request for lifting the duty on cotton yarns from two talers per centner to five was resisted by the weavers of Prussia (the Rhineland) and Silesia.[93]

Cotton yarns and iron were the critical items. Shortly after the formation of the Zollverein a trend toward protection was seen to be under way.[94] The Leipzig consul reported a new duty on iron to the Board of Trade in February 1837 and observed that the switch from imports of cotton cloth to imports of yarn pointed in the direction of ultimate exclusion of both.[95] Bowring's letter of August 1839 noted that the manufacturing interest was growing stronger, that the existing position was untenable, and that tariffs would be raised under the growing demands and increasing power of the manufacturing states, or would be lowered by an alliance between the agricultural and commercial interests.[96]

Open agitation for protection began two and one-half years after the formation of the Zollverein, when the south pushed for duties on cotton yarns. Linen yarns and cloth went on the agenda in 1839 and iron, protection for which was sought by Silesian and west German ironwork owners, began in 1842.[97] But these groups lacked decisive power. The Prussian landed nobility covered its position by citing the interests of consumers,[98] and Prince Smith, the expatriate leader of the doctrinaire free traders, in turn tried to identify free trade and low tariffs with the international free-trade movement rather than with the export interests of the Junkers.[99] The tariff on iron was raised in 1844, those on cotton yarns and linen yarns in 1846. Von Delbrück presents in detail the background of the latter increases: he starts with the bureaucratic investigations into linen, cotton, wool, and soda, with their negative recommendation; continues through the negotiations, in which Prussia was ranged against any increase and all the others in favor; and concludes that the Prussian plenipotentiary to the Zollverein conference was right in not vetoing the increase, as he could have done, since a compromise was more important than the rationally correct measure of this or that tariff.[100] The head of the Prussian Handelsamt (commerce office) was not satisfied with the outcome of the conference, but had to accept it.

From 1846 on, the direction of Zollverein tariffs was downward, aided first by the repeal of the Corn Laws and second by the Cobden-Chevalier treaty. With the increases of the 1840s and English reductions the Zollverein tariff, which had started as one of the lowest in Europe, had become relatively high. Von Delbrück was one of the doctrinaire free traders in the Prussian civil service and remarked in 1863 that he had been trying for a reduction in the tariff on pig iron for seven years, since the tariff reform of 1856, which reordered but did not lower duty schedules. He also wanted a reduction in the tariff on cotton cloth; duties on woolens were no longer needed. The opportunity came with the announcement of the Anglo-French treaty. He noted that Austria had gone from prohibitions to tariffs, that the Netherlands had reformed its tariffs with a 5-percent maximum on industrial production, and that the levels of Italian duties were lower than those in Germany. "Could we stay away from this movement? We could not."[101]

Bismarck was no barrier to the Junker bureaucracy. His view about tariff negotiations was expressed in 1879 in the question, "Who got the better of the bargain?" Trade treaties, he believed, were nothing in themselves but an expression of friendship. His economic conscience at this time, he said later, was in the hands of others.[102] Moreover, he had two political ends that a trade treaty with France might serve: to gain her friendship in the Danish question (which led up to the Prussian war of 1864); and to isolate Austria, which was bidding for a role in the German confederation.[103] Austrian tariffs were high. The lower the levels of the Zollverein, the more difficulty she would have in joining and bidding against Prussia for influence. The Zollverein followed the 1863 treaty with France with a series of others.

Exports of grain from Prussia, Pomerania, and Mecklenberg to London as a percentage of total English imports hit a peak in 1862 at the time of the Civil War[104] and proceeded down thereafter as American supplies took over. The free-trade movement nonetheless continued. Only hesitation prevented a move to complete free trade at the peak of the boom in 1873.[105] There is debate about whether or not the crash later in the year triggered off the return to protection in 1879. Victory in 1871 had enlarged competition in iron and cotton textiles by including Alsace and

Lorraine in the new German empire. Radical free traders and large farmers achieved the reduction in duties on raw iron in 1873 and passed legislative provision for complete removal in 1877.[106] But Lambi notes that *Gewerbefreiheit* (freedom of occupation) had caused dissatisfaction and in some versions subsumed free trade.[107] By 1875 the iron interests were organizing to resist the scheduled elimination of iron duties in 1877.

The difference between the 1873 depression, which led to tariffs, and the 1857 crisis, which did not, lay in (*a*) the fact that the interests were not cohesive in the earlier period, and (*b*) that Britain did not keep on lowering duties in the later period as it had in the first.[108] On the first score the Verein Deutscher Eisen- und Stahl Industrielle was formed in 1873, after vertical integration of steel back to iron mining had removed the opposition between the producers and the consumers of iron. This supports the view of the effectiveness of concentrated interests in achieving their tariff goals when scattered interests will not—though again it has nothing to do with representative democracy. On the other hand, the free traders also organized; in 1868 the Kongress Nord-Deutscher Landwirte was organized, and in 1871 it was broadened to cover all Germany. In 1872 a Deutsche Landwirtschaftsrat was formed.[109] Many of these organizations and the once free-trade Congress of German Economists were subverted and converted to protection after 1875, but a new Union for the Promotion of Free Trade was formed in September 1876.[110] German economic interests as a whole became organized, and the struggle was among interests concentrated on both sides.

Abandonment of the opposition of the landed interests is perhaps critical. Consumers of iron in machinery, they opposed tariffs on iron up to 1875, but with the decline in the price of grain and the threat of imports, their opposition collapsed. It might have been possible to support tariffs for grain and free trade for iron, but inconsistency is open to attack. After von Delbrück's resignation or discharge in April 1876, Bismarck forged the alliance of bread and iron. As widely recounted, he had strong domestic political motives for higher tariffs on this occasion, as contrasted with his international political gains from lower tariffs up to 1875.

In general, however, the German case conforms to the Stolper-Samuelson explanation: the abundant factor wants free trade; when it becomes relatively scarce, through a gain in manufacturing at home and an expansion of agriculture abroad, it shifts to wanting tariffs. Doctrine was largely on the side of free trade. List's advocacy of national economy had little or no political force. His ultimate goal was always free trade, and his early proposal of 10-percent duties on colonial goods, 15-percent on Continental, and 50-percent on British was more anti-British than national.[111] In the 1840s he was regarded in Germany, or at least by the Prussians, as a polemicist whose views were offered for sale.[112] Bismarck is often regarded as the arch-villian of the 1879 reversal of Zollverein low tariffs, but it is hard to see that his role was a major one.

Italian moves in the direction of free trade prior to 1850 were tentative and scattered. The abandonment of the policy of supply in Tuscany in the eighteenth century has been mentioned earlier, as well as the removal of prohibitions on the export of raw silk in Piedmont, Lombardy, and Veneto. Lombard and Venetian tariff policies were largely imposed by Austria, which was perhaps not wholly indifferent to local interests and to the promotion of industry.[113] Piedmont concluded a series of trade treaties with the larger states, especially France and Britain, and in 1847–1848 explored a tariff union with Tuscany and the papal states.[114] But the major initiatives were taken after Cavour became minister of agriculture, industry, and commerce, then minister of finance (1851), and then prime minister (1852). The low tariffs that Cavour achieved for the Kingdom of Sardinia were subsequently extended to Italy as a whole after its unification in 1860 under Cavour's leadership and were followed by a series of trade agreements lowering import duties still further.

As a young man, Cavour had visited France and Britain—once in 1833–1835 and again in 1842–1843. Like Chevalier, whose lectures he attended during the second visit, he was interested in growth through banks, public works, and especially market forces encouraged by freedom of trade. He knew Babbage, Nassau Senior, Cobden, de Tocqueville, Sismondi, Cherbuliez, Michelet, Pellegrino Rossi (an Italian free-trader, resident in Paris), Chevalier, and Faucher, and wrote long papers on English Poor Laws, the Irish question, and the Corn Laws.

Cavour was attacked as a doctrinaire who deserted a tried and effective system to follow an abstract theory,[115] but has been defended by biographers as having "a genius for the opportune."[116] His fifty-two speeches on the tariff question as finance minister had high educational quality, says Thayer, and achieved an economic revolution. There are views that Cavour's successful pressure for free trade represented economic interests. He was a large landowner, and the low tariff has been said to "reflect clearly the interests of the large landowners."[117] Piedmont agriculture was related to western European markets for rice, silks, wine, and hides.[118] The application of Piedmont's low tariff to all of Italy has been said to have assured the interests of the ruling classes of Britain and France.[119]

For the most part, however, it seems evident that in following low-tariff policies in the Kingdom of Sardinia in the early 1850s and in Italy after unification in 1860, Cavour was operating on the basis of a theory. His views were widely shared. Prodi notes that the liberal faith in freedom through the market in 1860 not only triumphed but remained sure and irrefutable. There were some like Cappellari who wanted to reduce tariffs slowly as industry was getting ready to export, as in England, and like Martello who was conscious of the differences between Italy and England and elastic in his application of Adam Smith to Italy.[120] For the most part, however, the tariff problem was ignored in Italy until the inquiry of 1870. Industrialists, led by the wool manufacturer Rossi, disliked the Piedmont low tariff and especially the twenty or more trade treaties that followed. Limited transport over land meant, however, that there was no unified domestic market for local manufacturers to exploit.

Clough[121] observes that the advantages that were supposed to devolve automatically from the free movement of goods in international commerce did not seem to accrue to Italy. For one thing, loss of custom revenues upset the finances of first Sardinia and then Italy, despite a vigorous expansion of trade.[122] Customs duties had provided 14.7 million lire out of a total revenue of 69.4 million.[123] Secondly, the balance of payments turned adverse, partly—perhaps mainly—as a result of Cavour's and his successors' programs of public works. Piedmont ran up a large debt, which later devolved on the Kingdom of Italy. In 1866 it became necessary to halt redemption of the lira in gold, and the depreciation of the currency during the *corso forzoso* (forced circulation) alleviated some of the effects of competitive imports. But the spread of the railroad in the 1860s and the low tariff policies proved ruinous to industry, especially in the south. The Sardinian tariff schedule by and large was at the same level as those of Modena, Parma, and Tuscany, well below that of Lombardy in most goods, though higher in others, but far below the levels of the papal states and especially of the Kingdom of the Two Sicilies (Naples).[124] After a long period when the country was "strangely deaf" to the troubles caused by the low tariff,[125] the Commission of Inquiry was launched in 1870, the tariff was raised in 1878, and a new system of high tariffs on industry, modified by trade agreements favoring agriculture, was instituted in its place.[126]

My first conclusion from this survey was that free trade in Europe in the period 1820 to 1875 had many different causes. Whereas after 1879 countries reacted quite differently to the single stimulus of the fall in the price of wheat—England liquidating its agriculture, France and Germany imposing tariffs (though for different political and sociological reasons), Italy emigrating (in violation of the assumptions of classical economics), and Denmark transforming from producing grain for export to importing it as an input in the production of dairy products, bacon, and eggs— before that, the countries of Europe all responded to different stimuli in the same way. Free trade was part of a general response to the breakdown of the manor and guild system. This was especially true of the removal of restrictions on exports and export taxes, which limited freedom of producers. As more and conflicting interests came into contention, the task of sorting them out became too complex for government (as shown in *Gewerbeförderung* in Baden and the refinement of the Navigation Laws in England) and it became desirable to sweep them all away.

Part of the stimulus came from the direct self-interest of particular dominant groups, illustrated particularly by the First Hand in the Netherlands. In Britain, free trade emerged as a doctrine from the political economists, with a variety of rationalizations to sustain it in particular applications: antimonopoly effects, increased real wages, higher profits, increased allocative efficiency, increased productivity through innovation required by import competition. In France, the lead in the direction of free trade came less from export interests than from industrial interests using imported materials and equipment as inputs, though the drive to free trade after 1846 required overcoming the weight of the vested interests by strong governmental leadership, motivated by political gain in international politics. The German case was more straightforward: free trade was in the interest of the grain-exporting and timber-producing classes, who were politically dominant in Prussia and who partly bought off and partly overwhelmed the rest of the country. The Italian case seems to be one in which doctrines developed abroad, which were dominant in England and in a minority position in France, were imported by strong political leadership and imposed on a relatively disorganized political body.

Second thoughts raise questions. The movement to free trade in the 1850s in the Netherlands, Belgium, Spain, Portugal, Denmark, Norway, and Sweden, along with the countries discussed in detail, suggests the possibility that Europe as a whole was motivated by ideological considerations rather than economic interests. That Louis Napoleon and Bismarck would use trade treaties to gain ends in foreign policy suggests that free trade was valued for itself, and that moves toward it would earn approval. Viewed in this perspective, the countries of Europe in this period should not be considered as independent economies whose reactions to various phenomena can properly be compared, but rather as a single entity that moved to free trade for ideological or perhaps better doctrinal reasons. Manchester and the English political economists persuaded Britain, which persuaded Europe—by precept and example. Economic theories of representative democracy, or constitutional monarchy, or even absolute monarchy may explain some cases of tariff changes. They are of little help in western Europe between the Napoleonic wars and the Great Depression.

Notes

1. See Pincus, "A Positive Theory of Tariff Formation." For the theory of collective goods see Breton, *Economic Theory of Representative Democracy*; Olson, *Logic of Collective Action*; and, introducing leadership, Froelich et al., *Political Leadership and Collective Action*. Froelich and his colleagues view leaders as political entrepreneurs, interested in maximizing their "surplus" or profit in providing collective goods against taxes, extortions, donations, or purchases.

2. Cited by Gerschenkron, *Bread and Democracy*, p. 65.

3. Helleiner, *Free Trade and Frustration*, p. 63.

4. Johnson, "Economic Theory of Protectionism," p. 118.

5. Stuart, *Free Trade in Tuscany*, p. 24.

6. Fischer, *Der Staat und Industrialisierung*.

7. Bulferetti and Costanti, *Industria e Commercio in Liguria*, pp. 495–501.

8. Wright, *Free Trade and Protection*, pp. 58–59.

9. Ibid., p. 112.

10. Ibid., p. 139.

11. Ibid., p. 113.

12. Porter, *Progress of the Nation*, chap. 16.

13. Bäsing, *Das goldene Delta*, p. 85.

14. MacGregor, *Germany under Frederick William IV*, p. 246.

15. Bulferetti and Costanti, *Industria e Commercio in Liguria*, chap. 2.

16. Bowring, "Prussian Commercial Union," p. 38.

17. Wright, *Free Trade and Protection*, p. 124.

18. Böhme, *Frankfurt und Hamburg*, chap. 1.

19. Checkland, *The Gladstones*, pp. 139, 333.

20. Crouzet, "Western Europe and Great Britain," p. 120.

21. Bläsing, *Das goldene Delta*, p. 83.

22. Heaton, *Economic History of Europe*, pp. 398–399.

23. Semmel, *Rise of Free Trade Imperialism*, pp. 181 ff.

24. Brebner, "Laissez-Faire and State Intervention," pp. 254–256.

25. Huskisson, *Speeches*, p. 328.

26. Ibid., pp. 503–505.

27. Labracherie, *Michel Chevalier*, p. 131.

28. Whyte, *Early Life and Letters of Cavour*, p. 131.

29. Select Committee on Export of Tools and Machinery, "Report," p. 12.

30. Wright, *Free Trade and Protection*, p. 130.

31. Select Committee on Exportation of Machinery, "First Report," p. 44.

32. Babbage, *The Economy of Machinery*, p. 363.

33. Polanyi, *The Great Transformation*, p. 136.

34. Select Committee on Exportation of Machinery, "Second Report," p. xx.

35. Ibid., p. xiv.

36. Babbage, *The Economy of Machinery*, p. 364.

37. Musson, "The 'Manchester School,' " p. 49.

38. Chambers, *Workshop of the World*, chap. 1.

39. "The Imperialism of Free Trade."

40. Polanyi, *The Great Transformation*, pp. 133–137.

41. Moore, "Corn Laws and High Farming."

42. Polanyi, *The Great Transformation*, pp. 152–153.

43. *Speeches on Questions of Public Policy*, pp. 4, 18.

44. Ibid., p. 57.

45. The Corn Laws "inflict the greatest amount of evil on the manufacturing and commercial community" (ibid., p. 57). "Silversmiths and jewellers get orders not from the Duke of Buckingham but from Manchester, from Glasgow or Liverpool or some other emporium of manufactures" (ibid., p. 90).

46. Ibid., p. 106.

47. Chambers, *Workshop of the World*, p. 71.

48. *Speeches*, p. 70.

49. Ibid., p. 100.

50. Ibid., p. 103.

51. *High Farming*, p. 374.

52. Moore, "Corn Laws and High Farming."

53. Bowring, "Prussian Commercial Union," p. 55.

54. Brown, *Board of Trade*, pp. 135, 171 ff.

55. Testimony of Thomas Ashton, in Select Committee on Exportation of Machinery, "First Report, " par. 235.

56. MacGregor, *Germany under Frederick William IV*, p. 68.

57. Bowring, "Prussian Commercial Union," p. 287.

58. Select Committee on Import Duties, "Minutes of Evidence, " p. 59, par. 782.

59. Semmel, *Rise of Free Trade Imperialism*, p. 149.

60. Platt, *Finance, Trade and Politics*, p. 87.

61. Clapham, "Last Years of the Navigation Acts," p. 161.

62. Woodham-Smith, *The Great Hunger.*

63. Cited by Semmel, *Rise of Free Trade Imperialism*, p. 207.

64. List, cited by Fielden, "Rise and Fall of Free Trade," p. 85.

65. Ibid., p. 78.

66. Gouraud, *La Politique commerciale de la France*, p. 198.

67. Ibid., p. 208.

68. Amé, *Les Tarifs de douanes*, vol. 1, pp. 170–174.

69. Lévy-Leboyer, *Histoire économique et sociale*, p. 96.

70. Augé-Laribé, *La Politique agricole*, p. 66.

71. *Histoire économique et sociale*, p. 92.

72. Lutfalla, "Aux origines du libéralisme économique," pp. 500, 515, 517.

73. Lévy-Leboyer, *Histoire économique et sociale*, p. 95.

74. Chevalier, *Cours d'économie politique*, p. 538.

75. Labracherie, *Michel Chevalier*, pp. 130–131.

76. Pollard and Holmes, *Documents of European Economic History*, vol 1, pp. 384–386.

77. Chevalier, *Cours d'économie politique*, p. 521.

78. Illasu, "The Cobden-Chevalier Commercial Treaty," p. 80.

79. Rist, "Une Expérience française," p. 937.

80. Dunham, *Anglo-French Treaty of Commerce*, p. 179.

81. Rosenberg, *Die Weltwirtschaftskrise*, pp. 24–26.

82. Most lists of treaties are given separately by country. For an overview, see Pollard, *European Economic Integration*, p. 117. The impact of repeal of the timber duties and the Navigation Acts in stimulating export-led growth in Scandinavia is treated by Norman, "Trade Liberalization and Industrial Growth." The stimulus to shipping in Norway and to timber

exports in Sweden led via linkages to industrialization, which the free-trade imperialists were seeking to avoid.

83. Dunham, *Anglo-French Treaty of Commerce,* p. 333.

84. Consumers of imported materials and machinery are not included here. But Lhomme's view was that the state adopted free trade because it loved the *grande bourgeoisie* and knew its interests better than the members did; that the *grande bourgeoisie* recognized this fact and agreed with the tariff reductions except for a few intransigent protectionists like Pouyer-Quartier. See Lhomme, *La Grande Bourgeoisie au pouvoir,* p. 179. It is, however, impossible for me to accept this rationalization.

85. Huskisson, *Speeches,* p. 131; Pollard, *European Economic Integration,* p. 112.

86. Jacob, *Agriculture, Manufactures, Statistics and Society,* pp. 201–202.

87. Fischer, *Der Staat und Industrialisierung,* pp. 128, 134.

88. Pollard and Holmes, *Documents of Economic History,* vol. 1, p. 374.

89. MacGregor, *Germany under Frederick William IV,* p. 6.

90. Olson and Zeckhauser, "An Economic Theory of Alliances." For a view emphasizing the revenue aspects of the Zollverein, especially savings in the costs of collection and the reduction in smuggling, see Dumke, "Political Economy of Economic Integration." Revenues available from the Zollverein permitted the petty princes to maintain their rule without democratic concessions to bourgeois interests.

91. Pollard, *European Economic Integration,* p. 112.

92. Von Delbrück, *Lebenserinnerungen,* vol. 1, pp. 142–144.

93. Fischer, *Der Staat und Industrialisierung,* p. 136.

94. Dawson, *Protection in Germany,* p. 20.

95. Brown, *Board of Trade,* p. 113.

96. Bowring, "Prussian Commercial Union," p. 287.

97. Von Delbrück, *Lebenserinnerungen,* vol. 1, p. 147.

98. Rosenberg, *Die Weltwirtschaftskrise,* p. 207.

99. Henderson, *Britain and Industrial Europe,* p. 171.

100. Von Delbrück, *Lebenserinnerungen,* vol. 1, pp. 162–164.

101. Ibid., p. 200.

102. Dawson, *Protection in Germany,* p. 21.

103. Lambi, *Free Trade and Protection,* p. 5.

104. Zorn, "Wirtschafts- und socialgeschichtliche Zusammenhänge," p. 296.

105. Barkin, *Controversy over German Industrialization,* p. 33.

106. Ibid.

107. *Free Trade and Protection,* pp. 83, 113.

108. Rosenberg, *Die Weltwirtschaftskrise*, p. 195.

109. Lambi, *Free Trade and Protection*, p. 57.

110. Ibid., p. 191.

111. Williams, *British Commercial Policy*, p. 199.

112. Thiedig, *Englands Übergang zum Freihandel*, pp. 31–32.

113. Greenfield, *Economics and Liberalism*, p. 113.

114. Clough, *Economic History of Modern Italy*, p. 27.

115. Whyte, *Political Life and Letters of Cavour*, p. 73.

116. Thayer, *Life and Times of Cavour*, p. 133.

117. Pedone, "La Politica del commercio-estere," in Fua, *Le Sviluppo Economico in Italia*, vol. 2, p. 242.

118. Castronovo, *Economia e societa in Piemonte*, p. 16.

119. Mori, quoted by Luzzato, *L'Economia italiana*, vol. 1, p. 28n.

120. Prodi, "Il Protezionismo," pp. 1–10.

121. *Economic History of Modern Italy*, p. 114.

122. Sachs, *L'Italie*, p. 748.

123. Norsa and Pozzo, *Imposte e tasse in Piemonte*, pp. 16, 17.

124. Parravicini, *Archivo economico*, p. 326.

125. Luzzato, *L'Economia italiana*, p. 28.

126. Coppa, "The Italian Tariff."

References

Amé, Léon. *Etudes sur les tarifs de douanes et sur les traités de commerce.* Vols. 1 and 2. Paris: Imprimerie nationale, 1874.

Augé-Laribé, Michel. *La politique agricole de la France de 1880 à 1940.* Paris: Presses universitaires de France, 1950.

Babbage, Charles. *The Economy of Machinery and Manufactures.* 4th. ed. London: Charles Knight, 1835.

Barkin, Kenneth D. *The Controversy over German Industrialization.* Chicago: University of Chicago Press, 1970.

Bläsing, Joachim F. E. *Das goldene Delta und sein eisernes Hinterland, 1815–1841, von niederländische-preussischen zu deutsch niederländischen Wirtschaft-beziehungen.* Leiden: H. E. Stenfert Kreese, 1973.

Böhme, Holmut. *Frankfurt und Hamburg, des deutsches Reiches Silber- und Goldloch und die allerenglische Stadt des Kontinents.* Frankfurt: Europaiches Verlags-anstalt, 1968.

Bowring, John. "Report on the Prussian Commercial Union, 1840." In *Parliamentary Papers.* Vol. 21, 1840.

Brebner, J. Bartlett. "Laissez-faire and State Intervention in Nineteenth-Century Britain." In E. M. Carus-Wilson, ed., *Essays in Economic History.* Vol. 3, London: Edward Arnold, 1962, 252–262.

Breton, Albert. *The Economic Theory of Representative Democracy.* Chicago: Aldine, 1974.

Brown, Lucy. *The Board of Trade and the Free-Trade Movement, 1830–1842.* Oxford: Clarendon Press, 1958.

Bulferetti, Luigi, and Claudio Costanti. *Industria commercio in Liguria nell' età del Risorgimento (1700–1861).* Milan: Banca Commerciale Italiana, 1965.

Caird, Sir James. *High Farming ... The Best Substitute for Protection.* Pamphlet, 1848, cited in Lord Ernle, *English Farming, Past and Present.* 4th ed. Longmans, Green, 1937, 374.

Castronovo, Valerie. *Economia e società in Piemonte dell' unità al 1914.* Milan: Banca Commerciale Italiana, 1969.

Chambers, J. D. *The Workshop of the World, British Economic History, 1820–1890.* 2nd ed. London: Oxford University Press, 1969.

Checkland, S. G. *The Gladstones: A Family Biography, 1784–1851.* Cambridge: Cambridge University Press, 1971.

Chevalier, Michel. *Cours d'économie politique, fait à Collège de France.* Vols. 1–3. 2nd ed. n. pl., 1855.

Clapham, J. H. "The Last Years of the Navigation Acts." in E. M. Carus-Wilson ed. *Essays in Economic History.* Vol. 3. London: Edward Arnold, 1962, 144–178.

Clough, Shephard B. *The Economic History of Modern Italy.* New York: Columbia University Press, 1964.

Cobden, Richard. *Speeches on Questions of Public Policy.* John Bright and James E. Thorold-Rogers, eds. Vol. 1. London: Macmillan, 1870.

Coppa, Frank J. "The Italian Tariff and the Conflict between Agriculture and Industry: The Commercial Policy of Liberal Italy, 1860–1922." *Journal of Economic History* 30 (1970): 742–769.

Crouzet, François. "Western Europe and Great Britain: Catching up in the First Half of the Nineteenth Century." in A. J. Youngson, ed., *Economic Development in the Long Run.* London: Allen & Unwin, 1972, 98–125.

Dawson, William H. *Protection in Germany: A History of German Fiscal Policy During the Nineteenth Century.* London: P. S. King & Son, 1904.

Delbruck, Rudolph von. *Lebenserrinnerungen.* Vols. 1 and 2. Leipzig: Duncker und Humblot, 1905.

Dumke, Rolf H. "The Political Economy of Economic Integration: The Case of the Zollverein of 1834." Queen's University *Discussion Paper* no. 153 presented to the Canadian Economic Association June 5, 1974.

Dunham, Arthur L. *The Anglo-French Treaty of 1860 and the Progress of the Industrial Revolution in France.* Ann Arbor: University of Michigan Press, 1930.

Fielden, Kenneth. "The Rise and Fall of Free Trade." In C. J. Bartlett, ed., *Britain Pre-eminent: Studies in British World Influence in the Nineteenth Century.* London: Macmillan, 1969, 76—100.

Fischer, Wolfram. *Der Staat und die Anfänge der Industrialisierung in Baden, 1800—1850.* Berlin: Duncker u. Humblot, 1962.

Froelich, N., J. A. Oppenheimer, and O. R. Young. *Political Leadership and Collective Action.* Princeton, N.J.: Princeton University Press, 1971.

Gallagher, John, and Ronald Robinson. "The Imperialism of Free Trade." *Economic History Review,* ser. 2, 6 (1952): 1—15.

Gershenkrom, Alexander. *Bread and Democracy in Germany.* Berkeley: University of California Press, 1943.

Gouraud, Charles. *Histoire de la politique commerciale de la France et son influence sur le progrès de la richesse publique depuis les moyen ages jusqu'à nos jours.* vols. 1 and 2. Paris: August Durand, 1854.

Greenfield, Kent Roberts. *Economics and Liberalism in the Risorgimento: A Study of Nationalism in Lombardy, 1814—1848.* Baltimore: Johns Hopkins Press, 1965.

Heaton, Herbert. *Economic History of Europe.* New York: Harper, 1936.

Helleiner Karl F. *Free Trade and Frustation: Anglo-Austrian Negotiations, 1860—70.* Toronto: University of Toronto Press, 1873.

Henderson, W. O. *Britain and Industrial Europe, 1750—1870: Studies in British Influence on the Industrial Revolution in Western Europe.* Liverpool, Liverpool University Press, 1954.

Huskisson, William. *The Speeches of the Right Honorable William Huskisson.* London: John Murray, 1832.

Illasu, A. A. "The Cobden-Chevalier Commercial Treaty of 1860." *Historical Journal* 14 (1971), 67—98.

Jacob, William. *A View of the Agriculture, Manufactures, Statistics and Society, in the State of Germany and Parts of Holland and France, taken during a journey through those countries in 1819.* London: John Murray, 1820.

Johnson, Harry, G. "An Economic Theory of Protectionism, Tariff Bargaining and the Formation of Customs Unions." *Journal of Political Economy* 73 (1965): 256—283.

Labracherie, Pierre. *Michel Chevalier et ses idées economiques,* Paris: Sicart, 1929.

Lambi, Ivo Nikolai. *Free Trade and Protection in Germany, 1868—1879.* Wiesbaden: Franz Steiner Verlag, 1963.

Lévy-Leboyer, Maurice. *Histoire économique et sociale de la France depuis 1848.* Les Cours de Droit, Institut d'études politiques, 1951—52.

Lhomme, J. *La Grande Bourgeosie au pouvoir, 1830—1880.* Paris: Presses universitaires de France, 1960.

Lutfalla, Michel. "Aux origines de la libéralisme économique de la France." *Revue d'histoire économique et sociale* 50 (1972): 494—517.

Luzzatto, Gino. *L'Economia italiana dal 1861 al 19114.* Vol. 1, 1861—1894. Milan: Banca Commerciale Italiana, 1963.

MacGregor, John. *Germany, Her Resources, Government, Union of Customs and Power under Frederick William IV.* London: Whittaker, 1848.

Moore, D. C. "The Corn Laws and High Farming." *Economic History Review,* ser. 2, 18 (1965): 544–561.

Musson, A. E. "The Manchester School and Exportation of Machinery." *Business History* 14 (1972): 17–50.

Norman, Victor D. "Trade Liberalization and Industrial Growth: The Impact of British Trade Liberalization in the 1840s on Industrialization in the Scandinavian Countries." Cambridge, Mass.: MIT Press, 1970.

Norsa, Paolo, and Mario Pozzo. *Imposte e tasse in Piemonte durante il periode cavouriano.* Turin: Museo nationale del Risorgimento, 1961.

Olson, Mancur. *The Logic of Collective Action: Public Goods and the Theory of Groups.* Rev. ed. Cambridge, Mass.: Harvard University Press, 1971.

Olson, Mancur, and Richard Zeckhauser. "An Economic Theory of Alliances." *Review of Economics and Statistics* 48 (1966): 266–279.

Parravicini, Giannino. *Archivo economico dell' unificazione italiana.* Turin: ILTE, 1958.

Pedone, Antonio. "La political del commercio-estere." In Giorgio Fua, ed., *Le sviluppo economico in Italia.* Vol. 2. Milan: France Angelli, 1969.

Pincus, Jonathan J. *A Positive Theory of Tariff Formation Applied to Nineteenth-Century United States.* New York: Columbia University Press, 1973.

Platt, D. C. M. *Trade and Politics in British Foreign Policy, 1815–1914.* Oxford: Clarendon Press, 1968.

Polanyi, Karl. *The Great Transformation.* New York: Farrar and Rinehart, 1944.

Pollard, Sidney. *European Economic Integration, 1815–1870.* New York: Harcourt Brace Jovanovich, 1974.

Pollard, Sidney, and C. Holmes. *Documents of European Economic History.* Vol. 2. New York: St. Martin's, 1968.

Prodi, Romano. "Il Proteccionismo nella politica e nell' industria italiana dall' unificazione al 1886." *Nuovo Rivista Storia.* 1–2 (1966): 1–74.

Rist, Marcel. "Une experience française de libération des échanges au dix-neuvième siècle: le traité de 1860." *Revue d'économie politique* 66 (1956): 908–963.

Rosenberg, Hans. *Der Weltwirtschaftkrise von 1857–1859.* Stuttgart-Berlin: Verlag von W. Kohlhammer, 1924.

Select Committee on Import Duties. "Minutes of Evidence," 15 July 1840. *Parliamentary Papers, Reports of Committees.* Vol. 5, 1840.

Select Committee on Laws Relating to the Export of Tools and Machinery. "Report." 30 June 1825, *Parliamentary Papers, Reports of Committees,* vol. 5, 1825.

Semmel, Bernard. *The Rise of Free Trade Imperialism: Classical Political, Economy, the Empire of Free Trade and Imperialism, 1750–1850.* Cambridge: Cambridge University Press, 1970.

Stuart, James Montgomery. *The History of Free Trade in Tuscany, with Remarks on Its Progress in the Rest of Italy.* London: Cassell, Potter and Galpin, 1876.

Thayer, William Roscoe. *The Life and Times of Cavour,* Boston: Houghton Mifflin, 1921.

Thiedig, Werner. *Englands Übergang zum Freihandel und die deutsche Handelspolitik, 1840–1856.* 40-page summary of thesis, Giessen, n. p., 1927.

Whyte, A. J. *Early Life and Letters of Cavour, 1810–1848.* London: Oxford University Press, 1925.

Whyte, A. J. *The Political Life and Letters of Cavour, 1848–1861.* Oxford: Clarendon Press, 1930.

Williams, Judith Blow. *British Commerical Policy and Trade Expansion, 1750–1850.* London: Oxford University Press, 1973.

Woodham-Smith, Cecil. *The Great Hunger: Ireland, 1845–1849.* New York: Harper and Row, 1962.

Wright Carl Major. *Free Trade and Protection in the Netherlands, 1816–1839: A Study of the First Benelux.* Cambridge: Cambridge University Press, 1955.

Zorn, Wolfgang. "Wirtschaft und Politik in deutschen Imperialismus. " In W. Abel, K. Borchardt, H. Kellenbenz, and W. Zorn, eds. *Wirtschaft, Geschichte und Wirtschaftsgeschichte.* Stuttgart: Gustav Fischer Verlag, 1955, 340–354.

Economic Growth

6   Germany's Overtaking of England, 1806 to 1914

The subject of economic rivalry has renewed relevance in the last third of the twentieth century, when American hegemony in economic matters is slipping.[1] An inevitable corollary is the question of which if any new economic power will take the place of the United States on the world stage: Japan? Germany? China? A dark horse like Brazil? A Toynbee view of the world may be too rigid, but it is not without value to study economic growth and development in comparative terms, emphasizing not only catching up[2] but also falling back and decline. One could focus equally well on the outstripping of the United Provinces of Holland by Britain in the eighteenth century, the rivalry of Germany and the United States vis-à-vis Britain in the period after 1850, or the rapid advance of Japan relative to the United States from 1955. The choice for this chapter is to focus on the catching or possible overtaking of Britain by Germany in the nineteenth century, or from 1806 after the Battle of Jena to 1914, prior to World War I.

Germany as Apprentice, 1806 to 1848

The major emphasis of the chapter is on German economic development, and only the last quarter is on decline in Britain. I shall follow to some degree Rostow's breakdown of German economic growth: 1806 to 1850 for the "preconditions," 1850 to 1872 for the "takeoff," and 1873 to 1913 for the "drive to maturity"; this is not to accept a Rostovian theory of "stages" or to worry much about the question of timing, which occupies so much space in Hardach's useful article.[3] Whether one selects the Zollverein or the revolution of 1848 as the turning point preceding what Gerschenkron would call the "great spurt" is of little consequence so long as it is well understood what was happening when.

It is worth spending a moment to explore what is meant, if anything, by such expressions as "overtaking," "catching up," and "falling behind." One could use measures of overall income or income per capita, although the well-known difficulties of comparing different national incomes in real terms give one pause. Leaving those difficulties aside, we can say that Germany overtook Britain in real income per capita only in the 1960s, and not at all in the nineteenth century. A crude measure of growth is the percentage of employment in agriculture. By this yardstick Britain is still far ahead of Germany. Or perhaps one ought to measure not output so much as consumption; this favors Britain in the short run because of her smaller proportion of income used for investment. One can take overall or per capita measures, or rates of change; there are economists who bring Samuel Johnson up to date by asserting that the first derivative is the last refuge of a scoundrel. Or the growth of productivity per weighted index of factor inputs. Or capacity to transform, that is, to adapt to changes in economic variables. Or capacity to develop new industries. A less subtle measure would relate to economic power defined in some sense such as Hawtrey used[4]—the ability to deliver firepower at a distance, a definition that peculiarly favored the insular position of Britain with her big navy. Or steel production. Or the rate of growth in competitive export markets. Or foreign lending. On each of these measures there will be somewhat different results. Germany never caught up with Britain in agriculture, textiles, shipping, or overseas banking. In the development of new industries, Germany was pressing her hard in the 1880s; in steel, in the 1890s. German overall investment overtook British in the 1870s. By Rostovian stages the German takeoff occurred sixty to seventy years after the British,[5] but the end of the drive to maturity becomes simultaneous.

The question is one of substance, and it was asked as early as 1827 by one Johann Conrad Fischer—a Swiss, to be sure, but one who spoke for Central Europe or the Continent as a whole: "Out of what origin and through what means has not industry but the spirit and the idea of industry and its kind and manner arisen in England and when will the continent come to a knowledge of its power and a culmination will be reached in England?"[6] Fischer first visited England in 1794 at the age of twenty-one, and for the last time in 1851. The biggest changes, in his view—he was a metallurgist who started out as a coppersmith and ended independently discovering crucible steel, so that he probably knew little of cotton textiles —occurred between 1794 and 1814. In the earlier year, Britain had nothing that the Continent lacked except the steam engine. In 1814 progress had been made in numerous industries, and changes taken place that he had not suspected. The British (by the 1820s) were masters of the Continent in fire, reflecting the advantages of physics and chemistry.[7] The Napoleonic wars were a hothouse of developments in metallurgy and machinery for Britain, but not for the Continent, and put Britain far ahead of, say, Germany.

Parenthetically, this brings up another moot issue of economic overtaking—whether Britain overtook France only during the Napoleonic wars or, rather, early in the eighteenth century. New research by Crouzet, Lévy-Leboyer, and others suggests that there was no enormous development gap between France and Britain prior to the Napoleonic wars, and that France if anything grew faster than Britain during the previous fourscore years, after having been even with her in 1685 and fallen behind in the period from the Revocation of the Edict of Nantes to John Law.[8] During the wars themselves Britain clearly outstripped France; but my intuition tells me to be skeptical about the conclusion that the gap, if any, was really very small in 1780 or favored France. France was ahead in a number of lines, such as glass and fine porcelain, but she had experienced no fundamental commercial or agricultural revolution, as Britain had, nor the first ten years of the industrial revolution. Moreover, French topography and balanced regions inhibited the joining of various parts of the country into a national market, as had occurred for a number of products in Britain. The rapid expansion of foreign trade had been superficial. Specialization and exchange were noteworthy to Adam Smith in 1776, who observed that Birmingham and Sheffield were three times as efficient as the Continent—an order of magnitude that admits little doubt—and competition under the Eden Treaty of 1786 proved painful to French producers in textiles (apart from silk), and porcelain, iron, and hardware to an extent that made continuation of the treaty, had not the French Revolution intervened, highly doubtful. A study of levels of output and income per capita in France and in England at various points in the eighteenth century and again in, say, 1820 would be highly valuable as an addition to our knowledge. I have little doubt that it would show Britain decisively ahead. But to return to Germany.

The Germans impressed Mme de Stael in 1810 as sluggish—poets and thinkers, musicians and metaphysicians. By 1910, says Lowie, they were the Yankees of Europe.[9] The early retardation is commented on widely, and frequently given a numerical estimate. In 1800, a German writing an English friend said that business in his country was in the same condition as that in Britain of seventy to a hundred years before.[10] Benaerts put Germany in 1820 fifty years behind on the road to the machine age,[11] but later indicated that with the help of foreign ideas, foreign capital equipment, and a distinctive German role, the country made up in twenty years an industrial lag of half a century.[12] In the Rhineland the lag in cotton spinning is said to have lengthened from ten years in 1800 to twenty in 1850.[13] Part of this phenomenon was the result of inadequate capital, which made it difficult for plants started under the Continental system to survive when British industry regained access to the market. Part was today's familiar problem of a widening gap between the developed countries and the less developed, with faster growth in the former. Britain was growing rapidly, and Germany had not yet gotten going.

German handicaps were many. Agriculture was still caught in the grip of the manorial system, three-field rotation, and compulsory crop selection (*Flurzwang*). There had been improvement in agriculture,[14] but no agricultural revolution. Industrial production was organized by guilds, patents, privileges. Commerce was stunted.[15]

The freeing of the serfs by vom Stein and Hardenberg was a direct consequence of the defeat of Prussia at Jena in 1806. In the occupied territories of the Rhineland, Napoleon had directly commuted peasant services to rents. His effect in the east was indirect, because the aristocracy felt the need to respond to the desires of the masses of suppressed serfs in order to get support for the war. The process was drawn out, and in the course of it land in the east ended up in Junker hands, whereas in the west the peasant controlled the land with a burden of debt or dues.

As in agriculture, so in handicraft. Napoleon broke up the system in the west, destroying guilds, secularizing church lands, and introducing more modern commercial law. In the south and east the process was a prolonged one and reached its culmination only with the revolution of 1848, which established *Gewerbefreiheit*, or occupational choice. Earlier *Gewerbeförderung* had had its positive as well as its negative side. The entrepreneur who had been awarded a privilege or patent, occasionally a site, buildings, or even capital, was regulated as to quality of output, limited in the amount of wood he could consume, needed permission to export, and the like. Foreign enterprise was controlled. The system carried the seeds of its own decay. As Fischer points out for Baden, complications became endless.[16] Improved transport made for overlap and conflict among the regulations of the locality, the Grand Duchy, and later the Zollverein. The ambiguities of patent laws were cited by an inventor in 1835 as one reason why Germany was a hundred years behind England.[17] But the system of discrimination, privileges, and exemptions proved so difficult to administer that it had to be swept away and Gewerbefreiheit substituted.

Freedom of occupation was introduced in Berlin as early as 1810, along with an employment tax devised by the French and reutilized by Hardenberg to repair the damaged finances of the state.

As noted earlier, the role of commerce in Germany in this period was limited. There were Hanseatic cities—Hamburg, Bremen, and Lübeck—which did a thriving external business in the Baltic, the North Sea, and across the Atlantic, though not in the Mediterranean where the British navy refused to protect German shipping against pirates and the Germans had no protection of their own. An earlier Hansastadt, Cologne, had slipped in position as oceangoing ships became larger and could no longer readily ascend the Rhine. Cologne's international position declined to that of being a satellite of first Antwerp, then Rotterdam and Amsterdam. The internationally oriented Hansa cities and Frankfurt, another externally oriented city, had limited connections with the interior. Hamburg built a tradition of being an English, rather than a German, city and was the last independent unit to join the Zollverein—doing so by conversion from a free port, and "not without repugnance,"[18] some seventeen years after it had joined the empire.

Frankfurt gave up earlier—in 1836, only two years after the Zollverein was established. Its international mercantile and banking traditions went far back to its role as a site for fairs on a medieval trade route on the ford of the Franks over the Main. These traditions were still powerful in 1810 when French occupation officials burned 185 chests of English goods owned by Frankfurt merchants in front of the town gates, only to have the Frankfurt bankers refuse to renew the discount on French bills, which produced bankruptcies in Strasbourg, Nancy, Rheims, and elsewhere.[19] The Continental system was soon overturned, but Britain continued to count on Frankfurt as a base, along with Hamburg, from which to smuggle goods into Prussia and other German states. With the formation of the Zollverein, new pressures arose to trade more with the German states and less with the outside; and in 1836, four hundred Frankfurt merchants, the "new men," voted to join the Prussian customs union, having been offered a favorable bargain on the division of customs receipts and special provision for admission of foreign goods to the fair despite the opposition of the lords of the Senate, the stock exchange, and the "English goods" party. The Hansa cities and Hanover were disgusted with Frankfurt's action, and more than one British observer considered that the city lost by the action.[20]

In 1790 three hundred rulers in Germany levied tolls as they pleased,[21] and there were eighteen hundred customs frontiers; between Strasbourg and the Dutch frontier on the Rhine were thirty customs houses. The process that led to the Zollverein started with the Prussian tariff of 1818. It was a low tariff, strongly influenced by the views of the Physiocrats and of Adam Smith. Smith's views were highly popular among the Prussian bureaucracy, and constituted a sort of bible, so much so that the provincial leader Vincke wrote in 1796 that he made it a practice to start each day by reading a passage from *The Wealth of Nations*.[22] Mercantilism in the early Prussian setting had meant monopolies, privileges, prohibitions, premiums, and subsidies to achieve export surpluses, rather than the construction of internal markets with emphasis on uniform coinage, codes of commercial law, and standards. Even with the liberal tariff rates of 1818, the merchant class in Germany developed slowly, thus forgoing the benefit from a commercial revolution in rationality and calculation on the one hand, plus capital formation on the other. But while a commercial revolution facilitates industrialization, it is neither sufficient—as the case of Holland illustrates—nor necessary—as Germany proves.

Gerschenkron's theory of backwardness calls for the state to substitute in backward countries for the initiative that came in Britain from a widespread entrepreneurial class. Part of the task is to clear away barriers, as just indicated. Part of the effort of the state, however, had negative effects in the provision of patents and privileges that inhibited enterprise. Still, a number of positive steps were taken in general and industrial education, in stimulating technical advances, in guiding certain industries such as mining, and in the provision of capital, especially to ailing industry, via *Seehandlung*, a state corporation engaged in finance and trade, not unlike the British East India Company of the nineteenth century.

The educational drive took place at all levels: against illiteracy, to reform the gymnasium and to develop new universities, and to teach industrial skills. Like the French, the Germans responded to defeat with educational reform. After Jena the drive was so enormous that in 1819 Jacob stated that many students could not find situations which required their attainments.[23] Not only were new schools and universities built, but their principles changed. There was a decline in theology and a rise in science, and a connection established by Humboldt between research and teaching.[24] The role of mathematics was expanded. All this took place during a period when science and technology were excluded from the curriculum of Oxford and Cambridge and left to the Scottish universities, the dissenting academies, and as an avenue for social advancement of the marginal nonconformist members of the Lunar Society of Birmingham or the Philosophical and Literary Society of Manchester. The British traveler

Banfield, in the Rhineland in 1848, observed that "education of people is a powerful influence on development of industry—and a most material and beneficial influence on the industrial occupations." He went further and made the "bold assertion" that the inhabitants of the Rhineland districts of Prussia, Nassau, Hesse-Darmstadt (with few exceptions), and Baden formed a mass of the best-educated inhabitants of Europe. There were 124 gymnasia in Prussia, 17 in the Rhenish Provinces alone. But the elementary schools were what the Prussians with most reason prided themselves on.[25]

The universities were created in Berlin, Breslau, Greifswald, Bonn, Halle, and Königsberg in Prussia, in competition with Göttingen, Tübingen, Heidelberg, and the like. Established in separate principalities, which had been reduced under Napoleonic occupation from three hundred to sixty-five or so, they provided competition and widespread initiative at the intellectual level.

One of the most famous institutions was the *Gewerbeinstitut* established by Beuth in Berlin, which trained artisans in 1820. It brought machinery from Britain, distributed subventions and prizes, and stimulated the growth of four shops. Borsig, the locomotive manufacturer of Berlin, along with Freund in steam engines, Egells in machinery, and Hollauer and Ehling in mechanical working, was a graduate of the Gewerbeinstitut. He dedicated his twenty-fourth locomotive to his old teacher, Beuth,[26] who had provided him with machinery on more than one occasion; perhaps helped to arrange a mortgage from Seehandlung to buy a factory; and submitted his forty-fourth locomotive to the 1844 Berlin Exhibition where it was a success.[27] All the technical schools, the 1871 *Jubelfest* of the *Gewerbeschule* noted, produced 3,500 technicians in fifty years, who "began in these years their superiority over the British."[28] Technical universities followed along after the Gewerbeinstitut. Hardach mentions that their establishment owed something to the spirit of competition among German states, as Karlsruhe in 1825 was followed by Darmstadt in 1826, Munich in 1827, Dresden in 1828, Stuttgart in 1829, and Hanover in 1831.[29]

Gewerbeförderung involved more than education. Bright young engineers were sent to England to study. As early as 1785 Bückling worked at Boulton and Watt "as a spy" to study the application of the steam engine to mines, and made a second trip in 1794 to bring back pieces of machinery and a British engineer. The latter, Richard, worked for thirty years in Silesian mining, making elevators and pumps.[30] Beuth himself made several trips to England, Belgium and Holland, and his Gewerbeinstitut gave

Egells 1,000 talers in 1817 to travel and work as a mechanic in England. When it proved difficult to find work, Egells asked for a greater subvention and received it, staying on for two years before starting his machine foundry in Berlin in 1821. Beuth bought a great deal of machinery in England, with capital provided by Seehandlung.

Industry, says Redlich,[31] needed spies to acquire machinery. Machine methods were secret at the company level, and prohibitions were imposed by Britain on the export of models, drawings, and machinery. "Even a man of the rank and ethical greatness of Baron vom Stein used dubious methods on his trips to England to acquire industrial knowledge."[32] But there was often little need to spy or to bribe local workers to obtain information. Fischer, the Swiss metallurgist mentioned earlier, had letters to Wedgwood, Lee, Faraday, Perkins, and the Woolich arsenal, and possessed an impressive personality and technical wisdom that his host often wished to obtain. He seems never to have had difficulty in learning about technical advances.[33]

Diffusion of technology took place largely via visits of German entrepreneurs and artisans to Britain, plus the short or long stays in Germany of British industrialists. Wilkinson, who had worked in Le Creusot in France in 1785, later came to Breslau to establish an iron foundry. From the Rhineland visits were paid to France, Belgium, and Holland as well as to Britain. In Baden there were visits back and forth to Switzerland and Alsace. In 1830 German chemists from Liebig to Kekulé went to Paris to study under Gay-Lussac, Frémy, and Berthollet "because they preferred the practical, laboratory-centered approach to the sterile idealism of the German universities at that time."[34] The situation later changed in both countries.

Not only in technical subjects, but also in banking, German young people went abroad to learn (or came from abroad to practice). Oppenheim was a French Jew, expelled from France at the time of the Restoration, brother-in-law of the French banker Fould, and closely connected with Isaac and Emile Pereire. He established an important private bank in Cologne. David Hansemann had lived abroad for seven years after 1810, traveling everywhere in Europe and bringing back ideas for insurance companies and chambers of commerce, as well as banking. Mevissen, Camphausen, and von der Heydt, the great names of mid-century German banking, lived and worked abroad for varying lengths of time—in France, Belgium, and England—and acquired both technique and ideas, in the case of Mevissen notions about limited liability and expansionist technocratic principles of the Saint Simoniens. There was a danger. The Junker

Yorck said about Stein, "That man to our sorrow has been in Britain and brings thence his principles of government; but the institutions established in the course of centuries in Great Britain whose wealth rests on naval strength, commerce and factories, must be acclimated to our poor Prussian agriculture."[35]

In addition to these steps toward economic growth taken in response to Napoleon during the occupation and after the defeat, the German, or in some instances the Prussian, economy responded directly to Britain in several ways. The largest impact came in 1819 with the British Corn Laws' worsening of the terms of trade of Prussia, which normally sold sizable amounts of grain and wood to Britain. Hit by substantial harvests in 1822 and 1823, as well as by the Corn Laws, the price of grain fell continuously from 1817 to 1825 by more than two-thirds. The Junker farming aristocracy was in difficulty. Land prices fell, mortgages rose, and with them foreclosures. State banks entered to assist. Writing at the end of the century, Ucke compared the agriculture depression of the 1820s with that of the 1880s and claimed it was worse.[36] Recovery set in at the end of the 1820s. Many people in East and West Prussia thought the depression in agriculture was the result of natural phenomena, including the destruction of crops by hailstorms and animals, but others blamed the British.

The Zollverein is usually thought of as more a political than an economic step, with Prussia taking the lead to promote her political authority and accepting an unduly small share of the revenues from the common pool as the price of her leadership. Bowring in 1840 noted that in Germany the move was generally felt to have been a first step in the germanization of the people.[37] That the leader of an alliance bears a disproportionate share of the costs, or receives too small a share of the benefits, is a finding of modern political theory and the principle of the "free rider," which states that those states less directly concerned in an alliance are able to pay less, or get more, than their proportionate share.[38] More recently an economic-political reason has been found for Zollverein: the gains to the participating states from reducing the cost of managing their customs borders.[39]

Many but not all British, however, regarded Zollverein as an attack on the Corn Laws. Bowring states that the Zollverein was not "formed in hostility to the commercial interests of other states, it was not intended prematurely to create a manufacturing population in rivalry with or opposition to the manufacturing aptitudes of Great Britain," but he adds that if "in the natural progress of things, the tariffs of the Zollverein have become hostile to the importation of foreign, and especially of British, produce, it is because [of] *our* laws."[40] Other views have been noted: Evans—"The Zollverein is the product of our destructive policy"; Palmerston—"One of the motives of Prussia in Zollverein was to induce England to diminish the duties on wheat and timber"; Bowring—"We have made the Germans trade with each other because we would not buy from them."[41] But British commercial policy was not all malign. In 1824 Britain signed a treaty with Prussia that removed discrimination against her in shipping. By 1828 Huskisson was starting to dismantle the restrictions on the export of machinery, which were swept away in 1842 along with reductions of tariffs. In 1846, of course, the Corn Laws fell; and by the mid-fifties, Germany was supplying 25 percent of wheat imports to Britain compared to 18 percent from the United States.[42]

British policy was directed against the Zollverein. Hanover, which was allied to the British crown, refused to consent to any sacrifice to facilitate the expansion of German trade.[43] A tax league was formed in 1834 among Austria, Hanover, Brunswick, Oldenburg, and the Hansa cities to counter the fiscal benefits of the Zollverein. Brunswick withdrew in 1844 to join the Zollverein, and by 1851 Hanover itself yielded to Prussian political pressure and economic enticements. Hanover was slow also in acquiescing to designs for railroad connections across its territory and in lifting its tolls on the Elbe, whether encouraged or not in these views by Britain.

In addition to restricting Prussian and other German exports until the 1840s, Britain made life hard for nascent German industry through her own exports. There were accusations of dumping immediately after the Congress of Vienna, and again in the early 1840s. The Zollverein was widely regarded as a response to this dumping. In an industry such as linen, where the Silesian cottage industry was driven to despair by the machine-spun yarns of Leeds and Belfast, not to mention the competition of cheap cotton textiles, the response was adulteration on the one hand and starvation on the other.

Linen provides a telling contrast between British and German growth in the first quarter of the nineteenth century. Prussia imposed a tariff on textiles, clothing, hardware, sugar, and coffee in 1821, and the British retaliated by enacting a tariff on raw linen. This led to mechanization of the British industry, with the aid of the Girard (French) machines,[44] and little further need for cloth imports from Germany. Germany tried to respond to machine yarns by lowering price, underbidding, and using cotton in linen mixtures. "Schmoller says with irony that 'the only technical progress they made was in disguising cotton so that hardly the most practiced eye could distinguish it from pure linen.' "[45] Linen declined from 23 percent by value of total German exports in 1828 to 11 percent in 1837, 9 percent in 1850, and 3 percent in 1864.[46]

There was continuous pressure for higher tariffs in the Zollverein, continuously resisted by Prussia. Changes in tariffs required a unanimous vote, and Prussia could apply a veto to any upward movement that threatened the export interests of the Junker decision makers. Palmerston had threatened retaliation against the Zollverein's formation in 1833.[47] Prussia was wary of substantial tariff increases on English iron, which appeared on the market in increasing quantities in the late 1830s and early 1840s, and on cotton yarn. But the Leipzig consul reported a new duty on iron to the Board of Trade in February 1837 and observed that the switch from imports of cloth to imports of yarn pointed to the ultimate exclusion of both.[48]

In some views, the Zollverein tariff increases of 1844 on iron and of 1846 on cotton yarns were significant policy actions designed to accelerate industrialization in what Crouzet, quoting Lévy-Leboyer, regards as the typical Continental as opposed to the British manner—upstream, rather than downstream—that is, industrialization that progressed from finished goods to components and inputs, rather than from iron to steel to machinery, or from yarn to cloth to clothing.[49] British manufacturers originally tried to prevent exports of yarn to inhibit weaving abroad, and for a long while managed to restrict exports of machinery. A strong case can be made that the repeal of the Corn Laws was "free-trade imperialism," to halt the move to industrialization on the Continent by enlarging the market for agricultural produce and primary materials.[50] But von Delbrück's account of the increases of 1844 and 1846 makes them appear as small concessions by Prussia to the other states, and almost accidental. In any event, Switzerland industrialized in the same directions as Germany without benefit of protection.

In addition to the connections through trade, the economic fortunes of Germany and Britain were tied through investment. Soon after the Napoleonic wars Prussia borrowed in London—in 1822 and 1832.[51] Between those dates a conversion loan was issued in London for Prussia by the Rothschilds. Thereafter for a time the flow of capital moved in the other direction, through amortization, and possibly through positive lending. Borchardt tends to doubt that Berlin exported capital on balance during the early 1840s,[52] and most sources agree that late in the decade there were capital imports in the form of subscription to railroad securities and investments in Rhenish mines, iron foundries, and nonferrous metalworks.

These connections were at best sporadic. Brockhage was surprised to find capital exports before 1850[53] and to determine that the Berlin capital market achieved importance at all. Frankfurt was the market par excellence for state loans, Hamburg for commercial lending, and Cologne for industrial loans. Political disintegration and the absence of a well-developed communication and transport network kept the capital market fragmented —a handicap to development theoretically analyzed in recent years by Shaw[54] and McKinnon[55] and already historically well understood by Borchardt[56]—and led to dealings with foreign sources of supply in both directions. The occasional purchase of foreign bonds seems to have been a result of lack of domestic investment opportunities, rather than a cause. The development of railroads after 1842 changed all this, along with the associated expansion of deposit banking after 1851.

The level of living in Germany to 1850 seems not to have risen perceptibly—though the data are even less reliable than those for the British standard-of-living controversy. Moreover, it is likely that total output per capita had not risen greatly, so that there were no substantial profits (for instance, from textiles, iron, agriculture, or commerce) available for capital formation, as there were in Britain. But the groundwork was being laid. The extension of the market took place in two ways—Zollverein on the one hand, and development of the railroad network on the other. These had trade-diversion as well as trade-creation effects, and the development of the railroads produced linkages to the iron and machinery industries. Even before the railroad, however, mechanization was under way, as Bowring observed:[57] "In some respects Germany may boast superiority to Great Britain in her means for manufactures. The arts of design and their application ... are more successfully wrought and worked; chemical knowledge is farther advanced than with us. Steam-engines are found on all sides, and mechanical improvements have made rapid strides, and have served to open a wide field for the characteristic development of German intelligence; which, if not specially distinguished for invention and discovery, seems particularly fitted to laborious and thoughtful application, and for the unwearied pursuit of any object which strongly interests its attention." But new industries were embryonic, as evidenced by the foundation of Siemens and Halske, the union of a military engineer and an artisan, in 1847.

The disruptions caused by the transition from the traditional economy to the market, which Britain had undergone earlier with the Luddites, along with the unrest led by Cobbett, Peterloo, and later the Chartists, were disturbing Germany in the late forties. These upheavals resulted from the dissolution of the guild system, the beginnings of factory work, and the dismissal of casual labor from the countryside as agriculture reorganized—combined with the potato crop failure and high food prices. By 1850 social unrest had been dissipated, partly through substantial emigration; the bourgeoisie had made its peace with the Hohenzollerns; and rising national consciousness was producing a motive for industrialization.

Germany was resolved to industrialize, but in a different way than Britain. It was felt that British industrialization had been socially disastrous for unprotected groups like women and children working in mines and factories, and unesthetic insofar as it led to belching chimneys, grimy villages, and squalid jerry-built housing. The sentiment was rooted in the Junker agriculturalist's distaste for the city with its egotism and immoderate ambition, speculation, and greed.[58] Even liberal thought had misgivings about industrial society with its blemishes of poor housing, alcoholism, and prostitution.[59] Part of the view was based on visits to England, part on anti-British prejudice. But industrialization was on its way. The period from 1820 to 1848 has been described as an "undynamic time, almost untouched by the breath of the capitalist spirit."[60]

Economic rivalry touches the emotions. In the seventeenth century, Britain was notorious for her hatred of the Dutch, "the abominable rival,"[61] and from that century there remains in the English language a series of expressions that use the adjective "Dutch" in an uncomplimentary way.[62] Kehr claimed that every connection with England in the 1840s was hailed in Germany[63] but this seems exaggerated in the light of Engels' "Die Lage der arbeitenden Klasse in England," as Tilly points out.[64] Love and hate were doubtless both involved.[65] If Kehr was right for the 1840s, however, the sentiment favorable to England was not to last, any more than the economy was to remain undynamic.

Germany as Journeyman, 1850 to 1871

In his theory of backwardness, Gerschenkron states that the greater the backwardness, (1) the sharper the kink and the more sustained the subsequent spurt; (2) the greater the stress on producers' goods; (3) the greater the scale of industrial plant and enterprise; (4) the greater the pressure on consumption levels of the populace; (5) the less active agriculture as a market for industrial goods and as a source of increased productivity; and (6) the more active the role of banks and beyond that of the state.[66] This is a more developed, if terse, statement than his earlier formulations, which concentrated on banks and government; it still leaves no room for the development of commerce, which presumably assisted economic development in the British case, but led nowhere in the case of the Netherlands.[67] Nor do foreign entrepreneurs, technology, or capital have a place in it. Britain, the first country to experience the industrial revolution, is the benchmark. In order of backwardness in Gerschenkron's schema come France, Germany, Italy, and Russia. France relies more on banks than government, Russia at the other end of the spectrum more on government than banks. Germany and Italy lie between.

The role of government in Germany was largely confined in the first half of the nineteenth century to clearing away the heritage of traditional society and preparing the groundwork for advance through education, support of technological acquisitions, and some limited capital formation. For the most part, government advanced the economic interest of the Junker aristocracy and pursued national political ends. Despite the mining engineer service, the German government was far from the technocratic planning agency represented by the Corps des ponts et chaussées in France, or the Saint-Simonien tradition. In fact it opposed the extension of banks. Tilly's study of "Financial Institutions and Industrialization in the Rhineland" concludes that, contrary to Henderson (and Gerschenkron) on the state and industrialization, Prussia hindered the Rhineland, and it was "decentralized, profit-oriented, decision-making by bankers which had to overcome the opposition of the state to industry." He goes further and asserts that Gerschenkron's thesis cannot be supported, since the Bank of Darmstadt failed to develop Hesse, Baden, and Württemberg.[68]

It may be doubted that the bankers' decisions were in fact decentralized. Oppenheim, Hansemann, Mevissen, von der Heydt in Cologne; Bleichroeder, Mendelssohn in Berlin; Rothschild in Frankfurt were tied into one another's activities, as well as into industry. Mevissen was an officer or director of six banks, eight industrial corporations, and a railroad.[69] He admitted that the government wanted to develop industry, but to keep it in tutelage.[70] His intimate friend, Vierson, had eight directorships further.

Government, moreover, opposed the development of banking. The first breakthrough came when the Schaaffhausen'scher Bankverein began to fail and was allowed to reorganize as a joint-stock bank in 1848. This was the first, and Mevissen used the new form to explore new means of financing. Subsequent requests for permission to start further banks were turned down by the Prussian government in Berlin, although Blumberg asserts that 1848 moderated the Prussian government opposition to companies.[71] It was not until 1851, when Hansemann found a loophole in the law, that large banks could be organized along the lines of a *Kommanditgesellschaft*, with silent partners and transferable shares rather than stockholders. Five years later a series of such banks was formed, six in Prussia alone and others elsewhere in Germany. The episode is parallel to the conclusion by Thomas Joplin in 1833 that the law of 1826, prohibiting note-issue banks within 65 miles of London, could not be applied to joint-stock banks which did not issue notes—a conclusion that broke through the restriction set up by the Bank of England. The movement took place twenty years later in Germany.

Mevissen and Oppenheim had intimate French associations and were early aware of the departure represented by the establishment of the Crédit mobilier in Paris in 1852. In 1853 they founded the Bank of Darmstadt, with some French, but mostly Cologne, money. Darmstadt was chosen because it lay outside Prussia, the government of which had rejected a request to establish the Bank of Berlin (and refused to allow the Schaaffhausen'scher Bankverein to transfer from Cologne to Berlin on the ground that anything not explicitly provided in the articles of incorporation was expressly forbidden).[72] In addition, Darmstadt was near Frankfurt, a financial center, which also refused permission to locate within its jurisdiction. The Darmstädter was intensely active, with agencies all over Germany and ultimately in Vienna and New York. At the end of 1856 Mevissen said that Germany, which had lagged a century behind France and England, had now surpassed them, thanks to the Darmstädter.[73] The judgment was premature in timing and excessive in causation. Böhme quotes Engels that Germany was not yet up to the English standard in 1860, but altogether changed from the past[74] and expanding rapidly.

The emphasis on banks and government as a substitute for entrepreneurship in Germany is perhaps a little overdone. German entrepreneurs were different from the British in their political backwardness. Kisch points out that the merchant-manufacturers of the Wupper Valley were devoid of political power.[75] It is claimed that the lack of power stems from the fact that they were scattered about in separate states.[76] Whatever the reason, whereas in Britain in 1865, 23 percent of the Members of Parliament were merchants and industrialists and 29.2 percent more were financial men, German entrepreneurs from all three sources in the Reichstag of 1871 amounted only to 8 percent of the total.[77] Merchants governed the Hansa cities such as Hamburg, but their grasp was limited. When the revolution of 1848 had run its course, the bourgeois classes, including the bankers to be sure, became frightened of the proletariat and let themselves be bluffed out of real political reform, both in the Frankfurt parliament and in separate constitutional crises, as in Hamburg. Regardless of their political weakness, however, the merchant class did provide recruits for the ranks of industrial entrepreneurship, especially in the Rhineland and Westphalia.

Krupp's ancestors were well-to-do merchants, as were those of the Haniel family in coal and ultimately iron. The textile industry on both banks of the Rhine was run by manufacturers who developed out of merchants. A few ironmasters came from the ranks of artisans, as did entrepreneurs in machinery. Chemists came from the drug business. All flourished more or less without government support, although with the assistance of banks, except in the case of Krupp. (He went to the money-lenders in the early 1840s, but not to the banks.) Moreover, the government occasionally singled out a would-be businessman, as it did in the case of a director of a company for the production of railway materials, who had taken part in the 1848 uprising. It threatened to withdraw the concession and the company collapsed. The year 1848 is said to have changed the attitude of the Prussian government to companies, on the ground that heavy industry was necessary in the interest of the state, and heavy industry required financing through limited liability.[78] In some views, the traditional antipathy of the landed aristocrats to industry was overcome only later, after the demonstration by Krupp in 1870 of his usefulness to German armed might.

Blumberg has provided the backgrounds of the professions of the 480 founders of 61 companies: 32 percent of them were merchants; 14 percent manufacturers, in which class I believe are included artisans who produce goods for the market by fairly primitive means; 12 percent state officials; 11 percent bankers; 7 percent large landholders; and 1.3 percent military. The figures were rather consistent by industry and region, except that artisans were sharply underrepresented in mining in Silesia—5 percent against 15 percent nationally. The rest were scattered or unknown.[79] One may find the list of the backgrounds interesting for the small number of merchants as compared, for example, with Britain, or because merchants have such a prominent position after all that has been said about backwardness. The role of the state officials is remarkable since even under the backwardness thesis, the state assists in industrialization qua state and not through the formation of enterprises by state officials in an individual capacity.[80]

Wutzmer emphasizes the merchant origins of Prussian industrial entrepreneurship in the 1840s, although in many cases the merchant roots go farther back, as do significant instances of entrepreneurship. The case of Schmölder in Rheydt, who imported British yarn in the 1840s but started in 1846 with 113,000 talers in capital, a mill site, and a row of machines to undertake spinning,[81] is matched sixty years earlier by Brügelmann, "the prototype of a Schumpeterian entrepreneur," who in 1780 smuggled a spinning machine from Arkwright's factory to Elberfeld, built in 1783 a five-story water-powered spinning mill for 20,000 Rhein talers, and shortly set up weaving and dyeing facilities.[82] Import substitution, with or without smuggling, was a classic mode of development.

Moreover, after industrialization had gone a certain distance, innovation was possible. In the first half of the nineteenth century Britain took over inventions from the Continent, including the Girard machine for spinning flax, the Jacquard loom for fancy patterns in silk—both from France—and as early as 1810 the Friedrich König printing press from Germany.[83] By the late 1840s Germany was innovating in electrical equipment, as well as rapidly applying British inventions and innovations. In the second half of the century Solingen factories—the largest with eight hundred men—were pioneers in the process of forging cutlery by mechanical methods instead of by hand, a process that Sheffield was slow to adopt.[84] The turnabout may be compressed into a shorter period of time if one notes Krupp's visit to Liverpool in 1839 to observe a rolling mill for copper plates, and the purchase in 1851 by Elkington of Birmingham of a Krupp machine for the mass production of spoons and forks.[85]

Import substitution occurred somewhat earlier in locomotives, with the assistance of the government that has already been described. Borsig's first locomotive was built in 1841. In that year there were only twenty locomotives in service in Germany, all foreign made. (An earlier 1840 locomotive, made by Poensgen at Aachen with the help of an English mechanic Dobbs, went out of service in 1841.) The major suppliers were Stephenson and Company of Newcastle, Robert Sharp of Manchester, and Norris of Philadelphia—a make preferred by the nascent Prussian railways. Borsig took a Norris model in 1841, perfected it, delivered it to the Berlin-Anhalt line in July of that year, and outperformed a British rival. In 1843, on the Berlin-Stettin line, another Borsig model beat an English make.[86] Borsig's forty-fourth locomotive, submitted to the Berlin Exhibition of 1844, won a prize on the basis of using less water than other machines, thus saving fuel, and costing less—12,000 talers as against 12,900.

By 1846 there were more German than foreign machines on the German railroad lines. By the end of 1847 Borsig had delivered 187 locomotives to German lines, out of a total park of 332. In 1846 and 1847 alone, it furnished 128 out of 187 machines. The turning point in import substitution was 1847, with imports of 30 machines from abroad representing the maximum. From 1848 to 1854 Borsig produced 335 locomotives (instead of 187 as in the previous decade), other German firms 65, and all foreign firms together 37. No foreign locomotives at all were bought in 1854; in that year Borsig sold 6 machines to Poland and 4 to Denmark. Import subsitution is complete when the industry moves to exporting.[87] Of the 1,036 locomotives produced from 1864 to 1869 by Borsig, one-quarter were exported, notably to Russia, Austria, and Scandinavia.[88]

The locomotive industry of Germany is interesting not only as a case study in import substitution, but also for the light it throws on the advantages of market disintegration. Borsig in Berlin was by all odds the dominant supplier in Germany, but tariffs, especially discrimination against Prussian suppliers by other political entities, provided sheltered markets in which local machinery manufacturers could get a start. Until 1867 Borsig had a virtual monopoly in Prussia, excluding the Rhineland. German companies outside Prussia delivered only 6 locomotives to Prussian railroads in 1861. On the other hand, 3 small railroad lines in the Rhineland had no Borsig locomotives and the Bergische-Märkische line only 4 of its park of 16. Outside of Prussia, however, there were machinery producers who went in for locomotive construction in Aachen (Regnier and Poncelet, plus Dobbs and Poensgen), Sterkade (Jacobi, Haniel, and Huyssen), Buckau (the Magdeburg-Hamburg steamship company), Munich (Maffei), Württemberg (Maschinenfabrik Esslingen), Kassel (Henschel), Hanover (Hanomag), and Stettin (Wöhlert, Schwarzkopf, Stettinger A. G.). Maffei of Munich was helped by being located in a large state that discriminated in its favor (as Prussia did for Borsig); Henschel and Maschinenfabrik Esslingen specialized in industrial locomotives for short hauls in plant yards and in powerful engines for mountain traction, including some innovative engines such as an Esslingen engine with six axles.

In other industries German producers successfully imitated and ultimately improved on English methods. The British introduced the first coke-oven in 1832. German foundries started to substitute coke for charcoal in about 1840 and achieved decisive success in 1852-1853.[89] Krupp's reputation in steel was based on perfecting French and English discoveries, especially the rapid development of Bessemer after 1856. The Thomas process developed in England in 1878 was avidly sought after by many manufacturers in France and Germany, though by none in Britain. The controversy among Burn, Hopkins and Burnham, Andrews and Brunner, Temin, McClosky, and others over whether it was economically feasible to cut back on acid Martin and expand basic openhearth in the Sheffield area is touched upon later. For myself, I am not intellectually satisfied by static models of profit maximization in a given state of the arts when the growth process is advanced by dynamic adaptation of new technology to given situations.

Imitation, followed by adaptation, followed by innovation are at their most conspicuous in the synthetic dye industry. Beer's account,[90] which is closely followed by such scholars of the chemical industry as Hohenberg and of technical change as Lilley, is well known and there is little need to reproduce it at lengh. Perkins made the initial breakthrough in aniline purple dye in 1856 at the Royal College of Chemistry in London. A student of Liebig named Hofmann, who had been brought to the Royal College in 1845 by the prince consort, went on in the search for other colors as Perkins withdrew from industrial research into pure academic work. Other discoveries took place in France and Britain, and these two countries were still on top in the Paris Exhibition of 1867. But France was falling rapidly behind: her bankers were unwilling to finance research, her patent laws were unfavorable, and, as Beer puts it, the French were poor at drudgery and preferred to search for ideas rather than processes. Perkins made a fortune and sold out at the age of thirty-five (he had been eighteen when he made his discovery) to devote his time to pure science. In 1865 Hoffmann went back to Germany to the University of Berlin to set up a methodical attack on synthetics. A new patent law sought by the industry helped in 1876. University and synthetic-dye companies teamed up, laboratories organized larger and larger battalions. Having started out in imitation, the German chemical industry remained to innovate.

The rise of German industrial output in the 1850s had significant impact on international movements of the factors of production that affected British-German relations. In the question of migration the British direct role was small, to be sure. There were three avenues for emigrants from Germany to the Western Hemisphere, via Hamburg and London or Liverpool, direct from Bremen, or overland to Cherbourg and thence by boat. The social turmoil of the 1840s—the dissolution of traditional agricultural ties, the collapse of the guild system, and the rise of the factory, all combined with the cholera of the 1840s and potato disease and poor crops—led to a swelling movement abroad. For the most part, the emigration was limited to artisans and peasants with some means to pay the passage. Whole villages would sell the forest to the nobles and head for America.[91] There is a tradition in the United States that this migration was in response to political oppression leading to and after the revolution of 1848, but this is overstated. The desire to escape military conscription was a contributory factor, and several hundred political refugees came to the United States after 1848. Largely, however, it was the agricultural depression in the years after 1845 that fed the emigration once it had started; what was remarkable was the manner in which it dried up under the blast of expansion. A standard question in migration analysis is whether the push was greater than the pull. German emigration reached 250,000 in the year 1854 after successive bad harvests from 1850 to 1853 and then dropped away to 100,000 in 1855 to 1857 with a good harvest and rapidly expanding industrial employment.[92] "The emigration from Germany was the most important single factor leading Germany to enter the North Atlantic trades" in competition with Britain.[93]

The indirect connection of this migration with England is that many of the emigrants went to dominions like Canada and Australia, or the former colony represented by the United States, and formed new, largely non-German loyalties. Britain's head start in world settlement of open spaces meant that there was no possibility of German migrants establishing Wakefield-like colonies or independent countries in which they exerted large influence to support the fatherland. When Germany acquired colonies later on, they were in native-populated and resource-poor areas in Africa, or islands in the Pacific, useful for coaling stations and a few colonial goods, but far from the dominions and the United States, which offered England large markets in peacetime and military support in war. Even after World War I, Hjalmar Schacht was continuously grumbling about Germany's lack of colonies. Germany is said to have overcome its inferiority complex with respect to French, Belgian, and especially British industry at the end of the 1850s and the beginning of the 1860s,[94] but there was always a sense of injustice that German emigrants were lost to the old country, whereas British emigrants located all over the world supported the homeland.

The other direct connection between Britain and Germany in factor movements concerned capital inflow. There is some debate about whether French, Belgian, and British capital exports to Germany were significant in the railroad investment boom of the 1840s, or only in the 1850s when investment shifted to coal, iron, and steel. Brockhage quotes contemporary observers on both sides of the question of whether foreign investors, especially British, bought German railroad paper.[95] One who believed it did not, Rother of Seehandlung, was possibly in a good position to judge. On the other hand, a modern study suggests that as much as 5 million talers (15 million marks) a year might have been investment in railroads; estimates total capital imports in the 1840s as 17 million talers; but asserts, against the weight of evidence, that capital imports stopped shortly after 1850.[96] The dominant current view is that capital imports were not important before 1850[97] and perhaps not important afterward either—contrary to what Haussherr, Jenks, Blumberg, Cameron, Legge, and Fischer (for Baden) say[98]—but were concentrated in mining. Benaerts gives the total mining to 1857 as 100 million marks (33 million talers),[99] presents extensive lists, and even sets out a *cri de coeur* from Gustav Mevissen published in the Köln-Neu-Essener Gewerbeverein Festschrift of 1852:

This field of action so productive, mining, a source scarcely explored in our national wealth, that our country, for lack of the spirit of enterprise has decided not to exploit, threatens more and more in these last few years to become the object of foreign speculation. It is a notorious fact that in the Rhineland for several years, many mining pits have been acquired for the account of French and English capitalists and are going to be exploited for their profit.... The treasures which the soil of our country embraces thus serve to augment the capitalistic preponderance that foreigners already possess elsewhere and to nourish the foreign capitalist through the fruit of German labor. It would seem to be in the supreme interest of our economy to keep for it as much as possible not only of the remuneration, but also of the capital.[100]

This statement is contemporary with the 1970s in spirit, if not in rhetoric—translated from German to French and from French to English —in the spirit of *Überfremdung*. A book published in 1924 with Überfremdung in the title mentions that there were 49 companies in mining and ore production controlled from abroad, for a total of 140 million gold marks (26 Belgian, 13 English, 6 French, 4 Dutch), having begun in 1851 and with investments taking place mostly in the 1850s and 1860s.[101]

Of particular interest in this experience is the fact that by and large it unwound without the intervention of the government policy. This sounds surprising by today's analysis of the multinational corporation. Direct foreign investments have been compared first with trees, which are long-lived, and then with redwoods. Some early direct investments follow that pattern, but with a difference from today's multinational corporation. So great were difficulties of communication that the investor, with his money, settled down abroad and ultimately became a citizen. Thus Thomas Mulvaney, who raised capital in Dublin for investment in what were called the Hibernia and the Shamrock mines (founded in 1856–1857) and who pioneered in new techniques for bracing the mine shaft with iron instead of brick, became a resident of Westphalia. For the most part, however, the investments were simply bought out. Some of the railroad securities were acquired in nationalization measures. It may be that the industrial banks, like the Darmstädter, founded the year after Mevissen's complaint about the German lack of spirit of enterprise, made a special point of buying up foreign holdings—although there is no evidence, and French investments in Ruhr coal continued as late as 1908 with the purpose of securing coking coal for the de Wendel interests in Lorraine.[102] It would seem rather that as companies came up for sale they went to the highest bidders. In the 1850s these proved to be foreign investors in a number of cases: beginning in the 1860s,[103] the highest bidder was generally a German enterprise except in special cases such as the Phoenix, "one of those pompous Paris speculative enterprises,"[104] or the cases above in which de Wendel wanted to buy into the coke cartel and was probably forced to pay a high price.

Foreign capital thus apparently played only a modest role in German economic development, despite Cameron's claim,[105] and its role in coal and iron lasted only briefly in the 1850s and part of the 1860s.

The 1850s saw a further step in the direction of Anglo-German rivalry as the All-English City of Hamburg began to assert its independence from London, and British banking houses missed a chance to keep Hamburg in its sphere of influence. The Hamburg-American Packet Line AG (Hapag) was created in 1848, but shifted out of sail into steam in 1856. (The North German Lloyd Company of Bremen, which was more truly a transatlantic company, was founded in 1857.) Although London remained the world's leading port, Hamburg was on its way to becoming the most important port on the Continent and began to import raw sugar, coffee, and other tropical products directly, instead of over London.[106] Hamburg finance staked out a position of some importance in Scandinavia, which had been a British preserve, especially after the Crimean war[107]—an expansion that was, in 1857, destined to produce difficulty.

The panic of 1857 started with the collapse of a small bank in the U.S. Midwest, spread through the falling price of wheat to Liverpool, then London, to Scandinavia, where English credits were called, and then to Hamburg, which had extended large-scale credits to Sweden. As a number of large trading and banking houses stood on the verge of collapse, Hamburg emissaries sought loans from Rothschild, Baring, and Hambro in London, Fould in Paris, and also in Amsterdam, Copenhagen, Brussels,

Berlin, Dresden, and Hanover.[108] Bank rates went to 10 percent, and ship captains hesitated to unload their wares because merchant houses might be unwilling to pay the freight.[109] The last two loan rejections had come from Fould in Paris ("Your dispatch is not sufficiently clear") and from the Hamburg ambassador at Berlin ("Bruck and the Emperor are not ambitious financially"), when the minister at Vienna cabled that the Austrians were providing a loan in the form of needed cash, in silver, which came to be called the Silver Train. It amounted to 12 million mark banco (plus another 4 million private credit to M. M. Warburg & Co., whose brother-in-law Schiff of the Austrian Credit-Anstalt had helped plead the case).[110] The episode was part of Hamburg's maturation. Böhme notes that the crisis kept coming back into the discussion of both Hamburgers and non-Hamburgers when discussing exchange, and even reading about it would make peoples' hair stand on end. Thereafter Hamburg merchants became more sophisticated and specialized more fully by banking, shipping, or trade.[111] It seems unlikely that Britain had a real opportunity to rediscount in the crisis for the Hamburg banks, at that rudimentary stage of the development of the international banking system. But international finance proved to be one more dimension in which German interests achieved comparatively early independence, if not rivalry.[112] Germany was again somewhat slowed down industrially by the financial crisis of May 1866, which started over the German-Austrian war and deepened after the outbreak of crisis in England when Overend, Gurney & Co. failed. Germany's recovery was speedy, and after the successful war against France its expansion was rapid.

It is of great interest that Prussia and Germany held to free trade ideals during all of the 1860s and in fact to 1875. The reasons were not analytical but ideological. The Junkers still clung to free-trade doctrines, and until Rudolph von Delbrück was dropped or voluntarily resigned as the president of the imperial chancellery in April 1876, these views dominated the civil service. Bismarck was interested in free trade less for its economic than for its diplomatic advantages. Low tariffs discomfited Austria with its exposed inefficient manufacturing, and prevented it from joining the Zollverein and rivaling Prussian leadership among the southern tier of German states.

With the conclusion of the Anglo-French Commercial Treaty of 1860, moreover, there was a competitive reason to join the movement to free trade, and this Prussia did in a trade agreement with France. A subsequent agreement with Russia carried an implied threat of favoring Russian over Austrian feed grains. In addition to the Stolper-Samuelson argument for free trade, which the Junkers subconsciously favored, there were the additional needs to keep up with Britain and to keep down Austria.

However, the Junker market in Britain was not to be sustained despite the repeal of the Corn Laws. Grain grew from 8 percent of German exports in 1828 to 11.5 percent in 1837 to 15.2 percent in 1850, while linen exports were falling, under the pressure of competition from Leeds, Belfast, and cotton textiles, from 23.4 to 11.1 to 8.9 percent.[113] But the gain did not last. It would be poetically just if the story told by Lambi that the Danish blockade of the Baltic and Hamburg during the war of 1864 over Schleswig and Holstein started the downfall.[114] The Junkers were for war and for grain exports. By choosing the former, they would have lost the latter (in this formulation). Bondi gives a figure for 1864 of grain as 7.3 percent of German exports, rising to 8.3 percent in 1869, which would support the view (his figures are given only for separate disjointed years). Despite Sering, on whom Lambi relies, there is little evidence for this contention. Knowledgeable historians are aware of a brief blockade of German exports by Denmark in the revolution of 1848, which had no lasting effects. It is likely that the loss of the British grain market by East Prussia was the result rather of American expansion, especially after the Civil War when the railroad was built west and veterans were given homesteads in the Northwest territories that now make up Minnesota and Nebraska. Whatever the reason, the German share of the British grain market compared to the American dropped precipitously after the end of the Civil War after peaking in 1861-1862:[115]

	German states	United States
1856 to 1860	25.9%	18.0%
1871 to 1875	8.2%	40.9%
1875	2.9%	60.2%

(From Lambi, *Free Trade and Protection*, pp. 10, 133.)

We may conclude by noting the economic implications of Prussia's three wars of the 1860s (if 1870 belongs to the 1860s), against Denmark, Austria, and France. Rostow makes a great deal of nationalism as a "most important and powerful motive force in the transition from traditional to modern societies,"[116] but he refers to "reactive nationalism—reacting against intrusion from more advanced nations" and, insofar as Germany is concerned, to the defeat at Jena in 1806. Again "it was German nationalism which stole the revolution of 1848 at Frankfurt and made the framework within which the German take-off occurred—the Junkers and men of the East, more than the men of trade and the liberals of the West."[117] To Harry Johnson, nationalism is a public good of collective consumption, rather than an investment that yields output in dedication to work and expansion.[118] In the German case, though it is difficult to make much of Rostow's statement that takeoff owed more to the Junkers than to the industrialists, it is fair to say that military success led to economic drive and expansion. The defeat of Austria in 1866 clinched the support of the southern tier. Victory over France stilled the last vestige of dissent of the "English" city, Hamburg, and made Prussian leadership in the newly founded Reich unanimous.

Germany as Master, 1873 to 1913

The smashing victory of Prussia over France in 1870 touched off a short-lived boom based on (1) unification of the German states under Prussian leadership; (2) receipt of a substantial sum in cash—742 million marks of gold, silver, and French and German banknotes—under the Franco-Prussian indemnity; (3) unification of German money with bimetallism giving way to the gold standard; but above all (4) a nationalist euphoria that produced a speculative rise in prices of commodities and securities. In the course of the transfer of the full indemnity of 5 billion marks, Germany accumulated 90 million in short-term claims on London. When the Jay Cooke failure in the United States led to a liquidity squeeze, the withdrawal of this amount precipitated the recession of 1873 and ushered in the Great Depression in England. After the collapse of stock markets, first in Vienna, then in Berlin and Frankfurt, the German economy was quiescent for a few years, accumulating strength for the expansion of the 1880s and 1890s. Britain, on the other hand, experienced a continuation of the investment boom of the early 1870s into and immediately past the middle of the decade. It then settled into depression in the 1880s. The contrast of German and British experience in the 1880s and 1890s produced the sense in both countries that Germany was catching up with and even overtaking Britain in economic expansion.

Even though it does not bear directly on our theme, it will be useful to observe the change in German tariff policy in 1879. This "fateful turning point,"[119] one of the most important in the history of modern Germany,"[120] was accomplished by the switch of the Junkers from alliance with the commercial interests of the northern cities to alliance with heavy industry. The ultimate cause was the loss of export markets for grain and the threat of imports. There is considerable discussion in the literature on whether the 1873 depression produced the change of attitude. Lambi says yes;[121] Barkin says no.[122] Gerschenkron notes that the depression increased the protectionism of industry,[123] but this was always high. Epstein perhaps has the point right: that the depression discredited laissez-faire and encouraged the organization of pressure groups, such as the Zentralverband deutscher Industrieller (1876). There was some good in the tariff; it prevented Germany from becoming a lopsided industrial country like England and required Bismarck in the political maneuvering to abandon his fight against the Catholics with whom he became allied.[124] Still, the shift consolidated all the anachronistic elements in the system at the top and buried the subservient interests that were hurt by the tariff under this feudal leadership. The peasant who benefited from cheap grain to feed his animals followed the leadership of the Junker who grew only grain. The small metal processors took their cue from the large vertically integrated processors who owned iron and made common cause with the iron interests.

The change took place with bewildering speed after 1877. Up to that time, Prussia and the Zollverein had been for low tariffs. The nationalist Friederich List was always opposed to tariffs on agriculture and, as an infant-industry protectionist, saw the ultimate end of protection in free trade. Tariffs had been raised on textiles and iron products in the 1840s, when Prussia yielded her principles and interests to accommodate the other members of the Zollverein. A later attempt to raise duties on manufactures in the 1850s obtained a grudging consent from Prussia to appease the southern tier. Britain started to intervene, but her ally Brunswick inside the Zollverein provided the necessary veto.[125] The single-veto system applicable to all members was abandoned in 1867 when the Zollverein was reorganized, but Prussia retained a presidential veto. Prussia was firmly wedded to liberal principles at the time, and the reduction of duties in connection with the trade agreement in France in 1862 was extended in the 1868 treaty with Austria, when duties were reduced on iron, cotton cloth, linen, chemicals, and wines.[126]

The boom of the early 1870s led to a movement to reduce still further the import duties on iron and to eliminate them altogether on iron manufactures (thus producing negative rates of protection for the latter). The iron producers were aided in resisting this pressure by the French system of "titres d'acquit à caution" for iron exported gross (while iron was imported on balance into France). This was regarded in Germany as an export subsidy. The device, later employed by the Germans in maintaining the export of grain when the country was on balance an importer, enabled exporters near the border in one part of the country to raise their price above the world level by selling certificates attesting to their exports to importers, who in turn used them to pay the duty. In this way exporters received and importers had to pay a price above the world market. As such it was a subsidy to export, but not one that lowered the price of an existing exporter.

The acquisition of Alsace-Lorraine in 1871 hurt the cotton interests of Saxony by bringing Mulhouse into the Zollverein. In iron ore it benefited the producers of iron and steel by providing them with a cheap source of iron—the French minette ores—and temporarily eliminating the supply of a commercial rival, until further exploration on the French side of the new border uncovered broad new fields. (While Germany was winning World War I, industrial war aims included acquisition of Briey-Longwy to add to the gains of 1871.)[127] At the peak of the boom the decision was taken to lower duties on iron—but later. Free-traders pressed for reduction, but with the passage of time the case for lowering tariffs weakened as the depression grew, and increasingly a positive case was expressed to raise the duties on iron. In 1876 Rudolph Delbrück, president of the imperialist chancellery under Bismarck, "resigned." As he was in good health and had no apparent reason, it seems evident that he was dismissed, rather than submitted his resignation voluntarily, because as a strong free-trader he inhibited the change of policy that was building in Bismarck's mind.

If the tariff did not have its origin largely in depression, it further had little to do with subsequent recovery. Overall it may be said to have slowed down expansion by tending to hold on the farm some of the thousands who were fleeing to the mines of the Ruhr and Silesia or the factories of Berlin. (Very quickly in the 1880s the problems of the Junkers were not solely those of falling prices and declining exports, on the side of demand, but also the supply of labor.) It also reduced real incomes and effective demands on workers and iron processors. The tariff may, however, have made some contribution to growth through higher profits for integrated iron and steel producers.

A more likely candidate for the role of contributor to growth is the German propensity to form cartels, concerns, and trusts. This tendency to amalgamate, to look after joint interests—in German, *Kartellfähigkeit*[128]— was an established German tradition. The Rheinisch Westfälische Kohlen Syndikat had a 33-paragraph agreement at the time of its formation in 1835. (A still older coal cartel, of course, was the famous Newcastle Vend of the seventeenth century in Britain.) The depression of 1873 led to rapid formation of cartels. Only 6 agreements have been traced to earlier than 1870, 14 to the period up to 1877. Thereafter many cartels were formed, 350 to the turn of the century, of which 275 survived,[129] and 1,500 to 1925.[130]

Of greater interest than the cartels is the push for vertical integration, a movement very different from what was happening in Britain. At a very early stage the steel industry of the Ruhr, supported by banks of the Ruhr, went backward into coal mining, later into the production of iron ore, then forward into machinery. Siemens and Halske bought a copper mine in 1864 and were encouraged by the prosperity of 1871 to move more widely into raw materials.[131] In the dyestuff industry one step on the way to the formation of the I. G. Farben trust occurred when three of the seven companies that ultimately participated got together to buy a coal mine.[132] Earlier the separate companies had branched into drug making, when they discovered that they had the raw materials and equipment to make active compounds, and into heavy chemicals to make themselves independent of other producers (and to save money).[133] In contrast with the British propensity to have separate stages of production separately owned, in Germany vertical integration was a common practice.

Moreover, the rise of large industrial organizations saw the elimination of the merchant. As Siemens in 1871 bought a shopful of equipment from the United States because of long delivery dates in Germany—five or six months—and set up an "American shop" with mass production methods, it began to change selling methods. Siemens decided to write to customers in advance of producing their "constructions," and to put pressure on them to order them as Siemens indicated, without alteration, to get them cheaply, well-made, and quickly.[134] This direct selling, in contrast to marketing through merchants, enabled the company to work out technical improvements acceptable to its customers, with an optimization that took into account both performance and cost, as contrasted with Britain where the merchant, standing between producer and customer, often impeded technical progress, telling the producer, "They don't want them like that," and the customer, "They don't make them like that."[135]

Until about 1885, according to Beer,[136] German dye companies marketed abroad through wholesalers whom, however, they permitted to carry the line of only one firm. From 1885 on, dyestuffs moved to direct selling, with firms wholesaling their own products, sending salesmen and consultants abroad to establish local sales corporations headed by Germans but otherwise employing local personnel.[137]

All this time the quality of German goods was improving. From slavish imitation and adulteration in the first half of the century, German industry was moving to autonomy—not always, as it happens, in a straight line. At the Great Exhibition of 1851, Britain led the world,[138] but Krupp exhibited a six-pounder cannon and a steel casting of 4,300 pounds.[139] In 1855 at the Paris Exhibition Krupp had a twelve-pound cannon, lighter than the French bronze and able to fire 3,000 rounds without buckling, and also a 10,000-pound steel casting.[140] Borsig won a prize for locomotives at Paris in 1855.[141]

The path of improvement was not always wide or steady. In Paris in 1865, German products were distinguished by being shoddy and cheap. The showing was regarded as a disaster for German exporters. In 1868 the Paris World Exhibition brought no significant success to the exporters of Barmen and Elberfeld,[142] although the inferiority against British goods observable in 1851 had been overcome.

The German exhibit at the Centennial Exhibition at Philadelphia was regarded as disastrously ineffective, with German goods cheap and poor except for Krupp artillery, which consisted of killing machines.[143] Even the chief German Commissioner to the Exhibition denounced his compatriots' showing.[144] Thereafter the performance changed rapidly. By the end of the century German products were scoring triumphs at Chicago in 1893, and at Paris in 1900 and 1901.[145]

Some shoddy goods were disguised as British, and from as early as the 1830s a number of British manufacturers were continuously engaged in litigation to protect trademarks. In the mid-1880s, complaints against foreign, and especially German, frauds against British trademarks blew into such a storm that the Merchandise Marks Act of 1887 was passed by Parliament, requiring imported goods to be marked to indicate their country of origin.[146] The law forbade misrepresentation and required that foreign goods marked with the name of an English dealer carry indication or place name of their foreign origin as well. The mark "Made in Germany," later the title of a book excoriating slipshod British commercial methods,[147] surprised the British by the ubiquity of goods available in Britain and in Europe, goods of rapidly rising quality. It quickly became apparent that the defensive measure had boomeranged and aided the offensive. Like Japanese goods in the twentieth century, which started out with a reputation for inferiority, and British woolens in the eighteenth century, German wares ultimately became known for their solid quality.

A similar defensive measure backfired somewhat later. In 1909, smarting under the import competition of German dyestuffs and chemicals, the

British government enacted legislation requiring that patents be worked or licensed. This had the effect of encouraging foreign firms to establish subsidiaries in England and produce dyes on the basis of imported intermediate goods, rather than stimulating British production. Most of the British consumption of dyes continued to be imported—80 percent—and a large part from domestic production was the output of foreign-owned firms.[148]

The last quarter of the century saw German goods squeeze British products out of a number of markets. Historians who denigrate the climacteric and the alleged failure of the Victorian entrepreneur tend to explain the relative decline in British exports to the Continent and to the United States in terms of the rise of protection. This explanation is not proof against the mass of evidence adduced by Hoffman of German gains at British expense, or faster than Britain, in a series of markets in Latin America and the Middle and Far East, outside of the colonies. Hoffman asserts that it is difficult to exaggerate the commercial preponderance of Britain in the 1880s and 1890s.[149] By 1900 pushy German exporters, giving undue lines of credit, selling in any quantity, and descending to the "petty ways and details of a shop,"[150] but also providing special rail and sea through-rates where these helped, were eating into British markets.

The difference in economic vitality is suggested by the difference in reaction to foreign tariffs: the British typically accepted exclusion from the foreign market as the Welsh tinmakers[151] and the Nottingham and Leicester hosiery trade[152] did after the United States McKinley tariff of 1890. The German reaction tended to be different and to consist in a search for new goods that could, at given costs, surmount or circumvent the barrier. Baron von Richthofen told Sir Francis Lascelles in 1900 that he was not disturbed by a possible increase in Chinese tariffs, stating: "Germany has had considerable experience in dealing with countries which imposed a high tariff, such as the United States and the South American Republics," and found that "it was quite possible to carry on a large business in spite of such tariffs."[153]

This equanimity in the face of prospective tariff increases was not maintained for long. In 1900 Canada adopted imperial preference, and Sir Joseph Chamberlain and a tariff reform movement advocated imperial preference on a wider scale for the entire empire. Germany took the occasion to denounce the 1865 trade treaty with Britain on the ground that it provided England with most-favored nation (MFN) treatment, not only for the mother country but also for the dominions. Furthermore, Germany threatened to withdraw MFN treatment on her own from the United

Kingdom and other dominions than Canada, from whom she did withdraw it. The German press followed the progress of the Trade Reform debate in Britain with avid interest and the strong conviction that reform would lead to a decline of German prosperity.[154] One of the reasons for the construction of the German navy was to keep doors open, to maintain colonies, and to guard against an unfavorable trade conspiracy. (Germany had never fully recovered from the exclusion of German ships from the Mediterranean in the 1830s, or the refusal of a British cruiser to come to the aid of a Prussian merchantman captured by pirates and held for ransom back in 1815.)[155] When he tried to negotiate the forestalling of the war in 1913 and 1914, Ballin laid down as one of the conditions of German cooperation that Britain continue to adhere to free trade, "a commitment so valuable to German commerce."[156] Brentano, the free-trader, put the issue sharply in political-economic terms: "What good is a fleet to protect our goods when foreign countries can raise tariffs against us," adding "and we can reduce our exports through our own tariffs."[157]

A number of observers insist that the 1850s were the watershed of German economic development and the period when Germany made its major gains in closing the gap with the British economy.[158] The period 1873 to 1896, moreover, is characterized as the Great Depression, in Germany as well as in Britain, to judge from the overall statistics. There is nonetheless good reason to maintain that the later period was the one in which German economic growth, and especially structural change, brought about a forward economic spurt that put Germany in a class with Britain as a major economic power, even if it did not bring the German economy entirely abreast of the British.

To break down the period, there were three short depressions—1873 to 1878, 1882 to 1886, and 1890 to 1894—and three recovery periods—1879 to 1882, 1886 to 1889, plus the period from 1894 to 1896. There were two especially good years, according to Spiethoff, 1889 and 1896, as contrasted with ten from 1849 to 1873.[159] Agriculture was depressed, but that no longer mattered in the overall economic position—though it was politically decisive. The movement off the farm became a flood. At the end of the 1870s Germany was still an agricultural country, with the majority living on the land. The proportion of the working force in agriculture, however, declined from 43.5 percent in 1882 to 36 percent in 1895. One and a half million emigrated, and vast numbers moved from agriculture in the east to mining in the west, a unique long-distance internal migration, as contrasted with short-range migration within Britain and France (except to Paris in the case of France).[160]

While the rate of growth was slower than in the earlier and subsequent periods, there were great additions to efficiency of plant and productivity of labor, creative innovations in business methods, and a wholesale adoption of improvements in technology and organization.[161] The number of artisans grew from 2.88 million to 2.93 million between 1882 and 1895, but middle-sized industry (from 5 to 50 workers) grew from 1.39 million to 2.45 million, and large industry (over 50) from 1.61 million to 3.04 million. Within the last group giant firms of more than 1,000 workers increased from 213,000 to 449.000. This was the period of growth of new industries in chemicals and electricity and the forward push of heavy industry that led Germany to match British output in iron and steel in the 1890s.

The upsurge in industry from 1894 to 1896 produced a halt in emigration, which echoed that of 1854 to 1855.[162] What is new and contrasts sharply with experience in Britain is the similar halt in foreign lending from Germany in the 1880s, at a time when British loans, especially to the Argentine, were flourishing.

The years 1871 to 1873 in Germany produced a boom in both domestic and foreign investment. The foreign-investment boom went in considerable degree to Russia. According to one estimate, in the mid-1880s Germany owned six-tenths of the sizable Russian debt of 6.25 billion rubles (about 3 billion marks). It is characteristic of neophyte foreign lenders (such as the United States in the 1930s) that foreign lending is positively correlated with the domestic cycle and not counterposed to it. These loans helped Germany find a prominent place in the Russian market for heavy goods—60 to 65 percent of imported pig iron, 50 percent of steel, 50 percent of instruments, and 70 percent of agricultural machinery. Beginning in 1886, however, German investment houses sold their Russian securities, or let them run off as the maturities of 1871–1873 were converted by a French loan of 1889. Berlin sold while Paris bought Russian securities,[163] which accounts for the curious phenomenon that French lending of billions of francs to Russia was accompanied by an export surplus only one-twelfth of that amount.[164] The halt of German lending to Russia had political overtones associated with the rise of Russian tariffs on pig iron in 1884–1885 and again in 1887, breaking out in general industrial protection and a tariff war in 1891 and 1893.[165] But Girault, the historian of French lending to Russia, is persuaded (no doubt rightly) that Berlin bankers would have been willing to refinance the Russian loans if the price had been right. Abundant French capital and the need for funds to finance German expansion cut off the flow of capital abroad, as the boom was to do to the emigration of workers in a few years. In Britain lending abroad continued to grow to a peak in 1913.

It is tempting to suggest that large-scale foreign lending—by the Dutch in the eighteenth century, the British at the end of the nineteenth, and the United States from 1958—is a symptom of industrial decline.

At about the middle of the 1890s the commercial and industrial rivalry of Germany with England broke out into more conscious political and military competition. On each side there was sharp awareness of the economic and military moves of the other. There is no need to detail the exact sequence of political steps leading to war, but it is of considerable interest to trace the relationship of various economic groups to the rising nationalism in Germany, and the German hatred of England, which rapidly replaced the earlier sense of inferiority.

Bankers, merchants, the Hansa cities, and the agrarians had little economic reason to oppose Britain. Independence was sought, but not mastery; Hamburg and Bremen had worked for direct commercial links with overseas areas and for independence in shipping to all parts of the world. The Deutsche Bank in 1872 was founded with the express purpose of freeing German trade from dependence on British banking. The same interests of banking, shipping, and trade sought colonies, especially after 1885. And the agrarian interests were socially scornful of British bourgeois commercial and industrial mentality, as well as distrustful of the processes of industrialization that led to grime, slums, a proletariat, and social unrest. In the initial stages these groups opposed building the fleet. Hansa cities and bankers were friendly to Britain and believed that their commercial success depended on British prosperity and commitment to free trade, and particularly on the avoidance of tariff reform. Agrarians opposed the navy on two social grounds: because the army was the senior and aristocratic service in Germany, and because of the tension in the 1890s between the industrial and the agrarian state. The Kanitz Bill called for raising grain prices to the 1850–1890 average and holding labor on the farm; the agrarians at one stage argued, *kein Kanitz, keine Kähne*— no Kanitz motion, not a single barge for the navy.[166]

A series of nationalist organizations was formed: the Kolonialverein in 1887, the Alldeutsche Verband in 1891, and the Flottenverein in 1898. Gradually they were taken over by the steel interests, and gradually in turn they won the support of the merchant classes, Hansa cities, bankers, and Junkers. Up to 1897 Hamburg opposed naval construction, wondering what a navy would do against free-trade England. By the fall of that year its opinion had swung over.[167] The banker von der Heydt withdrew from the Alldeutsche Verband shortly after its founding in 1891, because of its enmity to England. Only 18 percent of the members of the organization were entrepreneurs, and only one-quarter in all were businessmen. As the decade wore on, however, the banking community began to ally itself with nationalism; the proprietor of the Bleichchröder Bank, P. von Schwabach, although British consul general in Berlin, was a member of both the Alldeutsche Verband and the Flottenverein.[168] The Bankhaus Mendelssohn was closely allied with the Flottenverein. Kehr, who is a political polemicist, maintains that the banks stopped opposing the fleet with the second naval building law of 1900.

Agrarian opposition to the fleet is said to have faded as a result of the Boer War, in which the Germans as a whole sided strongly with the Boers and against Britain. The modern analogue of the Boer War in the United States was of course the long and unpopular conflict in Vietnam.

In due course commercial rivalry, colonies, shipping, financial competition with Britain in such regions as the Middle East, big steel, and naval building were all fused in a harmonious, highly nationalist relationship. In 1913, on the occasion of the twenty-fifth anniversary of Kaiser Wilhelm II's accession to the imperial throne, plans were made for the foundation of the Königliche Institut für Seeverkehr und Weltwirtschaft, located in Kiel, which was to be dedicated to the study of world trade. (These plans were finally realized in 1914, and in 1919 the buildings were bought from Krupp for a nominal sum.) There were merchants and bankers like Ballin and Warburg of Hamburg who did not share in the rapidly spreading hatred of England; they formed part of a rapidly dwindling minority.

Hardach ascribes the rise of anglophobia to the years 1850 to 1873.[169] In that period the warnings in Germany to avoid anglicization of the economy, which had been weak and isolated in the first half of the century, accumulated force. But the intensity of feeling grew sharply beginning in the 1880s and reached a peak at the end of the century, at a time when Britain in its turn felt threatened by German commercial rivalry. The *Agrarstaat* versus *Industriestaat* debate brought the English example to the fore. With their scornful contrast between *Händler und Helden* (tradesmen and heroes), the Junkers finally turned their detestation of the city and industry against the British as a means of preserving their position of leadership. Big steel prospered on this diet. "For conservatives, agrarians, bureaucrats and academics, their social inferiority to England, partly living, partly unconscious, was decisive in the rejection of England"[170]— with ultimately fateful consequences.

British Slowdown after 1875

There is no doubt that German economic growth after 1873 was fast, faster than that of Great Britain. The question that is unsettled is whether the British economy slowed down, suffered a "climacteric"—a maturing or aging process—and lost its capacity to adapt and to respond to economic signals. Answers to the question turn partly on methodology and separate the traditional economic historians from the "new," who use explicit economic models and econometric analysis.

It is perhaps foolhardy of one who is neither an econometrician nor a bona fide economic historian to enter the debate, a literary economist who is more historical economist than economic historian, interested in testing economic models against historical fact more than using particular economic models to understand history. Nevertheless, it seems to me important to try to resolve the conflict. The traditional economic historians—with some distinguished exceptions—tend to believe that Britain slowed down after 1875 for reasons that Landes summarizes as social and institutional[171] and Habakkuk ascribes to the early start and the complexity of the industrial structure.[172] The new economic historians, on the other hand, tend to conclude from their models and regressions that the British economy, and especially British industry, did as well throughout the period as it was able, given the constraints of exogenous conditions, that it maximized profits—with limited exceptions—and that where it failed to adopt foreign innovations or domestic inventions, there were sound reasons of lack of profitability to explain it.

The methodological issue turns on whether one argues by example, as Saul and Richardson assert is true of traditional economic historians,[173] or whether the econometricians draw out of their models little more than the assumption they put in to begin with, as can perhaps be claimed. In a private letter McCloskey says that the use of evidence by traditional economic historians at a casual level is much below the standards to which their profession holds up the medieval historians, who of course have to rely on much less copious information. As a tu quoque reply, one can suggest that econometrics runs the risk of circular reasoning. It is perhaps a mistake to go outside the scope of Germany and Britain, but I have been struck by the triviality of Fogel's finding that railroads made little contribution to the economic growth of the United States after he assumed that both railroads and canals had constant-cost functions.[174] If two processes have constant costs over the whole range of possible outputs and are both in use at a given time, one (or the other) can be thrown away. In the case of many of the essays in the book edited by McCloskey,[175] and in his own study of British iron and steel,[176] if one assumes a competitive model in which technical change is exogenous it is quite easy to find in the usual case that companies were maximizing. The McCloskey demonstration in iron and steel goes further than this, to be sure, into comparative rates of labor productivity. But no consideration is given to the possible relevance of a model in which firms "satisficed" rather than maximized profits; or maximized a function that included among its arguments the desire for a quiet life; or maximized profits competitively in a model in which among the ways to maximize profits were to alter technology so as to reduce costs, economize on a scarce resource, make more effective use of an abundant resource, or reorder institutions (such as substituting direct selling for the merchant) in an effort to overcome barriers to still higher profits. As Pollard has said,[177] there are questions of dynamics. In a static model the problem is to maximize some function within given constraints. But dynamic models are available in which it is possible to break down such constraints. Bottlenecks can be limiting in a static model, or stimulating in a dynamic one.[178] Which is relevant in a given case is a question of judgment. The new economics seems usually to choose the static model.

Some years ago, John R. Meyer ascribed the slowdown of British growth to the falling off of export demand.[179] He constructed an input-output table for the British economy on the basis of the Census of Manufactures data for 1907 and suggested that if export demand had grown from 1875 to 1913 at the same rate as it had in the third quarter of the century, British growth would have been much higher. But an input-output table for a given year with its fixed coefficients is evidently an inappropriate tool to use over a forty-year period of changing technology, and the inference that demand must always come from the same place to sustain the same rate of growth is surely unacceptable. Britain in this period had too high a rate of growth of exports, rather than too low, since exports of standard goods to the countries of the empire enabled the economy to evade the exigencies of dynamic change, away from cotton textiles, iron and steel rails, galvanized iron sheets, and the like, to production for export or for the home market of the products of the new industries. It should be added that McCloskey is not attracted to the Meyer explanation based on demand.[180]

Whatever the shortcomings of the new economic history, what is required of more traditional methods, if they are not to be casual empiricism or anecdotal history—two highly pejorative characterizations?

There is nothing wrong with the use of illustrative examples, provided that the generalizations they decorate or illuminate are soundly drawn from a representative sample of the universe under discussion, and that they properly illustrate the point. The use of an example presupposes that the scholar has first undertaken a study of the total body of material under discussion, or a carefully drawn and representative sample, and that the example is suggestive of a mean or model case, and not one or three standard deviations away—or a boundary case.

It is not necessary to recite the numbers that illustrate the faster growth of Germany than Britain during the forty years prior to 1914, nor to do more than recapitulate the useful discussion of Landes, already referred to, from which McCloskey and the new economic historians (plus a few more traditional economic historians such as Saul) are dissenting. If we take the statistics as read, the Landes argument consists in dismissing objective reasons for British backwardness—lack of resources, smaller population, high wages, and availability of capital, and stressing rather the disadvantages of the head start, with interrelatedness of technical capital increments; running down of entrepreneurial vigor after the founder's generation; scarcity of venture capital; and lack of technical education.[181] Saul regards the notion of technical decline between 1851 and 1867 as "entirely mistaken" and cites evidence of "brilliant newcomers," "pioneering first-generation firms," the rise of the bicycle industry to world dominance in ten years, and "strikingly good performance" in stationary engines.[182]

The provision of example and counterexample without description of the entire population from which the samples are drawn is a vapid procedure. For a Marshall of Leeds illustration, in which the second generation crippled the most efficient flax-spinning plant in the world in 1848 and the third generation brought it to bankruptcy in 1881,[183] one can counter with a Pilkington illustration where the new generation provided a vigorous sales effort, adopted Siemens gas-fired tank furnaces, and met foreign competition.[184] It is not enough to cite the failure of old companies—Hawks Crawshaw, Maudlays, Boulton & Watt, and Napier[185]—if new firms are rising to take their place. Nor is it appropriate for McCloskey to cite Lowthian Bell as an example of a trained scientist in the steel industry of Britain,[186] whereas Erickson indicates that he was the only one or at best one of two.[187] Or to claim with Temin that the steel industry failed to innovate or sustain technical progress because of lack of demand[188] without noting the failure of the tinplate industry to change its scale or technique over a hundred years despite an expansion of demand by one hundred fifty times between 1800 and 1891—and of exports by four times between 1872 and 1891.[189]

The following succinct discussion will cover several dimensions of the problem: technical change, including invention, innovation, and imitation, and within the group the speed of solving technical problems, overcoming technical difficulties, or adopting a process that is dominant; the advantages and disadvantages of specialization, including the merchant system, the independent engineer, and their opposites—direct buying and selling and vertical integration—and related to both, the role of industrial standards; and lastly the Victorian entrepreneur and his education, including its technical content.

Technical Change

In the period from 1770 to at least 1851, technical change took place in Britain and imitation, with delay, took place on the Continent. A variety of cases has been cited earlier, including those in which inventions occurred in Europe, but the first useful applications were taken up in Britain: the König printing press, the Girard flax spinner, the Jacquard loom. In the period after 1875 the record is replete with the statement of new industries where innovations occurred in Europe or the United States, even when the invention was given birth in Britain; German imitation of British innovation was rapid, whereas British imitation of Germany was slow. It is only necessary to cite Bessemer, Gilchrist Thomas (and the French and German races to Britain to obtain the patents), mauve dyes, and the Parsons steam turbine on one side; and the diesel engine, Solvay process, hot blast coke ovens, Linotype, turret lathe, Owens Bottling machine, tabor molding machine, Northrop automatic loom, ring spindles, three-phase current, and reduction of aluminum on the other.

The classic case of course is the British delay in adopting the Gilchrist Thomas process and developing East Midland ores. McCloskey maintains that it was not profitable within the existing technology, the state of demand, and the location of the ores in relation to consuming centers.[190] The question arises, however, why it was necessary to wait from 1878 to 1915 until the Americans solved the technical problem—as far as the Northhamptonshire ores of Stewart and Lloyd at Corby were concerned.[191] A problem of coking fines at Frodingham did not find full solution for thirty years.[192] The experience of United Steel at Appleby-Frodingham in the 1920s and 1930s is not relevant to our subject, as McCloskey points out in relation to Clapham's strictures,[193] but it is of interest to note that the annual reports of United Steel point out that while Frodingham was fully employed and making substantial profits in each year from 1923 to 1928,[194] and again in the 1930s, expansion there was not undertaken until late in the 1930s.[195]

The record has further examples: the tunnel kiln developed for pottery in 1912, which took forty years to become general;[196] and the 100-inch twin grinders and continuous twin polisher at Pilkington's plate glass which took "the short time of seventeen years" to develop.[197] The defenders of United Steel speak of "necessary time lags" and claim that technical change takes time.[198] In the earlier stages of the industrial revolution, however, enormous changes were crowded into relatively few years—the cotton textiles in the 1760s, iron and steel in the 1850s, shipbuilding in the 1880s. By contrast the late nineteenth and early twentieth century performance of Britain seems deliberate.

As noted, there were successes: textile machinery, specialty steel, bicycles, machine tools for bicycles, paints, explosives, pharmaceuticals, soap, and the Parsons steam turbine (though it was ultimately surpassed by the Curtis, Rateau, and Zoelly turbines). In bicycles, moreover, there was speed. The new industry of Coventry and Birmingham rose to world dominance in ten years and responded positively to the financial setback of 1897.[199] This approaches the hub of the question. In a static model, depressions hurt; in a dynamic one, they evoke creative response from which come growth and profits. The contrast is between the Keynesian and the Schumpeterian models. In most industries, Britain followed the former.

A significant question is whether the British entrepreneur failed to understand the importance of research and development (R&D), as Richardson claims is true of the chemical industry and the British nation in general,[200] or was unsuccessful at it. Failure can be the consequence of general ineffectuality, or of one critical error at an important turning point. Richardson supports the view that R & D were held in low esteem in Britain by citing numbers of patents there and in Germany.[201] In other industries one can find statements of scorn for innovation in general,[202] and industries bemused with past successes that ignored new developments, as in steam, which inhibited interest in internal combustion, or groups of engineers who failed to be aroused by striking events: for example, the English electrical engineers' failure to respond to the long-distance demonstration of transmission of three-phase current.[203] But there are instances on the other side, where there was great interest but a wrong choice, notably heroic and successful efforts to improve the Leblanc soda process when it should have been abandoned; and example after example of attempts to adopt or adapt machinery, which failed for want of competence. An early example is the effort of James Marshall in the 1850s and 1860s to change from mechanical retting of flax for linen, and to make effective use of the Schlumberger combing machine. Efforts were extensive but unsuccessful and in the end, in 1874, the French equipment was discarded.[204] Byatt cites instances of companies that failed to overcome teething troubles in electric lighting and in electric supply, and abandoned the fields.[205] Experiments undertaken by the Brush company with the Swedish Ljundström machine proved to be "expensive."[206] It is difficult to devise an adequate classification scheme to enable one to weigh how much lack of Schumpeterian response at the end of the century was the result of disinterest, gross errors, or low levels of competence. Presumably all three obtained, as well as cases of effective entrepreneurial innovation.

There remains the competitive model in which research activity is not undertaken because it does not pay; it is more profitable to let others invent and innovate and to imitate slowly because the mean of the probability distribution of going down the wrong path is high. To the Chicago school, in which everyone is always maximizing profits, this explanation for limited invention, innovation, and slow imitation or solution of production problems is appealing. One particular form of the argument is that skilled labor was so cheap in Britain that it did not pay to innovate or imitate in labor-saving techniques.[207] But this argument can run either way, depending on whether one uses a static or a dynamic model. Cheap skilled labor will enable a country to build complex machinery in a static model, obviate the necessity for so doing in a dynamic one. In the same way that one can find economic historians saying that high wages are good[208] or bad[209] or for growth, high or low prices, more or less exports and imports, and the like can stimulate or retard depending upon the model chosen.

The new economics, moreover, might have been expected to take note of the finding that economic growth has a large residual component, whether investment in human capital, technical change, or learning by doing. At the very least, speed of imitation of innovations that can be recognized as likely to be successful has a payoff. The return to electricity may be less when there is a gas network for lighting; the Leblanc process should be abandoned when it is clear that the Solvay method dominates it, even though economies are being achieved in the former,[210] and solution of the problems of the East Midlands ores has a high payoff after the Thomas process shows the way. When the "residual" is so large a contribution to growth, the a priori view that technical change does not pay is difficult to accept.

Specialization and Standardization

Standardization achieves economies of scale in production. In contrast, thirty grades of low-grade poplins, when the ultimate user can distinguish at best three grades;[211] two hundred types of axle boxes and forty different handbrakes; fifty different systems of electrical supply, twenty-four voltages, and ten different frequencies; one hundred twenty-two channel and angle sections in steel when the Germans made thirty four;[212] "an almost unbelievable lack of standardization" on the part of British makers of plows;[213] and other examples all suggest difficulties in achieving scale economies. Specialization is limited by the size of the market, to be sure, but the question is not wholly out of the hands of the entrepreneur if he succeeds in achieving standardization of design. For this purpose he needs to have direct contact with the consumer. A filter in the form of a system of merchants or consulting engineers is likely to prevent technical change that settles on a standard design, which in turn optimizes economies of production and efficiency in use.

In a static model the merchant is efficient because he prevents the diseconomy of too large an administrative scale and permits specialization. The producer specializes in production; the merchant in selling. Each looks after his end of the process independently. Without technological change, the disintegration works—although Allen believes that in cotton, it works well in expansion but poorly when demand is declining.[214] When the time comes to contemplate change, however, the merchant acts as a filter between producer and consumer, preventing them from getting together to agree on how the product should be modified to enable it to be produced as cheaply as possible within the requirements of the consumer. The great specialization of Britain, which was a strength as new products became refined in such industries as cotton textiles, became a handicap when the problem was to streamline, simplify, and standardize. When companies rose to national size in the United States, they tended to give up dependence on wholesalers and jobbers and go in for direct selling.[215] At an early stage in American retailing, department stores stopped reliance on commission merchants and turned to direct buying, first through permanent agents, then by sending buyers to the producers even in Europe. The abandonment of the merchant by Siemens and the chemical companies in Germany in the 1880s has been mentioned.[216] Hohenberg's thesis is that the chemical industry could grow in size and profitability only by educating the consumer companies in the use of intermediate goods, and, for fertilizers, by educating the ultimate consumer.[217] In the third quarter of the twentieth century a distinction is made between hardware and software, the latter needed for the effective use of the former. In a merchant system software must be kept to a minimum because it requires direct selling by "commercial engineers."

It is not only the merchant who filters and screens effective communication between producer and user. The wrong type of engineer can equally impede standardization. Railroad lines with superintending engineers laid down specific standards for locomotives, based on professional judgments, which prevented British companies from producing stock models on a mass basis.[218] Consulting engineers hired by municipalities ordering electric lighting systems laid down rigid specifications with heavy penalty clauses, which inhibited fixing standards.[219] Saul generalizes this experience and notes that in northeastern England Charles Mertz both provided electrical supply and acted as the consulting engineer, without separation of function, with the result that electrification achieved its most notable progress in the area where he concentrated.[220] Vertical integration, which brought the merchant and the design function under the same roof with production, offered the opportunity for achieving standardization of design, or the provision of special modifications for special needs—which the British economy lacked. But only the opportunity. A laissez-faire system with many small companies, and no organization of the trade or dominant companies, lacks a mechanism for setting standards unless government is willing to undertake it. In Britain Parliament laid down the Standard Gauge Act in 1846, but failed to apply it to the Great Western Railroad. For the most part the public good of standards was provided in Germany and the United States by large companies. "The big firms rammed it through."[221] Contrast the British example with that of two large firms in Germany. Each British municipality hired its own consulting engineer with his own idea and ordered a specially designed system. In Germany, Siemens responded rapidly in the 1890s to AEG's demonstration of the superiority of high-voltage, three-phase alternating current, and the two firms offered the public an identical standardized product.

One municipal engineer in Glasgow, John Young, pushed through the use of the overhead trolley at the end of the nineteenth century. Whereas in France, standardization in this field came from the outstanding producing company (Thomson-Huston), which operated some tramway lines but

made its profits on equipment, the dynamism of Glasgow under the leadership of one individual seems to have enabled the street railway industry
to avoid the proliferation of standards found in most other items of
municipal equipment.[222]

The clash between the old economic history and the new is sharply
revealed in steel and the role played by the merchant system. Old-
fashioned economic history, which the new history dismisses summarily,
ascribes a role in slowing down technological change and maintaining
exports of standardized rails, galvanized sheets, and the like to the dominance of the industry by merchants, "gradually less suited" to the needs
of the industry,[223] with no technical capacity, and responsible for a large
part of domestic and home sales.[224] The industry was competitive, says
McCloskey, and while steel users based their judgments of steel qualities
not on chemical analysis but on experience and reputation, they were
right in preferring first wrought to cast iron, then mild steel to hard steel,
and then acid open-hearth to basic Bessemer. The fact that the admiralty
fastened on the acid-basic difference rather than the open-hearth/
Bessemer, and rejected basic open-hearth steel for ships until well into the
First World War, is not explained. By implication there is no need for an
institutional arrangement that links up producer and consumer without
intermediaries. Technical information circulates perfectly when developed
and made public, and price is all that is needed to direct choices. Contemporary observers who complain that producers and consumers are failing
to take advantage of their opportunities, on the other hand, lack an appreciation of the effectiveness of competitive markets. It is not explained
why these observers lack information, whereas consumers and producers
have all they need.

The issue then is one of the existence or absence of market failure. The
new economic historians believe markets work. Apart from a rare case like
the Leblanc process, competition, adequacy of information, and rational
behavior result in economic solutions. Externalities, like the dissemination
of technical information through direct selling (software) and public
goods like standards, are not needed; continuous profit maximization with
adequate foresight is forthcoming under any and all circumstances. The
alternative view for which a great deal of qualitative evidence exists, but
which is difficult if not impossible to pose in quantitative form, is that
at one level, everyone is maximizing subject to constraints; but at a
less tautological and trivial level, periods of rapid technical change may
lead to market failure through a lack of positive externalities and public
goods, through institutions that inhibit profit maximization and, as the

next section proposes to show, through actors who maximize objective functions other than profits.

The Victorian Entrepreneur

First, a small point. In a 1970 paper,[225] McCloskey uses macroeconomic statistics of productivity in Britain to suggest that Coppock was wrong in trying to correct the dating of the climacteric from the 1870s to the 1890s,[226] and that in fact it should be brought forward to the first decade of the twentieth century. It was not the Victorian entrepreneur who failed but the Edwardian. (Later it proved to be the case that no entrepreneur at all failed.) McCloskey's conclusion seems to rest on a failure to understand Coppock's argument, which turns on the choice of deflators for converting money to real income. McCloskey seems to believe that Coppocks's criticism was based on the difference in weights of the price deflator between one based on national product and one based on value added. He suggests that these are the same, and of course this is correct. But Coppock's actual position rests on the difference, in an open economy with changing terms of trade, between income produced and income consumed. In the 1880s and 1890s income consumed was rising rapidly because of improvement in the terms of trade. Income produced, however, did less well. If instead of a deflator for national income, one for net national product were used, the climacteric is pushed back before the 1880s. The period from 1900 to 1913 is one of declining income despite improved output because of worsening terms of trade, and not one of newly arrived entrepreneurial failure.

Timing aside, there is the question of whether in three generations from clogs to clogs the British entrepreneur was spoiled by success and failed to develop from a brilliant amateur, who achieved the industrial revolution, into an accomplished professional technical manager, who kept it going.

The new economic historians have a powerful a priori argument on their side. It is insufficient to point out the decline of firms. It is possible for firms to decline, for family firms to fail, and for the sons of self-made men to go to Oxford and Cambridge and then into the professions or government rather than business, without economic decline or even a slowdown of growth, so long as those who leave industry are replaced by newcomers. It is not gross movements that count, but net; and not the quality of old owner-managers, but the average quality, including dynamism, of industrial managers as a whole. Everything said about the interest in the quiet life, trustee securities, three-day weekends in the country, and the like is of no importance if the *élan vital* of industry is maintained on balance by a flow of recruits.

There were newcomers. Saul points to them in textile machinery, high-speed engines, machine tools, bicycles, soap, alkalis, electrical companies.[227] And there were successes for old firms in hydraulic machinery and the like. But many firms in electrical products and chemicals were foreign, as were a number of critical technical people in various companies—in automobiles,[228] Short in Dick, Kerr and Co.,[229] and Levenstein and Dreyfus in dyestuffs.[230] It would appear that the number of domestic newcomers was not sufficient to fill the ranks left by those departing.

In *Economic Growth in France and Britain* I put together a table of nineteenth-century business dynasties drawn from *Fortunes Made in Business*, which showed that sons, grandsons, and great-grandsons were drawn more and more out of business into Parliament and other forms of public life.[231] The list could have been made much longer for public life had I not wanted other indications of change of interest including education, religion, charitable works, and the like. It would be interesting to extend the list also to include the movement out of industry into the professions.

Habakkuk cites the case of William Morris, who started in the automobile business because his father could not afford to send him to the university to study medicine.[232] This is highly evocative of the last half of the eighteenth century, when entrepreneurs were recruited in large part from the ranks of Dissenters and Scots who were prevented from studying at Oxford and Cambridge, and thus from qualifying for the professions. A century later the barrier of religion in education and the professions had been broken down. Civil service, the law, medicine, and even engineering as an independent profession were recruiting many of the dynamic individuals who would have been available for the ranks of industry in the eighteenth century.

A recent paper by Thackray notes that science was studied by such persons as the members of the Philosophical and Literary Society of Manchester in the eighteenth century, not for the purpose of solving industrial problems, as the conventional wisdom has it, but to achieve social advance.[233] Successful manufacturers would study spiders, and not for what they could learn about weaving from them. Thackray's thesis is that the provincial scientific societies—outside of the Royal Society in London—had the function of legitimizing marginal men. In this they were successful. The first generation, which was self-educated and successful in business, turned to science in middle age, but to study such nonuseful subjects as (at that time) astronomy. The second generation in a modal family would be educated at Edinburgh and engage to some degree in business, but mostly study science. The third generation, however, converted to anglicanism, attended public school and Oxford or Cambridge, engaged in political life, lived in the country, and stayed in society. This same third generation moved to put more science into Oxford and Cambridge, especially Cambridge, and to support Darwin, Huxley, and technical education—for others. There was great interest in scientific and technical education, but few engaged in practical applications.

Musgrave claims that science and technological education were not on the agenda of Victorian Britain.[234] The statement seems exaggerated if one contemplates the Select Committee on Scientific Instruction (1868), the Royal Commission on Scientific Instruction and the Advancement of Science (1870–1875), the reorganization of the Royal School of Mines (1882), the Royal Commission on Technical Instruction (1883), the Technical Instruction Act of 1889, its finance with whiskey money in 1891, and so on, including the expansion of examinations in mathematics, chemistry both practical and theoretical, and metallurgy, between 1875 and 1895. The question of technical and scientific instruction was not addressed in Britain in the eighteenth century, as in France, or in the first half of the nineteenth century, as in Germany; but as German competition rose, it was by no means overlooked. More apposite is Cotgrove's view that the social structure did not favor technical education of the elite for application in business.[235] There was widespread support for the idea of technical education, little opportunity to achieve social advance by means of it.

The contrast is with France, where established firms were identified with the Ecole polytechnique, with the Ecole centrale des arts et manufactures, and even certain banking families who went, generation after generation, to the Hautes Etudes commerciales. This is not to claim that French technical education was admirably suited for success in business: its Cartesian quality, emphasis on mathematics, and elitism produced a succession of brilliant and arrogant technocrats who did best in the army and public works and less well, unless they had apprenticed abroad, in the family firm. Nonetheless, the point of contrast is that scientific and technical education were approved *for* the elite in France, *by* the elite in Britain. If a son was intended for trade, he would not be sent to the public school or the university.[236] Leadership in industry was left to "players," while "gentlemen" went into public life, the civil service, the professions—

medicine, law, ministry, the military services—or rusticated. This explains why in steel, an industry where most of the leading manufacturers were recruited from sons of businessmen and gentry, including professionals, the average age of these sons was rising rapidly between 1865 and 1895—the mean from 38 to 46 and later to as high as 55, and the lower limit of the third quartile from 54 to 65.[237]

The brilliant newcomers in bicycles, from whose ranks came most of the less brilliant newcomers in automobiles (apart from William Morris), rose from the players as did Lever in soap. The gentlemen failed to furnish an adequate number of new recruits for industry, and in fact drew them off. The supply of replacements was insufficient. This is why, while it was possible for British industry as a whole to continue to grow while given firms were declining, and a number of large firms were emerging to industry dominance—Distillers Company, Imperial Tobacco, Courtaulds, J. P. Coats, Bryant and May, in addition to those already mentioned—on the whole, growth was unspectacular.

But it is time to return to the question of Germany. When did Germany overtake Britain? Certainly not until well after World War II. Rapid growth of the German economy as a whole, and leadership in new industries at the end of the nineteenth century were not sufficient to offset the long lag in efficiency in agriculture, textiles, shipping, banking, and foreign investments. In a world of S-curves, more rapid growth of one country than another does not inevitably mean overtaking via linear extrapolation, so that the slower growing country should resign like a chess master who loses a pawn against a peer. Much can supervene to delay an outcome that is in any case inevitable. The United States can perhaps take some comfort in this thought as it contemplates Japan. But not much.

Notes

1. This chapter is based on four lectures given in Professor S. B. Saul's seminar in economic history at the University of Edinburgh in January 1974. The superficial excuse for choosing the topic is set out in the first paragraph. The underlying reason is that in 1971 I read German economic history for four months at the Institut für Weltwirtschaft at the University of Kiel, and the seminar afforded an opportunity to organize that material.

2. Crouzet, "Western Europe and Great Britain," pp. 98 ff.

3. Rostow, *Stages of Economic Growth*; Hardach, "German Economic Historiography," pp. 60–61, 66–70.

4. *Economic Aspects of Sovereignty*.

5. Kocka, *Unternehmungsverwaltung und Angestelltenschaft*, vol. 2, p. 79.

6. Redlich, "Frühindustrielle Unternehmer," p. 408. (Translations of all quotations in this chapter taken from non-English sources are my own.)

7. For the contemporaneous view of another German-Swiss engineer, J. G. Bodmer, who visited Birmingham in 1816–1817 and found some unevenness in British development, with much handwork of a primitive kind side by side with much more elaborate technical process, see Court, *Rise of the Midland Industries*.

8. Crouzet, "Croissances comparées," pp. 139, 147, 150.

9. *The German People*, pp. 50–52.

10. Ritter, *Die Rolle des Staates*, p. 34.

11. *Les Origines de la grande industrie allemande*, p. 119.

12. Ibid., p. 369.

13. Adelmann, "Structural Change," p. 88.

14. Abel, *Geschichte der deutschen Landwirtschaft*, pp. 258 ff.

15. The absence of commerce is stressed by William Jacob, a visitor to Germany in 1819. Of Münster, he says "little commerce" (*Agriculture, Manufactures, Statistics and Society*, p. 94); further, "Commerce, of Hanover inconsiderable despite connection to Bremen" (p. 116); "Berlin is not a commercial city, there is no great enterprise, and no great efforts diverted to make it become one" (p. 204); "A body of merchants and manufacturers, who by their capital give employment to numerous workmen, and who like country gentlemen are too rich to be dependent on the smiles or frowns of the court, is not to be found in Prussia" (p. 225).

16. *Der Staat und Industrialisierung*, p. 49.

17. Ibid., p. 90.

18. Benaerts, *Les Origines de la grande industrie allemande*, p. 57.

19. Riesser, *The Great German Banks*, p. 39.

20. Böhme, *Frankfurt und Hamburg*, p. 172; Banfield, *Industry of the Rhine*, ser. 2, p. 196; Bowring, "Prussian Commercial Union," p. 38.

21. Henderson, *Britain and Industrial Europe*, p. 92.

22. Von Bodelschwingh, *Leben des Ober-Präsidenten Vincke*, p. 96.

23. *Agriculture, Manufactures, Statistics and Society*, p. 231.

24. Ritter, *Die Rolle des Staates*, p. 25.

25. Banfield, *Industry of the Rhine*, ser. 2, pp. 222, 224.

26. Ritter, *Die Rolle des Staates*, p. 25.

27. Benaerts, *Borsig et les locomotives en Allemagne*, p. 51.

28. Ritter, *Die Rolle des Staates*, p. 25.

29. "German Economic Historiography," p. 77.

30. Benaerts, *Les Origines de la grande industrie allemande*, p. 344.

31. "Frühindustrielle Unternehmer," p. 342.

32. Ibid.

33. Ibid., p. 368.

34. Hohenberg, *Chemicals in Western Europe*, p. 68.

35. Benaerts, *Les Origines de la grande industrie allemande*, p. 337.

36. *Die Agrarkrise in Preussen*, p. 32.

37. "Prussian Commercial Union," p. 7.

38. Froelich et al., *Political Leadership and Collective Action*; Olson and Zeckhauser, "An Economic Theory of Alliance," pp. 266 ff.

39. Dumke, "Political Economy of Economic Integration."

40. "Prussian Commercial Union," p. 2.

41. Benaerts, *Les Origines de la grande industrie allemande*, p. 74.

42. Lambi, *Free Trade and Protection*, p. 20.

43. Benaerts, *Les Origines de la grande industrie allemande*, p. 66.

44. Williams, *British Commercial Policy*, p. 200.

45. Blumberg, "Geschichte der deutschen Leinenindustrie," p. 99.

46. Bondi, *Deutschlands Aussenhandel*, p. 146.

47. Ibid., p. 44.

48. Brown, *Board of Trade*, p. 113.

49. Crouzet, "Western Europe and Great Britain," pp. 121–122.

50. Semmel, *Rise of Free Trade Imperialism*.

51. Brockhage, *Zur Entwicklung des preussischdeutschen Kapitalexports*, pt. 1, pp. 106, 117, 128.

52. "Zur Frage des Kapitalmangels," p. 412.

53. *Zur Entwicklung des preussischdeutschen Kapitalexports*, pt. 1, p. 52.

54. *Financial Deepening*.

55. *Money and Capital*.

56. "Zur Frage des Kapitalmangels."

57. "Prussian Commercial Union," p. 38.

58. Barkin, *Controversy over German Industrialization*, pp. 150 ff.

59. Ibid., p. 132.

60. Hardach, "German Economic Historiography," p. 51.

61. Wilson, *Anglo-Dutch Commerce*, p. 29.

62. For instance, a "Dutch uncle" is not an uncle, but a harsh and overbearing elder; a "Dutch treat" is not a treat, but an event in which the guest pays his own way; "Dutch courage" is alcohol; "Dutch arithmetic" results in a total larger than the constituent entries; a

"Dutch wife" is a pillow; a "Dutch concert" is cacophony; a "Dutch nightingale" is a frog; and so on. Even the opprobrious term "boor" in English is the neutral word in Dutch for a farmer.

63. "Imperialismus and deutscher Schlachtflottenbau," p. 295.

64. Tilly, "Los von England," p. 182.

65. Hardach, "Anglomanie und Anglophobie," pp. 153 ff.

66. Gerschenkron, "Typology of Industrial Development," pp. 499 ff.

67. Rostow, "Beginnings of Modern Growth," p. 573, n. 45.

68. Tilly, *Financial Institutions*, p. 138.

69. Blumberg, "Die Finanzierung der Neugründungen," p. 199.

70. Benaerts, *Les Origines de la grande industrie allemande*, p. 256.

71. "Die Finanzierung der Neugründungen," p. 174.

72. Riesser, *The Great German Banks*, p. 509.

73. Benaerts, *Les Origines de la grande industrie allemande*, p. 277.

74. Böhme, *Prolegomena*, p. 54.

75. "From Monopoly to Laissez-Faire," p. 390.

76. Zunkel, *Der rheinische-westfälische Unternehmer*, p. 252.

77. Ibid., p. 189.

78. Blumberg, "Die Finanzierung der Neugründungen," p. 174.

79. Ibid., p. 196.

80. Details for a few companies (Blumberg, "Die Finanzierung der Neugründungen," pp. 201 ff; Zunkel, *Der rheinische-westfälische Unternehmer*, p. 52) suggest that differences existed between manufacturing and mining, and between the Rhineland and Silesia, with mining and Silesia having the greater numbers of government officials among the original shareholders.

81. Wutzmur, "Die Herkunft der industrielle Bourgeoisie Preussens," p. 148.

82. Kisch, "From Monopoly to Laissez-Faire," pp. 400 ff.

83. Henderson, *Britain and Industrial Europe*, p. 161. On the question of British invention and innovation in the first half of the nineteenth century, consider the statement by Porter, *Progress of the Nation*, p. 262: "Some part of our cotton-spinning is of foreign invention; but the state of mechanical arts not being sufficiently advanced for that purpose in their own countries, the inventors have been obliged to resort to English workshops for the means of perfecting their conceptions."

84. Clapham, *Economic Development of France and Germany*, p. 288.

85. Henderson, *Britain and Industrial Europe*, p. 161.

86. Benaerts, *Borsig et les locomotives en allemagne*, pp. 48–51.

87. Ibid., pp. 51 ff.

88. Ibid., p. 40.

89. Benaerts, *Les Origines de la grande industrie allemande*, p. 358.

90. *Emergence of the German Dye Industry*.

91. Walker, *Germany and the Emigration*, p. 77.

92. Wiskemann, *Hamburg und die Welthandelspolitik*, p. 186.

93. Sturmey, *British Shipping and World Competition*, p. 17.

94. Aycoberry, "Probleme der Sozialschichtung in Köln," p. 513.

95. *Zur Entwicklung des preussischdeutschen Kapitalexports*, pt. 1, pp. 220 ff.

96. Von Borries, *Deutschlands Aussenhandel*, pp. 238 ff.

97. Semmel, *Rise of Free Trade Imperialism*; p. 412.

98. Ibid.

99. *Les Origines de la grande industrie allemande*, p. 353.

100. Ibid.

101. Legge, *Kapital- und Verwaltungsüberfremdung*, p. 45.

102. Sédillot, *La Maison de Wendel*, p. 250.

103. Benaerts, *Les Origines de la grande industrie allemande*, p. 355; but see Legge, *Kapital- und Verwaltungsüberfremdung*, p. 46, who dates the return flow as 1875.

104. Cameron, *France and the Economic Development of Europe*, p. 395.

105. Ibid., p. 403.

106. Wiskemann, *Hamburg und die Welthandelspolitik*, p. 189.

107. Rosenberg, *Die Weltwirtschaftskrise*, p. 128.

108. Böhme, *Frankfurt und Hamburg*, p. 235.

109. Ibid., pp. 266 ff.

110. Rosenbaum, "M. M. Warburg & Co.," p. 126.

111. Böhme, *Frankfurt und Hamburg*, pp. 272–273.

112. A previous example of import substitution can be seen in the period 1830 to 1850, as Rhineland banks began at an early stage to compete with Dutch banks for the finance of Rhenish linen and cotton exports and by 1850 had replaced them (Adelmann, "Structural Change," p. 89).

113. Bondi, *Deutschlands Aussenhandel*, p. 146.

114. Lambi, *Free Trade and Protection*, p. 19.

115. Zorn, "Wirtschafts- und sozialgeschichtliche Zusammenhänge," p. 259.

116. *Stages of Economic Growth*, p. 26.

117. Ibid., p. 27.

118. "Efficiency and Welfare Implications," pp. 49–50.

119. Epstein, "Socio-economic History," p. 111.

120. Lambi, *Free Trade and Protection*, p. 340.

121. Ibid., p. 73.

122. *Controversy over German Industrialization*, p. 33.

123. *Bread and Democracy*, p. 42.

124. Epstein, "Socio-economic History," p. 111.

125. Williams, *British Commercial Policy*, p. 200.

126. Barkin, *Controversy over German Industrialization*, p. 33.

127. Cecil, *Albert Ballin*, p. 264.

128. Levy, *Industrial Germany*, p. 7.

129. Clapham, *Economic Development of France and Germany*, p. 311.

130. Levy, *Industrial Germany*, p. 15.

131. Kocka, *Unternehmungsverwaltung und Angestelltenschaft*, p. 125.

132. Beer, *German Dye Industry*, p. 130.

133. Ibid., p. 99.

134. Kocka, *Unternehmungsverwaltung und Angestelltenschaft*, p. 128.

135. Kindleberger, *Economic Growth in France and Britain*, p. 148.

136. *German Dye Industry*, p. 95.

137. Ibid., p. 96.

138. J. C. Fischer, the Swiss-German metallurgist who visited England frequently between 1794 and 1851, when he was 78 regarded the 1851 exhibition as the peak of materialist development and felt obliged to say, "That's enough, let us quiet down so that we can once again hear the human spirit" (Redlich, "Frühindustrielle Unternehmer," p. 407).

139. Batty, *The House of Krupp*, p. 61.

140. Ibid., pp. 62 ff.

141. Benaerts, *Borsig et les locomotives en allemagne*, p. 22.

142. Köllmann, *Sozialgeschichte der Stadt Barmen*, pp. 44–45.

143. Beer, *German Dye Industry*, p. 110.

144. Hoffman, *Great Britain and German Trade Rivalry*, p. 77.

145. Beer, *German Dye Industry*, p. 110; Hoffman, *Great Britain and German Trade Rivalry*, p. 119.

146. Hoffman, *Great Britain and German Trade Rivalry*, pp. 45 ff.

147. By E. E. Williams.

148. Beer, *German Dye Industry*, p. 47.

149. Hoffman, *Great Britain and German Trade Rivalry*, p. 168.

150. Ibid., p. 177.

151. Minchinton, *British Tinplate Industry*, pp. 63–71.

152. Saul, *Studies in British Overseas Trade*, pp. 160–161.

153. Hoffman, *Great Britain and German Trade Rivalry*, p. 185.

154. Ibid., p. 285.

155. Bondi, *Deutschlands Aussenhandel*, vol. 5, p. 53.

156. Cecil, *Albert Ballin*, p. 171.

157. Kehr, "Imperialismus und deutscher Schlachtflottenbau."

158. Benaerts, *Les Origines de la grande industrie allemandle*, p. 626.

159. Rosenberg, *Grosse Depression*, vol. 2, p. 55.

160. Böhme, *Prolegomena*, p. 85.

161. Rosenberg, "Political and Social Consequences of the Great Depression," p. 59.

162. Inoki, "Aspects of German Peasant Emigration," p. 214.

163. Girault, *Empruntes russes*, pp. 139 ff.

164. White, *French International Accounts*.

165. Barkin, *Controversy over German Industrialization*, p. 75.

166. Kehr, *Der Primat der Innenpolitik*, p. 135.

167. Ibid., pp. 133–134.

168. Zorn, "Wirtschaft und Politik," p. 353.

169. "German Economic Historiography."

170. Fogel, *Railroads and American Economic Growth*.

171. In McCloskey, *Essays on a Mature Economy*.

172. McCloskey, *Economic Maturity and Entrepreneurial Decline*.

173. In McCloskey, *Essays on a Mature Economy*, p. 106.

174. Fogel, *Railroads and American Economic Growth*.

175. *Essays on a Mature Economy*.

176. *Economic Maturity and Entrepreneurial Decline*.

177. McCloskey, *Essays on a Mature Economy*, p. 106.

178. Kindleberger, *Economic Growth in France and Britain*, p. 325.

179. "An Input-Output Approach," pp. 12–15.

180. McCloskey, "Did Victorian Britain Fail?" pp. 446 ff.

181. Saul, "Engineering Industry," p. 191.

182. Ibid., pp. 192, 206, 215, 216.

183. Rimmer, *Marshall of Leeds*.

184. Barker, "Glass Industry," p. 318.

185. Saul, "Engineering Industry," pp. 187, 233.

186. *Economic Maturity and Entrepreneurial Decline*, p. 56, note.

187. *British Industrialists*, pp. 35, 59.

188. "Relative Decline of the British Steel Industry," pp. 140 ff.

189. Minchinton, *British Tinplate Industry*, pp. 24, 29.

190. *Essays on a Mature Economy*.

191. Burn, *Economic History of Steelmaking*, p. 169, note.

192. Andrews and Brunner, *Capital Development in Steel*, p. 135.

193. "Did Victorian Britain Fail?" p. 447.

194. Andrews and Brunner, *Capital Development in Steel*, pp. 125–130.

195. Ibid., pp. 204–207.

196. Carter and Williams, *Industry and Technical Progress*, p. 206.

197. Cook, *Effects of Mergers*, p. 305.

198. Andrews and Brunner, *Capital Development in Steel*, p. 96.

199. Saul, "Engineering Industry," p. 215. The bicycle industry rose in Coventry on the ruins of the ribbon trade, which had been overwhelmed by French competition consequent to the Anglo-French Commercial Treaty of 1860. It took advantage of cheap labor from the prostrate textile industry and skilled labor previously engaged in watch- and clockmaking. See Prest, *Industrial Revolution in Coventry*, p. 4.

200. Richardson, "Chemicals," p. 302.

201. Ibid.

202. Burn, *Economic History of Steelmaking*, p. 296; Minchinton, *British Tinplate Industry*, p. 195.

203. Byatt, "Electrical Products," p. 252.

204. Rimmer, *Marshall of Leeds*, pp. 265, 267.

205. "Electrical Products," pp. 245, 249.

206. Saul, "Engineering Industry," p. 207.

207. Harley, "Skilled Labour," pp. 391 ff.

208. Crouzet, "Croissances comparées," pp. 139. ff.

209. Mokyr, "Industrial Revolution," pp. 365 ff.

210. The drawn-out replacement of the Leblanc by the Solvay process in the production of caustic, bleach, and soda ash is one of the few examples of nonprofit-maximizing behavior found by the new economic historians. See Lindert and Trace, "Yardsticks for Victorian Entrepreneurs," pp. 239 ff. A post–World War I example has been presented by Henning and Trace, "Britain and the Motorship," pp. 353 ff. They conclude that it would have been profitable for British shipowners like Danish to shift to motorships, but the decision and actions to change were taken much more slowly.

211. Robson, *Cotton Industry in Britain*, pp. 92–95.

212. Landes, "Technological Change," p. 495.

213. Saul, "Engineering Industry," p. 212.

214. *British Industries and Their Organization*, pp. 229, 238. This author believes that Lancashire was slow in adopting mechanical improvements—ring spindles, automatic looms, and high-speed winding (p. 247)—but a later economic historian argues that the failure of the industry in the interwar period cannot be blamed on technological backwardness or entrepreneurial ineptitude (Sandberg, *Lancashire in Decline*).

215. Chandler, *Strategy and Structure*.

216. The absence of a highly developed commercial network of merchants outside the Rhineland and the Hanseatic cities may have been a benefit for Germany in an age of technological complexity, since it required emerging firms to perform the merchanting functions (assembling inputs and marketing outputs) largely by themselves. This accounts for the larger average size of German, compared with British, firms.

217. *Chemicals in Western Europe*.

218. Saul, "Engineering Industry." p. 202.

219. Byatt, "Electrical Products," pp. 269, 272.

220. Byatt, "Electrical Products," p. 272; Saul, "Engineering Industry," p. 231 ff.

221. Burn, *Economic History of Steelmaking*, p. 199.

222. See McKay, *Tramways and Trolleys*, pp. 181–184.

223. Burnham and Hoskins, *Iron and Steel in Britain*, p. 80.

224. Ibid., pp. 210–211.

225. "Did Victorian Britain Fail?"

226. Coppock, "Climacteric of the 1890's," pp. 1 ff.

227. "Engineering Industry," pp. 192, 200, 206, 213. See also Byatt, "Electrical Products," pp. 244 ff.

228. Saul, "Engineering Industry," p. 226.

229. Byatt, "Electrical Products," p. 255.

230. Richardson, "Chemicals," p. 287.

231. *Economic Growth in France and Britain*, pp. 128 ff.

232. Habakkuk, *American and British Technology*, p. 191.

233. Thackray, "Natural Knowledge in Cultural Context," pp. 672 ff.

234. *Technical Change and Education*, p. 120.

235. *Technical Education and Social Change*.

236. Coleman, "Gentlemen and Players," pp. 105–107.

237. Erickson, *British Industrialists*, pp. 12, 73.

References

Abel, Wilhelm. *Geschichte der deutsche Landwirtschaft von frühen Mittelalter bis zum 19. Jahrhundert*. Deutsche Agrargeschichte 2., Stuttgart, 1962.

Adelmann Gerhard. "Structural Change in the Rhenish Linen and Cotton Trades at the Outset of Industrialization." In F. Crouzet, W. H. Chaloner, and F. Stern, eds., *Essays in European Economic History, 1789–1914*. New York: St. Martins, 1970, 82–97.

Allen, G. C. *British Industries and Their Organization*. 2nd ed. London: Longmans, Green, 1939.

Andrews, P. W. S., and Elizabeth Brunner. *Capital Development in Steel: A Study of the United Steel Companies, Ltd.* Oxford: Basil Blackwell, 1952.

Aycoberry, Pierre. "Probleme der Sozialschichtung in Köln im Zeitalter der Fruhindustrialisierung." In W. Fischer, ed., *Wirtschafts- und sozialgeschichtliche Probleme der frühen Industrialisierung*. Berlin: Colloquium Verlag, 1968, 512–528.

Banfield, Thomas C. *Industry of the Rhine*. Ser. 1. *Agriculture*, 1846, ser. 2, *Manufactures*, 1848. New York: Agustus Kelley, 1969.

Barker, T. C. "The Glass Industry." in D. H. Aldcroft, ed., *The Development of British Industry and Foreign Competition, 1875–1914*. London: Allen & Unwin, 1966, 307–325.

Barkin, Kenneth D. *The Controversy over German Industrialization, 1890–1902*. Chicago: University of Chicago Press, 1970.

Batty, Peter. *The House of Krupp*. London: Secker and Warburg, 1967.

Beer, John Joseph. *The Emergence of the German Dye Industry*. Urbana: University of Illinois Press, 1959.

Benaerts, Pierre. *Börsig et les débuts de la fabrication des locomotives en Allemagne*. Paris: Editions F. H. Turot, 1933.

Benaerts, Pierre. *Les origines de la grande industrie allemande*. Paris: Editions F. H. Turot, 1933.

Blumberg, Horst. "Die Finanzierung der Neugrunden und Erweiterungen von Industriebetrieben in Form der Aktiengesellschaften während der fünftiger Jahrhunderrts in Deutschland, am Beispiel des preussichen Verhältnisse erlaütert." In Hans Mottek, ed., *Studien zur Geschichte der industriellen Revolution in Deutschland*. Berlin: Akademie Verlag, 1960, 65–145.

Bodelschwingh, E. von. *Leben des Ober-Präsidenten Vincke, nach seier Tagebüchern bearbeitet*. Vol. 1. Berlin: Georg Reiner, 1853.

Böhme, Helmut. *Frankfurt und Hamburg, des deutsches Reiches Silber- und Goldloch und die allerenglischste Stadt des Kontinent*. Frankfurt: Europaïsche Verlaganstalt, 1968.

Böhme, Helmut. *Prolegomena zu einer Sozial- und Wirtschaftsgeschichte Deutschlands, in 19. und 20. Jahrhundert*. Frankfurt: Suhrkamp Verlag, 1968.

Bondi, Gerhard. *Deutschlands Aussenhandel, 1815–1870*. Berlin: Akademie Verlag, 1958.

Borchardt, Knut. "Zur Frage des Kapitalmangels in der ersten Halfte des 19. Jahrhunderts in Deutschland." In *Jahrbücher für Nationalökonomie und Statistik* 173 (1961): 401–421.

Borries, Bodo von. *Deutschlands Aussenhandel, 1836 bis 1856*. Stuttgart: Gustav Fischer Verlag, 1970.

Bowring, John. "Report on the German Commercial Union, 1840." In *British Parliamentary Papers*. Vol. 21, 1850.

Brockhage, Bernhard. *Zur Entwicklung des preussischdeutschen Kapitalexports*. Leipzig: Duncker u. Humblot, 1910.

Brown, Lucy. *The Board of Trade and the Free Trade Movement, 1830–1842*. Oxford: Clarendon Press, 1958.

Burn, Duncan L. *Economic History of Steelmaking, 1867–1939*, Cambridge: Cambridge University Press, 1940.

Burnham, T. F., and C. O. Hoskins. *Iron and Steel in Britain, 1870–1930*. London: Allen & Unwin, 1943.

Byatt I. C. R. "Electrical Products." in D. H. Aldcroft, ed., *The Development of British Industry and Foreign Competition, 1875–1914*. London: Allen & Unwin, 1968, 273–268.

Cameron, Rondo. *France and the Economic Development of Europe*. Princeton: Princeton University Press, 1961.

Carter, C. F., and B. R. Williams. *Industry and Technical Progress: Factors Governing the Speed of Application of Science*. London: Oxford University Press, 1957.

Cecil, Lamar. *Albert Ballin: Business and Politics in Imperial Germany*. Princeton: Princeton University Press, 1967.

Chandler, Alfred D. *Strategy and Structure: Chapters in the History of Industrial Enterprise*. Cambridge, Mass.: Harvard University Press, 1962.

Clapham, J. H. *The Economic Development of France and Germany, 1815–1914*, 4th ed., Cambridge: Cambridge University Press, 1953.

Coleman, D. C. "Gentlemen and Players." *Economic History Review* 25 (1973): 92–116.

Cook, P. Lesley. *Effects of Mergers: Six Studies with the Collaboration of Ruth Cohen*. London: Allen & Unwin, 1958.

Cotgrove, Stephen E. *Technical Education and Social Change*. London: Allen & Unwin, 1958.

Court, W. H. B. *The Rise of the Midland Industries, 1600–1838*. London: Oxford University Press, 1938.

Crouzet, François. "Croissances comparées de l'Angleterre et de la France au XVIIIe siècle: essai d'analyse comparée de deux croissances économiques." R. M. Hartwell, ed., *The Causes of the Industrial Revolution in England*. London: Methuen, 1967, 139–174.

Crouzet, François. "Western Europe and Great Britain: 'Catching up' in the First Half of the Nineteenth Century," in A. J. Youngson, ed., *Economic Development in the Long Run*. London: Allen & Unwin, 1972, 98–125.

Dumke, Rolf H. "The Political Economy of Economic Integration: The Case of the Zollverein of 1834." Queen's University Discussion Paper no. 153, presented to the Canadian Economics Association, June 5, 1974.

Epstein, Kalus. "The Socio-Economic History of the Second German Empire." *Review of Politics* 29 (1967): 100–112.

Erickson, Charlotte. *British Industrialists: Steel and Hosiery, 1850–1950*. Cambridge: Cambridge University Press, 1959.

Fischer, Wolfram. *Der Stadt und die Anfänge der Industrialisierung in Baden, 1800–1850*. Berlin: Duncker u. Humblot, 1962.

Fogel, Robert W. *Railroads and American Economic Growth: Essays in Economic History*. Baltimore: Johns Hopkins University Press, 1964.

Froelich, N., J. A. Oppenheimer, and O. R. Young. *Political Leadership and Collective Action*. Princeton: Princeton University Press, 1971.

Gerschenkron, Alexander. "Typology of Industrial Development as a Tool of Analysis." In *Second International Conference on Economic History*, Paris/The Hague: Mouton, 1965, 487–505.

Girault, René. *Empruntes russes et investissements français en Russie, 1887–1914*. Paris: A. Colin, 1971.

Gouraud, Charles. *Histoire de la politique commerciale de la France et son influence sur le progrès de la richesse publique depuis les moyen ages jusqu'à nos jours*. Vols. 1 and 2. Paris: August Durand, 1854.

Habakkuk, H. J. *American and British Technology in the Nineteenth Century*. Cambridge: Cambridge University Press, 1962.

Hardach. K. W. "Anglomanie und Anglophobie während der industriellen Revolution in Deutschland." *Schmollers Jahrbuch* 91 (1971): 153–181.

Hardach, K. W. "Some Remarks on German Economic Historiography and its Understanding of the Industrial Revolution in Germany." *Journal of European Economic History* 1 (1972): 37–99.

Harley, C. K. "Skilled Labor and the Choice of Techniques in Edwardian Industry," *Explorations in Economic History*, ser. 2, 2 (1973/74): 391–414.

Hawtrey, R. G. *Economic Aspects of Sovereignty*. 2nd ed. London: Longmans, Green, 1952.

Henderson, W. O. *Britain and Industrial Europe, 1750–1870: Studies on the Industrial Revolution in Western Europe*. Liverpool: University Press, 1954.

Henning, Graydon R., and Keith Trace. "Britain and the Motorship: A Case of the Delayed Adoption of a New Technology," *Journal of Economic History* 35 (1975): 353–385.

Hoffman, Ross J. S. *Great Britain and the German Trade Rivalry, 1875–1914*, Philadelphia: University of Pennsylvania Press, 1933.

Hohenberg, Paul M. *Chemicals in Western Europe, 1850–1914: An Economic Study of Technical Change*. Chicago: Rand McNally, 1967.

Jacob, William. *A View of the Agriculture, Manufactures, Statistics, and Society in the State of Germany and Parts of Holland and France, taken during a journey through those countries in 1819.* London: John Murray, 1820.

Johnson, Harry G. "The Efficiency and Welfare Implications of the International Corporation." In C. P. Kindleberger, ed., *The International Corporation,* Cambridge, Mass.: MIT Press, 1970.

Kehr, Eckhart. *Der Primat der Innenpolitik: gesammelte Aufsätze zur preussisch-deutschen Sozialgeschichte im 19. und 20. Jahrhundert.* H. U. Wehler, ed. Berlin: Walter de Gruyter, 1965.

Kehr, Eckhart. "Imperialismus und deutscher Schlachtflottenbau." Excerpts from *Schlachtflottenbau und Parteipolitik, Berlin, 1930.* In H. U. Wehler, ed., *Imperialismus.* Cologne and Berlin: Kiepenhener u. Witsch, 1970, 289–308.

Kindleberger, Charles P. *Economic Growth in France and Britain, 1851–1950.* Cambridge, Mass.: Harvard University Press, 1964.

Kisch, Herbert. "From Monopoly to Laissez-Faire: The Early Growth of the Wupper Valley Textile Trades." *Journal of European Economic History,* Fall 1972, 298–407.

Kocka, Jürgen. *Unternehmungsverwaltung und Angestelltenschaft am Beispiel Siemens, 1847–1914: zum Verhältnis von Kapitalismus und Burokratie in der deutschen Industrialisierung.* Stuttgart: Ernst Klett Verlag, 1969.

Köllmann, Wolfgang. *Sozialgeschichte der Stadt Barmen in 19. Jahrhundert.* Tübingen: J. C. B. Mohr (Paul Siebeck), 1960.

Lambi, Ivo Nikolai. *Free Trade and Protection in Germany, 1868–1879.* Wiesbaden: Franz Steiner Verlag, 1963.

Landes, David S. "Technological Change and the Development of Western Europe, 1750–1914." In *The Cambridge Economic History of Europe.* VI, *The Industrial Revolution and After: Incomes, Population and Technological Change.* Cambridge: Cambridge Universiy Press, vol. 1, 274–601.

Legge, Joseph. *Kapital- und Verwaltungsüberfremdung bei der Industrie und der Vehrkehrsanstalten Deutschlands von 1800 bis 1923/24,* Halberstadt: Meyer, 1924.

Lindert, Peter H., and Peter Trace. "Yardsticks for Victorian Entrepreneurs." In D. N. McCloskey, ed., *Essays in a Mature Economy: Britain after 1840.* Princeton: Princeton University Press, 1971.

Lowie, Robert H. *The German People, A Social Portrait of 1914.* New York: Rinehart, 1946.

McCloskey, D. N. "Did Victorian Britain Fail?", *Economic History Review* 23 (1970): 446–459.

McCloskey, D. N. *Economic Maturity and Entrepreneurial Decline: British Iron and Steel, 1870–1913.* Cambridge, Mass.: Harvard University Press, 1973.

McCloskey, D. N., ed., *Essays on a Mature Economy: Britain after 1840.* Princeton: Princeton University Press, 1971.

McKinnon, Ronald I. *Money and Capital in Economic Development.* Washington, D.C.: Brookings Institution, 1973.

Meyer, John R. "An Input-Output Approach to Evaluating the Influence of Exports on British Industrial Production in the Late 19th Century." *Explorations in Entrepreneurial History* 8 (1955): 12–34.

Minchinton, W. E. *The British Tinplate Industry: A History*. Oxford: Clarendon Press, 1957.

Mokyr, Joel. "The Industrial Revolution in the Low Countries in the First Half of the Nineteenth Century: A Comparative Case Study." *Journal of Economic History* 34 (1974): 365–391.

Musgrave, P. W. *Technical Change, the Labor Force and Education: A Study of the British and German Iron and Steel Industries, 1860–1964*. Oxford: Pergamon Press, 1967.

Olson, Mancur, and Richard Zeckhauser. "An Economic Theory of Alliances." *Review of Economics and Statistics* 48 (1966): 266–279.

Porter, G. R. *The Progress of the Nation*. New ed. London: John Murray, 1847.

Prest, John. *The Industrial Revolution in Coventry*. London: Oxford University Press, 1960.

Redlich, Fritz. "Frühindustrielle Unternehmer und ihre Probleme in Lichte ihrer Selbtszeugnisse." In W. Fischer, ed., *Wirtschafts- und Sozialschichtliche Probleme der frühen Industrialisierung*. Berlin: Colloquium Verlag, 1968, 239–413.

Richardson, H. W. "Chemicals." In D. H. Aldcroft, ed., *The Development of British Industry and Foreign Competition 1875–1914*. London: Allen & Unwin, 274–306.

Riesser, Jacob. *The Great German Banks and their Concentration, in Connection with the Economic Development of Germany*. Washington, D.C.: U.S. Government Printing Office (National Monetary Commission), 1913.

Rimmer, W. C. *Marshall of Leeds, Flaxspinners, 1788–1886*. Cambridge: Cambridge University Press, 1960.

Ritter, Ulrich Peter. *Die Rolle des Staates in der Industrialisierung*. Berlin: Duncker u. Humblot, 1961.

Robson, William A. *The Civil Service in Britain and France*, London: Hogarth, 1956.

Rosenbaum, Eduard. "M. M. Warburg & Co., Merchant Bankers of Hamburg: A Survey of the First 140 years, 1798 to 1938." Reprinted from Leon Baeck, Institute of Jews from Germany, *Yearbook VII*. London, 1962.

Rosenberg, Hans. *Bie Weltwirtschaftskrise von 1857–59*. Stuttgart-Berlin: Verlag von W. Kohlhammer, 1934.

Rosenberg, Hans. "Political and Social Consequences of the Great Depression of 1873–1896 in Central Europe." *Economic History Review* 13 (1943): 56–73.

Rostow, Walt W. "The Beginnings of Modern Growth in Europe: An Essay in Synthesis." *Journal of Economic History* 33 (1973): 547–580.

Rostow, Walt W. *The Stages of Economic Growth*. Cambridge: Cambridge University Press, 1960.

Saul, S. B. *Studies in British Overseas Trade, 1870–1914*. Liverpool: Liverpool University Press, 1960.

Saul, S. B. "The Engineering Industry." In D. H. Aldcroft, ed., *The Development of British Industry, 1875–1914*. London: Allen & Unwin, 1968, 186–277.

Sédillot, Rene. *La Maison de Wendel de mille sept cents quatre à nos jours*. Paris: privately printed, 1958.

Semmel, Bernard. *The Rise of Free Trade Imperialism: Classical Political Economy, the Empire of Free Trade, and Imperialism, 1750–1850*. Cambridge: Cambridge University Press, 1970.

Shaw, Edward S. *Financial Deepening in Economic Development*. New York: Oxford University Press, 1973.

Sturmey, S. G. *British Shipping and World Competition*. London: Athlone Press, 1962.

Temin, Peter. "The Relative Decline of the British Steel Industry, 1880–1913." In Henry Rosovsky, ed., *Industrialization in Two Systems: Essays in Honor of Alexander Gerschenkron*. New York: Wiley, 1966.

Thackray, A. "Natural Knowledge in Cultural Context: The Manchester Model." *American Historical Review* 79 (1974), 671–684.

Tilly, Richard H. *Financial Institutions and Industrialization in the Rhineland. 1815–1870*. Madison: University of Wisconsin Press, 1966.

Tilly, Richard H. "Los von England: Probleme des Nationalismus in der deutschen Wirtschaftsgeschichte." *Zeitschrift für das gesamte Staatswissenschaft* 124 (1968): 179–196.

Ucke, Arnold. *Die Agrarkrise in Preussen während zwangiger Jahre dieses Jahrhundert*, Halle: Max Niemeyer, 1888.

Vernon, Raymond, *Metropolis 1985*, Cambridge, Mass.: Harvard University Press, 1960.

Walker, Mack. *Germany and the Emigration, 1816–1885*. Cambridge, Mass.: Harvard University Press, 1964.

Williams, Judith Blow. *British Commercial Policy and Trade Expansion, 1750–1850*. London: Oxford University Press, 1973.

Wilson, Charles. *Anglo-Dutch Commerce and Finance in the Eighteenth Century*. Cambridge: Cambridge University Press, 1941.

Wiskemann, Erwin. *Hamburg und die Welthandelspolitik von den Anfängen zur Gegenwart*. Hamburg: Friederischen, de Gruyter, 1929.

Wutsmer, Heinz. "Die Herkunft der industrielle Bougeoisie Preussens in den vierziger Jahren des 19. Jahrhundert." In Hans Mottek, ed., *Studien zur Geschichte der industriellen Revolution in Deutschland*. Berlin: Akademie Verlag, 1960, 145–165.

Zorn, Wolfgang. "Wirtschafts- und socialgeschichtliche Zusammenhänge der deutschen Reichsgrundüngszeit (1850–1879). In Helmut Böhme, ed., *Probleme der Reichsgrundüngszeit, 1848–1879*. Cologne-Berlin: Kiepenheuer u. Witsch, 1968.

Zunkel, Friederich. *Der rheinische-westfälische Unternehmer, 1834–1879, ein Beitrag zur Geschichte deutsche Bürgertums in 19. Jahrhundert*. Cologne and Opladen: Westdeutcher Verlag, 1962.

7   The Aging Economy

I am enormously honored by the Institut für Weltwirtschaft which I persist in thinking of as the Institut für Seeverkehr and Weltwirtschaft, a name that had to be changed, I suspect, when aviation became general. I first learned of the Institute when I read some of the inordinately long Enquêteteausschuss, produced in the 1920s by, among others, Gerhard Colm, the first winner of the Bernhard Harms Prize, and a man much loved and honored in the United States. I later had the good fortune to spend four months in 1971 in Kiel, living at the Haus Welt-Club, and using the Institute's magnificent library to read German economic history. Those were golden months, and I feel very much at home.

The Harms Prize is given in international economics, which makes me feel a bit of an impostor as for years I have been beating a retreat out of international economics as such, and into economic history, or, as I prefer to call it, historical economics. It is sometimes possible to combine international economics and economic history, as I hope to demonstrate. But the aging professor, like the aging economy, may have lost an old comparative advantage in a field now full of innovations such as distortions, effective rates of protection, growth theory, macro-economic policies under flexible exchange rates, econometric testing and the like, and find a need to transform along the production possibilities curve to find a new good (or rather service) that he is capable of exporting in competitive markets.

My choice of a topic for this occasion was only partly stimulated by these narcissistic reflections on the passage of time. I have for some years been interested in economic maturity, as contrasted with the economic

Lecture given by the author when he was awarded the Bernhard Harms Prize at the Institut für Weltwirtschaft, Kiel, July 5, 1978, and published in *Weltwirtschaftliches Archiv*, vol. 114, no. 3 (1978).

adolescence associated with development economics. At the Institut für Weltwirtschaft in 1971, studying Germany's rise to economic maturity, I chose to contrast it with the British "Climacteric," or falling back. In a paper in a popular periodical, I compared the position of the United States today with that of Britain in 1890 or 1900, although this has been called "Spenglerian nonsense." But most of all, I suspect, I was moved at the time of Professor Giersch's invitation, by the advice of Lord Kaldor, contained in an interview in *Le Figaro* (February 18–19, 1978) under the headline "Only Protection Can Save England." Kaldor argued that there should be tariffs for aging economies, comparable to the infant-industry tariff for young countries. The ordinary response of the international-trade economist is to transform along the production-possibilities curve, i.e. to adjust, perhaps with adjustment assistance. If you can no longer do international economics in the fast company of dynamic growing economists, find something else worthwhile to do, by which I mean something with a positive price, even economic history. Kaldor suggests instead that the country ought to keep on doing what it is doing, in the old way, cutting off the competition of the market by tariff or other barriers.

Observe first that this advice applies best to import-competing activities and means cutting down on access to new and cheaper goods and services from abroad. We shall address somewhat later the question of demonstration effect that may arise in this connection. But protection does not help with export activities unless the country can find one or more other countries to join with it in a bloc that discriminates against the outside world. Such a suggestion has been made, that the developed countries trade mainly among themselves, retaining the production of textiles, shoes, electronic apparatus, shipbuilding, automobiles and the like, while the developing countries compete with each other, but not with the developed world, in products that they have normally purchased in Europe, North America and Japan. I return to this suggestion below. Note now, however, the difficulties that were faced by Britain in trying to forge an Empire or Commonwealth preference scheme to assure outlets for its exports. As Drummond's brilliant study shows, the customers of the aging economy were not prepared to continue to buy its high-priced and dated-quality brand of products when there were cheaper and up-to-date alternatives available, and when the young partners themselves wanted to take over lines of production that their aging partner sought to reserve for herself (Drummond, 1974). The aging professor of international economics may retain with protection 1950 theory and statistical testing for the economics he buys from the outside—thus turning rapidly away from most of the articles in today's leading journals. To whom does he sell if he wants to export? Happily universities have a friendly toler-ance for and loyalty to their old staffs, a tolerance and a loyalty that would have undergone change, I suspect, if the mandatory retirement age for tenured staff had been raised in the United States from 65 to 70.

Apart from the difficulty about exporting, Kaldor's advice may apply better to individuals than to entire economies. Individuals, like old dogs, are often incapable of learning new tricks. With a limited time horizon, however, and terminal conditions under which their intellectual capital can safely be consumed in its entirety, they had perhaps in some cases better do what they know how to do, even though the price for it be declining, and repulse the efforts of those who would urge that they maintain productivity by transforming into better-paid lines, peopled by the young with higher productivity. But individuals and dogs are mortal. Aging economies have no choice but to carry on, without contemplation of any terminal stage. A society is not an organism that dies at the end of its reproductive cycle, but rather a branch in the evolutionary tree. Such branches survive only by adaptation, and by giving up the old specializa-tion and returning to a simple undifferentiated form to specialize in new ways.

Perhaps before I get much further I should define a little more precisely what I mean by "aging." There is here a grave danger of circular reason-ing, defining aging in terms of certain characteristics, and then deriving the characteristics from the "fact" of aging. I shall ask you to accept the hypothesis that growing economies, like many other structures, proceed along a path described by the Gompertz or S-curve, starting slowly, pick-ing up speed in growth, gradually slowing down, and then levelling off or declining. The process is often repeated, with new Gompertz curves at some stage growing out of the old. I shall not identify the early stages with Rostow's (1960) preconditions, take-off, drive to maturity; you are free to do so if you choose. But at the last stage I definitely part company with Rostow, who postulates a stage of high-level mass consumption of durable goods, that presumably lasts forever as the economy lives happily ever after, whereas I am more interested in the capacity of the economy to respond to changes in economic conditions. It is this that seems to me to slow down with aging.

In the writing of economic history, a fundamental choice is when to use a static, and when a dynamic economic model. The infant-industry model is on the whole dynamic. A tariff increases profits in the industry, expands scale, and through learning-by-doing or economies of scale, the industry shifts its supply curve downward and to the right. Until Arrow discovered learning-by-doing, something which international-trade economists understood by intuition, theory told us that there could be no declining-cost curve since it was incompatible with perfect competition (Arrow, 1962). In all competitive static models, supply curves slope upward.

The difference between static and dynamic models is illustrated by the contrast, suggested some years ago by Henry Wallich (1960) in his *Monetary Problems of an Export Economy*, between Keynesian and Schumpeterian models. In a Keynesian model, increased demand raises income, decreased demand reduces it. In a Schumpeterian economy, on the other hand, reduced demand stimulates the entrepreneur to innovate and reduce costs. The shift of the demand curve to the left and down often kicks off a displacement of the supply curve to the right and down, which may maintain or even increase income (Wallich, 1960). On the basis of these two types of analysis, I concluded some years ago (1961) that increased exports, decreased exports, increased imports (perhaps through lower tariffs), decreased imports (perhaps through higher tariffs)—all or any can either stimulate growth or slow it down. For example, increased exports may stimulate growth through the Keynesian multiplier/accelerator, or reduce it by diverting attention from the necessity of the economy to adapt to new technological conditions, as, in Britain at the end of the nineteenth century, increased exports of iron and steel rails, galvanized iron roofing, cotton textiles, etc. to poorer markets, undermined the evident necessity to face effectively the new industries of electricity and chemicals, or to adopt new processes in old industries, like Gilchrist Thomas in steelmaking. Economic historians using econometric models have had no difficulty in showing that Britain at the turn of the century was not well suited to undertake certain changes (McCloskey 1971). Prices of some needed inputs were too high; in other cases demands were too low. The reasoning implied static models. What remains unanswered is why the historians chose static instead of dynamic models in which disproportions and other adversity lead to innovation and cost reduction. The lowering of the tariff on silk by William Huskisson in the 1820s forced the British industry to improve productivity the better to reduce French imports, and it did so, a fact widely noted by the Saint-Simonists in France who favored tariff reductions, and by Cavour in Italy. Cavour in fact used the dynamic argument that tariff reductions stimulate growth as a basis for his low-tariff policies in Piedmont in the 1840s and 1850s, and for Italy in 1860, with unhappy results in the latter instance. As a British civil servant told a friend of mine asking about the stimulation of industry anticipated from

British entry into the Common Market: "Not every kick in the pants gal-
vanizes; some merely hurt."

The foreign-trade aspects of aging permit a return to an old interest of
mine, the terms of trade, and venturing the thought that aging economies
are like adolescent ones in another respect, their preoccupation with the
terms of trade. To equate changes in the terms of trade with changes in
welfare, of course, is another instance of partial-equilibrium analysis, taking other things as equal when they may have changed, or perhaps should
have changed. In the *Terms of Trade* (1956), I concluded that it was true
that developing countries experienced declining terms of trade, but not
for the reasons advanced by Prebisch, based on the differential market
behavior of primary products and manufactured goods. LDCs were typically unable or unwilling to transform in response to price changes. When
prices fell, they were left stranded in unrewarding industries and occupations; when prices rose—at least until the advent of OPEC—easy entry
for mature competitors brought them down again. Easy entry and difficult
exit constitute a formula for declining terms of trade that may apply to
aging economies as well as to those starting up the Gompertz curve. But
it is not the terms of trade that count. Most economies in the full vigor of
health have no idea what their terms of trade are. Preoccupation with the
terms of trade is a form of economic hypochondria, like the frequent taking of one's temperature. To the healthy economy, price changes are a
signal to adjust; to the economy that finds adjustment difficult, they
appear to be changes in welfare, or the balance of payments, or both
(Kindleberger, 1956).

The question of static and dynamic models has a macro- as well as a
micro-economic component. All economists agree that micro- and macroeconomic questions should be separated as far as possible, and that tariffs,
for example, should be used to improve the balance of payments only
with the greatest reluctance, as a second- or more nearly fifth- or sixth-
best policy, since tariffs are a micro-economic tool, and the balance of
payments a macro-economic target. None the less, I remain impressed by
how rapidly young growing countries respond to tariff reductions in
overcoming transitional balance-of-payments deficits, and how slowly do
aging countries. From history take the response of Britain to the repeal of
the Corn Laws in 1846 or of France to the reduction in tariffs under the
Anglo-French (Cobden–Chevalier) treaty of 1860. The latter, to be sure,
was a reciprocal agreement, so that exports were stimulated along with
imports. As a young country in the 1840s, however, Britain scorned the
necessity to have tariff reductions reciprocal. Economic theory taught that

the balance of payments embodied an adjustment mechanism; an increase in imports would lead to an increase in exports. And so it proved. The balance of payments righted itself very quickly. There were, to be sure, many factors at work; discoveries of gold in California and Australia, the boom in foreign lending to India, rapid growth after 1848 on the Continent. If you need a purer case, closer to our time, recall that Germany in 1956 sought to correct its strong balance-of-payments surplus with a unilateral reduction in tariffs. The current-account surplus barely took notice. You may regard this as proof of low elasticities, or, like me, as part proof of the absorption theory of balance-of-payments adjustment, while dismissing the income effect of the tariff change which would tend to lower income and savings. It follows, in either case, that raising tariffs—unless to prohibitive levels—is not likely to improve the balance of payments much in an aging economy, nor are reductions likely to worsen them in a young and dynamic one.

This brings me to the savings question, which is a complex one with many dimensions. First, it makes an enormous difference to savings whether an old or aging country, or individual, is poor or rich. I start with individuals. Most people have to reduce their consumption as they get old, and at the same time run balance-of-payments deficits, i.e. consume their capital, because productivity falls off more than consumption, and they lack a substantial flow of income from investments. Luckily in most cases that appetite for consumption declines to some extent as well. For those without much in the way of savings, or lacking transfers from the state, consumption may have to fall a great deal. Not so the rich; they may run balance-of-payments deficits and draw on wealth, unless they have their hearts set on leaving a big estate, but in a very few cases, income from property is so substantial that while savings decline they remain positive to the end.

In countries, as in individuals—though generalization is fraught with danger—it makes a considerable difference whether a country has accumulated substantial claims on other countries through foreign investment, and has not dissipated them, for example by drawing them down to fight a war, and how substantial its demonstration effect is.

Rapid growth in leading countries is often associated with the acquisition of foreign claims, although interest in international finance may itself be an early sign of aging, like the first lock of gray hair. Venice, Genoa, Antwerp, Amsterdam, London and New York were first mercantile and then financial centers. The transition from trade to finance, first at home and then abroad, was usually made smoothly, and finance flourished as

commerce began to wilt under intense competition from younger economies. Amsterdam in the latter half of the eighteenth century, Britain in the
second half or perhaps the last third of the nineteenth century, and the
United States thus far in the last third of the twentieth century were in
various degrees slipping in industry and trade, but going strong in international banking. It is worth noting that in the last quarter of the nineteenth century Germany had ambitions in international finance, and
sought to rival Britain in this field, as well as in commerce. But the
domestic boom was so intense that from time to time it proved desirable
to sell off foreign investments—Argentine bonds to Britain, and Russian
bonds to France, for example—to stoke the fires of investment at home.
Dynamic early middle age, that is, does not accumulate foreign claims but
builds capital at home; successful late middle age makes the transition
from home to foreign investment.

It is hard to say what would happen if a country aged with its foreign
capital intact since Amsterdam and Britain, at least, spent large portions of
their foreign wealth in the Napoleonic and two world wars, respectively.
Even without war, however, there is likely to be serious capital consumption from the aging process because of demonstration effect. I suggested
that the passion of individuals for consumption may cool with age. The
generalization is dangerous, since the propensity to consume may shift
upward in at least two items of consumption: tourism and medical expense, as opposed to such items as household goods and other durables,
especially books, where the problem becomes one of decumulation rather
than the accumulation of youth. For countries, however, the demonstration effect that Nurkse detected in developing countries that seek to consume and invest in excess of income may play a role. A few with long
memories may remember the economic writings of Lord (then Sir Geoffrey) Crowther in dollar shortage. His explanation ran in terms of goods
produced by the United States that the rest of the world had to have "no
matter what they cost." Crowther pioneered in the sort of comparison
between individuals and economies that I am indulging in today, even
reciting Shakespeare's seven stages of man from the infant "mewling, and
puking in the Nurse's arms," to the old man "sans teeth, sans eyes, sans
taste, sans every thing." He surely exaggerated the price inelasticity of
British import demand for trucks, airplanes, earth-moving equipment,
computers and the like, but the point is a relevant one (Crowther, 1957).
The fact that a country loses its capacity to innovate and to transform
smoothly and effectively from one industry in which it is losing comparative advantage to another does not mean that it will not want to continue

to share in the consumption of the new goods of the world. Or the point may be put in terms of the Duesenberry effect. Loss of capacity in countries to produce effectively does not necessarily go hand in hand with loss of appetite for continued high consumption. The best illustration of this generalization, I suspect, and one which is fateful in many respects, is the unwillingness, or inability, of the United States to adopt an effective program of conserving energy.

Let us return to the saving functions. Aging seems to me to be critical to the question of personal savings at the national level, although again the discussion runs the risk of circular reasoning. The fact that saving out of disposal income is close to 25 percent in Japan, 15 percent in Germany, 7 percent in the United States and 5 percent in Britain is doubtless a function of such institutions as the thirteenth monthly paycheck and the rudimentary state of social security in Japan, flourishing instalment credit in Britain and the United States, as opposed to Germany and Japan, and the like, but the institutions themselves reflect the fact that Germany and Japan are future-oriented, interested in accumulation, social advancement, building for later generations, whereas in the United States and Britain there is more attention to the present. In an interesting paper on modern Germany, Karl Hardach (1977) has tried to dispel the "myth" of German interest in hard work and saving, pointing to the strong propensity for tourism. But the travel is paid for in advance, out of savings, whereas in the United States and Britain, vacations are more likely to be requited with credit cards. In the steady state, with no growth, it makes no difference whether one pays now or later, since equal numbers are saving and dissaving equal amounts. With continuous growth in income and consumption, however, the use of credit to finance consumption leads to continuously mounting consumer credit, and dissaving net, whereas saving in advance of consumption piles up savings.

I should perhaps insert a paragraph here on the aging of population, and the ratios of working to total population in young, middle-aged and aging countries, but I lack the requisite demographic capacity. I suspect that in very young and very old countries, the ratio is low for different reasons—because of large numbers of children under 15 years of age in young countries, and large numbers over 64 in the old. Between the two, in countries that have finished their Malthusian revolution, but have not yet accumulated a thick layer of gray-haireds over 64, the ratio is at its highest, with important effects on productivity, creativity, savings, etc. But I am incompetent to do more than to pose the issue.

As always in discussing economic history, I am reminded of my friend Alexander Gerschenkron, with his debatable and debated theory of backwardness. You will remember his generalization that the more backward a country is as it starts the process of economic development, the more it relies on banks and government instead of leaving the direction of economic activity to the private market and its entrepreneurs. Other aspects of the theory are that backward countries are more likely to start with heavy instead of light industry, with large firms instead of small (Gerschenkron, 1962).

One need not here settle the validity of these views on backward developing countries. The question is how they apply to aging ones. I have a hard time in discerning a particular role for banks. For young countries banks may be, in the Saint-Simonist phrase, a stimulus and a regulator, a motor and a brake, with the emphasis on the first of the two effects in each instance (Vergeot, 1918). In growing economies of early middle age, banks may shift to a more regulatory role, although the statement runs the risk of implicit theorizing. For aging and old economies, it is hard to find a useful generalization about banks.

More can be said about government, however. I am partial to a vacuum-filling theory of government. I refer not simply to public goods, such as lighthouses, roads, parks, etc., where the consumption of each individual, short of a level of congestion, leaves the consumption of others unaffected, nor to natural monopolies like public utilities where the choice between government regulation and government ownership and operation is often a close one. Even in what are normally thought of as private goods, with competition possible, government may enter because the private market is not discharging the function well. The failure of the market may produce private diseconomies—uneducated, sick and slum-dwellers—which public action is designed to eliminate. Wagner's law that the role of government increases with time may apply to all countries. The portion of national income passing through government hands is substantial in Germany and Japan. But one cannot help but be struck by how more and more functions are being turned over to government in Britain and the United States because of dissatisfaction with the performance of the market. The forms taken are more nearly nationalization in Britain, regulation in the United States. It may be that Germany and Japan started along the Wagner path at higher levels of government intervention than did Britain and the United States, partly because of backwardness, and are therefore now, at different stages of aging, at roughly the same government-to-private-activity ratio. In any event, I suspect that aging economies find the private market less and less able to discharge particular functions effectively and call on government to take them over. The evidence is incomplete, but one is well advised to be sceptical, whether government can successfully fill the vacuum in housing, health care, education, steel, coal, shipbuilding, etc.

It is perhaps injudicious of me to disclose that Gerschenkron has been working on time preference in relation to backwardness, with the hypothesis that the more backward the country, the more it thinks of the present, and the less willing it is to take heed for the morrow. Again in my opinion, age resembles extreme youth, with the addition that it is interested in the past (as well as the present) more than the future. Vigorous middle age is, as indicated earlier, future-oriented, which supports the propensity to save, lowers the rate of interest, spurs investment, stimulates growth. There may be cultural dimensions to living in the past, such as preoccupation with history, literature, the performing arts and the like. I doubt that there is an economic equivalent to such dimensions, overall, but surely the focus is relevant for technical change and for income distribution. Aging economies are dominated by *positions acquises*, a French expression not well rendered in English as "vested interests." It means the Duesenberry effect in consumption, maintaining expenditure at the expense of saving when income falters. It is especially relevant to a decline in risk-taking, clinging to old techniques even when new and more economical are available, resistance to rationalization, a propensity for featherbedding, maintaining old wage differentials that have become technologically obsolete. A problem in Western Europe and the United States is whether it will be possible to change the wage structure so as to attract sufficient numbers of workers to the menial and dirty jobs of street-cleaning, rubbish disposal, hospital orderlies, dishwashing in hotels and the like, without letting loose more inflation as traditionally-skilled workers agitate to maintain differentials. The world of the future is surely going to have to alter the wage structure. In aging economies, the attempt is likely to be inflationary.

But I have gone on perhaps too long with diagnosis. If I reject the Kaldor remedy of bundling up the aging economy in blankets and rolling it in its wheelchair into the sunshine, what do I have in mind for therapy and prognosis, particularly if it should turn out that there is no fountain of youth to be found by an economic Ponce de León?

The world economy is facing a serious crisis. In the last few years I have been studying financial crises, and there are some financial aspects to

the present position. I refer today, however, to the more intractable problems of structural adjustment, the need to adapt to the diffusion of world
technology not only in textiles, shoes, synthetic fibers, electronic components, but also in steel, shipbuilding, oil refining, petrochemicals, precision
instruments, and a host of other industries. In 1954, Sir Donald MacDougall made the startling statement that automobiles would be the textiles
of tomorrow (MacDougall, 1954). He was perhaps a little ahead of his
time, but he was surely right, as we see Brazil making Volkswagens, and
even sending parts to Germany, Ford bodies being stamped out in South
Korea, and countries everywhere gearing up to reproduce the successful
Japanese drive into the world automobile market. Labor-intensive manufacturing is going abroad. Where technological change is still advancing
in developed countries, it runs along capital-intensive lines. As such it
may bring certain processes back from developing to developed countries
but without providing much in the way of employment. At the OECD
Meeting on Technology in Paris in 1977, Christopher Freeman put the
point dramatically that the advanced countries now face the necessity to
slim down their manufacturing sectors in terms of employment, as they
once slimmed down the agricultural.

   I mentioned earlier the proposal by André Grjebine (1978) for a division of world trade primarily into that within two blocs, the developed
countries on the one hand, and the developing on the other. Some few
products would be traded between the blocs—oil and a few metals from
the developing countries, plus coffee, tea and cocoa, against wheat, cotton, wool and advanced manufactures like computers and aircraft from the
developed. For the most part, however, the developing world would produce its own high-cost manufactures, and the developed world retain its
high-cost labor-intensive sectors. This is customs union, with trade diversion instead of trade creation, on a global scale, and I find the picture
appalling. It is fair to say that Grjebine recommends the policy as an improvement on what he anticipates will be the probable course of events:
high national protection. Protection by blocs in his judgment preserves
more competition and lower costs than seems to him otherwise likely.
The problems posed by this solution are too many to explore: where to
put intermediate countries, the necessity to redistribute resources within
rather than between blocs, the choice of what commodities to trade
between blocs and how, the intensification of the possibility of global
economic warfare. Grjebine has surely made a contribution in illuminating
the problem. I hope his solution will appeal to few.

The alternative to Kaldor's protection for the single country and Grje-bine's new order based on two world customs unions is evidently adap-tation, what Carl Major Wright (1939) called *Economic Adaptation to a Changing World Market*. Where individuals cannot adapt, their contracts can be bought up, and they can be pensioned off early. There are no pen-sion schemes available to national economies, so this choice is not open. Moreover, adjustment assistance below the level of the nation, while the subject of some talk, thus far has failed to demonstrate successful action.

The process of reducing sectors is difficult in democracies because the old large sectors relinquish political power more slowly than they are forced by the market to give up economic rewards. Engel's law and eco-nomic growth produce the result that agriculture is overrepresented in legislative assemblies. Obsolete retailing (and manufacturing) industries can muster political support as the Robinson–Patman Act on behalf of retail-price maintenance, the similar movement in Germany, Poujadism in France, etc., amply testify. Railroad unions in the United States spent sub-stantial amounts of money to demonstrate that the presence of the extra "fireman" in the locomotive, retained long after there was a fire to be tended, increases the chances of avoiding accidents by some small but finite amount, but without mentioning featherbedding, and without a rea-sonable calculation of cost and benefit.

Adaptation is difficult, and it is possible that some fashions are not worth adapting to. It is discouraging for people of my generation to be told in stores when we ask for a certain item: "We haven't stocked that for 20 years." A stopped clock is right twice a day. If some of us refuse to adapt to the latest fashion and maintain the same styles with respect to haircuts and face-hair that were *à la mode* in the 1930s, we shall be back in style before too long. It is not self-evident that following the fashions in dress and comportment is vital to happiness in all cases.

Some may think I am making too heavy weather of the aging problem and that it can be handled by some simple rule, in the case of the aging economy, such as a fixed money supply, or one growing at a constant rate, or clean floating of the exchange rate, or leaving resource allocation entirely to the market, or turning it over entirely to indicative planners. I do not deny that optimal monetary, exchange, competitive, and even interventionist policies will help, but contend that the achievement of optimal policies becomes more difficult with aging. It is tempting to sug-gest that the adaptability of the economy that is a function of age is more important that the content of policies within a wide margin of variation, but I stop short of that. It is important to recognize that the success of policies is a function of things other than age.

In discussing economic development, my colleague Everett Hagen (1962) has focused on "the will to achieve." It is presumably stronger in the younger person than in the aging or old. But it is affected in other ways as well. McClelland (1961), from whom Hagen has derived some of his inspiration, relates the need for achievement (or N-achievement) in the individual to the family situation from which he or she springs. A man with a strong mother and a weak father tends to have a stronger N-achievement than one with parents in the converse situation. For nations much may depend upon the degree of social cohesion or purpose, in turn affected by victory or defeat in war. Denmark responded to the fall of the price of wheat in the 1880s, I have asserted (1978), in a dynamic way—rather than the static liquidation of the agricultural sector that took place in Britain—switching from exports to imports of grain as an input in new industries of dairy products and meat production, partly as a result of its defeat by Germany in 1864, and of loss of territory, falling back on a more densely settled country. The experience of Germany and Japan with their economic miracles after World War II is not wholly dissimilar. Victory in both world wars made Britain, and to a lesser degree France, feel that they had earned a higher standard of living, and compounded, I would think, the problems of simple aging. I suspect that defeat is a solvent that melts old ideas and old resistances, whereas victory strengthens the pressure groups and vested interests that make adaptation difficult.

The consolidation of individuals into groups that fight to protect their interests has gone far in democracies and threatens stability, as is widely recognized, but also threatens adaptability. It is often necessary for groups to take what Walker has called "extra-market action" to protect themselves against exploitation, but such action can quickly turn into exploitation of others. It would be idle to multiply examples, but John Lindsay's retreat before the vested interests of New York may serve. When all groups demand 110 percent of the national income, and government is unable to resist them, 10 percent inflation is inevitable. The shift of responsibility from the individual to the group has a strong tendency to run wild through logrolling and the fallacy of composition, with the action of each to protect itself assuring the hurt of all. But to ask individual groups to sacrifice their possible class advantage in the interest of the total is interpreted as yielding to the interests of other groups, and becomes a counsel of perfection. Leading with one's chin is a game-theoretic recipe for disaster.

Some years ago there was an intense debate in Britain over the disadvantages of the headstart. Those who thought the headstart entailed disadvantages argued interrelatedness of capital structures, which meant that to change equipment at one stage of a process you had to change all (Frankel, 1955), or the failure of markets always to articulate linked investments in different states of a vertically integrated process where the stages were owned by different capitalists and the division of costs and benefits was uncertain, as in joint costs, joint products and the like (Kindleberger, 1964, ch. 7). Much more could have been said of the burden of an economy's historical memory, which inhibits it on occasion from sensible action: the burden of the German memory of inflation of 1923, still flourishing today, or of the British unemployment after the 1925 return of sterling to par. John Jewkes insisted that if an existing obsolete capital structure was in the way it could be torn down. Bygones are bygones. Sunk costs are to be forgotten. For him there was no disadvantages in the headstart. New starts could be undertaken at any time (Jewkes, 1946).

This gets to the heart of the matter. I doubt that the past is so easily discarded, and especially not the collective memories that inhibit, or the groups with *positions acquises* that fight to resist loss of income and especially of status. The physical past is not so important, as Europe discovered after the destruction of World War II. But how to wipe out collective memories and how, especially, to devise means to move from class responsibility to the responsibility of the individual? Defeat in war seems to have done it in the past, if my hunch is correct, but the price is an impossible one.

One may well say that the problem is one for political science, but politicians more and more address their promises to pressure groups rather than to the good sense of the individual; or for sociology, although that science seems better at description that at shaping society and can tell us mostly, for example, that we have moved in selecting individuals for economic roles from status to achievement and back to status again. Or perhaps we could derive inspiration from evangelical religion and contemplate how entire societies can be "born again," and return to a state of innocence in which the individual was responsible for his behavior and his achievement. At the moment we seem to be in the unhappy position where progress is made by class action, rather than individual effort and it is permissible to think that all developing nations become rich, all blacks and women equal to white men, all students learned, by a stroke of the pen, rather than by unremitting effort. I hear myself founding querulous and shrill the way my father sounded in the days of the New Deal. These may be the maunderings of galloping senility, but I think we need a fountain of youth to dissolve the social arteriosclerotic structures in the body politic. William James sought a "Moral Equivalent of War" the better to focus society on single objectives. Perhaps we need rather to find a "Sociological Equivalent of Defeat."

References

Arrow, Kenneth J. (1962), "The Economic Implications of Learning by Doing," *Review of Economic Studies*, vol. 29, pp. 155–73.

Crowther, Sir Geoffrey (1957), *Balances and Imbalances of Payments*, The George H. Leatherbee Lectures, Boston.

Drummond, Ian M. (1974), *Imperial Economic Policy, 1917–1939. Studies in Expansion and Protection*, London.

Frankel, Marvin (1955), "Obsolescence and Technological Change in a Maturing Economy," *American Economic Review*, vol. 45, pp. 296–319.

Gerschenkron, Alexander (1962), *Economic Backwardness in Historical Perspective. A Book of Essays*, Cambridge, Mass.

Grjebine, André (1978), "Vers une autonomie concertée des régions du monde," *Revue d'Economie Politique*, vol. 88, pp. 250–68.

Hagen, Everett E. (1962), *On the Theory of Social Change: How Economic Growth Begins*. The Dorsey Series in Anthropology and Sociology, Homewood, Ill.

Hardach, Karl (1977), "Germany, 1914–1970," in Carlo M. Cipolla ed., *Contemporary Economies*. The Fontana Economic History of Europe, vol. 6, Hassocks, New York, part I.

Jewkes, John (1946), "Is British Industry Inefficient?" *The Manchester School of Economic and Social Studies*, vol. 14, pp. 1–16.

Kindleberger, Charles P. (1956), with the Assistance of Herman G. van der Tak and Jaroslav Vanek, *The Terms of Trade: A European Case Study*, Technology Press Books in the Social Sciences, New York, London.

Kindleberger, Charles P. (1961), "Foreign Trade and Economic Growth, Lessons from Britain and France, 1850 to 1913," *Economic History Review*, vol. 14, pp. 289–305.

Kindleberger, Charles P. (1964), *Economic Growth in France and Britain, 1851–1950*, Cambridge, Mass.

Kindleberger, Charles P. (1978), "Group Behavior and International Trade," in Kindleberger, *Economic Response, Comparative Studies in Trade, Finance, and Growth*, Cambridge, Mass.; first published in 1951.

MacDougall, Donald (1954), "A Lecture on the Dollar Problem," *Economica* (new series) vol. 21, pp. 185–200.

McClelland, David C. (1961), *The Achieving Society*, Princeton, NJ.

McCloskey, Donald N., ed. (1971), *Essays on a Mature Economy: Britain after 1840,* Papers and Proceedings of the Mathematical Social Science Board Conference on the New Economic History of Britain, 1840–1930, held at Harvard University, 1–3 September 1970 London.

Rostow, W. W. (1960), *The Stages of Economic Growth,* Cambridge.

Vergeot, J. B. (1918), *Le Crédit comme stimulant et régulateur de l'industrie. La conception saint-simonienne, ses réalisations, son application au problème bancaire d'après-guerre,* Paris.

Wallich, Henry C. (1960), *Monetary Problems of an Export Economy, The Cuban Experience, 1914–1947,* Harvard Economic Studies, vol. 88, Cambridge, Mass.

Wright, Carl Major (1939), *Economic Adaptation to a Changing World Market,* Copenhagen.

8

Standards as Public, Collective, and Private Goods

I

Adam Smith postulated three types of public goods: safety, justice and public works which it would not pay private individuals to produce, all three summed up in the word *magistracy*, which was the necessary prerequisite for free trade (1776, pp. 653, 669, 681–2).[1] Magistracy can be extended from this group or made to include within it such elusive "goods" as macroeconomic stability, redistribution of national income, the monetary system, and of interest here, standards of various sorts. Standards of measurement—whether linear, weight, bulk, temperature, time or value (i.e. the unit-of-account function of money) clearly fall within Samuelson's definition of public goods in that they are available for use by all and that use by any one economic actor does not reduce the amount available to others (1954). In fact they are a strong form of public good in that they have economies of scale. The more producers and consumers use a given standard, the more each gains from use by others through gains in comparability and interchangeability.

My concern goes beyond standards of weights, measures, temperature, time and value, though they play important roles in what follows, to include standards determined by various groups—governments, trade or professional associations, and even companies—limiting the characteristics of goods or products, and to deal with the setting, diffusion, and changing of standards.

II

At least two classes of standards can be distinguished: those designed to reduce transactions costs, and those in which there are physical economies

A seminar paper given to the Institute for International Economic Studies. University of Stockholm 16 November 1982 and published in *Kyklos*, vol. 36, Fasc. 3, 1983, pp. 377–95.

external to the firm. Under transactions costs can be included not only the ease of concluding transactions because both parties to a deal mutually recognize what is being dealt in, but also the prevention of adulteration, short measure, or short weight, debasement and the like that may make a transaction unsatisfactory to one of the parties. In recent times the state has set standards of weights and measures and maintained surveillance to see that they were adhered to. In the Middle Ages, the cloth guild of Florence controlled yardsticks (Origo, 1957, p. 77). Linear measure in retail trade is today probably left to the consumer to patrol, but most cities check up on the more complex machines to weigh, say, meat, to ensure against short weight. Quality counts as well as quantity. In the Middle Ages most trade was conducted on consignment because the buyer wanted to inspect the merchandise to check for quality (de Roover, 1966, p. 143). Some goods today are incapable of being described in a standard designation because of the unevenness of nature or manmade uniqueness. On this account diamond, furs, wool, race horses, art and antiques are sold in quantity only at auctions after inspections. Where possible, however, transaction costs on commodities are reduced by standardizing quality by grades. At a primitive stage of international trade, India sold cotton in the famine created by the American Civil War full of dirt (Landes, 1958, p. 71), and Turkish wheat entering world markets for the first time in the early 1950s was said to suffer from an admixture of stones and dead mice. Standardization and grading, resulting in such short-hand descriptions as middling cotton, 1 3/8ths inch staple, No. 2 medium-grain rice, Straits quality tin, Santos No. 4 coffee, prime western slab zinc, etc. save time in description, allow for conventional discounts or premiums for divergences from the standard, and permit trading over distance without inspection. There may be provision for testing, as in taking a core sample of a loaded railway car of wheat. Where standards of quality can be established, however, trade is expedited and transaction costs reduced.

Some standards are imposed by government in the interest of the consumer, notably in the testing of drugs and inspection of meat. For the most part, however, standardization was originally undertaken by merchants. In a previous paper, I have suggested that a distinction could be made between the gains-from-trade merchant who arbitraged goods in their existing condition, buying cheap and selling dear, and the value-added merchant who was especially interested in upgrading and controlling quality (1978a, pp. 37–8). These are ideal types and in actual practice most merchants combined the two functions. Part of the value added of such a stapling centre as Amsterdam in the seventeenth and eighteenth centuries was the sorting, grading, packing and storing undertaken by the Second Hand after the First Hand of great merchants had brought the goods to the entrepot centre. Adam Smith's belief that the merchant exchanging corn from Königsberg for wine from Portugal brought both to Amsterdam because he felt uneasy separated from his capital and wanted to see it badly enough to be willing to pay the double charge of loading and unloading (1776, pp. 421–2) was based on a complete misunderstanding of this central point. The merchant had a strong interest in ensuring that the goods were sorted by grade and conformed to the qualities demanded. The "gentlemen merchants" of Leeds paid more attention to quality of the woolens they bought than to price (Wilson, 1971, pp. 56–7). It had been especially efficient to do so two or three centuries early at a time when goods were sold at semi-annual or quarterly fairs, or shipped in an annual convoy to such a destination as Newfoundland, since goods rejected by the buyer would tie up the merchant's capital for an extended period.

The function of the merchant in commercial development in fixing and maintaining standards of quality is underlined when one contemplates the difficulties encountered in quality by Socialist countries, where producer performance and bonuses are usually related to quantities of output, which, given goods shortages, does not have to meet a rigorous quality test in the market. Competitive markets that clear allow consumers to reject altogether or to price down low-quality output, and thus provide strong incentives to merchants to enforce quality control on producers.

Governments and merchants are of course not the only instruments for standardization. When Denmark entered the international (largely British) market for butter at the end of the nineteenth century, much of its output was so-called "peasant butter" of uneven taste and texture. Before this could be sold in quantity abroad, it had to be upgraded to the quality of "manor butter," a process carried out, after the invention of the cream separator, through a newly-created institution, the marketing cooperative. This had the advantage of allowing production to continue on the small labour-intensive scale of the family farm, while marketing, after standardization and grading of eggs, bacon, and cheese, as well as butter, was done on an efficient large scale (Faber, 1931). These standards were of course collective, as contrasted with public, goods or the quasi-private goods of merchant standards. The twentieth-century equivalent of such collective goods is the control by wine-growers of the labelling of champagne and other "appellations contrôlées" wines from particular regions. Here the standards are set by the vintners but enforced by government in an effort to protect consumers from adulteration on the one hand and to limit competition on the other.

After a certain stage of development and for certain classes of goods the efforts of merchants to standardize and grade output can become dysfunctional. It was said that the wholesale merchants dealing in cotton goods in Lancashire in the twentieth century maintained 34 grades of poplins when the ultimate user could distinguish at most three different qualities (Robson, 1957, pp. 92–5). In the British machine-tool trade, merchants have been regarded as inhibiting quality change and the development of new tools by standing between the producer and the consumer, telling the producer with an idea for a new machine "They don't want them like that," and the customer looking for a new device "They don't make them like that" (Beesley and Throup, 1958, pp. 380ff). Chandler (1962) notes that when the local and regional corporation in the United States grew to national size at the end of the nineteenth century, it gave up the services of independent wholesalers and jobbers and drew the marketing function back into the firm so as to maintain direct contact with customers. Without the interposition of the merchant, it was possible for producer and consumer to explore together possible improvements and their costs and benefits. This gain seems to have outweighed the diseconomies of scale in administration from combining in one company such different functions as production and marketing.

Machine tools were long an industry in transition from standardized lathes, milling machines, grinders and the like to special machines for special purposes. Between these limits a large and growing class of goods exists in which the hardware is standardized but requires instruction or software for its effective use. The claim has been made that the need for software first developed in the chemical industry at the end of the nineteenth century as instruction in the use of nitrate fertilizers was necessary to prevent the peasant-farmer from blowing himself up (Hohenberg, 1967). In today's world complex manufactured products lead naturally to the spread of the multinational corporation as products require instruction in use and repair, plus depots of spare parts, both leading to the creation in each national market of subsidiaries that evolve with some high degree of probability into local manufacture (Carlson, 1978). The standards set by makers of automobiles, electrical appliances, other durable consumer goods and industrial equipment are private goods, supported by advertizing to reinforce the claims for quality, rather than collective or public goods. The maintenance of these quality standards has perhaps little effect in economizing on transactions costs except where a customer satisfied with a given product is content to replace it with the same item from the same producer without search.

Where government lays down standards for the protection of ignorant consumers it may do so in the interest of producers, as Lindblom asserts was true both for meat inspection and for pure food and drugs, with policy formulated by business control parading as democratic reform without an important contribution from popular demand (1977, p. 191). If this be true, an ostensible public good is effectively a collective good, although the two sorts of good can be complementary. Similar examples can be found in land zoning, with perhaps different private groups having different interests in the outcome of zoning decisions, and policy leading to standards with costs and benefits that have particular distributions. Governmental standards may also turn out to be dubious public goods and at the same time collective bads, as in building codes designed to protect the public from shoddy construction, but frequently piling up requirements, such as provision for handicapped persons in areas where few if any exist, at costs which are only casually considered and prove to be exorbitant. Governmental standards of this sort for the protection of consumers or investors are difficult to bring under the rubric of "reducing transactions costs" and perhaps deserve a separate category.

To return to standards set directly by producer or marketer, they save transactions costs in improving recognition and avoiding buyer dissatisfaction, with perhaps the disability of impeding quality changes if merchants inhibit exchange of information between producer and consumer. But standardization can reduce transaction costs in other ways, notably in standardization of working time, of statistics, and of monies. The saving in transactions costs, it may be noted, may well involve other types of costs which in particular cases exceed the transactions benefit.

Milton Friedman once applied the analogy of daylight saving time to flexible exchange rates. Instead of changing our habits when we wish to extend the hours of daylight, we change our clocks. By the same token we should change exchange rates instead of trying to change prices and wages (1953). He neglected to point out that to be efficient, daylight saving time has to be adopted for an entire zone at once, and optimally for all time zones around the world by the same amount on the same day of the year. When New York is in touch with London or San Francisco or Singapore or Bahrein, exchange rates for time zones must be fixed (Kindleberger, 1981, pp. 34–41). The point can be generalized: standardization of working time facilitates transactions by having people on the assembly line or in offices that need to interact available to work together.

There is no such necessity for novelists or scholars, but for factory or office workers there is likely to be, despite the heavy costs in excess capacity in buildings and equipment, in transport congestion, and to the extent that everyone takes a holiday in the same weeks or month, in resort facilities. The Soviet Union experiment with varying the day or days of rest within the week, and currently popular proposals in the west for "flexitime" working arrangements focus on one cost of standardized work days, weeks, months and years, but neglect the benefits. Standardized worktime in the factory makes possible the simultaneous or sequential application of labour to materials; in urban occupations where interpersonal communication at a high level is needed, as in advertising, law, finance and administration, it makes it likely that the person needed will be found when sought at his or her desk (Vernon, 1960; Winston, 1982).

Standardization of economic information reduces transactions costs in various ways for the most part too obvious to require illustration. The European Economic Community had to establish a common tariff nomenclature before it could impose a common tariff. Comparison and aggregation of national trade data require standardization of trade statistics whether by the Hague convention of 1913, the interwar League of Nations standard, or the United Nations Standard International Trade Classification (SITC). Today the United Nations and such bodies as the International Monetary Fund, the World Bank and other specialized agencies, national governments, their ministries and statistical bureaus, private research organizations, and individual scholars like Kuznets, Leontief, Friedman and Schwartz, Maizels, Bairoch, Rostow etc. spent countless hours and sums trying to make statistical series comparable both between countries and over time. The difficulty inherent in the process is that national statistics are shaped to separate country's conditions and needs, and statistical series over time encounter changes in underlying conditions of population, technology, resources, products and tastes which require changes in their composition. The index-number problem is insoluble both in time series and in cross-sectional analysis, despite the powerful sophisticated methods which have been brought to bear on it.

Finally in this listing is the need for money as a measure and as a medium of exchange. As a unit of account, money reduces transactions costs by assisting comparisons, converting, as is well known, the $N(N - 1)/2$ comparisons of a barter system to $N - 1$. Hayek (1977) and Vaubel (1979) neglect the unit-of-account function of money when they recommend the innovation of private competitive monies. They believe they take care of the objection that two or more would be subject to Gresham's law by allowing the several private monies to be traded against one another at varying prices. With monies varying in price, however—within a country and even between countries—there is in my view no national (or international) money in the sense of a standard suitable for measurements. A fixed conversion coefficient between metres and yards permits measurement to take place in either. When the relationship between the yard and the metre fluctuates, however, the public good of a standard of measurement is lost.

Even the medium-of-exchange and store-of-value functions of money that Vaubel believes should be left to the private market as private goods, subject to the prescription of *caveat emptor*, pose problems in transactions costs. The state has two reasons to set a money standard. In the first place, there is strong historical evidence that not all members of society possess the capacity adequately to safeguard their own interests. This is the reason for standards of pure food and drugs, honest measure, tolerable limits of bacteria in the water at bathing beaches and public swimming pools, enforced by the state. The state, moreover, lays down and seeks to enforce strong rules against counterfeiting or debasement of money of other sorts, such as writing bad cheques. The Federal Deposit Insurance Corporation sets limits of insured deposits, originally $10,000, then $40,000 and now $100,000, because small depositors presumably lack the capacity to judge the safety of a given bank, whereas the possessor of wealth is held responsible for protecting his own money.

In addition to this function of protection, standardization of the medium of exchange saves transaction costs. It took four months to test and count the 1,200,000 escudo ransom of the sons of Francis I in 1529—40,000 escudos more being demanded because of imperfect coins (Vilar, 1976, p. 174). To economize on weighing and assaying specie in Italy in the Middle Ages, and up to the nineteenth century in the Eastern Mediterranean, banks accumulated coin in purses marked with the amounts contained, and dealt in them without recounting, with the state levying heavy penalties against any overstatement of the amount (Udovitch, 1979, p. 174; Marlowe, 1974, p. 153). "Bank money" developed in the seventeenth century, consisting of transferable deposits of coin in the public banks of Genoa, Venice, Amsterdam, Hamburg, etc. with the bank certifying to the existence on deposit of specie of the requisite weight and fineness (Van Dillen, 1934). Bank money in Amsterdam normally traded at a premium of 3 to 5 per cent above the equivalent coin, the premium testifying to the transaction saving in testing and counting (Smith, 1776, p. 452). As unit of account, and to a great extent in the medium-of-exchange and store-of-value functions, standardization of money—a process that has been continuing in Darwinian fashion for centuries—provides a public good that reduces transactions costs.

III

Standardization can produce physical economies as well as savings in transactions, though not necessarily in total cost. In production, the saving may lie in economies of scale through repetitive production and in the reduction of down time for changing patterns and shifting materials. In use—more often perhaps of intermediate than of final goods—the benefit is in interchangeability of equipment. A classic example is the standard railway gauge of 4 feet 8 1/2 inches, believed by tradition to have originally represented the width of the hind end of a Norfolk mule used to pull coal wagons on wooden rails. In 1846 the British Parliament enacted the Gauge Act requiring all railroads to conform to the standard gauge. The Great Western Railway that operated from London to Devon and Cornwall and had started with a gauge width of five feet resisted strenuously on the ground that its wider gauge was superior to the standard adopted, producing a smoother, more stable and safer ride. As the Great Western acquired other railroads through purchase and merger it widened their gauges by 3 1/2 inches and equipped the acquired locomotives and wagons with new axles. Cargo moving on other railroads from the Midlands to the Southwest had to be transhipped at Gloucester from standard to wide-gauge wagons, and vice-versa for shipments in the other direction. After holding out for half a century, the Great Western finally yielded to the inevitable and adopted the standard gauge in the 1890s.

Railway-gauge problems have also been prominent in wars involving Russia with a wide gauge and Germany with the standard (adopted by most countries), and in the separate states of Australia. In the Russo–German case, the Germans for a time shifted one track inward on sleepers as they conquered Russian territory in World Wars I and II, and then adopted locomotive and wagon axles with an extra wheel to fit the wider size to make transfers possible without relaying track. In Australia each state kept to its own gauge until after the middle of the present century, forcing most interstate cargo to be carried by sea between settlements along the coast, and interstate shipments by rail to be reloaded from one system to the other.

Many manufacturing processes in Britain escaped standardization for lack of government efforts, those of a trade association, or the pressures of a dominant firm. It has been said that there were 200 types of axle boxes, 40 different handbrakes in railway wagons, perhaps 200 sizes and specifications for manhole covers. The Railway Clearinghouse laid down regulations for equipping privately-owned cars with automatic brakes, but most railroads built their own stock to their own standards (Parkhouse, 1951). There were 122 channel and angle sections in England, when the Germans had reduced their number to 32 (Landes, 1965, p. 495), and "an almost unbelievable lack of standardization" on the part of British manufacturers of ploughs (Saul, 1968, p. 212). In World War I Britain was found to have 70 electricity generating companies with 50 different systems of supply, 24 voltages and 10 different frequencies (Plummer, 1937, p. 21). British automobiles adopted the precedent of trains and drove on the left of the road with the driver in the right-hand side of the front seat, whereas virtually all other countries changed over to the American standard of left-hand drive cars on the right-hand lane of dual roads.

Standardization between firms allows for greater interchangeability of equipment not only in such items as railroad locomotives and rolling stock, but also savings for the consumer if, say, the change from 78 revolutions per minute for records and record-players is made entirely to 33 r.p.m. long-playing records, instead of one company, R.C.A., adopting for a time a different standard of 45 r.p.m. French resistance to the adoption of the United States standard in colour television of a minimum number of lines per inch and attempt to spread its own finer but more complex and difficult to maintain standard evoke echoes of the holdout of the Great Western railway except that in this case it succeeded in getting its standard adopted in Europe. It is a general phenomenon that the first major firm in the field in a country has a relatively free hand in setting the standard. This may, however, prove later to be less than optimal but at such time difficult to displace.

In Britain some part of the explanation for the lack of standardization that would have constituted a collective good for an industry lay in the numbers of small companies making a virtually simultaneous start in an industry, with none sufficiently in advance to induce others to follow its lead. In addition, both railroads and cities hired own consulting engineers with pride in their professional competence who chose specifications for railway or municipal equipment as if they were architects designing unique structures, without attention to possible external economies (Saul, 1968). (The adoption of separate building codes for cities and towns in the United States has the same origin in local pride of authorship and the same result in preventing the achievement of economies of scale in many aspects of the construction industry, though there may be some basis for regional differences—south and north, wet and dry, and the like.) There were exceptions in the British case. In tramways, John Young was a dynamic municipal engineer who persuaded the entire country to follow his standard type of overhead trolley, enabling manufacturers to gain production economies of scale (McKay, 1976, pp. 181–4). By contrast standardization in Germany and France was achieved by the success of a dominant firm in each country so far in the lead that it forced the competition to follow. Charles Mertz of Northeastern England was both a consulting engineer and a supplier of electrical equipment who achieved standardization of electricity production and distribution in the area in which he operated (Saul, 1968, pp. 231ff; Byatt, 1968, p. 272). He was of course aided by starting some time after the initial introduction of electricity in the south of England, and was able to profit from the example of that region's troubles.

Where a company is far in the lead, as the American Telephone and Telegraph Company or IBM in computers, there is strong pressure on the rest of the industry to make its equipment compatible, leading to the private and collective good of standardization, although for the lead company which may be partially displaced, the standardization might be regarded as a private bad. In international trade Jacques Drèze has explained why Belgium, a small country unable by itself to get economies of scale in its market, has to concentrate on the production of standardized commodities that can be sold in world markets, for example, semi-finished iron and steel bars, rods, shapes, wire and the like, flat glass, intermediate chemical products such as soda ash and urea, electric wiring harnesses used interchangeably on many models of foreign automobiles (1960).

Standardization may also be desirable within an organization for physical reasons. Armies, navies, air forces find it desirable to focus on a few types of weapons in order to reduce numbers of spare parts to be maintained, and to simplify the training and operations of users and repairers. What is self-evident for such a large organization as an army applies as well to firms, to railroads for locomotives, bus companies, fleets of taxis or rental cars, etc. If the equipment wears out a little at a time, and technical progress or model changes continue in the industry, the company faces a difficult choice between heterogeneous equipment or lumpy capital expenditures, which choice may or may not be assisted by the possibility of selling obsolete serviceable equipment in a second-hand market.

A variety of defences of advertising have been put forward, notably the dissemination of information, the gaining of consumer loyalty through product recognition, appealing to consumers directly over the heads of wholesalers, jobbers and retailers (Kaldor, 1951). For consumer loyalty it is important for the company to set and maintain high standards and quality control and to persuade the public that a brand name is a guarantee of quality. Brand loyalty based on such belief is an intangible asset, included on the balance sheet under good will. Sophisticated methods of testing and quality control are required along with advertising to eliminate "lemons" (equipment that performs inadequately or requires excessive maintenance and repair), short measure, or disappointment to public expectations in other ways. Generic foodstuffs and drugs which are cheaper than branded articles encounter difficulty where a brand name is believed to be a guarantee of quality. To the extent that generic products are gaining on higher-priced branded products, it is possible that the consumer attaches an implicit guarantee of standard quality to the retail dispenser.

IV

Standards may be imposed by government, by trade or professional association, dominant firm, or in some cases be altogether missing. Where they exist with important economies in transaction costs or physical economies of scale, or don't exist but would be useful, they are difficult to change, or to adopt late in an industry's life, because of lumpiness. A substantial capital investment is likely to be required for a smaller monetary gain over time. With perfect information on costs and benefits, and well-functioning capital markets the decision as to whether or not to change standards is readily made by a single decision-maker with due attention to discounting future benefits by some appropriate rate of interest. In practice, with many firms in an industry, the difficulties are likely to be great, partly because of the free-rider problem that inhibits the production of public goods: each firm, household, individual waits to undertake to change the standard until the rest of society has conformed and the costs and benefits to the single unit are clarified. The various forms that resistance may take can be illustrated, beyond the Great Western railway and French television already cited, with reference to right- and left-hand drives for automobiles, and the metric system in France, Britain and the United States.

Trains in Britain used the left track, and those of Sweden, Switzerland and the United Kingdom (at a minimum) still do. When automobiles came along, the British clung to the left-hand side of the road, whereas the United States chose the right-hand side. (The question was undoubtedly decided state by state, but once the first few states adopted a common standard the rest followed without question. The practice of driving on one side or the other with horses and horse-drawn vehicles may have been a factor affecting the choice in Britain and the United States, but I lack information.) When the United States moved into mass production and export of automobiles, the American left-hand drive car, appropriate to a right-hand traffic pattern, came to dominate foreign countries. Pressure for standardization was significant among contiguous countries, although a few like Austria and Sweden, held out in the British pattern. For the British Isles, with no highways running directly to foreign countries—prior to completion of the Channel tunnel—it was easy to keep to an idiosyncratic standard since there was no necessity to change sides of the road in continuous travel. A certain cost was incurred in having to have special assembly lines for left-hand drive cars sold abroad, or right-hand cars purchased from abroad, and in accidents from drivers who intuitively turned the wrong way or pedestrians who looked the wrong way. The extra cost of foreign right-hand-drive cars may have been enjoyed, however, as a non-tariff-barrier.

Sweden shifted from the left to the right side of the road after a long drawn-out process of study and decision-making. Royal Commissions studied the question once in the 1930s, and again in 1946, both with negative decisions, a national referendum voted against change in the 1950s, and a positive decision was taken only at the end of the 1960s. The early commissions thought the costs—presumably the transitional heterogeneity of the carpark as well as the more serious necessity to discharge passengers of trams and buses on the street rather than on the sidewalk—outweighed the benefits of moderately cheaper cars and a common standard with neighbouring countries. Increasing internationalization of automotive purchases and sales and of automotive travel finally tipped the decision the other way. It is of some interest that the national referendum voted overwhelmingly against change.

In Austria, I believe, there was little pressure for change up to 1938 when, after *Anschluss*, Hitler ordered the change to be made overnight. Confusion was substantial, and doubtless accidents, but an absolute authority, interested in uniformity throughout the country, decreed that it be done without ado. The contrast between the close and drawn-out decision in Sweden, made without difficulty in a democratic society, and one put into effect without discussion suggests the limits of experience in changing standards.

The French change from the weights and measures of the *Ancien Régime* to a metric system, including among the measures money, reveals a process with something of both elements, along with a failure, the decimalization of time. The basis for the metric system was laid in the seventeenth century, and with the support of the French Academy of Science, put into effect by Talleyrand who got it through the Estates General of the French Revolution. The legislation was introduced in 1790; commissions were appointed for weights and measures on the one hand and time on the other. Both were adopted. Decimal time beginning with year one from 22 September 1794 and the 12 months of thirty days each: *Vendémiaire, Brumaire, Frimaire*, etc., weeks of 10 days was adopted partly to break down the Christian system of Sundays and holy days. It lasted only ten to twelve years. Decimal time with 10 hours of 100 minutes each per day survived far less—failing to survive for two years (Carrigan, 1968). Weights and measures needed a Revolution to effect a drastic change. The substitution of the decimal *franc germinal* for the *livre* (pound) *tournois*, divided into *sous* and *deniers* (nominally equivalent to shillings and pence), a quasi duo-decimal system that went back to the Romans was perhaps more readily put into effect in 1803 under Napoleon because of the collapse of the *assignats* in 1795.

Somewhat like the Gauge Act of 1846, however, it was one thing to order the standard changed and another to have the change accomplished. In his book *From Peasants into Frenchman* (1976), Eugen Weber points out that the French peasant was still using the old measures as late as 1870, when he began to be integrated into the rest of France by virtue of military service on the one hand and national norms laid down for education on the other. The process seems extended, but it is understandable to those who are aware that the change from the old to the new franc, decreed by President de Gaulle in 1958 at the ratio of 100 to 1, is still ignored by many French today. Children and tourists quickly began to calculate in new francs, the children learning in school, the tourists starting with *tabula rasa*. People who grew up under the old franc, however, mostly cling to 10,000 francs when foreigners would say 100.

A generation for the new franc, seventy years for the *franc germinal* of 1803 were slight as compared with the century and a half for the British to adopt a system of decimal money. Immediately after the Napoleonic wars there were pressures to join the French in adoption of the decimal system. A Royal Commission in the 1840s recommended early action. Indeed, the minting of the two shilling florin was undertaken in 1847 as the first step toward a decimal money—one tenth of a pound as compared with the half crown which was a binary one eighth of a pound. Throughout Europe in the middle of the nineteenth century country after country was falling in line with the decimalization of money—Belgium, Germany, Italy, Spain, Sweden, Switzerland, although the Swedish decision lagged behind others for a time because of the objections of clergymen. A new committee was appointed in Britain in the 1850s to rubber-stamp the decision to follow suit. It happened, however, to contain the opinionated monetarist, Lord Overstone, who objected to decimalization largely because it involved change. By adroit manoeuvring he blocked the decision which was not taken favourably until a century later when computerization somewhat increased the benefits of the change (O'Brien, 1971, Vol. 1, pp. 52–9; Vol. 3, appendices D and E).

Lord Overstone's stated objections to decimalization were based on technical grounds on the one hand, and on the distribution of costs and benefits on the other. Technically he made such points as that a system of 1000 mils, which would have been required because 100th of a pound (2.4 d) would have been too large for the smallest coin, was inferior to a system of 960 farthings (1/4 d), since 27 numbers can be divided into 960 without a remainder and only 15 into 1000. He also felt that it would have been necessary to change the normal system of counting since he found it awkward to quote a price of, say, 10 pennies for a dozen eggs. As to distribution of costs and benefits, he acknowledged that the change would benefit banking, insurance, and finance of all sorts for which reckoning, especially of percentages, would be eased, but felt that the change in money would be hard on the lower classes and the poor. While Overstone was generous in gifts to charity, it is not evident that he had an intimate knowledge of these groups. In general he opposed change. Final British action in 1951 was taken after Australia and New Zealand had adopted decimalization, and long after the change had been made in Canada and South Africa.

The United States is today engaged in the process of changing, especially linear and liquid measurements and temperatures from the British to the continental decimal standard, doing it with deliberate slowness and increasingly meeting resistance from politically conservative groups who oppose change, especially change that involves adopting foreign standards. To an amateur in such matters, it seems to have been psychologically wrong to proceed so slowly, posting temperatures in public places both in Fahrenheit and in Celsius, and distances and speeds both in kilometres and in miles. The process of change requires the public first to convert from the new to the old, and, when the new becomes sufficiently familiar, to stop converting and use just the new. If both measures are given simultaneously, the necessity to convert is eliminated, and the second stage of relying on the new scales to economize on conversion may not be reached. It may be in the short run, however, that the benefits of a common set of measures between the United States and the rest of the world are declining as neomercantilism spreads, and that the benefits appear to decline as the costs seem heavier.

V

Apart from international statistical standards which have to be changed anyway and where countries have a strong motive to agree, it is hard to think of international standards that did not start out as the public good of some particular country, usually one with high international standing because of its economic and/or military power. During World War II, the United States and the United Kingdom harmonized the pitch of the screw thread between them to make screws of the same size interchangeable. Since the economy of the United States was several times that of Britain, the most costly changes were made by the latter. The Justinian and Gregorian calendars in macro-temporal measurement were produced by Rome and adopted generally in Europe and throughout its colonies, though not by Russia or the Moslem world. Greenwich mean time became the world standard when Britain ruled the waves. As noted, decimalization emerged from France, the gold standard from Britain, and the dollar-exchange standard from the United States, the last with some political holdouts such as France. It is not a random result that international air traffic, where the benefits of a common standard of communication are high, communicates in English, except for the one expression for planes in distress, "M'aidez," which is usually transliterated into "Mayday." Like a dominant corporation in a new industry producing steel shapes, left-hand drive automobiles, IBM 360 computers, the big countries 'ram it through'.

When countries are more evenly matched in size and importance, agreement on international standards for output, regulations, taxation etc. is likely to lag or to be weakened in compromise. The original Rome treaty envisaged not only abolition of tariffs on trade within the Community but also the harmonization of excise taxes, regulations and the like so that trucks and railroad cars carrying goods would not have to stop at the frontier. This freedom of movement for goods remains to be achieved. Local standards may be retained and new ones such as the requirement that cars in Sweden be equipped with windshield wipers for the head-lights imposed as non-tariff barriers. In joint activities such as the European airbus, the equipment of NATO, the pooling of research in space and nuclear physics, the principle of allocating work to the low-cost source has been compromised in favour of the *juste retour* in which each country gets a share of output allocated to it according to its financial contribution. The possibility exists that the Common Market may end up like early British industry with only limited harmonization and inter-changeability as the free rider or the holdout hoping to have its standard adopted, making easy adoption of common standards impossible. Merchants were responsible for most standardization at the international level in earlier times, though some international standards were imposed by strong governments, and a few by the power of superior performance. In today's world in highly competitive national markets and in the international economy with no one country any longer leading or dominant, there is risk of market failure in the sense of failure to adopt widely accepted standards in new goods, to keep old standards up to date as improvements become possible, and especially to achieve the international public good of world standards.

Note

1. This paper brings together, extends and generalizes a number of previous observations on the subject (Kindleberger, 1964, pp. 149–52, 1978a, pp. 137, 228ff., 1978b, pp. 6–7, 1982, pp. 203–16). The analysis and illustrations accordingly are to a considerable extent repetitious.

References

Beesley, M. E. and Troup, G. W., "The Machine-Tool Industry," in: Duncan Burn (ed.), *The Structure of British Industry*, 2 vols., Cambridge: Cambridge University Press, vol. 1, pp. 359–92.

Byatt, I. C. R., "Electrical Products," in, Aldcroft, D. H. (ed.), *The Development of British Industry and Foreign Competition, 1875–1914*, London: George Allen & Unwin, pp. 238–73.

Carlson, Sune, 'Company Policies for International Expansion: The Swedish Experience', in, Agmon, Tamir and Kindleberger, C. P. (eds), *Multinationals from Small Countries* Cambridge, Mass.: MIT Press, pp. 49–71.

Carrigan, Jr., R. A., "Decimal Time," *American Scientist*, Vol. 66 (1978), no. 3, May–June, pp. 305–13.

Chandler, Alfred D. *Strategy and Structure: Chapters in the History of Industrial Enterprise*, Cambridge, Mass.: Harvard University Press, 1962.

de Roover, Raymond, *The Rise and Fall of the Medici Bank*, New York: W. W. Norton, 1966.

Drèze, Jacques, "Quelques réflexions sereines sur l'adaptation de l'industrie belge au Marché Commun," *Comptes rendus des Travaux de la Société Royale d'Economie Politique de Belgique*, no. 275, 1960.

Faber, Harald, *Co-operation in Danish Agriculture*, 2nd ed., London: Longmans Green, 1931.

Friedman, Milton, "The Case for Flexible Exchange Rates," in, Friedman, M. *Essays in Positive Economics*, Chicago: University of Chicago Press, 1953, pp. 157–203.

Hayek, F. A., *Choice in Currency: A Way to Stop Inflation*, London: Institute of Economic Affairs, Occasional Paper no. 48, 1977.

Hohenberg, Paul M., *Chemicals in Western Europe, 1850–1914: An Economic Study of Technical Change*, Chicago: Rand McNally, 1967.

Kaldor, Nicholas, "The Economic Aspects of Advertising," *Review of Economic Studies*, vol. 28 (1951), pp. 1–27.

Kindleberger, C. P., *Economic Growth in France and Britain, 1851–1950*, Cambridge, Mass.: Harvard University Press, 1964.

————, *Economic Response: Comparative Studies in Trade, Finance and Growth*, Cambridge, Mass.: Harvard University Press, 1978a.

————, "Government and International Trade," Princeton, NJ: Essays in International Finance, no. 129, 1978b.

————, *International Money*, London: George Allen & Unwin, 1981.

————, "International Monetary Reform in the Nineteenth Century," in, Cooper, R. N. *et al. International Monetary System under Flexible Exchange Rates*, Lexington, Mass.: Ballinger, 1982.

Landes, David S., *Bankers and Pashas*, Cambridge, Mass.: Harvard University Press, 1958.

————, "Technological Change and the Development of Western Europe, 1750–1914," in, *The Cambridge Economic History of Europe*, VI. Vol. 1, Cambridge: Cambridge University Press, 1965, pp. 274–601.

Lindblom, Charles E., *Politics and Markets: The World's Political–Economic System*, New York: Basic Books, 1977.

Marlowe, John (pseudonym), *Spoiling the Egyptians*, London: Deutsch, 1974.

McKay, John P., *Tramways and Trolleys: The Rise of Urban Mass Transport in Europe*, Princeton, NJ: Princeton University Press, 1976.

O'Brien, D. P. (ed.), *The Correspondence of Lord Overstone*, 3 vols., Cambridge: Cambridge University Press, 1971.

Origo, Iris, *The Merchant of Prato*, New York: Knopf, 1957.

Parkhouse, S. E., "Railway Freight Rolling Stock," *Journal of the Institute of Transort*, vol. 24 (1951), pp. 211–18, 242.

Plummer, Alfred, *New British Industries in the Twentieth Century*, London: Pitman, 1937.

Robson, R., *The Cotton Industry in Britain*, London: Macmillan, 1957.

Samuelson, Paul A., "The Pure Theory of Public Expenditure," *The Review of Economics and Statistics*, vol. 36 (1954), pp. 387–9, reproduced in *The Collected Scientific Papers of Paul A. Samuelson*, Vol. 2, Cambridge, Mass.: The MIT Press, 1966, pp. 1223–5.

Saul, S. B., "The Engineering Industry," in, Aldcroft, D. H. (ed.), *The Development of British Industry and Foreign Competition, 1875–1914*, London: George Allen & Unwin, 1968.

Smith, Adam, *An Inquiry into the Nature and Causes of the Wealth of Nations*, 1776 (Cannan ed.), New York: Modern Library, 1937.

Udovitch, Abraham, L., "Bankers without Banks: Commerce, Banking and Society in the Islamic World of the Middle Ages," Center for Medieval and Renaissance Studies: *The Dawn of Modern Banking*, New Haven: Yale University Press, 1979, pp. 255–74.

Van Dillen, J. G. (ed.), *History of the Principal Public Banks*, The Hague: Martinus Nijhoff, 1934.

Vaubel, Roland, "Free Currency Competition," *Weltwirtschaftliches Archiv*, vol. 113 (1977), pp. 435–59.

Vernon, Raymond, *Metropolis, 1985*, Cambridge, Mass.: Harvard University Press, 1960.

Vilar, Pierre, *A History of Gold and Money, 1450–1920*, London: NLB, 1976 (Spanish original 1969).

Weber, Eugen, *From Peasants into Frenchmen*, Stanford: Stanford University Press, 1976.

Wilson R. G., *Gentlemen Merchants: The Merchant Community of Leeds, 1700–1830*, Manchester: Manchester University Press, 1971.

Winston, Gordon, *The Timing of Economic Activities*, New York: Cambridge University Press, 1982.

Finance

9   The Dollar and World Liquidity: A Minority View

with Emile Despres and
Walter S. Salant

Three American economists, each outside government service but each with influence in official Washington, here put forward a dissenting view on the prime current issue of international payments. We believe that the analysis is of profound importance and must be taken into account even by those who would balk at some of the conclusions. Our own remaining reservation is appended briefly.

The consensus in Europe and the USA on the US balance of payments and world liquidity runs about like this:

(1) Abundant liquidity has been provided since the Second World War less by newly mined gold than by the increase in liquid dollar assets generated by US balance-of-payments deficits.

(2) These deficits are no longer available as a generator of liquidity because the accumulation of dollars has gone so far that it has undermined confidence in the dollar.

(3) To halt the present creeping decline in liquidity through central-bank conversions of dollars into gold, and to forestall headlong flight from the dollar, it is necessary above all else to correct the US deficit.

(4) When the deficit has been corrected, the growth of world reserves may, or probably will, become inadequate. Hence there is a need for planning new means of adding to world reserves—along the lines suggested by Triffin, Bernstein, Roosa, Stamp, Giscard and others.[1]

So much is widely agreed. There is a difference in tactics between those who would correct the US balance of payments by raising interest rates—bankers on both sides of the ocean and European central bankers—and those in the USA who would correct it, if necessary, by capital restrictions, so that tight money in the USA may be avoided while labor and other resources are still idle. There is also a difference of emphasis between the Continentals, who urge adjustment (proposition 3 above), and the Anglo-Saxons, who stress the need for more liquidity (proposition 4). British voices urge more liquidity now, rather than in the future. But with these exceptions, the lines of analysis converge.

Four Counter Propositions

There is room, however, for a minority view which would oppose this agreement with a sharply differing analysis. In outline, it asserts the following counter propositions:

(1) While the USA has provided the world with liquid dollar assets in the postwar period by capital outflow and aid exceeding its current account surplus, in most years this excess has not reflected a deficit in a sense representing disequilibrium. The outflow of US capital and aid has filled not one but two needs. First, it has supplied goods and services to the rest of the world. But secondly, to the extent that its loans to foreigners are offset by foreigners putting their own money into liquid dollar assets, the USA has not overinvested but has supplied financial intermediary services. The "deficit" has reflected largely the second process, in which the USA has been lending, mostly at long and intermediate term, and borrowing short. This financial intermediation, in turn, performs two functions: it supplies loans and investment funds to foreign enterprises which have to pay more domestically to borrow long-term money and which cannot get the amounts they want at any price, and it supplies liquidity to foreign asset-holders, who receive less for placing their short-term deposits at home. Essentially, this is a trade in liquidity, which is profitable to both sides. Differences in their liquidity preferences (that is, in their willingness to hold their financial assets in long-term rather than in quickly encashable forms and to have short-term rather than long-term liabilities outstanding against them) create differing margins between short-term and long-term interest rates. This in turn creates scope for trade in financial assets, just as differing comparative costs create the scope for mutually profitable trade in goods. This trade in financial assets has been an important ingredient of economic growth outside the USA.

(2) Such lack of confidence in the dollar as now exists has been generated by the attitudes of government officials, central bankers, academic economists and journalists, and reflects their failure to understand the

implications of this intermediary function. Despite some contagion from these sources, the private market retains confidence in the dollar, as increases in private holdings of liquid dollar assets show. Private speculation in gold is simply the result of the known attitudes and actions of governmental officials and central bankers.

(3) With capital markets unrestricted, attempts to correct the "deficit" by ordinary macro-economic weapons are likely to fail. It may be possible to expand the current account surplus at first by deflation of US income and prices relative to those of Europe, but gross financial capital flows will still exceed real transfer of goods and services (that is, involve financial intermediation, lending long-term funds to Europe in exchange for short-term deposits) so long as capital formation remains high in Europe. A moderate rise of interest rates in the USA will have only a small effect on the net capital outflow. A drastic rise might cut the net outflow substantially, but only by tightening money in *Europe* enough to stop economic growth, and this would cut the USA's current account surplus. Correcting the US deficit by taxes and other controls on capital, which is being attempted on both sides of the Atlantic, is likely either to fail, or to succeed by impeding international capital flows so much as to cut European investment and growth.

(4) While it is desirable to supplement gold with an internationally created reserve asset, the conventional analysis leading to this remedy concentrates excessively on a country's external liquidity; it takes insufficient account of the demands of savers for internal liquidity and of borrowers in the same country for long-term funds. The international private capital market, properly understood, provides both external liquidity to a country and the kinds of assets and liabilities that private savers and borrowers want and cannot get at home. Most plans to create an international reserve asset, however, are addressed only to external liquidity problems which in many cases, and especially in Europe today, are the less important issue.

With agreement between the USA and Europe—but without it if necessary—it would be possible to develop a monetary system which provided the external liquidity that is needed and also recognized the role of international financial intermediation in world economic growth.

Europe Needs Dollars

Analytical support and elaboration of this minority view is presented in numbered sections, conforming to the propositions advanced above as an alternative to the consensus.

(1) The idea that the balance of payments of a country is in disequilibrium if it is in deficit on the liquidity (US Department of Commerce) definition is not appropriate to a country with a large and open capital market that is performing the function of a financial intermediary. Banks and other financial intermediaries, unlike traders, are paid to give up liquidity. The USA is no more in deficit when it lends long and borrows short than is a bank when it makes a loan and enters a deposit on its books.

Financial intermediation is an important function in a monetary economy. Savers want liquid assets; borrowers investing in fixed capital expansion are happier with funded rather than quick liabilities. Insofar as the gap is not bridged, capital formation is held down. Europeans borrow from the USA, and Americans are willing to pay higher prices for European assets than European investors will, partly because capital is more readily available in the USA than in Europe, but mainly because liquidity preference in Europe is higher and because capital markets in Europe are much less well organized, more monopolistically controlled, and just plain smaller than in the USA. With unrestricted capital markets, the European savers who want cash and the borrowers who prefer to extend their liabilities into the future can both be satisfied when the US capital market lends long and borrows short and when it accepts smaller margins between its rates for borrowing short and lending short. European borrowers of good credit standing will seek to borrow in New York (or in the Eurodollar market, which is a mere extension of New York) when rates of interest are lower on dollar loans than on loans in European currencies, or when the amounts required are greater than their domestic capital markets can provide. But when interferences prevent foreign intermediaries from bridging the gap, and when domestic private intermediaries cannot bridge it while the public authorities will not, borrowing possibilities are cut, and investment and growth are cut with it.

The effects are not confined to Europe, or even to the advanced countries. Slower European growth means lower demand for primary products imported from the less developed countries. Preoccupation of the USA, Britain, and now Germany with their balances of payments dims the outlook for foreign aid and worsens the climate for trade liberalization. And the American capital controls are bound to reduce the access of less developed countries to private capital and bond loans in the USA—and indirectly in Europe.

(2) It may be objected that no bank can keep lending if its depositors are unwilling to hold its liabilities. True. But savings can never be put to productive use if the owners of wealth are unwilling to hold financial

assets and insist on what they consider a more "ultimate" means of payment. If the bank is sound, the trouble comes from the depositors' irrationality. The remedy is to have a lender of last resort to cope with the effects of their attitudes or, better, to educate them or, if neither is possible, to make the alternative asset (which, against the dollar, is gold) less attractive or less available. To prevent the bank from pursuing unsound policies—if it really tends to do so—it is not necessary to allow a run on it. The depositors can have their say in less destructive ways, for example through participating in the management of the bank of last resort or through agreement on the scale of the financial intermediation.

The nervousness of monetary authorities and academic economists is a consequence of the way they define a deficit and the connotations they attach to it. No bank could survive in such an analytical world. If financial authorities calculated a balance of payments for New York *vis-à-vis* the interior of the USA, they would find it in serious "deficit," since short-term claims of the rest of the country on New York mount each year. If they applied their present view of international finance, they would impose restrictions on New York's bank loans to the interior and on its purchases of new bond and stock issues. Similarly, the balance of payments of the US financial sector consists almost entirely of above-the-line disbursements and therefore nearly equal "deficits." Between 1947 and 1964 the liquid liabilities (demand and time deposits) of member banks of the Federal Reserve System alone increased from $110 billion to $238 billion. This increase of $128 billion, or 116 per cent, was not matched by an equal absolute or even proportionate increase in cash reserves. Indeed, these reserves increased only $1.6 billion, or 8 per cent. Yet nobody regards this cumulated "deficit" of over $126 billion as cause for alarm.

The private market has not been alarmed about the international position of the dollar in relation to other currencies or the liquidity of the USA. Although there has been private speculation in gold against the dollar, it has been induced largely by reluctance of some central banks to accumulate dollars. The dollar is the world's standard of value; the Eurodollar market dominates capital markets in Europe, and the foreign dollar bond market has easily outdistanced the unit-of-account bond and the European "parallel bond." As one looks at sterling and the major Continental currencies, it is hard to imagine any one of them stronger than the dollar today, five years from now, or twenty years hence. Admittedly, short-term destabilizing speculation against the dollar is possible, largely as a consequence of errors of official and speculative judgment. It can be contained, however, by gold outflows and support from other central banks, or by allowing the dollar to find its own level in world exchange markets, buttressed by the combination of high productivity and responsible fiscal and monetary policy in the USA. In the longer run, as now in the short, the dollar is strong, not weak.

(3) Since the US "deficit" is the result of liquidity exchanges or financial intermediation, it will persist as long as capital movement is free, European capital markets remain narrower and less competitive than that of the USA, liquidity preferences differ between the USA and Europe, and capital formation in Western Europe remains vigorous. In these circumstances, an effort to adjust the current account to the capital outflow is futile. The deficit can be best attacked by perfecting and eventually integrating European capital markets and moderating the European asset-holder's insistence on liquidity, understandable though the latter may be after half a century of wars, inflations and capital levies.

An attempt to halt the capital outflow by raising interest rates in the USA either would have little effect over any prolonged period or else would cripple European growth. With European capital markets joined to New York by substantial movements of short-term funds and bonds, the rate structure in the world as a whole will be set by the major financial center, in this instance New York. Interest-rate changes in the outlying centers will have an impact on capital flows to them. Higher interest rates in New York will raise rates in the world as a whole.

The effort is now being made to "correct the deficit" by restricting capital movements. Success in this effort is dubious, however, for two reasons.

Money Is Fungible

In the first place, money is fungible. Costless to store and to transport, it is the easiest commodity to arbitrage in time and in space. Discriminating capital restrictions are only partly effective, as the USA is currently learning. Some funds that are prevented from going directly to Europe will reach there by way of the less developed countries or via the favored few countries like Canada and Japan, which are accorded access to the New York financial market because they depend upon it for capital and for liquidity. These leaks in the dam will increase as time passes, and the present system of discriminatory controls will become unworkable in the long run. The USA will have to choose between abandoning the whole effort or plugging the leaks. Plugging the leaks, in turn, means that it must either get the countries in whose favor it discriminates to impose their own restrictions or withdraw the preferences it now gives them. Accordingly, the choices in the long run are between no restrictions, restrictions on all outflows, and establishment of what is in effect a dollar bloc, or a dollar-sterling bloc, within which funds move freely but which applies uniform controls against movements to all nonbloc countries.

In the second place, it is not enough to restrain the outflow of US-owned capital. As Germany and Switzerland have found, to keep US funds at home widens the spreads between short-term and long-term rates in Europe and also the spreads between the short-term rates at which European financial intermediaries borrow and lend, and so encourages repatriation of European capital already in the USA. For Europe, this effectively offsets restrictions on capital inflows. "Home is where they have to take you in." It would be possible for the USA to block the outflow of foreign capital—possible but contrary to tradition. If this door is left open, the $57 billion of foreign capital in the USA permit substantial net capital outflows, even without an outflow of US capital. Although it would require powerful forces indeed to induce foreign holders to dispose of most of their American investments, they might dispose of enough to permit the "deficit" to continue for a long time.

(4) Capital restrictions to correct the deficit, even if feasible, would still leave unanswered a fundamental question. Is it wise to destroy an efficient system of providing internal and external liquidity—the international capital market—and substitute for it one or another contrived device of limited flexibility for creating additions to international reserve assets alone? In the crisis of 1963, Italy borrowed $1.6 billion in the Euro-dollar market; under the Bernstein plan it would have had access to less than one-tenth of the incremental created liquidity of say $1 billion a year, perhaps $75 million in one year—a derisible amount. It would be the stuff of tragedy for the world's authorities laboriously to obtain agreement on a planned method of providing international reserve assets if that method, through analytical error, unwittingly destroyed an important source of liquid funds for European savers and of loans for European borrowers, and a flexible instrument for the international provision of liquidity. Moreover, agreement on a way of creating additional international reserve assets will not necessarily end the danger that foreigners, under the influence of conventional analysis, will want to convert dollars into gold whenever they see what they consider a "deficit."

But, it will be objected, the fears of the European authorities about the dollar are facts of life, and the USA must adjust to them. Several points may be made by way of comment.

Europe Squeezes Itself

In the first place, the European authorities must be learning how much international trade in financial claims means to their economies, now that it has been reduced. Europe has discovered that liquidity in the form of large international reserves bears no necessary relationship to ability to supply savers with liquid assets or industrial borrowers with long-term funds in countries where financial intermediation is inadequately performed and which are cut off from the world capital market. Financial authorities in Italy, France and even Germany have lately been trying to moderate the high interest rates which reflect strong domestic liquidity preference and the wide margins between the rates at which their intermediaries borrow and lend, as well as (in the case of Germany) their own policies. Having scant success in getting households, banks or private intermediaries to buy long-term securities, these authorities are increasingly entering the market themselves. Investment is declining: in Germany with long-term interest rates touching 8 per cent for the best borrowers, in Italy despite Bank of Italy purchases of industrial securities, and in France where government bonds are issued to provide capital to a limited list of industrial investors. It is ironic that US firms seem able to borrow in Europe more easily than European firms, as they continue investing in Europe while abiding by their government's program of voluntary capital restraint. Given their liquid capital strength in the USA, they have no objection to borrowing short, and command a preferred status when they choose to borrow long. But their operations in Europe put pressure on European long-term rates and enhance the incentive of other European borrowers and US lenders to evade the restrictions.

Europe's own capital markets cannot equal that of the USA in breadth, liquidity and competitiveness in the foreseeable future. Europe must therefore choose between an open international capital market, using fiscal policy to impose any needed restraints, and use of monetary restraint with an insulated capital market. The second alternative involves serious dangers. Without substantial European government lending to industry, which is unlikely, the terms on which long-term money would be available may cause industrial stagnation.

The first choice is the more constructive one, but it can work only if its implications are understood in both Europe and the USA. The USA, too, has failed to appreciate the role of New York in the world monetary system and has acquiesced in the Continental view of the US payments position. It must be recognized that trading in financial assets with the USA means a US "deficit"; US capital provides not only goods and services, but liquid assets to Europe, which means European acquisition of dollars. Moreover, the amount of dollars that private savers in Europe will want to acquire for transactions and as a partial offset to debts in dollars, and for other purposes, will increase. This increase in privately held dollars will involve a rising trend in the US deficit on the Department of Commerce definition, though no deficit on the Bernstein Committee definition.

But that is not all. The new liquid saving in Europe which is matched by European borrowing in the USA is not likely to be held largely in dollars, and certainly will not be held entirely so. Savers typically want liquidity in their own currencies, and so do banks. If household and commercial banks want to hold liquid assets at home rather than securities or liquid assets in dollars, the counterpart of foreign borrowing by industry must be held by the central bank of their country in dollars, or converted into gold. This implies a deficit for the USA even on the Bernstein Committee definition.

Whether householders and banks want to hold dollars or their own national currencies, the effect is the same: both alternatives now frighten the USA as well as Europe. They should not. And they would not if it were recognized that financial intermediation implies a decline in the liquidity of the intermediary as much when the intermediation is being performed in another country as when it is being performed domestically. An annual growth in Europe's dollar-holdings averaging, perhaps $1\frac{1}{2}$ to $2 billion a year or perhaps more for a long time is normal expansion for a bank the size of the USA with a fast-growing world as its body of customers. To the extent that European capital markets achieve greater breadth, liquidity and competitiveness, the rates of increase in these dollar holdings consistent with given rates of world economic growth would of course be lower than when these markets have their present deficiencies. But whatever rate of growth in these dollar holdings is needed, the point is that they not only provide external liquidity to other countries, but are a necessary counterpart of the intermediation which provides liquidity to Europe's savers and financial institutions. Recognition of this fact would end central-bank conversions of dollars into gold, the resulting creeping decline of official reserves, and the disruption of capital flows to which it has led.

It must be admitted that free private capital markets are sometimes destabilizing. When they are, the correct response is determined governmental counteraction to support the currency that is under pressure until the crisis has been weathered. Walter Bagehot's dictum of 1870 still stands: In a crisis, discount freely. Owned reserves cannot provide for these eventualities, as IMF experience amply demonstrates. Amounts agreed in advance are almost certain to be too little, and they tip the hand of the authorities to the speculators. The rule is discount freely, and tidy up afterwards, transferring outstanding liabilities to the IMF, the General Arrangements to Borrow, or even into funded government-to-government debts such as were used to wind up the European Payments Union. Owned reserves or readily available discounting privileges on the scale needed to guard against these crises of confidence would be inflationary in periods of calm.

Let the Gold Go

Mutual recognition of the role of dollar holdings would provide the most desirable solution, but if, nevertheless, Europe unwisely chooses to convert dollars into gold, the USA could restore a reserve-currency system, even without European cooperation in reinterpreting deficits and lifting capital restrictions. The decision would call for cool heads in the USA. The real problem is to build a strong international monetary mechanism resting on credit, with gold occupying, at most, a subordinate position. Because the dollar is in a special position as a world currency, the USA can bring about this change through its own action. Several ways in which it can do so have been proposed, including widening the margin around parity at which it buys and sells gold, reducing the price at which it buys gold, and otherwise depriving gold of its present unlimited convertibility into dollars. The USA would have to allow its gold stock to run down as low as European monetary authorities chose to take it. If they took it all, which is unlikely, the USA would have no alternative but to allow the dollar to depreciate until the capital flow came to a halt, or, much more likely, until the European countries decided to stop the depreciation by holding the dollars they were unwilling to hold before. If this outcome constituted a serious possibility, it seems evident that European countries would cease conversion of dollars into gold well short of the last few billions.

   This strategy has been characterized by *The Economist* as the "new nationalism" in the USA. It can reasonably be interpreted, however, as internationalism. It would enable the USA to preserve the international capital market and thereby protect the rate of world economic growth, even without European cooperation.

While US–European co-operation in maintaining the international capital market is the preferable route, it requires recognizing that an effective, smoothly functioning international capital market is itself an instrument of world economic growth, not a nuisance which can be disposed of and the function of which can be transferred to new or extended intergovernmental institutions, and it requires abandoning on both sides of the Atlantic the view that a US deficit, whether on the Department of Commerce or the Bernstein Committee definition, is not compatible with equilibrium. Abandonment of this view, in turn, requires facing up to the fact that the economic analysis of the textbooks—derived from the writing and the world of David Hume and modified only by trimmings—is no longer adequate in a world that is increasingly moving (apart from government interferences) toward an integrated capital and money market. In these circumstances the main requirement of international monetary reform is to preserve and improve the efficiency of the private capital market while building protection against its performing in a destabilizing fashion.

The majority view has been gaining strength since 1958, when Triffin first asserted that the dollar and the world were in trouble. Between 1958 and 1965 world output and trade virtually doubled, the US dollar recovered from a slight overvaluation, and the gold hoarders have foregone large earnings and capital gains. Having been wrong in 1958 on the near-term position, the consensus may be more wrong today, when its diagnosis and prognosis are being followed. But this time the generally accepted analysis can lead to a brake on European growth. Its error may be expensive, not only for Europe but for the whole world.

Where We Disagree[2]

Certainly America's deficit represents above all a provision of banking services to other financially less mature countries. Certainly the current attempts to dam up the provision of these banking services threaten constriction for world trade and investment. Certainly one can see no quick replacement for those services, least of all through new official forms of international reserves (from Triffin to Cru). But that was never their intended function. The function of new forms of international credit is not to replace private international lending, but to reinforce it—by warding off the threat of a run on the bank. This is the function of a central bank domestically. Commercial banks have been able to operate as banks and lend long while borrowing short only because of this newly created cash and this ever open rediscount window. Why then can one suppose banking functions can be extended internationally without any such equivalent source of international cash? Britain's own experience in running down its international cash ratio to low fractions provides a warning example that America is bound to heed.

We do not, therefore, see the institution of international credit on an organized basis as merely an optional extra in a working payments system. It is the view that America can, even at this late stage of the day, perform all its old international financing functions without such international support that we have termed "the new nationalism." Certainly America should not wed itself inextricably to its present gold buying and selling policy. It may be in the end that jolting the dollar as well as the pound off their present pegs turn out to be the one way in which radical moves to an international monetary order can be launched. What seems unrealistic is to suppose, as our contributors do, that prospects of a possible dollar depreciation will actually uphold the present function of the dollar as a reserve currency by making central banks more willing to hold it. It is this contingent possibility that has surely made them increasingly reluctant about dollar liquidity.

Notes

1. For one of many good discussions of the proposals by Triffin, Bernstein and Stamp, as well as others not mentioned above, see *Plans for Reform of the International Monetary System* by Fritz Machlup, Special Paper in International Economics no. 3, revised March 1964 (International Finance Section, Department of Economics, Princeton University). See also Herbert Grubel (ed.), *World Monetary Reform: Plans and Issues* (Stanford, Calif.: Stanford University Press, 1963). For Robert V. Roosa's present views, see his *Monetary Reform for the World Economy* (New York: Harper & Row, for Council on Foreign Relations, 1965). An English translation of the suggestions by M. Valéry Giscard d'Estaing, made when he was Minister of Finance and Economic Affairs of France, may be found in various speeches published under the title *Statements Made by M. Valéry Giscard d'Estaing on International Monetary Problems*, Collection Ouvertures Economiques (Paris: L'Economie, 1965).

2. By *The Economist*.

Measuring Equilibrium in
the Balance of Payments

I

It is tempting to suggest that we should abolish balance-of-payments statistics. Two of the world's strongest currencies—the pound sterling prior to 1913 and the Swiss franc today—lacked a complete statement of the position. New York as a financial center has only a limited idea of the network of its financial flows *vis-à-vis* the rest of the country. Textbooks insist that governmental authorities need balance-of-payments data to guide changes in monetary, fiscal exchange, commercial and other policies, although journalists and speculators seem to react to the data more sensitively than do governments. *Realpolitik* makes clear, however, that balance-of-payments figures are collected and published, and that it is impossible to discontinue the process. The question then is how to present them.

The question arises particularly for a country—the USA—which has a large international financial role. It was the recognition of the importance of this role which started the process of recasting the definition of equilibrium which led to the "liquidity definition." The liquidity definition is easily attacked as appropriate to a firm which has inadvertently taken on substantial financial commitments, and quite inappropriate to an established financial center. The critic, however, is frequently met with the demand for a measure of his own. A growing number of economists insist that no one measure can be accepted,[1] but this position again meets insistence on a single number by government, journalism and the public. Machlup (1964, pp. 140–166) and Cooper (1966) have shown that the numbers for a given year can give a wide range of answers based on different definitions. Neither writer explicitly considered the balance of payments of a financial center. This chapter seeks to recapitulate the evolution of definitions of balance-of-payments equilibrium in summary fashion and to choose an appropriate definition for a financial center.[2] It concludes that there is no single number which can be given to noneconomists, and that they should be given, at a minimum, two measures: the change in the country's net claims on foreign countries, and the *ex ante* change in gross reserves. Neither is satisfactory. Together they are no substitute for detailed analysis of the position, but they are an improvement on any single number.

II

Equilibrium is that state of the balance of payments of a country, or of the world, for a given set of parameters, which can be sustained without intervention. The parameters involved are national incomes, price levels, and behind them tastes, resources and the production functions for the current account, and on capital account, propensities to invest and save, liquidity preferences, money supplies, and the views of the value of a country's currency, relative to alternative assets, taken by individuals and by monetary authorities. When any of these parameters change, the equilibrium position of the balance of payments changes. When it fails to adjust, or overadjusts, there is disequilibrium. Deficits cannot be sustained because a country will ultimately exhaust its liquid assets or borrowing capacity. Surpluses in the balance of payments of a country are more easily supported but put pressure on other countries, and other parameters, in the system.

In this chapter, balance-of-payments equilibrium relates to the position of a single country, primarily the USA. US equilibrium is evidently affected by changes in other countries, both separately and in the world as a whole. It is also related to the world payment system. But equilibrium for particular countries need not imply equilibrium for the system. The system's equilibrium, for example, may require the net of the surpluses and deficits of the separate countries to be either zero, given adequate reserves, or a substantial surplus. The criteria for determining balance-of-payments equilibrium, therefore, may or may not converge with those of the system as a whole.

III

The analysis uses a simple notation and arranges symbols in simple identities or equations.

X = exports of goods and services (absolute value),

M = imports of goods and services (absolute value),

T = remittances, pensions, and government aid to foreign recipients (receipts minus),

I = increase in inventories of internationally traded goods (decrease minus),

LTC = long-term capital outflow (inflow minus),

STC = short-term capital outflow (inflow minus),

G = net increase in gold, gold tranche at the IMF, holdings of convertible currencies (decrease minus).

The variables can be subdivided into a number of components indicated by subscripts:

US   = owned by United States residents,

f   = owned by foreign residents,

mon   = monetary,

nonmon = nonmonetary,

p   = private

o   = official

$ = dollar area.

The balance of payments always balances. This is expressed:

$$X - M - T - LTC - STC - G = 0. \tag{1}$$

If both types of capital record outflows, and there is a gain in gold, exports must exceed imports and transfers by the total amount of foreign investment, which includes the increase in gold. If the sum of the foreign investment item, LTC, STC, and G, is not positive, however, balance requires that $X \leq M + T$.

To measure equilibrium, a selected group of items in the total balance must sum to zero. Since the balance always balances, this means that the remaining items also add up to zero. Where the zero is placed is the same as the position of the horizontal line separating the selected items from the others when the balance of payments is arranged vertically. If the items on the left-hand side of the equation (above the line) are positive, there is a surplus; if they are negative, there is a deficit. In theory, the autonomous items in the balance of payments are assembled on the left-hand side of the equation, and the compensatory items on the right (below the line).

Mercantilist Balance

In the mercantilist period, prior to Hume and Smith, equilibrium was regarded as current-account balance,

$$X - M = 0 = G. \tag{2}$$

Little or no notice was taken of capital movements because they were small. The object of policy—as in some countries during recent periods— was to have a surplus and to gain gold.

Basic Balance

With the introduction of capital movements on a substantial scale, it was no longer possible to think of the current account as the sole autonomous variable. Basic equilibrium, expressed in equation (3a), required a current-account surplus to balance an outflow of long-term capital (or a current-account deficit to balance an inflow), and the algebraic sum of gold and short-term capital movements to be zero.[3]

$$X - M - LTC = 0 = STC + G. \tag{3a}$$

This is the measure adopted by Nurkse in his celebrated article on balance-of-payments equilibrium (1945). The designation of this balance as "basic" occurred in the 1950s. Cooper (1966, p. 384) notes that "it represents an attempt to measure the underlying trends, abstracting from such 'volatile' transactions as short-term capital movements." This is a later rationalization. Initially, basic balance grew out of the preoccupation of economists with the transfer problem. With international capital markets imperfectly joined, the question was whether autonomous capital movements were fully transferred in goods and services. Both autonomous and adjusting variables can be found within the left-hand side of the equation. In the ordinary formulation of the transfer problem, as in the equation (3b), the question was whether the current account developed in such a way as to transfer the autonomous long-term capital movement.

$$LTC - (X - M) = 0 = -STC - G. \tag{3b}$$

The version in equation (3a) better fits the views of Keynes, who, in debate with Ohlin, took the view that the current-account balance was the autonomous (sticky) variable, to which the capital movement should adjust in equilibrium (Keynes, 1929).

Basic balance was used as a criterion of equilibrium in the USA in the early 1950s and is used in Britain today.[4] It was applied by Salant and his associates (Salant *et al.*, 1963) to the USA in their attempt to forecast the balance of payments of the USA in 1968. In these cases, the criterion was used not to measure transfer but to abstract from volatile items. In fact, it seemed a little old-fashioned when a well-known economist recently referred to the balance-of-payments problem of the USA as a transfer problem (Machlup, 1964, pp. 374–95). The transfer formulation of equilibrium assumes that there are only two markets to be cleared internationally, securities and goods and services. Research on the nineteenth-century experience suggests that, when the USA and London were intimately connected, at least three markets had to be cleared simultaneously, goods and services, securities, and money (Williamson, 1964). The three markets can clear *ex ante* even if the net balance on securities does not exactly match that in goods and services.

Balance, Including Inventories of Internationally Traded Products

An adequate balance-of-payments definition of equilibrium requires that the variables in the payments equation be linked to one another in a way which can be sustained. If there is a rapid fluctuation of internationally traded commodities, this will not be true, as the world found out in the USA, in 1936–7, and in postwar Europe in the early 1950s. Increases in such inventories can be put among autonomous variables on the left-hand side, as in equation (4a), or regarded as the equivalent of international reserves, among compensatory items on the right, as in equation (4b).

$$X - (M - I) - LTC = 0 = STC + G, \qquad (4a)$$

$$X - M - LTC = 0 = STC + G - I. \qquad (4b)$$

While important for countries such as Britain and the Netherlands, the point about inventories is normally of little consequence for the USA and will be dropped hereafter.

The Dollar Shortage

In the immediate postwar period, with production thoroughly dislocated in Europe and the Far East, and only the USA capable of substantial production, the US basic balance showed large surpluses. Moreover, international capital markets had broken down, and the flow of official capital through the Bretton Woods and other institutions was insufficient to meet reconstruction needs. Accordingly, the US government undertook substantial transfers on official account. These were initially recorded on the right-hand side of the equation (below the line) as compensatory items (under the original formulation of the IMF), as:

$$X - M - LTC = T_0 + STC + G \neq 0. \tag{5a}$$

This formulation was accepted until Machlup pointed out that there was no unambiguous basis for putting official transfers among compensatory items (Machlup, 1950). It was just as true, and *ex post* truer, to say that foreign aid made possible the US export surplus, as to say that the foreign aid financed the European and Japanese import surpluses. Government transfers thus joined private transfers (up to now not made explicit) on the left-hand side of the equation, as:

$$X - M - T - LTC = 0 = STC + G. \tag{5b}$$

Ex Ante and *Ex Post* Balances

Machlup's point can be generalized and extended to include various constraints stipulated by Nurkse (1945) about unemployment and trade policy or implied by the Department of Commerce when it corrects the balance of payments for "special transactions." The best statement is by Cooper (1966). The balance of payments may be viewed both *ex ante* and *ex post*: *ex ante*, with or without the application of various policies and special measures of window-dressing or cosmetics, and *ex post*, only with the actual policies and measures applied. Nurkse chose to view stable equilibrium as a condition which excluded mass unemployment and tariff or other trade restrictions imposed for balance-of-payments purposes. Machlup (1958) characterized this as "disguised politics," although since the discussion was explicit the criticism seems harsh. *Ex ante* imbalance may be forestalled by policies which produce *ex post* balance as measured by the chosen equation. There is more than one possible way to reckon *ex ante* balance; an exact analogy is furnished by the federal budget. *Ex ante* and *ex post* budget surpluses or deficits may differ because of special measures to accelerate or delay receipts or expenditures, and *ex ante* there are the administrative budget based on current legislation, the budget assuming the passage of certain legislative proposals, the full-employment budget, etc.

Special transactions—debt repayments, Roosa bonds, special investments under military agreements,—not to mention tied loans, capital movements restricted (after a fashion) by the Interest Equalization Tax (IET), Gore amendment, and Mandatory Credit Restraint Program (MCRP)—raise similar questions. An *ex post* statement showing equilibrium is likely to conceal *ex ante* disequilibrium, which is impossible to calculate without measurement of the separate effects and their action on other variables in the system and on each other.

Liquidity Balance

With economic recovery in Europe in the 1950s, and having rebuilt their capital of fixed assets and inventories, various countries reconstituted their international reserves, largely in the form of dollars. About 1955, concerned over the gradually mounting volume of US liabilities to foreigners, the Department of Commerce, under the direction of Walther Lederer, chief of the Balance of Payments Division, altered the definition of equilibrium. The objective was to show changes in the liquidity position of the country. Flows of short-term capital were divided into two parts, movements of US capital which went above the line and changes in foreign liquid capital (consisting of all US short-term liabilities to foreigners and all foreign holdings of US government securities, whatever their maturity) which went below the line. Equilibrium was defined:

$$X - M - T - LTC - STC_{US} = 0 = STC_f + G. \tag{6}$$

US short-term capital outflow was put above the line, on the grounds that the assets could not be readily mobilized in case of trouble. Increases in foreign short-term claims, largely dollar deposits in New York banks, were regarded as the equivalent of a loss of gold because they were thought to be subject to sudden withdrawal, and were put below the line.

The liquidity definition has been widely criticized on technical, analytical and factual grounds. Technically, as one of many possible examples, it makes no sense to count the minimum balance held against a New York bank loan to a Japanese borrower as subject to withdrawal, when its maintenance is a condition of the loan. Analytically, US claims on foreigners can be arrayed in a distribution based on the degree of their liquidity, and foreign claims on the USA arrayed on the basis of their susceptibility to withdrawal. The means of the distributions and their variance are of interest in both cases, but it is clearly wrong to imply that all foreigners will withdraw their deposits before any foreign assets can be liquidated. A similar point has been made many times regarding the susceptibility to flight of foreign holders of dollars, and domestic holders; if one counts potential claims on the gold stock of the USA as actual claims, one should deduct some sizeable portion of the US money supply. In fact, US banks did succeed in bringing back to the USA and borrowing abroad $2.5 billion in a single month, during the credit crunch of August 1966. These monies represented some US short-term claims regarded under the Department of Commerce definition as unavailable, plus some of the cash held in the Eurodollar market by subsidiaries of US firms, which was recorded in earlier balance-of-payments statements as direct investment, or long-term capital.

The liquidity definition is appropriate to a crisis but not to the steady state. It is well known that bank reserves suffer from the dilemma that in ordinary times none are needed, and that in crisis 100 per cent reserves are hardly sufficient. But to adopt a crisis definition for day-to-day operation of a financial system is evidently calculated to put the system out of business.

Exchange-market Capital, Open-market Capital, and Capital Sensitive to Monetary Stimuli

Strenuous objection to the Department of Commerce definition was raised on all sides. Three alternative formulations, all slightly different, may be treated together, those of Gardner (1961), Triffin (1962) and Lary (1961, 1963). All three criticized the notion of putting increases in US claims on foreigners above the line, and foreign claims on the USA below the line. The alternative criteria developed were broadly similar. Gardner and Triffin sought to put below the line those capital items which were volatile and handled in organized capital markets,[5] as distinct from, for example, direct investment or credits on short-term capital accounts used to finance merchandise trade. For Lary, the criterion for position was sensitivity to monetary conditions and policies, with insensitive items above and sensitive items below. The three alternative formulations may be illustrated by equation (7), representing the Lary version:

$$X - M - T - LTC_{\mathrm{nonmon}} - STC_{\mathrm{nonmon}} = 0 = LTC_{\mathrm{mon}} + STC_{\mathrm{mon}} + G. \quad (7)$$

The difficulty with these suggestions is that they are nonoperational. Economics has no definite answer as to what forms of capital movement are and which are not sensitive to interest-rate differences, to changes in interest-rate differences (Branson, 1968), or to monetary conditions and policies.[6] In seeking to work out an exchange-market definition, Gardner reverted to the autonomous/compensatory distinction of the IMF but failed to escape the Machlup criticism of that position. Lary himself criticized the "open-market capital" concept of Gardner and Triffin as looser than "sensitivity to monetary policy" and of less operational significance (1963, p. 158). The Department of Commerce definition was rejected, but no acceptable alternative was developed.

Balance on Official Reserve Transactions

Persistent deficits on the liquidity basis and persistent criticism of that basis led in 1963 to the appointment of a committee to review balance-of-payments statistics and to comment on their adequacy as 'a measure of the problem and a framework within which to consider policy alternatives' (Review Committee, 1965, p. iii). The committee made a number of suggestions for refining and improving the statistics, but its major contribution was a new formula for measuring the balance of payments. Foreign short-term capital was divided between private and official, with the former above the line and the latter below the line, as:

$$X - M - T - LTC - STC_p = 0 = STC_{f_0} + G. \tag{8}$$

Since all US short-term capital is private, there is no need to separate US from private foreign short-term funds.

The rationale of the new definition was that foreign private banks, companies and individuals are willing holders of dollars, whereas foreign officials are not. It also assumes that one can distinguish private from official ownership of dollar balances in New York. None of these assumptions is warranted.

In the first place, both private and official foreign holders of dollars may be regarded at a given point in time as solving a portfolio-balancing problem. The problems of each group of holders differ, because of differences in their objective functions and in the alternative assets available to them. However, it is extremely unlikely (virtually impossible) that all private holders would want to hold continuously the amount of dollars they have in their possession at a given point in time, and that all official holders are eager to convert all their dollar balances into a different asset, such as gold.

The concept makes good sense at the margin. Private balances grow slowly; when such balances grow, it is an indication, subject to the second assumption to be discussed, that there is an increased demand for dollars.

On the other hand, official holdings of dollars may reach an upper limit beyond which authorities are reluctant to go; any increase in holdings should be regarded as unwanted. The nature of statistical presentations, covering a succession of years, however, prevents making the useful distinction between inframarginal and marginal holdings.

Secondly, the balance on official transactions is widely criticized because of the difficulty in distinguishing the ownership of funds in New York. Balances in private hands may be beneficially owned by foreign central banks which have undertaken spot sales against forward purchases of dollars as a device for taking funds out of the domestic money market. Or foreign official dollars may have been sold forward, so that in effect they are held for private account.[7]

Thirdly, table 10.1 below shows that the balance on official transactions is considerably more volatile than the basic and liquidity balances. This is partly the result of arbitrary changes in the division of foreign funds between official and private accounts, and partly the consequence of its shift from above to below the line of such items as Roosa bonds. But the volatility of the measure made it impossible for government, even apart from strong bureaucratic inertia, to shift from the liquidity definition to the official definition. For a time both were used. Later, the official definition fell into disuse, and the liquidity definition again dominated the field.

Another reason for academic disinterest in the official definition, along with the three criticisms above, was that it failed to take account of the role of an international financial center.

IV

Lary introduced the concept of the USA as a banker into the discussion, though he made very little of it and was, in fact, somewhat skeptical of the analogy (1963, p. 147, n. 13). When the analogy is pursued however, it becomes apparent that the liquidity-balance definition of equilibrium in the balance of payments is inappropriate. An ordinary trading or producing firm may calculate a quick-asset ratio of liquid assets to short-term liabilities and regard any worsening of the ratio (especially any increase in demand liabilities) as disequilibrating. Perhaps the view that no assets other than gold and convertible currencies are liquid is extreme. But the liquidity-balance definition could be defensible if the USA could be regarded as a firm.

Since the USA is more than a firm, however, the question arises as to the appropriate definition of balance-of-payments equilibrium for a bank.

Table 10.1
Various Measures of the Surplus (+) or Deficit (−) of the Balance of Payments of the USA, 1958–67 (in billions of dollars)

Measure	1958	1959	1960	1961	1962	1963	1964	1965	1966	1967	1968
Basic balance	−3.7	−5.7	−1.7	−0.7	−1.8	−2.2	0.0	−2.0	−1.0	−2.7	n.a.*
Liquidity balance	−3.4	−3.9	−3.9	−2.4	−2.2	−2.7	−2.8	−1.3	−1.4	−3.6	+0.2
Balance on Official Reserve Transactions	n.a.	n.a.	−3.4	−1.3	−2.7	−2.0	−1.5	−1.3	+0.2	−3.4	+1.6
Loss of reserves	−2.3	−1.0	−2.1	−0.6	−1.5	−0.4	−0.2	−1.2	−0.6	−0.1	+0.9
Net-worth balance	−1.1	−2.7	+0.5	+2.0	+1.3	+1.4	+4.0	+2.6	+0.6	−0.6	n.a.

Sources: Basic balance: 1958–9, Salant *et al.* (1963); 1960–3, Review Committee (1965); 1964–8, computed from Department of Commerce data. Liquidity and Official reserve balances: 1958, Department of Commerce. Loss of reserves and net-worth balance: 1958, computed from Department of Commerce data.

*n.a. = not available.

Whereas firms normally have a quick-asset ratio of two and one-half or three to one, the reserve ratios of banks run much less than one, for example, one to five. In ordinary circumstances, bank liabilities are not paid off, as is true of those firms, but remain in existence, passing from hand to hand as money. It makes no sense to say that a bank which adds to its assets and to its deposits in some reasonable pattern is in deficit.

The art of banking is to maintain enough liquidity to meet the demands of depositors. This involves forecasting the pattern of deposit activity. The Department of Commerce liquidity definition of disequilibrium implies that no deposits will be kept in the bank. The balance on official transactions assumes that private depositors are steady customers, whereas monetary authorities are anxious to withdraw their accounts. A third rule of thumb for dividing owners of foreign balances in the USA is whether or not they belong to the dollar area.

Dollar-area Balance

This concept of balance, put forward by Bergsten (1968, 1972) places increases in foreign balances owned by dollar-area countries above the line, whether private or official. In notation, the definition is summed up by

$$X - M - T - LTC - STC_{US} - STC_{f_\$} = 0 = STC_{f_{non-\$}} + G. \tag{9}$$

The distinction has long been made in Britain between sterling-area and nonsterling-area balances. However, since the British define balance-of-payments equilibrium in terms of basic balance rather than in terms of a liquidity definition, the distinction has played no role in formal balance-of-payments analysis. The concept of the dollar area, however, is less widely accepted. Canada and Japan, for which exceptions to the IET and the voluntary and mandatory credit restraint programs have been made, are clearly in the dollar area, if such can be said to exist. France, which converted dollar balances into gold at the rate of $300 million a month in the spring of 1965, is not in a dollar area (despite the fact that the dollar is used by the Bank of France as a vehicle currency). Presumably Germany is in a dollar area, on the basis of an agreement not to buy gold from the USA, even though the IET and MCRP apply to it.

A definition of equilibrium in terms of areas of ownership of dollar balances is helpful in one respect. It clears up an ancient ambiguity, under some definitions (such as basic balance), in cases when a reserve currency country lost gold "without running a deficit." Suppose Germany is in the dollar area and France is not, and France has a surplus against Germany. This results in a transfer of dollars from Germany to France, which converts them into gold, and the USA loses reserves, although it is not itself in deficit. The complaint implicit in this statement is no longer acceptable under the dollar-area definition of balance. A banker loses deposits when his depositors, taken as a group, have deficits. The appropriate deficit is that of the currency area as a whole. Britain can lose reserves either when she lives beyond her means or when other members of the sterling area, as a group, live beyond their means. Definitions of equilibrium which fail to take into account the deficits of members of the currency area with countries not belonging to the area are too limited.

If the dollar area were an organization with well-defined rules regarding access to dollar credit and unlimited willingness to hold dollar balances, it might be appropriate to operate with an equilibrium definition of this sort. But there is no formal dollar area, and good reason why there should not be. The dollar became established as a reserve currency by an evolutionary process which took advantage of the use of currency as a unit of account, medium of exchange, and store of value. It can function as a reserve currency only when it performs these functions. To formalize the institutions just as the market and the authorities begin to question how much they can count on the continued discharge of the functions might well lead to breakdown (Triffin, 1968, p. 14). Sufficient political reasons also militate against dividing the world, outside the Sino-Soviet bloc, into dollar, sterling, and gold blocs.

Loss of Reserves

If it makes little sense to measure the balance-of-payments deficit of a financial center by attempting to forecast how much of its deposit liabilities it may expect to retain and how much to lose, there is at least one clear *ex post* definition: a country has a surplus when it gains gross reserves or a deficit when it loses them. This definition is illustrated thus:

$$X - M - T - LTC - STC = 0 = G. \tag{10}$$

This brings full circle to the mercantilist version of disequilibrium loss of gold (and IMF gold and supergold tranche, plus convertible currencies). It is impossible to forecast how many dollars members or nonmembers of the dollar area will want to have as working balances, as precautionary balances, and as a store of wealth. But if they have too many, they can convert the excess into gold. Whatever the belief about adjustment, the test of whether the country is overdoing lending, investing, monetary expansion, and the like is whether other countries are using dollars to gain gold or selling gold to gain dollars. Rather than measuring adjustment directly, it is possible to measure it indirectly, via conversions of reserves from one asset to another (the "confidence" problem in the trilogy of adjustment, confidence and liquidity [International Study Group, 1964]).

The actual gold losses of the USA in recent years are distorted, of course, by a variety of devices undertaken by the treasury to forestall gold sales, and by some juggling of the books to disguise them. In a situation such as that of Britain in November 1967, one would want to know not only changes in reserves but also the volume of contracts in forward dollars sold to prevent an outflow of capital; such an accumulation of contracts could be regarded as a first charge against reserves actually on hand. In measuring the position of a bank, one should not only count its deposits with the Federal Reserve but also subtract from them borrowings and rediscounts at the Federal Reserve bank.

Use of reserve losses, suitably corrected, as a measure of the deficit makes it unnecessary to try to forecast the behavior of a multitude of variables which do not lend themselves to accurate forecasting. Moreover, it appeals to common sense, a rare basis for checking analytical concepts but not altogether a useless one. Even sophisticated economists slip into thinking in this mode.[8]

There are, however, several difficulties in using reserve losses as a measure of deficit. As liabilities build up, reserves should grow in some appropriate proportion. Their failure to do so gave rise to the liquidity problem which inspired the SDRs. Secondly, and important in an opposing sense in measuring the cumulative deficit of the USA, a bank (or a financial center) can have excess reserves. One should count loss of reserves as deficit only from the point where reserves are some suitable proportion of liabilities. Thirdly, of course, changes in confidence change the need for reserves against a given quantity of liabilities. In seeking to guard against this third danger, the liquidity definition of balance-of-payments equilibrium has precipitated crises; when banks show that they are worried about their liquidity, they terrify their depositors.

Net-worth Balance

The final concept of equilibrium in this list is also an elementary one and turns on the question of whether a country (or family) is living beyond its means. We may call it the net-worth balance, although it measures changes in net worth rather than the amount of net worth. This concept, set out in equation (11), is what most observers have in mind when they think of a deficit:

$$X - M - T = 0 = LTC + STC + G. \tag{11}$$

In a world of no transfers or capital movements, it is the equivalent of equation (2). Jacques Rueff implied something like this definition when he criticized the reserve-currency standard by suggesting that he would order more suits if his tailor would lend him back the money he paid for them (Rueff and Hirsch, 1965, p. 3). Most economists have gone to great trouble to explain that the US balance-of-payments problem results not from overspending on imports but from overspending relative to foreign investment or from overinvesting (for example, Hansen, 1965).

The net-worth balance as measured from annual balance-of-payments data is a highly limited concept. It makes no adjustment for changes in asset valuation or in domestic assets. Conservative accounting procedure calls for revaluation only when assets decline in value, in accordance with the "cost or market, whichever is lower" criterion. The point about domestic assets is more fundamental. A financial center, which expects large gross movements of capital, should presumably lend net abroad at a fairly steady rate, so that its foreign assets mount with its domestic assets. But a less developed country may be said to be in disequilibrium if it borrows for consumption, and in balance if its foreign liabilities are matched by its domestic assets. Because of this, net-worth balance is less appropriate than basic balance for a growing country and the concept is not one that symmetrically adds to zero for the world.

If there are limitations on the generality of net-worth balance, and if it focuses on solvency rather than on liquidity, the concept is still very much worth watching in this country. In his testimony before the Republican balance-of-payments seminar in January 1968, Triffin dismissed other calculations of balance-of-payments deficits and drew attention to the 'major point' that the net-worth balance had deteriorated from $4 billion surplus in 1964 to a rate of—$200 million a year in 1967 (corrected for the entire year to—$600 million). This was "a reversal of more than $4 billion in our current position" (Triffin, 1968, p. 7).[9]

V

Different balance-of-payments concepts apply to nonreserve and reserve currency countries (Birnbaum, 1968). If we move from the level of the country to smaller units, we can distinguish the balance-of-payments problems of firms and banks. These can be illustrated by comparing successive balance sheets on the assumption that there is no payout of dividends. It is the contention of this chapter that there is no single measure of surplus or deficit for a firm or a bank, and that the problem is still different for financial centers.

The major relevant concepts for a firm are changes in net worth, the debt-equity ratio, and the quick asset ratio. Any two of these elements may move in a different direction from the other. Thus if a firm adds to fixed assets through a short-term bank loan and through plowed-back profits, its net-worth position improves but its quick-asset position worsens, and its debt-equity ratio can move in any direction, depending on relative amounts.

Nor is any single measure available for a bank. The ratio of reserves to deposits is perhaps the most usual liquidity measure, but reserves may or may not include secondary reserves along with cash, and may be gross or net of borrowed federal funds and rediscounts. Some allowance must be made for excess reserves which may decline without causing alarm. The measures do not inevitably move together. Moreover, the reserve ratio, however calculated, can improve when the capital-deposit ratio worsens. Changes in net worth are also significant, especially where one has the consolidated balance sheet of a conglomerate corporation which is both a trading or manufacturing firm or bank.

Along with other financial intermediaries, a bank is not in deficit when it lends long and accepts deposits, although it can certainly overdo such intermediation. When banks are grouped into financial centers, and these centers are linked, one must expect gross lending and borrowing between them. This may take the form of lending long and borrowing short, lending largely to firms, and borrowing from banks (even from central banks when the financial centers are in different countries), as borrowing firms interested in access to cheaper credit scan a wider horizon than savers interested in higher returns on savings. The larger financial center is not necessarily experiencing a balance-of-payments deficit in a meaningful sense if it adds to long lending and short borrowing in a given year, although there are limits beyond which it is dangerous to continue such practices.[10]

A particular problem presents itself when monetary policies of two financial centers are conducted independently but capital is mobile between them. If the smaller center raises its interest rates, for example, some firms

whose normal habitat for loans is the local center will shift their borrowing to the foreign center. Since they need local currency for spending,
they will sell it to banks, which may in turn sell it to central banks. The
banks with increased external funds may invest them in long-term securities in the larger center, which results in an exchange of one type of long-
term borrowing (firms borrowing from banks) against another (banks
buying securities, presumably issued by governments). Another possibility is that the smaller financial center will lower its interest rates again, restore the customary spread in rates between the centers, and undo the
excessive borrowing abroad by local firms. What is inappropriate, however, is to have the combination of long-term firm borrowing and short-
term bank lending regarded as a consequence of monetary or fiscal policy
in the larger financial center. It results from an inappropriate rate structure
between joined financial centers.

How then does one measure the balance-of-payments position of a
country like the USA, which is a "firm," a "bank," and a "financial center"?
As a firm, the most significant measure is the net-worth balance. This is
the criterion for adjustment, in the sense of living beyond one's means.
Basic balance would be appropriate when capital markets are not so
closely joined as to give rise to international financial intermediation.
When such intermediation takes place, however, some long-term lending
or borrowing is of a purely financial type, the lending country providing
liquidity to the borrowing country, rather than real resources. Because
there is no objective basis for determining how much of the lending
should be transferred in goods, and how much in other forms, one must
rely on subjective judgments. Changes in the net-worth balance, as shown
in table 10.1, however, give a better idea of the balance-of-payments position of a country than changes in basic balance, because of fluctuations in
financial intermediation. If it be assumed that the USA has an excess of
savings over domestic needs for investment, relative to the rest of the
world, the net-worth balance of the USA should perhaps be close to $3–
$4 billion surplus. On this showing, the balance-of-payments was in sub-
stantial deficit in 1959 and again in 1967 and 1968. It was in surplus in
1964 and 1965.

Confidence in a bank is measured by whether it is losing or gaining
reserves. It would be useful to have an *ex ante* measure of the state of confidence. In actuality, we have only the *ex post* measure. It is easy to forgive
the authorities for frustrating (through special measures) and disguising
gold losses, since so much of the confidence of other monetary authorities
is based on the superficial *ex post* measure. The real improvement in the

ex ante position from the two-price system for gold adopted in March 1968 may be thoroughly disguised by relying on *ex post* statistics.

The liquidity position of a large financial center, however, is virtually impossible to measure in a meaningful way, especially if one insists on sharp discontinuities between those assets and liabilities which count in the sum and those which do not. Much better is a ratio (or an array of ratios) of primary reserves to demand liabilities (plus foreign-held assets of great liquidity, like government bonds), primary plus secondary reserves to demand and time deposits, and so on. Measured in all these ways, and even after allowance for excess reserves, the reserve ratio of the USA has been declining, so that the effort of US authorities to expand primary reserves through SDRs is understandable.

But the balance of payments of a financial center joined to other centers, where all try to operate independent monetary policies, will have erratic changes in the volume of international financial intermediation which have little meaning for the underlying competitive position of the countries, and would have little significance for confidence in one or another currency if the changes were understood. It is important to recognize the serious deterioration in the net-worth balance after 1966, brought on by spending abroad for Vietnam, inflation arising from the budget deficit at home, and a serious deterioration in the competitive position of the USA in foreign markets. A separate factor was the substantial inflow of European capital into US securities, especially mutual funds, in 1967 and 1968, some part of which may have been matched by an increase in domestic assets. Changes in confidence which result in central banks, speculators and investors switching between gold and dollars are also important (and here recent events have produced a large improvement). What is of limited significance, however, is the churning about of long- and short-term funds between the New York dollar, the Eurodollar and other money and capital markets of Europe, while the authorities and market institutions are finding an equilibrium structure of interest rates among them. This is what the liquidity and official transactions measures of the US balance of payments reflect. They are dysfunctional.

Notes

1. See, for example, Bernstein (1968, p. 7): "The balance of payments deficit cannot be measured, it can only be analyzed;" and Cooper (1966, p. 389): "Those who do not understand the important differences and variations among concepts have no right to have placed in their hands for use a *single* concept 'with no ifs, buts or maybes,' on the same principle that children should not be given real guns until they are taught how to use them properly."

2. For simplicity, no notice will be taken of a long list of small, troublesome, statistical points, such as how to handle errors and omissions, Roosa bonds, prepayments, and the like. These complications are for the most part assumed away in the analysis.

3. In some formulations, it is added that both should be small, on the grounds that a large flow of gold balanced by an appropriate movement of short-term capital is likely to be self-corrective, and hence not a steady state appropriate to equilibrium (Kindleberger, 1953, p. 402). This links the criterion to that in equation (10) on page 231.

4. Cooper (1968, p. 150) states "Selection of an *ex post* measure of equilibrium in a country's balance of payments is notoriously difficult, especially for a country that acts as an international banking center. A measure which gives some idea of underlying developments is the balance on current and long-term capital."

5. Compare this with Ingram (1962), who argues that long-term capital assets can be used as balancing items, and McKinnon and Oates (1966), who explore the implications of a single long-term asset serving as an internationally mobile security.

6. Gardner, Triffin and Lary categorized direct investment as non-open market or non-sensitive to monetary stimuli. French economists, however, believe that the outflow of direct investment capital from the USA is a result of inflationary monetary expansion.

7. To be sure, if the private counterparty to the official forward sale of dollars is a pure speculator, the ultimate conclusion of the contract will consist in an undoing of the original transaction.

8. For example, compare Bernstein (1968, p. 3): "We have a balance of payments problem. The external evidence of this balance of payments problem is that in the last ten years our gold reserves dropped over ten billion. It is interesting to note that the gold reserves of the United States on January 1, 1958 were slightly larger than they were on December 31, 1950. The real balance of payments problem, therefore, is a ten-year problem."

9. So far as I can ascertain, however, Triffin did not comment favorably on the improvement in the net-worth balance of $7 billion between 1959 and 1964. The existence of a variety of balance-of-payments definitions makes it possible for an observer always to be grave, or optimistic, according to his temperament.

10. A number of writers make a distinction between a deficit, which is simply a departure from zero of a given number of variables in the balance of payments, and disequilibrium, which is an excessive deficit. On this view there is no need for concern. The analogy is to a small deficit in the budget of the US government, which is supportable with *ex ante* savings, where a large deficit might not be. But the semantics make it difficult to regard a perpetual deficit as supportable, because of the analogy to household, where such a deficit is not supportable because of limits to available credit.

References

Bergsten, C. Fred, "Taking the monetary initiative," *Foreign Affairs* (July 1968), pp. 217–32; and *Reforming the Dollar: An International Monetary Policy for the US* (New York: Council on Foreign Relations, 1972).

Bernstein, Edward M., Republican Balance-of-Payments Seminar, remarks of Hon. Charles E. Goodell, *Congressional Record* (reprint) (5 February 1968).

Birnbaum, Eugene A., "Gold and the international monetary system: an orderly reform," *Essays in International Finance*, no. 66 (Princeton, NJ: Princeton University Press, April 1968), p. 6.

Branson, William H., *Financial Capital Flows in the U.S. Balance of Payments* (Amsterdam: North-Holland, 1968).

Cooper, Richard N., "The balance of payments in review," *Journal of Political Economy*, vol. 74, no. 4 (August 1966), pp. 379–95.

Cooper, R. N., "The Balance of payments," in Richard Caves *et al.*, *Britain's Economic Prospects* (Washington, DC: Brookings Institution, 1968).

Gardner, Walter R., "An exchange-market analysis of the U.S. balance of payments," IMF, *Staff Papers* (May 1961), pp. 195–211.

Hansen, Alvin H., *The Dollar and the International Monetary System* (New York: McGraw-Hill, 1965).

Ingram, James, "A proposal for financial integration in the Atlantic Community," in *Factors Affecting the United States Balance of Payments*, US Congress, Joint Economic Committee, 87th Cong., 2d sess. (Washington, DC: Government Printing Office, 1962).

International Study Group, *International Monetary Arrangements: The Problem of Choice*, Report on the Deliberations of an International Study Group of Thirty-two Economists (Princeton, NJ: International Finance Section, 1964).

Keynes, J. M., "The German transfer problem," *Economic Journal*, vol. 39, no. 1 (March 1929), pp. 1–7. Reprinted in American Economic Association, *Readings in the Theory of International Trade* (Philadelphia, Pa.: Blakiston, 1949), pp. 161–9.

Kindleberger, C. P., *International Economics* (Homewood, Ill.: Richard D. Irwin, 1953).

Lary, Hal. B., "Disturbances and adjustments in recent U.S. balance-of-payments experience," *American Economic Review, Papers and Proceedings*, vol. 51, no. 2 (May 1961), pp. 417–29.

Lary, Hal. B., *Problems of the United States as World Trader and Banker* (New York: National Bureau of Economic Research, 1963).

Machlup, Fritz, "Three concepts of the balance of payments and the so-called dollar short-age," *Economic Journal*, vol. 60, no. 1 (March 1950), pp. 46–68. Reprinted in F. Machlup, *International Payments, Debts and Gold* (New York: Scribner's, 1964), pp. 69–92.

Machlup Fritz, "Equilibrium and disequilibrium: misplaced concreteness and disguised politics," *Economic Journal*, vol. 68, no. 1 (March 1958), pp. 1–24. Reprinted in F. Machlup, *International Payments, Debts and Gold* (New York: Scribner's, 1964), pp. 110–35.

Machlup, Fritz, *International Payments, Debts and Gold* (New York: Scribner's, 1964).

McKinnon, Ronald I. and Oates, Wallace E., "The implications of international economic integration for monetary, fiscal and exchange-rate policy," *Princeton Studies in International Finance*, no. 16 (1966).

Nurske, Ragnar, "Conditions of international monetary equilibrium," *Essays in International Finance*, no. 4 (Princeton, NJ: Princeton University Press, Spring 1945). Reprinted in American Economic Association, *Readings in the Theory of International Trade* (Philadelphia, Pa.: Blakiston, 1949), pp. 3–34.

Review Committee for the Balance of Payments Statistics to the US Bureau of the Budget, *The Balance of Payments Statistics of the United States, A Review and Appraisal* (Washington, DC: Government Printing Office, 1965).

Rueff, Jacques and Hirsch, Fred, "The role and rule of gold: an argument," *Essays in International Finance*, no. 47 (Princeton, NJ: Princeton University Press, June 1965).

Salant, Walter S. *et al.*, *The United States Balance of Payments in 1958* (Washington, DC: The Brookings Institution, 1963).

Triffin, Robert, "The presentation of U.S. balance of payments statistics," *Proceedings of the Business and Economics Statistics Section (1961)* (Washington, DC: American Statistical Association, 1962).

Triffin, Robert, Republican Balance-of-Payments Seminar, remarks of Hon. Charles E. Goodell, *Congressional Record* (reprint) (5 February 1968).

Williamson, Jeffrey G., *American Growth and the Balance of Payments, 1820–1913* (Chapel Hill, NC: University of North Carolina Press, 1964).

11   The Formation of Financial Centers

It is a curious fact that the formation of financial centers is no longer studied in economics, perhaps because it falls between two stools. Urban and regional economics, which concern themselves with cities, discuss the location of commerce, industry, and housing but rarely that of finance. (Exceptions should perhaps be made for Canada[1] and for France.[2]) Pred's study of urban growth in the United States deals exclusively with commerce and industry, with no mention of banking or financial markets.[3] A 1973 survey of U.S. urban economics mentioned finance only once in the text and referred to no work on the subject in a bibliography of 438 items.[4] Only the study of the New York metropolitan area led by Vernon devotes attention to it.[5] At the same time, a vigorous new literature on money and capital markets and their role in economic development takes no interest in geographical location or the relationships among financial centers.[6] Apart from a sentence or two, one would think that the money and capital market was spread evenly throughout a given country.

The "geography of finance," to borrow Kerr's phrase, is relevant to contemporary issues as well as being of considerable historical interest. Contemporary relevance is provided partly by the tasks of building money and capital markets in developing countries, which McKinnon[7] and Shaw[8] regard as vital to economic development—more important, indeed, than foreign aid or export expansion. Among developed countries there is the issue of which center, if any, will emerge as the leading money and capital market of the European Economic Community if it achieves monetary integration. Economic analysis may not be equal to the task of predicting the answer to this question, or of recommending the policy measures a government or intergovenmental body should follow if it wishes to affect the outcome of the market process.[9]

Historically, an explanation is needed about why money and capital markets were centered at the capital in Great Britain, France, and Germany, but not in Italy, Switzerland, Canada, the United States, or Australia. One can formulate an aspect of the issue as a riddle: What do the Midlands Bank, the Crédit lyonnais, and Dresdner Bank, the Banca Tiberina, the Bank of Nova Scotia, and the First Boston Corporation have in common? The answer: Their executive offices are located in a different place from that implied by their names—the Midlands Bank in London, the Crédit lyonnais in Paris, the Dresdner Bank in Berlin (from 1892 to 1945), the Banca Tiberina (after 1987) in Turin (not along the Tiber), the Bank of Nova Scotia in Toronto, and the First Boston Corporation in New York. The two historical curiosities can be combined. A year after the Midlands Bank transferred its headquarters from Birmingham to London in 1891, there was a simultaneous movement of the Schaffhausen'schen Bankverein from Cologne to Berlin (that is, from a provincial city to the capital) and of the Eidgenössische Bank from Bern, the capital, to Zurich. The affinity of finance and location is underlined by the fact that so many banks have places rather than functions (such as Merchants, Farmers) in their names. (Private banks, where confidence is all-important, are named for people.)

A historical approach is also called for, because if analysts have little interest in spatial finance, the same cannot be said of their grandfathers. Two generations ago, before and after World War I, economics displayed an interest in the functions of and relations among financial centers that is rare in current research. Fanno had a chapter on the centralization process in banking and money markets that included geographic centralization.[10] Powell presented a detailed account of the processes by which congeries of isolated banks were formed into a financial structure centered on London, with many physiological analogies, including natural selection and survival of the fittest.[11] The most highly developed analysis, however, was provided by Gras, the economic historian, who described the stages of development from village and town to metropolitan economy, specifying the development of specialized financial institutions as a metropolitan function.[12]

In the pages that follow, a comparative analysis is presented in literary rather than statistical or econometric form. It is perhaps unnecessary to defend the comparative method after having shown that the administrative capital sometimes serves as the financial center and sometimes does not. I go further, however, and suggest that the study of single cases, valuable as it is, frequently tempts the economic historian to rely too heavily on single analytical models and that the comparative method, for limited problems at least, is of value in showing what is general and what special in historic process. The qualification that the comparative method is most

effective with limited problems—as a rule, of a partial-equilibrium sort—
reflects concern that, as the analyst moves from one country, society, polity, or economy to another, general-equilibrium issues like business cycles,
stages of growth, and backwardness embody too many degrees of freedom to enable him to generalize with confidence.

That the comparative historical account is qualitative rather than quantitative derives from the limitations of the writer, the magnitude of the
task of deriving comparable data from a wide number of countries, and an
interest more in process than in detailed outcome. Even such an impressive study as that of Goldsmith, which shows conclusively that financial
machinery becomes more elaborate as a country grows in productive
process, does not examine the detailed processes, particularly the spatial
ones.[13] Extending this study to measure the process described would
make it unduly long.

The next section of this chapter briefly reviews the literature on the
location of cities and their functions, the roles of money and capital markets in the development process, and the evolution of banks and banking.
Its main purpose is to identify the economies inherent in a central organization of financial markets and banking machinery, and to show why
financial centers tend to be organized spatially in a hierarchy, with a single center as the keystone of the arch. The description is limited largely
to banks and banking, with little explicit attention to other elements of
money and capital markets. Some reference is made to clearinghouses,
stock exchanges, government and private security markets, mortgages,
foreign bonds, and insurance, though none to factoring, consumer finance,
or pension funds. As economic growth proceeds, the importance of banks
as financial intermediaries diminishes relative to other institutions, but it is
always strategic.

This concentration on the why of a single financial center is followed
by seven case studies designed to show the processes by which a given
locality is chosen. I deal with England, France, and Germany, where the
political capital became the financial center as well. The contrast between
the English and French centers, on the one hand, and the German, on the
other, is provided by their respective political histories, especially the late
unification of Germany in 1870, which furnishes a sort of "instant replay"
of the process. Later sections deal with the Italian and Swiss examples,
each with late unification, in 1860 and 1848 respectively, but different
from the German case because the financial center turns out to be a city
different from the political capital. Canada and the United States furnish
examples of financial centers that are emerging in countries developed

from the wilderness; here again, the political and financial leadership chose different sites. The Canadian experience is of particular interest. The country felt obliged to free itself successively from money- and capital-market reliance on London and New York, experienced two shifts of the financial center, from Halifax to Montreal, then—long-drawn-out and still incomplete—from Montreal to Toronto. Lately, moreover, a relatively independent market has begun to develop in Vancouver.

The final section deals in summary fashion with the question of a world financial center, arching over and connecting indirectly national money and capital markets. London held the position during most of the nineteenth century, though with challenges from France and Germany. In the twentieth century a shift to New York occurred, and a second shift is now in progress from New York to the Eurodollar market. That market is spread all over the world; but its heart, to use a well-worn image, beats in the American and British banks in London. I conclude by seeking to use the lessons derived from the historical studies to throw light on the question of whether a financial center for the European Economic Community will emerge, and if so where.

Banking Development and the Metropolis

A recent spate of books has focused anew on the role of banking in economic development. Two of the earliest writers in the field were Hoselitz and Gerschenkron, who emphasized especially the role of the Crédit mobilier, founded in 1852, in stimulating rapid industrial expansion in France.[14] German banking was said to be as powerful as the steam engine.[15] These leads were followed up and developed by Cameron, in his own book on France and in the case studies he edited.[16] Some of these cases, particularly Austria, Italy, and Spain, suggested that banking may or may not make a positive contribution to economic development, depending not on the personal qualities of the bankers but on the "structural characteristics of the system, and the laws, regulations and customs."[17] The contribution of the Crédit mobilier to the industrial development of France has also been downgraded;[18] its interests, and those of many of its imitators, lay in speculation, not in industrial growth.

Much of this historical literature, however, focused on banking as an agent of growth through stimulation of demand. By contrast, the analytical contributions of Goldsmith, McKinnon, and Shaw emphasize the role of banking in mobilizing and allocating liquid resources. Goldsmith points out that the development of financial intermediaries "accelerates economic

growth and improves economic performance to the extent that it facilitates the migration of funds to the best user, i.e. to the place in the economic system where the funds will find the highest social return."[19] Shaw
equates "deep" with "liberalized" finance, which opens the way to superior allocations of savings by widening and diversifying the financial markets in which investment opportunities compete for the savings flow. In
his only reference to space, he goes on: "The market for savings is
extended.... Local capital markets can be integrated into a common market, and new opportunities for pooling savings and specializing in investment are created."[20] McKinnon's emphasis is on raising the rate of
interest on financial capital to equality with the rate of interest on real
capital.[21] This makes it worthwhile for entrepreneurs to save in money
form for later investment and increases the availability of external finance;
entrepreneurs who would otherwise be limited to their own savings are
thereby enabled to start businesses sooner and on a larger scale. Financing
trade and production at a rate of interest equal to the return on real assets
is a shot in the arm to development. Integration of capital markets eliminates local and sectoral monopoly and monopsony, but especially stimulates the formation of savings and its pooling.[22] Here is an echo of
Powell's reference to banking as a "magnet which pulls out hoards."[23]

As noted, these discussions of banking innovation and financial intermediation or deepening lack a spatial dimension. Financial centers are
needed not only to balance through time the savings and investments of
individual entrepreneurs and to transfer financial capital from savers to
investors, but also to effect payments and to transfer savings between
places. Banking and financial centers perform a medium-of-exchange function and an interspatial store-of-value function. Single payments between
separate points in a country are made most efficiently through a center,
and both seasonal and long-run surpluses and deficits of financial savings
are best matched in a center. Furthermore, the specialized functions of
international payments and foreign lending or borrowing are typically
best performed at one central place that is also the specialized center for
domestic interregional payments. (This is not always the case. For twenty
years after Berlin became the undisputed center for German domestic
finance, Hamburg continued its role as the leading city for foreign-trade
finance.)

To limit ourselves again to domestic interregional payments, the efficiency of a single center is akin to the contribution to utility of a single
numeraire. Each locality deals not with each other locality in making and
receiving payments, but with a single center; $n - 1$ conduits are needed

instead of $n(n-1)/2$. Small localities are typically clustered about a provincial financial center but are linked to others through the central financial market. When country clearing was established in London in 1858, the National Provincial Bank thought it "preposterous" for a bank at Manchester to collect a check on Newcastle upon Tyne through London.[24] At that time, the National Provincial Bank had offices in Manchester and Newcastle, whereas its banking office in London was opened only in 1866. Later, however, the National Provincial Bank must have cleared among its branches through a central point such as London. French centralization of distribution through Paris has been much criticized; the efficiency of central clearing for such purposes as moving artichokes from Dijon to Bordeaux obviously declines as costs of transport rise. But for money payments, there can be no doubt of the efficiency of a central financial market as the apex of a national system, and of a single international market as the apex of national financial centers. An African student once complained to me that Latin American payments to a country such as Kenya were made in dollar checks on New York; he was persuaded that the system was devised to enable imperialist extortionists to exploit the periphery. He found incredible the truth that the centralization of payments and use of a vehicle currency are efficient.

As an efficient system of payment develops, utilizing the medium-of-exchange function of banking, firms find themselves able to economize on working balances by centralizing them at the metropolitan pivot. Companies above a certain size tend to establish financial offices in the metropolis to deal in financial markets as well as to finance a larger flow of payments with smaller working balances. Increasingly competitive security markets provide larger and cheaper security issues for those who need capital, as well as more liquid investments for lenders. Economies of scale are found not only in the medium-of-exchange and store-of-value functions of money, but also in the standard-of-deferred-payment function insofar as it relates to loans, discounts, and bond issues.[25]

The origins of banking are diverse. Elementary textbooks imply that they can be traced mainly to the storage function of goldsmiths, but this is oversimplification. The goldsmiths in England, congregated in London, were an important source of private banking, but by no means as important as merchant houses. Other bankers originated as scriveners or notaries, tax receivers or tax farmers who lent out funds being held for remittance to the treasury, court bankers who provided advances and personal services to profligate princes, and industrial companies that paid wages in tokens, moving a stage beyond the truck system (payments in commodities), and found that the tokens remained in circulation. Some manufacturers lent out business profits rather than plowing them back in industrial expansion. But the majority of bankers started as merchants, gradually becoming specialized in the financial side of commerce. Ten of fourteen private bankers in Liverpool—a commercial city, to be sure— sprang from wholesale houses.[26] Often a merchant devised a system for making or collecting payments at a distance and was asked to perform such services for others. The Bank of England was started during the Nine Years' War by wine merchants who, as they sold their stocks and had no opportunity to replace them, found themselves with liquid capital. Beer also resulted in capital accumulation that in a number of instances led the brewer into banking.

Both banking and commerce involve the overcoming of distance, and the geographical pattern of banking was linked to commerce. Cities are typically located at a break in transport; such a break must lie across a trade route.[27] London, Paris, Cologne, Rome, and Montreal lie on major rivers at the first ford or shallow part up from the sea. Berlin lies at the point of transshipment for bulk cargoes moving from the Oder to the Elbe.[28] Lyons and Frankfurt were historic fair towns on international cara- van trails, and the *furt* in Frankfurt stands for ford—the ford of the Franks on the river Main. As we shall see, the coming of the railroad, a major in- novation in transport in the nineteenth century, changed the character of banking and the location of some financial centers, and only timely action by communities to influence the shape of the railroad network prevented other changes adverse to them.

Not all commodities are identical in their impact on transport or the location of financial activity. It is possible to construct a "staple theory" of finance, at least for the early stages of banking development, to explain the particular impact of different commodities on the size and pattern of financial flows. Seasonality of financial requirements is one aspect; unique production processes, a need for bought inputs, and time needed to con- sume outputs are others. Ports are dominated by particular commodities financed in certain ways: Liverpool by cotton and wheat, Glasgow by sugar and tobacco, Cherbourg by cotton, Bremen by cotton and coffee (financed in London), and so on. This in turn affects their financial development.

The mechanism by which the location of a city, the transport network, and the economic characteristics of the goods and services in which an area specialized, determined the financial pattern was partly Darwinian and partly the result of deliberate action by government or private indi- viduals. The Darwinian evolution of the banking pattern is illustrated by depressions that wiped out both badly located banks and bankers and those who were well located but incautious. State policy is reflected by the centralizing policies of the Bank of France and French government, which in 1848 eliminated the provincial banks established during the 1830s, and by the decentralizing pressures in Canada and the United States. The strength of regional banking in France in the period before World War I was in spite of, not owing to, state action—which typically operated at that time to discourage regional autonomy. At the private level, local action fostered means of transport and opposed rival financial centers. Of great interest, banks, bankers, corporation head offices, and the like deliberately changed locations, often saving face by professing loyalty to their birthplace. Goldstein and Moses describe Webber's game-theoretic model of location decisions under uncertainty with the assumption that "once the firm is located, it is impossible to relocate."[29] For banks, as will be evident later, such an assumption lacks historical validity.

Some allowance must also be made for pure accident. I am informed by Juan Linz that Bilbao flourishes in Spain as the second financial center outside of Madrid because Prieto, the Socialist finance minister in the 1930s, came from that region and saved its banks while allowing those of Barcelona to fail. The history of European and North American banking is filled with accounts of bankers' quarrels based on personal, social, political, and religious differences, which may or may not be superficial rationalizations of deep-seated economic forces.

In terms of Harold Innis' "staple theory," which ascribes economic outcomes to the characteristics of different commodities or products that dominate economic life at any one time, banking starts out to serve the needs of sovereigns and nobles; develops in connection with commerce; then, less personally, with governmental finance; next with transport, including shipping, canals, turnpikes, and railroads; then with industry; and finally with intermediation in insurance, mortgages, consumer finance, factoring, pension funds, and the like. In a highly developed setting like New York or London, the money market in a broad sense includes (*a*) a money market with many specialized segments for commercial paper, acceptances, collateral loans, treasury bills, federal funds (in New York), certificates of indebtedness, and the like, and (*b*) a capital market, both private and governmental, dealing in new issues and secondary distribution, together with (*c*) trading in commodities, foreign exchange, bullion (in London, Paris, and Zurich), and, to a lesser degree, ships and ship charters, and insurance.[30] The borrowing and lending pattern starts locally and extends to a national center, with perhaps intermediate regional stops, finally becoming international. Specialization grows in instruments and functions and by hierarchical market. Inflations, depressions, wars, and the like distort or intensify the pattern.

The hierarchical character of financial specialization was originally discussed in 1922 by an economic historian, N. S. B. Gras, who developed a theory of stages of metropolitan development in which finance was the apex.[31] There is a national credit market in a country, but it is spatially concentrated in a hierarchical pattern. As summarized by Duncan,[32] Gras traces through four phases the growth of the metropolis to serve a hinterland: (a) commerce, (b) industry, (c) transport, (d) finance. Finance is more concentrated than commerce, industry or residence. In 1929, four counties had one-quarter of the savings deposits in the United States—a poor measure of financial concentration—whereas eleven counties shared one-quarter of retail sales, and twenty-seven counties shared one-fourth of the population.[33] In 1955, New York had $4.4 billion of nonlocal loans, compared with $1.2 billion for Chicago and $490 million for San Francisco—another measure of metropolitan character.[34] Similar data for Canada in the 1960s are given later in this chapter.

Cities, according to Vernon, attract industries or services in which there is great uncertainty and need for face-to-face contact, those in which speed of interaction is a requisite.[35] Unstandardized outputs lead to agglomeration as a convenience for the shopper. The port of New York attracted the wholesalers, who pulled in the financial institutions, which attracted the central offices of national corporations.[36] A detailed study of New York's financial functions supports this view and discusses the external economies arising from specialization, joint facilities, and the services of other industries such as printing.[37] Shopping convenience is mentioned, but perhaps too little is made of the fact that the broader the financial market, the greater the liquidity of security issues, with the result that lenders and borrowers from other regions will transfer to that market their gross demands and supplies, not just net excess demand or supply. The borrower pays a lower rate of interest and/or is able to issue a larger loan. The lender acquires a qualitatively different investment because it is traded on a broader secondary market, which is why he is willing and often eager to accept a lower interest rate.[38] Insurance companies are less centralized than most other segments of the money and capital market because of a pronounced preference by consumers in the United States for locally issued insurance policies.[39]

In addition to economies, there are diseconomies that work against centralization and favor regional markets. The foremost is cost of information, which gives local credit markets an advantage in dealing with small firms in an area. Unfamiliarity with local personalities and character may discourage central money and capital markets from lending locally. The difference in time is another diseconomy of centralization that has supported the growth of North American markets as against European, the Eurocurrency market as against New York, and the West Coast of North America as against Toronto-Montreal and New York. Direct communication by telephone or telex must be simultaneous; when it spans many time zones, it involves a dislocation of the working day for at least one party. This is another specific illustration of the cost of dealing in finance at a distance; the foremost is the loss of information obtainable only with face-to-face contact. Still a third diseconomy of centralization is crowding, which made for the building of hundreds of offices in midtown Manhattan after World War II and induced one bank, the First National City Bank, to move its head office from downtown to midtown Manhattan. The same phenomenon had been evident in London, with a banking community in the West End of London, separate from the city, for the convenience of wealthy clients in Mayfair. The London and Westminster Bank, formed in 1836, communicated through its name that it was one of the few banks that operated in both the city and the West End.

Not a diseconomy so much as a discrimination is the tendency of governments and private persons to favor their compatriots over foreigners, even at the expense of higher cost or lower profit—an implicit or explicit mercantilist attitude.

Up to a certain high degree of concentration, positive externalities and economies of scale appear to outweigh diseconomies and favor centralization. The continuous reduction in the costs and difficulties of transport and communication over the last two hundred years has favored the formation of a single world financial market.

London as the Financial Center of England

Prior to about 1750 there was little country banking in England. Large incorporated banks existed in Scotland, and the Bank of England was established in London in 1694; there were also many private bankers there. The Bank of England had a monopoly of joint-stock banking in England. Private banks were allowed to issue notes, but their size was limited by the fact that they could have no more than six partners.

Beginning about 1750 there was an upsurge of banks in the country. The dozen or so existing at that time doubled by 1772 and reached four hundred by 1800.[40] Bankers with large families or trusted relatives tended to establish a separate firm in the city in addition to one in the country. The father of the four Baring brothers had come to Exeter from Germany as a wool and serge merchant and had gone into banking in 1717; fifty years later the brothers divided up—two in London and two in Exeter.[41] And Abel Smith II, son of the tax receiver Thomas Smith who remitted funds to London through his connections as a mercer with goldsmith bankers, started a Nottinghamshire bank in 1757, a London bank in 1758, a Lincoln bank in 1775, and a bank at Hull for the Russian trade in 1784.[42] Much of the activity of these banks was remittance. Landlords living in London received their rent twice a year in May and November, so that the banks were called upon at these times to provide London bills.[43] The West End banks, which served the landed interests, were particularly involved in government securities.[44] In addition, in prosperous times country banks accumulated deposits which they remitted to London for investment. Testifying before the Bullion Committee in 1810, Mr. Richardson, a bill broker, said:

In some parts of the country there is little circulation of bills drawn on London, as in Norfolk, Essex, Sussex, etc. . . . I receive bills to a considerable extent from Lancashire in particular, and remit them to Norfolk &c where the bankers have large lodgments and much money to advance on bills of discount.[45]

Bagehot added in 1873 that the distribution of the bill-brokers' customers remained much the same after sixty years,[46] and his text speaks of funds from agricultural counties such as Somersetshire and Hampshire, with good land but no manufactures or trade, being invested in the discount of bills from Yorkshire and Lancashire.[47]

The numerous country banks, hard hit by the deflation following the Napoleonic wars, generated a campaign, led primarily by Thomas Joplin, a timber merchant from Newcastle, for adoption of the Scottish system of joint-stock (incorporated) banking with branches. The panic of 1825, in which many small country banks disappeared, brought the adoption of joint-stock banking in 1826; but within a radius of 65 miles from London the privilege of issuing notes was reserved to the Bank of England. (The bank sought to provide an element of stability for the country banks by opening branches outside the 65-mile area.) With the renewal of the bank's charter in 1833, further legislation was required. This was interpreted, against the wishes of the Bank of England, as permitting joint-stock banks of deposit, if not joint-stock banks of note issue, within 65 miles of London. The result was the establishment outside the radius of many banks with the right of note issue. Inside the area only a few banks were started, as the issuing of notes was deemed the principal source of profit. The outstanding one, which survives today, is the London and Westminster.

The other four of the five great joint-stock banks of 1967 (reduced to four by the merger of the National Provincial with the London and Westminster in 1968) were originally provincial. Lloyds was started as a private bank in 1765 in Birmingham by a successful Quaker metal trader. Members of the family set up a London firm in 1770; the last partner of both the London and Birmingham houses died in 1807. The Birmingham bank remained private until 1865, when it began a series of mergers and amalgamations that converted it from a provincial to a city and national institution. Mergers of 1884 with two private banks (Messrs. Barnett, Hoares, Hambury, and Lloyd; and Bosanquet, Salt and Co.) brought the bank effectively to London. The head office remained in Birmingham, but the center of gravity shifted rapidly to London.[48] The need to acquire branches and to establish the bank of London came from difficulties in balancing the demand and supply for investments. In 1866 a shareholder was opposed to branching, but the chairman pointed to the need to attract funds.[49] Then, as the branch movement grew and banks were acquired in areas of surplus funds, the opposite necessity to find an outlet for funds in London became imperative—a process of unbalanced growth. According to Sayers, "A main attraction for joining Lombard Street was the prospect for fuller and more remunerative employment of surplus cash."[50] Integration of the national capital market can be seen in the tension caused by the original practice of paying 2.5 percent on deposits in Birmingham, while in Lombard Street the rate varied with the bank rate. When the bank rate rose above 4 percent, some depositors were tempted to move cash to London. This tendency existed before amalgamation with the London banks, but became accentuated thereafter. Only much later, in 1920, when a 7-percent bank rate had made the London rate apply far out into the country, was the problem resolved by establishing a single deposit rate for the entire bank.[51]

The history of Midlands Bank is similar to that of Lloyds. It started early, in 1836, as a joint-stock bank, but moved slowly, acquiring only six branches in the next fifty years, all near Birmingham. By 1889 it had absorbed eight provincial banks, including substantial ones in Lancashire and Wales. At this point the Birmingham Banking Company, another smaller rival of Lloyds, followed Lloyds' example in acquiring a London connection.[52] Like modern multinational corporations, which invest defensively, following the leader to prevent it from stealing a march, the Midlands Bank merged with the Central Bank of London in the same year. So as not to offend Birmingham, it was stated that the London bank had imposed among its conditions "a sine qua non that the head office must be in London, and half-yearly meetings of stockholders in January in Birmingham and July in London." The Baring crisis of 1890 sped the process of amalgamation when Lord Goschen, chancellor of the exchequer, shocked the banks by calling their reserves inadequate. By October 1898 the business of the Midlands was judged ill-balanced: "Our country business is out of all proportion to our Metropolitan business," and the head office was too small. This was corrected by merging with the City Bank of London.[53] The bank's biographers regard the process as the outcome of an irresistible trend in English banking; Surrey and Kent and the suburbs of London—not the agricultural counties this time—were lending surplus funds to the industrial areas of the Midlands and the West Riding (Yorkshire). The head office was the channel through which resources flowed far more efficiently than under the old agency and bill system.[54] There was danger for local banks which became too heavily involved in separate industries: Bradford in wool, Oldham in cotton, Sheffield in steel.[55]

On occasion, however, there was safety in being off by oneself. Prior to its merger with the Midlands, the Bank of Wales had little trouble in the crises of 1857 and 1866, largely because its business was predominantly Welsh.[56] On the other hand, the Northumberland and Durham Bank failed in 1857—whether, as one story has it, because the bank had loaned almost £1 million of its £2.5 million assets to a single company, Derwent & Co., which was working mineral rights owned by the bank's Jonathan Richardson,[57] or because £250,000 of small bills on Newcastle shopkeepers, probably good in themselves, were not discountable outside Newcastle.[58] Integration is good in good times; in bad times, it is good if you have the trouble and the rest of the world helps, bad if the trouble originates outside and is communicated inward.

The National Provincial Bank and Barclays developed differently. The National Provincial was organized as a joint-stock company in 1833, with £1 million of capital, a board in London, but banking operations in a series of branches outside the 65-mile limit. Some existing banks were taken over; many new ones were created. The geographical spread was wide: Gloucester, Stockton, Darlington, Kingsbridge, Manchester, Ramsgate, Newcastle, Emlyn, and so forth. As Withers notes, "In those days of slow communication and transport it must have required no ordinary courage … in an era of political and industrial unrest and wild speculative fever, to open for business, and to establish liabilities in places as remote as Darlington in the north and Exeter in the west."[59] The provincial banks were given a certain amount of local autonomy but were under the general management of London. In 1866, when the bank had 122 offices, it opened for business in London. This involved giving up the right to issue notes.

The calculations that led to this decision—to exchange the right of note issue amounting to nearly £450,000 for banking operations in London—have not been made explicit. The rise of railroad communication, development of London clearing, and, after the Bank Act of 1844, spread of payment by check rather than by notes, plus the development of limited liability for banks as well as other shareholders in 1857 and 1862, may all have played a role. In 1858 the National Provincial was opposed to clearing in London and to the substitution of checks for country banker drafts and notes.[60] By 1865 it found the trends irresistible. If the testimony of other banking histories is applicable, the London agency banks were probably earning profits on a surplus of funds generated in the branch network; the branch banks could appropriate the profit by investing the funds themselves. It would be interesting to know whether the decision was influenced by the possibility of improving intrabank settlements in London.

The last of the giant joint-stock banks, Barclays, was created in 1896 from an amalgamation of twenty private banks then doing business in various parts of England, with histories stretching back many generations. The three largest were Barclay, Bevan, Tritton, Ransom, Bouverie & Co. of London, itself a merger of a city and a West End bank; Gurney and Co. of Norwich; and Jonathan Backhouse of Darlington. Seven of the twenty original banks were firms in which there were Gurney interests. The merger combined a valuable London business with strong connections in the eastern counties, the southwest, and the northwest.[61] Amalgamation reflected the view that the day of the private general banker was ending and that national networks both made for efficiency in payments and protected the banker from undue dependence on other banks for funds or outlets. In particular, country banks with considerable surpluses of funds to invest required assured outlets, partly in the industrial counties but partly abroad. The necessary division of surplus funds could be made only in a central capital market, with the net excess of each branch-banking network made available for lending abroad through the discount market and the stock exchange.

In concluding the discussion of England, it is hardly necessary to explain how London became the metropolitan apex of the financial network. Whether with the correspondent system, the Bank of England branches in the provinces, or the nationally spread joint-stock banks with their head offices also in the provinces, the system had no choice but to center in London. London had an ancient banking tradition and it was a major port, the capital seat, and the hub of the railroad network; all forces were brought to bear on this locality, which was itself somewhat divided between the city and the West End. The different banking systems in Ireland and Scotland reached across their boundaries and linked up with London.

After the railroad was built in 1830, London was accessible from all parts of the country. Howard Lloyd went to London from Birmingham one day a week from 1884 to 1902 and, after his retirement in that year, attended a weekly board meeting from his country place until his death in 1920.[62] In 1899 one partner of Smiths spent three days a week at Nottingham and one each at London, Newark, and Mansfield.[63]

London was not the only port; much foreign banking business had been conducted through Liverpool, the cotton and grain port, and through Glasgow and Dundee, which specialized respectively in tobacco and jute. The centralization process occurred through failure, merger, or a change of headquarters. Three American banks, the so-called W-banks—Wiggins, Wildes, and Wilson—failed in the crisis of 1837,[64] and the Bank of Liverpool did not survive the crisis of 1857; the Royal Bank of Liverpool failed in 1847 and stopped payment a second time in 1867. W. & J. Brown & Co., which remained afloat in 1837, added British capital and opened a London branch during the Civil War, when cotton was scarce; it closed down the Liverpool operation in 1889. Other Liverpool banks were absorbed at the end of the century, like the Liverpool Union Bank, which was taken over by Lloyds in 1900. The takeover required courage, Sayers states, as Liverpool valued its independence.[65] When Lloyds tried to absorb the Manchester and Liverpool District Bank in 1903, there was an outcry. The *Manchester Guardian* protested that the "strongest, best conducted and most prosperous of the so-called country banks should not lose its identity."[66] Financing was separated from the handling of commodities and concentrated away from the port of entry. Henry Bell, who became general manager of Lloyds in 1913, had started his banking career in a private bank in Liverpool. He worked for a time with the Liverpool Union Bank, where he gained experience in the financing of cotton, corn, timber, and provisions. When the Liverpool Union was taken over by

Lloyds, he was soon transferred to the head office in Birmingham, and in 1903 was transferred again to manage the City office in Lombard Street. There he turned his Liverpool experience in commodity finance to such good account that he ended up as general manager of the entire Lloyds Bank.[67] Successful men, management, and techniques all converge upon the center.

Two of the smaller national joint-stock banks survived into the 1960s, with head offices in Lancashire but large London branches. The Manchester and Liverpool District Bank kept its identity until 1962, despite amalgamations, but changed its name to District Bank in 1924 when it achieved national status. By the same token, the Bank of Liverpool grew through merger to national scope, permitting its acquisitions to retain their original London agents, until in 1918 it was dealing with five private bankers. It then merged with Martin's Limited, with a head office in Liverpool but a separate board in London. In due course, after a death, the parochial name was altered to Martin's Bank.[68]

As they became national, banks experimented with various degrees of uniformity of practice and decentralization.[69] In the end, "the principal characteristic of the British money market is the decentralization of granting credit, while at the same time the various banking institutions are closely connected by the placing of their actual reserve in the hands of one note-issuing bank."[70]

That coiner of physical images, Ellis T. Powell, quoted the 1858 Select Committee on the tendency of deposits to gravitate to London, the center of commercial activity, adding, "The expression 'gravitates' is singularly felicitous, though it is possible that the Committee did not realize how rapidly the mechanism of the Money Market was being modelled on the lines of the Solar system."[71]

Paris in France

The development of banking in France differed sharply from that in England. Centralization had been a feature of French life since the time of Louis XIV, but the French Revolution scattered banking back to its origins in Geneva or Germany, or overseas. With the peace these merchant banks returned to Paris; they began to slough off speculation in merchandise and to open subsidiaries in ports such as Le Havre to finance imports of cotton.[72] Apart from the ports, however, the development of credit markets was slow and they were poorly integrated. Emile Pereire wrote in 1834 that there were no banks outside of Paris, in contrast with England, which had five or six hundred.[73] The disconnected character of money and capital markets is illustrated by the fact that Dijon paid 9 or 10 percent for discounts, while Paris paid 4 percent and Lyons as little as 3 percent.[74] Lyons, however, found money tight each spring when it paid for silk from Italy. The seasonal tightness applied to all of rural France, which shipped funds to Paris in the first half of the year and got them back with the harvest after August.[75]

Napoleon, who established the Bank of France at the turn of the century, sought to unify the national credit system by establishing subsidiaries of the bank in the provinces to improve the circulation of specie and drafts. With the Restoration, the Bank of France abandoned this policy on two grounds, the difficulty of finding the local buyers for Bank of France stock needed to qualify as regents of the provincial *comptoirs*, and the scarcity of three-name paper, which was all the bank would rediscount. The alternative was to establish regional banks to mobilize local savings more effectively. Such banks got off to a good start in Rouen, Nantes, and Bordeaux—all ports—and others were begun in the 1830s in Le Havre, Lille, Lyons, Marseille, and Dijon, but under restrictions. The Bank of France decided that it needed a monopoly of the note issue and limited the regional banks on the paper they could discount, the size of the notes they could issue, and the ability to redeem notes in Paris.[76] In the financial crisis of 1848 the Bank of France allowed the regional banks to fail, so as to take over the note issue, and returned to a program of comptoirs.

One of the fundamental reasons for developing local institutions was the fear that the Bank of France would order the provinces to restrict credit in a crisis without regard for local conditions.[77] As we have seen in the case of England, however, integration and separation can each be a help or a hindrance in periods of stress, depending upon where the liquidity squeeze strikes.

With a fractured national market, some localities experienced unique conditions owing to specialized foreign relations. While Paris served as an intermediary between sources of capital such as Vienna, Frankfurt, Strasbourg, and Basel and outlets such as Rouen, Saint-Quentin, and Ghent, Lyons had its special connection with Geneva, and Mulhouse with Basel.[78] Marseille was continuously bled for specie by Spain, Corsica, Algiers, and the Black Sea.[79]

In contrast with these cities, which were linked into two or more banking networks, the countryside went its own way. Bankers were often landed proprietors rather than merchants, with an interest in lending to agriculture and in equipping large estates, but they were dominated by security, prudence, tradition, and routine. The banking leadership was in Paris, and the small country banks chose not to follow it.[80]

With the foundation of the Crédit mobilier and the large credit banks—the Crédit lyonnais, Société générale, Comptoir d'escompte, and others—in the 1850s and 1860s, the money and capital market of France became better interconnected but no less centralized with the passage of time. The Crédit mobilier and the Société générale started in Paris and undertook large-scale lending for railroads, ports, and other public works, but did not finance local industrial activity. Established in the silk capital at the entrepôt for foreign trade to Switzerland and Italy, the Crédit lyonnais spread out a network of branches—first in the Languedoc and then throughout the country—to draw funds not to Lyons but to Paris. The history of the bank is discussed in detail in two books, one an account of the years from 1863 to 1882,[81] the other one of the few studies of credit networks by a geographer.[82]

Bouvier follows with great precision the move of the bank from Lyons to Paris. Started by Henri Germain, son of a silk manufacturer, who received a substantial dowry from his wife, daughter of another silk family, its early investments were industrial and regional. Most were in difficulty by 1870. In some cases, such as the widely discussed firm La Fuchsine, manufacturers of a synthetic dye, the difficulties of the firm were intensified by the greed of the bank in seeking quick profit rather than careful development. Mme Germain died in 1867, and M. Germain was remarried in 1869 to a Parisian. He was elected to the Chamber of Deputies, and this required his presence in Paris. Bit by bit he spent a greater proportion of his time in Paris. He did not visit the head office in Lyons once during 1881, and the head office was actually shifted to Paris in 1882. Even in 1879, the head of the subagency at Béziers asked whether he could not deal directly with Paris rather than going through Lyons.

In 1871 the bank made very large profits in the Thiers rente. From then on its task was to collect savings from all France, but especially from the Lyons hinterland, to funnel to Paris for investment in foreign bonds. "Drainage" (with a French pronunciation) was the function of the branch network, the accumulation of deposits. Towns like Grenoble, Annecy, and Creusot, which had thriving industry and building and needed loans, were to be avoided. Loans were provided to commerce, the fruitgrower, the cattle feeder, and the abbatoir, but not to industry. The minister of finance made the same objection in relation to Lille in 1835: "It is rate that banks adapt to and prosper in cities of factories. There is little hope of keeping the notes of the bank in circulation for very long."[83]

The change in the personal interests of Henri Germain from Lyons to Paris are of course symptomatic rather than causal. The decline in silk manufacturing in the Lyons area reduced the demand for finance and left Lyons "a gold mine for savings." Germain and the *hauts banquiers* of Paris, Geneva, and Italy who started the bank with him were interested only in lending to large and established industry, as was true of Paris banking generally. Where such loans were not available, foreign loans served instead.

Little change in this process was produced by the rise of the so-called "industrial banks," or *banques d'affaires*, founded in the 1870s. Most disappeared in the Great Depression or in the crash of 1882, which also engulfed the Union générale. Those that survived did so by hoarding their profits on the Thiers rente. With recovery, from 1896 on, moreover, their investments were highly similar to those of the deposit banks, in foreign bonds and established companies.

Under these circumstances the demand for local credit had to be filled locally in regional credit markets, which sprang up in competition with the national market. In 1910, and again in 1929, small regional banks that had not merged with or been driven under by the large Paris-led firms organized to resist the domination of the center. In 1910 the four-hundred-member Syndicat central des banques de province met at Bordeaux.[84] In 1929 the Crédit industriel et commercial, in cooperation with several other institutions, organized the Union des banques régionales pour le crédit industriel.[85] The movement flourished, particularly in the north, in Lorraine, and in Haute Savoie.

In the north, the Crédit du nord emerged as one of the strongest of the regional banks in France. With its head office in Lille in 1848, it established a few branches—Armentières in 1878, Tourcoing in 1884, and Paris in 1889, before expanding more rapidly after 1894.[86] It is of particular interest that it remained a regional bank and did not move its head office to Paris. Other vital regional capital markets in Lorraine and Haute Savoie undertook to finance the expansion of Briey iron ore after 1870 and the development of hydroelectric power generation, aluminum, and other electric metallurgical and electric chemical industries.[87] The Charpenay bank failed in 1931, receiving no assistance from the Bank of France. A well-known writer on French banking has accused the Bank of France of fostering greater centralization in the twentieth century by actively competing with the regional banks for local paper.[88] The small regional banks were able to compete with the national institutions because their deposits were mostly at term, as opposed to sight, and they were able to maintain much lower reserve ratios, in some cases as low as 3 to 4 percent, against 12 percent or so for the larger banks.[89]

Beyond the private and deposit banks, centralization of the capital market in France was accentuated by government institutions, not only the Bank of France but also such national institutions as the Crédit foncier (1852), Crédit agricole (1860), and Caisses d'epargne (1881, later merged with the Caisse de dépôts et de consignations). To this day, savings banks do not invest locally, as is generally the case in the United States, but divert their funds to Paris, where they are administered by a single decision-making unit, most recently as an adjunct to the planning process.

The choice of Paris over other central locations need not be explained. Tradition, administrative centralization, the communication network laid out in a star with Paris as the center, all attest to the pull of the capital. Apart from the regional banks, there was no resistance to the centripetal force. By 1900 the Lyons bourse had been left behind and was characterized as a museum piece, despite some revival during the German occupation of France in 1940 to 1942, when it was in the unoccupied zone.[90] After World War II the movement continued, with the transfer to Paris in the single year 1950 of the head offices of three major Lyons companies, including the Comptoir de textile artificiel, whose president continued to live in Lyons but worked in Paris during the week.[91] The movement of international, largely American companies to France in the 1950s and 1960s accentuated the trend and finally elicited a program to move industry and head offices out of Paris to the provinces.

Berlin in Germany

The emergence of a single financial center in Germany has taken place twice, on both occasions in connection with war: first, in the rise to dominance of Berlin over Cologne, Frankfurt, Darmstadt, Dresden, Leipzig, and Hamburg after the victory of Prussia over France in 1871; and, second, in the gradual emergence of Frankfurt as the financial capital of West Germany, following the isolation of Berlin at the end of World War II. In both instances the process was partly political and partly economic.

Prior to 1870 Germany was made up of at least thirty principalities, republics, and kingdoms. These varied in size from cities like Frankfurt and Hamburg to the large state of Prussia, which encompassed a wide area from Frankfurt north to the sea and then east—including East Prussia and Silesia—with its capital at Berlin. Prior to the reduction of internal barriers in 1818, the establishment of the Zollverein in 1834, and the construction of the railroad in the 1840s, the constituent elements of Prussia often pursued separate policies because of physical separation. Private banks were local—the Rothschilds in Frankfurt, the Oppenheims in Cologne, Bleichröder and Mendelssohn in Berlin, Heine and Warburg in Hamburg. Beginning with the creation of the Schaffhausen'schen Bankverein in 1848 on the ruins of Schaffhausen & Co., which had failed, two waves of bank formation took place, from 1850 to 1857 and from 1866 to 1873, from the victory of Prussia over Austria to the onset of the Great Depression, with hardly any pause for the Franco-Prussian War in 1870.[92]

In a passing moment of absent-mindedness, the Prussian government in 1848 granted the Schaffhausen'schen Bankverein permission to create an incorporated bank. But when the bank sought to grow by adding to its capital and moving to Berlin in 1853, it was refused permission.[93] Its by-laws did not specifically provide for branches. Tilly states that Berlin in the 1850s was the ideal place to start a bank, although he fails to say why—presumably because of its security activity in the finance of railroads.[94] To get around the refusal of the Prussian government to permit further incorporated banks, Cologne financiers, led by the Oppenheims and Gustav Mevissen and with French financial support, started the Bank für Handel und Industrie, known as the Darmstädter Bank, in Darmstadt, Hesse, a few miles from Frankfurt-am-Main and outside Prussian jurisdiction, where money was plentiful. The statutes were for the most part copied from those of the Schaffhausen'schen Bankverein charter of 1848, but went beyond these to include provisions patterned after the Crédit mobilier of 1852, permitting loans and participations for its own account, underwriting, issuance of bonds, and powers to effect mergers and consolidations of various companies.[95] The bank quickly opened an agency in Frankfurt and followed that with agencies in Mainz, Berlin, Heilbronn, Mannheim, Breslau, Leipsig, and, considerably later, in Hamburg and Stuttgart.[96] The Frankfurt agency was converted to a branch in 1864.

In 1856 another way was found around the Prussian refusal to grant bank charters, by using the form of Kommanditgesellschaft auf Aktien, a limited partnership with transferable shares.[97] Scores of banks were created, among them the conversion of the private bank of Hansemann, founded in 1851, into the Diskontogesellschaft, the Berliner Handelsgesellschaft (both of them in Berlin and both with Cologne money), the Norddeutsche Bank, and the Deutsche Vereinsbank at Hamburg.[98]

The participation of Cologne bankers in operations in Darmstadt and Berlin, and via them throughout the German states, raises the question whether there was a national German or at least a Prussian-Saxon money and capital market as early as the 1850s. Cologne had no security market of its own, finding it easier to use Berlin and Frankfurt, or even Brussels and Paris.[99] At this stage Frankfurt and Berlin specialized in security markets: Frankfurt loaned to princes, towns, and foreign states, but not to industry and not for railroads.[100] The thesis of Tilly's study of the Rhineland banks is that German industrialization of the period was achieved not through the careful planning of an efficient state bureaucracy but in "thousands of profit-oriented decisions made by capitalist entrepreneurs operating throughout Prussia"—and especially in the Rhineland.[101] The implication is that the decisions were decentralized. Karl Marx said of Germany that there was "no Isaac Pereire but hundreds of Mevissens on the top of more Crédit mobiliers than Germany has princes."[102] But Mevissen was himself the president of the Darmstädter Bank, Luxemburg Bank, Schaffhausen'schen Bankverein, Bank für Suddeutschland, Kölner Privatbank, and the Berlin Handelsgesellschaft, in addition to being president of a railroad, and he sat on the boards of six mines and two industrial companies, typically as chairman of the executive committee.[103] Other Cologne bankers like Hansemann, Camphausen, and Oppenheim moved freely between banking in Berlin and Cologne and business operations in the Ruhr. Eichborn was a banker in Berlin and an industrialist in Silesia. Private bankers such as Bleichröder and Mendelssohn in Berlin worked alongside the joint-stock banks and corporations, especially in the issuance of securities.[104] For Prussia, at least, and for Germany as a whole, excluding Bavaria, Württemburg, Baden in the south, and the Hansa cities in the north, the banking network solidified rapidly in the 1850s.

Hamburg was different. It clung longer to merchant banking and was slower to specialize than other parts of Germany. Its interests lay in foreign trade, in shipping, and in overseas finance rather than in domestic railroads and coal and steel. Regarded by the rest of Germany as the "English city," and itself disdainful of Prussian leadership until the successes of 1870, its banking was tied more closely to London than to Berlin. In 1857 this foreign connection almost led to disaster. The speculative excess in grain produced a crisis that spread from New York to Liverpool to London to Scandinavia to Hamburg, where a number of private houses could not meet their obligations and ship captains were unwilling to discharge their freight for fear of not being paid. Appeals for a silver loan were made to Rothschild, Baring, and Hambro in London; to Fould and Napoleon III in Paris; and to Amsterdam, Copenhagen, Brussels, Dresden, Hanover, and Berlin.[105] Fould, who was the father-in-law of Heine, the Hamburg banker, telegraphed back: "Your dispatch is not sufficiently clear." The Berlin ambassador indicated that Brück and the Kaiser would not help. At the last minute, as an anti-Berlin gesture, the Austrian government sent a train with 12 million talers of silver, known as the *Silberzug*, which saved the private banks of Merck, Godeffroy, Donner, John, Berenberg, and Gossler & Co. after the discount rate had reached 10 percent.[106] Shortly thereafter, Hamburg moved to specialized banking and the foundation of joint-stock banks, the Norddeutscher Bank and the Commerz- und Diskontobank.

With Prussian successes in the 1860s, German banking became increasingly concentrated in Berlin. The defeat of Austria deprived Frankfurt of its counterweight against the power of Prussia; from having been an imperial city and a free city, it became, in Böhme's expression, a Prussian provincial city. The functions of the Frankfurter bourse in dealing with state loans passed to Berlin. Among private banks Bleichröder, Mendelssohn, and Warshauer in Berlin flourished in their security dealings, while Bethmann, Erlanger, and Rothschild in Frankfurt found their clientele shrinking.[107] It seems evident that the ascendancy of Berlin over Frankfurt was political, but there are other explanations—the nimbleness and skill of the Berlin bankers[108] and the greater importance of railroad issues over those of state entities.[109] Each contains a portion of the truth. But Berlin had not made its start by specializing exclusively in railroad securities: the Prussian State Bank and the affiliated Seehandlung had undertaken some industrial development finance well before 1840. Nor had Frankfurt monopolized state issues. After the fire of 1842 Hamburg floated a loan of 34.4 million mark banco through one Hamburg and two Berlin houses. Issued in Berlin, much of the original amount was bought in Hamburg, and all had been repatriated by 1846.[110] Berlin was thus a capital market for more than Prussia before 1850.

When the Reich was founded by unifying Prussia and the other German states, the several monies in circulation were consolidated by adoption of the mark; the several banks of issue were absorbed into the Preussische Staatsbank, which emerged in 1875 as the Reichsbank. In the boom that immediately followed victory, however, there was a rash of bank creations, the most important new banks being the Deutsche Bank in Berlin and the Dresdner Bank in Dresden, both in 1872. The Deutsche Bank was started by a group including Adalbert Delbrück and Ludwig Bamberger, the former a private banker, the latter a member of the Zollverein Parliament and an economic expert who had worked in Paris banks during an exile after 1848. The bank's founders wrote to Bismarck in February 1870 indicating their intention to devote the bank to foreign trade. Outside the

United States, the finance of world trade at that time was in the hands of the French and British. Georg von Siemens, a cousin of the electrical-equipment manufacturer, was general manager of the Deutsche Bank. He was completely persuaded of the high national purpose of making German trade independent of British credit and of filling "the gap in finance of external trade."[111] The bank was located in Berlin, "the importance of which is indicated by the eagerness with which the Frankfurt capital market comes to meet it."[112] It also enlisted some Hamburg capital.[113]

In actuality the Deutsche Bank had little success in foreign finance and found it impossible to operate in that field from Berlin. Its first step in March 1871 was to open a branch in London, in cooperation with two Frankfurt banks. It then established branches in Bremen and Hamburg in 1871 and 1872, respectively, "because of the difference in foreign exchange in inland and coastal towns, and the rather sharp differences in inner and coastal trading practices."[114] Von Siemens' biographer insists that the requirements of overseas trade were decisive for the foundation of the Deutsche Bank but notes that business was not limited to foreign trade; he justifies expansion on the domestic front by the need to have the bank's acceptance signature widely recognized.[115] In the crisis of 1873 a number of banks failed and the Deutsche Bank took over several of them. In the beginning it restricted itself to state loans, communal loans, and railroad securities and held back from founding industries and issuing securities. Gradually, however, it built a syndicate of banks to move into industrial finance and underwriting. The finance of foreign trade was forgotten or put aside because of the need to build domestic roots;[116] lending to foreign borrowers, but not finance of German foreign trade, was undertaken in the 1890s. Foreign-trade finance remained the province of the Hansa cities, particularly Hamburg with its strong ties to London.

Victory in 1871 brought to the capital the Därmstadter Bank from Hesse and the Mitteldeutsche Creditbank from Frankfurt. The crash of 1873 produced a lull in the movement, and then came the Dresdner Bank in 1882, the Schaffhausen'schen Bankverein in 1892, the Commerz- und Diskonto Bank from Hamburg in 1892. Whale comments that these Berlin offices were at first only branches but soon grew to be coordinate head offices that rather eclipsed the original head offices.[117] The process is set forth in more detail in the centennial volume of the Commerz Bank.[118] The Mitteldeutsche Creditbank, which had started in Sachische Meiningen in 1856 because it had been refused permission to locate in Frankfurt, opened its Berlin office, as noted, in 1871. From 1889 on it began a policy of building local branches both in Frankfurt and in Berlin. By 1905 there were six such offices in Frankfurt, including Hoechst and Offenbach-am-Main, and seventeen in Berlin. These numbers reflect "the gradual shift of weight to the capital and the squeezing out of Frankfurt from its leading position as bank and stock exchange city."[119] When Anton Gustav Wittekind retired in 1912 after forty years of leadership, two successors were appointed, one in Berlin and one in Frankfurt.

The move of the Commerz Bank from Hamburg to Berlin was more complex, as befitted a surrender by the possessor of a proud heritage. Founded in Hamburg in 1870, the Commerz Bank saw its early hopes dashed by the crisis of 1873. Deciding to follow the fashion of the times and found a subsidiary in Berlin, it absorbed the private banking house J. Dreyfus and Co. of Frankfurt-am-Main, which had acquired a Berlin subsidiary in 1891. The merger gave rise to some competition in Frankfurt, but the Commerz Bank's chief interest from the first had been in Berlin. In 1899 it embarked on a policy of branch offices in Berlin, followed by more branches in Hamburg. The Frankfurt office of J. Dreyfus was given up in 1897 in favor of a *commandite* with the reconstituted firm. Even this was ended in 1908. In 1905 the Commerz Bank merged with the Berlin Handelsbank, bringing it a head office for its subsidiary and fourteen deposit branches. By 1914 the bank had eighteen branches in Hamburg and forty-four in Berlin.[120]

Riesser attacks a statement that banks in Germany differed from those in Britain in that the British banks moved from the provinces to London, whereas those in Germany moved from the capital to the provinces.[121] The latter process started only after 1897, when the big banks had finished moving to Berlin. Then came the filling out of the national system in directions and areas hitherto neglected, exactly as individual British banks had done.[122]

German experience differed from that of the rest of the Continent and North America in that the metropolitan financial center for the country did not also serve for intermetropolitan dealings. Berlin had borrowed and lent abroad in the first half of the century, when the German capital market was fragmented, just as had Frankfurt, Cologne, Hamburg, and Augsburg.[123] With the unification of the German capital market after 1871, domestic functions focused on Berlin and finance of foreign trade on Hamburg. The Diskontogesellschaft had worked closely with the Norddeutsche Bank of Hamburg since the early 1860s. Although the Deutsche Bank established a Hamburg subsidiary in 1872, it became effectively interested in overseas operations only in 1886.[124] The Darmstädter

Bank opened a subsidiary in Hamburg in 1890, the Dresdner in 1892, and the Mitteldeutsche in 1896. Wiskemann observes that Bismarck's interest in capital exports was not exclusively political.[125] The "imperialistic phase" of German capital lending began after his dismissal. However much it might rival Britain in shipping and in direct rather than entrepôt purchasing, Hamburg did not challenge London in finance, whether from inability or disinclination.

The position of Berlin as a transfer point for transport between the Elbe and Oder rivers and its subsequent development as a railroad center have been mentioned. Friedrich List characterized it as an important communications center as early as 1833.[126] Two scholars, one a social historian, the other an economic historian, have suggested that part of Berlin's importance lay in the fact that it was midway between the Ruhr and Upper Silesia.[127] Borchardt's other reasons seem more compelling—the concentration there of the Prussian authorities, the German imperial authorities, and the central bank, and the preference of associations and other organizations for that city, its easy access to Hamburg, and the like. The German geographer W. Christaller developed the theory that a central location tends to be chosen as a metropolis, but this view has since been discredited by the abundance of counterexamples, such as New York and London.[128] Even to the extent that the central-place theory retains validity, there is no reason why it should be central between heavy industries that are competitive rather than complementary. The break-in-transport theory of metropolitan location requires connections between intercommunicating portions of a common hinterland, not a point on the ridge of equal delivered prices between competitive suppliers.

After World War II, with the isolation of Berlin and the formation of zones of occupation, the major banks were broken up. In 1945 the Deutsche Bank, for example, was divided into ten branch institutes in the three western zones of occupation. With the relaxation of Allied control in 1952, these were amalgamated into three regional banks, the Süddeutsche Bank in Frankfurt, the Rheinische-Westfälische Bank (later Deutsche Bank West) in Düsseldorf, and the Norddeutsche Bank in Hamburg. When permission was granted in 1957, these three were reunited into the Deutsche Bank AG, with a legal seat at Frankfurt but with three "central offices" remaining in the three cities indicated, each of which had several members on the common management committee. In the mid-1960s the central office in Hamburg was reduced in status. In 1974 Frankfurt dominated Düsseldorf on the board of directors, with eight directors to Düsseldorf's five, and weekly board meetings held mainly in Frankfurt. The general secretary of the Deutsche Bank explained that Frankfurt had become the main focus of the bank because of the city's status as the most important financial center of postwar Germany. The Bundesbank was there, the Frankfurt bourse had the greatest turnover of all the exchanges in the German Republic, and both of the other so-called Grossbanken had their head offices in Frankfurt.[129]

In the same fashion, the Commerz Bank of Hamburg was divided into ten successors, reassembled into three in 1952, and into one in 1958. Various directories in the 1960s gave the location of its head office as Düsseldorf. In 1974 the head office was in Frankfurt.

It is of some interest that Cologne, the city nearest to Bonn, the postwar capital of the German Republic, was never in contention. Düsseldorf, which gave Frankfurt the greatest competition, is the trading and financial city of the Ruhr, with its heavy industry. Hamburg and Frankfurt were chosen by the British and American authorities respectively as the seats of their occupation forces in Germany. After the moratorium on foreign investment in Germany was removed, the head offices of American-owned multinational corporations gravitated to Frankfurt, partly because of its large and efficient international airport and partly because of the American governmental presence there, although the decisive element in that presence was shortly moved to Bonn.

The fragmentation of German financial (and political) areas and their reunification in West Germany reflect the U.S. political preoccupation with decentralization and the reality of the forces pushing in the direction of a single financial center. In the initial stages U.S. policy harbored, or at least fostered, the illusion that each of the ten *Länder* might have a central bank and a separate monetary policy. When the occupation forces were withdrawn, Land banks were quickly unified in a Bank Deutsche Länder, later transformed into the Bundesbank. The American effort at decentralization represented an idealistic (ideologic?), interesting, but futile experiment.

Italy—Turin, Florence, Rome, or Milan?

In her account of the rise of the New York money market, Myers states: "There occurred a separation between the political and financial capitals which is peculiar to America. In Europe the two are generally the same: London, Paris, Berlin are the seats both of government and of the money market."[130] Milan, Zurich, and Amsterdam attest to the fact that this is not always the case. As we shall see, moreover, the formation of the Italian financial center was more complex than this statement implies.

Italy, of course, had an ancient tradition in banking. Venice and Florence were banking centers in the Renaissance; Lombard Street in London was named after immigrant bankers from Milan and its surrounding area. In the late eighteenth century, when port cities were banking centers, Genoa, the capital of Liguria, was a flourishing trading town with a developed financial community. There was a smaller financial community down the coast at Leghorn. With its magnificent port, Naples was the commercial and financial center of the Kingdom of Two Sicilies, with the whole south of Italy as its hinterland. Its importance is indicated by the fact that the Rothschilds established a branch of their house there after the Napoleonic wars.

As the northern city-states lacked a substantial hinterland,[131] the small city-states declined, and Italy reached the middle of the nineteenth century without a substantial banking center in the north outside of Genoa. As late as 1844, Genovese were convinced that Turin could not become a banking center.[132] Attempts to create banks in Milan failed between 1821 and 1847, and Lombardy had to rely on capital imports from France during the period of seasonal financial stringency caused by silk.[133] With the unification of Italy in 1860 under the leadership of Count Cavour of Piedmont, Turin became the capital of Italy, and the banking center as well. Lombardy, which had been liberated by the Kingdom of Sardinia in the course of the unification struggle with Austria, held back from whole-hearted support of "Italy" and insisted on local autonomy. Rome and the papal states were not to be acquired until 1870.

The financial difficulties of the regime led to foreign borrowing and to the selling off of royal and church land. Rivalry developed in France between the Pereires and the Rothschilds over which could stake out a dominant position in Italy. Both were interested in banking and the finance of state and public works, largely railroads. Speculative fever in Paris stimulated the Crédit mobilier to found the Società Generale di Credito Mobiliare, and the Société de crédit industriel et commercial to start the Banca di Credito Italiano. The English ambassador joined the Ricasoli family of Florence to found the Banca Anglo-Italiana, again in Turin. In all, thirteen banks of ordinary credit (roughly equivalent to joint-stock banks in Britain or commercial banks in the United States) were founded in Turin from 1860 to 1866, including the notorious Banco Sconto e Sete (Bank of Discount and Silk). Elsewhere in the north there were three leading private banks in Genoa, four in Milan, and one in

Leghorn. In 1865 Florence became the capital. In 1866 de Boullay of Paris started a new bank in Florence, which sold American mortgages and shares in the tax collections of Lecce. It quickly suspended payments. The Credito Mobiliare, which for thirty years was to be the most important bank in Italy after the Banca Nazionale, the predecessor of the Bank of Italy, transferred its head office to Florence in 1865.[134]

Gerschenkron has ascribed the development of Italy after 1896 to the industrial investments of the Banca Commerciale Italiana and the Credito Italiano, which were founded with largely German funds.[135] The question inevitably arises why the Credito Mobiliare and the Banca di Credito Italiano did not produce the same result thirty years earlier. Cameron indicates that, if a banking system is to be effective, government must assure minimal conditions of both financial and political order and refrain from random ad hoc interference.[136] Cohen, who supports the Gerschenkron thesis for the end of the century,[137] explains the earlier failure by the poor development of financial institutions, their geographic limitation to the north and central parts of the country, and their general inefficiency.[138]

The banks of the 1860s were supported in 1871 and 1872 by a new wave of foreign banks, including the Banca Italo-Germanica, which started in Florence, moved to Rome, and developed branches in Naples, Milan, and later Trieste and Leghorn. This bank speculated unwisely and collapsed in 1874. Another with a similar experience was the Banca Austro-Italiana. Both names indicate that nationality was not a critical factor at this stage and that German banks as well as French banks could fail. Somewhat longer lived was the Banca Generale, founded in Rome in 1871 with Milanese and foreign capital.[139] Luzzatto comments that these bank failures were unimportant in an economy which was four-fifths agricultural and not integrated through cheap transport.[140] Losses were suffered mainly by foreign speculators, plus some Italians in Turin and Genoa, and, in minor measure, in Florence, Milan, and Leghorn.

Despite the abortive attempts to shift the financial center to Florence when it became the capital in 1865 and to Rome when the capital was finally established there in 1870, Piedmont and its capital, Turin, remained the financial center of the country from 1860 to 1890. The Banca Tiberina, which had close associations with the Banco Sconto e Sete, moved north from Rome in 1879 and maintained its legal seat in Turin until 1889.[141] Its purpose was to enlarge its capital for speculation in Roman real estate, and it sought capital not only from the Banco Sconto e Sete but also from the Banca Nazionale. In 1884 the Banca Napoletana was transformed with the help of the Banca Nazionale and new Genovese, Turin, and Swiss

capital into the Banca di Credito Meridionale for the purpose of investing
in Neapolitan real estate under the regulations of a law of the same
year.[142] The Credito Mobiliare seems to have moved back from Florence
to Turin to be in the action (although I find no explicit mention of a date)
and to have participated alongside the Banca Generale in lending to the
steel and shipbuilding complex at Terni, to railroads, and for housing,
especially in Rome. One of the six banks of issue, the Banca Romana was
also deeply involved in the financing of Roman expansion. The note circulation of the Banca Nazionale reached its limit in 1866 and the limit was
raised.[143] The Banca Tiberina began to fail and it was saved. Two matters
caused crisis to erupt—the tariff war with France in 1887, which pro-
voked the withdrawal of French capital, and the revelation that the Banca
Romana had violated its statutory note-issue limit, leading to a political
scandal. The result was the failure of the Credito Mobiliare and the Banca
Generale, the forced amalgamation of the seven banks of note issue
(including the Banca Nazionale and the Banca Romana) into the Bank of
Italy, and the collapse of Turin as the financial capital of Italy. The failure
of the Credito Mobiliare is sometimes ascribed to the death in 1885 of its
leader, Balduino. While he was alive, the bank's speculations were happy.
In his contemporary annual articles on Italian financial affairs, Pareto
blamed the failures on the fact that the banks engaged in affairs patron-
ized by the government; he advised the Banca Commerciale Italiana and
the Credito Italiano to refrain from such activity.[144] Under Balduino's
successor, Bassi, the Credito Mobiliare entered into building speculation
in Rome and Naples.[145] The Banca Generale lost heavily in Terni, in railroads (the Ferrovie Meridionale), in Milan, and in foreign investment.
Luzzatto notes that its Crédit mobilier-type operations were pursued from
the Rome head office, and that the Milan branch went in for strictly commercial banking.[146]

The wave of liquidation from 1887 to 1893 removed Turin from leadership and put Milan and Genoa ahead. The larger Lombard and Ligurian
banks built branches in Piedmont, including its capital, Turin, and Piedmont's depositors shifted their funds to them.[147] In the nineties the Banca
Commerciale Italiana was established in Milan; the Credito Italiano started
with its head office in Genoa and ultimately moved it to Milan.[148] The
former was purely German in origin, started by Bleichröder and the
Deutsche Bank. The latter took over the Milan remnant of the Banca
Generale and had German, Belgian, and Swiss stockholders. In 1898 a
Società Bancaria Milanese was started, was transformed into the firm

Weill-Schott Brothers and Co., and absorbed another private bank in Milan. It expanded rapidly in boom conditions, acquired the Banco Sconto e Sete in 1904, kept on expanding, and in 1907 was dominated by its Genovese group. The Bank of Italy supported it, being interested in developing a third large bank in Lombardy, in Liguria, and above all in Genoa. Bonelli notes that the bank lacked central direction, with its Milan office entirely unaware of the risks taken in Genoa.[149] When the international money market tightened in the crisis of 1907, the Società Bancaria Italiana, as it was now known, collapsed despite the efforts of Stringher of the Bank of Italy to save it. This left Milan as the undisputed financial center *in* Italy. The more interesting question is whether it was the financial center *of* Italy, that is, whether the Italian financial system was still unintegrated or had coalesced into a unified structure.

The critical questions in this abbreviated account of the geography of Italian banking from 1860 to the First World War are, Why was Rome not the financial center? If not Rome, why did Turin lose out to Milan? What role in the choice between Turin and Milan was played by the nationality of the foreign sources of capital and direction?

The reasons for the rejection of Rome seem evident. It became the capital late, it was badly located in relation to the productive parts of Italy, and its transport connections were poor. In no sense could it be called a metropolis with an economic hinterland for which it provided service. Rome, in fact, was a parasitical city. The church sucked income from the rest of Italy and the world, and the services it rendered in return were spiritual, and economically elusive. Savings were limited, the demand for capital for investment in housing very large. It was a sinkhole for capital, not a functioning pivot for allocating capital throughout the country.

The rise of Milan to pre-eminence over Turin has been attributed to the excesses and scandals of 1887 to 1893, the loss of prestige of France relative to Germany after 1871, the deep cleavage between France and Italy over the tariff agreement of 1887, and the political banking of Germany, with its Lombard connections. In my judgment, more cause should be attributed to the locational aspects. Turin got the jump on Milan with the Fréjus pass and the Mt. Cenis tunnel in 1870, the latter projected under Cavour in 1859 before unification. Cavour's policies concerning railroads, canals, and economic development generally gave the Kingdom of Sardinia (Piedmont and Sardinia) a head start in economic development, but easy access to France was a vital aspect. When the Gotthard tunnel was finished in 1882, the position of Piedmont was weakened and that of

Milan strengthened;[150] the completion of the Simplon tunnel in 1906 intensified the central character of Milan and the increasingly peripheral character of Piedmont.

A hypothesis emerging from this review is that Italian financial integration did not take place until 1893 and that it had an important role in the economic upsurge that occurred between then and World War I, much along the lines predicted by Shaw and McKinnon. Prior to that time the capital market was fragmented, despite a certain amount of branch banking, the active roles of the Banca Nazionale and the government, and the close connections of banks in Turin and Rome on a few investments (largely housing and such railroads as were left over by foreign investors). Such a hypothesis would explain why German Crédit mobilier-type banks succeeded in stimulating the Italian economy when French banks of the same character could not. Turin industry grew rapidly after 1893, but it was financed by the Banca Commerciale Italiano and the Credito Italiano, except for the automobile industry, which used the Turin bourse.[151] From 1860 to 1885 Italy, even central and northern Italy, was not an integrated financial market. When it became one, economic development spurted.

A Single Center in Switzerland?

Forty years ago Schwarzenbach made the case that Switzerland differed from France, England, and Holland in not having a single financial center but, rather, three: Zurich, Basel, and Geneva.

In contrast to other financial centers ... the money market in Switzerland is not concentrated in any one city. This fact is chiefly due to the political organization of Switzerland as a confederation of twenty-five states (cantons) which have wide powers of local government. As an outgrowth of territorial and historical factors, a strong individualism exists which is responsible for the lack of uniformity in the social and economic structure of the various states. Consequently there has developed no single preponderant business or financial center such as Paris in France, London in England, or Amsterdam in Holland.[152]

This statement was hardly true. Of the seven large commercial banks in being forty years ago, five had their largest office, if not the nominal head office, in Zurich and two in Basel;[155] of the seven stock exchanges, only Zurich, Basel, and Geneva were of any importance, and the Zurich turnover was from two to four times greater than that of Basel, with Geneva an also-ran.[154] Switzerland provides a classic case of the formation of a single financial center, since it started with many, of which Zurich was originally not particularly important compared with Geneva, Basel, Bern, or Winterthur. Zurich emerged as the financial center at the end of the nineteenth century, despite the connections and traditions of Geneva and Basel and the fact that the governmental seat was at Bern after confederation in 1848. Zurich's success can be ascribed to its focal location in the railroad age, especially after the building of the Gotthard tunnel, and to the pushiness of its bankers.

Geneva and Basel were old banking communities with long-established connections. Geneva's lines ran to Lyons, which had a great Swiss colony, the so-called *Nation suisse*,[155] and to Paris, where its Protestants mingled freely with the Huguenots and Jews of the *hautes banques* and the Bank of France. Many Parisian bankers had spent the Revolution and especially the Terror in Geneva, although others installed themselves in Zurich, Neuchâtel, Lausanne, or Winterthur.[156] With the return of peace, fifteen out of twenty-two hautes banques in Paris were said to be of Genevese origin.[157] The traditional names of Burchardt, Iselin, and Stahelin were long associated with Basel banking, lending to Switzerland generally but principally to Baden, as far north as Karlsruhe and Stuttgart, and to eastern France in competition with Paris, especially to Besançon, Mulhouse, Strasbourg, and Nancy.[158] Mulhouse was even called the daughter of Basel finance.[159]

Zurich had some tradition in foreign banking going back to 1750, but it was hardly a significant town one hundred years later. It was less important than Geneva or Basel and about on a par as an economic center with Winterthur, when it started its meteoric rise in 1850. Its population increased elevenfold between 1850 and 1910.[160] In World War I its position in the interior of the country, away from the belligerents' borders, resulted in the concentration there of international transactions.

Zurich's development can be illustrated by an account of the Union Bank of Switzerland, which was formed from an amalgamation in 1912 of the Bank of Winterthur, established in 1862, and the Toggenburger Bank, originally of Lichtensteig and later of St. Gallen in eastern Switzerland. The Bank of Winterthur started out bravely as a banque d'affaires in the boom of the 1860s, in discounts, industrial-security issuance, and railroad promotion. From the 1850s, Winterthur was connected by railroad with Zurich, Frauenfeld, Schaffhausen, and St. Gallen. The town fathers, proposing to make the city a center for storage and transshipment of goods, built a weighing house, a municipal granary, and a storage warehouse at the time they formed the Bank of Winterthur. By 1872 the bank was on a solid footing with a flourishing business throughout German Switzerland.

In 1873 the city embarked on a foolhardy scheme to build a "Swiss National Railway" in order to make Winterthur a link in the network running from Lake Constance to Lake Geneva, bypassing Zurich, Bern, and Lausanne. Part of the inspiration was pique against Zurich, the capital of the canton in which Winterthur was situated, and against Alfred Escher, "the strongest personality in economic and political life at the time,"[161] president of the Schweizerische Kreditanstalt, which he founded in 1856, president of the Northeastern Railroad, and later promoter of the Gotthard tunnel. The threat of Winterthur to Zurich and Escher was met by prompt and effective action by the Northeastern and Central railroads. The Swiss National Railway went bankrupt in 1878, and the city had to issue debt to make good its share of the loss when assets of the company in which 31 million Swiss francs had been invested were sold at auction to the Northeastern Railroad for less than 4 million.[162]

"If you can't lick them, join them." Already in the 1870s there had been a demand for the Bank of Winterthur to establish a foothold in the business center of Zurich. As Winterthur stagnated and Zurich flourished, the bank moved at the very end of the century to shift its center of gravity. In 1897 it acquired a participation in a Zurich banking and stockbrokerage firm, but this proved to be unsatisfactory and was given up in 1901. The bank then strove to overcome its prejudice against branches and in 1906 acquired the Bank of Baden's Zurich office, which had been established in the 1890s. Part of the stimulus was the rising strength of Escher's creation, the Swiss Credit Bank, growing with the city of Zurich, his success in railroading, and the threat of the Swiss Banking Corporation. The corporation, started in midcentury as a syndicate of private bankers calling itself the Bank Corporation, formed into a bank, the Basler Bankverein, in 1870. In 1895 it merged with the Zürcher Bankverein to form the Swiss Bank Corporation.[163] The Swiss Credit Bank and the Swiss Bank Corporation belonged to the "cartel of Swiss banks" formed in 1897 to place the loans of municipalities and cantons. The cartel excluded the Bank of Winterthur, which then formed a rival group. The Bank of Winterthur merged with the Toggensburger Bank of eastern Switzerland in 1912, started branching into French Switzerland in 1916, and went into Italian Switzerland in 1920. Its last penetrations into Basel and Bern occurred in 1920 and 1923.

A history of the bank, Union Bank of Switzerland, asserts that it was inevitable after the formation of the Zurich office that Zurich should become the heart and center of the institution. The "administrative offices" were kept in Winterthur and St. Gallen, and annual meetings of stockholders alternated between them from 1912 to 1945. There was one managing director for Winterthur and Zurich and one for Lichtensteig and St. Gallen; they acted alternately as chairman of the annual meeting. "Gradually the Toggensburger chairman for Lichtensteig and St. Gallen gave precedence to Winterthur, and after his death in 1921, the two-consul system fell into desuetude."[164] In World War I the foreign-exchange business of Zurich grew, and this encouraged the concentration of the Union Bank's commercial business in Zurich. Even before the war, that branch had been making rapid progress in the handling of its stockmarket and credit operations. A new building was completed in Zurich in 1917, and a year later the accounting department was moved there from Winterthur. From then on the board of directors held all its regular meetings in the Zurich building. In 1912 the management had comprised two ex-Winterthurers and two ex-Toggensburgers. One retired, and three new managers from Zurich were brought in, including the head manager, Paul Jaberg. Another death left the Zurich preponderance at three of five.[165]

Of further interest, the Swiss National Bank (the central bank, created in 1905 after a legislative proposal for its establishment had been rejected by referendum in 1894) has been domiciled in Bern since 1935, but effectively it is divided between Bern and Zurich. The seat of management is Zurich, and two of three departments are located there—discounts, foreign exchange, and secured loans in one, giro and auditing in the other. The third department in Bern deals with note issue, cash reserves, administration, and the fiscal agencies for the federal government and the federal railways.[166] This division of functions brings to Zurich all subjects that involve uncertainty and need for face-to-face communication (except those involving the federal government) and leaves routine questions— except possibly cash reserves—for another location.

There is a question today whether telex and the telephone have made Basel, Geneva, and Zurich one financial center, with no real distinction among them. Are the distances between Zurich and Basel and the language barrier, if one adds Geneva, so slight as to be negligible? I think not. Some American corporations, such as Investors Overseas Service, may have chosen Geneva because it has been a more international community than Zurich ever since the location there of the League of Nations in 1919. Moreover, the French-speaking atmosphere may be more attractive to international corporations than *Schwytzerdütsch* or even *schriften Deutsch*. But Zurich clearly dominates. The gnomes are the gnomes of Zurich, not of Switzerland. The location in Basel of the Bank for International Settlements—a 1930 decision dictated by the route of the railroad

—and in Geneva of the league and its successors, the Economic Commission for Europe and the European offices of the United Nations, keep those cities alive administratively and as banking centers. But Zurich is the focus.

Even had it not been for its traditional banking relations to France, Geneva would have held on to some (perhaps most) of its role as a distinct financial center because of the cultural differences between French- and German-speaking Switzerland. It is of interest to contemplate whether Geneva would have outstripped Zurich if *Suisse romande* had been larger and wealthier than the German-speaking parts. Lugano in a small way remains a separate financial community, linked to Italy by ease of communication as well as by language and separated from the rest of Switzerland by the Alps, however much tunneled. But Ticino is a very small proportion of total Switzerland. Geneva, the Vaud, Neuchâtel, and the other francophone portions are substantial both in numbers and economically. It is likely but not certain that cultural differences made for separation of financial functions.

Switzerland, I conclude, is not very different in financial agglomeration from other European cases. Tradition, the federal form of government, the seat of government in Bern, the international roles of Basel and Geneva, and the financial relations of those cities with particular hinterlands abroad, at least historically, were overwhelmed by the central location of Zurich at a crossroads. The crossroads was partly arbitrary and man-made, if we accept the Union Bank's account of the role of Escher, which I have not pursued in depth. Zurich benefited from the accident of World War I, which inhibited development of the two financial markets on the border; Geneva, with its relations with France, and Basel, connected to Germany exclusively after the loss by France of Alsace-Lorraine, may to some extent have neutralized each other. While there can be no doubt that Geneva and Basel are today closely connected with Zurich and with each other, Zurich is the financial capital of Switzerland, and an international money and capital market, though not the political capital, which is in Bern.

A final point: Measured by total assets, Zurich would stand out, but not so much as when measured by the assets of commercial or private banks. This is because of the large role of the cantonal banks, the first of which was established in Bern in 1834. Restricted to particular cantons, they do not move. Their total assets rose ahead of those of "discount banks" and "other banks" in the 1870s and by 1910 constituted four-fifths of the banking total.[167] But the cantonal banks put half their funds into mortgages, where the national market is less perfect than in bills of exchange, commercial loans, or stock-exchange securities. (In the 1960s, it took a difference of almost 2 full percentage points in savings-bank interest rates to move savings-bank funds from the East to the West Coast of the United States, indicating that in this capital market integration proceeds slowly.) The cantonal banks do not constitute so much an exception to these remarks as a different story.

Toronto vs Montreal in Canada

Initially, I intended to limit this exercise in comparative economic history to Europe, and thus to countries at broadly the same stage of development and with similar factor proportions. The more I considered Canada, however, the more I observed certain interesting and perhaps unique features. I therefore deal here with Canada, and later, as a companion piece, briefly with the United States.

Chartered banking in Canada began after the Napoleonic wars. The Bank of Montreal opened its doors in 1817 without a charter. The first chartered bank, according to Neufeld, was the Bank of New Brunswick, opened in 1820.[168] The centenary volume of the Bank of Montreal claims 1821 as the date for its charter, but royal assent was not received until 1822, putting the bank two years behind its New Brunswick neighbor.[169] Then quickly followed the formation of the Quebec Bank, the Bank of Canada (not the central bank started in 1936, but a Montreal bank established by American citizens), and the Bank of Upper Canada.

With a large Scottish population, initial Canadian practice followed the Scottish tradition of branch banking rather than the English, and the Bank of Montreal opened agencies in Quebec, Kingston, and York in the first year, 1817. Kingston and York (now Toronto) were in Upper Canada (now Ontario), so that the tension between Montreal and Toronto, or between the provinces of Quebec and Ontario, may be said to have started early. In the same year the Bank of Canada founded an agency in Kingston. The Bank of Montreal opened an agency in New York in 1853, the first such agency and one of only two as late as 1870.[170] The Bank of British North America was organized in London in 1836 and within a year opened branches in Toronto, Montreal, Quebec, St. John, Halifax, and St. John's, Newfoundland.[171]

While Montreal handled the export of furs and the import of general merchandise, Nova Scotia throve on shipbuilding from as early as 1761 to 1874, when wooden ships lost out to ironclads. The major banks in Nova

Scotia were the Halifax Banking Company, formed in 1825 from Collins, an earlier private bank; the Bank of Nova Scotia, organized in 1832 as a counterweight to the monopoly of the Halifax; and the Merchants Bank of Halifax (later the Royal Bank of Canada), proposed during the Civil War, when shipbuilding had its last expansion. The two largest firms, heavily indebted to the Merchants Bank, passed into receivership in 1885. The Merchants Bank "now realized that if enterprises of national importance were to be financed, the bank must become national in scope, with [sufficient] capital and reserves that its position could not be shaken by local losses."[172] The bank resolved in that year to extend its operations to Montreal and, after establishing a branch there, opened agencies in the east and west of the city.[173] In twelve years, the focus of the bank had shifted from Halifax to Montreal. In 1898 Duncan of the Halifax branch ceased to be in sole command of the bank, though he remained for one more year in charge of the head office in Halifax and the branches in the Maritimes and Newfoundland. With the upsurge of business the Montreal manager, Pease, was made general manager; the name was changed from the Merchants Bank of Halifax to the Royal Bank of Canada; branches were opened as far away as Vancouver; and some 5,000 new shares of $250 par were sold to prominent Americans. At the annual meeting of 1906 it was proposed to change the head office from Halifax to Montreal, "the natural center for expansion." This was accomplished the following year.[174]

The decision of the Bank of Nova Scotia took place more slowly. Again, a personnel change was the occasion:

One of the first important decisions made by the new general manager—a title which replaced the old Scotch form of "cashier" in 1898—was the removal of the Bank's executive office from Halifax to Toronto in March, 1900. The change was a natural outcome of the westward turn of events which followed closely on the linking of far-flung provinces by the Canadian Pacific and other railway systems and was a necessary step if the Bank were to play a leading role in the new prosperity and economy of the twentieth century. Many of its Maritime customers had already become dominion-wide concerns, and important connections which it had established in Ontario, Quebec and Winnipeg, necessitated banking facilities free from the delay attendant upon correspondence between these points and Halifax. It is a matter of pride to the citizens of Nova Scotia that the Bank still retains its head office in Halifax, and that year by year the shareholders meet on the fourth Wednesday in January in the Maritime home of their institution—now a splendid new building completed last year and fittingly used for the first time by the directors and shareholders at the hundredth annual meeting in January, 1932.[175]

At almost exactly the same time, in 1899, Max Aitken (later Lord Beaverbrook) became secretary to a Halifax firm at the age of twenty. He arranged a merger between the Commercial Bank of Windsor and the Union Bank of Halifax, which presumably transferred the focus of that bank's operations from Nova Scotia to Ontario. Later, he formed an investment concern, Royal Securities, in Halifax, which operated in new ventures, mergers, reorganizations, and the like. This was moved from Halifax to Montreal in 1906.[176]

Puzzling in the foregoing is the lack of a single magnet: Montreal, Toronto, Windsor, and again Montreal. It is tempting to say that Montreal was the attraction in 1887 when the Merchants Bank of Halifax (Royal Bank of Canada) made its decision, and delay in the case of the Bank of Nova Scotia produced a different choice because of developments between 1887 and 1900. Moreover, the choice of Windsor in 1899 is odd unless the Commercial Bank was Aitken's second or third choice for merger with the Union Bank. But then why Montreal again in 1906? And why, once the Royal Bank had established itself in Montreal and Toronto outstripped it—a supposition we are about to examine—why did not the Royal Bank or the Bank of Montreal move to Toronto? The Bank of Montreal declined relative to the Canadian Imperial Bank of Commerce, located in Toronto,[177] but presumably not enough to warrant the expense and wrench of transferring to the livelier site.

The decline of Halifax as an early financial center needs no further explanation, but the drawn-out resolution of the competition between Toronto and Montreal is perplexing. Toronto started to compete with Montreal in the 1850s, was beaten back in the 1860s when a financial crisis followed the end of the Civil War in the United States, and then began a long rise to rival status. With the western boom and the wave of British investment in Canada after 1896, Toronto gained further, even though much of the capital from London was handled through Montreal. After World War I, there were still further gains for Toronto but no clear-cut ascendancy. Toronto continued to gain and ultimately surpassed Montreal as a financial center, but the latter did not give way, as had Cologne, nineteenth-century Frankfurt, Lyons, Turin, Philadelphia, Baltimore, and Boston. The money market in Canada is said to be centered in "Toronto and Montreal," or reference is made to the interest differential between New York and "Montreal-Toronto."[178] The Royal Commission on Banking and Finance refers to foreign-exchange brokers of Montreal and Toronto, or to the dealer inventories of the secondary security market as "concentrated in Montreal and Toronto."[179] The Bank of Montreal and the Royal Bank retain their offices in Montreal, whereas the three smaller but faster-growing (till 1960) chartered banks—the Canadian Imperial Bank of Commerce, the Bank of Nova Scotia, and the Toronto-Dominion Bank—are headquartered in Toronto.[180] Since 1960 the Bank of Montreal and the Royal Bank have grown in total assets relative to the Toronto three, but with regard to security deals, the Royal Commission in 1964 observed:

The main volume of business has remained concentrated in Montreal and Toronto with the latter tending to grow in relative importance in response to the westward shift of Canadian economic activity and the replacement of overseas countries by the United States as the primary source of external capital.[181]

Yet Montreal is as close to New York as is Toronto and should not have suffered when New York replaced London as the source of overseas investment in stocks and bonds issued by Canadian entities.

Let us leave aside the question of whether Montreal or Toronto is the more important money and capital market for this or that financial instrument. The more interesting question is whether Toronto is emerging as the single financial center of Canada by a process drawn out at much greater length than in other countries, or whether the two centers have been stabilized in an exceptional cooperative relationship. In 1947 Masters wrote, "Rivals, their capital structures became and remained closely linked."[182] This has been the standard view until very recently. It now appears, however, that Toronto has overtaken and surpassed Montreal. So drawn out is the process, however, that Montreal banks seem to be under no pressure to move their head offices or their major money-market or foreign-exchange activities to the Ontario financial capital. The diseconomies of disarticulation are, in some inexplicable way, not very pressing.[183]

Gras distinguishes four stages—commerce, industry, transport, and finance—through which a town must pass en route to becoming a metropolis.[184] For the early period during which Toronto came out from under the shadow of Montreal, we are fortunate in having a history that explicitly uses Gras's model. Masters' study is focused on the period from 1850 to 1890, when Toronto triumphed over its other rivals and emerged as the dominant financial center of the province.[185] Along the way, there was a continuous struggle with Montreal, a struggle marked by the desire to avoid financial domination by New York.[186] The major episodes in that struggle were construction of the Grand Trunk railroad and the early Welland and St. Lawrence canals; transfer of the government account from the Bank of Upper Canada in Kingston to the Bank of Montreal in 1864; the failure of the former in 1866; the determination of E. H. King, general manager of the Bank of Montreal, to pattern banking legislation after the National Bank Act in the United States, shifting from branch to unit banking to keep ahead of challenging banks and requiring banks of issue to hold government debt, thus relieving the Bank of Montreal; and the struggle over the Canadian Pacific Railway terminus in the 1870s. The details are perhaps too complex for a non-Canadian readership. The central point is that in the 1860s Ontario was alarmed at the growing strength and dominance of the Bank of Montreal, which it believed to be draining loanable capital from Ontario to Montreal.[187] Determined to resist this development, Ontario made political efforts to bring transportation routes to and through Toronto, created and fostered banks such as the Bank of Commerce in 1866 and the Dominion Bank in 1870, and influenced banking legislation.[188] Toronto's population rose from 45,000 in 1861 to 210,000 by 1901, while Montreal's grew from 90,000 to 270,000. Thereafter, as money and migrants poured westward, Toronto continued to gain on Montreal, but not so much as to crush it as a financial center.

Several factors account for the rise of Toronto as a rival of Montreal in addition to the transport system, the development of the west, and policy initiatives by Torontonians. One is the shift of investment from railroads to mining. St. James Street in Montreal specialized in railroad securities, while Toronto specialized in mining stocks. In manufacturing, moreover, Montreal tends to have older industries: clothing, textiles, food and tobacco products, and railway equipment, as well as machinery and aircraft, whereas the Golden Horseshoe from Niagara to Toronto and around the western end of Lake Erie, the Torontonian hinterland, specializes in flour milling (old), steel, automobiles, agricultural implements, and electrochemical and electrometallurgical industries based on Niagara power.[189] Casual empiricism suggests that the income elasticity of Ontario's industry outweighs that of Quebec.

Another factor is the change in the source of external capital from Britain to the United States. Britain's gateway to Canada was naturally Montreal. New York had the choice of going up the Hudson all the way or turning west via the Erie Canal. Direct investment, however, strongly favored Toronto. Table 11.1, showing employment percentages in Canadian-, U.S.- and U.K.-owned firms in Canada indicates sharp differences by province. There is, of course, no assurance that the location of production facilities governs the location of head offices of investing

Table 11.1
Manufacturing employment in selected provinces of Canada, by nationality of control of firms, 1961 (percent of total).

	Canadian	United States	United Kingdom
Atlantic provinces	78.67	6.05	15.15
Quebec	75.95	16.84	6.35
Ontario	62.39	30.71	6.10
Canada	70.48	22.54	6.16

Source: Ray, "Regional Aspects of Foreign Ownership," p. 49.

companies, which in turn have an effect on the location of financial facilities. United States corporations could locate production facilities in Ontario but have Canadian corporate headquarters in Montreal, in communication with the U.S. head office in New York, but this pattern is unlikely. With New York virtually equidistant from Montreal and Toronto, it makes sense for companies such as General Motors, whose production facilities are in the Middle West and whose finance is in New York, to choose Toronto over Montreal in the interest of efficient communication between U.S. headquarters and Canadian production. Where a U.S. company has only a single factory in Canada, moreover, head office and plant are probably located together. Toronto may also be favored by U.S. businessmen because of the identity of language and the similarity of culture.

But what must be explained is less the rise of Toronto than the lack of greater decline of Montreal until the 1970s. Part of the explanation may lie in governmental policy, which urged the two main banks to keep their head offices in Montreal. Unlike the central bank's position in England, France, Germany, or Switzerland, but similar to that of the Bank of Italy in Rome, the Bank of Canada remains in the capital, Ottawa, where it was established in 1935. Ottawa is located in Ontario, but on the Quebec border. The Porter Commission notes that until recently the bank's senior personnel "have made only infrequent visits to the financial centers of Toronto and Montreal," and that visits of financial people to Ottawa, while always welcome, are made only for some specific purpose or complaint and do not provide the "frequency of contact needed."[190] The remark is addressed to the question of the efficient functioning of Canadian financial machinery, which requires frequent face-to-face contact among governmental and private financial decision makers. There are recent indications that the diffidence between central and commercial bankers noted by the Porter Commission has diminished or disappeared. It is perhaps

Table 11.2
Selected data for indicated metropolitan centers[a] in Canada, about 1961 (percent of Canadian total).

	Montreal	Toronto	Vancouver	Next ranking city
Population (1961)	11.6	10.0	4.3	2.6 (Winnipeg)
Population (1966)	12.2	10.7	4.4	2.5 (Winnipeg)
Service receipts and retail sales	13.4	13.8	5.4	3.1 (Winnipeg)
Value added in manufacturing	17.9	19.8	4.0	5.3 (Hamilton)
Checks cleared at clearinghouses	26.8	37.3	6.0	7.1 (Winnipeg)
Income tax paid	12.7	19.0	6.1	3.6 (Winnipeg)
Assets of leading corporations	38.1	36.7	6.3	5.0 (Calgary)
Value of stock-market transactions	26.3	67.1	6.3	0.2 (Calgary)
Domestic airline passenger traffic[b]	17.6	23.3	10.9	6.6 (Edmonton)

Source: Kerr, "Geography of Finance in Canada," tables 16-1 to 16-6, 16-8.
[a]Metropolitan census areas.
[b]Leading airports outbound plus inbound (1965).

going too far to read into the discussion a hint that the Bank of Canada remains in Ottawa because it is unable or unwilling (given the bicultural nature of the dominion) to choose between Toronto and Montreal.

Canada is one of the few countries where geographers as well as historians have studied metropolitan development, using the Gras model. Geographers, along with economists, are surprised that relations between Toronto and Montreal have for so long been complementary rather than competitive, and that the country fails to conform to the model of metropolitan primacy. In population the ratio of the largest to the next largest city is 1.2 in Canada, compared with 2.3 in the United States and 7.5 in France.[191] Almost 350 miles apart, Toronto and Montreal overwhelm the rest of Canada but not each other, as table 11.2 shows. Financial concentration reaches more than 90 percent in the two cities in stock-market activity, and here Toronto is far ahead. In all else, it has been a draw.

Geographic analysis throws more light on the separate claims of Toronto and Montreal to metropolitan supremacy by comparing the inbound and outbound passenger traffic of the two cities with that of other major Canadian cities. The nul hypothesis is that such traffic will conform to the gravity model, in which predicted traffic between any two cities is

Table 11.3
Pairs of cities with high positive and negative residuals.[a]

High positive residuals in descending order of importance	High negative residuals in descending order of importance
Toronto—Vancouver	London—Windsor
St. John's—Halifax	Sudbury—Quebec
Toronto—Winnipeg	Sudbury—St. John's
Toronto—Calgary	Sudbury—Fort William
Toronto—Edmonton	Sudbury—Regina
Toronto—Halifax	Sudbury—Ottawa
Toronto—St. John's	Sudbury—Montreal
Vancouver—Winnipeg	Sudbury—Edmonton
Vancouver—Montreal	Ottawa—Montreal
Vancouver—Ottawa	Moncton—St. John's

Source: Kerr, "Metropolitan Dominance in Canada," table 16-11.
[a]Calculated by relating airline passenger traffic of the cities to the product of their populations divided by the square of the distance between them.

some constant times the product of the two populations divided by the square of the distance between them. The model predicts well for most pairs,[192] but high residuals—positive and negative—have significance (see table 11.3). The residuals suggest that Toronto has particularly close relations with distant cities, and that Sudbury, a large mining town, has limited relations with the cities nearby, presumably because it is specialized and because it deals with the world through Toronto. It is equally of interest that St. John's and Halifax have heavy interaction in the provinces, probably because they are so removed from other centers, whereas London and Windsor, both important manufacturing towns, deal little with each other, presumably because their relations go through Toronto. Airplane traffic is not as useful an index of financial interaction as check clearings would be, but it throws an oblique light on the phenomenon.

The centripetal tendencies in Canada, then, are less forceful and much slower than those observed in Europe.[193] Canada first detached its monetary and capital relations from London and turned them toward New York. Montreal balanced between London and New York. Toronto then rose to assert independence from Montreal, with some duality: "One group of finance capitalists were to continue to shuttle back and forth between Toronto and Montreal, while others, including mining men, were to be just as solicitous in cultivating the New York market."[194] The dominion built up "Toronto-Montreal" as a counterweight to New York, fostering a market in Treasury bills in the 1950s and a day-loan market, which enabled the Bank of Canada to control the money supply by internal operations rather than resort to New York funds.

In the same fashion, under the leadership of the Bank of British Columbia, Vancouver has set out to build its own money and capital market; in its foreign-exchange operations, it deals in U.S. dollars directly with banks in Seattle, San Francisco, and Los Angeles, rather than through Toronto-Montreal.[195] One reason, of course, is the difference in time zone, and distance (that is, the cost of wire services) may be another. It is paradoxical, except perhaps in terms of differences in rates of growth, that Canadian banks should abandon one coast—Nova Scotia—and cultivate the other.

The arguments for and against regional financial independence are summed up in a sentence from the Porter report apropos of stock markets, but applicable in general to money and capital markets:

While a single national exchange would concentrate all trading, cause the markets to be broader and more resilient and might reduce trading costs per unit, it would fail to take account of the country's significant regional variety and of the need of local exchanges to provide a center for the shares of smaller and less nationally-known companies.[196]

Contrast this with the remark quoted earlier from the Royal Bank's fiftieth anniversary celebration volume that if "enterprises of national importance were to be financed, the bank must become national in scope, with [sufficient] capital and reserves that its position could not be shaken by local losses."[197]

New York as the Financial Center of the United States

The rise of New York as the financial center of the United States, winning out initially over Boston, Philadelphia, and Baltimore in the first quarter of the nineteenth century, and beating back, so to speak, later challenges from Chicago and St. Louis, is sufficiently familiar that it need not occupy us for long. It is, moreover, well chronicled in Albion,[198] Gras,[199] and Myers[200] and has been more recently analyzed in Robbins and Terleckyj.[201] Of the financial dominance of New York since 1825 there is no doubt. The remarkable feature is that it was maintained despite persistent attempts to defeat it—from the early efforts of rival cities, the Second Bank of the United States in Philadelphia, and the National Bank Act of 1863 to the attempt embodied in the Federal Reserve Act of 1913. Economies of scale in money and finance proved stronger than the institutional enactments against them.

Prior to the end of the Napoleonic wars, there was no clear ascendancy of one North Atlantic American port over the others. Each had its hinterland. After 1815, well before the completion of the Erie Canal, New York took steps to pull ahead. British supplies accumulated during the war were dumped there. When commission merchants threatened to hold them back for higher prices, New York enacted an auction law that made all sales final and forbade withdrawing goods once offered for sale. Jobbers, wholesalers, and country merchants flocked to the port. In 1818 a New York merchant started the first liner service, by sailing packet to Liverpool; a ship left promptly on schedule whether it had a full cargo or not. These actions created a demand for sterling. To provide a supply, merchants, shippers, and bankers—at that time indistinguishable from one another—sought the financing of cotton and grain. Planters, always needing to buy more land and slaves, were continuously in debt. New York bankers advanced them funds to ensure that cotton bound for Liverpool from New Orleans, Mobile, Savannah, or Charleston would be shipped coastwise to New York and then across, a diversion of 200 miles which after 1850 proved physically unnecessary. The Erie Canal, projected in 1818, was finished in 1825. That same year New York bankers advanced a large loan to the state of Ohio to divert the grain trade from the Ohio and Mississippi rivers to the canal and New York.[202] Baltimore was slow in building the Chesapeake and Ohio Canal. It was still under construction when the opportunity came to build the Baltimore and Ohio Railroad. Philadelphia tried to meet the competition with the Main Line Railroad, built between 1827 and 1837. But this route was clumsy and inefficient. It ran by rail from the city to the Susquehanna River and by boat to the Alleghenies, with produce hauled over the mountains by stationary engine. By 1842 Boston had tunneled the Berkshires with the Boston and Albany Railroad but still had to rely on the Erie Canal for western produce. Supplementing the canal by the New York Central on a water-level route, New York stayed ahead.[203] When Andrew Jackson destroyed Philadelphia's Second Bank of the United States in 1836, New York's position was assured.

A good illustration of the pull to New York is the experience of Alexander Brown and Sons of Baltimore. The father came to the United States from Ulster in 1800, opened an Irish-linen warehouse in Baltimore in that year, and distributed bulky goods through Maryland and Virginia. He took William, one of his four sons, into partnership in Baltimore in 1805, sought to open a branch in Philadelphia in 1806 and again in 1809, but succeeded through his son John only in 1818. By this time William was in Liverpool, and Liverpool and Philadelphia had outstripped Baltimore. By 1825 it was clear that New York was the most interesting center, and in that year son James opened Brown Brothers & Co., primarily to promote the interests of the Liverpool house, William and James Brown & Co. While Baltimore remained the head of the family enterprises until Alexander's death in 1834, for the last years of his life the backbone of the commission business was the sale in New York or shipment to Liverpool of the cotton sent by southern correspondents. The first New York circular of Brown Brothers & Co. in 1825 indicated correspondents in New Orleans, Mobile, Charleston, Savannah, and Huntsville.[204]

Others to desert Baltimore were George W. Peabody, Elisha Riggs, and William W. Corcoran. Peabody, originally from Boston, teamed up with Riggs to serve as London commission agent. The American end of Peabody and Riggs moved to New York in the late 1830s and subsequently broke up, with Peabody founding in London the firm that later developed into J. P. Morgan & Co.[205] Riggs then went into the securities business with Corcoran and at some stage, probably at the time of the Mexican War, both moved to Washington to deal in U.S. securities. Here is the direct pull of the capital. Note, however, that neither made an optimal choice in terms of maximizing wealth; the Riggs Bank and the Corcoran securities business, while profitable, remained small compared with New York operations.

New York attracted people as well as goods and money. Most came from Connecticut and Massachusetts (south of Cape Cod and west of Worcester, beyond which the pull of Boston dominated), with few, apart from the Stevens family, from New Jersey. New Englanders captured the New York port about 1820 and dominated its business until after the Civil War.[206] The analogue is with the Scots in banking and accounting in London. While I have no definitive explanation for the divergent behavior of New Jersey and Connecticut, the answer is likely to be found in the different character of the soil, flat and relatively rich on the one hand, hilly and rocky on the other.

As New York became the financial center of the country, the practice developed of maintaining bankers' balances in the city. A substantial seasonal movement had to be handled. New York funds were built up during the harvest and movement of crops and drawn down during the rest of the year. New York funds bore a premium exchange rate over those in Philadelphia and other centers, a fact that was resented by other parts of the country. Measures were taken by states to prevent the drain of funds to New York; for example, Connecticut in 1848 required a minimum reserve of 10 percent in vault cash, in 1854 prohibited lending out of state more than one-quarter of a bank's capital and surplus, and required that loans be made within the state up to the amount of capital and surplus before any could be loaned outside. None of these devices proved effective. Country banks found New York paper and deposits among the safest and most reliable investments. As in England, provision was made in New York State for the redemption of notes issued by country banks either at their seats or in New York, Troy, or Albany, a further incentive to build up New York balances.[207] The city served as an intermediary between Europe and the south and west, and balanced the country movement of cash on a seasonal basis as well.

The National Bank Act of 1863 furnished legal recognition of the New York banks' role as the ultimate banking reserve of the country. The original legislation provided that country banks could keep as little as two-fifths of the mandatory 25 percent reserve in vault cash and deposit the remainder in a national bank in one of eight cities: Boston, Providence, New York, Philadelphia, Cincinnati, New Orleans, Chicago, and St. Louis. Banks in the eight cities had to hold their entire reserve in currency. This was hard on the reserve cities outside New York; they normally kept funds in New York, but now had to hold only currency reserves. Revision of the law in 1864 provided for eighteen "redemption cities," enlarged from the previous list, and allowed banks in those cities to keep half their 25 percent reserve in New York. "Country banks" were permitted to maintain two-fifths in deposits in a national bank in any redemption city. In effect, New York was a central reserve city and the other seventeen were reserve cities.[208]

In 1887 the legislation was amended again to permit any city of more than 200,000 inhabitants to become a central reserve city. Chicago and St. Louis accepted, "determined to wrest from New York its prestige and financial preeminence."[209] St. Louis complained to little avail that merchants making payments to other cities bought drafts on New York rather than sending checks on St. Louis banks.[210] Bank balances rose rapidly in the two cities, but those in New York did not slow down. Chicago and St. Louis attracted deposits from their areas, but cities even farther west and farther south kept correspondent balances in New York.

The Federal Reserve Act of 1913 represented an extension of resistance to the financial domination of New York. Gras in 1922 said it "struck a heavy but not a death blow."[211] The statement seems exaggerated even for its time. New York remained the leading financial center, unchallenged by the eleven places chosen as regional centers for the other districts. Because branch banking was permitted in California, individual institutions like the Bank of America grew to be among the largest in the country, though the New York State requirement of unit banking failed to prevent New York banks from dominating the country in size and number.

The Federal Reserve Act was based on the theory that regional money and capital markets would develop around the locations of the twelve district banks. The act implicitly contemplated separate monetary policies for the twelve districts. A structure of rates developed, the lowest rates being charged customers in New York, for example, with higher rates as size of city decreased and as one moved from north and east to south and west.[212] Fluctuations in the rate were wider in New York than in the outlying portions of the market.[213] But there was only one money market and only one monetary policy, focused on New York. Discount and open-market policies were unified. New York's facilities were more specialized, more competitive, and more available to other regions. Half the loans of New York City's banks were for borrowers outside the city, as contrasted with 8.2 percent for Chicago, 7.8 percent for Dallas, and 6.3 percent for San Francisco—the three nearest competitors.[214] New York was also the center for international finance.

Here is a clear example of economies of scale. The financial center was a port, but the connection of finance to ports had diminished. It was neither an administrative capital nor a central location. Its dominance continued in spite of the strong resistance implicit in populism, in spite of political steps to reduce its role, in spite of New York's own insistence on unit rather than branch banking, and in spite of efforts to create other financial centers by legislation.

The 1959 move of the head office of the First National City Bank from Wall Street to a midtown location on Park Avenue raised a series of new questions. Have the economies of centralization been exaggerated, or is modern communication reducing them? Is propinquity to corporate head offices for bank decision makers more important than ready access to other banks, law offices, and financial markets for Treasury bills, foreign exchange, commercial paper, stocks, bonds, and the like? The bank left the bulk of its check handing in downtown Manhattan, close to the other banks and the clearinghouse but far from headquarters. It was understood that this would create some problems. In London, City banks acquired West End banks (by merger rather than by building new branches in competition with existing institutions) to serve the convenience of nonfinancial clients. In New York, the same forces threatened to reverse the centralization process.

International Financial Centers

The same concentration that produces a single dominant financial center within a country (with the possible exception of Canada) tends to result in the emergence of a single worldwide center with the highly specialized functions of lending abroad and serving as a clearinghouse for payments among countries. Banks, brokers, security dealers, and the like establish branches in such centers. The process is similar to that which takes place within a country, although the barriers of exchange risk and higher transaction costs prevent it from being carried as far.

Court, merchant, and security banking spread internationally, as it did within countries, by the process of branching. Originally these functions were usually performed by large families of male members. The court banking performed by the five Rothschild brothers moved out after the Napoleonic wars to Vienna, Frankfurt, Naples, Paris, and London. Alexander Brown used his four sons to extend his merchant banking business from Baltimore to Philadelphia, New York, Boston, and Liverpool. (It has been suggested that one of the reasons for extending Alexander Brown and Sons in space, apart from efficiency, was that Alexander found it difficult to live near his most dynamic son, William.)[215] Early American bankers in France, such as Welles and Greene, who were associated with Welles cousins in Boston, went to Paris and Le Havre in 1817, and Fitch and Co. of New York established a branch with a brother in Marseille in the 1830s.[216] In the early 1860s, the eight Seligmann brothers went from New York and San Francisco to Frankfurt, Paris, and London (the central financial capitals rather than the ports) and to Amsterdam and New Orleans, largely to sell U.S. securities.[217] The Philadelphia banker Drexel, who had moved there in 1837 after dealing in foreign exchange in Louisville, Kentucky, had three sons. One of them, Joseph William Drexel, set up an allied firm in Paris in 1867. He teamed up with J. P. Morgan in New York in 1871 to provide a network for selling U.S. securities in Europe in close coopertion with his brothers in Philadelphia.[218]

It is not entirely clear that there was a dominant financial center in Europe prior to 1870. It seems doubtful that the economies of scale had extended far enough that one center existed. American banks went to London, Liverpool, Paris, and Marseille. London bankers established themselves in Paris, and Baring Brothers teamed up with Hope and Co. of Amsterdam. Prussia placed loans abroad in Hamburg, Frankfurt, Kassel, Leipzig, Amsterdam, and Genoa in the 1790s.[219] By 1820 it was borrowing in Amsterdam on foreign issues, and in Frankfurt on domestic; Amsterdam was the first trading city on the Continent for public loans— Prussian, Austrian, and Russian. Interest rates differed widely among financial centers.[220]

British foreign lending at short term was stimulated by the usury laws of 1571, which limited interest charged to a stipulated rate that successively declined from an original 10 percent to 8 percent in 1623, 6 percent in 1660, and finally 5 percent in 1713, until their repeal in 1854. Akin to the interest ceilings of Regulation Q in the United States (which did not apply to foreign time deposits, allowed foreign banks to earn high interest rates in New York, and enabled them to bid for dollar deposits, thus stimulating the movement of funds to the Eurodollar market in the late 1950s), acceptances on foreign bills permitted charging commissions as well as interest, thereby avoiding the usury laws, as some domestic borrowers complained.[221] By the time the usury laws were eliminated, this man-made distortion no longer had importance in stimulating the flow of British capital abroad, inasmuch as British savings exceeded domestic demand at going rates of interest and the efficiency of the London market kept transaction costs low.

By the mid-1820s Britain was a substantial exporter of capital on long-term account. In one view, Britain had a monopoly of capital exports until 1850, when France moved in, largely for *la gloire* (that is, capital exports in the service of national policies).[222] This view is not universally shared. Crick and Wadsworth express an opposite opinion:

During the early years of the 19th century, Paris had held pride of place as the principal international banking center, but subsequently London steadily overtook her.... After suspension of specie payments by the Bank of France in 1848, London banks became busier in international affairs, with more and more bills domiciled in London.[223]

Both statements seem insufficiently qualified. As Cameron has shown, French bankers experimented with international lending in the 1830s and 1840s but came into their own in foreign issues in the 1850s and 1860s, led by the Crédit mobilier and the Rothschild Paris house, which transferred their intense domestic rivalry to the international arena.[224] Whether London or Paris was the leader in the second quarter of the century, the role was contested during the twenty years after 1850, and Paris finally lost out:

All great communities have at times to pay large sums in cash, and of that cash a great store must be kept somewhere. Formerly there were two great stores in Europe, one was the Bank of France and one was the Bank of England. But since the suspension of specie payments by the Bank of France [in the war of 1870] its use as a reservoir of specie is at an end.... Accordingly London has become the sole great settling house of exchange transactions in Europe, instead of being formerly one of two. And this preeminence London will probably retain for it is a natural preeminence. The number of mercantile bills incalculably surpasses those drawn on any other city.... The pre-eminence of Paris partly rose from a distribution of political power.[225]

Even this statement, written immediately after the events of 1871 and 1872, is put too strongly. London emerged as the undisputed leader in international finance after 1873, especially outside the Continent, but Paris was by no means completely in the shadow.

The pivotal role of London was enhanced by the part it played in transferring the Franco-Prussian indemnity. The new German government ended up with substantial claims in sterling, which, along with the Vienna stock-market crash, helped to precipitate the Great Depression.[226]

Whether London focused so heavily on foreign lending that it neglected the provision of finance to domestic industry is a familiar issue, incapable of a clearcut answer. The presumption is that it did not. Numerous industries required large amounts of capital: for a long time, railroads; then shipping, iron and steel, cotton, banking, and finance; later coal, public utilities, and communications. The London Stock Exchange was responsive to the capital needs of these industries.[227] In addition, private companies went public in manufacturing and such profitable enterprises as brewing. Investors wanting trustee securities lost their taste for industrial shares and preferred foreign railroad and government bonds.[228] On the whole, however, domestic and foreign lending are complements, not substitutes, even though in the British case they were cyclically opposed.

After 1870 France did not contest British financial leadership. On the contrary, on such occasions as the Baring crisis of 1890 (when the London market was threatened with panic because of the failure of the major bank, Baring Brothers, which was deeply involved in speculation in Argentine land bonds), France supported London with a gold loan from the Bank of France to the Bank of England. While the apex of the financial system of the world was London, foreign balances were also maintained by central banks in Paris and Berlin, like provincial cities in a national system.

Germany's attempt at resistance, led by the Deutsche Bank, and its failure have been detailed earlier in this chapter. Hamburg was prepared to challenge London's pre-eminence in shipping and to support the German program of naval construction,[229] but not to contest the financial position of London. It had a special place in financing German trade and in providing a market for northern securities,[230] but it was too provincial vis-à-vis Berlin in domestic matters and vis-à-vis London in international ones. While the Deutsche Bank, with a few others, opened a branch in London, it contested British financial hegemony mainly in the narrow arena of the Ottoman empire, or took on the Italian clients of the weakened French.

New York's challenge to the dominance of London has been traced back to 1900. In his report for 1904 the U.S. Comptroller of the Currency recommended that national banks with more than $1 million of capital be allowed to accept bills of exchange and establish foreign branches. In the panic of 1907 American banks borrowed more than $100 million from Europe to overcome the inelasticity of the money supply. As a result, Abrahams states, it became clear that the American economy had grown too large to be carried by Europe and that an American solution was necessary.[231]

As in 1870, however, it was war that turned positions sharply. J. P. Morgan & Co. provided an early credit to the French government against gold deposited in the vault of the Morgan, Harjes bank in Paris. In 1916 three leading American banks, the Guaranty Trust, the Bankers Trust, and J. P. Morgan, organized a syndicate under which 175 American banks made loans under acceptance credits to 75 French firms. During World War I a number of commercial-bank branches that had been opened in France and Britain in the early years of the century were expanded and new ones were established, to serve both governmental finance and industry, but especially to handle monies for the U.S. Army.

Further branches were organized after the war in a massive expansion, which subsided after the 1920 boom. H. Parker Willis, in his Introduction to Phelps, spoke of the "unfavorable experience gained by some American banks which went hastily into foreign countries during the years 1919 and 1920."[232] Substantial foreign lending by Wall Street began with the success of the Dawes loan in 1924, but declined after June 1928 when the stock-market rise diverted attention to that outlet and tight money hit the domestic and foreign bond markets. Foreign, especially German, borrowing shifted to the short-term market and finance paper, slowed down in 1930, and stopped completely after the Standstill Agreement of July 1931.

From 1914 on London had difficulty maintaining its role as a center for foreign reserves and a source of short- and long-term credit. The rise of

New York produced two reactions—anguish at the loss of leadership and relief at the shifting of responsibility. The head of the London City and Midland Bank (as it was known then) "publicly wept" over the passing of sterling supremacy, while the head of the Hong Kong and Shanghai Bank was enthusiastic about the rise of New York credits, telling Benjamin Strong—"and most English bankers agreed with him"—that New York must carry some of the load for financing the world's commerce.[233]

I have dealt elsewhere[234] with the hiatus created in the interwar period by British inability to serve as a lender of last resort for Europe and by U.S. unwillingness, at least until the Tripartite Monetary Agreement of September 26, 1936, to take over the task. In this view the 1929 depression was the consequence of an ineffective transition of the financial center from London to New York. No new center rose to challenge the old ones and to wrest financial supremacy or responsibility from them. Instead, in this instance an old center lost the capacity to serve as the center of the world financial system, and the most promising candidate for the position was unwilling or unable to fulfill the responsibilities.

From 1936 on, and especially during World War II, the United States increasingly accepted world financial leadership. The first steps were governmental. The Anglo-American Financial Agreement of 1946 represented a "key currency" approach in which, first, sterling would be restored to health as a means of rebuilding the financial system, so that the sterling area could play an important, and possibly even coequal, role with the dollar. In the first Marshall Plan discussions, however, in June 1947, Clayton and Douglas rejected the suggestion of Bevin and Dalton that the United States undertake a new program of assistance to Britain, after which they would approach Europe in "financial partnership."[235] Gradually the New York market recovered its interest in lending abroad, at long term and short. New York was the world financial center from the early 1950s until the end of the decade, when the Eurodollar market began to develop.

As the emphasis in this chapter is historical, little will be said of the transition from New York as the leading financial center back to London as the principal location of the Eurodollar market, or of the breakdown of the Eurodollar market with the events of August 1971, the Smithsonian devaluation, and the floating period begun in February 1973. Several points about the process should be made, however. First, U.S. banks and security dealers increased the number and size of their European branches in the 1960s. Early in the decade the major efforts abroad of New York banks in London were as dealers in dollars seeking to escape first Regulation Q and later capital controls. In the crunch of 1966 and 1969–1970, however, a number of banks throughout the United States went to London not to lend but to be in position to borrow dollars to add to their reserve balances in the United States. Second, much of the foreign branching was defensive investment. Banks went abroad not so much to earn profits as to avoid losing clients; as American corporations moved abroad, their bankers went with them. Third, with the forced devaluation of the dollar in August 1971, the Smithsonian Agreement of December 1971, and the period of floating in response to adverse speculation beginning in February 1973, the Eurodollar bond market substantially dried up.

After the second devaluation, trade payments and long-term contracts came to be denominated in currencies other than dollars. While borrowers were willing to go short of dollars, private parties outside the United States were less willing to go long. In Eurocurrency and Eurobond markets, the dollar was less widely used. No single currency took its place, however; the deutsche mark, Swiss franc, Japanese yen, and, to a lesser extent, Dutch guilder and Belgian franc severally replaced the dollar as international money. As the dollar declined in world financial use, no other currency or center, for the time being at least, rose to take its place. The international payments mechanism thereby lost the efficiency that comes from centralizing payments.

One possibility is that the European Economic Community may develop as a money and capital market to replace the Eurodollar market in the world financial system.

A Financial Center for Europe?

Will European economic integration, specifically the formation of the European Economic Community, result sooner or later in geographic financial centralization? To pose the question is to review the forces that in the past have led to the formation of financial centers.

(1) *A European currency.* Is a European currency necessary to the development of an efficient money and capital market? The answer is almost certainly yes. The Segré report proposed to achieve an integrated money and capital market—presumably concentrated in space, although the issue was not addressed—by removing national restrictions on lending and harmonizing regulations.[236] The resultant market, however, would still have been divided by currency. The Werner report recognized that integration of financial institutions implies development of a single money,[237] although currencies having permanently fixed exchange rates,

by the Hicks theorem, are a single money in all but the trouble and expense of exchange transactions. In some views it is necessary to go further and develop common long-term assets that are included in the portfolios of participating nations.

The London capital market operates in sterling, while New York and the Eurodollar markets operate in dollars. The movement toward world financial integration has been set back by currency realignments and floating. The development of a European capital market serving world as well as European needs probably requires a European currency.

History suggests that this is conveniently accomplished by taking an existing money and converting others onto it. In Germany, the Prussian thaler was adopted after conversion from silver to gold, but it was called the "mark" after the currency used in Hamburg. In Italy, the process was more complex and involved reduction of ten separate currencies to four and then to one, the one being the new lira of Piedmont, which had taken the lead during the political unification. The process took a decade.[238] If a national currency—say, the deutsche mark—is chosen as the basis for new currency called the *ecu* (both an acronym for European Currency Unit and an ancient French coin), it might confer an advantage on the established financial center associated with the chosen currency, in this case Frankfurt. It is likely that Berlin benefited from the choice of the Prussian thaler and Turin from that of the Piedmont lira.

An attempt to create an entirely new currency would presumably not affect the ultimate choice of a particular financial center, assuming that the currency was successfully established and the agglomeration process envisaged actually took place. Some unexpected side effects would probably occur. There is, of course, the question of whether the public would in fact go over to the synthetic currency. The 1958 conversion of the old to the new franc by dividing by 100 affected children and tourists more than it did the French population, which continued for a number of years to use the old franc as a unit of account. On the other hand, the conversion of sterling to the decimal system in 1970 was relatively painless. Money is established not by fiat but by public acceptance, and public acceptance in nine countries of a synthetic new money cannot be guaranteed. Such acceptance is necessary, however, to the creation of a single financial center.

(2) *A central bank.* The development of a European money ultimately requires a European central bank, and meanwhile a pooling of foreign-exchange reserves. It is not evident that the latter must have a physical embodiment and staff; the former will. If a single central bank—the Bank

of England, the Bank of France, the Bundesbank, or any other—were chosen as the European central bank and other central banks were merged into it, its existing location might well have an effect on the ultimate choice by the market of a physical center. The example of the Bank of Italy in Rome, far from the financial center in Milan, makes this uncertain, however.

In any case history suggests that the choice of one among a number of competing centers is normally evaded in the process of merging banks. The new European central bank would probably begin as a "federal reserve" system in which the various central banks started as separate units but ultimately became fully articulated subordinate parts. The managing board might be located in a nonfinancial center comparable to Washington, Ottawa, or Bern. With the passage of time one regional bank would come to dominate the others, as New York dominates Boston, Philadelphia, and Richmond. Location of the board in a place like Strasbourg, for instance, would probably have little attractive force.

(3) *An administrative capital.* If the administrative machinery of the European Economic Community, including the European central bank, were located in an existing financial center, it would be likely to serve as a magnet to other financial institutions and to attract them into a single primary location. The creation of a new capital would surely not, as Rome, Bern, Washington, Ottawa, Canberra, and a host of other examples testify. Other factors would have to be at least neutral—with enough tradition, savings available for investment throughout the Community, and the like. This suggests an interesting question: If France persuaded the EEC to choose Paris over Brussels as its capital, would France's strong postwar tradition in opposition to foreign lending stand in the way of financial concentration?

(4) *Tradition.* Tradition and skill favor London as the financial center, but it is doubtful that these are enough. Savings are also necessary, so that dealers can make a market, lend when the rest of the market is borrowing, and sell out of inventory when the rest of the market is buying. London's success in capturing the lion's share of the Euromoney market arose from the presence there of major branches of U.S. banks, which provided savings. British savings are limited in amount; are concentrated in institutionalized form, such as insurance and pension funds that no longer flow into foreign investment; and are in any case held at home by investment controls. It is conceivable but unlikely that skill and tradition are enough to bring the European financial center to London on the basis of brokerage, with the British participants not taking a position. The

Interbank Research Organization, studying the future of London as an international financial center, recognizes that Britain is unlikely to be a major exporter of capital but proposes that it operate as an entrepôt, with Europe as its hinterland.[239] The picture is not persuasive.

(5) *Economies of scale.* Clustering develops when the high risks of an activity can be reduced by continuous interchange of information.[240] It is possible but expensive to communicate by telephone and telex, and many financial functions involving uncertainty are better performed face-to-face. Robbins and Terleckyj note that the central financial district of lower Manhattan minimizes communications costs.[241] In 1960 a financial house with 120 lines to New York houses would have paid $420 monthly rental if located in New York, $230,000 if in Chicago, and $640,000 if in Los Angeles. While presumably communications costs have declined in the intervening years (costs are not so high as to prevent the head offices of a limited number of banks from being located in Toronto and Montreal in Canada, or Basel and Zurich in Switzerland), they are not likely to be so low as to eliminate all tendency to clustering. A network of banks located in all the financial capitals of Europe—London, Paris, Frankfurt, Amsterdam, Brussels, Milan, and Zurich—would not be cheap.

Note the unimportance of clustering for new security issues. Syndicates in new issues comprise firms located virtually everywhere. But secondary markets must be concentrated so as to eliminate the need to search over wide distances for price information or to maintain continuous interchange. While long-distance arbitrage does take place in some securities, such as kaffirs (gold-mining stocks) between London and Johannesberg and between major European markets and New York, the number of securities handled in this manner is limited; efficiency in handling a large number of issues is sacrificed to efficiency in handling a diffuse market through arbitrage.

Robinson has said that the secondary market is unimportant for corporate bonds, as most investors keep them until they mature or are otherwise retired.[242] This does not seem to be borne out for the Eurobond market, if one can judge by the number of articles devoted to "the major weakness of the Euro-bond market ... trading rather than issuing."[243] In addition, costs of the continuous exchange of price information among traders must be covered. The six leading traders—three of them American firms—were located in London, Brussels, Geneva, and Zurich in 1969; today the leaders are in Frankfurt, Paris, Luxembourg, and some centers in Canada and the United States.[244] Furthermore, there are problems of delays in payment and delivery of bonds. To meet these, the Morgan

Guaranty Trust Company organized "Euroclear" in Brussels in 1968, Barclays Bank International founded Eurobond Clearing House in London in 1969, and a group of Luxembourg banks organized a Center of Delivery of Euro-Securities in Luxembourg (CEDEL) in 1971. That such arrangements were unsatisfactory is indicated by these events: (*a*) Barclays Bank Internatioal abandoned the Eurobond Clearing House and substituted a different system of Registered Depository Receipts;[245] (*b*) Euroclear and CEDEL agreed to collaboration after long negotiations sponsored by the Association of International Bond Dealers; and (*c*) the Morgan Guaranty Trust Company decided to sell Euroclear while making an agreement to render it banking services for five years. This last step represents an improvement by eliminating the control of the clearinghouse by a single bank. At the time it was stated that the number of participants in Euroclear had risen from 74 in 1968 to 376 in 1972.[246]

In 1971 Kohn suggested that there was no need for a single center for the secondary market—"the true marketplace."[247] While "in any particular time one locale is more attractive than another," he said,[248] the market really has no center at all—not London or Luxembourg, Frankfurt or Brussels, Paris or Geneva; it is a mistake to expect all market makers to buy or sell freely in all circumstances. This verdict seems appropriate only for a period of transition or flux before an efficient centralized system has been developed. Another possibility is that the secondary market for securities could be linked up among widely separate centers by a computer-based system of bid and asked prices, supported by a regional system of security depositories. In the United States, the National Association of Security Dealers started the first of these in 1971 and the Depository Trust Company of New York, with eight regional depositories in six states, provided the second in 1973. Although it is far from clear what volume of security dealings would be necessary to cover the capital expense of establishing such a system in Europe, it seems likely that in time there will be no need for a central location for secondary markets in securities.

Other centripetal forces remain, especially the need for face-to-face communication with bankers, lawyers, security dealers, and borrowers and lenders. Telephone and telex have moderated these centralizing tendencies but have not destroyed them. Nor is the picture telephone likely to provide a substitute for face-to-face communication in the flesh.

The achievement of economies of scale in a concentrated center—an evolutionary and time-consuming process, as the historical record shows—has been disrupted by the 1971–1974 currency realignments and floating. When and if a European currency is established or the Eurodollar recovers strength and is reestablished as international money, the need for scale economies is likely to lead ultimately to agglomeration. Present participants in the Eurocurrency and Eurobond markets may be content to remain where they are and deal with one another by telex and telephone (this is more likely for the Eurocurrency market and for new issues than for the secondary market), but new entrants will be drawn to optimal locations, probably a single place. Banks and security dealers located in many centers will cut down on the less efficient locations in periods of recession and expand the efficient ones when recovery comes, in spite of the decline in cost of communication. While the experience of Euroclear, CEDEL, and Barclay's suggests that the choice lies between Brussels and London, the outcome is likely to depend on other factors. Economies of scale predict one center, but not which one.

(6) *A central location.* The Christaller view that the metropolis chosen as the financial center must be centrally located[249] probably holds at the extremes: Edinburgh, Copenhagen, Rome need not apply. It cannot count for much in Europe among London, Paris, Frankfurt, Brussels, or Amsterdam (or Geneva or Zurich if Switzerland were to join the European Economic Community). Probably even Hamburg or Munich would not be ruled out for failing to stand at the epicenter.

But need the European financial center be in Europe? Could it again be New York, with London, Paris, Frankfurt, and the rest linked to one another by means of their connections with Wall Street? Can Europe be integrated financially by an outside center, as it is to some degree integrated in the field of labor by Mediterranean workers who have no roots in any one place, and in industry by American corporations that are more mobile than their European counterparts? Such an outcome is possible and, as indicated, there is some interest in the United States in developing policies to restore New York to world financial leadership. The immediate outlook is not propitious, given the dim view the world takes of the dollar. Over a longer view, moreover, the time differences round the world make a European center, rather than one in North America or Asia, more efficient in integrating European financial markets.

(7) *Transport.* While metropolitan centers have grown at breaks in transport, it is usually possible today to adjust transport to function. A few communities, like Wellington, New Zealand, are so hemmed in between mountains and sea that a major airport can be developed only at exorbitant expense. Small cities may have difficulty supporting the costly transport facilities necessary for effective communication. Existing facili-

ties are likely to be taken into account to avoid constructing new ones. On the whole, however, there are few limits among European cities.

(8) *Headquarters of multinational corporations.* Might banks, perhaps starting with U.S. banks, drift into a single center or build up their offices in such a center, perhaps putting those offices in charge of European branches, if a number of multinational corporations, particularly those of U.S. ownership, were to congregate? The reason for attributing particular behavior to foreign corporations and foreign banks is that, in the context of European integration, they are more mobile than "native" corporations and banks. American corporations in Canada are likely to be located in a more economic pattern than Canadian corporations, since the latter will resist leaving the places in which they started. In Canada, however, the location of the U.S. parent corporation may cast an economic shadow across the border, as Ray has suggested.[250] The location of U.S. subsidiaries in Europe is likely to reflect no such influence. French corporations, by contrast, may move their headquarters from Lyons to Paris, but they are unlikely to continue further to London, Brussels, or Frankfurt.

What governs the choice of location for the headquarters of an American firm in Europe? Initially, investment was often made in Britain, on the basis of similarity of language and culture; in a particular country from which forebears of the firm's decision makers had migrated to the United States; or in centers thought to be agreeable, especially Paris. Later, but before the Common Market, it was frequently judged necessary to produce in each country in which the firm wanted to sell: "To sell in France, produce in France." The advent of the Common Market, and the conversion of the Six into the Nine, has changed this less than had been anticipated. With time, however, and as the European Economic Community seems more solid and less ephemeral, other firms may follow the pattern of IBM, which is said to have rationalized its production to take advantage of the elimination of tariffs, or of Ford Motor Company, whose major facilities exchange parts between Antwerp and Cologne.

What is relevant, however, is not the location of production facilities but of company headquarters. In Germany after World War II, companies were attracted to the American military headquarters in Frankfurt. Today more and more American companies seem to develop an affinity for the headquarters of the Commission of the European Communities in Brussels.[251] Sales headquarters may be divided culturally between Latin and Germanic countries, in some cases splitting Switzerland between two European headquarters. Financial headquarters of some companies have been located in London. Where a company has one headquarters, and it was not established in the last fifteen years in Brussels, it has typically been where the firm has its largest production facilities, or in London or Paris. If there is a trend, it is probably to Brussels.

With one exception, major American banks in Europe have not designated any one branch to head up their European network. London, Brussels, Paris, Frankfurt, Zurich, Geneva, and Rome report separately to the head office, and coordination among them is directed from New York. It is not evident that this is efficient. It is likely, rather, that the matter will be allowed to continue unresolved, pending the emergence of a particular location as the dominant center.

(9) *Culture.* For cultural reasons a single financial center may not emerge. Cultural factors perhaps contributed to the stalemate between Toronto and Montreal and, according to some authors, to the survival of Basel and Geneva as financial centers in spite of the competition from Zurich. French corporations stay in Paris, Belgian in Brussels, Dutch in Amsterdam, and German in Düsseldorf, Hamburg, and Frankfurt. International cooperation among such banks as the Crédit lyonnais, the Banca Commerciale Italiana, the Deutsche Bank, and Morgan Guaranty Trust remains voluntary for separate deals; there is no true merger, with unified decision making. Historical evidence predicts that the emergence of a true financial center would be preceded by takeovers, mergers, and amalgamations, but in the last fifteen years these have been few.

This is perhaps the crux. If there is no integration beyond tariff removal and collaboration in international economic negotiation, there will be no single European financial center apart from the world system. Like the banks in the hinterland of St. Louis and Chicago that kept correspondent balances in New York, European financial institutions will operate partly within the Community and partly outside. During the period of the Eurodollar, the separate financial markets of the Six were more effectively joined with the Eurodollar market than they were with one another. If a European center emerges as the apex of the world hierarchical system and Europe does not achieve effective integration, sections of the capital market in Europe may even be linked to the center through outside connections, as part of the world feeder system.

(10) *Policy.* Governmental policy can accelerate or slow down the emergence of a given city as the primary financial center, but it can probably not change the outcome. Pushing too hard for centralization will create resistance, while strong efforts at decentralization can be overcome by private forces. It is uncertain whether the United States could recreate in New York a financial center for the world after its maladroit handling

of the troubles of the dollar. Whether the Swiss or German authorities can prevent their financial capitals from being developed to serve as a world center is less uncertain. It is difficult to use exchange control to prevent inflows of hot money, but governments can forbid development of the positive institutions that will effectively employ foreign monies in domestic and foreign lending.

Policy requires more than governmental agreement. The Segré report on the unification of the European capital market was widely praised, but nothing happened. No European country was deeply committed to building a well-functioning European capital market. Accordingly, I predict—very tentatively—that Brussels will emerge as the financial center of the European Economic Community, for the following reasons. It serves as headquarters for the commission; it attracts foreign corporations and will ultimately attract foreign and European banks; and it tolerates the world intellectual medium of exchange, the English language. The process will be long and drawn out, for commitment to European integration does not go deep. France will push the advantages of Paris as the federal administrative center, and incidentally the center for financial institutions, but with little likelihood of consent from the other members. Sterling is too weak, and British savings too unavailable, to advance London's claim for consideration. While the advantages of centralization are less compelling than they were in the middle of the nineteenth century, they still exist. Thus I predict that, despite cultural resistance and only with difficulty, centralization will take place, but not before the late 1980s.

Notes

1. Kerr, "Geography of Finance" and "Metropolitan Dominance in Canada."

2. Labasse, *Les Capitaux et la région*.

3. Pred, *Spatial Dynamics*.

4. Goldstein and Moses, "A Survey of Urban Economics."

5. Vernon, *Metropolis, 1985*.

6. Goldsmith, *Financial Structure and Development*; McKinnon, *Money and Capital*; Sametz, *Financial Development*; Shaw, *Financial Deepening*.

7. *Money and Capital*.

8. *Financial Deepening*.

9. An up-to-date report on the subject is Interbank Research Organisation, *The Future of London*. There are, moreover, indications that the U.S. government is interested in contemplating the steps that would be required to restore the supremacy of New York as the leading world financial center.

10. Fanno, *La Banche e il mercato monetario*.

11. Powell, *Evolution of the Money Market*.

12. Gras, *Introduction of Economic History*, chaps. 5 and 6.

13. Goldsmith, *Financial Structure and Development*.

14. Gerschenkron, "Economic Backwardness" (1952); Hoselitz, "Entrepreneurship and Capital Formation."

15. Gerschenkron, *Economic Backwardness* (1962).

16. Cameron, *France and the Economic Development of Europe; Banking in the Early Stages of Industrialization; Banking and Economic Development*.

17. Cameron, *Banking and Economic Development*, p. 8.

18. Fohlen, "France, 1700–1914," vol. 4, p. 37.

19. Goldsmith, *Financial Structure and Development*, p. 400.

20. Shaw, *Financial Deepening*, p. 10.

21. McKinnon, *Money and Capital*.

22. Shaw, *Financial Deepening*.

23. Powell, *Evolution of the Money Market*, p. 274.

24. Taylor, *Gilletts, Bankers at Banbury*, p. 229.

25. I cannot refrain from pointing out that these economies tend to be lost in the international system when there are fluctuating exchange rates, no international money, and a disintegrated international capital market.

26. Pressnell, *Country Banking*, p. 49.

27. Duncan et al., *Metropolis and Region*, p. 39.

28. Henning, "Standorte und Spezialisierung."

29. Goldstein and Moses, "A Survey of Urban Economics," p. 485, n. 40.

30. Madden and Nadler, *International Money Markets*, p. 110.

31. Gras, *Introduction to Economic History*.

32. Duncan et al., *Metropolis and Region*, p. 84.

33. McKenzie, *The Metropolitan Community*, 1933, p. 62.

34. Duncan et al., *Metropolis and Region*, p. 117.

35. Vernon, *Metropolis*, 1985, pp. 70, 73.

36. Ibid., p. 80.

37. Robbins and Terleckyj, *Money Metropolis*, p. 38.

38. Kindleberger, "European Integration," pp. 191–192.

39. Robbins and Terleckyj, *Money Metropolis*, chap. 6.

40. Bisschop, *Rise of the London Money Market*, pp. 150, 163.

41. Wechsberg, *The Merchant Bankers*, p. 102.

42. Leighton-Boyce, *Smiths, the Bankers*, p. 20.

43. Bisschop, *Rise of the London Money Market*, p. 156.

44. Anderson, "The Attorney and the Early Capital Market," p. 251.

45. Bagehot, *Lombard Street*, p. 138.

46. Ibid., p. 140.

47. Ibid., p. 6.

48. Sayers, *Lloyds Banks*, p. 35. The general manager from 1871 to 1902, Howard Lloyd, went to London from Birmingham once a week after 1884; his successor made it his business to concentrate the head office in London (ibid., p. 50). From 1899 the board met alternately in Birmingham and London, and by 1910 met only in London (ibid., p. 272).

49. Ibid., p. 237.

50. Ibid., p. 269.

51. Ibid., pp. 165, 270. References to the ability and willingness of depositors to move funds between the provinces and London are found elsewhere in Sayers' account of Lloyds for Birmingham (ibid., p. 110), and Leighton-Boyce's account of Nottingham (*Smiths, the Bankers*, p. 36).

52. Crick and Wadsworth, *Joint-Stock Banking*, p. 311.

53. Ibid., pp. 312, 316.

54. Ibid., pp. 329, 342.

55. Ibid., p. 345.

56. Ibid., p. 188.

57. Gregory, *Westminster Bank*, p. 184.

58. Powell, *Evolution of the Money Market*, p. 286.

59. Withers, *National Provincial Bank*, pp. 61, 62.

60. Taylor, *Gilletts, Bankers at Banbury*, p. 229.

61. Matthews and Tuke, *History of Barclay's Bank*, pp. 1–9.

62. Sayers, *Lloyds Bank*, p. 50.

63. Leighton-Boyce, *Smiths, the Bankers*, p. 279.

64. Hidy, *George Peabody*, p. 84.

65. Sayers, *Lloyds Bank*, p. 261.

66. Ibid., p. 263.

67. Ibid., pp. 79–80.

68. Chandler, *Four Centuries of Banking*, vol. 1, pp. 420 ff.

69. Leighton-Boyce, *Smiths, the Bankers*, p. 279; Sayers, *Lloyds Bank*, pp. 58, 232.

70. Bisschop, *Rise of the London Money Market*, p. 217.

71. Powell, *Evolution of the Money Market*, pp. 370, 372.

72. Lévy-Leboyer, *Les Banques européennes*, pp. 436–437.

73. Bigo, *Les Banques françaises*, p. 21.

74. Gille, *La Banque en France*, pp. 57, 77.

75. Bigo, *Les Banques françaises*, p. 101.

76. Gille, *La Banque en France*, pp. 1–101.

77. Ibid., p. 24.

78. Lévy-Leboyer, *Les Banques européennes*, p. 429.

79. Gille, *La Banque en France*, pp. 67–68.

80. Thuillier, "Pour une histoire bancaire régionale," p. 512.

81. Bouvier, *Le Crédit lyonnais*.

82. Labasse, *Les Capitaux et la région*.

83. Gille, *La Banque en France*, p. 36.

84. Brocard, "Les Marchés financiers du province," p. 106.

85. Madden and Nadler, *International Money Markets*, p. 327.

86. *Crédit du nord centenaire*.

87. Buffet, *Du régionalisme au nationalisme financier*; Charpenay, *Les Banques régionalistes*.

88. Dauphin-Meunier, *La Banque de France*, pp. 165–166.

89. Fanno, *Le Banche e il mercato monetario*, p. 74.

90. Labasse, *Les Capitaux et la région*, p. 446.

91. Ibid., pp. 493, 500.

92. Helfferich, *Georg von Siemens*, p. 30.

93. Riesser, *The Great German Banks*, p. 509.

94. Tilly, *Financial Institutions*, p. 115.

95. Cameron, "Founding the Bank of Darmstadt"; Riesser, *The Great German Banks*, pp. 56–57.

96. Benaerts, *Les Origines de la grande industrie allemande*, p. 275.

97. Compare the British episode of 1833 (described earlier in this chapter) when joint-stock banks were created in England within 65 miles of London, over the objection of the Bank of England, through the discovery of a loophole in the 1826 law.

98. Tilly, *Financial Institutions*, p. 115.

99. Ibid., p. 118.

100. Böhme, *Deutschlands Weg zur Grossmacht*, p. 219; *Frankfurt und Hamburg*, pp. 151–153. For a discussion of the Frankfurt money and capital market more generally, see Heyn, "Private Banking and Industrialization."

101. Tilly, *Financial Institutions*, p. 138.

102. Quoted by Blumberg, "Die Finanzierung der Neugründungen," p. 172.

103. Ibid., pp. 199–200.

104. Landes, "The Bleichröder Bank," p. 206.

105. Böhme, *Frankfurt und Hamburg*, p. 254.

106. Ibid., pp. 266–270; Rosenberg, *Die Weltwirtschaftskrise*, pp. 128 ff.

107. Böhme, *Deutschlands Weg zur Grossmacht*, p. 219; *Frankfurt und Hamburg*, p. 236.

108. Helfferich, *Georg von Siemens*, p. 27.

109. Brockhage, *Zur Entwicklung des preussischdeutschen Kapitalexports*, p. 56.

110. Ibid., pp. 208–209.

111. Helfferich, *Georg von Siemens*, pp. 31, 38, 41.

112. Ibid., p. 34.

113. Wiskemann, *Hamburg und die Welthandelspolitik*, p. 206.

114. Helfferich, *Georg von Siemens*, p. 43.

115. Ibid., p. 58.

116. Ibid., p. 111.

117. Whale, *Joint-Stock Banking in Germany*, pp. 27–28.

118. *Hundert Jahre im Dienst der Deutschen Wirtschaft*.

119. Ibid., p. 42.

120. Ibid., p. 48.

121. Riesser, *The Great German Banks*, p. 654.

122. In 1900, for example, the Midlands Bank, finding itself with few branches south of a London-Bath line, created a network in the area (Crick and Wadsworth, *Joint-Stock Banking*, p. 341).

123. Brockhage, *Zur Entwicklung des preussischdeutschen Kapitalexports*.

124. Wiskemann, *Hamburg und die Welthandelspolitik*, p. 237.

125. Ibid., p. 238.

126. Baar, "Probleme der industriellen Revolution," p. 531.

127. Böhme, *Deutschlands Weg zur Grossmacht*, p. 333; Borchardt, "Industrial Revolution in Germany," p. 152.

128. Duncan et al., *Metropolis and Region*, p. 81.

129. Deutsche Bank, letter of Jan. 25, 1973, Seidenzahl, *100 Jahre Deutsche Bank*, pp. 375 ff.; Wechsberg, *The Merchant Bankers*, pp. 260 ff.

130. Myers, *New York Money Market*, p. 6.

131. Luzzatto, *Storia economica*, p. 160.

132. Romani, *Italia nel secolo XIX*, p. 591.

133. Greenfield, *Economics and Liberalism*, p. 142.

134. Luzzatto, *L'economia italiana*, pp. 63 ff.

135. Gerschenkron, *Continuity in History*, p. 88.

136. Cameron, *Banking and Economic Development*, p. 18.

137. Cohen, "Financing Industrialization."

138. Cohen, in Cameron, *Banking and Economic Development*, p. 60.

139. Clough, *Economic History of Modern Italy*, p. 125.

140. Luzzatto, *L'economia italiana*, p. 105.

141. Clough, *Economic History of Modern Italy*, p. 12.

142. Luzzatto, *L'economia italiana*, pp. 211–212.

143. Smith, *Italy*, p. 163.

144. Pareto, *Le Marché financier italien 1894*, p. 59.

145. Luzzatto, *L'economia italiana*, p. 266.

146. Ibid., p. 250. An earlier failure of the Banca di Milano was the result of the failure in 1882 of the Union générále of Paris, which had created it.

147. Fanno, *Le Banche e il mercato monetario*, p. 92n.

148. Luzzatto, *Storia economica*, p. 465.

149. Bonelli, *La Crisi del 1907*, pp. 29–37.

150. There is irony in the fact that the Banca di Torino (the Società delle Ferrovie de Gottardo) helped finance the Gotthard route (Castronovo, *Economia e societa in Piemonte*, p. 116).

151. Ibid., pp. 200 ff., 215 ff., 243.

152. Schwarzenbach, "The Swiss Money Market," pp. 482–483.

153. Ibid., p. 497.

154. Ibid., p. 519.

155. Iklé, *Switzerland*, p. 10.

156. Lévy-Leboyer, *Les Banques européennes*, pp. 425, 431.

157. Ibid., p. 432n.

158. Iklé, *Switzerland*, p. 14.

159. Gille, *La Banque en France*, p. 88.

160. *Union Bank of Switzerland*, p. 55.

161. Iklé, *Switzerland*, p. 18.

162. *Union Bank of Switzerland*, pp. 38—39.

163. Iklé, *Switzerland*, p. 15.

164. *Union Bank of Switzerland*, p. 74.

165. Ibid., pp. 86—88, 132.

166. Schwarzenbach, "The Swiss Money Market," pp. 484—486.

167. Jöhr, *Die schweizerischen Notenbanken*, p. 457.

168. Neufeld, *Financial System of Canada*, p. 39.

169. Bank of Montreal, *Centenary*, p. 14.

170. Neufeld, *Financial System of Canada*, p. 123.

171. Ross, *Canadian Bank of Commerce*, vol. 1, p. 22.

172. *Royal Bank of Canada*, p. 17.

173. It is significant that in the same year, poised on the brink of decline, Halifax established the first clearinghouse in Canada; this example was quickly followed by Montreal (1889), Toronto and Hamilton (1891), and Winnipeg (Jamieson, *Chartered Banking in Canada*, p. 25).

174. Ibid., pp. 17—24.

175. *Bank of Nova Scotia*, pp. 81, 83.

176. Neufeld, *Financial System of Canada*, pp. 488—489.

177. Ibid., p. 573.

178. Botha, "Canadian Money Market," pp. 138, 143.

179. *Report*, pp. 294—315.

180. For size in selected years from 1870 to 1970, see Neufeld, *Financial System of Canada*, table 4.6, p. 98.

181. Royal Commission on Banking and Finance, *Report*, p. 343.

182. *Rise of Toronto*, p. 211.

183. As this study was being prepared for publication, Dr. Irving Silver of the Canadian Ministry of State for Urban Affairs kindly called my attention to an article that appeared in the *Montreal Gazette* on May 28, 1974. It reported that a study by Professor Andre Ryba of the University of Montreal established that stock-market, money-market, bond-market, and banking activities are all gradually shifting to Toronto. In particular, both the Royal Bank of Canada and the Bank of Montreal have shifted their "vital money market 'trading desks' to Toronto."

184. Gras, *Introduction to Economic History*.

185. Masters, *Rise of Toronto*.

186. Glazebrook, *Story of Toronto*, pp. 193—194.

187. Masters, *Rise of Toronto*, p. 59.

188. Ibid., p. 97.

189. Ray, "Regional Aspects of Foreign Ownership," pp. 40, 41.

190. Royal Commission on Banking and Finance, *Report*, pp. 322–323.

191. Kerr, "Metropolitan Dominance in Canada," p. 538.

192. Ibid., p. 545.

193. Note that in Australia there are two main money markets—an old one, Melbourne, and a new one, Sydney, with "Sydney tending to become the more important of the two, partly because the Head Office of the Reserve Bank is there" (Wilson, "Australian Money Market," p. 49). This case is worth comparing with that of Canada and may help determine the role in the slow rise of Toronto played by the cultural differences between French Montreal and British Toronto.

194. Masters, *Rise of Toronto*, p. 212.

195. Botha, "Canadian Money Market," pp. 138–143; Eaton and Bond, "Canada's Newest Money Market," p. 15.

196. Royal Commission on Banking and Finance, *Report*, p. 344.

197. *Royal Bank of Canada*, p. 17.

198. Albion, *Rise of New York Port*.

199. Gras, *Introduction to Economic History*.

200. Myers, *New York Money Market*.

201. Robbins and Terleckyj, *Money Metropolis*.

202. Albion, *Rise of New York Port*, pp. 1–93.

203. Ibid., pp. 378–381.

204. Kouwenhoven, *Partners in Banking*, pp. 20–31.

205. Hidy, "George Peabody," pp. 15, 95, 136, 237.

206. Albion, *Rise of New York Port*, pp. 238–242.

207. Myers, *New York Money Market*, chap. 6.

208. Ibid., chap. 11.

209. Ibid., p. 240.

210. Gras, *Introduction to Economic History*, p. 266.

211. Ibid.

212. Lösch, *Economics of Location*, pp. 461 ff; Riefler, *Money Rates and Money Markets*, pp. 65, 72.

213. Riefler, *Money Rates and Money Markets*, p. 74.

214. Robbins and Terleckyj, *Money Metropolis*, p. 85.

215. Brown, *A Hundred Years of Merchant Banking*.

216. Redlich, *American Banking, Men and Ideas*, pt. 2, p. 60.

217. *In Memoriam, Jesse Seligmann*, p. 115.

218. Hopkinson, *Drexel & Co.*

219. Brockhage, *Zur Entwicklung des preussischdeutschen Kapitalexports*, pp. 34–35.

220. Ibid., p. 54.

221. Leighton-Boyce, *Smiths, the Bankers*, pp. 10, 61, 205.

222. Rosenberg, *Die Weltwirtschaftskrise*, p. 38.

223. Crick and Wadsworth, *Joint-Stock Banking*, p. 307.

224. Cameron, *France and the Economic Development of Europe*.

225. Bagehot, *Lombard Street*, p. 16.

226. Newbold, "Beginnings of World Crisis," p. 438.

227. Jeffrys, "Business Organisation in Great Britain," pp. 62, 121.

228. Kindleberger, *Economic Growth in France and Britain*, pp. 61–64.

229. Cecil, *Albert Ballin*.

230. Wiskemann, *Hamburg und die Welthandelspolitik*, p. 273.

231. Abrahams, "Foreign Expansion of American Finance," p. 10.

232. *Foreign Expansion of American Banks*, p. iii.

233. Abrahams, "Foreign Expansion of American Finance," p. 53.

234. Kindleberger, *The World in Depression*.

235. U.S. Department of State, *Foreign Relations*, vol. 3, pp. 269, 272.

236. *Development of a European Capital Market*.

237. "Report to the Council and the Commission on the Realization by Stages of Economic and Monetary Union."

238. De Mattia, *L'unificazione monetaria italiana*; Luzzatto, *L'economia italiana*, pp. 60 ff.

239. Interbank Research Organization, *The Future of London*, pp. 1–8.

240. Robbins and Terleckyj, *Money Metropolis*, p. 35.

241. Ibid.

242. Robinson, *Money and Capital Markets*, pp. 19, 202.

243. Yassukovich, "International Capital Market"; see also Low, "Improving the Secondary Market"; Lutz, "Problems of the Secondary Market."

244. Low, "Improving the Secondary Market," pp. 1157–1158.

245. McRae, "Barclay's Euro-clearing System."

246. Low, "Euroclear Opens Up," p. 31.

247. Kohn, "Eurobonds," p. 70.

248. Ibid., p. 68.

249. Duncan et al., *Metropolis and Region*.

250. "U.S. Manufacturing Subsidiaries in Canada."

251. "In all, some 450 international companies have their main European offices in Brussels, a total rivalled only by Paris" (International Research Organisation, *The Future of London*, pp. 22). And following them, two American banks—the Chase Manhattan and the Security Pacific—have located their European headquarters in Brussels rather than London.

References

Abrahams, Paul P. "The Foreign Expansion of American Finance and Its Relation to Foreign Economic Politics of the United States, 1907–1921." New York: Arno Press, 1974.

Albion, Robert Greenhaigh. *The Rise of New York Port (1815–1860)*. New York: Scribners, 1939.

Anderson, B. L. "The Attorney and the Early Capital Market in Lancashire." In François Crouzet, ed., *Capital Formation in the Industrial Revolution*. London: Methuen, 1972.

Baar, Lothar. "Probleme der industriellen Revolution in grosstädtischen Industriezentren: das Berliner Beispiel." In W. Fischer, ed., *Wirtschafts- und sozialgeschichtliche Probleme der frühen Industrialisierung*. Berlin: Colloquium Verlag, 1968, 529–542.

Bagehot, *Lombard Street: A Description of the Money Market*. New York: Scribner, Armstrong, 1873.

Bank of Montreal. *The Centenary of the Bank of Montreal, 1817–1917*. Montreal: privately printed, 1917.

Bank of Nova Scotia, 1832–1952. Toronto: privately printed, 1932.

Bigo, Robert. *Les Banques françaises au cours du XIX⁰ siècle*. Paris: Sirey, 1947.

Bisschop, W. R. *The Rise of the London Money Market, 1640–1826*. London: Frank Cass, 1968.

Blumberg, Horst. "Die Finanzierung der Neugründungen under Erweiterungen von Industriebetrieben in Form der Aktiengesellschaften während der fünfziger Jahrhunderts in Deutschland." In Hans Mottek, ed., *Studien zur Geschiche der industriellen Revolution in Deutschland*. Berlin: Akademie Verlag, 1960, 165–208.

Böhme, Helmut. *Deutschlands Weg zur Grossmacht, Studien zum Verhältnis von Wirtschadt und Staat während Reichsgründungzeit, 1848–1881*. Cologne: Kiepenheuer u. Witsch, 1966.

Böhme, Helmut. *Frankfurt und Hamburg, des deutsche Reiches Silber- und Goldloch und die allerenglischste Stadt des Kontinents*. Frankfurt: Europaïsche Verlag-anstalt, 1968.

Bonelli, Franco. *La Crisi del 1907: Una tappa dello sviluppo industriale in Italia*. Turin: Fondazione Luigi Einaudi, 1971.

Borchardt, Knut. "The Industrial Revolution in Germany, 1700–1914." in C. M. Cipolla, ed., *The Fontana Economic History of Europe*. Vol. 4. N.p.: Collins/Fontana, 1972, 76–160.

Botha, D. J. J. "The Canadian Money Market: 1, Institutional Development." *South African Journal of Economics* 40 (1972): 118—143.

Bouvier, Jean. *Le Crédit Lyonnais de 1863 à 1882: les années de formation d'une banque des dépôts.* Vols. 1 and 2. Paris: SEVPEN, 1961.

Broccard, Lucien. "Les marchés financiers de province." In A. Aupetit et al., *Les grands marchés financiers.* Paris: Alcan, 1917, 105—152.

Brockhage, Bernhard. *Zur Entwicklung des preussischdeutschen Kapitalexports,* Leipzig: Duncker u. Humbolt, 1910.

Brown, John Crosby. *A Hundred Years of Merchant Banking: A History of Brown Brothers & Co.* New York: privately printed, 1909.

Cameron, Rondo. *France and the Economic Development of Europe.* Princeton: Princeton University Press, 1961.

Cameron, Rondo, with the collaboration of Olga Crisp, Hugh T. Patrick, and Richard Tilly. *Banking in the Early Stages of Industrialization: A Comparative Study.* New York: Oxford University Press, 1967.

Cameron, Rondo, ed. *Banking and Economic Development: Some Lessons of History.* New York: Oxford University Press, 1971.

Castronovo, Valerie. *Economia e società in Piemonte dell' unità al 1914.* Milan: Banca Commerciale Italiana, 1969.

Cecil, Lamar. *Albert Ballin: Business and Politics in Imperial Germany.* Princeton: Princeton University Press, 1967.

Chandler, George. *Four Centuries of Banking (Martin's Bank).* London: Batsford, vol. 1, 1964; vol. 2, 1968.

Clough, Shepherd B. *The Economic History of Modern Italy.* New York: Columbia University Press, 1964.

Crédit du nord centenaire. Lille: privately printed, 1948.

Crick, W. F., and J. E. Wadsworth. *A Hundred Years of Joint-Stock Banking (Midlands Bank).* London: Hodder & Stoughton, 1967.

Dauphin-Meunier, A., *La Banque de France.* Paris: Gallimard, 1936.

Dumke, Rolf H. "The Political Economy of Economic Integration: The Case of the Zollverein of 1834." Queen's University Discussion Paper no. 153, presented to the Canadian Economics Association, June 5, 1974.

Duncan, O. D., et al. *Metropolis and Region.* Baltimore: Johns Hopkins University Press, 1960.

Eaton, G. Howard, and David E. Bond. "Canada's Newest Money Market—Vancouver," *Canadian Banker* 77 (1970): 14—15.

Fanno, Marco. *Le Banche e il mercato monetario.* Rome: Athenaem, 1913.

Fohlen, Claude. "France, 1700—1914." in C. M. Cipolla, ed. *The Fontana Economic History of Europe.* Vol. 4. N.p., Collins/Fontana, 1972, 7—75.

Gerschenkron, Alexander. "Economic Backwardness in Historical Perspective." In B. F. Hoselitz, ed., *The Progress of Underdeveloped Areas.* Chicago: University of Chicago Press, 1952.

Gille, Bertrand. *La banque en France au XIXe siècle: recherches historiques*, Geneva: Librairie Droz, 1970.

Glazebrook, G. P. de T. *The Story of Toronto*. Toronto: University of Toronto Press, 1971.

Goldsmith, R. G. *Financial Structure and Development*. New Haven, Conn.: Yale University Press, 1969.

Goldstein, Gerald S., and Leon N. Moses. "A Survey of Urban Economics." *Journal of Economic Literature* 11 (1973): 473–515.

Gras, N. S. B. *An Introduction to Economic History*. New York: Harper, 1922.

Greenfield, Kent Roberts. *Economics and Liberalism in the Risorgimento: A Study of Nationalism in Lombardy, 1814–1848*, Baltimore: Johns Hopkins Press, 1965.

Gregory, T. E. *The Westminister Bank during a Century*. Vols. 1 and 2, London: Westminister Bank, 1956.

Helfferich, Karl. *Georg von Siemens, Ein Lebensbild aus Deutschlands grosser Zeit*. Revised and abridged edition of the 1921–23 work in 3 vols. Krefeld: Richard Serpe, 1956.

Henning, Friederich-Wilhelm. "Standorte und Spezialisierung des Handels und Transportwesen in des Mark Brandenburg um 1800." *Scripta Mercatura*, 1971, 1–44.

Heyn, Udo E. "Private Banking and Industrialization: The Case of Frankfurt-am-Main, 1825–1875." Ph.D. dissertation, University of Wisconsin, 1969.

Hidy, Muriel E. "George Peabody: Merchant and Financier, 1829–1854." New York: Arno Press, 1974.

Hopkinson, Edward, Jr. *Drexel & Co. over a Century of History*. New York: Newcomen Society of North America, 1952.

Hoselitz, Bert F. "Entrepreneurship and Capital Formation in France and Britain since 1700." In *Capital Formation and Economic Growth*. Princeton: Princeton University Press (for the National Bureau of Economic Research), 1956.

Hundert Jahre im Dienst der deutschen Wirtschaft: ein Rüblick zur Erinnering an die Gründung der mitteldeutschen Creditbank. Frankfurt-am-Main, privately printed, 1956.

Iklé, Max. *Switzerland: An International Banking and Finance Center*. Stroudsberg, Penn.: Dowden, Hutchunson & Ross, 1972.

In Memoriam, Jesse Seligmann. New York: privately printed, 1894.

Interbank Research Organization. *The Future of London as an International Financial Centre*. London: HSMO, 1973.

Jamison, A. B. *Chartered Banking in Canada*. Toronto: Ryerson, 1955.

Jeffrys, J. B. "Trends in Business Organization in Great Britain since 1890, with Special Reference to the Financial Structure of the Companies, the Mechanism of Investment, and the Relations between the Shareholder and the Company. Doctoral dissertation, London School of Economics, 1938.

Jöhr, Adolf. *Die schweizerischen Notenbanken, 1826–1913*. Zurich: Orell Füssli, 1915.

Kerr, Donald P. "Metropolitan Dominance in Canada." In John Warkentin, ed., *Geographical Interpretation of Canada*. Toronto: Methuen, 1967, 531–555.

Kerr, Donald P. "Some Aspects of the Geography of Finance in Canada." *Canadian Geography* 9 (1965): 175–192.

Kindleberger, Charles P. *Economic Growth in France and Britain, 1851–1950*. Cambridge, Mass.: Harvard University Press, 1964.

Kindleberger, Charles P. "European Integration and the Development of a Single Financial Center for Long-Term Capital," *Weltwirtschaftliches Archiv* 90 (1963): 189–219.

Kindleberger, Charles P. *The World in Depression, 1929–1939*. Berkeley: University of California Press, 1973.

Kohn, Eric D. "Euro-bonds—What Sort of Market?" *Euromoney* 3 (1971): 68–70.

Kouwenhoven, John A. *Partners in Banking: An Historical Portrait of a Great Private Bank, Brown Brothers, Harriman & Co. 1818–1968*. New York: Doubleday, 1968.

Labasse, Jean. *Les capitaux et la région, étude geograohique: essai sur le commerce et la circulation des capitaux dans la région lyonnaise*. Paris: Colin, 1955.

Landes, David S. "The Bleichroeder Bank: An Interim Report." In *Yearbook V*, publication of the Leo Baeck Institute. London: East and West Library, 1960, 201–220.

Leighton-Boyce, J. A. S. L. *Smiths, the Bankers, 1658–1958*. London: National Provincial Bank, 1958.

Lévy-Leboyer, Maurice. *Les banques européenes et 1'industrialization internatioale dans la première moitié du XIXᵉ siècle*. Paris: Presses universitaires de France, 1964.

Lösch, August. *The Economics of Location*. New Haven, Conn.: Yale University Press, 1954.

Low, William F. "Euroclear Opens Up." *Euromoney* 4 (1972): 31, 33.

Low, William F. "Improving the Secondary Market." *The Banker* (1972): 1157–1159.

Lowie, Robert H. *The German People, A Social Portrait of 1914*. New York: Rinehart, 1946.

Lutz, Alfred. "Problems of the Secondary Market—Has It really Come of Age?" *Euromoney* 5 (1973): 19, 21.

Luzzatto, Gino. *L'economia italiana dal 1860 al 1914*. Vol. 1 (*1861–1894*). Milan: Banca Commerciale Italiana, 1963.

Luzzatto, Gino. *Storia economica dell'età moderna et contemporanea*. Vol. 2. Padua: CEDAN, 1960.

McKenzie, R. D. *The Metropolitan Community*. New York: McGraw-Hill, 1953.

McKinnon, Ronald I. *Money and Capital in Economic Development*. Washington, D.C.: Brookings Institution, 1973.

McRae, Hamish. "Barclay's Euro-clearing System, Mark II." *Euromoney* 4 (1972): 33.

Madden John T., and Marcus Nadler. *The International Money Market*. New York: Prentice-Hall, 1935.

Masters, D. C. *The Rise of Toronto, 1850–1890*. Toronto: University of Toronto Press, 1947.

Matthews, P. W., and Anthony W. Tuke. *History of Barclay's Bank, Ltd*. London: Blades and Blades, 1926.

Myers, Margaret G. *The New York Money Market*. Vol. 1. New York: Columbia University Press, 1931. Reprinted 1971.

Neufeld, E. P. *The Financial System of Canada, Its Growth and Development*. New York: St. Martin's 1972.

Newbold, J. T. W. "The Beginnings of the World Crisis, 1873–1896." *Economic History* 2 (1932): 422–441.

Pareto, Vilfredo. *Le Marché financier italien, 1891–1899*. Annual articles. Reprinted, Geneva: Droz, 1965.

Powell, Ellis T. *The Evolution of the Money Market (1384–1913): An Historical and Analytical Study of the Rise and Development of Finance as a Central Coordinating Force*. London: Financial News, 1915. Reprinted, New York: Augustus Kelley, 1966.

Pred, Allan R. *The Spatial Dynamics of U.S. Urban-industrial Growth, 1900–1914: Interpretive and Theortical Essays*. Cambridge, Mass.: Harvard University Press, 1966.

Presnell L. S. *Country Banking in the Industrial Revolution*. Oxford: Clarendon Press, 1957.

Ray, D. Michael. "Regional Aspects of Foreign Ownership of Manufacturing in Canada." Waterloo, Canada: unpublished paper for the Task Force on the Structure of Canadian Industry (Watkins Committee), 1967.

Ray, D. Michael. "The Location of United States Manufacturing Subsidiaries in Canada." *Economic Geography* 47 (1971): 389–400.

Redlich, Fritz. The *Molding of American Banking, Men and Ideas*. New York: Hafner, 1951.

Riefler, Winfield W. *Money Rates and Money Markets in the United States*. New York: Harper, 1930.

Riesser, Jacob. *The Great German Banks and Their Concentration, in Connection with the Economic Development of Germany*. Washington, D.C.: U.S. Government Printing Office (National Monetary Commission), 1911.

Robbins, Sidney M., and Nestor E. Terleckyi. *Momey Metropolis: A Location Study of the Financial Activities in the New York Region*, Cambridge, Mass.: Harvard University Press, 1960.

Robinson, Roland I. *Money and Capital Markets*. New York: McGraw-Hill, 1964.

Romani, Mario. *Storia economica d'Italia nel secolo XIX, 1815–1914*. Vol. 1. Milan: Dott. A. Giuffre Editora, 1968.

Rosenberg, Hans. *Die Weltwirtschaftskrise von 1857–1859*, Stuttgart-Berlin: Verlag von W. Kohlhammer, 1934.

Ross, Victor A. *A History of the Canadian Bank of Commerce*, Toronto: Oxford University Press, vol. 1, 1920, vol. 2, 1922.

Royal Bank of Canada, Fiftieth Anniversary, 1865–1919. Montreal: privately printed, 1920.

Royal Commission on Banking and Finance. *Report* (Porter Report). Ottawa: Queen's Printer, 1964.

Sametz, Arnold W., ed. *Financial Development and Economic Growth*. New York: New York University Press, 1972.

Sayers, R. S. *Lloyds Bank in the History of English Banking*. Oxford: Clarendon Press, 1957.

Schwartzenbach, Ernst. "The Swiss Money Market." in J. T. Madden and M. Nadler, eds., *The International Money Market*. New York: Prentice-Hall, 1935, 481–523.

[Segré Report] *The Development of a European Capital Market*. Brussels: European Economic Community, 1967.

Seidenzahl, Fritz. *100 Jahre Deutsche Bank, 1870–1970*, Frankfurt-am-Main: Deutsche Bank, 1970.

Shaw, Edward S. *Financial Deepening in Economic Development*. New York: Oxford University Press, 1973.

Smith, Denis Mack. *Italy: A Modern History*. Ann Arbor: University of Michigan Press, 1959.

Taylor, Audrey M. *Gilletts, Bankers at Banbury and Oxford: A Study in Local Economic History*, Oxford: Clarendon Press, 1964.

Thuillier, Guy. "Pour une histoire bancaire régionale: Nivernais de 1800 à 1880," *Annales, économies, sociétés, civilisations* 10 (1955): 494–512.

Tilly, Richard H. *Financial Institutions and Industrialization in the Rhineland, 1815–1870*. Madison: University of Wisconsin Press, 1966.

Union Bank of Switzerland, 1862, 1912, 1962. Zurich: privately printed, 1962.

Vernon, Raymond. *Metropolis, 1985*. Cambridge, Mass.: Harvard University Press, 1960.

Wechsberg, Joseph. *The Merchant Bankers*. Boston: Little Brown, 1966.

[Werner Report] "Report to the Council and the Commission on the Realization by Stages of Economic and Monetary Union." European Community *Bulletin*, suppl. 11, 1970.

Whale F. Barrett. *Joint-Stock Banking in Germany: A Study in German Credit Banks before and after the War*. London: Cass, 1930. Reprinted New York: Augustus Kelley, 1968.

Wilson, J. S. G. "The Australian Money Market." Banca Nazionale del Lavoro *Quarterly Review* 104 (1975): 46–59.

Wiskemann, Erwin. *Hamburg und die Welthandelspolitik von den Anfängen bis zur Gegenwart*. Hamburg: Friederischen, de Gruyter, 1929.

Withers, Hartley. *National Provincial Bank*. London: privately printed, 1933.

12   Anatomy of a Typical Crisis

History vs. Economics

For historians each event is unique. Economics, however, maintains that forces in society and nature behave in repetitive ways. History is particular; economics is general. In the chapters that follow, we shall set out various phases of speculative manias leading to crisis and collapse, with a wealth of historical explanation. In this chapter we are interested in the underlying economic model of a general financial crisis.

Note that we are not presenting here a model of the business cycle. The business cycle involves a full revolution of the economic wheel, while boom and bust deal only with that portion of the cycle covering the final upswing and the initial downturn. Nor are we concerned with the periodicity of both cycles and crises. Such a discussion would broaden the subject to different kinds of cycles: the Kitchin cycle of thirty-nine months, based on the rhythm of fluctuations in business inventories; the Juglar cycle of seven or eight years, related to business investment in plant and equipment; the Kuznets cycle of twenty years, from population changes from generation to generation and the resultant rise and fall in the construction of housing; and possibly the more dubious and elusive Kondratieff cycle, set off by major inventions such as the railroad and the automobile.[1] Along with other observers, we note the spacing of crises ten years apart in the first half of the nineteenth century (1816, 1826, 1837, 1847, 1857, 1866), before the timing became more ragged. We make no attempt to explain this rhythm, beyond suggesting that some time must elapse after one speculative mania that ends in crisis before investors have sufficiently recovered from their losses and disillusionment to be willing to take a flyer again.

The Model

We start with the model of Hyman Minsky, a man with a reputation among monetary theorists for being particularly pessimistic, even lugubrious, in his emphasis on the fragility of the monetary system and its propensity to disaster.[2] Although Minsky is a monetary theorist rather than an economic historian, his model lends itself effectively to the interpretation of economic and financial history. Indeed, in its emphasis on the instability of the credit system, it is a lineal descendant of a model, set out with personal variations, by a host of classical economists including John Stuart Mill, Alfred Marshall, Knut Wicksell, and Irving Fisher. Like Fisher, Minsky attaches great importance to the role of debt structures in causing financial difficulties, and especially debt contracted to leverage the acquisition of speculative assets for subsequent resale.

According to Minsky, events leading up to a crisis start with a "displacement," some exogenous, outside shock to the macroeconomic system. The nature of this displacement varies from one speculative boom to another. It may be the outbreak or end of a war, a bumper harvest or crop failure, the widespread adoption of an invention with pervasive effects—canals, railroads, the automobile—some political event or surprising financial success, or a debt conversion that precipitously lowers interest rates. An unanticipated change of monetary policy might constitute such a displacement, and some economists who think markets have it right and governments wrong blame "policy-switching" for some financial instability.[3] But whatever the source of the displacement, if it is sufficiently large and pervasive, it will alter the economic outlook by changing profit opportunities in at least one important sector of the economy. Displacement brings opportunities for profit in some new or existing lines, and closes out others. As a result, business firms and individuals with savings or credit seek to take advantage of the former and retreat from the latter. If the new opportunities dominate those that lose, investment and production pick up. A boom is under way.

In Minsky's model, the boom is fed by an expansion of bank credit that enlarges the total money supply. Banks typically can expand money, whether by the issue of bank notes under earlier institutional arrangements, or by lending in the form of additions to bank deposits. Bank credit is, or at least has been, notoriously unstable, and the Minsky model rests squarely on that fact. This feature of the Minsky model is incorporated in what follows, but we go further. Before banks had evolved, and afterward, additional means of payment to fuel a speculative mania were available in the virtually infinitely expansible nature of personal credit. For a given banking system at a given time, monetary means of payment may be expanded not only within the existing system of banks, but also by the formation of new banks, the development of new credit instruments, and the expansion of personal credit outside of banks. Crucial questions of policy turn on how to control all these avenues of monetary expansion. But even if the instability of old and potential new banks were corrected, instability of personal credit would remain to provide means of payment to finance the boom, given a sufficiently thorough-going stimulus.

Let us assume, then, that the urge to speculate is present and is transmuted into effective demand for goods or financial assets. After a time, increased demand presses against the capacity to produce goods or the supply of existing financial assets. Prices increase, giving rise to new profit opportunities and attracting still further firms and investors. Positive feedback develops, as new investment leads to increases in income that stimulate further investment and further income increases. At this stage we may well get what Minsky calls "euphoria." Speculation for price increases is added to investment for production and sale. If this process builds up, the result is often, though not inevitably, what Adam Smith and his contemporaries called "overtrading."

Overtrading is by no means a clear concept. It may involve pure speculation for a price rise, an overestimate of prospective returns, or excessive "gearing."[4] Pure speculation, of course, involves buying for resale rather than use in the case of commodities, or for resale rather than income in the case of financial assets. Overestimation of profits comes from euphoria, affects firms engaged in the productive and distributive processes, and requires no explanation. Excessive gearing arises from cash requirements which are low relative both to the prevailing price of a good or asset and to possible changes in its price. It means buying on margin, or by installments, under circumstances in which one can sell the asset and transfer with it the obligation to make future payments. As firms or households see others making profits from speculative purchases and resales, they tend to follow: "Monkey see, monkey do." In my talks about financial crisis over the last decade, I have polished one line that always gets a nervous laugh: "There is nothing so disturbing to one's well-being and judgment as to see a friend get rich."[5] When the number of firms and households indulging in these practices grows large, bringing in segments of the population that are normally aloof from such ventures, speculation for profit leads away from normal, rational behavior to what has been described as "manias" or "bubbles." The word *mania* emphasizes the irrationality; *bubble* foreshadows the bursting. In the technical language of some economists, a bubble is any deviation from "fundamentals," whether up or down, leading to the possibility and even the reality of negative bubbles, which rather gets away from the thrust of the metaphor. More often small price variations about fundamental values (as prices) are called "noise." In this book, a bubble is an upward price movement over an extended range that then implodes. An extended negative bubble is a crash.

As we shall see in the next chapter, the object of speculation may vary widely from one mania or bubble to the next. It may involve primary products, especially those imported from afar (where the exact conditions of supply and demand are not known in detail), or goods manufactured for export to distant markets, domestic and foreign securities of various kinds, contracts to buy or sell goods or securities, land in the country or city, houses, office buildings, shopping centers, condominiums, foreign exchange. At a late stage, speculation tends to detach itself from really valuable objects and turn to delusive ones. A larger and larger group of people seeks to become rich without a real understanding of the processes involved. Not surprisingly, swindlers and catchpenny schemes flourish.

Although Minsky's model is limited to a single country, overtrading has historically tended to spread from one country to another. The conduits are many. Internationally traded commodities and assets that go up in price in one market will rise in others through arbitrage. The foreign-trade multiplier communicates income changes in a given country to others through increased or decreased imports. Capital flows constitute a third link. Money flows of gold, silver (under the gold standard or bimetallism), or foreign exchange are a fourth. And there are purely psychological connections, as when investor euphoria or pessimism in one country infects investors in others. The declines in prices on October 24 and 29, 1929, and October 19, 1987, were practically instantaneous in all financial markets (except Japan), far faster than can be accounted for by arbitrage, income changes, capital flows, or money movements.

Observe with respect to the money movements that in an ideal world, a gain of specie for one country would be matched by a corresponding loss for another, and the resulting expansion in the first case would be offset by the contraction in the second. In the real world, however, while the boom in the first country may gain speed from the increase in the supply of reserves, or "high-powered money," it may also rise in the second despite the loss in monetary reserves, as investors respond to rising prices and profits abroad by joining in the speculative chase. In other words, the potential contraction from the shrinkage on the monetary side may be overwhelmed by the increase in speculative interest and the rise in demand. For the two countries together, in any event, the credit system is stretched tighter.

As the speculative boom continues, interest rates, velocity of circulation, and prices all continue to mount. At some stage, a few insiders decide to take their profits and sell out. At the top of the market there is hesitation, as new recruits to speculation are balanced by insiders who withdraw. Prices begin to level off. There may then ensue an uneasy period of "financial distress." The term comes from corporate finance, where a firm is said to be in financial distress when it must contemplate the possibility, perhaps only a remote one, that it will not be able to meet its liabilities.[6] For an economy as a whole, the equivalent is the awareness on the part of a considerable segment of the speculating community that a rush for liquidity—to get out of other assets and into money—may develop, with disastrous consequences for the prices of goods and securities, and leaving some speculative borrowers unable to pay off their loans. As distress persists, speculators realize, gradually or suddenly, that the market cannot go higher. It is time to withdraw. The race out of real or long-term financial assets and into money may turn into a stampede.

The specific signal that precipitates the crisis may be the failure of a bank or firm stretched too tight, the revelation of a swindle or defalcation by someone who sought to escape distress by dishonest means, or a fall in the price of the primary object of speculation as it, at first alone, is seen to be overpriced. In any case, the rush is on. Prices decline. Bankruptcies increase. Liquidation sometimes is orderly, but more frequently degenerates into panic as the realization spreads that there is only so much money, not enough to enable everyone to sell out at the top. The word for this stage—again, not from Minsky—is *revulsion*. Revulsion against commodities or securities leads banks to cease lending on the collateral of such assets. In the early nineteenth century this condition was known as *discredit*. Overtrading, revulsion, discredit—all these terms have a musty, old-fashioned flavor. They are imprecise, but they do convey a graphic picture.

Revulsion and discredit may go so far as to lead to panic (or as the Germans put it, *Torschlusspanik*, "door-shut-panic"), with people crowding to get through the door before it slams shut. The panic feeds on itself, as did the speculation, until one or more of three things happen: (1) prices fall so low that people are again tempted to move back into less liquid assets; (2) trade is cut off by setting limits on price declines, shut-ting down exchanges, or otherwise closing trading (the device has come to be known as a "circuit breaker," from the Nicholas Brady report to the U.S. government on the stock market implosion of 1987, earlier applied to trading on commodity exchanges, which is cut off for the rest of the day when a commodity has fallen in price by a given percentage in a single session); or (3) a lender of last resort succeeds in convincing the market that money will be made available in sufficient volume to meet the demand for cash. Confidence may be restored even if a large volume of money is not issued against other assets; the mere knowledge that one can get money is frequently sufficient to moderate or eliminate the desire.

Whether or not there should be a lender of last resort is a matter of some debate. Those who oppose the function argue that it encourages speculation in the first place. Supporters worry more about the current crisis than about forestalling some future one. There is also a question of the place for an international lender of last resort. In domestic crises, gov-ernment or the central bank (when there is one) has responsibility. At the international level, there is neither a world government nor any world bank adequately equipped to serve as a lender of last resort, although some would contend that the International Monetary Fund since Bretton Woods in 1944 is capable of discharging the role.

Dilemmas, debates, doubts, questions abound. We shall have more to say about these questions later on.

The Validity of the Model

The general validity of the Minsky model will be established in detail in the chapters that follow. At this stage we simply want to argue against three contrary positions. The first maintains either that each crisis is unique, a product of a unique set of circumstances, or that there are such wide differences among economic crises as a class that they should be broken down into various species, each with its own particular features. We dismiss without argument the monetarist position mentioned in the last chapter that a distinction should be made between "real" (or "true") and "pseudo" financial crises. The second position is that while the Minsky model may have been true of some earlier time, today things are different. This argument cites structural changes in the institutional underpinnings of the economy, including the rise of the corporation, the emergence of big labor unions and big government, modern banking, speedier communications, and so on, and so on. These changes, it is alleged, make a model of crises based on the instability of credit uninteresting except to antiquarians. This view has of course received less support since the financial troubles of the 1980s in Third World debt, office buildings, luxury apartments, shopping malls, and the like, especially in the oil-producing areas of the Southwest, and since the 508-point drop in the Dow-Jones industrial average on October 19, 1987.

The third position is that there can be no bubbles because market prices reflect fundamentals, and that sharp falls in prices frequently reflect "policy switching" by government or central banks. Where there are no fundamentals to claim attention, and an alleged bubble appears to be the result of herd behavior, positive feedback or bandwagon effects—credulous suckers following smart insiders—econometrians who believe in the efficient market hypothesis tend to suggest that the model is "misspecified," i.e. that something was going on not taken into account by the theory, and that more research is called for.[7] Some of the research ignored by those with this belief is offered in this book.

The issue cannot of course be resolved to the satisfaction of everyone. Truth is multidimensional, and on issues of this kind, differences of approach to truth can be justified on the basis of taste or depth of perception. The argument here is that the basic pattern of displacement, overtrading, monetary expansion, revulsion, and discredit, generalized in modern terms by the use of the Minsky model, describes the nature of capitalistic economies well enough to direct our attention to crucial problems of economic policy.

Take first the contrary view that each crisis is unique, a product of a series of historical accidents. This has been said about 1848 and about 1929,[8] and is implied by the series of historical accounts of separate crises referred to throughout this text. There is much to support the view. Individual features of any one crisis will differ from those of another: the nature of the displacement, the object or objects of speculation, the form of credit expansion, the ingenuity of the swindlers, the nature of the incident that touches off revulsion. But if one may borrow a French phrase, the more something changes, the more it remains the same. Details proliferate; structure abides. Our interest in this chapter is structure; in future chapters, details will engage us.

More compelling is the suggestion that the genus "crises" should be divided into species labeled commercial, industrial, monetary, banking, fiscal, financial (in the sense of financial markets), and so on, or into groups called local, regional, national, and international. Taxonomies along such lines abound. Although there is something to be said for such classification, we reject it for two reasons. In the first place, we are concerned primarily with international financial crises involving a number of critical elements—speculation, monetary expansion, a rise in the prices of assets followed by a sharp fall, and a rush into money. Crises that fall outside these dimensions do not, on the whole, concern us, and there are enough within the category to suggest that the broad genus is worthy of study. Second, this book is sufficiently occupied with general features; to penetrate to deeper levels would overburden the analysis by burying it in detail.

A more cogent attack on the model used here comes from the late Alvin Hansen, who claimed that something closely akin to it applied satisfactorily to the world economy prior to the middle of the nineteenth century but then underwent a sea change:

Theories based on uncertainty of the market, on speculation in commodities, on "overtrading," on the excesses of bank credit, on the psychology of traders and merchants, did indeed reasonably fit the early "mercantile" or commercial phase of modern capitalism. But as the nineteenth century wore on, captains of industry ... became the main outlets for funds seeking a profitable return through savings and investments.[9]

In the book from which this quotation is drawn, Hansen was setting out to explain the business cycle. Before getting to the Keynesian analysis, of which he was a foremost expositor, he wanted to clear away earlier explanations. In my judgment, he was wrong—not about the rise of the modern corporation or the importance of savings and investment, but on the corollary that these required the dismissal of the earlier views on speculation in commodities and securities and on instability in credit and prices. It is understandable that Hansen's attention was drawn to savings and investment and the forces that lay behind them, but ignoring uncertainty, speculation, and instability does not mean that they had disappeared.

The heart of this book is that the Keynesian theory is incomplete, and not merely because it ignores the money supply. Monetarism is incomplete, too. A synthesis of Keynesianism and monetarism, such as the Hansen–Hicks IS–LM curves that bring together the investment-saving (IS) and liquidity-money (LM) relationships, remains incomplete, even when it brings in production and prices (as does the most up-to-date macroeconomic analysis), if it leaves out the instability of expectations, speculation, and credit and the role of leveraged speculation in various assets. The Keynesian and Friedmanite schools, along with most modern macroeconomic theories that synthesize them, are perhaps not so much wrong as incomplete. At the same time, the omissions under particular circumstances may be so critical as to make both Keynesianism and monetarism misleading.

The Model's Relevance Today

One place where the model surely applies today is foreign-exchange markets, in which prices rise and fall in wide swings, despite sizable intervention in the market by monetary authorities, and in which exchange speculation has brought large losses to some firms and some banks while others have made substantial trading profits. Financial crisis has been avoided, but in the opinion of some observers, not by much.

Again, contemplate the enormous external debt of the developing countries, built up not only since the rise of oil prices but importantly—a widely ignored fact—in the several years before that time. This occurred as multinational banks swollen with dollars created through a serious mistake in monetary policy (that is, cheap money initiated in the United States to help with Nixon's presidential reelection campaign while the Deutsche Bundesbank was tightening money to curb inflation) tumbled over one another in trying to uncover new foreign borrowers and practically forced money on the less-developed countries (LDCs). Some of the chickens have already come home to roost, in defaults by Zaire and Peru; others such as Argentina, Brazil, and Mexico have had close calls and been forced from time to time to postpone debt service and negotiate debt rescheduling. In this area of syndicated bank lending the world was in distress as early as 1978, although it failed to identify that condition until the Mexican debt crisis of August 1982. On that occasion the United States acted as a lender of last resort with advanced purchases of a billion dollars' worth of oil for the strategic stockpile and a billion-dollar bridging loan from the Federal Reserve Bank of New York until the International Monetary Fund could work out a debt rescheduling. Muddling through has continued thereafter, despite calls from various quarters for a definitive solution of Third World debt by means of a massive write-off.

Other more recent examples can be found in the Japanese stock and real-estate markets in 1988–90 and in mutual fund investments in "emerging markets" in 1993, many of which—especially the Mexican again—collapsed in 1994. Some attention to this fairly current experience is paid below.

The model also applies in the domestic sphere. The biggest economic problem of the late 1980s and 1990s inheres in the twin deficits in the U.S. balance of payments and in the government budget. These clearly outweigh in importance the various speculative bubbles in the United States of the decade that have raised prices to giddy heights from which sharp falls, speculator bankruptcies, and bank failures are not impossible. Overtrading, followed by revulsion and possibly discredit, is by no means a relic of a distant past.

I therefore insist that the model cannot be dismissed out of hand, as Hansen tried to do. But I look back, not ahead. This is a work in financial history, not economic forecasting. The world seems not to have learned from experience in the past. It may do so in future.

Notes

1. Joseph A. Schumpeter, *Business Cycles: A Theoretical, Historical and Statistical Analysis of the Capitalist Process* (New York: McGraw-Hill, 1939), vol. 1, chap. 4, esp. pp. 161ff.

2. Hyman P. Minsky, *John Maynard Keynes* (New York: Columbia University Press, 1975); and idem, "The Financial Instability Hypothesis: Capitalistic Processes and the Behavior of the Economy," in C. P. Kindleberger and J.-P. Laffargue, eds., *Financial Crises: Theory, History and Policy* (Cambridge: Cambridge University Press, 1982), pp. 13–29.

3. Robert D. Flood and Peter M. Garber, *Speculative Bubbles, Speculative Attacks, and Policy Switching* (Cambridge, Mass.: MIT Press, 1994).

4. See R. C. O. Matthews, "Public Policy and Monetary Expenditure," in Thomas Wilson and Andrew S. Skinner, eds., *The Market and the State: Essays in Honour of Adam Smith* (Oxford: Oxford University Press, Clarendon Press, 1976), p. 336.

5. See James B. Stewart, *Den of Thieves* (New York: Touchstone Books [Simon & Schuster], 1991, 1992), p. 97: "What really fueled the takeover boom [in the 1980s] was the sight of other people making money, big money, by buying and selling companies."

6. M. J. Gordon, "Toward a Theory of Financial Distress," *Journal of Finance*, vol. 26 (May 1971), pp. 347–56.

7. See Flood and Garber, pp. 73–4, 85, 96, 98 etc.

8. See C. P. Kindleberger, *The World in Depression, 1929–1939*, 2nd ed. (Berkeley: University of California Press, 1986), pp. 1–3.

9. Alvin Hansen, *Business Cycles and National Income* (New York: W. W. Norton, 1957), p. 226.

13   Gresham's Law

1   Introduction

Once again in this lecture I am going to give the name of a "law" to
something that is miscalled. Gresham's law—that bad money drives good
money out of circulation—is misnamed because the empirical uniformity
was not discovered by Gresham at all. It was wrongly attributed to him in
1857 by Henry D. McLeod. Raymond de Roover tells us that the principle was already well known in 1550, having been stated by Nicolaus
Copernicus in his essay on coinage of 1525.[1] Louis Wolowski traces the
idea back to Nicholas Oresme, Bishop of Lisieux in France, who wrote *De
Moneta* in 1360 or so, attacking monetary debasement and asserting that
the king had no right to change the weight or fineness of coins, or the
bimetallic ratio.[2] An obscure British writer, Humphrey Holt, complained
in 1551 that debased coins were driving good heavy coins abroad and
pushing up prices. This was the year in which Sir Thomas Gresham went
to Antwerp as a private merchant and royal factor, or financial agent of
the Crown, paying out the service of old debts, buying ordnance against
new, and handling specie payments. As is so often the case, the rich, prominent man gets the credit for well-known theories devised by others.

It is of course too late to change the appellation of Gresham's law to
the Oresme, the Copernican or the Holt law. I want, moreover, to widen
the scope of Gresham's law first to two monies, and then beyond it to
discuss market instability, whether for different monies, as in bimetallism,
for notes and coins, two central-bank reserve assets, and the like, to two
different sorts of assets more generally, and especially to money on the
one hand, and real or other types of financial assets on the other. Gresham's law thus extended is a highly useful analytical model for the economic historian to keep in his toolbox, although as the theme of these
lectures warns, it is but one among many, rather than a universal solvent,
or sovereign remedy, like holy relics or North American snake oil.

Gresham's law gained acceptance in a period when most money was silver and the problem lay in the difficulty of keeping good and bad coins together in circulation side by side. Coins that had been sweated, clipped, rubbed, worn or otherwise reduced in weight, or adulterated by addition of other metals and subtraction of silver would be spent quickly. Good coins would be hoarded or shipped abroad where they were sold for their specie weight rather than their nominal value.

Discussion of Gresham's law in this generation has mostly concerned the gold-exchange standard, under which central-bank reserves consisted of gold, foreign exchange convertible into gold, or both, and the trade-off runs between an appropriate supply of international money on the one hand, and its instability with two sorts of reserves on the other. Earlier, the issue arose mainly in connection with bimetallism, where again instability from having two monies—gold and silver—was judged acceptable or unacceptable depending upon one's judgment as to the significance of instability on the one hand and a larger money supply on the other. The trade-off between quantity and stability, however, fails to get to the root of the issue. There is the further vital point that the same money does not always serve with equal efficiency in all uses. More monies may be needed not only to get the quantity right, but to provide the appropriate monies for the different purposes for which they are most suitable.

In the Middle Ages, three metals were used as money—to ignore the sporadic and occasional use of salt, pepper, barter, book entries, tokens, truck, bank notes and bills of exchange—namely copper, silver and gold. Copper was required for small retail transactions of simple folk, but did not suit as well the larger expenditures of middle-class and noble households that used silver, nor the still larger transactions of great merchants that were most efficiently settled in bills of exchange, but where these were unavailable, in gold. Gold was useless for the peasant or craftsman; copper, as Swedish merchants and banks learned the hard way, was a most awkward money for use in settling international imbalances.[3] In France, copper was legal tender up to 1/40th of debts to assist those receiving it to pass it along, but the royal Treasury still found itself overwhelmed with more than it could use. The *Régie des Postes* under Napoleon I, for example, received 9 millions out of its 10 million livres of annual receipts in copper.[4] And of course Gresham's-law problems grew as one moved from metallic monies to bills of exchange, bank notes, deposits, certificates of deposits, and the like. All are money, or may be under appropriate definitions. Most have a comparative advantage in one or another use. The problem is to ensure that they are continuously convertible into one another at fixed rates, the fixed rates being the essence of being able to continue counting them as money.

2 Market Instability for Different Monies

If we move a slight distance from money, Gresham's law could be extended to cover many kinds of assets in portfolios, with the problem to ensure that money can be exchanged for the assets, or the assets for money, and if not at fixed prices, at least at prices that do not careen about wildly. This issue will be dealt with later; bimetallism will be examined first, then the convertibility of notes into coin and deposits into notes, and finally the gold-exchange standard and the pure exchange standard will be touched upon.

Gold has always had a certain magical quality to it, familiar from the Midas legend, and evoked by the heading in one of Keynes' chapters in *The Treatise on Money*, and again in *Essays in Persuasion*, "*auri sacra fames*", or the sacred mystique of gold.[5] Silver may not arouse such deeply psychoanalytical feelings. For the most part, in the last century or two, the contest has been between the gold standard as such, and bimetallism. A number of poorer countries, notably India, China, and Mexico, have embraced the silver standard in the past as Europe had done until 1700 or so; American experiments in raising the price of silver under the New Deal to appease the silver Senators proved deeply disturbing to China and Mexico which were then still on the silver standard.[6]

In 1819 a number of Britons urged that the country resume specie payments in silver, not gold. A number more seem to have preferred the bimetallic standard but fell back on gold as a second-best solution so as to avoid rendering comfort to the monetary cranks who urged against resumption and in favour of continued inconvertibility.[7] In the 1850s in California and Australia gold discoveries threatened to cheapen gold relative to silver and gave rise in France to three successive commissions investigating the monetary standard problem. One member of the commissions, Michel Chevalier, recommended demonetizing gold and moving to the silver standard, as opposed to one member, Esquirou de Parieu, recommending demonetizing silver and the remaining four members coming out for retention of bimetallism.[8] One metallic money as a rule meant gold, adopted by Britain *de facto* in 1774, and *de jure* 42 years later. Two monies meant bimetallism, with gold and silver coins circulating side by side at some fixed mint ratio. Problems arose from many sides; from the fact that mint ratios might differ between countries, although this was not serious so long as transport costs were fairly high and kept the export and import points of the two metals wide apart; from uneven debasement of coins in the separate metals; and especially from changes in production in gold and silver reflecting the accidental effects of discoveries and new mining processes. I say "accidental," although it should be recalled that the age of exploration, initiated by Henry the Navigator of Portugal and culminating in Columbus' discovery of America, was a response, conscious or subconscious, to the 15th-century shortage of specie, brought about by the need to export metal to the Levant in payment for import surpluses.[9]

The ratios at which gold and silver have been coined and thus exchanged for one another have ranged widely. The easily available records beginning in the 13th century show the ratio falling from about $12\frac{1}{2}$ silver to 1 of gold in 1244, to a little over 11 to 1 just before Columbus' discovery. With gold pouring in from Brazil in the first half of the sixteenth century, the ratio fell to 5 to 1. The subsequent flood of silver from the mines of Mexico and Peru tilted the ratio back to more than 15 to 1. In 1717, when Sir Isaac Newton was Master of the Mint in London, a price of gold was set that lasted 200 years. Dominant money at the time was silver. The gold standard began in Britain when silver was demonetized, except for coins, *de facto* in 1774, *de jure* in 1816.[10] Bimetallism was retained in France, with frequent fine adjustments in the 18th century under Turgot and Mirabeau, leading, after the monetary difficulties of the Revolution, to the establishment of the franc under the Law of 7 Germinal (1803). Paris became the European pivot for gold and silver. It came to the aid of London in the crisis of 1825, for example, exchanging gold largely in sovereigns for silver when the Bank of England was having difficulty in keeping its notes convertible into gold coin.[11] The gold discoveries in California and Australia proved less disturbing than Michel Chevalier thought would be the case because gold arriving from overseas in London was rapidly shipped to Paris which offset its impact on the quantity of money in Western Europe by losing silver to the Far East. In 1860 when silver was overvalued, the Bank of France exchanged £2 million of silver for gold with the Bank of England in order to have enough gold on hand to avoid paying out silver. For it to have paid out silver would have caused a run on bank notes exchanged for silver.[12] Again in 1876 the Bank of France was embarrassed by having its principal reserve in the appreciated metal—this time gold—but resolved the issue not through acquiring and paying out silver, but by abandoning bimetallism for the gold standard.[13]

The discoveries in California and Australia yielded as much gold in ten years as had been produced in the 356 years between 1492 and 1848.[14] A somewhat different calculation by Knut Wicksell concludes that in the 25 years after 1851 the world produced as much gold as in the previous 250.[15] Whatever the calculation, the discoveries led to an intense discussion in France of the wisdom of bimetallism, as already indicated, and in particular a sharp debate between the bimetallist Louis Wolowski and the monometallist Michel Chevalier. Ludwig Bamberger, who was in France at the time, stated that men lose their wits about two things, love and bimetallism.[16] Forty years later the polemic between Karl Helfferich, monometallist, and Otto Arendt, the leading German supporter of the Junker bimetallist position, became so heated that Arendt sued Helfferich for slander (but had his suit thrown out of court).[17] In the debate with Chevalier, Wolowski used some striking metaphors. He quotes Molière's *Le Malade Imaginaire*: "Me, cut off an arm, pluck out an eye, in order to get along better. What a beautiful operation—make myself blind and crippled."[18] And he quotes another bimetallist, Cernuschi, who asked: "The world offers two fuels; is it necessary to proscribe wood because one burns coal?"[19]

These rhetorical questions may be said to pose the issue. If two monies are complements, and more is better than less, as agrarian interests like the Junkers in Germany and the Populists in the United States believed, then two monies are better than one. If, on the other hand, the two monies are substitutes, and expectations as to which is the more valuable tilt back and forth and lead to hoarding or exporting one, stepping up the spending of the other, one is better than two. Some monometallists, and hard money men who oppose the use of bank notes, or of foreign exchange as central-bank reserves along with specie, base their opposition to two monies on fear of inflation. Some bimetallists objected to the gold standard for fear of deflation, notably the eloquent William Jennings Bryan. The Gresham's-law question ignores the appropriate quantity of money, that is regarded as separable, and focuses on instability. Walter Bagehot held that bimetallism was not a currency of two metals, but a system of alternative currencies.[20] A defender of bimetallism like Wolowski calls it not a double standard, but double money.[21] Rhetorical tricks abounded. Alfred Marshall sought to overcome the instability and at the same time gain the advantage of a larger monetary base by proposing "symmetallism," in which gold and silver would be always combined in coins and bullion in the same proportions—though this suggestion probably underestimated the ease of melting down the alloy and separating the metals if the market price diverged from the implicit ratio of the combination.[22] A similar proposal in effect was put forward to stabilize the gold-exchange standard by the Dutch economist, S. Posthuma, who recommended a rule that central banks should hold, pay out and accept gold and foreign exchange in their international reserves in an agreed fixed proportion.[23] Both these ideas rely on John Hicks' theorem that two commodities always traded at the same price may be regarded as one. An early attempt to stabilize the overvalued metal is found in the order issued by Charles V of Spain in 1514 that all bills of exchange be paid two-thirds in gold to make up for a decline in the circulation of gold coin.[24]

Bimetallism broke down after 1875, whether because of the discovery of the Comstock lode in Nevada in 1859, the new electrolytic process of recovering silver from lower-grade ores, the large-scale export of silver from Italy preceding the *corso forzoso* of 1866, the precipitous German switch from bimetallism to the gold standard after receiving the 500 million mark metallic portion of the indemnity after the Franco-Prussian war largely in gold, and dumping silver on the world markets, or some combination of the above. Long before this, however, Gresham's law had been tested many times in the convertibility of bank notes into coin.

3   Market Instability and Bank-Note Convertibility

Maintenance of bank-note convertibility is not perhaps exactly the same issue as that posed by two types of metallic money, since paper money has a comparative advantage over coin in terms of convenience and ease in counting, guarding, transporting. It is well to remember that in the early days of banking, bank deposits generally went to a small premium over coin because of this advantage and because of the implicit guarantee by the bank that the metallic reserves against the deposits consisted of the appropriate weight and fineness.[25] Moreover, paper and specie are not additive as are gold and silver, if the paper money is issued against reserves of coin or bullion rather than circulating side by side with it. Nonetheless, the principle is the same and the instability question is central. Instability can also be found between bank deposits and notes, bank deposits and specie, deposits of one bank and those of others. It is seldom that one finds instability between different denominations of bank notes issued by the same authority and in virtually infinitely elastic supply, but Gresham's law generalized a limited distance—I go further later—holds that there may be instability between any two forms of money. Wolowski summarizes Gresham's law in the expression *"le papier chasse le numéraire"* (paper money drives out specie), but one can find opposite cases in addition to the premium of paper over coin under early deposit banking just mentioned. Forrest Hill of the University of Texas tells me that during the 1860s when the rest of the United States was on the greenback standard because of the Civil War, California remained on gold for local payments and maintained a market in greenbacks needed for some payments to the federal government. In this instance, the strong currency drove out the weak, or gold chased paper, and Professor Hill regards it as the opposite of the traditional formulation of Gresham's law.[26]

It is perhaps far-fetched to subsume the Banking School vs. the Currency School debate of the first half of the 19th century in Britain under the heading of Gresham's law, or the comparable modern debate of monetarists vs. Keynesians, but something of a case could be made for so doing. Like the bimetallists, the Banking School, Keynesians and expansionists on the whole do not give much weight to instability, and are more interested in enlarging the money supply, increasing spending, expanding incomes and employment. The Currency School and some monetarists worry somewhat about inflation, but are also concerned with instability and maintaining convertibility.[27] Convertibility of one money into another, of money into assets, and of normally marketable assets into money is the touchstone. When such convertibility is maintained, Gresham's law is held at bay. Monetary debate in the 19th century spent endless hours and countless pages discussing the conditions under which convertibility could be maintained, and forced circulation of bank notes avoided, whether by a 100 per cent reserve at the margin above a fiduciary issue, as under the Bank Act of 1844 in Britain, or a fractional reserve system, such as the *de facto* ratio of bank notes no more than three times the specie reserves of the Bank of France. A few unreconstructed fundamentalists opposed bank notes altogether—Henri Cernuschi in France wanted to limit them to amounts of specie on deposit in a reversion to 100 per cent deposit banking of the 17th century.[28] The agrarian radical, William Cobbett, in England opposed banking altogether,[29] and President Jackson in the United States was at the same time a populist who wanted monetary expansion, and a gold bug who opposed both banks and bank notes.[30]

The Gresham's-law clash between coin and bank notes ended inevitably in the demonetization of coin except for small transactions, and then with a substantial element of seignorage. Bank notes (and deposits) became established as the real money. Demonetization of gold, like that of silver, took time and proceeded in stages. Gold coin coexisted with bank notes in periods of calm only among grandfathers at Christmas, and in the stockings of French peasants, for whom, remembering John Law, the *assignats* and the inflations of two world wars, there was never any calm. In moments of agitation, gold would be sought as a hedge against the uncertain value of notes and bank deposits. There was never enough on such occasions. When the deflationary troubles came in the United States in 1933, the run on banks made it necessary to call in gold at the old price, and forbid further private possession. Coin and bullion were forbidden to foreign-exchange arbitrageurs in March 1968, when the two-tier system was established, with one price for gold among central banks and another for private holders (outside the United States). In August 1971, the United States refused to convert dollars into gold. With the gradual auctioning off of the gold stocks of the International Monetary Fund and the Federal Reserve System demonetization became virtually complete. Gold was reduced to a commodity—and a highly speculative one at that. With no fixed price, it ceased to be money, and paper reigns supreme.

It should be observed once again that two monies are symmetrically unstable and not that specie always drives out paper. The "Golden Avalanche" of 1936–37, occurred when the price of gold had been raised from \$20.67 to \$35.00 and many participants in financial markets, including not a few central banks, thought gold was priced too highly. Dollars were bought in the not-so-rational expectation that the gold price would be lowered again, and gold poured into the United States for months until the steadiness of the United States Treasury and its refusal to lower the gold price became evident.[31]

4   Market Instability and Two Central-Bank Reserve Currencies

En route to demonetization of gold, Gresham's law made itself felt in two aspects of international money, in the clash between gold and foreign exchange in central-bank reserves, and in the clash between two reserve currencies. The gold-exchange standard developed well before World War I (as Peter Lindert has demonstrated).[32] It was promoted by Montagu Norman of the Bank of England at the Genoa conference after that war.[33] After World War II it was submitted to strong attack by Robert Triffin and Jacques Rueff. Triffin called the system absurd and self-destroying on the ground that it encouraged the reserve centre to over-issue its money.[34] Rueff thought it inflationary and providing unfair advantage in seignorage to the reserve-centre country.[35] Neither emphasized the instability under Gresham's law which the existence of two international monies implies, although both proposed replacing the gold-exchange standard with a single money. Triffin wanted to establish a newly-created internationally-operated paper money, with gold demonetized and dollars funded into the new money through the International Monetary Fund, much the sort of process now contemplated in the so-called Substitution Account at the International Monetary Fund. Rueff favoured a return to the pure gold standard, with gold revalued to provide a liquid replacement for the dollars expelled from the system, and countries committed thereafter to settle all balances in gold.

Neither Triffin nor Rueff recognized that in any system with one money that proves to be not completely satisfactory in all uses, the market will create additional money or moneys to suit its needs. In particular, if the national money of the leading country in international financial intercourse is excluded from official reserves in favour of an artificially-created reserve unit or repriced gold, it is virtually inevitable that the market will choose sooner or later to hold at least some reserves in foreign exchange which is spendable. The gold-exchange standard grew up because of the convenience of maintaining reserves in a form that can be used directly, without the necessity to convert them first. For the most part the market chooses to ignore the distinction Triffin and Rueff sought between a reserve currency and a vehicle currency. National money of the leading economic country has a comparative advantage over a pure reserve unit insofar as it can be spent directly. It is virtually impossible to limit international monies to one unless that money is accepted in monetary transactions in the major countries of the world. If officials decree only one international money, the market will produce more, and by so doing reintroduce Gresham's law. With two international reserve centres, the instability threat of Gresham's law is more pressing perhaps than with gold and one national dominant money. If we may abstract from gold and silver and postulate a world where sterling and dollars are used as international monies, there is inevitable latent instability. I do not mean to exaggerate. Sterling, dollar, franc, and other national money blocs may co-exist under reasonable conditions of stability, so long as each financial centre can discharge the necessary functions. But should the capacity of a currency like the pound to finance trade and provide capital look less certain for any reason—whether because of a climacteric in productivity, capital losses during a war, overvaluation of its exchange rate, or any other reason—independent countries belonging to no bloc, and some countries whose ties to the bloc are weak, will turn to other financial centres to fulfil their needs. Paris and London competed for preeminence as the world financial centre during the 19th century, with London's dominance established finally, in the view of most observers, when France went off gold during the Franco-Prussian war.[36] New York's rivalry with London began sometime before or during World War I in the judgment of most historians,[37] but I have found an expression of American braggadocio in challenging London as early as the crisis of 1857.[38] Today with the dollar weak, there is no immediately viable alternative in the Special Drawing Right or the European Currency Unit, but if and when one is produced by official negotiation, or a national currency such as the Deutschmark, the Swiss franc, the Japanese yen is preferred by the market and permitted to be held abroad, Gresham's-law instability will return. Some holders will convert; others will do it more subtly, spending the weak currency and collecting payments in the strong. The present position with the dollar weak and gold demonetized seems anomalous. My reading of history leads me to the conclusion that it will not persist long, and by long I mean five to ten years.

Foreign-exchange crises can be assimilated to Gresham's law, with the two monies representing one national money on the one hand, and all other currencies into which it is convertible on the other. As in other instances, the crisis comes from a change in expectations. It may be belated, or come slowly, or suddenly result from an untoward event, but what happens is that a currency thought strong is seen to be weak, or the contrary, and people rush out of or into the domestic money. In the classic German hyper-inflation, the currency initially depreciated slowly, as Germans and foreigners thought it would be restored to par, and then rapidly as their initial hopes and expectations were proved to be false.[39] The market may be composed of insiders and outsiders, each with different perceptions, the outsiders catching on only slowly to what the insiders are doing. The first to buy get low prices, and the first to sell get high, whereas the outsiders tend to buy high and sell cheap, thus losing money. Of course national monies need not be unstable simply because there are other monies into which they are convertible. I do not insist that Gresham's law always applies, so much as that it is always a possibility. History is replete with illustrations.

The issue arises especially in connection with flexible exchange rates. Many economists assert that there can be no such thing as destabilizing speculation, that markets are rational and daily set prices that take into account all possible available information, so that there is no overshooting of prices upward or downward, no sudden reversals of views, no price changes in absence of changes in the objective situation. The record of the exchange market since the adoption of floating in March 1973 would seem to belie that view, but to pursue the subject would lead me too far afield. I should like to state some of my beliefs on this issue: (i) with flexible exchange rates there is no international money, so that the costs and benefits of international money are escaped and lost respectively; (ii) clean floating (or allowing the flexible exchange rate system to produce any exchange rate it chooses without intervention by the authorities) is an unworkable rule. I could go further and say that all strict rules are unworkable, but that too would lead me astray. For the moment I should like to say that intervention by the authorities in the determination of the exchange rate under a floating exchange rate regime is as inescapable as a lender of last resort in periods of domestic financial crisis.

To summarize, I claim that Gresham's law, which holds that two monies are unstable over time since the weak one drives the stronger into hoarding, is a fact of life virtually impossible to overcome because of the impossibility of settling for long on one money. There are two reasons for this. One money cannot discharge effectively all the tasks that money is needed for. The money that suits one task may not fit another. In addition, if authorities attempt to fix the money supply, or leave it to nature to fix it by adopting a specific metal as money, the market will from time to time create new monies because it wants more. Metallic money led to banks and bank notes. The Bank Act of 1844, that fixed the supply of bank notes, stimulated the use of bills of exchange and bank deposits as money. If one fixes a certain M_i as money, and the market becomes excited, it will create an additional money M_j. The authorities insist on money as exogenous and fixed; if so the market will find new ways to monetize debt and make money endogenous and elastic and these new monies give us more than one money, paving the way for Gresham's law, and latent instability.

5   Real and Financial Assets: A Generalized Market Instability Problem

I now leave the field of exclusively monetary questions and widen the discussion to include other financial assets, and even real assets such as commodities, buildings and land. My contention is that a phenomenon so much like Gresham's law as to be included under its general heading may apply (but not necessarily) when money, other financial assets and real assets are not complements in a portfolio but substitutes because of expectations that their relative prices will change. As in the discussion of

Gresham's law limited to money, we are dealing with crisis phenomena. Crises are not endemic; economies are not always unstable. I assert rather that crises may occur, and that history shows they have occurred. An economic theory that had no room for the instability implicit in Gresham's law would be incomplete, as would a view of economic history that assumed all markets were always in stable equilibrium.

Monetary economists assume that the demand for money is stable. They apply this in balance-of-payments analysis by suggesting that when the supply falls short of demand, people sell goods or securities abroad to build up their money stocks, and when supply at home exceeds demand, they spend the excess money on foreign goods or buy foreign securities to bring the supply of money down to the demand. This is of course a long-run view. In the short run, it makes little sense to vary output and spending to stabilize the supply of money when the evident function of money as a store for value is to bridge over discrepancies between income and spending. Moreover, the long-run view of monetarism that the demand for money is stable is sometimes falsified when people's expectations of the relative worth of money and other assets change, and households and businesses rush out of money into real and other financial assets, or out of real and other financial assets into money—in a sort of Gresham's law pattern of behaviour that leads them to dump one sort of asset for another.

In this sense the model is an ancient one. Adam Smith and John Stuart Mill called it overtrading, leading to revulsion and discredit.[40] Overtrading can take place in bonds, both foreign and domestic, stocks, real estate, both urban and rural, commodities, foreign-exchange (as already noted), particular forms of investment such as canals, railways, office buildings, shopping centres, holiday houses and the like. Lord Overstone is quoted by Walter Bagehot as having a somewhat longer sequence: "quiescence, next improvement, growing confidence, prosperity, excitement, overtrading, CONVULSION [Bagehot's capitals], pressure, stagnation, distress, ending again in quiescence,"[41] that amounts to much the same thing.[42] Crises have been fewer in Britain after 1866, and in 1873 the British may have avoided one by fine tuning when the Bank of England discount rate was changed 24 times in a single year. But other countries and even Britain have had a number—1873 in Austria, Germany and the United States, 1882 and 1888 in France, 1890 in Britain, 1893 in the United States, 1907 in Italy and the United States, 1920 in Britain, and again the United States in 1929, 1937.... There have been frequent foreign-exchange crises since World War II, and small bubbles in lending

for 747 mothballed airplanes, oil tankers moored in Norwegian fjords or
Greek bays, Real Estate Investment Trusts (REITS) and more recently mortgages, consumer credit, loans to less developed countries, and the gold
bubble of last autumn 1979 and this winter 1979–1980, that reminded
many commentators of the tulip mania of 1636, a third of a millennium
earlier, and the silver bubble of spring 1980. Some event occurs, expectations are formed, they go too far, the market overshoots, and then gradually, or suddenly, expectations are revised by a few or by the many, and
the rush into some less liquid financial asset (than money) comes to a halt
and the rush out of it into money begins. It may be thought that the difference between these financial crises and Gresham's law is considerable
and, if pressed, I should have to concede that it may be so. With two
monies, the official price is wrong, so that the market rushes to take advantage of it by spending the undervalued and hoarding the overvalued.
With financial or commodity crises, there is no official price to be wrong.
But there is something not too wide of that, that is, a sudden change in
expectations which makes the old price in the market wrong, and a rush
to get out of the overvalued security, asset or commodity into the safer
one, money, before the price of the overvalued asset collapses.

Economic history teaches us that when Gresham's law relates to monies
the possible remedies are several: 1) shift the mint price of the two metals
nearer to the market price; 2) demonetize all but one of the monies; 3)
increase the supply of the scarce money to show that you have enough to
meet all contingencies; 4) increase the supply of the overvalued currency
to ensure that you can meet all likely demands on the central bank with
that and need not pay out the undervalued currency that guarantees profits to those who obtain it. Demonetizing all but one money, as already
noted, has the awkwardness that it is unlikely that a single money—gold,
silver, paper, foreign exchange—will meet all the money needs of the
society. Increasing the supply of the scarce currency can be done from
time to time by borrowing or swaps, but there are limits. Suspending local
limits on paying out the abundant currency was the standard means of
handling banking panics in Britain in the 19th century. The technique was
to suspend the Bank Act of 1844 which required the Bank of England to
maintain a fixed amount of gold against its bank-note liabilities. More
generally in panics where there is a rush out of real and long-term financial assets into money, the means of allaying the panic is for the lender of
last resort to make money freely available. Reassurance that other assets
can be converted into money induces many asset holders to cease trying
to convert them into cash. It is the prospect of a limit that excites panic

selling, the fear that there will be no money left when it comes one's time
to sell.

There is the view that markets always work well, and that there is no
need for a lender of last resort. The historical response to this claim is to
point to the facts of financial crises in history, and to emphasize that at
the time, while the crises might in theory cure themselves if left alone, the
authorities are rarely willing to take the risk that a given crisis will not. By
some sort of revealed historical preference, the lender of last resort moves
in panic, to provide the liquidity so desperately needed as judged by contemporaneous observers. William Huskisson said of December 1825, "We
were within a few hours of a state of barter."[43] Clapham writing on the
same panic said "It was as the Duke said of Waterloo, 'a damned nice
thing'—the nearest run thing you ever saw in your life."[44]

It may well be that contemporaneous observers exaggerate the disasters
that would ensue from failing to halt the panic. In 1933, the Bank Holiday
in the United States was widely noted to have produced not dismay on
the part of the public, but a relaxation of the inchoate financial fears of
the previous months, and even a sort of carnival spirit that came from the
release of tension. But I would argue that the possibility of sudden
changes in expectations and normal relationships between the values of
assets—in a sort of extension and generalization of Gresham's law—calls
for an awareness of the role of the lender of last resort, at national and
international levels, and that to dismiss such possibilities is irresponsibly
to ignore the lessons of history.

Finally I should like to return to the narrower view of Gresham's law,
and by way of conclusion re-emphasize the dilemma in which it puts us.
With two or more monies, we are subject to the instability of Gresham's
law. Any attempt to limit ourselves to one money is likely to be thwarted
by the market's need for different monies for different purpose and its
capacity to create them.

The market's capacity to create new monies raises an issue of monetary
theory which has long been dormant but is nonetheless important to bear
in mind. At the turn of this century, an issue of monetary theory centred
on whether money was the creation of the state which typically had a
monopoly of minting, often of issuing bank notes through its central
bank, and regulated banks and through them deposits, or whether money
was what money did, i.e. was a creation of the market. Knapp held to a
state theory of money. The usage school held oppositely that while the
state proposed, the market disposed. Money was what people used in
making payments. On this showing, if the state issued a ukase that gold

alone was money, the market could frustrate that decision by making payments with bank notes, bank deposits, bills of exchange, or other instruments. If the state then seeks to escape the clutches of Gresham's law by establishing a single money, this will work for money, provided that Knapp was right, and money is what the state determines it to be, but not for the instability of sudden panicky switches back and forth between money and other assets. If the usage school is right, however, as seems likely to me, the state can decree that there be one money, but the market can make more, thereby raising the possibility of Gresham-law instability, as switches occur between or among the various monies.

Under fixed exchange rates, despite Jacques Rueff's belief in gold settlements, the inconvenience of gold or Special Drawing Rights, or even the European Currency Unit, is virtually certain to make some national money superior for settling international payments, thus resulting in at least two monies, gold and a dominant national money. Since economies that wax may also wane, as the Gompertz curve derived from Engel's law in the first lecture makes clear, the dominant money that serves well for international payments at one time, may not suit so well in another era, thus inducing the market to switch over time to another currency. With two reserve currencies, Gresham's law is on the loose in another area. Reference can be made to the increasing unsuitability of the dollar as international money, and the attempt in the European Monetary System to create a viable alternative. The transition period between the world on the dollar standard and a shift to the ECU will be fraught with Gresham-law instability.

Perhaps Gresham's law and the possibility of instability have been overemphasized, for I maintain that for the most part markets are stable, and monies are stable. I only warn that Gresham's law explains a great deal of economic history. And it seems to me foolhardy to think of monetary reform as if Gresham's law could be wished away.

In his pamphlet on "A Universal Money" based on a series of articles in *The Economist* in 1868, Walter Bagehot started out proposing one universal money, and then backed off, thinking that it would take too much political will to integrate the pound, dollar, German mark on the one side and the Latin Monetary Union on the other:

I fear the attempt to found a universal money is not possible now; I think it would fail because of its size. But I believe we could get as far as two moneys, two leading commercial currencies, which nations could one by one join as they chose, and which, in after time, might be combined; and though this may fall short of theoretical perfection, to the practical English mind it may seem the more probable for that very reason.[45]

I like the hint of the optimum currency area in the mention of size, and of John Williams' "key-currency" concept in the mention of "leading commercial currencies." But I would suggest to Walter Bagehot, and to the European Economic Community as its members set up the European Currency Unit, that economic history warns against the dangers of ignoring Sir Thomas Gresham's law, even if Gresham did not originally propound it.

Notes

1. Raymond Adrien de Roover, *Gresham on Foreign Exchange*, Cambridge, Mass.: Harvard University Press, 1949, pp. 91–2.

2. Ludwig (Louis) Franciszek Michal Raimond Wolowski, *La Question monétaire*, Second edition, Paris: Guillaumin, 1869, p. 19.

3. Eli F. Heckscher, "The Bank of Sweden in its Connection with the Bank of Amsterdam," in J. G. Van Dillen, ed., *History of the Principal Public Banks*, The Hague: Martinus Nijhoff, 1934, pp. 161–89, see pp. 179–80.

4. François Nicolas Mollien, *Mémoires d'un Ministre du Trésor Public, 1780–1815*, Paris: Fournier, 1845, tôme III, p. 171.

5. John Maynard Keynes, *A Treatise on Money*, London, Macmillan 1930, vol. II, Chapter 35; *Essays in Persuasion*, New York: London, Macmillan, 1932, p. 181; respectively reprinted in *The Collected Writings of John Maynard Keynes*, vol. VI, *A Treatise on Money: The Pure Theory of Money*, Chapter 35 and vol. IX *Essays in Persuasion*, p. 248, London: Macmillan, 1971 and 1972.

6. See Charles P. Kindleberger, *The World in Depression, 1929–1939*, Berkeley: University of California Press; London: Allen Lane, The Penguin Press, 1973, p. 235.

7. The secondary sources are a little confused as to which economists or economic amateurs favoured silver and which bimetallism. Smart states that the Earl of Lauderdale favoured silver over gold (William Smart, *Economic Annals of the Nineteenth Century*, vol. 1, *1801–1820*, London: Macmillan, 1910–1971; reprinted New York: Augustus M. Kelley, 1964, pp. 478, 622). In one discussion, Fetter notes that the Earl of Lauderdale introduced a resolution for bimetallism (Frank Whitson Fetter, *Development of British Monetary Orthodoxy, 1797–1875*, Cambridge, Mass.: Harvard University Press, 1965, p. 9). In a more recent work he observes that Alexander Baring, Peter King, the Earl of Lauderdale, Poulett Thompson, and Sir Robert Richard Torrens, in principle supporters of a silver standard or of bimetallism, held back because of their strong opposition to inconvertible paper money (Frank Whitson Fetter, *The Economist in Parliament, 1780–1868*, Durham, N.C.: Duke University Press, 1980, p. 95).

8. Louis Wolowski, *La Question monétaire, op. cit.*, pp. 187–8.

9. Ralph Davis, *The Rise of the Atlantic Economies*, Ithaca: Cornell University Press, 1973, pp. 4, 7. See also Pierre Vilar, *A History of Gold and Money, 1450–1920*, translated from the 1969 French edition by Judith White, London: NLB, 1976, pp. 45, 47, 63; first published as *Oro y Moneda en la Historia, 1450–1920*, Barcelona: Ediciones Ariel, 1969.

10. United States Senate, *International Monetary Conference*, held in Paris, in August 1878, under the auspices of the Ministry of Foreign Affairs of the Republic of France, Senate Executive Document No. 58, 45th Congress, Third Session, Washington D.C.: Government Printing Office, 1879, p. 619; reprinted New York: Arno Press, 1979.

11. Sir John Clapham, *The Bank of England: A History*, Cambridge: Cambridge University Press, 1945, vol. 2, p. 100.

12. Walter Bagehot, "The Effects of the Resumption of Specie Payments in France on the Price of Silver," in *The Silver Question*, IV, *The Economist*, vol. XXXIV, 18th March 1876; reprinted in *The Collected Works of Walter Bagehot*, edited by Norman St John-Stevas, London: The Economist, 1978, vol. X, pp. 150–5, *see* p. 150.

13. *Ibid.*, p. 152, and United States Senate, *op. cit.* 207n.

14. Michel Chevalier, *On the Probable Fall in the Value of Gold: The Commercial and Social Consequences which may Ensue, and the Measures which it Invites*, translated from the French, with Preface, by Richard Corben, Manchester: Alexander Ireland & Co., London: W. H. Smith and Son; Edinburg: Adam and Charles Black, Third edition, 1859, p. VI.

15. Knut Wicksell, *Lectures on Political Economy*, vol. II, *Money*, New York: Macmillan; London: G. Routledge & Sons, 1935, p. 37.

16. Quoted by Paul H. Emden, *Money Powers of Europe in the Nineteenth and Twentieth Centuries*, New York: D. Appleton-Century, 1938, p. V.

17. John G. Williamson, *Karl Helfferich, 1872–1924, Economist, Financier, Politician*, Princeton: Princeton University Press, 1971, pp. 33–5.

18. Louis Wolowski, *La Question monétaire, op. cit.*, p. 91n.

19. *Ibid.*, p. 217.

20. Walter Bagehot, "Bimetallism," in *The Silver Question*, XVII, *The Economist*, vol. XXXIV, 30th December 1876; reprinted in *The Collected Works of Walter Bagehot, op. cit.*, pp. 215–17, see p. 216.

21. Louis Wolowski, *La Question monétaire, op. cit.*, p. 207.

22. Alfred Marshall, *Money, Credit and Commerce*, London: Macmillan, 1923, pp. 64–7.

23. Suardus Posthuma, "The International Monetary System," *Banca Nazionale del Lavoro Quarterly Review*, No. 66, September 1963, pp. 239–61.

24. Frank C. Spooner, *The International Economy and Monetary Movements in France, 1493–1725*, Cambridge, Mass.: Harvard University Press, 1972, p. 133.

25. J. G. Van Dillen, "The Bank of Amsterdam," in J. G. Van Dillen, ed., *History of the Principal Public Banks, op. cit.*, pp. 91–2.

26. Conversation with Professor Forrest Hill, Austin, Texas, 2nd April 1979.

27. See Charles P. Kindleberger, "Keynesianism vs. Monetarism in the eighteenth and nineteenth centuries," in *History of Political Economy*, vol. 12, No. 4, Winter 1980, pp. 499–523.

28. See the testimony of Garnier-Pages, Ministère des Finances et Ministère de l'Agriculture, du Commerce et des Travaux Publics, *Enquête sur les principes et les faits généraux qui régissent la circulation monétaire et fiduciaire*, Paris: Imprimerie Impériale, 1867, tome II, p. 43.

29. Michel Chevalier, *Lettres sur l'Amérique du Nord*, Third edition, Pairs: Gosselin, 1838, vol. 1, p. 73 note.

30. *Ibid.*, vol. 1, p. 223.

31. Frank D. Graham and Charles R. Whittlesey, *Golden Avalanche*, Princeton: Princeton University Press, 1939; reprinted New York: Arno Press, 1979.

32. Peter H. Lindert, "Key Currencies and Gold, 1900–1913," Department of Economics, Princeton University, N.J.: *Princeton Studies in International Finance*, No. 24, August 1969.

33. Sir Henry Clay, *Lord Norman*, London: Macmillan, 1957; reprinted New York: Arno Press, 1979, p. 137.

34. Robert Triffin, *Gold and the Dollar Crisis*, New Haven: Yale University Press, 1960.

35. Jacques Rueff and Fred Hirsch, "The Role and the Rule of Gold: An Argument," Department of Economics, Princeton University, *Essays in International Finance*, No. 47, June 1965.

36. See Walter Bagehot, *Lombard Street. A Description of the Money Market*, Chapter II, "A General View of Lombard Street," London: H. S. King, 1873; reprinted in *The Collected Works of Walter Bagehot, op. cit.*, vol. IX, pp. 58–68, see pp. 63–4.

37. See, for example, Paul P. Abrahams, *The Foreign Expansion of American Finance and its Relationship to the Foreign Economic Policies of the United States, 1907–1921*, New York: Arno Press, 1974, and Kathleen Burk, "J. M. Keynes and the Exchange Rate Crisis of July 1917," in *Economic History Review*, vol. XXXII, No. 3, August 1979, pp. 405–16, see p. 409.

38. See "the late struggle of 1857 was in a great degree between New York and London, and has terminated to the advantage of the former city. And the time must ere long arrive, when New York, and not London, will become the financial center not only of the New World, but also to a great extent, of the Old World" from the *New York Herald*, "The Revolution of 1857—Its Causes and Results," in David Morier Evans, *The History of the Commercial Crisis, 1857–1858, and the Stock Exchange Panic of 1859*, London: Groombridge and Sons, 1859; reprinted New York: Augustus M. Kelley, 1969, p. 114.

39. See League of Nations, Economic, Financial and Transit Department, *The Course and Control of Inflation. A Review of Monetary Experience in Europe after World War I*, A Report written by Ragnar Nurkse, League of Nations, 1946, p. 47.

40. See Adam Smith, *An Inquiry into the Nature and Causes of the Wealth of Nations*, two volumes, London: Printed for W. Strahan and T. Cadell, 1776. The Edition quoted is the text edited by Edwin Cannan and published by Methuen & Co, London: Fourth edition, 1935 p. 406; John Stuart Mill, *Principles of Political Economy, with some of their applications to social philosophy*, First edition in two volumes, London: John W. Parker, 1848; The edition quoted is the text edited by W. J. Ashley, London: Longmans Green & Co., 1909, pp. 631–734.

41. Walter Bagehot, "Investments," *Inquirer*, vol. XI, No. 526, July 31 1852, p. 482; reprinted in *The Collected Works of Walter Bagehot, op. cit.*, vol. IX, pp. 272–5; see pp. 272–3.

42. O'Brien calls this one of the first statements of the trade cycle. It is contained in Lord Overstone (then Samuel Jones Loyd), *Reflections Suggested by a Perusal of Mr. J. Horsley Palmer's pamphlet on the Causes and Consequences of the Pressure on the Money Market*. London: Pelham Richardson, 1837. See Denis Patrick O'Brien, "Introduction" in Denis Patrick O'Brien, ed., *The Correspondence of Lord Overstone*, Cambridge: Cambridge University Press, 1971, vol. 1, p. 63.

43. William Smart, *Economic Annals of the Nineteenth Century*, vol. ii, *1821–1830*, London: Macmillan, 1910–1917; New York: Kelley Reprints, 1964, p. 299.

44. Sir John Clapham, *The Bank of England: A History*, vol. ii, *1797–1914*, Cambridge: Cambridge University Press, 1945, p. 101.

45. Walter Bagehot, *A Universal Money*, (*A Practical Plan for assimilating the English and American money, as a step towards a Universal Money*), London: Longmans, 1869; reprinted in *The Collected Works of Walter Bagehot, op. cit.*, vol. xi, pp. 57–104, see "Preface," p. 66.

14 British Financial Reconstruction, 1815–1822 and 1918–1925

It may be regarded by some as ill-mannered to argue with Walt Rostow in honouring him. A superficial defence can be found in the modern statement that it doesn't make any difference what you say about a person as long as you mention him frequently and spell his name correctly. More fundamentally, Professor Rostow has posed an interesting and profound interpretation of a classic issue that is worth illuminating.

In the first place, in *The World Economy* (1978, pp. xlii, xliii), he states:

For some, at least, monetary affairs will appear to have been slighted. In the analysis of the pre-1914 era monetary affairs appear only when I believe they left a significant impact on the course of events, e.g. transmitting the effects of bad harvests in the eighteenth and nineteenth centuries; in helping create the settings for cyclical crises and then (in Britain at least), cushioning their impact; in stimulating, under the gold standard, the inflationary diversion of resources to gold mining. In the post-1918 world of more conscious monetary policies, they emerge on a stage in the 1920s with the French devaluation and the British return at the old rate, as well as the failure of the United States to accept its responsibilities for the trade and monetary structure of the world economy. After 1945, the rise and fall of the Bretton Woods system forms (*sic*), of course, part of the narrative.

Nevertheless it should be underlined that the view taken here of the course of production and prices—in cycles, trend periods, and in the process of growth itself—would regard the non-monetary factors as paramount.... Men and societies have devised and evolved monetary systems which more or less met their deeper needs and purposes as they conceived them. Different monetary policies, at different times and places, might have yielded somewhat different results than history now records. The same could be said with equal or greater strength about fiscal policies. But down to 1914 modern concepts of monetary and fiscal policy did not exist, except perhaps in a few unorthodox minds; and prevailing notions reordered the monetary system substantially passive and responsive.

Reprinted with permission from Charles P. Kindleberger and Guido di Tella (eds), *Economics in the Long View: Essays in Honour of W. W. Rostow.* Vol. 3: *Applications and Cases, Part II* (London: Macmillan, 1982), pp. 105–20.

In a subsequent essay reviewing the new monetarism, he defends this position at length, insists that pre-1914 monetary systems were passive and flexible, and sides once more with the Thomas Tooke position, against David Ricardo, that price changes emanate from the supply side through costs and output changes (1980).

I have a difficult time with these propositions, and especially with the notions: (1) That there was a major discontinuity in 1914; and (2) the pre-1918 world was less conscious of monetary problems than the post-1918 and that the modern concepts of monetary and fiscal policy did not exist theretofore. The more usual view is that monetary orthodoxy goes back at least to 1797, or, if you prefer, to Thornton and Ricardo in 1802 and 1809 (Fetter, 1965; Morgan, 1943). But the inspiration of this paper comes secondly from Rostow's sharp reaction to a remark I made in his seminar at the University of Texas at Austin, shortly after having read A. W. Acworth's *Financial Reconstruction in England, 1815–1822* (1925), suggesting close parallelism between Britain, 1815 to 1822 and 1918 to 1925. Analogues run between the Bullion Report (1810/1978) and the Cunliffe Report (1925/1978); the postwar booms of 1814 and 1919, followed by collapse in 1816 and 1920, and then recovery for a couple of years in both cases; the Parliamentary committee report favouring resumption in 1819 and the Chamberlain–Bradbury report of 1924; the Peterloo "massacre" of 1819 and the coal strike of 1925 plus the General Strike of 1926; deflation following for four more years to 1823 after resumption in 1819, for six years until the 1931 depreciation in the case of 1925. Rostow denied that the troubles of 1815 to 1822 were anything like those of 1918 to 1925 or 1931. The latter were monetary, the former non-monetary. One could cite weightier authority than Acworth who says in his preface that he has "refrained from pointing comparisons, contrasts with the last seven years" (1925, p. v.), for example T. E. Gregory in his introduction to Tooke's *History of Prices* (1928), who states:

If the economic and, in particular the monetary problems we are facing today have a startling resemblance to those which were the subject-matter of contention for two generations a century ago, the experience of the Napoleonic and post-Napoleonic days has an interest for us in two respects. The two periods illumine one another, and we can pass from the depreciated exchanges of 1797–1819 to those of 1914–1925 ... with the feeling that our comprehension of the past and present is increased by comparing one with the other.

But these volumes have a renewed interest in another ... respect. The interpretation of the events of the period ... gave rise to an intellectual conflict in which now one side, now the other seemed for a time to have carried off the final victory.

It is true that the major participants in the decision to stabilise the pound seem not to have thought about the analogy—*pace* Acworth. I recall no reference to it in Keynes (1930, 1932, 1933), Leith-Ross (1968), Grigg (1948), the Moggridge accounts (1969, 1972), the Norman biographies— Clay (1957/1978), Boyle (1967)—or Howson (1975). A peek is worth two finesses, however, so I wrote to Moggridge and asked. He kindly replied that only Hawtrey evoked the analogy between 1819 and 1925, and he did so several times. Nonetheless there seems to be enough evidence to reopen the question, to indict, if not at this stage to convict.

If I were more ambitious, I might try to extend the analogy to the British recoinage of silver in 1696, which involved appreciation and depression (Hawtrey, 1927, pp. 290 ff), or that of Demaretz in France in 1715 when the *livre* was raised from 20 to 14 to the *louis d'or* (Lüthy, 1959, I, p. 281). I urge these extensions on the reader, not excluding Professor Rostow.

Apart from the closeness of the 1815/1918 analogy, it is hard to accept the suggestion that money and banking were passive and accommodating. Resumption was subject to "extremely heated controversy," particularly as it was accompanied by sharp deflation, probably intensified by the decision in 1821 to return to a full gold-coin standard instead of Ricardo's bullion plan (O'Brien, 1971, I, p. 71). The decision to resume gold payments was postponed at least six times. Nor did all but a few unorthodox minds agree on policy choices. There were clearly many who were unorthodox —William Cobbett who detested paper money, the national debt and banks; Sir John Sinclair, who "went off in all directions at once, as he so often did," wanted a large note issue but was concerned about the "coinage of paper money" (Fetter, 1965, pp. 22, 29); the eighth Earl of Lauderdale, an advocate of silver money, or at best bimetallism, a perpetual Cassandra of the economic situation in England (*ibid.*, p. 15). In his review of a book by Lord King, Francis Horner, the chairman of the Committee that wrote the Bullion Report of 1810 stated: "In great commercial cities, opinions have been avowed by persons who ought to be acquainted with the money trade that precious metals are unnecessary and that the provisions of the law of 1797 should be made permanent" (*ibid.*, p. 56). On the other side of the debate, Wheatley was, if penetrating and original, an extreme bullionist who held that monetary expansion had no effect on output, and foreign payments no impact on the exchange rate because of frictionless real transfer (*ibid.*, p. 38). Most participants in the discussion, however, were prepared to concede some merit to the opposite case. Ricardo would have advocated devaluation if the pound had been depreciated in 1819 by 30 per cent, as it had been in 1813 (Viner, 1937,

p. 205n.). "Even so ardent a disciple of Ricardo as McCulloch thought the old par a mistake" (*ibid.*, p. 175). Thomas Attwood of the Birmingham School, who resisted resumption and wanted monetary expansion, would halt such expansion whenever it was sufficient to call every labourer into action; any further stimulus would be nugatory or injurious (*ibid.*, p. 212n.). Even Tooke, says Gregory, was *never* (his italics) an extreme bullionist (1928, p. 16). He was however a good hater (*ibid.*, p. 120), a magnificent controversialist, with a thesis to uphold and an enemy to vanquish.

Rostow, of course, has been over this ground years ago. He wrote Part I of Volume I of the classic Gayer, Rostow and Schwartz, *Growth and Fluctuations of the British Economy, 1790–1850* (1953, I, p. vi). In this work he broke down restriction from 1797 to 1819 into a series of short periods, largely, for our purposes, 1803 to 1806, 1807 to 1811, 1812 to 1816, and 1817 to 1821, and submitted each one to an identical period-by-period analysis of prices, foreign trade, investment, industry and agriculture, finance and labour. Finance was only one factor out of six, and that taken up penultimately. Moreover, he follows Tooke closely. I counted 10 long quotations from that authority in the 110 pages, in addition to 60-plus citations. Tooke's time periods are somewhat different, 1799–1803, 1804–8, 1809–13, 1814–18, and 1819–22, and his schema is divided in three: the effect of the seasons, which discusses the harvest; the effect of war, dealing largely with the need to finance British and foreign troops fighting the French; and finally currency, which in his view essentially has nothing to do with prices or the exchange rate. Rostow follows him and Silberling (1924) in the analysis of the exchange rate. Extraordinary expenses abroad consist of bills and specie remitted for British armies, subsidies and loans for allies, and grain imports of more than £2 million in any year. The sum of these tracks very well with the price of silver and the exchange rate on Hamburg, as Viner shows (1937, p. 143), and the depreciation of the pound is not markedly different whether one takes the premium of the market above the mint gold price, the premium on silver, or the Hamburg exchange rate. Tooke and Rostow have a solid victory in this over many of the bullionists, including especially Ricardo and Wheatley, who dismissed extraordinary foreign expenditures as a source of depreciation because they assumed a frictionless transfer mechanism. The directors of the Bank of England on the other hand were also wrong in telling the Bullion Committee that foreign payments led to a 100 per cent loss of specie. But the division of the period into short subperiods leads to overemphasis of the short run and neglect of the truths of the long.

Tooke has little difficulty in indicating a whole series of years at the beginnings and ends of his mini-periods when currency issues and prices were going in different directions. In some of his more ironic passages, he goes down into quarters and months, finding, for example, that the gold premium and the exchange rate were improving in the spring of 1814 when the circulation was rising, and that prices collapsed in the spring of 1819 when the Bank of England circulation was still unchanged (1838, II, pp. 80–1, 96–7). I shall have something more to say about these speculative periods later. For the moment, however, one should observe that if 1797 to 1822 is divided into one expansionary and inflationary period from 1797, and particularly from 1808 to 1814, followed by deflation to 1822, as Viner does (1937, chs iii, iv), it would have been evident that the sum of Bank of England commercial paper under discount and advances to the government rose from a low of £14.1 millions in 1798 to £41.4 millions in 1815 (*ibid.*, p. 167); and that thereafter total advances (a somewhat different concept) declined from £42.9 millions in 1814 (£42.5 million in 1815) to £14.8 millions in 1824. To focus on the short run and leads and lags neglects long-run truth. Bank of England circulation is not a good measure of the money supply for a number of reasons—the debated question whether the note issues of the country banks are substitutes or complements for notes of the Bank; the even more hotly debated issue whether or not to count £1 and £2 notes, issued for the first time to conserve gold early in the war, and replaced by gold coin at an unknown rate beginning in 1816; and the gradually evolving role of deposits at the Bank.

It is none of our tasks to resolve these questions and decide by how much the money supply rose to 1814, and fell thereafter, or whether in fact the Bank responded passively, as Tooke and his Banking School believe it should and did, or whether the Bank behaved perversely in following the real-bills doctrine erroneously up to 1814, and then, beginning to get ready for resumption, withdrawing money and stockpiling gold. It is enough to point out the analogy between the two periods, 100-plus years apart, and to suggest that, if anything, economic analysis of the resumption issue was more sophisticated after the peace of Vienna than after Versailles.

Modern monetary theory may have been said to have begun with Henry Thornton's *An Enquiry into the Nature and Effect of the Paper Credit of Great Britain* in 1802 rather than in 1936 with Keynes' *General Theory.* Thornton not only developed the doctrine of the lender of last resort, well before Bagehot, but he also had a nice sense of the long run and the short. Much of the work is devoted to the quantity theory which he later brought to his shared authorship of the Bullion Report (1810/1978), but he also warned against too-precipitous contraction of the Bank of England circulation which may well produce convulsions leading to outflows of specie, rather than the inflow predicted by the monetary theory of the balance of payments (1802/1962, pp. 116, 122, 226–7). Tooke admired *Paper Credit*, he asserted, and called Thornton profoundly acquainted with the principles and details of banking, adding, however, that he had not necessarily, from his occupation as a banker, any knowledge of markets (1838, I, pp. 313–14). The remark could be turned against Tooke, who was a merchant and business man, in insurance and docks, but whose understanding of banking came from the perspective of a customer, rather than the inside.

Unlike 1925, when there was little or no organised opposition to the return of sterling to par, and only the somewhat chaotic and unconvincing arguments of Keynes and McKenna (Moggridge, 1972, pp. 42 ff), two groups opposed resumption in 1819 and earlier, and wanted it reversed in subsequent years. In numbers and position they were so prominent that it is hard to characterise them as "a few unorthodox minds." The Birmingham School was interested in employment, maintaining an embryonic Keynesian view (of the 1930s, not 1920s) that expansion of bank circulation was necessary to increase employment and that it was impossible to achieve such expansion with resumption. The agriculturalists had what was close to a Populist position, with emphasis on higher prices to lighten the burden of debt, both mortgage and national debt, the service of which required high taxation. It even contained a bimetallist, who sometimes appears to be in favour of the silver standard, the Earl of Lauderdale (Smart, 1911/1964, I, pp. 478, 622) who was the sole member of the 1819 Lords Committee to vote against resumption (Fetter, 1965, p. 93 note). In this he was a precursor of the Junkers who favoured bimetallism for Germany at the end of the century (Williamson, 1971, p. 21), and of course the American Populists of William Jennings Bryan's day.

It does not seem to me to be entirely correct to say that the Birmingham School had no interest in the inequity between creditor and debtor from inflation and deflation (Fetter, 1965, p. 75; Checkland, 1948, p. 3). Checkland himself notes that Thomas Attwood conceded the case for resumption, provided all debts and obligations would be adjusted (1948, p. 5; Viner, 1937, p. 186). He further talked in terms of stabilising money in terms of wheat, all prices, the rate of interest, or the wages of agricultural labour, all but the third of which comes close to the agricultural position. But the main interest of Birmingham was employment.

There was no doubt that Birmingham was hurt by real factors. War expenditure had been cut, particularly affecting the city that manufactured small arms, hardware, and the "toy trade." Machinery was displacing handwork. Exports had been reduced not only by the miscalculations of 1814, comparable to those of 1919, but by tariff increases in the United States and on the Continent. Britain had made rather feeble efforts to guarantee entry of her products in the territory of her wartime allies, seeking, like the United States in the Lend-Lease settlements nearly a century and a half later, to use its bargaining power for trade advantage. It did not succeed (Sherwig, 1969, p. 311). The failure was complained of contemporaneously by Brougham and in 1835 by Cogden (Acworth, 1925, pp. 121–2). A Birmingham petition of labourers, with 11,000 signatures collected in 48 hours, was presented by Brougham to Parliament in 1817, complaining that the city was unemployed or down to 2 to 3 days work a week. Another petition of Birmingham citizens in 1820, drafted by the banker Thomas Attwood, called for a reconsideration of resumption. (These petitions have left a less lasting impression in history than the well-known petition of the Merchants of London for freer trade, presented in 1820 too, written by Thomas Tooke, and presented to Parliament by Alexander Baring [Smart, 1911/1964, I, pp. 744–7].) A motion for repeal was introduced into the House of Commons by Baring, and was defeated twice, the second time on a roll-call vote of 141–27. In the course of the debate, Edward Ellice said he would have preferred resumption at £5 10s for gold, compared to the parity price of £3 17s 10$\frac{1}{2}$d. This would have been a depreciation of more than 40 per cent (Fetter, 1965, pp. 100–1). Lord Folkestone for the agriculturalists would have settled for £4 0s 6d in 1819. Tooke states that undertaking resumption at the market price of 1819 "however *palpably unjust*, would have least have been *intelligible*" (1838, II, p. 65, his italics). In 1828 Mr Denison said the proper course to be taken in 1819 was not widely agreed. He held to £4 10s or £4 15s while a colleague in the House of Commons, agreeing with a noble Lord in the other House (Lord Lauderdale?) thought that it ought to be £5 5s or £5 10s (*ibid.*, II, pp. 67, 68). Thomas Attwood himself wanted abandonment of the gold standard altogether, but failing that he sought devaluation by raising the price of gold to £8, qualified to £6 in 1821 and to £5 in 1826 (Checkland, 1948, p. 15). The first number qualifies as unorthodox.

Here was a sharp contrast with 1925 when the issue was never posed in terms of alternative exchange rates but only resumption or no resumption at the price for gold set by Isaac Newton in 1717. It will also be remembered that, when Britain finally went off the gold standard in September, 1931, Tom Johnson, an ex-Labour minister, is said to have remarked "They never told us we could do that" (Moggridge, 1969, p. 9).

The problem of money as a standard of deferred payment for contracts came to national attention early when Lord King in 1811 for political reasons wrote a letter to his tenants giving them notice that he wanted his rents paid in gold equivalents because of the depreciation of paper currency. Paper currency had not been made legal tender officially because of the frightening example of the *assignats* in France, but the government responded to Lord King's initiative by legislation preventing Bank of England notes being received for a smaller sum than specified on the notes passed (Levi, 1880, pp. 123–33; Fetter, 1965, p. 59). When inflation turned to deflation, 'one William Cobbett' (*sic*, Smart, 1911/1964, I, p. 739) petitioned Parliament for relief by reducing his debt to its 1813 value. He had bought and improved an estate to the extent of £30,000, of which £13,000 was borrowed. With prices less than half their 1813 level "on account of the Resumption Act" he was about to be ruined. The petition was ignored, and he did lose his farm at Botley in Southampton (*Encyclopaedia Britannica*, 1970, V, p. 989). But Cobbett was more interested as a Radical in the problems of farm labourers and factory workers. He did not "hate Peel like Castlereagh and Pitt, but held him primarily responsible for severe distresses of common people. Returning to gold without any liquidation of debt charges or reduction of other burdens had been the main cause of semi-starvation …" (Cole, n.d., p. 396).

A short digression on Cobbett may be worthwhile, even though he is assuredly one of the few minds that Rostow characterises as unorthodox. In 1819 he had written from the United States, where he had taken refuge from the 1817 act repealing Habeas Corpus, that "resumption would result in a big fall in prices which would be universally ruinous … ruin to all who held stocks of goods or who owed large sums or who had heavy mortgages." Later, when the Resumption Act passed (and he had returned to Britain), he wrote saying that at least one million would die of hunger, that the act would never be completely carried out, and that, if it were so, he "would suffer Castlereagh to broil him alive while Sidmouth stirred the coals, and Canning stood by to make a jest of his groans" (Doubleday, 1847, pp. 248–9). A gridiron became his symbol and logograph for his newspaper, the *Political Register*. The key word in his promise is the word *completely*, meaning the need to eliminate the note issues of the country banks and the Bank of England (Fetter, 1965, p. 108) and do something about the burden of the national debt. A Feast of the Gridiron was promised to his Radical followers and held in April, 1826 (Cole, n.d., pp. 280–3). But by this time Cobbett had returned to his hatred of paper money, inspired by his reading of Thomas Paine's *Decline and Fall of the English System of Finance* (1796), and embodied in his *Paper against Gold* (1815), written when he was in Newgate prison for sedition. When prices were rising in 1824 and 1825, he tried to bring them down by urging trade unionists to convert paper money into gold at every opportunity, and trade unions to appoint a "gold man." In August 1832 he debated Thomas Attwood, the Birmingham expansionist, who wanted larger issues of paper money while Cobbett wanted to eliminate both paper money and debt. Attwood opened the debate before 1,400 people in a speech lasting four and a half hours, and Cobbett came back the next day with a moderate two hours of rebuttal (Cole, n.d., pp. 223, 263, 396–7). E. P. Thompson notes that it is not difficult to show that Cobbett had some very stupid and contradictory ideas but he quotes with approval Raymond Williams' attribution to Cobbett of an "extraordinary sureness of instinct" (1963, pp. 749, 758), and Cole calls him "largely right" (Cole, n.d., p. 280). Both men write, to be sure, from a leftist perspective.

The classical writers were by no means unaware of the problem of equity between creditor and debtor. Thornton said that the question of whether resumption should be undertaken or not turned on whether depreciation had lasted a long time, such as 15 or 20 years, during which bargains had been made in depreciated currency, or merely two or three years (1802/1962, p. 345). In 1802 when *Paper Credit* was written there had been but two years of 10 per cent or so depreciation (premium on the mint price of gold). This then subsided until 1809 when it rose to 40 or 50 per cent until 1814. What Thornton would have thought about the equity of resumption in 1819 in the light of this uneven record is an interesting puzzle but academic. He died in 1815. Ricardo and McCullogh were concerned less with mortgages and private bargains than with the national debt, as was a wide section of opinion in the 1810s. There was no such issue, so far as I am aware, in public opinion in the 1920s. Ricardo advocated a capital levy to restore equity. In 1817 the income tax had been abandoned, and in any case had not been progressive (Acworth, 1925, ch. v, esp. p. 57). In his first tract in economics, J. R. McCulloch proposed reduction of interest on the national debt because much of it had been advanced in depreciated currency (Smart, 1911/1964, I, p. 510).

This would not have affected the capital value of repayment of short-dated issues. Tooke was scornful of all such talk, especially in agricultural land: 'What it has since been the fashion to call an equitable adjustment of contracts means in reality an indemnification of bad speculations' (1838, I, p. 326). Nor did his heart bleed for the industrialists who suffered losses from the fall in prices of industrial goods, some running as high as 50 per cent upon the return of Napoleon from Elba:

That rise of prices of exportable produce and manufactures which proved so ephemeral as being founded upon the most unwarranted expectations of demand *in consequence of the peace* [his italics], and of the renewal of commercial intercourse with the Continent, has been the occasion of the most absurd conclusions conceivable.... The disastrous effects of these ill-judged and extravagantly extensive speculations began to manifest themselves in numerous failures which took place toward the end of 1814. (*ibid.*, vol. II, pp. 6–8)

The analogue, of course, is with the boomlet of 1920–1 when a great number of industries in Britain, notably cotton textiles, steel and shipping, went into debt at very high prices of output and capital assets that could not be sustained, and piled up interest charges that were a heavy burden for the rest of the decade (Pigou, 1948, p. 12; Youngson, 1960, pp. 25–6).

Speculation ran the prices of agricultural produce and exports up and down. It did the same with gold, silver and foreign exchange. Once resumption was in the offing, the premiums on gold, silver and Hamburg exchange declined sharply, so that the depreciation of sterling from par was less than 5 per cent. In 1924 after the change of government from Labour to the Conservative party, the pound sterling rose against the dollar to a depreciation of the order of 10 per cent. In these circumstances, the temptation to go the rest of the way is strong indeed. Tooke calls the gap a "trifling" distance or divergence (1838, II, pp. 65, 76). In commenting on Peel's view that failure to undertake resumption would have been a fraud on creditors Hawtrey uses the same word: "It would have been a mean-spirited course to go back on the century-old standard on account of so trifling a premium on gold" (1927, p. 351).

"Fraud" and "mean spirited" introduce into the question the moral issues which were present both in 1819 and in 1925. 'Defenders of the metallic standard contented themselves with an appeal to arbitrary dogmas and moral issues' (Viner, 1937, p. 216). Fetter quotes Brougham: 'To tamper with the public faith; to sully the honour of the country; to declare a national bankruptcy? Good God! Who in his senses would recommend it?' (1965, p. 105). Compare Sauvy on resumption in 1925: "A question of prestige, a question of dogma,... almost a question of honor" (1965,

p. 121). Another French view states that it came from the need to look the dollar in the eye ... "an affair of *amour propre* rather than monetary policy" (Perrot, 1955, p. 35).

Tooke initially held to the view that the elimination of the 3 or 4 per cent premium on gold or discount on sterling could not have reduced prices by more than that percentage (1838, I, p. 4). He later admitted that, by drawing gold from the Continent, Britain could have raised the price of gold, or lowered commodity prices on a world-wide basis. Ricardo had tried to limit the British demand for gold by urging that resumption take place on the bullion standard, so that convertibility would not be made into coin. This raises the issue of the £1 and £2 notes again, and how much gold was required to retire them from circulation. Tooke admits the possibility of deflation from this source but argues that the amounts of British gold and silver lost to or gained from the rest of the world never amounted to more than £12 to 15 million as contrasted with a world money supply of gold and silver somewhere between £1,200 and £2,000 million, or close to 1 per cent and surely no more than 2 per cent (1838, I, pp. 131–5). The counter to this contention is that the world was, for the most part, on the silver standard, and British gains and losses in gold were a much higher percentage of the world gold supply. Soetbeer's tables of the average ratio of gold to silver in Hamburg goes from 15.11 in 1817 to 15.95 in 1821 (US Senate, 1879/1978, p. 709), which suggests an increasing scarcity of gold, above that of world money in general. From the modern theoretical views of Mundell and Laffer embodied in the expression "World Monetarism," some pressure on the world money supply, more in gold currency than in silver, thus came from British gold acquisitions from 1819 on. Ricardo put this effect at 5 per cent, and agreed with Tooke that it was the result of Bank mismanagement, that is acceptance of the decision to redeem in coin as well as bullion (Viner, 1937, p. 175).

Insistence of the Banking School that it was real factors that produced these drastic up and down swings in prices, and especially series of crop failures or gluts in a row, encounters another serious objection, that all prices rise and fall more or less together. This is true in Britain, as between agricultural and industrial prices, and between Britain and the Continent, where general price levels rise and fall in wider swings than can be accounted for by exchange-rate differences, which in their turn, on the Banking School showing, were generated by extraordinary foreign payments—another real factor. On the other hand, the classical explanation is probably not much help here either. It was not that prices rose and fell with Bank of England policies of monetary expansion and contraction, although there was some of that as far as the government was concerned. There was some expansion up to 1814 to finance government, and some contraction when the government, in connection with resumption, acceded to the Bank's request to pay down its advance by £10 million. For the most part, however, and particularly for private discounts, the Bank was passive, as indeed the Banking School and the real-bill doctrine believed it should be. Speculation drove prices and prices drove money. As Temin explains in his discussion of the depression in the United States in 1929–33, it was not the LM curve which moved independently and reduced nominal income; it was the shift in spending, that IS curve, which reduced income and led to a decrease in the money supply (1976). A Currency School approach under which the attempt would have been made to limit fluctuations in money to those dictated by the state of the specie reserve would have moderated the swing of prices responding to speculation, but not eliminated them. Speculation in agricultural produce, agricultural land and export commodities responding to variations in harvest and to changes in the fortunes of war could be financed for some considerable distance on the up-side and without limit on the down by the possibility of monetising personal credit. The country-bank note issues responded in this way. Bills of exchange could equally do so. The fact that agricultural and industrial prices rose and fell together suggests that it was not variations in crops alone that affected prices, but that there were important forces working on the side of money as well, despite the passiveness of monetary policy.

The same issue arises with Europe. European prices rose and fell with British ones. Tooke attempts to rebut the argument that this bespeaks the primacy of monetary over real factors, advanced by Matthias Attwood, a London banker and brother of the Birmingham banker, Thomas Attwood, in debate on 10 July 1822 on Mr Western's motion to reconsider resumption, by stating that the same real factors were operative on the Continent as in Britain, and that in fact the decline of prices in 1819 originated on the Continent not England (1838, II, pp. 87, 89, 95). The charge has a familiar ring to those who recall the debate as to whether the financial crisis of 1836 originated in the United States or Britain, and the similar issue over 1929. It is evident that variations in weather can leap the Channel with little difficulty and that one can have long and short crops simultaneously in England and the Continent. The coincidence that the same real factors in industrial products would move non-agricultural prices in similar directions is hard to credit, unless speculation financed by monetised personal credit be regarded as a real instead of a monetary factor.

On these scores I find it hard to accept the view that

(a) monetary policies were more conscious after 1918 than before;

(b) that non-monetary factors are paramount in economic history (I propose to say more on this question at another time and place);

(c) that modern concepts of monetary policy did not exist down to 1914;

(d) that the monetary system was substantially passive and responsive; and

(e) that economic reconstruction after 1815 was altogether different from that after 1918.

I should perhaps go further, and suggest here, as I have in the case of eighteenth- and nineteenth-century France (1980), that the clash between monetarism and Keynesianism is an ancient one, going back at least to John Law a century before Henry Thornton. I expect it will still be around a century hence.

Perhaps I should give the last word to the Rostow of about 1941 who wrote:

During these years (1819–21) and in the following three decades there was much controversy on the allegedly deflationary consequences of the Act of 1819. These speculations (along with those of 1810) evoked perhaps the most fruitful monetary discussion of the nineteenth century. (Gayer *et al.* 1953, p. 165)

This would seem to dispose of the "few unorthodox minds."

References

Acworth, A. W. (1925), *Financial Reconstruction in England, 1815–1822* (London: P. S. King).

Boyle, Andrew (1967), *Montagu Norman* (London: Cassell).

Bullion Report (1810/1978), *Report from the Select Committee on the High Price of Gold Bullion*, Ordered by the House of Commons to be printed 8 June 1810; reprint edn. (New York: Arno Press, 1978).

Checkland, S. G. (1948), "The Birmingham Economists, 1815–1850," *Economic History Review*, 2nd ser., vol. 1, no. 1, pp. 1–19.

Clay, Sir Henry (1957/1978), *Lord Norman* (London, Macmillan); reprint edn. (New York: Arno).

Cole, G. D. H. (n.d.), *The Life of William Cobbett* (New York: Harcourt Brace, preface dated 1924).

Cunliffe Report (1925/1978), British Parliamentary Reports on International Finance, *The Cunliffe Committee and the Macmillan Committee (1931) Reports* (New York: Arno Press).

Doubleday, Thomas (1847), *A Financial, Monetary and Statistical History of England from the Revolution of 1688 to the Present Time* (London: Effingham, Wilson).

Fetter, Frank Whitson (1965), *Development of British Monetary Orthodoxy, 1797–1875* (Cambridge, Mass.: Harvard University Press).

Gayer, Arthur D., Rostow, W. W. and Schwartz, Anna Jacobson (1953), *The Growth and Fluctuation of the British Economy, 1790–1850. An Historical, Statistical and Theoretical Study of Britain's Economic Development* (Oxford: Clarendon Press; largely unchanged from the MS. of 1941).

Gregory, T. E. (1928), "Introduction" to Thomas Tooke and William Newmarch, *A History of Prices and of the State of Circulation from 1792 to 1856* (New York: Adelphi, 6 vols; reproduced from the original; first 2 vols originally 1838).

Grigg, P. J. (1948), *Prejudice and Judgement* (London: Jonathan Cape).

Hawtrey, R. G. (1919/1927), *Currency and Credit*, 3rd edn. (London: Longmans, Green).

Howson, Susan K. (1975), *Domestic Monetary Management in Britain, 1919–38* (Cambridge: Cambridge University Press).

Keynes, John Maynard (1930), *A Treatise on Money* (New York: Harcourt Brace, 2 vols).

Keynes, John Maynard (1932), *Essays in Persuasion* (New York: Harcourt Brace).

Keynes, John Maynard (1933/1951), *Essays in Biography*, new edn. with three additional essays (London: Hart-Davis).

Keynes, John Maynard (1936), *The General Theory of Employment, Interest and Money* (New York: Harcourt Brace).

Kindleberger, Charles P. (1980), "Keynesianism vs. Monetarism in Eighteenth- and Nineteenth-Century France," *History of Political Economy*, vol. 12, no 4 (Winter) pp. 499–523.

Leith-Ross, Sir Frederick (1968), *Money Talks. Fifty Years of International Finance* (London: Hutchinson).

Levi, Leone (1880), *The History of British Commerce* (London: Murray).

Li, Ming-Hsun (1963), *The Great Recoinage of 1696 to 1699* (London: Weidenfeld & Nicolson).

Lüthy, Herbert (1959), *La Banque protestante en France de la révocation de l'édit de Nantes à la révolution*. Vol. I: *Dispersion et regroupement (1685–1730)* (Paris: SEVPEN).

Moggridge, D. E. (1969), *The Return to Gold, 1925. The Formulation of Policy and its Critics* (Cambridge: Cambridge University Press).

Moggridge, D. E. (1972), *British Monetary Policy, 1924–1931. The Norman Conquest of $4.86* (Cambridge: Cambridge University Press).

Morgan, E. Victor (1943), *The Theory and Practice of Central Banking, 1797–1913* (Cambridge: Cambridge University Press).

O'Brien, D. P. (ed.) (1971), *The Correspondence of Lord Overstone* (Cambridge: Cambridge University Press, 3 vols).

Paine, Thomas (1796), *The Decline and Fall of the English System of Finance* (Paris: Hartley Adlard & Son).

Paine, Thomas (1815), *Paper against Gold* (London: J. M'Creery).

Perrot, Marguerite (1955), *La Monnaie et l'opinion publique en France et en Angleterre, 1924–36* (Paris: Colin).

Pigou, A. C. (1948), *Aspects of British Economic History, 1918–25* (London: Macmillan).

Rostow, W. W. (1978), *The World Economy* (Austin, Tex.: University of Texas Press).

Rostow, W. W. (1980), "Money and Prices: An Old Debate Revisited," in *Why the Poor Get Poorer and the Rich Slow Down: Essays in the Marshallian Long Period* (Austin, Tex.: University of Texas Press).

Sauvy, Alfred (1965), *Histoire économique de la France entre les deux guerres*. Vol. I: *1918–31* (Paris: Fayard).

Sherwig, John M. (1969), *Guineas and Gunpowder. British Foreign Aid in the Wars with France, 1793–1815* (Cambridge, Mass.: Harvard University Press).

Silberling, N. J. (1924), "Financial and Monetary Policy in Great Britain during the Napoleonic Wars," I, II, *Quarterly Journal of Economics*, vol. 38, pp. 214–23, 397–439.

Smart, William (1911/1964), *Economic Annals of the Nineteenth Century*. Vol. I: *1801–1820*; Vol. II: *1821–1830*, reprint edn. (New York: Kelley).

Temin, Peter (1976), *Did Monetary Forces Cause the Great Depression?* (New York: W. W. Norton).

Thompson, E. P. (1963), *The Making of the English Working Class* (New York: Knopf).

Thornton, Henry (1802/1962), *An Enquiry into the Nature and Effect of the Paper Credit of Great Britain, together with the Evidence*; edited with an introduction by F. A. Hayek (London: Frank Cass; reprint of 1939 edn., London: Allen & Unwin).

Tooke, Thomas and Newmarch, William (1838/1928), *A History of Prices and of the State Circulation from 1792 to 1856*, reproduced from the original with an introduction by T. E. Gregory (New York: Adelphi, n.d.; introduction dated 1928; 6 vols, first 2 vols originally 1838).

US Senate (1879/1978), *International Monetary Conference of 1878, Proceedings and Exhibits* (Washington, DC: USGPO); reprint edn (New York: Arno Press).

Vilar, Pierre (1976), *A History of Gold and Money, 1450–1920*, translated from the 1969 Spanish original by Judith White (London: New Left Books).

Viner, Jacob (1973), *Studies in the Theory of International Trade* (New York: Harper).

Williamson, John (1971), *Karl Helfferich, 1872–1924, Economist, Financier, Politician* (Princeton, NJ: Princeton University Press).

Youngson, A. J. (1960), *The British Economy, 1920–1957* (London: Allen & Unwin).

15

Intermediation, Disintermediation, and Direct Trading

I owe a large intellectual debt to Hyman Minsky who got me to think about instability in financial markets. It may be appropriate in a paper with this title to indicate that I got to Minsky's writings through the intermediation of Martin Mayer, author of *The Bankers* and many other popular works on the economy of our time. I mentioned my interest in financial crises, and Mayer asked whether I knew of Minsky's work. Like many an intermediary, he had, as far as I was concerned, a monopoly of information. After this information had been diffused, I have profited greatly over the years by dealing with Hy in "direct trading."

The concept of intermediation I propose to discuss is primarily economic and financial. Allow me, however, to display my interdisciplinary knowledge by noting that the idea is of greater applicability. Talcott Parsons somewhere wrote that governesses or nannies intermediate between parents and children, especially, I admit, in England. And that in the military, noncommissioned officers intermediate between commissioned officers and privates. To use a different social science, President Theodore Roosevelt intermediated between Japan and Czarist Russia in Portsmouth in 1905, as President Jimmy Carter did between Egypt and Israel at Camp David, and is attempting to do again, as I write, between Ethiopia and its former province, Eritrea, now independent.

Sometimes middlemen are not in the middle, so to speak. Michel Crozier's (1964) *The Bureaucratic Phenomenon* notes that face-to-face communication in governmental hierarchy in France is fraught with tension so that an official at level E will communicate with his superior at D by going above him and dealing through C. More nearly akin to economic and financial considerations is the public relations officer with a monopoly

Reprinted from Steven Fazzari and Dimitri B. Papadimitriou, eds., *Financial Conditions and Macroeconomic Performance: Essays in Honor of Hyman P. Minsky* (Armonk, N.Y.: M. E. Sharpe, 1992), 71–84.

of information who stands between high governmental or business officials and the public.

On a macrosociological level, the existence of a large middle class contributes to political stability as it narrows the gap for bright and aggressive members of the lower class to cross as they rise. The middle class also cushions the decline of the elite, including younger sons in a system of primogeniture, and reduces the risk of polarization of society.

To extend the sociological aspects of the subject one iota, observe that when children grow up they no longer need the intermediation of a nanny, if they ever did, and communicate with their parents, in direct trading, often with ruthless bluntness.

But let me narrow the focus to economics and finance. More than a quarter of a century ago, John Gurley and Edward Shaw (1960) produced a path-breaking book, *Money in a Theory of Finance*, which developed the theory of intermediation as the key to monetary and other financial institutions. As they viewed the process, financial structures in an economy developed in evolutionary fashion; from self-financing, to direct financing, to indirect financing through financial intermediaries. Some, but not overwhelming, attention was paid to disintermediation as a pathological process. They did not, however, envisage a further step, relevant today, of a return to direct financial contacts between borrower and lender when the advantage of the banking intermediary has been lost. I have in mind, especially, direct purchases of certificates of deposit and securities issued by large industrial corporations, bought by large pension funds and insurance companies. But first I want to extend the economic theory of intermediation to markets in general, and offer an analogy between goods markets and financial markets, using a bit of the economic history with which I have been keeping myself pleasantly occupied for some years. I will not test your patience by going back millennia in history, but start with such a stapling center as Amsterdam.

Amsterdam happened to be well located, close to the junction between the Atlantic (and the Mediterranean) and the Baltic and North Seas, handy to Britain, and connected by the Rhine and the Meuse to a vast hinterland. After the fall of Antwerp to Spanish attackers in 1585, Amsterdam became an entrepôt center. Its merchants were divided among the First, Second and Third Hand—from which we get these expressions. The First Hand, engaged in "distant trade," brought goods from abroad to the city and took them away again. The Second Hand broke bulk, stored goods, performed other intermediating functions, and repackaged the goods. Repackaging, for example, was necessary if grain from Danzig in Poland was not to explode under the hot Mediterranean sun as a consequence of spontaneous combustion, as it was being delivered say to Leghorn. Wines from Bordeaux were brought to Amsterdam in casks and sometimes bottled there, as free ports do today. The Third Hand sold at retail the small proportion of the total trade that remained in the United Provinces of Holland.

The First Hand had a monopoly of information and of capital; information as to what goods were available where, and what were wanted where. It intermediated by place and risk, and with the help of the Second Hand, by scale. The Second Hand also intermediated by social status, as it traded with the imperious leaders of the Dutch Republic—the First Hand —which clung tightly to power.

Adam Smith wrote the Bible for economists, *The Wealth of Nations*, and it is perhaps impious on my part to take exception to two of his remarks about merchants. In the first, he claimed that a little grocer in a seaport town had all the attributes of a great merchant except capital (1776, 112). This is far from the case as one contemplates the need to learn languages, and to acquire much wider knowledge of accounting, exchange rates, the qualities of goods, their prices, and the markets where they can be bought cheapest and sold at the highest prices. In the second, he stated that the merchant should normally be located at one end of a trade route or the other, in the instant case at Königsberg in East Prussia or Lisbon in Portugal, rather than midway between. But he stayed in Amsterdam and brought his goods there because he was uneasy at being separated from his capital and wanted it under his view, despite the double charges for loading and unloading along with some duties and customs (422). This explanation ignores the functions of intermediating by size and risk, and it assumes that the merchants were, at least in some degree, irrational. By calling attention to the extra charges of handling merchandise in an entrepôt center, however, Dr. Smith made clear the origins of direct trading when the monopoly of information of the great merchants had been dissipated by diffusion, and these costs could be saved.

But intermediation in trade does not persist. When the information monopoly that gave rise to it dissipates, direct trading is substituted for intermediation in goods. Exeter undertook to trade its serges directly to Spain, and Hull its woolen piece goods to Hamburg. London was for long the great exporter of raw materials from the Empire, but in due course, Scandinavia would trade directly with Australia, for example, and British reexports shrank to a small percentage of total exports from figures that previously approached 30 percent. Some intermediation in goods continues, to be sure, where simple processing was called for by the economics of transportation, especially downscaling the final delivery of goods shipped in bulk from the original source. Where it was possible to save handling and the middleman's profit, however, direct trade took over as knowledge of needs and availabilities was widely diffused.

Let me indulge in a bit of Ciceronian rhetoric and say I would enjoy going on discussing intermediation in trade and its replacement by direct trading if space permitted—the Hanseatic merchants, hated by the inland towns on the ground that the merchants set prices at which the towns had to trade and had the power to ruin a country (Moser 1944, 197); Sweden trying to bypass Lübeck in the seventeenth century by selling its copper directly to Amsterdam (Glamann 1971, 456); German and Italian merchants deserting the Lyons fairs at the end of the sixteenth century to exchange goods through the Alpine passes, escaping the heavy taxation of the French monarchy (Boyer-Xambeu, Deleplace, and Gillard 1986, 155); nineteenth-century British merchants who slowed down technical change in cotton yarns and machine tools, telling producers "they don't want them like that" while simultaneously telling customers "they don't make them like that" even though the elimination of the middleman would allow producer and buyer to discuss together and agree on the nature of improved quality and whether it was worth the cost (Kindleberger 1964, 148–49); and, the elimination of jobber and wholesaler by American corporations as they rose in scale from local to regional to national and took the marketing function into the firm for direct buying and selling (Chandler 1962).

Middlemen have long been excoriated and defended. Oscar Wilde said that a publisher is simply a useful middleman between author and reader with no right to express an opinion on the value of what he publishes, while Disraeli wrote "It is well known what a middleman is: he is one who bamboozles one party and plunders the other" (Cole 1989). A newspaper columnist on economics has felt the need to defend middlemen (Warsh 1989). I neither defend nor attack, but observe that intermediaries exist at an early stage of trade, and are usually replaced in due course by direct trade to save transport costs and one layer of profit. The market in the middle may have an artificial monopoly which it guards jealously, as did the Merchant Staplers of Britain selling wool on the continent (Braudel 1986, 448–49), or Danzig with the "privilege of being the only professional middlemen between Polish and West European merchants" (Federowicz 1976, 362). But competition nibbles away at most monopolies in goods, and monopolizing intermediators, as a rule, give way to direct trade.

Our interest, however, is in finance, not trade. Financial centers last longer than trade centers, I hypothesize, because the costs of transport in money—more generally transactions costs—are trivial compared with those in goods. Many trade centers, notably Amsterdam, London, and New York, shifted over from trade to financial intermediation when their informational monopolies in goods eroded and their appetite for risk diminished with rising wealth. But let me proceed more slowly by discussing the various bases for intermediating between borrower and lender.

One ancient basis had to do with social status. Nobles would be contaminated if they dealt directly with commoners, but had less hesitation in doing so through the intermediation of scriveners, notaries, goldsmiths, bankers; in France, *officers* and *financiers* who were holders of particular offices bought from the king. A rapid expansion of intermediary lending can be seen in comparative statics in the rise of the number of scriveners from "several" in the first decade of the seventeenth century to "at least 30 by 1630" (Parker 1974, 537).

One particular form of social intermediation was intimately bound up in risk—lending to the sovereign. The king could not be sued to collect unpaid debts owed by him, so that there was a need for special protection. This included lending on the crown jewels, the grant of a monopoly in the form of a tax, or the collateral of productive assets such as the silver mines of the Tyrol or the mercury mines of Almaden in Spain, both acquired by the Fuggers when their loans were defaulted on. The Spanish *asientos* (a form of loan to the King) were usually accompanied by a permit, which had value, to export silver. Or a member of the king's household, like Sir Stephen Fox in the court of Charles II, would borrow from the public to lend to the king, because the king was unlikely to welsh on a debt to an intimate (Clay 1978). Lionel Cranfield was a courtier of James I who lent to the monarch and borrowed to do so, including once from the merchant and early economic writer Thomas Mun, author of the great book, *England's Treasure by Forraign Trade*. One is surprised to find R. H. Tawney surprised to find that in 1641, financiers called upon to lend to the crown borrowed from others to be able to do so (1958, 107). And of course in France, many of those who paid the court large sums for offices to farm taxes or to take over various monopolies, like that in tobacco, borrowed from the public to obtain the needed capital (Dent 1973).

This antiquarian information has some relevance to the world of today because of the issue of syndicated bank debt by sovereign Third World countries. (This problem was discovered by most of the world in August 1982 when the Mexican debt crisis was revealed, but was apparent to academic observers more than half a decade earlier [see Goodman, ed., 1978]). There is something of a puzzle here that despite an impressive record of default by sovereign debtors, the investing public, including bankers who are presumably sophisticated in such matters, has often taken a childishly optimistic view of foreign government debt. I need not go back to the miserable record of Edward III of England whose defaults were said to have ruined the Bardi, Peruzzi, and Aicobaldi banks of Florence and Lucca (but see Hunt 1990) or to those of Philip II of Spain which undid the Fuggers, Welzers, and the bankers of Genoa. To a world that believes in any degree of rational expectations it is bizarre that French investors were trusting of Czarist Russia in the years from 1888 to 1913. A false analogy presumably was developed between lending to one's own sovereign, who could pay his debts by printing money, and lending to a foreign sovereign who lacks capacity to produce foreign exchange.

After intermediation by social status and to overcome sovereign immunity. I come to intermediation by place. In his classic, *Lombard Street*, Walter Bagehot discusses how the bankers of rich agricultural counties like Somersetshire and Hampshire discounted the bills of the industrial counties of Yorkshire and Lancashire ([1873] 1978, 53), illustrating the process with the testimony of a London bill broker before an 1810 Commission of Inquiry (ibid., 191–93). He claimed, moreover, that the practice still prevailed 60 years later, though in his introduction to Bagehot's *Collected Works*, R. S. Sayers denies it (ibid., 35, 193).

Intermediation by place took other forms. In England, areas with excess savings initially bought bills on places with deficits, through London brokers, but gradually they established a branch in London, or bought out an existing bank there. Banks needing money did the same to obtain funds. London banks in due course established national networks to bring savings efficiently from where they were abundant to where they were needed. For a time, provincial banks with a branch or subsidiary in London could pay depositors at the head office a fixed low rate of interest, whereas the London rate varied with bank rate. In time, the provincial depositors learned to move their funds to London when bank rate went to 4 percent or above. When enough depositors learned this, such a bank as Lloyds of Birmingham learned that it had to maintain a single deposit rate for the entire system (Sayers 1957, 165, 270).

In France, as Jean Bouvier's masterly account of the growth of the *Crédit lyonnais* tells us, Henri Germain started the bank in Lyons, which was heavy with capital accumulated in the silk business, went to Paris in due course to place the monies, and then built a network throughout France. The *Crédit lyonnais* favored those communities with excess savings, at the expense of those that were eager for loans, in order to accumulate funds to use in foreign lending. Deep students of my work on financial centers may remember the riddle: What do the Midland Bank, the Dresdener Bank, the Bank of Montreal, Bank of Nova Scotia, First Boston Corporation, and the *Crédit lyonnais* have in common? The answer is that the head office of each is located in a different city (or area) than that noted in the institution's name (1978, 67).

Place intermediation, through commercial banks in the United States, has been held back by rules against branch banking, rules now in process of being eased. Savings banks and savings and loan associations, both of which originally provided finance for home building, furnish a good example of the process. In the last decades of the nineteenth century, mortgage markets were regionally segmented by size of city and region, with a spread that ranged from 5.60 percent in cities within 25 miles of New England population centers with more than 100,000 people, to 9.76 percent for banks in the West within 25 miles of towns of 8,000 to 25,000 (Snowden 1988, 278). Such segmentation continued into the early twentieth century for savings institutions. There were some national players like insurance companies that were embarrassed when they felt it necessary to foreclose on farm mortgages in the 1930s, but these were not large enough to close the gap. With a wave of building in the West after World War II, especially in California, a number of thrifts in that state advertised in New York papers for deposits by mail at rates one percentage point or more above rates in the East. Further integration of the market for mortgage money came through Veterans Administration lending and the creation of the Federal National Mortgage Association and the Government National Mortgage Association, known familiarly as "Fannie Mae" and "Ginnie Mae," respectively. When savings bank disintermediation began in the late 1970s and early 1980s, savings banks replaced lost local deposits by borrowing on the national market for CDs. Most recently the packaging of mortgage lending has been undertaken by private as well as government institutions, and some of these packages of diversified mortgages (and automobile loans, installment and credit card paper, and in Britain, export credits) are sold internationally. The intermediation through risk involved in this diversification is discussed below. It is not clear to me whether the private "securitization" of mortgage loans is diversified as to place, like those of Fannie and Ginnie Mae, or are localized.

The securitization of mortgages involves intermediation by size as well as place, and in this instance there is no progression for the small borrower that leads on to direct trading. I do have an illustration of direct trading replacing intermediation in information, if not in mortgage money on houses. In 1974 in discussing the finance of offshore drilling for oil and gas, I asked a banker in Aberdeen whether he would seek information on the subject from his London correspondent who would get it from New York. The answer was that Aberdeen would deal directly with Houston.

Intermediation by size is wider and more commonplace than the foregoing illustration of securitization of mortgages, auto loans, installment paper, and the like. Typically people of small means deposit their savings with intermediaries who lend it in larger volume. This is the essence of the classic function of banks in the "mobilization of loan capital," to use an expression of Ehrenberg ([1895] 1928, 328–29). A strong element of intermediation by risk is involved, because the small saver is typically uninformed about the credit standing of the ultimate borrower and relies on the banking intermediary to lend only to creditworthy individuals and firms. The ignorance of the small depositor, as opposed to the reputed financial sophistication of the large, is of course the basis for limits on governmental deposit insurance in the United States, limits that have been increased with inflation and real wealth from $5,000, originally to $10,000, then $40,000, and now $100,000. There are, moreover, occasions, such as the financial crisis involving the Continental Illinois Bank, when the Federal Deposit Insurance Corporation has guaranteed foreign deposits of more than $100,000 in order to stop a run on a bank, making clear that the purpose of deposit insurance is more to stop runs—the extreme form of disintermediation—than it is to protect small savers. One could perhaps argue that wealthy foreigners may legitimately be more ignorant of the condition of American banks than U.S. residents, but the reasoning is not persuasive. As a classic example of intermediation by size, some years ago it was common knowledge that the Eurodollar market would not take deposits of less than $25,000, nor make loans below $1 million.

Intermediation by size occurs outside of banks in odd-lot houses that break bulk for small investors trading in securities in amounts of less than one hundred shares. At the other end of the scale, trading in lots of thousands of shares is mostly undertaken directly off the floor of the intermediating Stock Exchange, to get the benefit of lower or zero commissions.

Direct dealing between borrower and lender for large loans, cutting out the intermediation of banks, is one of the major innovations in finance in recent years, according to the Cross report (BIS 1986). Pension funds and insurance companies, dealing in large sums of money, are able to judge credit risks through treasurer departments peopled with finance analysts, and to lend with assured safety on certificates of deposit issued by non-financial companies or on securities placed directly with them. The banks have begun to miss out on a large portion of industrial loans for the larger companies, and this development is responsible for their intense lobbying for the repeal of the Glass-Steagall Act of 1933 that separated institutions into banks on the one hand, and investment houses on the other, forbidding banks to underwrite the issue of securities. Some of the smaller banks with a deep clientele of middle-size industrial companies with small financial staffs and a need for financial advice that banks traditionally provided, continue to do well. I vividly recall, however, hearing from the chief executive officer of a $400 million-a-year sales company—a big number at the time—that he refused to maintain a compensating balance at his bank, and when the bank president protested and justified such a balance on the ground of providing the company with a variety of services, he interrupted to say that the banks should charge the company for any service it asked for. He not only would not carry a compensating balance, but would, in fact, ride the float and make the treasurer's office in his company a profit center.

The loss of the loan business of large companies has led the banks to seek other sorts of business; some as more nearly "merchant banks," giving financial advice to various kinds of business for fees. Other banks began dealing in financial instruments such as swaps, repos, futures, and the like; still others providing accounting and transfer services to such institutions as mutual funds. In many instances, the loss of the ordinary run of large business loans has led banks to take more risky roads into construction loans, bridge loans for takeover firms, and junk bonds. It is not clear to me whether the surge in Third World debt in the 1970s was related to the shrinkage of ordinary loan outlets or not. In any case, the rise of direct trading between trade and industry on the one hand, and nonbank financial firms on the other has diverted a great many banks from their wonted paths into risky endeavors in which they now find themselves uncomfortable or worse.

The $100,000 limit on deposit insurance led to another form of intermediation by size that was less than salubrious for the economy as a whole; namely, the growth of deposit brokers who took large sums of deposit money and divided them into amounts of less than $100,000 to distribute among weak thrift institutions that had to pay more than

standard deposit rates to attract funds. The practice keeps third-rate institutions alive longer than they would otherwise remain. A high deposit
rate is normally a sign that the saving bank is in trouble, but the practice
of breaking bulk of large sums to provide the weak bank with extra protection is dysfunctional for the system as a whole. It both encourages risk
taking and paralyzes the conservative and well-managed thrifts through
disintermediation.

Bank competition for deposits led the way, from demand deposits that
earned no interest, to Negotiable Orders of Withdrawal (NOW) accounts
that did, thus depriving the banks of seignorage. Before the innovation,
demand depositors could have been regarded as exploited by banks,
which got something for nothing, or very little. Alternatively, demand
deposits could be viewed as providing needed liquidity, such liquidity
being a service rendered by the bank in time intermediation. Whichever
view one takes of non-interest-bearing demand deposits, their demise and
the need to "buy" deposits has reduced the earnings of banks on intermediation by size. Foreign banks in Paris which had to buy all their
deposits were at a strong disadvantage vis-à-vis domestic banks which
attracted the deposits of Frenchmen on which no interest was paid
(Koszul 1972). The shift to NOW accounts in the United States has meant
that domestic banks had to buy their deposits, as do foreign banks,
increasing the degree of international competition.

Banks intermediate not only by place and size of wealth holding, but
also by time and risk. For time, it is evident that savers and borrowers
have different time preferences. Savers want liquidity, borrowers to have
their debts stretched out in time. Banks intermediate by lending long and
borrowing short. They can provide liquidity to savers because not all
savers will want their money simultaneously—a diversification effect. J. K.
Price in discussing British overseas trade historically notes that wholesalers in Britain provided easy credit to exporters who, in turn, gave long
credits to their foreign customers. The lengths of credit were equivalent,
and most merchants had balance sheets dominated by accounts receivable
and debts owed, with little in the way of fixed capital (1989, 278). This
reflects a fairly primitive stage in financial development to such an extent
that it merits attention.

There was an era in which savings institutions narrowed the gap in
time between assets and deposits by requiring notice on deposit withdrawals. Commercial banks made sharp distinctions between demand and
time deposits. Fixed terms remain in effect, today, on certificates of deposit,
but most savings and time deposits are available on demand. And demand

deposits—NOW accounts—earn interest along with time deposits. The threat of disintermediation runs from bank deposits, both commercial and thrift, to money funds, which have the advantage over banks in that there are no legal reserve requirements. Most, too, allow a certain amount of check writing, or easy indirect access to the money on demand. The sharp rise in interest rates at the beginning of the 1980s led to outflows of money from banks to money funds from which it was loaned back to banks again, in certificates of deposits, at higher interest rates. This was not so much disintermediation, perhaps, as reintermediation.

An ironic point is worth mentioning. The small saver in a poor neighborhood generally left his money in savings banks at 5 or $5\frac{1}{2}$ percent interest, without realizing that money funds were available to pay higher returns. The sophistication that produced disintermediation from banks to money funds in prosperous cities and towns was absent in poor neighborhoods. Thus their savings banks, and similar institutions such as credit unions, continued to earn good returns in the 1980s, when the institutions that had been well located in terms of wealth suffered from disintermediation. With higher interest rates they lost deposits and had to borrow in the open market so as not to have to sell their fixed-rate assets —mortgages and bonds—at the lower prices produced by increases in interest rates.

Intermediation by time is still required, but is taking place increasingly through futures markets as opposed to direct dealing. Banks and nonfinancial firms can find that pattern of liquidity that suits them in terms of cash flows in and out through forward contracts that adjust the time profile of anticipated receipts and payments. There remain solvency risks in such contracts, but their use is to fine-tune liquidity. Some years ago I observed that a number of companies would adjust their time preferences as to liquidity through their own intermediation, borrowing long in the Eurobond market when they planned a project, and depositing the funds in the Eurodollar market, so as to have the funds on hand when they were needed. This could be regarded as a form of direct trading within the firm, with the cost of purchasing liquidity represented by the difference between the long- and short-term rates of interest.

Another form of direct trading is the practice of Japanese groups that combine banks and insurance companies with manufacturing and chemical companies so as to be certain to have a source of financing always available. This is a form of vertical integration that applies also in some industries, controlling sources of supply and outlets in order to avoid the risk of interruption from breakdown of the market for inputs or outputs. Where inputs are bulky and difficult to store, as in coal or oil, control through ownership was thought necessary since interruption could not be fore-stalled by the maintenance of sizable inventories. Some of this vertical integration varied with the business cycle, to be sure; oil companies being readier to own tankers in tight markets and to rely on the market when tanker rates were slack. The move to just-in-time scheduling of materials and components made possible by computers reduces, further, the need to store inputs, just as futures contracts make it less necessary to store cash.

Intermediation by risk is connected with that by time and size. The small saver lends to one intermediary who both accumulates savings for large loans, and diversifies by lending to more than one borrower. The diversification should reduce default risk, although if the intermediary is badly or dishonestly managed, perhaps excessively speculative in its investments, the depositor's presumed gain through reduced default risk from diversification is lost.

In addition to default risk, there is interest-rate risk. With a true time deposit, the depositor has a chance of gain when competitive interest rates decline, an opportunity-cost loss if they rise. The major interest-rate risk in intermediation, however, is that of the bank, as it lends long and borrows short. If its assets are in fixed-rate loans, securities, or mortgages for extended time periods, and interest rates rise, it may both lose deposi-tors and suffer reductions in the value of its assets, even though the latter loss may be disguised by continuing to carry the assets on the books at cost. In recent years, banks and other lenders have sought to escape interest-rate risk by changing the rates paid for deposits on the one hand, and those charged on loans and mortgages on the other. But of course variable rates do not reduce risk overall. They shift it from the bank to the depositor and the borrower.

In one view the role of the intermediary in reducing risk for the lender (or depositor) is less connected with information than with reputation (Terlizzese 1989). The good reputation of a bank or other intermediary rests in the belief of the depositor that the intermediary understands the nature of risks and how to manage them. That view has had to undergo modification when the carefree lending and buying of junk bonds follow-ing the 1982 deregulation of the thrifts was exposed to light. But of course information and reputation are closely connected.

International intermediation by reputation has come to attention recently with some striking examples. Christopher Platt has examined the books of the Baring Brothers bank in London in the 1840s and been struck by the fact that gross and net lending by Britain to France differed sharply since much of the French bonds issued in London were bought by Frenchmen. There were elements of size involved, to be sure, as the London bond market was larger than that in Paris, and hence more liquid. But French investors felt safer lending to their own government and new railroads through the City, rather than directly, on the basis that the city's reputation for financial acumen was greater. Later, London issued bonds for the Argentine government bought by Argentinians as well as by British and other investors. There was an element of exchange risk here, as there may have been in European issues of dollar bonds in New York after World War II bought by Europeans. Such risk was minimal in the London-French case of the 1840s given the long-established gold standard. Platt notes that the standard estimates for the British capital outflow before 1914 must be reduced considerably to make allowance for these purchases by the borrowing countries. While this is doubtless true for France and Argentina, there is not, so far as I am aware, evidence that similar differences between net and gross existed for dominion borrowers such as Australia, Canada, and New Zealand.

Somewhat further away from this lending from national creditors to a national debtor through the intermediation of an outside country is that seen by Bacha and Diaz-Alejandro (1982), in their well-known article "International Financial Intermediation: A Long and Tropical View." Here, firms and governments in Third World countries borrowed from U.S. banks at a time when wealth holders in those countries undertook to protect their capital by escaping foreign-exchange control and piling up deposits in U.S. banks, often the same ones. There was no intention on the part of, say Argentine or Mexican, capitalists to lend to their governments through foreign banks; it was nonetheless a form of international intermediation by size and exchange risk.

Still another form of international intermediation by reputation involving the Third World occurred after the OPEC price rise of 1973. One oil expert thought it would have been desirable for the OPEC countries to sell oil to nonoil Third World countries on credit terms (Levy 1982, 245, 266). The producing countries evidently thought otherwise, presumably on the ground that the credit standings of the importers were weaker than those of world-class banks. In consequence they sold only for dollars, with cash on the barrelhead, so to speak. This produced "recycling" as it was then called, but which, in our terms, is international intermediation by reputation, the OPEC countries lending to the Eurodollar market, and the Eurodollar banks lending to the Third World, both oil producers such as Mexico and Venezuela, and the importers.

I have pointed out that the displacement (to use Minsky's term), or exogenous shock, that gave rise to the lending in the first place antedated the November 1973 price rise by a couple of years. In 1970 and 1971, the United States tried to lower interest rates in the interest of President Nixon's reelection campaign at a time when the Bundesbank was tightening interest rates to curb inflation. Money poured out of the United States into the Eurodollar market. As interest rates fell, the world banks sought out new borrowers and found them in the Third World.

Intermediation then, by social status, place, time, and various sorts of risk, whether because of monopolized information or reputation, is continuously threatened by disintermediation, which may be intermediation through a different medium and by direct trading. I hazard the guess that intermediation by social status is a thing of the past, although the point about blue-collar neighborhoods being less subject to disintermediation than white-collar areas suggests a vestigial remnant of the effect. Intermediation by place would seem to be stretched to the limit in a world of ubiquitous computers connected by modems, facsimile machines, and copiers. That by time, and to a certain extent by risk, will compete with new financial instruments such as swaps, options, and the like. The troubles of the junk-bond market would appear to dampen the enthusiasm of some groups for intermediation by default risk, for example in the funds collected by leveraged buyout (LBO) firms to use as bridge loans or equity investment in takeovers.

While intermediation by size changes its form as pension funds and insurance companies achieve a scale where they trade directly with large borrowers issuing notes and securities, that for smaller amounts will doubtless continue. The banking function of providing financial services to smaller companies that choose not to build their own treasurer's department to cover all their financial needs will last. In theory, there should be an advantage in having an outside opinion to guard against intellectual autointoxication, but the herdlike behavior of financial markets in the 1980s raises the question whether outside opinion givers are independent of the waves of financial fashion.

It is likely that the size of companies moving to direct trading will shrink with time, but intermediation as a basic economic function is almost certainly here to stay. At the last minute, however, strong evidence of the loss of business to direct trading at major U.S. banks came with the second quarter of 1990 profit returns, and the efforts of Citicorp and Chase Manhattan to reduce their staffs.

The need for cost cutting is especially evident for banks like Chase and Citicorp, which have been hurt by a decline in wholesale lending and other financing for large corporations. While the banks still maintain expensive networks of foreign offices, corporate treasurers have learned how to borrow money more cheaply in the securities markets or from foreign banks. (*New York Times* 1990, 29)

An awareness of economic history might have forestalled the buildup now being trimmed down.

References

Bacha, Edmar Lisboa, and Carlos F. Diaz-Alejandro. 1982. *International Financial Intermediation: A Long and Tropical View*. Essays in International Finance, No. 147. Princeton, N.J.: Princeton University International Finance Section.

Bagehot, Walter. [1873] 1978. *Lombard Street*. In N. St. John-Stevas, ed., *The Collected Works of Walter Bagehot*, volume 9. London: *The Economist*, 45–233.

Bank for International Settlements. 1986. *Recent Innovations in International Banking*. The Cross Report, prepared by a study group established by the central banks of the Group of Ten countries. Basle: B.I.S.

Bouvier, Jean. 1961. *Le Crédit Lyonnais de 1863 à 1882: Les Années de Formation D'une Banque de Dépôts*, 2 volumes. Paris: SEVPEN.

Boyer-Xambeu, Marie-Therèse, Chislain Deleplace, and Lucien Gillard. 1986. *Monnaie Privée et Pouvoir des Princes*. Presses de la foundation nationales des sciences politiques.

Braudel, Fernand. 1986. *Civilization & Capitalism, 15th–18th Century*. Vol. 2. *The Wheels of Commerce*, (translated from the French by Sian Reynolds). New York: Harper & Row.

Chandler, Alfred D. 1962. *Strategy and Structure: Chapters in the History of Industrial Enterprise*. Cambridge, Mass: Harvard University Press.

Clay, Christopher. 1978. *Public Finance and Private Wealth: The Career of Sir Stephen Fox, 1627–1716*. Oxford: Clarendon Press.

Cole William Rossa. 1989. "Author and Editor Against the Publisher." *New York Times Book Review* (September 3): 1.

Crozier, Michel. 1964. *The Bureaucratic Phenomenon*. Chicago: University of Chicago Press.

Dent, Julian. 1973. *Crisis in Finance: Crown, Financiers and Society in Seventeenth-Century France*. New York: St. Martin's Press.

Federowicz, Jan K. 1988. "Anglo-Polish Commercial Relations in the First Half of the Seventeenth Century." *Journal of European Economic History* 5: 359–78.

Glamann, Kristof. 1971. "European Trade, 1500–1750." In *The Fontana Economic History of Europe: Volume 2, The Sixteenth and Seventeenth Centuries*, Carlo M. Cipolle, ed. Glasgow: Collins/Fontana, 427–526.

Goodman, Stephen, ed. 1978. *Financing and Risk in Developing Countries*. New York: Praeger.

Gurley, John G., and Edward S. Shaw. 1950. *Money in a Theory of Finance*. Washington, DC: Brookings Institution.

Hunt, Edward S. 1990. "A New Look at the Dealings of the Bardi and Peruzzi with Edward III." *Journal of Economic History* 50: 149–62.

Kindleberger, Charles P. 1964. *Economic Growth in France and Britain, 1851–1950*. Cambridge, Mass.: Harvard University Press.

———. 1978. *Economic Response: Comparative Studies in Trade, Finance and Growth*. Cambridge, Mass.: Harvard University Press.

Kozul, Jean-Pierre. 1970. "American Banks in Europe." In *The International Corporation: a Symposium*, C. P. Kindleberger, ed. Cambridge, Mass.: M.I.T. Press, 273–89.

Levy, Walter J. 1982. *Oil Strategy and Politics, 1941–1981*. Melvin A. Conant ed. Boulder, Colo.: Westview Press.

Moser, Justus. 1969. "Some Thoughts about the Decline of Commerce in Inland Towns." In *European Society in the Eighteenth Century*, Robert and Elborg Forster, eds. (translated by Gerhard Stalling). New York: Walker & Co., 185–89.

Parker, Geoffrey. 1974. "The Emergence of Modern Finance in Europe, 1500–1730." In *The Fontana Economic History of Europe, Volume 2, The Sixteenth and Seventeenth Centuries*, Carlo M. Cipolle, ed. Glasgow: Collins/Fontana.

Price, Jacob M. 1989. "What Did Merchants Do? Reflections on British Overseas Trade, 1660–1770." *The Journal of Economic History* 49: 267–84.

Platt, D. C. M. 1984. *Foreign Finance in Continental Europe and the USA, 1815–1870, Quantities, Origins, Functions & Distribution*. London: George Allen & Unwin.

Sayers, R. S. 1957. *Lloyds Bank in the History of English Banking*. Oxford: Clarendon Press.

———. 1978. Introduction to *The Collected Works of Walter Bagehot*, N. St. John-Stevas, ed., vol. 9. London: The Economist.

Snowden, Kenneth A. 1988. "Mortgage Lending and American Urbanization, 1880–1890." *The Journal of Economic History* 4: 273–86.

Tawney, R. H. 1958. *Business and Politics under James I: Lionel Cranfield as Merchant and Minister*. Cambridge: Cambridge University Press.

Terlizzese, Daniele. 1988. "Delegated Screening and Reputation in a Theory of Financial Intermediaries." *Temi di Discussione*, Banca d'Italia, No. 111.

Warsh, David. 1989. "In Defense of Middlemen." *The Boston Globe* (September 3): 33, 38.

Political Economy

16

The Politics of International Money and World Language

A Nationalistic Suggestion for Monetary Reform?

In 1966 I participated with two colleagues in writing an article in *The Economist* which set forth a minority view on "The Dollar and World Liquidity."[1] Its point was that the dollar-exchange standard would be a good international monetary system if it were understood: that a return to gold as advocated by the French, the adoption of a new international currency proposed by Triffin, or of a new international asset to supplement gold and dollars, under consideration by the Group of Ten, would each be contrived, artificial, and less efficient than the dollar standard, with liquidity supported by an international capital market centered on New York and its Eurodollar and Eurodollar-bond extensions. The dollar system could not work so long as European monetary authorities did not understand the international financial intermediation it performed, and converted dollars into gold. In the clutch, we thought, if these authorities did not see the intellectual force of the argument, they could be driven to an understanding of the system by the willingness of the USA to sell all its gold, and its unwillingness to buy it back in future. (We differ as to the wisdom of pushing along this line.)

Despite an explicit claim that it was international rather than nationalistic, our position has been widely criticized as the latter. *The Economist* itself appended a reservation in which it termed "the new nationalism" the 'view that America can, even at this late stage of the day, perform all its old international financing functions without ... international support....' Triffin has applauded some parts of the analysis and criticized its statistical underpinnings in an essay in *Essays in International Finance*, September

Reprinted with permission from *Essays in International Finance*, no. 61 (Princeton, NJ: Princeton University Press, August 1967).

1966, but is reported in seminars to have contrasted his international solution with our national one. The left-wing *Monthly Review* is generous
enough to regard us as having "long records as liberals reaching back to
New Deal days" but at the same time states that we advocate forcing an
"American" solution on the European rivals of the US capitalist class, and
characterizes the article as expressing "the American imperialist view in
its most nationalistic and aggressive form."

The purpose of this chapter is to elucidate the political aspects of the
economic solution proposed for the international monetary system, and
to make clear the incongruity between economic objectives and political
side-effects. It will call attention to certain measures and procedures
which, it is hoped, reduce the political unattractiveness of the economic
scheme we put forward. Finally, it suggests an analogy between money
and language in the international sphere which may be illuminating. The
basic question that will be left unanswered is whether economic efficiency
is less important in these matters than political appearances, which many
other observers would probably call political reality. It is possible that it
is, but economists are accustomed to having doubts. At the least, I would
insist that there is a tradeoff between economic inefficiency and political
appearances which must be explicitly evaluated to see whether the cost in
one is worth the benefit in the other.

The Prestige of Reserve Currencies

At the bottom of much of the European case against the dollar standard is
prestige. In the USA there is genuine confusion, arising from the definition of balance-of-payments deficit by the Department of Commerce,
which regards all assets other than gold acquired by the USA as illiquid
and all demand liabilities as about to be immediately presented for payment. There is some confusion in Europe, as when Jacques Rueff suggests
that the dollar-exchange standard permits the USA to consume beyond its
capacity to produce. This he suggested at a time when the US balance
of payments on current account reached close to record surpluses—still
short, however, of the full amount of US aid and foreign lending. There is
also some irrationality in the way that central banks hold gold and forego
earnings on assets denominated in foreign exchange based on an implicit
decision-rule that the central bank gets none of the benefits from foreign
earnings and all the blame in the event that the foreign currency is devalued. A sensible system would allow the central bank to weigh its
expectation of devaluation against the earnings foregone by holding gold,

perhaps by using earnings to set up reserves against future devaluation losses. But it is fair to say that much of the French case against the dollar-exchange standard is based on prestige, and much of the French case rubs off on other Europeans.

Prestige is expensive. It is expensive in earnings foregone on foreign-exchange reserves (corrected for a proper evaluation of the risk of loss through devaluation) and it is expensive in transactions costs.

The dollar is the world unit of account—the standard in which foreign-exchange reserves, agricultural prices in the Common Market, contributions to the United Nations budget, and a host of other international monetary items are measured. It is true that the Banque de France recently abandoned the practice of announcing its gains and losses of foreign reserves in dollars, and now states them only in francs, thus shifting to the press the trivial burden of calculating the dollar equivalents. The dollar is also the world's standard of deferred payment. After the imposition of the Interest Equalization Tax the dollar-bond market flourished in Europe at the expense of two European ways of borrowing money at long term: the unit-of-account bond, denominated in the Common Market units of account, equivalent to the dollar in value, but with fixed parities among all the European currencies, and the parallel issue, which appeared simultaneously in several European capital markets. When Europeans were borrowing in New York, there was some thought in economic circles that they were going short of the dollar in the expectation that in the long run the dollar would be devalued. This theory, however, ran into a fact that required a contrary interpretation: many of the European dollar bonds issued in New York and all those issued in Europe were bought by Europeans or foreigners with European accounts. In effect, the dollar has continued as the world's standard of value.

But it is as a medium of exchange that the efficiency of the dollar standard is the clearest. As foreign-exchange markets now stand, most transfers between currencies other than sterling or dollars go through sterling or dollars, and mostly through dollars. Gold is not used for making payments, but must be sold for currency for payments. It can be freely sold only in the London gold market and in the USA. While there are small markets for direct dealings between, say, French francs and Deutsche marks, most large transactions go through dollars or sterling. Working balances have to be held in dollars (and in sterling for the sterling area). The question is how large these working balances should be relative to the transactions costs of transferring reserves into and out of other assets.[2]

Part of the recent movement into gold—inch by inch on the part of most of the European central banks, in substantial strides of $300 million a month by the French for some months after May 1965—has perhaps been dictated by fear of dollar devaluation. But not much. It is hard to see how there can be much realistic belief that the dollar will be voluntarily devalued. If it were to be, it would get no exchange-rate benefit, since other currencies would be devalued simultaneously to restore exchange rates throughout the international monetary system and produce only a change in the price of gold. Since the USA opposes a change in the gold price, devaluation has a very low expected value.

Much of the movement to gold is an attempt to discipline the USA by inducing it, for example, to tighten interest rates. But since 1966, when this had been accomplished, there is no exchanging gold again for dollars. The application of pressure to change macroeconomic policies produces a once-and-for-all reduction in the volume of liquidity in the system, as US gold plus European dollars becomes European gold. But it also reduces the efficiency of the international monetary system and increases future transactions costs.

The final reason for holding gold instead of dollars is the prestige supposedly associated with it. The question here is why the USA should hold only gold in its reserves, when other countries hold gold and dollars in varying proportions. This is a useful question, but there is an answer. International currencies are not all of equal value as units of account, standards of deferred payment, and media of exchange. They stand in relationship to one another not as full equals, but in a hierarchical arrangement of ascending utility as international money. This is John H. Willams's concept of "key currencies," which he opposed to the Bretton Woods' concept (underlying the International Monetary Fund) that a country drawing exchange from the Fund would be as likely to draw one currency as another. It is Robert V. Roosa's concept of a vehicle currency. When he was Under Secretary of the Treasury, Mr Roosa promised in a speech that when the USA again had a surplus in its international accounts it would buy foreign currencies rather than gold. This action would multilateralize the exchange standard, and there are strong political reasons for doing so. In economic terms, however, it must be recognized that acquisitions by the USA of large amounts of sterling, French francs, Deutsche marks and lire, for example, would have a different economic impact than foreign dealings in dollars. That these countries do not buy and sell their currencies against gold at fixed prices is one aspect of this difference, but an unimportant one. More significant is that these currencies have behind them less price stability, smaller capital markets, and more limited capacities to supply incremental exports at relatively constant prices (though these differences are smaller than they used to be).

Considerations of prestige partly govern US policies with regard to international monetary reform. My reason for wanting to keep the dollar-exchange standard is efficiency, but I suspect that many Americans take the same position for reasons of prestige. The Italian suggestion that sterling and dollar liabilities should be internationalized at the IMF is unacceptable because of the added transactions introduced into the system, but will not be accepted for possibly very different reasons. The same is true of the Triffin plan for a new international currency.

United States policies immediately after the war were not dictated by prestige, however. Leadership at Bretton Woods, the Lend-lease settlement, the Marshall Plan, Point IV, the General Agreement on Tariffs and Trade, and so on, had their origins in the necessity to solve problems. Then, as now, this country was accused of throwing its weight around but, without the exercise of leadership, there is a good chance of accomplishing nothing, or even of weakening the international system through log-rolling. An example of the latter is the voting of the second tranche of UNNRA in August 1945 when the USA, with one vote in seventeen, had to agree to take over the Canadian share from the first tranche, shifting Austria and Italy from military relief to UNNRA to reduce the British share of the cost of aiding those countries, and providing relief to Byelorussia and the Ukraine, despite the fact that the USSR was a benefactor in UNNRA relief and not a recipient. It was this experience that induced the Department of State to insist that Marshall Plan assistance be organized so that the recipient countries entered into agreement with the USA both as a group and separately. It is this same difficulty that results in the frustration of the less developed countries at such a conference as the United Nations Conference on Trade and Development in Geneva in March 1964, where a large majority of the participating countries proposed schemes to be underwritten at the cost of a few. There is a continuous clash between multilateral policies that may make good politics but often end up in impossible economics, and unilateral policies that are politically less attractive but economically more feasible (if in some instances less than generous). This, however, is not a question of prestige but of feasibility.

The strength of the dollar as a world exchange standard lies in the international capital market operated in dollars. If the USA must cut itself off from the provision of capital to the world by reason of its worries about its balance of payments, the role of the dollar as a vehicle currency is seriously and perhaps fatally damaged. The capital market is a means of providing both real assets to the countries of the world with an adequate credit standing, and liquidity to firms and countries with real assets and credit standing but inadequate liquidity. The provision of real assets requires transfer of goods and services. The provision of liquidity calls for lending long and borrowing short. This is not American imperialistic taking-over of European and other capitalism, as the *Monthly Review* and some less ideological critics of US direct investment abroad think. I suspect that there has been some excessive American foreign investment which will prove, in time, not to be profitable. But in other instances, the American bond investors and American firms have provided capital, technology, and liquidity to borrowers and asset-holders abroad. For a bank to acquire an asset and a liability simultaneously is not, as a rule, imperialist penetration.

Internationalizing the Dollar

The foregoing may sound very nationalistic. But there are several international aspects of it which have been dealt with fleetingly and which are worth emphasizing. Firstly, in *The Economist* article it was indicated that the dollar-exchange standard needs to be underpinned by international arrangements like the Basle agreement of March 1961, which would provide discounting in a crisis. I should prefer to see a true international central bank, but doubt that there is sufficient consensus to make possible agreement on the appropriate kind of institution. To convert the IMF into a central bank, as is possible, requires abandonment of a fundamental feature of Bretton Woods and of the proposals for an international reserve unit: the provision of liquidity in advance of need by owned reserves. The great merit of the Basle agreement, and the crucial feature of an international central bank, is the availability of unlimited amounts of assistance through rediscounting in a period of crisis. Who does what for whom and who gets paid for it are settled after the event, not in advance, when the outline of possible events can be perceived only dimly. There has to be a broad understanding that the helped does not let the helpers suffer by reason of the help. When the crisis is over, the accumulated obligations can be transferred to the IMF or funded in long-term debts. An international central bank could make its own arrangements for repayment of rediscounts, and this would be a desirable improvement over the *ad hoc* arrangements now necessary. But the kind of international central bank that could be agreed upon at this stage of thinking about the international monetary system would almost undoubtedly have owned reserves, and only limited lines of credit. The volume of owned reserves is not a vital aspect of the system. Lines of credit must be unlimited, and hence conditional, since the character and scope of need for them are impossible to foresee accurately.

Secondly, the Basle arrangements mean mutual surveillance of swaps, lines of credit, borrowings, and so on. European insistence on knowing what the facts are is fully justified, and US and British resistance to such surveillance is not consistent with the provision of emergency discounting facilities.

Thirdly, in a system of international monetary arrangements of the sort I favor—a dollar-exchange system buttressed by informal Basle-type arrangements—the monetary policy of the major countries, say, the Group of Ten—should be determined internationally. Just as the Federal Reserve Act of 1913 took monetary policy from the New York banks and transferred it to a national body, in which New York, along with Washington, had a powerful voice, it is important now that rates of interest in the international capital market be determined internationally, on the basis of conditions in Europe and Japan, as well as in the USA. Instead of the Federal Open-Market Committee, which makes monetary policy for the USA, we need an Atlantic Open-Market Committee.

New York and Washington will still have a powerful voice in the determination of rates of interest and amounts of money. There is an asymmetry between the New York money and capital market and its Eurodollar extensions and the separate European capital markets, which are joined to each other not directly but through New York and the Eurodollar network. When one of the peripheral central banks—say, the Bank of Italy—changes its discount rate, it alters the spread between it and the others, but when the New York rate is changed, it alters the level of the total. The analogy with the Federal Reserve Banks of Minneapolis and New York is broadly accurate. Minneapolis can change the spread but not the level; New York can change the level but not the spread. In capital markets, as in foreign-exchange markets, subsidiary markets within the total can be ordered hierarchically. There is no way to escape the fact that the USA has major responsibility for the level of rates in the international money market. But it should and must consult those countries affected by the international market, and let policy be guided by some weighted impact of the views of all.

Multilateral versus Independent Diplomacy

The international politics of monetary arrangements are analogous to those of peace keeping. No expert on this topic, I must keep my discussion brief and suggestive. The need for bilateral as well as multilateral engagements in the Marshall Plan and in foreign aid is one example. The balance between the Assembly and the Security Council of the United Nations is another. There is a subtle line to be drawn between US intervention in Korea and Lebanon, which met with fairly general approval in the West, and those in the Dominican Republic and in Vietnam, which have not. The USA operated alone, but with the approval of the less developed countries, in blowing the whistle on the British and French attack on Suez in 1956. The United Nations peace-keeping operations in the Gaza strip and the Congo were financed by US loans, with Soviet and French abstention. The USSR was perhaps a little in advance of the USA in moving to halt the war between Pakistan and India. China, the USSR, and the USA are all working to prevent the spread of the war in Vietnam, deeply as they disagree on the resolution appropriate to that country.

In all these matters, the line between nationalism and internationalism is hard to draw, and perhaps not worth trying to draw. A pure internationalism that relied solely on the United Nations would cause the overburdened organization to explode in frustration. Pure nationalism, such as the ideologues suggested the USA should pursue in Vietnam, is hard to square with the picture as a whole. National leadership is inescapable, in my judgment, but can operate efficiently only in an international setting. And, where the international forms cannot be preserved in their purity, this does not mean nationalist dominance so much as a muddier form of internationalism, *ad hoc* or even in an old-fashioned balance-of-power guise.

English (or American) and the Dollar

However, the analogy which interests me most is that between the use of the dollar in international economics and the use of the English language in international intercourse more generally. Analogies are tempting, and dangerous because frequently misleading. But the dollar "talks," and English is the "coin" of international communication. The French like neither fact, which is understandable. But to seek to use newly created international money or a newly created international language would be patently inefficient.

Languages are ordered hierarchically. Like sterling, French used to dominate. Like the dollar, English does now. Frenchmen must learn English; it is not vital for Anglo-Saxons to learn French.

The analogy with the language quarrel in Belgium is exact. The Flemish must learn French, but the Walloons, despite their constitutional edict of equality between the languages and the legislative edict which requires civil servants to do so, do not learn or use Dutch. The Flemish are offended and begin to insist on Flemish, exactly as France has insisted that its representatives at international conferences, even when they know English perfectly, must speak only French and insist on all speeches in English being translated into French. The transactions costs of translation, including the misunderstanding in communication and the waste of time, are even more evident than the transactions costs of converting gold to dollars and dollars to gold, when it is dollars—not gold—that are necessary to transactions.

Etiemble's passionate attack on the intrusion of English into French, *Parlez-Vous Franglez?*, is at the same time amusing, hysterical and pathetic.

To gain its ends entirely, the dollar kills our language.... No one is ignorant of the fact that scarcely had they delivered France from Nazism, the Americans set about eliminating French as a working language at the United Nations.

I am not a "nationalist."

... The fact is that if France and Germany demanded tomorrow the conversion of its balances at the Federal Reserve Bank the United States would go bankrupt. Acknowledge that it is comforting. Doubtless one would have to be an idiot, a Stalinist or an anarchist to wish the collapse of the dollar: we would suffer from it. In any case, only an idiot would not profit from the improvement in our finances and refuse to signify to Wall Street that the time is past for compliance and servility.... Since Walter Lippman makes public that the American Treasury in weeks which were difficult for it obtained the support of foreign banks of issue "including especially that of France," then thanks to the numerous African states which it has freed from the yoke of colonialism, our country disposes in the United Nations and in UNESCO, of many friends and loyal adherents, since this year in the course of a general debate at the United Nations, 25 speeches were given in French against 35 in English or American, 15 in Spanish, 5 in Russian and 1 in Chinese, we are in a position to demand of the Yankees that they do not sabotage French any more in international organization.[3]

It is easy to imagine what is implied in a "sabotage" of French as a working language at the United Nations. Someone—presumably an Anglo-Saxon—at a working-committee meeting, observing that all the Francophones had a good command of English, suggested that the translation into French from English and possibly from French into English be dispensed with in the interest of efficiency. The transactions (translation) costs of simultaneous but especially of consecutive translation are highly inefficient, owing to loss of time or accuracy and of intimacy in two-way communication.

It is highly desirable for Americans and British to know enough French, German, Italian, Spanish, and perhaps Russian to be able to receive in those languages, or some of them, even if they transmit only in English. But world efficiency is achieved when all countries learn the same second language, just as when the different nationalities in India use English as a *lingua franca*. There is much to be said for the national unity which comes from one's own language, and this sometimes works, as Hebrew in Israel, and sometimes not, as Gaelic in Eire and Hindi in India. One's own currency is the native language, and foreign transactions are carried on in the vehicle currency of a common second language, the dollar.

It is hard on French, which used to be the language of diplomacy, to have lost this distinction, but it is a fact. In scientific writing, as in communication between international airplane and control tower, English is the universal language, except for the rescue call "Mayday" which Etiemble would have put in French as "M'aidez." But a common second language is efficient, rather than nationalist or imperialist.

The power of the dollar and the power of English represent *la force des choses* and not *la force des hommes*. This is not to gainsay the existence of unattractive nationals abroad—from virtually all countries. I recall particularly a *Chicago Tribune* reporter who got through Europe with two words: "Whiskey" and "Steak." But it is not nationalism which spreads the use of the dollar and the use of English; it is the ordinary search of the world for short cuts in getting things done. It is of some interest that most British are no longer anxious about the prestige of sterling, but content to let the dollar take over as a key currency. In language, however, the equivalent of a former vehicle language resigning itself to national use is not in evidence, as the French support billions of foreign aid each year in considerable part to keep their former colonies in the Francophone area.

The selection of the dollar as the *lingua franca* of international monetary arrangements, then, is not the work of men but of circumstances. Pointing to its utility involves positive, not normative, economics. Students of international politics must deplore the nationalistic overtones and would like to see the ultimate bastions of the system, and the means of producing policy, international.

But the analogy has one more aspect. The futility of a synthetic, deliberately created international medium of exchange is suggested by the analogy with Esperanto. This still commands a doughty band of true

believers, but their legions have thinned. A linguistics expert states that
Esperanto suffers from being inadequately planned as an international language. If he worked on it, he could devise a common language which
would be much better suited to the task. Our instinct tells us that this
is equally applicable to the myriad of plans—Triffin, Stamp, Postuma,
Roosa, Bernstein, Modigliani-Kenen, and all the rest—all of which have
strengths (and weaknesses) but also share the basic weakness that they
do not grow out of the day-to-day life of markets, as the dollar standard
based on New York has done, and likewise the Eurodollar.

Perhaps the Group of Ten's proposed International Reserve Unit,
denominated in dollars, can be compared with Basic English, which had a
brief fad and still has its faithful adherents but is gaining few new ones.

At the other extreme, the French view that the international money
system should re-enthrone gold as the international medium of exchange
resembles an appeal for a return to Latin as the *lingua franca* of international discourse, an appeal not without its nostalgic value for those
who admire ancient Rome and medieval culture, but one that is evidently
swimming against the stream of history, as the increasingly rapid abandonment of Latin in the Catholic Church testifies.

Finally, the many academic economists who recommend separating international money and capital markets by a system of flexible exchange
rates between national currencies in effect call for a return to Babel, with
foreign languages used by none save professional interpreters. This maxi-
mizes transactions costs and minimizes international discourse. A compromise between this and fixed exchange rates is possible: with separate
dollar, sterling (or dollar-sterling), franc, and ruble areas, each with many
countries having fixed exchange rates and speaking a common area language but with flexible exchange rates and full formal translation between
them. This has been proposed for the international monetary system
by Robert Mundell, and is implied by the French position on French
as an international working language. For those who like neat Cartesian
designs, it has much to recommend it.

But how can one make such a division of the world among the great
powers into spheres of influence stick, even if one has no misgivings
about its morality? An earlier paper by Mundell raised the central issue,
'What Is the Optimum Currency Area?' and the same question could
be put for languages. The rapid shrinkage of the world, however, makes
it impractical to try to maintain traditional currency and language areas
without infiltration of a single language and currency into a wider range
of human activity. The Organization of Petroleum Exporting Countries

(OPEC), consisting of Arab and Spanish-speaking states, inevitably reckons in dollars and discourses in English, and there is little that the statesmen of the major powers can do to prevent a succession of hundreds of similar steps toward reducing the costs of economic and social intercourse. In positive, not normative, terms the optimum currency and language area is rapidly expanding to the world.

In 1966, an Englishman named Horsfall Carter published a book called *Speaking European*,[4] a title patterned after a remark of Aristide Briand in 1936 apropos of Locarno. The ironic and politically very damaging fact is that the European language is English, or perhaps one should say American, just as the European unit in monetary affairs is the dollar. This is because the optimum language and currency areas today are not countries, nor continents, but the world, and because, for better or worse—and opinions differ on this—the choice of which language or which currency is made not on merit, or moral worth, but on size.

Notes

1. See Chapter 9 in this volume.

2. The extent of transactions costs for gold depends in part on where it is held, whether it is left abroad under earmark for later sale without the incurrence of shipping charges or brought home. It is of some interest that, after leaving in New York for many years the gold that might have to be sold for dollars, the French in the early 1960s started shipping it home. It can be argued that the advent of the ICBM made Paris as safe as New York in the event of world war, a consideration which had favored New York from about 1933 on.

3. René Etiemble, *Parlez-vous franglez?* (Paris: Gallimard, 1964), pp. 239–40, 293–5 (The translation is mine.)

4. W. Horsfall Carter, *Speaking European: The Anglo-Continental Cleavage* (London: George Allen & Unwin, 1966).

17

The International
Monetary Politics of a
Near-Great Power: Two
French Episodes, 1926–
1936 and 1960–1970

I

Students of international monetary relations have lately learned that their subject has, along with its technical intricacy, a high content of pure politics, and political scientists have begun to explore international relations beyond the usual confines of diplomatic and security questions into areas of technology and high finance (see, for example Rolfe, 1966; Kindleberger, 1967; Strange, 1970, 1971).[1] The production of testable hypotheses as to how various powers will behave politically in monetary affairs has hardly begun, however. Miss Strange has offered a taxonomy which divides currencies into "Top Currencies, Master Currencies, Passive or Neutral Currencies and Political or Negotiated Currencies" which combines elements of economic and political analysis (1971, p. 217). A number of historians have blamed the British crisis of 1931 on the small powers which converted sterling into gold in self-protection and helped to bring about the departure of the pound from gold (see, for example, Born, 1967; Hurst, 1932).

The hypothesis submitted to testing in this paper is that the international monetary politics of great powers and little powers are relatively simple compared with those of countries in between. Great powers, typically one great power, have responsibility for the stability of the international monetary system. Small countries with no power separately to affect the system have no such responsibility and are free to pursue the narrow national interest. In between, near-great powers face a difficult problem since they have power to hurt the system, generally insufficient power to steady it in the face of disruption on a wide scale, but are

A paper presented to the Economic History Society meeting at the University of Kent, Canterbury, England, 1972, and published in *Economic Notes*, vol. 1, no. 2–3 (Siena, 1972), pp. 30–44. Reprinted with permission of Monte dei Paschi di Siena.

tempted to pursue national goals which diverge from the interest of the system. The parts of the hypothesis applying to the great and the small powers are evidently widely challenged. The near-great powers especially contend that the great power purporting to act in the interest of the stability of the system is in reality motivated by self-interest which it confuses, deliberately or with self-hypnosis, with the broader world interest. On a high ethical plane, the small countries should adopt the Kantian Categorical Imperative, acting in ways which can be generalized, rather than pursue their national interest by means, which, if many small countries used them, would undermine the system. Since present interest attaches to such a near-great power as France, however, the validity of these parts of the hypothesis can be put aside, except insofar as it affects the behavior of near-great powers. The problem is the course of behavior of a country not strong enough to stabilize the system, but with ambitions and purposes of its own and sufficient strength to disturb it.

The question is examined historically with concise accounts of two periods when a case could be made that France rocked the international monetary boat for purposes of its own, in one case helping to capsize it. The first of these periods runs from the *de facto* stabilization of the French franc by Poincaré in 1926 to the Blum devaluation ten years later. The second covers the approximate decade from the de Gaulle stabilization of 1958 to the Pompidou devaluation of August 1969. In the first period, French national goals were largely of a security nature, although the economic aim of securing reparation from Germany played a significant role. In the second, French purposes included a change in the international monetary system itself, with a downgrading of the role of the dollar, a central place for gold, and a change in procedure for making international monetary decisions.

II

After World War I, the pound sterling was stabilized at its pre-war par in 1925, whereas the French franc, halted in its continuous depreciation by an heroic effort by Poincaré in July 1926, was stabilized *de facto* in the fall of 1926 and *de jure* in June 1928 at one-fifth of its pre-war value. The return to par overvalued the pound, weakened the British balance of payments and produced unemployment.[2] In the short run, however, it conveyed prestige on sterling. Poincaré thought long and hard when the French franc recovered in the fall of 1926 about letting it go all the way to par (Moreau, 1954, pp. 61, 94, 166, 184, etc.). Complaints from the automobile industry and from Léon Jouhaux, the leader of the CGT, as appreciation proceeded, turned the decision against any such course. The rate of 125 to the pound (roughly 4 cents) left the franc undervalued, although the decision was made with care.[3] In arriving at the rates, both Britain and France thought about national interests, rather than the impact of a disequilibrium cross-rate on the international monetary system. In the light of the pre-war position, however, there was more obligation on Britain to contemplate the wider interest than on France.

The overvaluation of the pound and undervaluation of the franc resulted in an accumulation of sterling (and later dollars) by France which altered the balance of financial power, weakened the international monetary system, and ultimately contributed to the world depression. A small part of the difficulty was the result of a technical point; beginning in the summer of 1927, the Bank of France held some sterling in the form of forward contracts with the Paris money market, which held sterling balances sold forward to the Bank of France. This made it appear that Bank of France (official) sterling was less than it really was, and further enabled the Bank of France, when the contracts ran off, to appear to convert into gold newly acquired rather than existing holdings of British exchange. The main problem was, however, first, that the French were somewhat antipathetical to Britain; second, that they chose to use their economic power for political purposes; and third, that in the final analysis, it was the British, not they, who were responsible for the stability of the system.

On the first score, the memoirs of Governor Moreau are highly revealing. As the apex of the hierarchical organization of the world economy, Governor Montagu Norman of the Bank of England thought it appropriate that the Bank of England organize the return to the gold standard of the other central banks in Europe. Governor Moreau was interested in competing for satellite central banks, and resented the efforts of the Bank of England. On frequent occasions, Governor Benjamin Strong of the Federal Reserve Bank had to be called in to lead a consortium to offer a stabilization loan to, for example, the National Bank of Poland. Moreau was conscious of the power which the Bank's sterling gave him over the Bank of England, and remarks on it frequently (1954, pp. 246, 250, 336, 488–9, etc.).

More significant was the difference between the British and the French over the use of the power of the lender to achieve political ends. The record is full of allegations of threats and calling of loans in the light of political rather than economic considerations. By no means can all be verified.

The French were hardly alone in attaching political conditions to economic loans. The Department of State had urged Wall Street not to lend to countries which failed to settle their war debts (Feis, 1950, pp. 20ff). Germany conditioned its participation in the Belgian stabilization loan on a rectification of the border at Eupen and Malmedy (Moreau, 1954, p. 76). Moreover, as noted, many of the accusations against France are debatable or unproved. The record, nonetheless, is a full one.

It is widely claimed, inconclusively, that the French threatened to withdraw credits from Germany when Schacht raised the questions of the return of German colonies and of the Polish corridor at the Young Plan discussions of Paris in April 1929 (Schacht, 1931, pp. 88–91).[4]

Leith-Ross of the British Treasury recounts in his memoirs that Quesnay of the Bank of France, supported by Francqui of Belgium and Pirelli of Italy, had reacted to Snowden's characterization of French demands for the division of reparations as "ridiculous and grotesque" by threatening to withdraw all French sterling from London (£240 million). Leith-Ross states that he rang for a messenger and directed him "Kindly show these gentlemen out," knowing that the Bank of France would certainly not want to see the collapse of sterling (1968, p. 124). This was in August 1929. Tight money in London, especially after the Hatry crisis of September 20, the day after the New York stock market peak, drew funds from New York and precipitated the crash. French opinion allows for the possibility that the spark that set off the explosion was the reaction to Snowden's abusive remark (Néré, 1968, p. 78).[5]

In the fall of 1930, the French press threatened the withdrawal of credits from Germany over a fancied slight—Germany hinting that it needed a loan to meet the withdrawals of capital which followed the National Socialist victory in the September elections, and then contracting it with Lee Higginson alone (Bennet, 1962). In the following spring, the accusation was made that France withdrew credits from Austria and Germany, over the Bruening initiative of Zollunion, a domestic political counter to the Nazi electoral gains. The facts of matter are in some confusion, and a recent investigator is doubtful (Bennet, 1962, p. 100).[6] But the French record on rescue loans for Austria and Germany is clear. They participated in the first Austrian credit, but insisted on political conditions. In the case of the second Austrian loan, Montagu Norman became angered at the French attitude, which he deplored, and went forward with a 50 million schilling loan to Austria for one week. It was not sufficient. A rescue loan for Germany did not get far. The French conditions of abandonment of the customs union with Austria and of the construction of the Panzerkreuzer were unacceptable to Bruening, looking desperately for foreign-policy successes to fend off the rising tide of National Socialism at home. While Stimson was for a loan, President Hoover and Secretary of the Treasury Ogden Mills felt that, with the Moratorium, they had gone as far as they could, and in particular were opposed to sending good money after bad, the essence of rescue operations. The British, weakened by withdrawals, explained that the "Bank of England had already lent quite as much as is entirely convenient" (Federal Reserve Bank of New York files, telegram, Norman to Harrison, 3 July 1931). There was no rescue loan and Germany joined Austria in blocking foreign credits.

There is no evidence that French officialdom contributed to the pressure on Britain which pushed that country off the gold standard in September 1931. On the contrary, the Bank of France joined the Federal Reserve Bank of New York in a rescue loan in August. Leith-Ross asserts that Moret, the governor of the Bank of France (successor to Moreau as of October 1928) was "very helpful," and the latter was in fact awarded a KBE in October 1931 (1968, p. 139). This may have been part compensation for the fact that the Bank of France lost heavily on the £62 million it had on deposit in London on September 21.

The loss on sterling converted the attitudes of France into those of a small country, concerned little with the stability of the monetary system and anxious about the safety of its dollar holdings. On September 21, Moret asked Governor Harrison of the Federal Reserve Bank of New York whether the Fed would object to the conversion of Bank of France dollars into gold. He was told that it would not. The next day the Bank of France converted $50 million (and the Bank of Belgium $106.6 million). Virtually daily thereafter the conversions continued. Moret explained politely the reasons for his concern—the British losses—and asked continuously whether his actions bothered the United States authorities. The loss of $775 million to all countries in the first three weeks did bother the Federal Reserve Bank, which was short of "free gold," but it proudly refused to acknowledge any inconvenience. Conversions died down only to be revived in January of 1932 in response to two events, the legislation indemnifying the Bank of France by the French government over the losses in Britain which awakened acute political concern, and a dispatch to the *Agence Economique* by Professor H. Parker Willis of Columbia University, characterizing the establishment of the Reconstruction Finance Corporation in the United States as inflationary. The Glass–Steagall bill passed in February relieved the gold situation in the United States, but only after the crisis had brought the United States, as Hoover said in the 1932 presidential campaign, within two weeks of going off the gold standard. A third flurry of conversion was started in March 1932, suspended briefly, resumed in April at $12.5 million a week. At the end of May when Moret indicated to Harrison that he wished to speed up the conversion, while avoiding "mischievous interpretations," it was suggested to him that he convert it all at once, and be done with the process. This he did on June 11, 1932. It was the bottom of the depression. (Federal Reserve Bank of New York files.)

One can argue, as do Friedman and Schwartz (1963, *passim*), that the responsibility for the world depression rests on mistaken monetary policy in the United States. The case in my judgement is thin. One can more readily blame the United States for cutting off foreign lending in 1928 just as the boom petered out, and putting strong deflationary pressure on Germany, Central Europe and the less developed countries—though it is difficult to imagine what positive steps this country could have undertaken to sustain lending. One can also fault the United States for raising tariffs as the depression began and for refusing to make rescue loans in time and in requisite amounts. The United States was far from ready to take responsibility for stabilizing the world economy. But the French actions in destabilizing for political advantage, in refusing rescue loans without impossible political conditions, and finally in cutting and running in the manner of a small country with no responsibility for the system compounded the felony.

III

After World War II French national finances were rather chaotic until de Gaulle came to power again in 1958 and devalued the franc for the second time, but successfully. The factors making for that success need not detain us, but the consequences were a positive balance of payments, rising claims in foreign currencies, largely dollars, and an interest in taking a significant role in shaping the evolving international monetary system.

As early as 1958, Professor Robert Triffin of Yale had been criticizing the gold-exchange standard, in which countries held reserves in currencies convertible into gold, as an absurdity (Triffin, 1960). In brief, his point was that holding reserves in the strongest currency induced the country that issued it to issue too much, with the result that the currency became weaker. This led to withdrawals and crisis. The view was well suited to French political interests. Sterling had been top currency, to use Susan Strange's not altogether suitable phrase, and now the dollar was. The French franc served a former colonial area, but enjoyed little international use outside it. French experts, and de Gaulle, attacked the gold-exchange standard, and especially the dollar standard. From the first 'dollar crisis' of the fall of 1960, to the 1969 devaluation of the French franc, French policies were directed to offering an alternative to a dollar-exchange system, and on occasion, to direct attack on the system.

It was recognized at the outset by Triffin and others that, if the dollar no longer served along with gold as an international asset, there would be a world shortage of international liquidity. Triffin proposed a new world central bank issuing a new international currency—an idea which had been advocated during the depression by Keynes and others. This would replace the International Monetary Fund, which did not issue permanent international money but rather made short-term loans which were repayable. The French view, expressed initially by Rueff, was that the price of gold should be raised to meet the liquidity need. In 1963 Giscard d'Estaing proposed the issuance of an international Currency Reserve Unit (CRU), the forerunner of the Special Drawing Right (SDR) which was ultimately adopted. Between the CRU as proposed by the French, and the SDR as adopted worldwide, however, there was this significant difference: the CRU, Giscard suggested, should be issued to every holder of gold in some proportion to his gold holdings. The alternative system, later adopted, and akin to the establishment of quotas in the IMF, was that countries should be issued the new international reserve unit in some proportion to their financial and trade strength. The French proposal was akin to raising the price of gold for central banks and had the disadvantage of encouraging central banks to convert exchange reserves into gold. In 1965 the French began exchanging dollars into gold as if in preparation for the issuance of CRU on the basis they suggested.

On February 4, 1965 President de Gaulle declared war on the dollar standard. He praised gold as "immutable, impartial and universal" and denounced the benefits which the United States derived from the use of the dollar as a reserve currency—the capacity to finance deficits, and in particular to buy foreign plants with money provided by the foreigners themselves.[7] The Bank of France began a rapid conversion of outstanding dollars into gold. In 1964, the French had been taking incremental increases in reserves in the form of gold rather than dollars, and these reserves increased from $3.4 billion at the end of May 1964 to $3.7 billion at the end of the year. Then began conversion of inframarginal dollars into gold to put pressure on the dollar-exchange standard. $1 billion in gold was gained in 1965 and another $500 million in the first nine months of 1966 before the French balance of payments turned adverse.[8] It was announced that henceforward Bank of France reserves would be published in francs, not dollars. In the fall of 1967, in the British crisis, the Bank of France withdrew from the gold pool supplying the hoarders, which had been created after the dollar troubles of 1960 (and in which the French contribution was very small), and further refused to participate in the rescue operations organized by the Group of 10 on behalf of the pound sterling. It is too much to say that France roiled the waters of British devaluation, but she fished them hard to obtain a change in the international monetary system along the hard-money lines already laid out. The effort failed. Britain's devaluation occurred without any change in the system, and when a change occurred in March 1968 it was taken without French participation, and in a direction contrary to French proposals. November 1967 was the peak of French efforts to remake the international monetary system along French economic and political lines.

In March 1968, a burst of gold hoarding led to the decision to institute a two-tier system for gold, with one price, $35 an ounce, for central banks, and a free market for hoarders where prices could rise in full as demand and supply willed, without intervention by the monetary authorities of the Club. The French were unable to denounce the scheme, since this would have committed them not to join the Club, and without membership it was not clear what the gold of the Bank of France was worth. As it turned out, this hesitation was wise, since the events of May and June led to sharp gold losses in July which were compounded by a capital outflow from France in the fall. At the end of March 1968 Michel Debré argued at Stockholm against the arrangements for issuing SDRs, which had been agreed in principle in Rio de Janeiro in September 1967. While he was speaking, the first student riots were taking place in Nanterre.

Successive strikes, first by students, then workers and in September by the middle class led to a crisis in November 1968, one year after the crisis in sterling. The French government cut back on nuclear tests, stretched out the *force de frappe* and the policy for all azimuths, but, in confrontation with the Germans who were unwilling to revalue upward, accepted the rescue operations organized by the Group of 10 and then refused to devalue. President de Gaulle characterized devaluation as absurd. The crisis it was said was international, not national, and the difficulty lay not in the French franc rate but in the whole international monetary system created at Bretton Woods, which was sick and headed for disaster. Reform was needed in the impartial gold standard. But in March 1969, the French government no longer thought it useful to raise the price of gold, which would only give windfall profits to gold speculators, and President de Gaulle, who repeated on March 6, 1969 that the franc would not be devalued, resigned at the end of April. During the period of holidays in August, the franc was devalued from 20.255 to 18.004 cents, or by 11 percent. France accepted her share of SDRs. The attack on the international monetary system, and its use of the dollar, was perhaps not ended. It was at least packed away into cold storage.[9]

IV

While there are broad similarities between the two experiences—extending as far as those between the Accord de Matignon of June 1936 and the Accord de Grenelle of June 1968, representing governmental capitulation to internal forces which made devaluation inevitable and ended the hope of international monetary success—there are significant differences as well. In the 1920s and '30s, the politics involved in monetary politics were low-level, conducted by Moreau, Quesnay, Rist and similar technical people. In the 1960s, the politics had moved higher to the level of the chief executive. Moreau kept in touch with Poincaré in 1926–28, as his diary makes clear, but it was he who issued the threats, or the Minister of Finance who withheld the loans, not the Prime Minister. President de Gaulle, on the other hand, discoursed freely on international monetary theory, not always, one suspects, with complete approval of his experts.

Secondly, the conversion of dollars was undertaken for economic reasons in the 1930s and for political in 1965 and 1966. The challenge to the dollar in the later period was comparable to the challenge to sterling in 1929, but for higher political stakes. Like that challenge, moreover, it is likely that de Gaulle was conscious of the dangers of pulling down the international monetary system, without achieving his positive ends. Just as Leith-Ross could stare down Quesnay, Franqui and Pirelli, confident in the conviction that France did not want to see the collapse of sterling, so the United States must have surely known that the French dollar conversions of 1965 were undertaken only because France believed that the

United States could resist them. The episode represents maneuvering, not warfare.

The near-great power finds itself in a cleft stick. If it cooperates in international monetary matters, as do Japan and Germany, it perpetuates the domination of one or more great powers; if it attacks the system *à l'outrance*, it threatens to bring it down around its ears. Isolation is an inadequate strategy, as the United States demonstrated persuasively in 1929 to 1931, and early intervention to produce change in the system either fails as in 1968 or destroys the world economy. The intermediate policy of cooperating until a country is strong enough to change the system and sustain a new one in the face of opposition requires a servility which proud nations find difficult to accede to. In international monetary matters, it would seem to be better to be dominant and accept the responsibility for making the system work, or small and able to ignore the public in favour of the private interest, rather than in between.

Notes

1. Straight historians as distinguished from economic historians have not ignored the politics of monetary problems. See, e.g., Bennet (1962) and Schwartz (1969).

2. For an account of the return to par, see Moggridge (1969).

3. Sauvy (1965, p. 99) calls the decision "an island of reason in an ocean of errors." For a defense of the rate and a discussion of its choice, see Rueff (1954, 1959).

4. Schacht's account is supported by remarks of Pierre Quesnay quoted in Clarke (1967, p. 165) and Lüke (1958, pp. 171–2). But the contemporary *Economist* (vol. 108, no. 4470, 4 May 1929, p. 966) is very doubtful.

5. Paul Einzig, the well-known English financial journalist, is another who believes that French withdrawals from Britain because of the Snowden–Cheron affair precipitated the Wall Street Crash. See Einzig (1935), pp. 172–4 and esp. p. 185. Note that "ridicule et grotesque" is much more abusive than "ridiculous and grotesque." Paul Schmidt, who was later Hitler's interpreter and who was present both for the Paris and the first Hague Young Plan conference, calls the former a poor translation for the latter (1949, p. 178).

6. But see Born (1967), pp. 56, 65, 66, who denies the allegation. Leith-Ross (1968, p. 144) suggested to Professor Charles Rist that France should lend to Austria on the condition that the government reformed the budget and added that France was always vaunting her financial power but seemed disinclined to use it except for political purposes. 'Professor Rist ... did not disagree with me.'

7. For a fuller statement on this point, see President de Gaulle's press conference of 27 November 1967, in e.g. *The New York Times*, 28 November 1967.

8. It is not without interest that when the French balance of payments did turn adverse, instead of selling gold, as implied by the statements praising the discipline furnished by the gold standard, France acquired dollars by borrowing them in Euro-dollar bond market

through nationalized companies. $30 million of Euro-dollar bonds were sold in January, June and October 1967 by Electricité de France, the Société Nationale des Chemins de Fer Français and the Caisse Nationale des Télécommunications, respectively.

9. The foregoing account has been put together from the contemporary press since there has been insufficient time to get an inside story from memoirs and documents. For an account of some of the French participants, see Fabra (*Le Monde*'s financial correspondent) (1968).

References

Bennet, Edward W. (1962), *Germany and the Diplomacy of the Financial Crisis, 1931* (Cambridge, Mass.: Harvard University Press).

Born, Karl Erich (1967), *Die deutsche Bankenkrise, 1931, Finanzen und Politik* (Munich: R. Piper & Co. Verlag).

Clarke, S. V. O. (1967), *Central Bank Cooperation, 1924–31* (New York: Federal Reserve Bank of New York).

Einzig, Paul (1935), *World Finance, 1914–35* (New York: Macmillan).

Fabra, Paul (1968), "The Moneymen of France," *Interplay*, January, pp. 37–40.

Feis, Herbert (1950), *The Diplomacy of the Dollar, 1919–1932* (New York: W. W. Norton).

Friedman, Milton and Schwartz, Anna Jacobson (1963), *A Monetary History of the United States 1867–1960* (Princeton, NJ: Princeton University Press).

Hurst, Willard (1932), "Holland, Switzerland and Belgium and the English Gold Crisis of 1931," *Journal of Political Economy*, vol. 40, no. 3 (June), pp. 638–60.

Kindleberger, C. P. (1967), "The Politics of Money and World Language," *Essays in International Finance*, No. 61 (Princeton, NJ, August).

Leith-Ross, Sir Frederick (1968), *Money Talks, Fifty Years of International Finance* (London: Hutchinson).

Lüke, Rolf E. (1958), *Von der Stabilisierung zur Krise* (Zurich: Polygraphischer Verlag).

Moggridge, D. E. (1969), *The Return to Gold, 1925: The Formulation of Economic Policy and its Critics* (Cambridge: Cambridge University Press).

Moreau, Émile (1954), *Souvenirs d'un gouverneur de la Banque de France. Histoire de la stabilisation du franc (1926–1928)* (Paris: Genin).

Néré, J. (1968), *La Crise de 1929* (Paris: Colin).

Rolfe, Sydney E. (1966), *Gold and World Power* (New York: Harper & Row).

Rueff, Jacques (1954), "Préface" to Emile Moreau, *Souvenirs d'un gouverneur de la Banque de France* (Paris: Genin).

Rueff, Jacques (1959), "Sur un point d'histoire: le niveau de la stabilisation Poincaré," *Revue d'économie politique*, 69e année (March–April), pp. 168–78.

Sauvy, Alfred (1965), *Histoire économique de la France entre les deux guerres*. Vol. I: *1918–1931* (Paris: Fayard).

Schacht, Hjalmar H. G. (1931), *The End of Reparations* (New York: Jonathan Cape and Harrison Smith).

Schmidt, Paul (1949), *Statist auf diplomatischen Bühne* (Bonn: Athenäum-Verlag).

Schwartz, Jordan (1969), *1933: Roosevelt's Decision, the United States and the Gold Standard* (New York: Chelsea House).

Strange, Susan (1970), *Sterling and British Policy: A Political Study of an International Currency in Decline* (London: Oxford University Press).

Strange, Susan (1971), "The Politics of International Currencies," *World Politics*, vol. 23, no. 2 (January), pp. 215–31.

Triffin, Robert (1960), *Gold and the Dollar Crisis* (New Haven, Conn.: Yale University Press).

18 An Explanation of the 1929 Depression

We return to the original questions: What produced the world depression of 1929 and why was it so widespread, so deep, so long? Was it caused by real or monetary factors? Did it originate in the United States, in Europe, in the primary-producing countries of the periphery, in the relations among them? Was the fatal weakness the nature of the international capitalist system or the way it was operated, that is, the policies pursued by governments? Were such policies, to the extent they were important, the consequence of ignorance, short-sightedness, or ill will? Were the depth and length of the depression a reflection of the strength of the shock to a relatively stable system, or were they a measure of the system's instability in the presence of a blow or series of blows of normal force (however measured)? Or—to bring the issue back among Paul Samuelson, Milton and Rose Friedman, and me—was the depression a fortuitous event, the consequence of deliberate and misguided monetary policy on the part of the U.S. Federal Reserve Board, or were its origins complex and international, involving both financial and real factors? Inevitably in drawing the threads together there will be a considerable amount of confirmation of preconceptions. I am open to the accusation of having selected statistics, facts, and incidents from the history of the decade which support a position chosen a priori. But I would claim that I have not knowingly suppressed any facts that do not fit the explanation that follows, nor ignored other explanations, such as U.S. monetary policy (Friedman), misuse of the gold standard (Robbins), mistaken deflation (Keynes), secular stagnation (Hansen), structural disequilibrium (Svennilson), and the like. The chapter is entitled "An Explanation," not "The Explanation."

The explanation of this book is that the 1929 depression was so wide, so deep, and so long because the international economic system was rendered unstable by British inability and U.S. unwillingness to assume responsibility for stabilizing it by discharging five functions:

(1) maintaining a relatively open market for distress goods;

(2) providing countercyclical, or at least stable, long-term lending;

(3) policing a relatively stable system of exchange rates;

(4) ensuring the coordination of macroeconomic policies;

(5) acting as a lender of last resort by discounting or otherwise providing liquidity in financial crisis.

These functions, I believe, must be organized and carried out by a single country that assumes responsibility for the system.[1] If this is done, and especially if the country serves as a lender of last resort in financial crisis, the economic system is ordinarily capable, in my opinion though not in that of others, of making adjustments to fairly serious dislocations by means of the market mechanism. There will be times when the structural dislocation is so far-reaching that more thoroughgoing measures are called for, such as the Marshall Plan and the British loan after the Second World War. D. E. Moggridge believes that the dislocation was so deep-seated in 1929 through 1931 that no rescue loans from France and the United States to Austria, Germany, and England would have served to halt the spiraling collapse of currencies.[2] The question is whether the shocks to the system—overproduction in primary products, French insistence on collecting reparations from Germany, U.S. demands for payment of war debts, overvaluation of the pound and undervaluation of the French franc, the halting of foreign lending by New York, the stock market crash, and the like—were so great that they would overwhelm any set of defenses; or whether, in the absence of some country willing and able to act as a stabilizer, any random shock to the system above some minimum level could set the unstable system off toward depression.

My contention is that the difficulty lay in considerable latent instability in the system and the absence of a stabilizer. Before the First World War, Britain stabilized the world by the discharge of the functions listed, more or less, and with the enormous help of gold standard mythology, which internalized both stable exchange rates and coordinated macroeconomic policies. There were occasions when Britain was either not involved or stood aside, as in 1873 when Central Europe and the United States shared a long depression.[3] In 1890, after five years of accelerated foreign lending, the London capital market suddenly stopped. The system was saved, after depression lasting from 1890 to 1895, by a deus ex machina in the form of a substantial flow of gold from the Rand mines of the Transvaal, discovered in 1886.[4] In 1929, 1930, and 1931 Britain could not act as a stabilizer, and the United States would not. When every country turned to protect its national private interest, the world public interest went down the drain, and with it the private interest of all.

Maintaining a Market for Distress Goods

Maintaining a market for distress goods can be regarded as another form of financing. Free trade has two dimensions: (1) to adapt domestic resources to changes in productive capacities abroad and (2) to keep the import market open in periods of stress. The first is more readily done by a rapidly growing country which needs to transfer resources out of less productive occupations and is willing to embrace the competition of imports. By holding firm to free trade during depression at some short-run cost to resources in import-competing lines, the second provides a market for surpluses accumulated abroad. Britain clung to free trade from 1846 (or some year thereafter, such as 1860, when all tariffs but those for revenue had been dismantled) until 1916. After 1873, although not growing rapidly, it continued to adhere to free trade since its declining industries were exporters rather than import-competers. Britain's tenacity in adhering to free trade in depression may have been born of cultural lag and the free trade tradition of Adam Smith rather than of conscious service to the world economy.

The contrast is with the Smoot-Hawley Tariff Act of 1930. At the first hint of trouble in agriculture, Hoover reached for the Republican household remedy, as Schumpeter characterized it, in the face of a recommendation of the World Economic Conference of 1927 that nations of the world should adopt a tariff truce. The action was important less for its impact on the U.S. balance of payments, or as conduct unbecoming a creditor nation, than for its irresponsibility. The congressional rabble enlarged protection from agriculture to primary products and manufactures of all kinds, and Hoover, despite more than thirty formal protests from other countries and the advice of 1,000 economists, signed the bill into law. This gave rise to (or at least did nothing to stop) a headlong stampede to protection and restriction on imports, each country trying to ward off deflationary pressure of imports, and all together ensuring such pressure through mutual restriction of exports. As with exchange depreciation to raise domestic prices, the gain for one country was a loss for all. With tariff retaliation and competitive depreciation, mutual losses were certain. The formula of tariff truce and exchange stabilization proposed for the World Economic Conference of 1933 offered no positive means of raising prices or expanding employment. It would nonetheless have been significant as a means of slowing further decline. With no major country providing a market for distress goods or willing to tolerate appreciation, much less offering to furnish long-term capital or discounting facilities to countries suffering from payment difficulties, the fallacy of composition with the whole less than the sum of its parts ensured that deflation would roll on.

Countercyclical Lending

In the nineteenth century Great Britain tended to lend abroad on a countercyclical basis, with some exceptions such as the 1890 episode already referred to.[5] But by and large, and especially after mid-century, foreign and domestic lending were maintained in counterpoint. Domestic recession stimulated foreign lending, while a boom at home caused both lending to be cut back and imports to be expanded, providing an export stimulus abroad in place of domestic investment with borrowed funds. Countercyclical lending stabilized the system.

In the 1920s, U.S. foreign lending was positively correlated with domestic investment, not counterpoised. The boom of the 1920s was accompanied by foreign lending; the depression of the 1930s saw the capital flow reversed. In *The United States and the World Economy*, written in 1943, Hal Lary recorded the fundamental fact that the United States cut down on imports and lending at the same time. The cut in lending actually preceded the stock market crash as investors were diverted from the boom in foreign bonds that followed the Dawes loan to the boom in domestic stocks dating from the spring of 1928. The deflationary pressure on Germany may be debated; the pressure on the less developed countries at the periphery is clear-cut.[6] As Table 1 shows, moreover, Britain joined the United States in reducing its lending in 1929 over 1928.

Stable Exchange Rates

Exchange rates were stable in the nineteenth century because of the gold standard. The price of gold was fixed in Britain in 1717 and in France in 1726 and maintai   with interruptions for war and crisis, until 1931 and 1928, respective   economists believe that the gold standard was managed by the Ba   England, with occasional help from the Bank of France, the Bank of   urg, and the State Bank of Russia. The system was accepted as an c   'ive fact, hardly subject to alteration. It was internalized and thus le   te.

When after the inflations of the First World War, exchange rates were either restored or adjusted, it was important to get them fixed at equilibrium levels. Attention was devoted to the problem. In most countries, economists worked at calculating purchasing power parities, without, however, always making adequate allowance for structural changes, such as the loss of overseas assets by Britain or the large volume of French capital that in 1926 was waiting abroad for the opportune moment to return to its normal habitat. Italy chose an exchange rate based almost entirely on prestige. The resulting pattern of rates put stress on the system.

Then came the depression and the response of many countries on the periphery, cut off from borrowing and facing sharply declining export prices and values, to depreciate their currencies. A certain amount of competitive exchange depreciation took place. Britain did not care how far the pound sank, but it created the Exchange Equalization Account to keep it from rising. The response of monetary authorities to the chaotic behavior of exchange rates in the 1930s was to adopt fixed rates at Bretton Woods in 1944 as a standard to prevent beggar-thy-neighbor tactics. When the set of rates came under stress as countries pursued independent macroeconomic policies, many economists came out in favor of floating. It was originally thought by many, and is still widely maintained by monetarists, that freely flexible exchange rates provide insulation from world conditions of instability for a given country. Experience both in the 1930s and in the 1970s, however, seems to indicate otherwise. In a world of deflation, as in the 1930s, flexible exchange rates with overshooting are deflationary. Depreciation leaves domestic prices unchanged and reduces prices in countries where exchange rates have appreciated. In a world of inflation, on the other hand, as in the 1970s, the ratchet works in the opposite sense: depreciation raises domestic prices; appreciation leaves foreign prices unchanged.

Economists have yet to agree on how best to achieve the optimal degree of exchange rate stability, steady in the short run, adjusted in the long as structural changes are called for and macroeconomic policies diverge. Nor is it clear how leadership would provide it today, though the United States dominated the Bretton Woods institutions until the early 1970s.

Coordination of Macroeconomic Policies

Like exchange rates, macroeconomic policies were coordinated more or less automatically in the nineteenth century under the gold standard. The

Bank of England had gradually developed techniques for management of the London money and capital markets, which communicated monetary policy to the rest of the country and the world. Fiscal policy scarcely existed in a world of balanced peacetime budgets, except as the shape of taxes changed. Such changes were designed for resource allocation and income redistribution, not for maintaining stability of national income.

The gold standard basically broke down in the interwar period when the United States and France, accumulating gold, sterilized it. Monetary policy was conducted largely for domestic purposes, except for the episode of 1927, which was later regarded as a mistake. German inflation in 1923 rendered that country paranoid about inflation. Positive fiscal policy was followed practically nowhere, not even in Sweden. And monetary policies went uncoordinated: it was "devil take the hindmost" or *sauve qui peut.*

Lender of Last Resort

The lender of last resort function has two dimensions, one domestic, one international. On the domestic front, it received timely attention. Montagu Norman of the Bank of England rescued the William Deacons Bank in January 1929. In October of that year, George Harrison of the Federal Reserve Bank of New York rushed into the breach with open market operations well in excess of the limits assigned him by the Federal Reserve Board in Washington in an effort to shore up the liquidity of the New York market. In Italy a variety of banks were saved secretly in 1930, well before the first bank panic in the United States in November and December of that year. The German record was less positive. A Social Democratic memorandum in July 1931 argued that the Reichsbank should undertake a new issue of banknotes without regard to the legal limits imposed by its gold and foreign exchange reserves, avoiding the danger of inflation by raising the discount rate. It undertook the latter, but not the former.[7] And the Danatbank was allowed to fail, a sin of omission regarded as incomprehensible from today's perspective.[8]

It was, however, in the international dimension that the lender of last resort was most conspicuously missing. The task is a difficult one at best, but Britain tried, up to the last 50 million schillings for Austria in June 1931, when the rest of the world had backed out. After that setback, Britain stood aside from a loan to Germany, while the French and Americans undertook one—"too little and too late," not to mention the stringent French political conditions. When it came England's turn to seek help, the

United States and France proceeded with one loan at a time—salami tactics, when the Bagehot prescription was to lend freely—and attached economic conditions to the second loan so severe that they brought the Labour government down. Conditionality in rescue loans raised in Third World negotiations with the IMF today is not a new problem.

British Leadership

Not until 1931 was it clear that Britain could not provide the leadership. In the early 1920s there were League of Nations programs for the stabilization of the currencies of Austria and Hungary. These were to a considerable extent British in spirit, with help of experts from Scandinavia, the Low Countries, and the dominions such as staffed the League of Nations Economic, Financial, and Transit Department. Later the Dawes and Young plans to settle German reparations were dominated by British experts, with Americans serving as front men to foster the British hope of tying reparations to war debts. By 1931 British capacity for leadership had gone. In small part it had been dissipated in puerile central bank quarrels between Norman and Moreau, although much of the competition for domination over the smaller central banks of Europe was the product of Moreau's imagination. (Benjamin Strong tried hard to arbitrate these quarrels, and his death in 1928 was a loss for the stability of the system.) More significant was the burden of French sterling balances, which inhibited Britain as a lender of last resort. At the World Economic Conference in 1933 it was clear that Britain had turned away from a leading world role, cultivating the Commonwealth and freedom to manage sterling, and largely leaving it to the United States to devise a world program.

Lack of U.S. Leadership

Revisionist historians, such as William A. Williams, insist that the United States undertook a leading world role, under Charles E. Hughes, as early as the Disarmament Conference of 1922.[9] It is difficult or impossible to find support for this position in the field of international economics, which holds with the conventional wisdom of such historians as E. H. Carr, that "in 1918, world leadership was offered, by almost universal consent, to the United States ... [and] was declined."[10] There was interest in the affairs of Europe in New York, in the Federal Reserve Bank of New York under Strong and Harrison, and in the financial community represented by such people as Dwight Morrow, Thomas Lamont, and Norman Davis. A few non–New Yorkers, such as Charles G. Dawes and Andrew Mellon, were brought into international finance and diplomacy. On the whole, however, the isolationism expressed by Henry Cabot Lodge in leading the rejection of the Versailles Treaty and U.S. adherence to the League of Nations typified the dominant sentiment. The United States was uncertain in its international role. It felt that the British were shrewder, more so-phisticated, more devious in their negotiating tactics, so that the United States came out of international conferences losers. Stimson would have been willing to undertake a major discounting operation to rescue the Reichsmark in July 1931; Hoover, Mellon, and (though from New York) Mills were opposed to sending good money after bad, as discounting calls for. In 1933 James Warburg, Moley, and presumably Woodin and Roosevelt still resisted sending good money after bad. Proposals for em-bryonic international monetary funds were legion, and even Britain pre-sented one officially. They were uniformly turned down with a lecture on how much the United States had already lost in unpaid war debts and the Standstill Agreement.[11] It was not until 1942 that Harry D. White began preparing a world plan for discussion at Bretton Woods—together with the plan of Lord Keynes—a world plan for limited discounting.

Cooperation

Clarke's conclusion that central bank cooperation was maintained up to mid-1928 but failed thereafter has already been dealt with in some detail. In summary, such cooperation as there was on matters such as hegemony over small central banks or the choice of an equilibrium exchange rate was inadequate before 1926, and the Bank of France supported the pound loy-ally (and expensively) in the late summer of 1931. A deeper question is whether cooperation as such would have been sufficient. In *America's Role in the World Economy*,[12] Alvin Hansen prescribed for the United States policies of maintenance of full employment at home and cooperation with international efforts at freer trade, restoring capital movements, improve-ment of the world monetary system, and so on. With the advantage of hindsight, it appears that more than cooperation was provided—namely, leadership—and that mere cooperation would not have built the institu-tions and policies of the Organization for Economic Cooperation and Development, Group of Ten, Bank for International Settlements, Interna-tional Monetary Fund, International Bank, General Agreement on Tariffs and Trade, and so on. As an acquaintance on the International Monetary Fund staff put it (admittedly to an American), if the United States did not take the leadership, nothing happened. Leadership may lack followership, and foolish or even sensible proposals may be defeated through lack of support. But the most sensible proposals emanating from small countries are valueless if they lack the capacity to carry them out and fail to enlist the countries that do. The World Economic Conference of 1933 did not lack ideas, as that of 1927 seems to have done. But the one country capable of leadership was bemused by domestic concerns and stood aside.

One special form of cooperation would have been joint Anglo-American leadership in the economic affairs of the world. The 1980s equivalent is the frequently proposed troika of Germany, Japan, and the United States, which could furnish the world leadership needed today now that American capacity or will to provide it alone has been dissipated. However, economists and political scientists usually agree that such arrangements, whether duopoly or bilateral monopoly, are unstable. Carr states explicitly that the hope for Pax Anglo-Saxonica was romantic and that Pax Americana "would be an easier contingency."[13] Vansittart, referring to the Standstill agreements and the German occupation of the Rhineland, wrote apropos of the World Economic Conference: "When action was required two years earlier, the two governments [British and American] sheltered behind each other like the British and French governments three years later."[14] With a duumvirate, a troika, or slightly wider forms of collective responsibility such as the Summit of Seven or the Group of Ten, the buck has no place to stop.

Changing Leaders

Friedman and Schwartz make a great deal of the role in the great depression of the shift of monetary leadership in the United States from New York to Washington.[15] They suggest that this sounds farfetched, since it is a "sound general principle that great events have great origins," but note that small events at times have large consequences through chain reactions and cumulative force. The universality of the asserted principle seems dubious to this observer;[16] the observation that shifts of the locus of leadership give rise to instability does not. Had they not focused so exclusively on monetary conditions in the United States, Friedman and Schwartz might have noted the accentuation of the depression that came with the transfer of the presidency from Hoover to Roosevelt (occurring after the money supply had been greatly enlarged) and the still more significant (in my judgment) transfer of leadership in the world economy from Whitehall to the White House.

This notion of the instability of a financial system with two centers, or of one where leadership is in the process of being dropped by one and picked up by another, is cited by Edward Nevin as crucial to the collapse of the gold standard in 1931. He quotes Sir Ernest Harvey's testimony before the Macmillan Committee: "such leadership as we possess has been affected by the position which America has gained," making a change in the ancient system as set out in the Macmillan Report, under which the bank rate regulated the reserve position of the United Kingdom, and other countries adjusted their positions to that of Britain. He then went on to say, "Better that a motorcar should be in charge of a poor driver than of two quite excellent drivers who are perpetually fighting to gain control of the vehicle."[17] The analogy of two excellent drivers fighting for control of the wheel may be more graphic than apposite. The instability seems rather to have come from the growing weakness of one driver and the lack of sufficient interest in the other. William Adams Brown, Jr., describes the gold standard of the period as "without a focal point," meaning that it had two, but the conclusions of his monumental work do not dwell on this critical aspect of the world economy.[18]

Role of the Small Countries and France

One passenger in the vehicle which did not lack interest was France. And one group which lacked responsibility—to discontinue the metaphor, or perhaps they should be regarded as passengers in the back seat—consisted of the smaller countries: Belgium, the Netherlands, Switzerland, and Scandinavia. The smaller countries can be disposed of first. They are sometimes blamed, as in Born's analysis, for having acted irresponsibly in, say, converting sterling into gold in the summer of 1931 or raising tariffs with alacrity after 1930. There is, however, no universally accepted standard of behavior for small countries. On one showing, they lack power to affect the outcome of great events and are therefore privileged to look after the private national interest rather than concern themselves with the public good of stability in the world economy as a whole. On a somewhat higher ethical level, the small countries may be held to the Kantian categorical imperative, which enjoins them to act only in ways that can be generalized. In such circumstances, of course, they would not have withdrawn credits from Austria in the spring of 1931, nor from Germany and Britain in the summer, nor from the United States in the autumn. The economist chooses between these standards perhaps on the basis of comparative cost. If the Netherlands had known the cost of leaving its sterling unconverted into gold, it seems unlikely that it would have done so, even at the risk of accelerating the collapse of the pound and deepening the world depression. It may be that such countries as Sweden, Canada, and New Zealand that set high standards of international conduct—in foreign aid, contributions to United Nations peacekeeping missions, etc.—do so solely for ethical reasons; or they may choose among occasions to take largely the opportunities that are relatively cheap. One may thus note that the small countries contributed substantially to the deflation by the speed with which they cut imports, depreciated, or converted sterling and dollars into gold, but find it hard to blame them for it.[19]

There is another aspect to the role of small countries: they could offer programs for recovery because they knew that the major cost of programs adopted would fall on other countries. Proposals for an embryonic international monetary fund in the Washington discussions preceding the World Economic Conference of 1933 were put forward by Poland, Turkey, Belgium, the ILO, and one was made by Britain, though this latter was quickly withdrawn when the United States frowned on it. Lacking resources to make these schemes effective, small countries were reduced to advisory roles without conviction, even when the proposals were sound. An essential ingredient of followership is to convince the leader that he is the author of the ideas that require the use of his resources.

The case of France is different. France sought power in its own national interest, without adequately taking into account the repercussions of its positions on world economic or political stability. Its intransigence in the matter of reparations or the attempt to attach political conditions to the second Austrian credit of June 1931 or the contemplated German loan of July of that year illustrate the position. Hurt in the depreciation of sterling in September, the Bank of France, under strong political pressure at home, converted its dollars into gold in the private national interest during 1931–32, all the while protesting its cooperation and concern for the interest of the United States. The rivalry between the Bank of France and the Bank of England over which should take over the leadership in restoring independence to central banks and stabilization of currencies in Eastern Europe would be pathetic, had it not run risks of instability for the system as a whole when the French threatened to withdraw balances from London.

Not quite big enough to have responsibility forced on it, nor small enough to afford the luxury of irresponsibility, the French position in the interwar period was unenviable. It had the power to act as a destabilizer, but it was insufficiently powerful to stabilize.[20] "Great Britain and the

United States together were the active nucleus that replaced the single centre of prewar days, but the position and policy of France actively affected their mutual as well as their joint relations to the outlying countries."[21] In these circumstances France could be (and was) blamed for upsetting the system when she had no capacity to take it over and run it in the presence of two larger powers, one feeble, the other irresponsible.

Public versus Private Interest

Cynicism suggests that leadership is fully rewarded for its pains in prestige and that no matter how much it protests its commitment to the public welfare, its fundamental concern is private. Bismarck insisted that free trade was the weapon of the dominant economy anxious to prevent others from following in its path. "The white man's burden" is an expression used today only in mockery. A country like France deliberately setting out to achieve prestige suggests that those with a concern for problem solving are either perfidious or self-deceiving. Nevertheless, there is a difference between accepting and declining responsibility for the way the system is run. The British accepted responsibility, although, as the 50 million schilling loan emphasizes, they were unable to discharge it. The French and the United States were unwilling to underwrite stability. Under Coolidge and Hoover, the United States refused to commit itself to any program of foreign reconstruction or currency stabilization, leaving these questions to the Federal Reserve System.[22] There was hardly any improvement in Roosevelt's commitment to the world economy until timidly in 1936, at the time of the Tripartite Monetary Pact, and ultimately during the Second World War. Inside France, as between France and the other leading powers, "all groups thought their opponents more united and dedicated than they were, and a concern for the general interest was virtually absent."[23]

Unable to cope with the public good, the British more and more turned their energy to the private. Keynes's advocacy of a tariff and the refusal to contemplate stabilization after 1931 are examples. One may find a hint or two in the documents that the initiative came from the dominions rather than Britain.[24] For a time, until well after the war, the British economics profession and public almost drew the lesson that each country should take care of itself without regard to external effects.

The point is illustrated in the memorandum written by Hubert Henderson at the British Treasury in 1943, entitled "International Economic

History of the Interwar Period."[25] This summarizes the crude view that the depression resulted from nationalism and tariffs, the collapse of world trade, bilateralism and preferences, and disregard of the advice of the League of Nations, leading to the conclusion that after the war there is need for the world to be more resolute in avoiding economic nationalism and attempting to construct a freely working economic system with international credits, the reduction of trade barriers, and the outlawry of qualitative regulation.[26] Henderson states that the history of the interwar period provides no support for this view. He opposes exchange depreciation: "There can be little doubt that the depreciation of the pound was in part responsible for the sharper fall in gold prices, and disillusionment is general in the United Kingdom and still more in the United States on the power of exchange depreciation to promote national recovery."[27]

But the conventional view is false in all essential respects. The old international order has broken down for good. Nothing but futility and frustration can come from the attempt to set it up again. Individual countries must be free to regulate their external economies effectively, using control of capital movements, quantitative regulation, preferences, autonomous credit policies, etc.[28]

This foot-dragging, which Keynes shared during the 1930s and until late in the war, is understandable. It misses the main lesson of the interwar years, however: that for the world economy to be stabilized, there has to be a stabilizer—one stabilizer.

Relevance to the 1980s and 1990s

Leadership is a word with negative connotations in the 1980s, when participation in decision making is regarded as more aesthetic. Much of the overtones of *der Führer* and *il Duce* remain. But if leadership is thought of as the provision of the public good of responsibility, rather than exploitation of followers or the private good of prestige, it remains a positive idea. It may one day be possible to pool sovereignties to limit the capacity of separate countries to work against the general interest; such pooling is virtually attained today in some of the functions needed to stabilize the world economic system, such as the Basel arrangements for swaps and short-term credits, which, pending a world central bank, serve as a world rediscounting mechanism in crisis. In this area, and in the world agencies for maintaining freer trade and a liberal flow of capital and aid, however, leadership is necessary in the absence of delegated authority. That of the

United States is slipping. It is not yet clear that the rising strength of Europe in an enlarged European Economic Community or of Japan will be accompanied by an assertion of leadership in providing a market for distress or aggressive goods, in stabilizing the international flow of capital, or in providing a discount mechanism for crisis. Presumably the Basel arrangements for the last will endure. There are indications that the European market for goods will remain ample, except in agriculture, which is an important exception from a world viewpoint. There is still some distance to go to stabilize the flow of capital countercyclically.

As the U.S. economic leadership in the world economy falters and Europe and Japan gather strength, three outcomes are politically stable, three unstable. Among the stable outcomes are continued or revived U.S. leadership, after the exchange controls of 1963 to 1968 and the recent wave of protectionism have been reversed; an assertion of leadership and assumption of responsibility for the stability of the world system by Europe, Japan, or some unsuspected third country such as Brazil; or an effective cession of economic sovereignty to international institutions: a world central bank, a world capital market, and an effective General Agreement on Tariffs and Trade. The last is the most attractive, but perhaps, because difficult, the least likely. As between the first two alternatives, the responsible citizen should be content with either, flipping a coin to decide, if the third alternative proves unavailable, simply to avoid the undesirable alternatives.

The three outcomes to be avoided because of their instability are: (1) the United States, Japan, and the EEC vying for leadership of the world economy, (2) one unable to lead and the others unwilling, as in 1929 to 1933, and (3) each retaining a veto over programs of stability or strengthening of the system without seeking to secure positive programs of its own. The articles of agreement of the International Monetary Fund (IMF) were set up to provide the United States with a veto over action it opposed. In the 1969 reform that legislated the addition of Special Drawing Rights (SDRs) to the monetary system, quotas of the IMF were adjusted to provide a veto to the EEC as well. This leaves open the possibility of stalemate, as in the United Nations Security Council, when two major powers are unable to agree. In the circumstances of the Security Council there is a danger of regressive spiral into war; the analogue in the economic field is stalemate—and depression.

The third positive alternative of international institutions with real authority and sovereignty remains pressing.

Notes

1. Political scientists refer to the leadership position of a single country as "hegemony." I prefer to think of it as responsibility. Hegemony may, however, be more realistic as well as more cynical. It should be noted that political scientists debate whether hegemony is needed for the maintenance of peace and of world economic stability. See Robert O. Keohane, *After Hegemony: Cooperation and Discord in the World Political Economy*, 1984. Keohane thinks that international regimes can substitute for hegemony. Regimes are institutionalized habits of cooperation. They are more precisely defined as "principles, norms, rules and decision-making procedures around which actor expectations converge in a given issue-area" (Stephen D. Krasner, "Structural Causes and Regime Consequences: Regimes as Intervening Variables," 1983, p. 1).

2. See his "Policy in the Crises of 1920 and 1929." Haberler agrees with the position taken here, that the aftermaths of the First and Second world wars called for different therapies because of differences in the extent of physical, economic, and political devastation and dislocation. See his "Die Weltwirtschaft und das internationale Währungssystem in der Zeit zwischen den beiden Weltkriegen," pp. 288–89. It may be remarked, however, that some years ago Haberler sided with those such as Roy Harrod, Friederich Lutz, Jacob Viner, and Senator Joseph Ball who opposed the notion of "dollar shortage," and in some instances the Marshall Plan, maintaining that stability and growth could be reestablished in Europe right after the war if countries would "halt the inflation and adjust the exchange rate." See the discussion in my *Dollar Shortage*, 1950, pp. 2–6.

For a largely political view that the two postwar eras are of the same piece, together with dissents, see Charles S. Maier, "The Two Postwar Eras and the Conditions for Stability in Twentieth-Century Europe," 1981, with comments by Stephen A. Schuker and me, and a reply by Maier.

3. See my *Manias, Panics, and Crashes*, p. 211.

4. See my "International Propagation of Financial Crises."

5. See my "The Cyclical Pattern of Long-Term Lending."

6. Fleisig, "The United States and the World Periphery in the Early Years of the Great Depression."

7. Holtfrerich, "Alternativen zu Brünings Wirtschaftspolitik in der Weltwirtschaftskrise," p. 6.

8. Irmler, "Bankenkrise und Vollbeschäftigungspolitik," p. 287.

9. See, for example, William Appleman Williams, *The Tragedy of American Diplomacy*, 1959, esp. ch. 4, "The Legend of Isolationism." Mr. Williams, a Marxist revisionist historian, states: "Hoover did not grasp the fact that the depression was a sign of stagnation in a corporate economy which was born during the civil war and came to maturity in the decade from 1895 to 1905" (p. 123); and: "From the fall of 1932 Roosevelt and Hull stressed the importance of foreign trade for domestic revival and expansion and for world wide relief of conditions which caused war and revolution" (p. 128). It is difficult to see how a historian could ignore such evidence as the First Inaugural Address, cited earlier, to be able to make such a statement about Roosevelt.

10. Edward Hallett Carr, *The Twenty Years' Crisis, 1919–1939: An Introduction to the Study of International Relations*, 1946, p. 234.

11. Pedersen blames the liquidity crisis of 1931 on the United States for its failure to support the German mark and, when that had been forced to suspend gold payments, for its failure to underwrite sterling. See "Some Notes on the Economic Policy of the United States During the Period 1919–1932," in his *Essays in Monetary Theory and Related Subjects*, pp. 208–9. This would be agreed today, and Professor Pedersen put it forward himself, as noted earlier, in 1933. As he himself points out, however (p. 210), the United States was acting with "the normal prejudices of the period."

12. Alvin Hansen, *America's Role in the World Economy*, 1945.

13. Carr, *The Twenty Year's Crisis, 1919–39*, pp. 233–34.

14. Vansittart, *The Mist Procession*, p. 466.

15. Friedman and Schwartz, *A Monetary History of the United States, 1867–1960*, p. 419.

16. Cf. Benjamin Franklin, *Maxims Prefixed to Poor Richard's Almanac*, 1757: "Little strokes fell great oaks" and "A little neglect may breed mischief: for want of a nail the shoe was lost; for want of a shoe the horse was lost; for want of a horse the rider was lost." The exception for cumulative feedback embraces the second quotation, but not the first.

17. Nevin, *The Mechanism of Cheap Money*, pp. 9n., 12, 14.

18. W. A. Brown, *The International Gold Standard Reinterpreted, 1914–34*, vol. 2, p. 781: "The essential difference between the international gold standard of 1928–29 and that of 1914 was that when the world returned to gold after the war it built its international financial system around a nucleus of London and New York, and not a single center." The title of his ch. 20 is "The Experiment of a Gold Exchange Standard without a Focal Point."

19. For an interesting political model of countries that are free-riders behind the leadership of others, see Norman Froelich and Joe A. Oppenheimer, "I Get Along with a Little Help from My Friends," 1970. But note (p. 119) that leadership is rewarded in this model rather than made to pay for the privilege, as implied where the responsibilities of leadership are maintaining an open market for goods, a countercyclical export of capital and a mechanism for rediscounting in crisis.

20. See my "International Monetary Politics of a Near-Great Power: Two French Episodes, 1926–36 and 1960–70," 1972.

21. W. A. Brown, *The International Gold Standard Reinterpreted, 1914–34*, p. 785.

22. Chandler, *Benjamin Strong*, p. 255.

23. Sauvy, *Histoire économique de la France entre les deux guerres*, vol. 1., p. 73.

24. See *Documents diplomatiques français, 1932–39*, 1967, vol. 3, no. 470, Bonnet to Paul-Boncour, July 9, 1933, p. 871: "One fact is evident: it is that Britain is not free. Its dominions and in particular Canada whose Prime Minister Bennett is a man of extraordinary violence have a predominant influence on her, to the point of modifying totally her opinion in the space of a few seconds." This is doubtless hyperbole. For an up-to-date account of the origins of imperial preference written by a Canadian, see Drummond, *Imperial Economic Policy, 1917–39*.

25. See Hubert D. Henderson, *The Interwar Years and Other Papers*, 1955, pp. 236–95.

26. Ibid., pp. 236, 290.

27. Ibid., pp. 260, 262; see also p. 291: "Of the various expedients which different governments employed in the 1930s, none produced more unfortunate results than deliberate exchange depreciation. It was the least helpful to the countries which tried it, and the most harmful to other countries."

28. Ibid., p. 293.

References

Brown, William Adams, Jr. *The International Gold Standard Re-interpreted, 1914–1934.* 2 vols. New York: National Bureau of Economic Research, 1940.

Carr, Edward Hallett. *The Twenty Years Crisis, 1919–1939: An Introduction to the Study of International Relations.* 2nd ed. London: Macmillan, 1946.

Chandler, Lesyer V. *Benjamin Strong, Central Banker.* Washington, D.C.: Brookings Institution, 1958.

Documents diplomatiques français, 1932–1939. 1st ser., 1932–35, vols. 1–3. Paris: Imprimerie Nationale, 1966; 2nd ser., 1936–39/Imprimerie Nationale, 1937.

Fleisig, Heywood W. "The United States and the World Periphery during the Early Years of the Great Depression." In Herman van der Wee, ed., *The Great Depression Re-visited: Essays on the Economics of the Thirties.* The Hague: Martinus Nijhoff, 1972.

Friedman, Milton, and Anna Jacobson Schwartz. *A Monetary History of the United States, 1867–1960.* Princeton: Princeton University Press, 1963.

Froelich, Norman, and Joe A. Oppenheimer. "I Get Along with a Little Help from My Friends." *World Politics* 23, no. 1 (October 1970): 104–120.

Haberler, Gottfried. "Die Weltwirtschaft und das internationale Währungssystem in der Zeit zwischen den beiden Weltkriegen." In Deutsche Bundesbank, *Währung und Wirtschaft in Deutschland, 1876–1975.* Frankfurt-am Main: Knapp, 1976, 205–248.

Hansen, Alvin H. *America's Role in the World Economy.* New York: W. W. Norton, 1945.

Henderson, Hubert D. *The Interwar Years and Other Papers.* Oxford: Clarendon, 1955.

Holtfrerich, Carl-Ludwig. "Alternativen zu Brünings Wirtschaftspolitik in der Weltwirtschaftskrise." *Frankfurter Historische Vortrage,* no. 9. Wiesbaden: Franz Steiner, 1982.

Irmler, Heinrich. "Bankenkrise und Vollbeschäftingungspolitik (1931–1936)." In Deutsche Bundesbank, *Währung und Wirtschaft in Deutschland, 1876–1975.* Frankfurt-am-Main: Knapp, 1976.

Keohane, Robert D. *After Hegemony: Cooperation and Discord in the World Political Economy.* Princeton: Princeton University Press, 1984.

Kindleberger, Charles P. *The Dollar Shortage.* Cambridge, Mass.: MIT Press, 1950.

Kindleberger, Charles P. "International Politics of a Near-Great Power: Two French Episodes, 1926–1936 and 1960–70." [Chapter 17 in this volume.]

Kindleberger, Charles P. *Manias, Panics and Crashes: A History of Financial Crises,* 1st ed., New York: Basic Books, 1978.

Kindleberger, Charles P. "The Cyclical Pattern of Long-Term Lending." In Mark Gersowitz, et al., *The Theory and Experience of Economic Development.* London: Allen and Unwin, 1982, 300–312.

Kindleberger, Charles P. "International Propagation of Financial Crises: The Experience of 1888–1893." In Wolfram Engels et al., eds., *International Capital Movements, Debt, and Monetary System.* Mainz: Hase & Koehler, 1984.

Maier, Charles S. "Two Postwar Eras and the Conditions for Stability in Twentieth Century Western Europe." *American Historial Review* 86, no. 1 (April 1971): 327–352.

Nevin, Edward. *The Mechanism of Cheap Money: A Study in British Monetary Policy, 1931–1939.* Cardiff: University of Wales Press, 1955.

Pedersen, Jørgen. *Essays in Monetary Theory and Related Subjects.* Copenhagen: Samfundsvidenkabeligt Forlag, 1975.

Sauvy, Alfred. *Histoire économique de la France entre les deux guerres.* Vol. 1: *1918–1931.* Paris: Fayard, 1965; vol. 2: *1931–1939.* Paris: Fayard, 1967.

Vansittart, Lord. *The Mist Procession: The Autobiography of Lord Vansittart.* London: Hutchinson, 1958.

Williams, William Appleman. *The Tragedy of American Diplomacy.* Cleveland: World Publishing, 1959.

19   Economic Responsibility

"Economic Responsibility" might be taken to be the extension of my collected essays in economic history, entitled *Economic Response.* Actually my interest is different. I propose to pursue a theme initially addressed in the Graham lecture at Princeton in 1977, and extended last year at the University of Rochester in the Gilbert lecture on "International Public Goods without International Government." The question I propose we think about is the extent to which under our mixed capitalist-government-intervention systems, the individual person, household, or firm is responsible for the system beyond the duty of conforming to explicit rules. Do we, that is, have an economic responsibility for the public as well as for our personal private welfare? I propose to discuss the issue first at the level of a national economy of households, firms and government, and then to apply the analysis to the world.

Let me start at the beginning with Adam Smith and his "obvious and simple system of natural liberty." Once this has been established, you remember

> Every man, as long as he does not violate the laws of justice, is left free to pursue his own interest in his own way.... The sovereign is completely discharged from a duty ... of superintending the industry of private people, and of directing it towards the employments most suitable to the interests of the society. According to the system of natural liberty, the sovereign has only three duties to attend ... first, the duty of protecting the society from the violence and invasion of other independent societies; secondly, the duty of protecting, as far as possible, every member of the society from the injustice or oppression of every other member of it, or the duty of establishing an exact administration of justice; and thirdly, the duty of erecting and maintaining certain public works and certain public institutions, which it can never be for the interest of any individual, or small numbers of

The Second Fred Hirsch Memorial Lecture. Warwick University, 6 March 1980, published in an abridged form in *Lloyds Bank Review*, October 1980, pp. 1–11.

individuals, to erect and maintain; because the profit could never repay the expense to any individual or small numbers of individuals, though it may frequently do much more than repay it to a great society.
(Book IV, Chapter IX)

Dr. Smith himself, of course, had reservations. In discussing corporations, he observed that private interests were too strong to allow the restoration of freedom of trade in Great Britain, stating that to expect it was as absurd as to expect an 'Oceana or Utopia should ever be established in it' (Book IV, Chapter II). He had some harsh words for the "mean rapacity, the monopolizing spirit of merchants and manufacturers, who neither are, nor ought to be the rulers of mankind"; and for the "sneaking arts of underling tradesmen" who employ chiefly their own customers, as opposed to "a great trader" who purchases goods only where they are cheapest and best. Implicit in these and similar passages is the admission that "natural liberty" may at least on occasion lead the economy astray.

Over two hundred years after *The Wealth of Nations* we still cling fairly generally to Smith's conclusions about the beneficent outcome of the market, although the analysis has been qualified and broadened in various ways. The theory of public goods implicit in his "certain public works and certain public institutions which it can never be for the interest of any individual or small number of individuals to erect," has been extended from magistracy or law and order, national defence, and roads and bridges to income distribution, where the market may yield a result unsatisfactory from the viewpoint of welfare, and to stabilization, where the fallacy of composition, of which more presently, means that individual households and firms, maximizing their private interest, may harm the general good. Moreover between the private goods of individuals and firms, and the public goods produced by the sovereign as an act of duty, there is room for collective goods, sought by aggregations of individuals or firms to advance the welfare of the particular group.

Smith's insight that it would not pay individuals or small groups of individuals to erect and maintain certain works or institutions has been generalized into the "free rider," who lacks adequate incentive to contribute or work for the production of public goods. Private and collective goods are produced because their benefits outweigh their costs to the producers; public goods are forthcoming because the sovereign fulfils his duty. In democracies, political scientists warn us, they may well be underproduced because of the free rider. Public goods are available for all to enjoy whether they bear an appropriate share of the transactions costs necessary to their production or not. The individual or firm maximizing its own welfare will hold back from carrying its share of the cost, unless it is forced to do so through the police powers of the state. If there are enough free riders, the bus never gets out of the garage.

Note that this theory holds that public goods are underproduced in democracy, or in monarchies where the sovereign is derelict in his duty, not for the reason Galbraith holds, that private goods are advertised and a gullible public buys too many of them. The public is rational and maximizing, rather than made up of sheeplike consumers who do not know their own interest. But the fallacy of composition brings it about that the whole may differ from the sum of its parts. Each free rider is rational and a maximizer; in the aggregate they fail to produce the public goods needed by the system.

The fallacy of composition was first borne in on me in the first edition of Samuelson's *Economics, An Introductory Analysis*, and in particular his treatment of the paradox of thrift. Thrift is good for the individual and the household—at least in a period of stable prices. But when everyone tries to save more, the economy may save less as it goes into recession and incomes fall. The problem is more general. Individuals pursuing their private and collective interests may interfere with one another. This is especially the case for collective goods, where an increase in monopoly profit reduces consumers' surplus and total consumption, and in free riding, where the individual conserving his energy for his own purposes inhibits the production of necessary public goods.

The Chicago school of sociological economics is using economic reasoning to illuminate a number of problems that were formerly dealt with by sociology or political science, for example, education, procreation, crime, voting in democracy. Rational, maximizing behaviour in this approach views, say the law in a detached fashion. One obeys the law if the mean of the probability distribution of being caught times the likely penalty of being convicted is greater than the benefit from ignoring the law. Or one departs from a short-run profitable action with untoward public consequences only if it should happen that the feedback of those consequences in the long-run is negative, and has a present discounted value, at some appropriate rate of interest, that is greater than the short-run profit that must be forgone. Government is provided by politicians who can earn higher returns in this fashion than by work in private industry, or by "leaders" who maximize a different argument in their objective function than income or wealth, perhaps *gloire*, immortality, lust for power, and similar non-economic drives.

I find the Chicago school altogether unpersuasive. As a counterexample to the theorem that profit maximization is all, let me suggest voting. Voting has positive transactions costs: one must take time and go to the polls. Moreover, the benefit of voting for the individual is derisory. Virtually no issues of consequence are decided by one vote. Accordingly, the costs to the single person outweigh the benefits and no rational person will take the trouble to vote. It is true that many people don't vote, and some nations, such as Australia, make voting compulsory in order to overcome the free rider. At times and places, votes will be bought as part of a collective good. For the most part, however, and within limits, people vote, and do so as a duty, as part of their political responsibility. What is more, while there are venal politicians in democracy, and in monarchies as well, many persons present themselves for elective office as a chance to serve the public.

My thesis is that economic, like political responsibility, takes two forms, one passive, obeying the law and acting in ways that can be generalized, to uphold the Categorical Imperative of Immanuel Kant and defeat the fallacy of composition; and an active form of positive leadership. Both are present in varying degrees and at various times in national economies and the world economy. An adequate supply of both is necessary if the economy is going to function well.

Before I pursue the argument, I wish to place on the record an admission of a strong prejudice in favour of market solutions to the greatest feasible extent. When it is working effectively, the market is a beautiful device for the decentralization of decision-making. Moreover, the analysis that underlies the defence of the market is highly useful as a pregnant hypothesis, to use Karl Popper's expression, serving to illuminate many problems in which behaviour can be analyzed as if (als ob) man responded in a rational way to income-maximizing motives. The presumption in favour of freedom for markets from regulation or intervention is perhaps weak, merely that the burden rests on people who oppose it to prove that they have a superior device for allocating factors of production to activities and the resultant outputs to end uses. The arguments in favour of the market are not conclusive, but merely that experience shows that, like marriage, honesty, democracy, old age and a few other tried and true institutions, it, while far from perfect, is better than the available alternatives.

The clash between the private market and government may perhaps be illustrated by the homely illustration of litter. The conduct may be prohibited by government, but the difficulties of enforcement are such that the chances of getting caught at, say, throwing a beer can from an automobile as adolescents in my country spend much of their time doing, mean that it is more economical for youth to defenestrate the empty container than to bring it home to the trash can (English translation, dustbin). Enlightened self-interest as a solution to the problem seems excluded, since one polluter or non-polluter in a beer can world would make so little difference—have such an exiguous feedback—that abstinence for the individual beer can ejector has no payoff. The state can require retailers to demand a deposit on beer containers which will be returned to the purchaser when the container is returned. This provides an economic incentive to withhold from littering. The difficulty here is that the collective interests of container-manufacturers, bottlers, and retail establishments dominate the public interest of the conservationists who find a countryside strewn with beer cans offensive. In the world of collective goods vs. public goods with free riders, the collective goods usually win, although container deposit laws have been passed in many states. The state can spend tax money to pick up beer cans along the highways and streets, and most do, albeit infrequently. A fifth means is education and peer-group pressure to instil the view that littering the highway is irresponsible behaviour.

I have deliberately chosen an unimportant issue, although it is one on which, living as I do in the country, I feel strongly. The essential point is that while self-interest within a framework of government regulation provides a useful first approximation to a description of the economic system, and even a working hypothesis for the solution of many economic problems, more is needed, and in particular a certain amount of self-restraint in some areas, voluntary compliance when enforcement cannot take us all the way in others, and active economic responsibility on behalf of the system as well.

Let me take the more serious problem of income tax. I am no tax expert, but it is clear that income tax in the United States, to the extent that it works well, relies on voluntary compliance. The Internal Revenue Service is completely inadequate to police the millions of tax returns, even with the help of social-security numbers and computers. Enforcement through audit or prosecution takes place from time to time, but on a scale so limited that there is strong incentive, at least for certain types of income, to fail to report it on cost–benefit grounds, the benefit of the tax saving being greater than the present discounted value of the chance of being caught times the penalty. There are indications that the tax system is breaking down in the United States, with a large black market in labour and goods, not to mention a white market in barter than seems to exist outside profit-and-loss statements in which income subject to taxation can be calculated. IRS lawyers work continuously to close old loopholes, while collective interests lobby to protect the old and create new.

So widespread have these collective interests become, with deductions from taxable income for interest payments, dependents, college tuition, medical expenses, old age, blindness, pensions, charitable contributions, taxes paid to other jurisdictions, expenditure for home insulation up to a limit, etc. that Joseph Pechman of the Brookings Institution has suggested that the slate be wiped clean of existing regulations and started again, taxing all income with no deductions, and reduced rates. The chances of such reform seem limited, given the fallacy of composition and the determination with which various groups protect their particular deduction, but history has at least two examples of regulation becoming so complex that it was no longer administrable and had to be abandoned. I refer to the Navigation Acts in Britain, repealed in 1847 when it was said that only three men in the Kingdom understood them in all their complexity, and the system of *Gewerbefoederung* or promotion of industry, with overlapping patents, privileges, concessions, monopolies, restrictions, prohibitions at the same time in Baden, which was swept away and replaced by *Gewerbefreiheit* or freedom of occupation. Collapsing voluntary compliance may be heading the income tax in the United States for disaster, such has overtaken those in France, Italy, Colombia, and many other countries, because it is cumulative. When groups interact, it is a mistake for one to act in the general interest if others do not. The problem is posed by game theory, or by the prisoner's dilemma. To act in the general interest when others do not is to be played for a sucker. How much voluntary compliance or economic responsibility is needed to make the system work is a difficult empirical question the answer to which may vary from problem to problem.

The fallacy of composition plus the need for equitable and consistent application of rules pose another problem. Most rules need exceptions for the hard cases. The difficulty is that the existence of loopholes for exceptional cases sooner or later attracts the attention of the run-of-the-mill participant for whom the rules were devised, who then claims the loophole for himself on the ground of non-discrimination. Numbered anonymous Swiss bank accounts served a laudable public purpose when they were illegally maintained by German Jews, fearful of expropriation. They are a threat to society when the system expands to accommodate criminals and other tax evaders, or I should say criminals including tax evaders. A small outlet for emigration is desirable in enabling citizens of a country thoroughly out of tune with the values of the society, and possibly persecuted for their behaviour, to leave. But to generalize emigration or immigration to make it available to anyone threatens to overwhelm or even destroy a state as the creation of the Berlin Wall in 1961, and the illegal inflow of Mexicans into the United States today demonstrate. Murray Weidenbaum has written in praise of tax havens, and there may be justification for them within highly restricted limits. Generalized, however, they destroy the state, and capacity to produce public goods, and enthrone individual self-interest together with economic irresponsibility.

The fallacy of composition for collective interests can be illustrated with organized business or organized labour. The latter had its origin in defence against the former, but as so often happens in multi-person games, two antagonists ultimately team up and war against a third, the consumer.

The individual litterbug can claim to have no impact on the beauty of the landscape except as the first beer can in a location attracts others, and the single taxpayer who fails to report income in cash, hardly affects the budget balance of a given year, but large trade unions can more readily be accused of achieving private gains at the expense of the public goods of price stability and sustained employment. Virtually every labour leader would deny that any union or combination of unions has responsibility for the economy as a whole. That is the task of government, they insist, even when their power frequently prevents the government from restraining unions. Or if the rise in the price of oil means that real national income must be reduced (in the United States), each union is likely to insist, along with all other organized groups in the society, that it is justified in seeking to ensure that none of the reduction falls on its members. Indexation, maintenance of wage differentials, exceptions to wage guidelines in collective bargains are the order of the day. In progressive industries, unions ask for the whole increase in productivity, while in lagging industries wages have to increase at the pace of the average to prevent loss of the work force. With no one willing to accept wages below the average increase in productivity, the average drifts upward. There is the view that Hans Boechler, Ludwig Rosenberg, and Otto Brenner in Germany after the war were responsible labour leaders who exercised great restraint in their wage demands in the short run to stimulate expansion, stability and greater rewards in the longer period. The alternative view, however, is that these union leaders were not so much responsible as their unions, after a decade or more of Hitler and war, were weak.

Or contemplate Sheik Yamani, the Saudi representative to the Organization of Petroleum Exporting Countries, who appears on a number of occasions in the last decade to have been trying to hold down the price of oil in the interest of world macroeconomic stability, as opposed to maximizing short-run returns. Again there is an alternative view, that reality differs from appearances, and that Yamani is a master of public relations fully committed to raising prices as fast as anyone else. It is nonetheless possible that a monopoly may set a price lower than that at which marginal cost equals marginal revenue as it worries about possible feedbacks, perhaps only that of encouragement to new entry, but conceivably that of world recession with its consequences on the long-run demand for oil.

Acting responsibly for unions or firms, however, has the disability implicit in the prisoner's dilemma. If unions hold wages, corporations may not behave in such magnanimous fashion but raise prices and profits anyhow, to make the short-run sacrifice of labour nugatory. Or as Saudi Arabia expands oil production to make up for some of the shortfall from turbulence in Iran, Kuwait among the low absorbers may cut its production further to thwart the attempt to hold down prices. Economic responsibility on the part of one actor may merely encourage greater short-run maximization in another, without achieving the public (and long-run private) purpose sought.

This is nowhere more strikingly illustrated than in the lender of last resort role that Hirsch illuminated in his striking paper on the 'Bagehot Problem' in the *Manchester School*. The issue is called 'moral risk' in the field of insurance. When an individual firm or household is fully insured, it has less incentive to be careful. Banks confident that they will be rescued if they get into trouble are less wary about staying out of it. The mean of the probability distribution of disaster may rise but the penalty arising from disaster is reduced. There are devices to correct for moral risk, deductible limits, and required self-insurance in the fields of fire and casualty. In life insurance, the policy holder presumably has a big stake in the outcome just as the pilot and crew have in the safe operation of airplanes—a fact from which I have often taken comfort. The insistence of government, central bank or an organization like the Federal Deposit Insurance Corporation in the United States that it will save only sound banks, and lend only on sound collateral is not persuasive. First, it is analytically awkward, confusing a general-equilibrium problem with a partial-equilibrium one; in a financial crisis with falling prices, soundness is a function of how fast the lender of last resort responds. The longer it waits, the further prices fall, and the less sound are banks and their collateral. Secondly, however, as the crisis deepens it is necessary to rescue the sinners with the faithful, since their fates are linked.

One answer to these game-theoretic problems is to have rules, spelled out with great clarity, as to how banks should invest their funds, and how insured policy holders should protect their property. In collective bargaining, the proposal is for a social contract under which each sector of society, and each segment of each sector, exercises great self-restraint in return for the promise of others to act similarly.

As in any cartel, the problem is in enforcement, how to prevent marginal units from chiselling or as I prefer to view it, competing. Swedish and Dutch experience with social contract goes further than that of most countries, but has been marked by wage drift, profit drift, and in the case of the Netherlands, wage explosion after an extended period of constraint. In addition there are serious problems of finding the appropriate initial conditions that represent a sort of stable equilibrium because they embody wage differentials agreeable to all. Most unions are likely to assert that once their prospective negotiations are completed with a hefty raise, providing all other collective arrangements are unchanged, and provided prices stabilize at their present level, they will be pleased to accede. But the fallacy of composition assures us that there is no time when all will agree that now is the exactly right time to enter into the social contract. Correcting lags of some wages behind others, in an attempt to get the differentials right, illustrates the problem at its clearest.

Thus far we have been discussing economic responsibility in terms of the fallacy of composition, with the implication that if a party is small and operates with no feedbacks or external effects, no fear of creating a precedent, and is unlikely to give rise to demand for equal treatment on the ground of consistency, it may be tolerable to permit free riders to take exceptions to general rules on the ground that no significant consequences would follow. This may be open to criticism on the ground that it allows the ends to justify the means, and that in law and in morality, small is big because precedents are set and consistency is needed. One cannot let small unions as in municipal transit get away with standard-breaking wage increases, because if any one group gets huge rents, all will insist on having them too. But there are two aspects of the question, related to what has just been said and to each other. What if the actors are large and conspicuous?

Large is almost definitionally equal to conspicuous, but not quite. It depends on the setting. Young people will behave differently in a big city than they do in their home village, because they are anonymous in the former and known in the latter. In New York, there is likely to be no feedback from loud and raucous conduct, provided one stays clear of the police, whereas if one were to behave the same way in Belmont or Lincoln, Massachusetts, the fact would be noticed, commented on, remembered. Observation affects behaviour—the Heisenberg principle applied to social science—in other ways. Some football players do better in the game on Saturday than they do in practice during the week, unobserved. And some firms behave more circumspectly when they loom large in a small town than when they fade into the background in a metropolis, or their actions may differ as between when they are, or are not, required to disclose their operations. It was long said of one major American corporation—I think General Electric, but that may be simply bad memory—that it was unwilling to have the only major factory in a small town because that inhibited its behaviour too drastically, as the community came to depend on it unduly. General Motors' response to the brouhaha raised in the early 1950s over its profits from the ownership of Holden Proprietary, Ltd. in Australia was to buy up the remaining minority stock and convert from a public to a private company which did not have to publish accounts—until that escape was cut off by Australian legislation requiring private companies owned by foreign corporations to publish regular reports. A number of years ago observers were struck that Edward S. Mason's book *Controlling World Trade* strongly condemned international cartels, but advocated the rather mild remedy of registration and disclosure of agreements. Presumably he thought that the content of international business agreements would differ substantially depending on whether or not the world—customers, potential competitors and governments—would or would not have access to the terms.

The small and anonymous individual or corporation is permitted a much wider range of conduct within the limits of legal proprieties than the large and conspicuous one. Some years ago, in 1960 the Ford Motor Company in the United States undertook to buy the minority stock in British Ford, for an amount equal to $360 million, if my memory serves, at a time when the balance of payments of the United States was weak, but there were no restrictions of any sort on capital outflows. The notion that a capital outflow of a given amount weakens the balance of payments by the same degree is of course partial-equilibrium analysis unacceptable in a general-equilibrium world. What the net effect on the balance of payments would have been could only be traced through by ascertaining how the monies were raised in the United States and what was done with them by the minority stockholders who sold out in Britain. Nonetheless the size of the operation produced a reaction by government and public alike, implying that the Ford Motor Company, conforming fully to the law, was less than responsible.

A similar episode occurred some years later in Britain when the Shell Oil Company tried to protect its assets by transferring more than £100 million abroad at a time when it was entirely legal but somewhat discomforting to the foreign-exchange position of this country. It too suffered a certain amount of obloquy. The current illustration in my country, although this slides over the issue of the social responsibility of corporations that I have been trying to stay clear of, concerns foreign direct investment in and business dealings with the Union of South Africa, the policies of which in respect of apartheid are widely judged in my country (and by me) to be obnoxious. Small companies are hardly troubled about the issue. Large ones with subsidiaries in that country are exposed to criticism by various groups—church, political, student—some with monies to invest, and some with university endowments, even though they are operating fully within the laws and policies of the government. We seem to be approaching the time when corporations and endowment funds are called upon to have their own foreign policy, necessarily more restrictive—since it cannot violate governmental limitations—than the foreign policy of the nation.

Size and conspicuousness are two dimensions affecting economic responsibility. Age and status are others. It is useful to distinguish between old money and new money, between the Establishment and the upstarts, between—at the level of individuals—the aristocracy or gentry and the *nouveaux riches*. Age, the Establishment and *noblesse* all *obligent*, i.e., have responsibilities that extend beyond those of the average citizen or firm. In the money dimension, of course, age and *noblesse* are highly correlated, apart perhaps from Southern Europe where inpecunious aristocrats are looking for heirs or heiresses to marry. The path to the gentry lay through business or financial success. But with gentlehood or aristocratic position went obligations along with perquisites. There is a certain amount of hypocrisy about this, and it is easy to be cynical about the Christmas baskets handed out by the lady of the manor which failed to deal effectively with any real social problem. Nonetheless, it seems to me useful to observe the greater responsibility of the successful than of the unsuccessful, and of the old successes as compared with the new.

It is suggested, for example, that Saudi Arabia has a major responsibility for the operations of the world economy, in holding down oil prices, providing foreign aid to developing countries, stabilizing the world monetary system, etc. etc. Anything that Saudi Arabia can readily do in these directions is of course highly welcome, especially in the moderation of oil-price increases mentioned early, but one must note that Saudi Arabia is a new boy in the school, not an old hand, and as such has its hands full coping with a variety of problems. Its responsibilities, apart from oil prices and refraining from rocking the world monetary boat, lie largely at home and in the region. My country, the Common Market and Japan cannot escape their responsibilities for the stability of the world economy by pointing to the new and enormous wealth of Saudi Arabia. Its problems are many, and its skilled hands limited in number.

A recent book by E. Digby Balzell, *Puritan Boston and Quaker Philadelphia*, speaks to the question of responsibility in a powerful way. Puritan Boston was a homogeneous city, hierarchically organized, intolerant, but with authority. It bred and trained (at Harvard) statesmen and leaders who served the city, state and nation. It was interested in money, but also in class pride, power, accomplishment. Quaker Philadelphia on the other hand went in for tolerant irresponsibility, more interested in making a fortune, but leading private and individualist lives rather than concerned with order and authority. To the Puritan the office of the magistrate was the highest secular calling, reinforcing rather than contradicting *noblesse oblige.* The Quaker, on the other hand, saw no need for magistrates, government or war if all men followed the ideals of the Sermon on the Mount. It was a prescription for anarchy. Into that void left by the Quakers with their first loyalty to the immediate family and the community, a union of such money-making, accumulating families, came political bosses and venal politics. The Quaker tradition shared with the Puritans the passive responsibility of obeying the laws, but they withdrew from active responsibility in making and administering them.

This leads us to a form of economic sociology diametrically opposed to sociological economics. The magistracy required to make the system work comes from the value-system, not from maximizing behaviour. Passive conformity to the spirit of the rules is part of the responsibility; readiness to take a role in enforcement and in adapting the rules to new circumstances is another, and more active part of it.

How does economic responsibility come into being? In my judgment it responds more to Keynes's law that demand creates its own supply than to Say's law that supply creates its own demand. My emphasis on size, prominence, position in society, the reactions of others, etc. suggests that it is pressure that pushes government into new functions, and peer pressure that pushes non-governmental bodies into positions and attitudes of responsibility. It is of great interest to me that in the nineteenth century and prior to the foundation of the Federal Reserve Act, the leading New York money market banks behaved differently than other banks in New York such as the trust companies and savings institutions, and than out-of-town banks of all descriptions. The larger group depended on the money-market leaders to provide them with cash in crisis, and the leaders knew what they were supposed to do, and prepared to meet the responsibility.

The conclusion is more general. More basic an incentive than maximizing income and wealth is obtaining the approval of one's peers. As David Riesman has suggested, most actors in today's society are outer-directed, conforming to the standards set sociologically in productive as well as consumption behaviour, and those that are inner-directed are merely running on the outer-directions received at an earlier stage and internalized. This last thought explains the responsibility of *noblesse oblige* and the responsibility of old money, although it must be admitted that some who might have been guided by tradition turn out to be more susceptible to the blandishments of the jet set in the outer-directed mode.

There is a problem here, however. To develop economic responsibility one must choose the right peer group. There is after all honour among thieves and one sociologist of my acquaintance explains much anti-responsible behaviour in France on the basis of the "delinquent peer groups" that grew up in that society in defence against strict parents and strict schools. People are drawn into academic life, business, the professions, government, and crime by choosing different models to ape, rather than each maximizing income and wealth—as the Chicago school would have it—in different ways. The point is neatly illustrated by the behaviour of two firms in the same industry toward high-level employees on their release from jail after serving sentences for criminal conspiracy against the anti-trust acts. Though the employees of the two firms had been convicted of conspiring together, one firm, seeking the approval of its employees for loyalty, gave their men a rousing welcome, new jobs and made them heroes. The other company, interested in being judged against a different standard, fired its group.

Economic responsibility at the national level, in this reasoning, is maximizing income and wealth within the constraints of avoiding behaviour which cannot be generalized, complying with the spirit as well as the letter of the law, watching feedbacks through the rest of society, and example-setting. Such responsibility is generated by success, but old success that has settled down and internalized class authority and pride. It is difficult to achieve in young economies, or aged ones, the former because responsible standards have not yet taken sufficient shape, the latter because there are too many groups struggling for collective goods and the fallacy of composition overwhelms them. Despite Adam Smith and the Chicago school, profit-maximizing economies having too few dedicated leaders, with insufficient individual commitment to voluntary compliance, and collective groups unprepared to restrain their demands, will not function. This seems to me the insight of Fred Hirsch in his book with John Goldthorpe on *The Political Economy of Inflation.*

I have not much space for economic responsibility on the international front, but this is hardly necessary as I have written a number of times of "leadership" in the world economy. In its active form, responsibility is leadership. François Perroux has written of dominance in international trade and investment, referring to the United States. Political scientists refer to the leadership role as "hegemony." On the left wing the expression is exploitation and neo-imperialism. In my judgment, Britain in the nineteenth century and the United States from perhaps the Tripartite Stabilization Agreement in September 1936 to the two-tier system in 1968 or the Connally *shocku* of August 1971 acted responsibly. It was in their interest to do so because of feedbacks and a low rate of interest on future trouble. There is a considerable question whether both countries benefited enormously from the position or paid something of a price in losing freedom of action, higher taxes for defence, carrying the free riders who held back paying a proportionate share of the world public goods of economic stability and peace.

The elements of economic leadership at the world level have been spelled out: an open market for distress goods, and a stockpile of accessible goods that are in short supply, in crisis only, not as a regular device for stabilizing prices; a counter-cyclical or at a minimum stable flow of capital (and aid) to maintain the flow of international purchasing power to all parts of the globe; management of exchange rates and of macroeconomic policies through the gold standard operation by the Bank of England in the nineteenth century, and the dollar standard of Bretton Woods after 1947; and finally the lender of last resort function, as illuminated by Fred Hirsch in "The Bagehot Problem," preventing deflation from spreading through the system by holding upright the critical domino—be it bank or money market at the right time. It was these requirements of responsibility that Britain could no longer discharge in the interwar period, and that the United States then hung back from that made the 1929 depression such a traumatic episode in world economic history.

I have not resolved in my own mind whether economic responsibility can be widely shared. Certainly at the moment when the United States capacity for leadership is diminishing and Germany and Japan are fully responsible in the passive sense like the Quakers, but unwilling to take a forward role, one cannot require small countries or the newly rich to undertake very much of the costs of maintaining the system. We are blessed by having few boat-rockers of the Bismarck–Hitler–Stalin–Hirohito—even de Gaulle stripe who would produce a drastic change in how the system operates. Iran, the PLO, Gaddafi, the New International Economic Order are not powerful enough to rock the system beyond the capacities of OECD countries to restore it to balance, provided that consensuses on policy rather than stalemate emerge rapidly. But such position as in the International Monetary Fund where the United States, and European Economic Community and the Committee of Twenty-four each has a veto suggests that active economic responsibility may be a scarce good in the years ahead.

Economic responsibility goes with military strength and an undue share in the costs of peacekeeping. Free riders are perhaps more noticeable in this area than in the economy, where a number of rules in trade, capital movements, payments and the like have been evolved and accepted as legitimate. Free ridership means that disproportionate costs must be borne by responsible nations, which must on occasion take care of the international or system interest at some expense in falling short of immediate goals. This is a departure from the hard-nosed school of international relations in political science, represented especially perhaps by Hans Morgenthau and Henry Kissinger, who believe that national interest and the balance of power constitute a stable system. Leadership, moreover, had overtones of the white man's burden, father knows best, the patronizing attitude of the lady of the manor with her Christmas baskets. The requirement, moreover, is for active, and not merely passive responsibility of the German–Japanese variety. With free riders, and the virtually certain emergency of thrusting newcomers, passivity is a recipe for disarray. The danger for world stability is the weakness of the dollar, the loss of dedication of the United States to the international system's interest, and the absence of candidates to fill the resultant vacua.

I beg you to excuse me from discussing Britain's responsibility to the European Community, and the price that is being charged for it. I hope, nonetheless, that I have interested you in the concept of economic responsibility as an essential ingredient of economic life, along with income and wealth maximization, and a legal framework in which every man, firm, bureaucrat and nation can pursue his, her or its interest.

20   International Public Goods without International Government

When the word of my prospective elevation to this exalted position first circulated at MIT at the end of March 1983, I happened to encounter Peter Temin in the library.[1] He offered congratulations, and added, "In your presidential address, skip the methodology. Tell them a story." This is the technique that he and Paul David used to great effect in the session on economic history at Dallas a year ago. I choose, however, to follow the lead of another historian, Donald McCloskey, who maintains that economics should be a conversation (1983).

In a recent paper, unpublished I believe, George Stigler discussed "the imperialism of economics," which, he claims, is invading and colonizing political science—through public choice theory and the economic theory of democracy—law, and perhaps especially sociology, where our soon-to-be president-elect, Gary Becker (1981), has extended the reach of economics into questions of the family, marriage, procreation, crime, and other subjects usually dealt with by the sociologist. "Imperialism" suggests super- and subordination, with economics on top, and raises the question whether as a profession we are not flirting with vainglory.

My interest has long been in trade, and I observe that economics imports from, as well as exports to, its sister social sciences. In public choice, we can perhaps explain after the event whose interest was served by a particular decision, but we need political science to be able to forecast which interest is likely to be served, whether that of the executive, the legislature, the bureaucracy, some pressure group—and which pressure group—or, in the odd instance, the voters. Individuals act in their own interest, let us grant, but a more general motive of emulation may be drawn from sociology as Adam Smith was aware in *The Wealth of Nations* (1776, p. 717), as well as in *The Theory of Moral Sentiments* (1759 (1808), I, p. 113). I want today to borrow one or two ideas from political philosophy, and to conduct a conversation with a new, impressive, and growing breed of political scientists working on international economic questions. The discussion falls into two loosely connected halves—the first dealing with what economists can, perhaps should and to some extent do, import from political philosophy and sociology; the second dealing more especially with international public goods.

I

That sharp and sometimes angry theorist, Frank Graham (1948), thought it a mistake to think of trade between nations. Trade took place between firms, he insisted. The fact that they were in different states was irrelevant so long as economic policy was appropriately minimal, consisting perhaps of free trade, annually balanced budgets, and the gold standard. But states may differentiate between firms, through such measures as tariffs, embargos, monetary, fiscal, and exchange rate policy which affect all firms within a given space, and this adds a political dimension (see my 1978 study). The essence may go deeper. In an early graduate quiz, I asked for the difference between domestic and international trade, expecting a Ricardian answer on factor mobility. One paper, however, held that domestic trade was among "us," whereas international trade was between "us" and "them." The student who wrote this (now escaped from economics and teaching international law at a leading university) had come from Cambridge University and a course with Harry Johnson. We go beyond this simple statement today in saying that nations are groups of people with common tastes in public goods (Richard Cooper, 1977). Geography discriminates between countries, as a hypothetical customs union between Iceland and New Zealand would demonstrate, and so do governments. Behind and alongside of governments, people discriminate.

Public goods, let me remind you, are that class of goods like public works where exclusion of consumers may be impossible, but in any event consumption of the good by one consuming unit—short of some level approaching congestion—does not exhaust its availability for others. They are typically underproduced—not, I believe, for the Galbraithian reason that private goods are advertised and public goods are not—but because the consumer who has access to the good anyhow has little reason to vote the taxes, or pay his or her appropriate share. Unless the consumer is a highly moral person, following the Kantian Categorical Imperative of acting in ways which can be generalized, he or she is apt to be a "free rider." The tendency for public goods to be underproduced is serious enough within a nation bound by some sort of social contract, and directed in public matters by a government with the power to impose and collect taxes. It is, I propose to argue in due course, a more serious problem in international political and economic relations in the absence of international government.

Adam Smith's list of public goods was limited to national defence, law and order, and public works that it would not pay individuals to produce for themselves. Most economists are prepared now to extend the list to include stabilization, regulation, and income redistribution (Cooper, 1977), even nationalism (Albert Breton, 1964), and standards that reduce transaction costs, including weights and measures, language, and money. Public goods were popular a decade ago. There is something of a tendency today, at least in political science, to draw back and claim that such institutions as open world markets are not public goods because countries can be excluded from them by discrimination. One monetarist goes so far as to maintain that money is not a public good, arguing, I believe, from the store-of-value function where possession by one individual denies possession by others, rather than from the unit-of-account function in which exclusion is impossible and exhaustion does not hold (Roland Vaubel, 1984).

II

Before addressing international public goods, I want to digress to suggest that there are other limits to the imperialist claims of economics. Social goods are not traded in markets, for example—honour, respect, dignity, love. In his address to the Columbia University Bicentennial Assembly, Sir Dennis Robertson asserted that what economists economize is love (1955, pp. 5–6). Michael Walzer (1983, pp. 101–2) has compiled a list of 'things' that contemporary moral philosophy will not tolerate being bought and sold: human beings, political power, criminal justice, freedom of expression, marriage and procreation rights (*pace* Becker), the right to leave the political community, exemptions from military service and jury duty, political office, basic services like police protection, desperate exchanges such as permission for women and children to work fourteen hours a day, prizes and honours, love and friendship, criminally noxious substances such as heroin. The inclusion of a number of items on the list is debatable, and history reveals that most of them have been traded on occasion in some cultures. The market, moreover, strikes two lawyers as a dubious device for making "tragic choices," like those in which scarcity confronts humanistic moral values, for example, allocating food in famine, children available for adoption, or organ transplants (Guido Calabrese and Philip Bobbit, 1978). It is difficult to dissent from Walzer's conclusion that a radically *laissez-faire* economy would be like a totalitarian state, treating every social good as if it were a commodity (1983, p. 119). There is, moreover, a similar remark from a founder of the Chicago school, Frank Knight, who said that the extreme economic man, maximizing every material interest, and the extreme Christian, loving his neighbour as himself, were alike in that neither had any friends.[2]

To admit social goods, not traded in markets, into our economic calculus does not call for altruism. Economists are reluctant to depend on self-denial to any degree (Kenneth Arrow, 1975, p. 22), and moral philosophers are not far behind. To a modern student of ethics, James Fishkin (1982, Chapter 2), obligations to others fall into three categories: minimal altruism, where the benefit to the receiver is substantial and the cost to the altruist low—the acts of a cheap Samaritan; acts of heroic sacrifice that are not called for; and a robust zone of indifference where one has no cause to be concerned over the effects of one's acts on others. This is for positive actions. Acts that harm others are proscribed by the Golden Rule. Adam Smith expressed the same viewpoint forcefully: "Every man is, no doubt, by nature first and principally recommended to his own care" (1759 (1808), I, p. 193), but goes on: "Although the ruin of our neighbour may affect us less than a very small misfortune of our own, we must not ruin him to prevent that small misfortune, or even to prevent our own ruin" (*ibid.*, p. 194). Does this prohibit us from playing zero-sum games or negative non-zero-sum games? In international trade, must we refrain from levying the optimum tariff? The optimum tariff works to self-interest mainly in the absence of retaliation, and if Adam Smith excludes hurting our neighbour, he recognizes that "as every man doth, so shall it be done to him, and retaliation seems to be the great law of nature" (*ibid.*, p. 191).

Note parenthetically that today's moral philosophers cover a wide territory either side of Fishkin, from Peter Singer (1972) at one extreme whose criterion of justice requires successive acts of altruism until the welfare of the recipient has risen to that of the giver which has fallen, to Robert Nozick (1974) at the other who believes that self-interest rules out altruism almost altogether.

III

Self-interest then is legitimate over a large zone of indifference provided that justice is served by our not hurting others. But the robust zone of indifference applies to strangers, and not to those with whom we have a special relationship, sharing collective goods. It does not apply in the family, the neighbourhood, in clubs, in the tribe, racial or religious group, or in the nation. There is some uncertainty whether it applies in regions within a country—New England, the West, the South—or to arrangements between countries short of the world level such as North America or the European Common Market. Collective goods involved here are distributed by mechanisms different from the market: gifts, grants, unequal exchange, sharing through a budget according to need, interest-free loans, inheritance, dowries, alimony, and the like all have a place. Membership in these groups is decided in various ways: by birth, by choice—as in moving into a certain neighbourhood or migrating between countries, by application for admission and acceptance. Walzer defends the right of countries to keep out would-be immigrants motivated by economic self-interest, but not those subjected to persecution: "The primary good that we distribute to one another is membership in some community" (1981; 1983, Chapter 2, p. 1). He argues, however, that states lack the right to keep members from emigrating if there is some other community ready to take them in. Clubs discriminate against outsiders. Neighbourhoods are more complex, being presumably open to anyone able to afford and find a place to live, but, in sociological reality, often exhibiting tendencies to attract their own kind and repel others, including harassment or unwritten or even legal restrictions against property ownership. The groupings are amorphous, but they exist.

The nature of the positive bonds that link families, neighbourhoods, tribes, regions, and nations is usually taken for granted and left unexplored, but the consequences are not. Albert Hirschman (1970), for example, makes a distinction between voice and exit: voice—speaking up and trying to persuade—being the appropriate action when one disagrees with the course followed by a group to which one belongs; and exit—resigning or refusal to buy the good or service—as a response to what one dislikes in the market. Adam Smith minimizes the difference between families and strangers, suggesting that affection is little more than habitual sympathy produced by propinquity; despite the greater thickness of blood than water, he claims that siblings educated at distances from one another experience a diminution of affection (1759 (1808) II, pp. 68–70). In arguing against Walzer's view that countries owe immigrants the right to become citizens, Judith Lichtenberg (1981) echoes Smith's view in saying that the crucial difference between members and strangers lies between those with whom one has face-to-face contact and those with whom one does not. An accident that kills someone in one's town or a neighbouring community is likely to be more moving than a catastrophe at the other end of the world in which hundreds or thousands die. Adam Smith goes further, comparing the loss of a little finger with a catastrophe that swallowed up China: '... if he lost his little finger he could not sleep, but for China he can snore ... provided he has never seen them' (*ibid.*, I, p. 317).

Some years ago in a book on the brain drain, Harry Johnson (1968) argued in favour of a cosmopolitan solution, encouraging emigration, and Don Patinkin (1968) for a national one. In discussing the Bhagwati scheme for taxing professional emigrants earning more abroad than at home, for the benefit of the poor sending country—saying this was akin to paying alimony in a divorce case for breaking a social taboo—I suggested (1977) that the Johnson position was equivalent to saying that a person should go where he or she could earn the highest return, while Patinkin said that people should stay where they belonged. Patinkin chided me privately for this interpretation, and it is admittedly oversimplified. But the difference between the Johnson and Patinkin positions, both emanating from Chicago, suggests the line between market and non-market areas in economics is shadowy.

In writing about the multinational corporation, I have from time to time suggested that host countries resist the intrusion of strangers because "... man in his elemental state is a peasant with a possessive love of his own turf; a mercantilist who favours exports over imports; a populist who distrusts banks, especially foreign banks; a monopolist who abhors competition; a xenophobe who feels threatened by strangers and foreigners" (1984, p. 39), usually adding that it is the task of international economics to extirpate these primitive instincts and to teach cosmopolitanism. The fact that some of these reactions remain at a late stage in the educational process can be tested by the device of asking students on examinations, *seriatim*, a series of questions:

Do you advocate free trade, or at least is there a strong presumption in its favour?

Do you advocate the free international movement of portfolio capital?

... of corporate capital in foreign direct investment?

... free migration of students and professional labour?

... immigration of relatives of persons permanently resident in this country?

... free migration for all?

(It is desirable to feed these questions to the victims one at a time without revealing the whole list before the first answer is given and to take up the replies to the first questions so that there is no chance to go back and amend early answers.) There will be sophisticated answers expatiating on the second, third, and fourth-best if the marginal conditions for a Pareto optimal solution are not met, and I would particularly excuse a James Meade (1955) solution that would limit immigration from countries that have not accomplished their Malthusian revolution, on the ground that their emigrants will be replaced, so that free immigration will reduce world income per capita, if not world income as a whole. Most economists and non-economists alike would agree, however, that goods are less intrusive than money, money less so than corporations with control over *our* economic decisions.[3] Intellectuals with whom we identify are hardly intrusive at all. Most of us grant that relatives must be permitted to come together. On the other hand, free migration of labour in general poses a threat to the national identity. The Swiss cut off immigration, despite the appeals of business for more labour, when immigrants constituted one-third of the labour force. In Germany, separate localities felt threatened and stopped inward migration when immigrants reached 12 per cent of the resident population. Feelings differed, of course, depending upon the origin of the migrants and their appearance, language, and religion.

One early venture of international economics into this line of investigation was Robert Mundell's 'optimum currency area' (1961), initiating a discussion of how large the area for a single currency should be, that can readily be extended to economics in general and to other social sciences. Mundell defined an optimum currency area as one where labour moved freely within the area, but not between it and other areas, taking us back to the Ricardian criterion distinguishing domestic from foreign trade: factor mobility within but not between countries. In neither case is the discontinuity in mobility explained. Perhaps something is owed to low transport costs, but additionally, factor mobility requires a group with such strong social cohesion that those moving are willing to shift, and those at the receiving end are content to receive them.

Ronald McKinnon (1963) offered a different criterion: an optimum currency area was one that traded intensively at home, but only to a limited extent abroad. This implied that tastes within a country are homogeneous for traded goods (as well as for public goods), and that regionally specialized production had grown up to serve those tastes. The Mundell and McKinnon criteria do not necessarily converge: on Mundell's standard, Canada is too big to be an optimum currency area, because of limited movement between Quebec and the English-speaking parts of Canada, and the comparative isolation of the Maritimes and Vancouver. On McKinnon's criterion, however, it was too small because so much of its trade is with the United States.

If one broadens the issue from the optimum currency area to economics more generally and to the other social sciences, anomalies arise from the divergence between the optimum economic area, which on efficiency grounds I take to be the world, and the optimum social unit, one that gives the individual a sense of belonging and counting—which is much smaller. In shifting to the optimum political unit, at least two problems arise, one related to the nature of the ties, the other to the ambitions of its members. To take the second point first, for a nation bent on glory—led by a Bismarck or a de Gaulle—bigger is better; whereas if one is merely trying to get along without trouble, like, say, Denmark, small is beautiful enough.

On the first issue, political ties vary widely. There are leagues, alliances, commonwealths, confederations, federations, provinces, states, principalities, kingdoms. Some lesser units are 'united' in varying degrees, as in the United Provinces of the Netherlands, the United States of America, the United Kingdom of Great Britain, and Northern Ireland. The North in the American Civil War was a union, as the Union of Socialist Soviet Republics asserts it is. The small amount of literature I have explored in examining the differences among these forms is not very conclusive, but perhaps the main distinction is between the single state that is centralized, and federations that are loosely joined, with greater powers at the local level. Designations are not always congruent with reality: the Federal German Republic is highly unified, despite the efforts of the occupation powers after World War II to spread political power widely; the Federal Reserve System was created as a loose agglomeration of twelve regional money markets but quickly fused into a single system in World War I. Centralization and federalization have reflections in demography and in finance. City populations in unified states follow a Pareto-skewed distribution with a single dominant city like London, Paris or Vienna, and no close rival among the tail of smaller cities and towns. In federations the distribution of cities is log normal (Brian Berry, 1961). Parallel to the demographic division is the financial. Paris has 91.3 per cent of French bank clearings; London 87 per cent of those for Britain. The contrast is with Canada: Toronto, 37.3 per cent; Montreal, 25.5 per cent; Vancouver, 6.5 per cent. Between these extremes lies Japan with Tokyo 51.2 per cent and Osaka 19.7 per cent (Jean Labasse, 1974, pp. 144–5).

One explanation for differences between centralized and federal states is historical: where larger states were formed later from unification of lesser units, administrative and financial functions were already being discharged at the local level, reducing the need for centralized services. This hypothesis faces the difficult counterexamples of Italy and Germany, unified out of smaller units in the second half of the nineteenth century, that quickly centralized administrative and financial functions, in Rome and Milan for Italy, and in Berlin for Germany. Another explanation runs in terms of size, with larger states necessarily federal because of the difficulty of providing administration to local units over long distances. This fits Canada, Australia, the United States, perhaps India, but fails to account for Switzerland, unless size is a proxy for maintaining a dense network of communication, and division of valleys by high mountains produces barriers equivalent to those of continental states. If the mathematically minded reader needs an analogue, think of federal states as decomposable matrices.

The difference between a single state and a federation may be illustrated with two examples. Some years ago, Seymour Harris (1952) wrote a book on New England in which he claimed that the area got a raw deal from the rest of the country because it paid more in taxes to the federal government than it received in federal expenditure. This thesis implicitly violated the distinction between a budget and a market: in a market equal values are exchanged. A budget, on the other hand, is a device expressing the cohesion of a sharing group with monies raised according to one standard, perhaps ability to pay, and expenditure distributed according to another, some combination of efficiency and need. The other example, equally shocking to an international trade economist, was the notion of the *juste retour*, or fair return, propounded by France in connection with expenditure for joint projects in Europe. France insisted that all monies contributed by her be spent in France. Tied sales are a third- or fourth-best device to limit balance-of-payments deficits for a given contribution to joint efforts, or to maximize the contribution for a given deficit. They are inefficient rather than fair.

IV

But I want to move on to the geopolitical unit that produces public goods. It is a cliché that these have increased in size as costs of transport and communication have declined. Under the eighteenth-century Poor Law in England, the parish resisted immigration from neighbouring par-

ishes because of reluctance to share with outsiders. Fernand Braudel
(1982) and Sir John Hicks (1969) have each expatiated on the rise of the
size of the economic unit from the city-state to the nation-state. National
and international markets for goods and money grew slowly, with entrepot centres that intermediated between buyers and sellers surviving in
money—cheap to move in space—and largely disappearing for goods
where costs of transport were high and could be saved by direct selling,
rather than relaying goods through fairs in the Middle Ages and later
through cities such as Amsterdam, Hamburg, Frankfurt, and London. The
hub-and-spoke system recently discovered in airplane travel and still in
place for money has long been superceded in goods. Caroline Isard and
Walter Isard's (1945) point that the most pervasive changes in the economy came from innovations in transport and communications remains
valid: contemplate the rudder (in place of the steering oar), fore-and-aft
sails; the turnpike; canal; railroad (despite Robert Fogel, 1964); the steamship; iron-clad ship; telegraph; telephone; refrigerator ship; radio; airplane;
bulk carrier; jet airplane; satellite television. The numbers of people
brought into face-to-face contact across continents and hemispheres has
increased exponentially. It is true, to be sure, as was said about a well-
known governor and presidential candidate, that it was impossible to dis-
like him until one got to know him, and increases in mobility and communications have been accompanied by separatism: of the Walloons from
the Flemish in Belgium, of Scotland and Wales in the United Kingdom (to
pass over the troubled Irish question), and of the *Québecois* in Canada.[4]
But it is easier than in Adam Smith's day to imagine ourselves in the circumstances of the Chinese, the inhabitants of the Sahelian desert in Africa,
or the tornado-struck islands of Bangladesh as we see them nightly on our
television screens via satellite. Do wider communication and transport
change the production and distribution of public goods?

Conflicts between economics and political science abound, and many
arise from the fact that goods, money, corporations, and people are
mobile, whereas the state is fixed. The increase in mobility produced
by innovations in transport and communication during and after World
War II led some of us to conclude that the nation-state was in difficulty. A
reaction occurred in the 1970s.

It is significant that Raymond Vernon's influential book *Sovereignty
at Bay* (1971), showing the multinational corporation ascendant over the
state, was followed by his *Storm over Multinationals* (1977) in which the
position is reversed. Cooper's *The Economics of Interdependence* (1968) was
followed by an upsurge of interest in national autonomy, decoupling, and

pluralism among political scientists, most of whom approve the nation-state and have as heroes, if they will forgive me, not Adam Smith and Woodrow Wilson, but Otto von Bismarck and perhaps even Charles de Gaulle. The tension remains, however. Mobility limits the state's capacity to enforce its writ in taxation, in foreign policy, in standards on such matters as antitrust, pure food and drugs, insider trading in securities, and the like. Mobility undermines social cohesion through the easy intrusion of different nationalities, races, religions, and traditions into the body politic.

V

I come at long last to international public goods. The primary one is peace. Economists are poorly qualified to discuss how, after war, peace is restored and maintained. Most of us reject the Marxian view that war grows directly out of capitalism, and as ordinary citizens and amateur students of history are prepared to agree that peace may be provided by a dominant world power—Pax Romana or Pax Britannica—or by balance-of-power manoeuvring, although that seems accident prone. Among the more audacious economists producing an economic theory or set of theories on war is Walt Rostow (1960, pp. 108 ff.). There are views that ascribe war to population pressure, to ambitious rulers aggressively seeking power, and to complex miscalculation. How these are to be avoided or contained is a question primarily for political science.

In the economic sphere, various international public goods have been identified: an open trading system, including freedom of the seas, well-defined property rights, standards of weights and measures that may include international money, or fixed exchange rates, and the like. Those that have interested me especially in a study of the 1929 depression and other financial and economic crises have been trading systems, international money, capital flows, consistent macroeconomic policies in periods of tranquillity, and as a source of crisis management when needed. By the last I mean the maintenance of open markets in glut and a source of supplies in acute shortage, plus a lender of last resort in acute financial crisis (see my 1973 book, revised 1986).

Public goods are produced domestically by government, unless the government agenda is blocked in stalemate among competing distributional coalitions as described by Mancur Olson (1982). Voluntary provision of public goods is plagued by the free rider. In the international sphere where there is no world government, the question remains how public goods are produced. Ralph Bryant is one of the few economists who has discussed the public good element in international cooperation. His vocabulary is different from that of the political scientists: their "regimes" are his "supranational traffic regulations" (1980, p. 470), and he expects leadership in cooperation in monetary and fiscal policy from supranational institutions such as the International Monetary Fund (p. 481). I find this doubtful on the basis of the interwar record of such institutions as the League of Nations.

Political science in this field has produced two schools: the realists who hold to a national-interest theory of international politics, and the moralists, whom Robert Keohane prefers to call "institutionalists" (1984, p. 7). Realists maintain that international public goods are produced, if at all, by the leading power, a so-called "hegemon," that is willing to bear an undue part of the short-run costs of these goods, either because it regards itself as gaining in the long run, because it is paid in a different coin such as prestige, glory, immortality, or some combination of the two. Institutionalists recognize that hegemonic leaders emerge from time to time in the world economy and typically set in motion habits of international cooperation, called "regimes," which consist of 'principles, norms, rules and decision-making procedures around which the expectations of international actors converge in given issue areas' (Stephen Krasner, 1983, p. 1). Under British hegemony, the regimes of free trade and the gold standard developed more or less unconsciously. With subsequent American hegemony, a more purposeful process of institution making was undertaken, with agreement at Bretton Woods, on tariffs and trade, the Organization for Economic Cooperation and Development, and the like. Political scientists recognize that regimes are more readily maintained than established since marginal costs are below average costs; as hegemonic periods come to an end with the waning of the leading country's economic vitality, new regimes needed to meet new problems are difficult to create. Cooper (1985) has written of the eighty years it took to create and get functioning the World Health Organization despite the clear benefits to all countries from controlling the spread of disease. And it takes work to maintain regimes; in the absence of infusions of attention and money, they tend in the long run to decay.

I originally suggested that the 1929 depression was allowed to run unchecked because there was no leading country able and willing to take responsibility for crisis management, halting beggar-thy-neighbour policies from 1930, and especially acting as a lender of last resort to prevent the serious run on the Creditanstalt in May 1931 spreading, as it did, to Germany, Britain, Japan, the United States, and ultimately to the gold bloc. Britain, the leading economic power of the nineteenth century, was unable to halt the run; the United States, which might have had the ability, possibly assisted by France, was unwilling. This view has been rejected by one economic historian who holds that the troubles of the interwar period were more deep-seated, and that what was needed was more fundamental therapy than maintaining open markets and providing a lender of last resort, something, that is, akin to the heroic public good after World War II, the Marshall Plan (D. E. Moggridge, 1982). That may have been true, though there is no way I see that the issue can be settled. Leadership at an earlier stage in the 1920s, presumably furnished by the United States with some cost in foregone receipts on war-debt account, might have resolved the war-debt-reparations-commercial-debt tangle that proved so destabilizing after the 1929 stock market crash. I conclude that the existence of an international lender of last resort made the financial crises of 1825, 1836, 1847, 1866, and 1907 more or less ephemeral, like summer storms, whereas its absence in 1873, 1890, and 1929 produced deep depressions—shortened in the 1890 case by the *deus ex machina* of gold production from the Rand. Again there is room for disagreement.

The point of all this is that after about 1971, the United States, like Britain from about 1890, has shrunk in economic might relative to the world as a whole, and more importantly, has lost the appetite for providing international economic public goods—open markets in times of glut, supplies in times of acute shortage, steady flows of capital to developing countries, international money, coordination of macroeconomic policy and last-resort lending. The contraction of concern from the world to the nation is general, and applies to economists as well as to politicians and the public. In reading recent books on macroeconomic policy by leading governmental economists under both Democratic and Republican administrations, the late Arthur Okun (1981) and Herbert Stein (1984), I have been struck by how little attention the authors paid to international repercussions. The same observation has been made by Ralph Bryant (1980, p. xviii) and by the British economist R. C. O. Matthews, reviewing Arjo Klamer's *Conversations with Economists* ... (1985, p. 621). There has been a recent upsurge of interest in the international dimension because of the connections among the federal deficit, the exchange rate for the dollar, and the balance-of-payments deficit, but the focus of this interest is almost exclusively on what the connections mean for US interest rates, industrial policy, growth, and wealth. The international impact is largely ignored, bearing out the truth in former German Chancellor Helmut Schmidt's statement that 'the United States seems completely un-conscious of the economic effects of its policies on the Alliance' (1984, p. 27).

Some of the discussion of international regimes by political scientists verges on what my teacher, Wesley Clair Mitchell, used to call "implicit theorizing," that is, convenient *ad hoc* theoretical explanations to fit given facts that lack generality. Charles Lipson (1985), for example, suggested that the slippage in US hegemony in the 1970s resulted in a loss of the international public good of secure property rights and therefore in the widespread nationalization of foreign direct investment. He went on to say that the reason less developed countries (*LDCs*) did not default on their debts to bank syndicates was that bank lending was "better institu-tionalized," "a smaller group," "better protected by legal remedies" (pp. 136, 158, 170). He was surprised that the decline of British hegemony in the interwar period did not result in more *LDC* aggression against foreign property (p. 191), but failed to observe the widespread default on foreign bonds in the 1930s, despite the organization of international finance. In my judgment Keohane exaggerates the efficacy and importance of the international regime in oil that was formed after the first OPEC oil shock of 1973 (see his Chapter 10). The crisis caused by the Yom Kippur em-bargo of the Netherlands was to my mind shockingly mishandled by governments, and the public good of crisis management was left to the private multinational oil companies. The formation of the International Energy Agency was a classic operation in locking the barn door after the horse had been stolen.

Between national self-interest and the provision of international public goods, there is an intermediate position: indifference to both. An interest-ing contrast has been observed in the 1930s between Britain which forced Argentina into a bilateral payments agreement (the Roca–Runciman Agreement of 1933) in order to take advantage of its monopsony posi-tion, and the United States that had a similar opportunity *vis-à-vis* Brazil but ignored it (Marcelo de Paiva Abreu, 1984).

It is fairly clear from the historical record that economic hegemony runs down in decay—in the British case after 1913 and the United States about 1971—leading Felix Rohatyn (1984) to say that the American cen-tury lasted only twenty years. The Nixon shock of 1973 in cutting off soya bean exports to Japan—a significant harm to an ally for a small gain to this country—was the act of a bad Samaritan. The import surcharge of the same year may have been required to move the dollar out from the position of the nth currency when only $n - 1$ countries are free to fix their exchange rates, but it would have been possible to start with the later attempt at cooperation that resulted in the Smithsonian agreement. This is especially true when so much of the case against the 1971 exchange rate was the result of the easy-money policy of the Federal Reserve System under Chairman Arthur Burns, at a time when the Bundesbank was tightening its money market/go-it-alone policies of both banks that flooded the world with dollars.

The present US administration claims to be working for open trade and does fairly well in resisting appeals for protection. The positive push for a Reagan round of trade liberalization in services and agriculture, however, is in pursuit of a national and not an international public good. The regime in capital movements—the World Bank, the regional development banks and that in last-resort lending orchestrated by the IMF—seems to be working, with bridging loans and an *ad hoc* purchase of oil from Mexico for the US stockpile in 1982 when the IMF finds itself unable to move fast enough. But there are signs of dissension that may spell trouble. The June 1985 bridging loan for Argentina was declined by Germany and Switzerland on the grounds that Argentina had not been sufficiently austere and that its problems were not a threat to the world financial system (*New York Times*, 15 June 1985, p. 1). The Japanese contribution, moreover, was said to have been small, although no figures were given.

What I worry about mostly is exchange policy and macroeconomic coordination. The US Treasury under Donald Regan was committed to the policy of neglect, presumably benign, but in any event ideological. And the commitment to consultative macroeconomic policies in annual summit meetings of seven heads of state has become a shadow play, a dog-and-pony show, a series of photo opportunities—whatever you choose to call them—with ceremony substituted for substance. The 1950s and 1960s, when serious discussions were held at the lowly level of Working Party No. 3 of the OECD, were superior because the United States and other countries took them seriously.

I am a realist when it comes to regimes. It seems to me that the momentum set in motion by a hegemonic power—if we must use that expression, I prefer to think of leadership or responsibility—runs down pretty quickly unless it is sustained by powerful commitment. The IMF and World Bank were agreed at Bretton Woods largely as a result of the US Treasury: the forms were international, the substance was dictated by a single country (Armand van Dormel, 1978). In the early days of the IMF, Frank Southard told me, if the United States made no proposal, nothing happened. Today the same is true of the European Economic Community: unless Germany and France see eye-to-eye, which is infrequent, nothing happens. Proposals of great technical appeal from individuals or small countries are not welcomed as the preparatory phases of the World Economic Conference of 1933 demonstrated (see my 1973 book, pp. 210–14). There needs to be positive leadership, backed by resources and a readiness to make some sacrifice in the international interest.

The leadership role is not applauded. When the United States accused the rest of the world of being free riders, Andrew Shonfield countercharged the United States of being a "hard rider," "hustling and bullying the Europeans," "kicking over chairs when it did not get its way" (1976, pp. 86, 88, 102). Furnishing the dollar to the world as international money has brought the United States an accusation of extracting seignorage, although the facts that the dollar is not a monopoly currency and that foreign holdings earn market rates of interest deflect that criticism in sophisticated quarters.

Neglect can verge on sabotage. When the European central banks collaborated to hold the dollar down at the end of February 1985, the conspicuous failure of the United States to participate on a significant scale encouraged speculators not to cover long positions. A former trader for the Federal Reserve Bank of New York has expressed concern that the habits of central bank cooperation and US official intimacy with the workings of the foreign-exchange market that have been built up over thirty years are being squandered for ideological reasons (Scott Pardee, 1964, p. 2).

Regimes are clearly more attractive in political terms than hegemony, or even than leadership with its overtones of the German *Führerprinzip* or of Italy's *Il Duce*, if not necessarily more so than responsibility. Polycentralism, pluralism, cooperation, equality, partnership, decoupling, self-reliance, and autonomy all have resonance. But it is hard to accept the view, so appealing to the political right, that the path to achieve cooperation is a tit-for-tat strategy, applied in a repetitive game, that teaches the other player or players to cooperate (Robert Axelrod, 1984). As Tibor Scitovsky demonstrated years ago (1937), this path can readily end by wiping out trade altogether. Hierarchical arrangements are being examined by economic theorists studying the organization of firms, but for less cosmic purposes than would be served by political and economic organization of the production of international public goods (Raj Sah and Joseph Stiglitz, 1985).

Minding one's own business—operating in the robust zone of indifference—is a sound rule on trend when macroeconomic variables are more or less stable. To the economist it means reliance on the market to the extent that the conditions for a Pareto optimum solution are broadly met. But the fallacy of composition remains a threat, and one cannot count on the Categorical Imperative. Markets work most of the time, as a positive-sum game in which the gain for one does not imply a loss for another. Experience teaches, however, that crises may arise. When they do, the rule changes from government and public indifference to the production of public goods by leadership or by a standby regime.

Leadership or responsibility limited to crises encounters another problem: how to keep the machinery for handling crises from obsolescence. In crisis one needs forceful and intelligent people, capable of making decisions with speed under pressure. It is sometimes said that the Japanese practice of decision by consensus with ideas coming up from below, makes it hard for that country to discharge in timely fashion the responsibilities of world leadership. In Marcus Goodrich's *Delilah* (1941), the amiable practice of fraternization between a watch officer and enlisted men on the bridge of the destroyer proved dangerous in a typhoon since the men had fallen into the habit of discussing the officer's orders. The paradox is that the attributes needed in crisis tend to atrophy in quiet times; for example in the control room of a Three Mile Island nuclear power plant.

Let me conclude by emphasizing once again my concern that politicians, economists, and political scientists may come to believe that the system should be run at all times by rules, including regimes, not people. Rules are desirable on trend. In crisis the need is for decision. I quote once more the letter of Sir Robert Peel of June 1844 a propos of the Bank Charter Act of that year:

My Confidence is unshaken that we have taken all the Precautions which Legislation can prudently take against the Recurrence of a pecuniary Crisis. It may occur in spite of our Precautions; and if it be necessary to assume a grave Responsibility, I dare say men will be found willing to assume such a Responsibility. (*Parliamentary Papers*, 1857, 1969, p. xxix)

Notes

1. I have benefited from comments and suggestions on an earlier draft from Susan Okin, Walt W. Rostow, Walter S. Salant, and Robert M. Solow. A paper with the same title before translation, but with a different coverage was written in 1980, and has appeared in French (1980).

2. This at least is oral tradition. I have been unable to find a specific reference in Knight (1936), or Knight and Thornton Merriam (1947).

3. If the intrusiveness of goods is less than that of corporations from abroad, it is perhaps anomalous that the standard of friendly international dealings exemplified in treaties of

Friendship, Commerce, and Navigation is less hospitable for goods than for corporations. Foreign corporations in theory are given national treatment; goods only that of the most-favoured nation. In practice, many countries ignore the commitment to national treatment and discriminate both against foreign corporations as a class, and among those of different nationality.

4. Tastes in public goods can of course differ within countries. A striking comparison is furnished in E. Digby Baltzell's *Puritan Boston and Quaker Philadelphia* (1979). Boston is characterized as intolerant, extremely homogeneous, ascetic, philanthropic, and devoted to social and political responsibility. Philadelphia, on the other hand, was an ethnic and religious melting pot, materialistic, believing in money making, and shunning power and responsibility. Boston produced four presidents of the United States, including one non-Puritan affected by the values of the city, Philadelphia none. Social scientists are wary of ascribing social responses to national (or urban) character. There may nonetheless be occasions when it is inescapable.

References

Arrow, Kenneth J., "Gift and Exchanges," in Edmund S. Phelps (ed.), *Altruism, Morality and Economic Theory*, New York: Russell Sage Foundation, 1975.

Axelrod, Robert, *The Evolution of Cooperation*, New York: Basic Books, 1984.

Baltzell, E. Digby, *Puritan Boston and Quaker Philadelphia: Two Protestant Ethics and the Spirit of Class Authority and Leadership*, New York: Free Press 1979.

Becker, Gary, *A Treatise on the Family*, Cambridge: Harvard University Press, 1981.

Berry, Brian J. L., "City-Size Distribution and Economic Development," *Economic Development and Cultural Change*, July 1961, 9, pp. 573–88.

Braudel, Fernand, *Civilization and Capitalism* (15th–18th Century), vol. 2, *The Wheels of Commerce*, translated from the French by Sian Reynolds, New York: Harper and Row, 1982.

Breton, Albert, 'The Economics of Nationalism,' *Journal of Political Economy*, August 1964, 72, pp. 376–86.

Bryant, Ralph C., *Money and Monetary Policy in Independent Nations*, Washington: The Brookings Institution, 1980.

Calabrese, Guido and Bobbitt, Philip, *Tragic Choices*, New York: W.W. Norton, 1978.

Cooper, Richard N., *The Economics of Interdependence: Economic Policy in the Atlantic Community*, New York: McGraw-Hill, 1968.

———, "World-Wide vs Regional Integration: Is There an Optimal Size of the Integrated Area?" in Fritz Machlup (ed.), *Economic Integration: Worldwide, Regional, Sectoral*, New York: Halstead, 1977.

———, "International Economic Cooperation: Is it Desirable? Is it Likely?" *Bulletin*, American Academy of Arts and Sciences, November 1985, 39, pp. 11–35.

de Paiva Abreu, Marcelo, "Argentina and Brazil During the 1930s: The Impact of British and American Economic Policies," in Rosemary Thorp (ed.), *Latin America in the 1930s: The Role of the Periphery in World Crisis*, London: Macmillan, 1984.

Fishkin, James S., *The Limits of Obligation*, New Haven: Yale University Press 1982.

Fogel, Robert W., *Railroads and American Economic Growth: Essays in Econometric History*, Baltimore: Johns Hopkins Press, 1964.

Goodrich, Marcus, *Delilah*, New York: Farrar & Rinehart, 1941.

Graham, Frank D., *The Theory of International Values*, Princeton: Princeton University Press, 1948.

Harris, Seymour E., *The Economics of New England: Case Study of an Older Area*, Cambridge: Harvard University Press, 1965.

Hicks, John R., *A Theory of Economic History*, London: Oxford University Press, 1969.

Hirschman, Albert O., *Exit, Voice and Loyalty*, Cambridge: Harvard University Press, 1970.

Isard, Caroline and Isard, Walter, "Economic Implications of Aircraft," *Quarterly Journal of Economics*, February 1945, 59, pp. 145–69.

Johnson, Harry G., "An 'Internationalist' Model," in Walter Adams, (ed.), *The Brain Drain*, New York: Macmillan, 1968.

Keohane, Robert O., *After Hegemony: Cooperation and Discord in the World Political Economy*, Princeton: Princeton University Press, 1984.

Kindleberger, Charles P., *The World in Depression 1929–1939*, Berkeley: University of California Press, 1973.

———, "Internationalist and Nationalist Models in the Analysis of the Brain Drain: Progress and Unsolved Problems," *Minerva*, Winter 1977, 15, pp. 553–61.

———, "Government and International Trade," *Essays in International Finance*, No. 129, International Finance Section, Princeton University, 1978.

———, *Multinational Excursions*, Cambridge, MIT Press, 1984.

———, "Des biens public internationaux en l'absence d'un government international," in *Croissance, échange et monnaie en économie international Mélange en l'honneur de Monsieur le Professeur Jean Weiller*, Paris: Economica, 1985.

Knight, Frank H., *The Ethics of Competition and Other Essays*, London: George Allen & Unwin, 1936.

———, and Merriam, Thornton, W., *The Economic Order and Religion*, London: Kegan Paul, Trend, Trubner, 1947.

Krasner, Stephen D., *International Regimes*, Ithaca: Cornell University Press, 1983.

Labasse, Jean, *L'espace financier: analyze géographique*, Paris; Colin, 1974.

Lichtenberg, Judith, "National Boundaries and Moral Boundaries," in Peter G. Brown and Henry Shue (eds), *Boundaries: National Autonomy and Its Limits*, Totowa: Rowman and Littlefield, 1981.

Lipson, Charles, *Standing Guard: Protecting Foreign Capital in the Nineteenth and Twentieth Centuries*, Berkeley: University of California Press, 1985.

McCloskey, Donald N., "The Rhetoric of Economics," *Journal of Economic Literature*, June 1983, 21, pp. 481–517.

McKinnon, Ronald I., "Optimum Currency Areas," *American Economic Review*, September 1963, 53, pp. 717–25.

Matthews, R. C. O., Review of Arjo Klamer, *Conversations with Economists ... 1983, Journal of Economic Literature*, June 1985, 23, pp. 621–22.

Meade, James E., *The Theory of International Economic Policy*, Vol. II, *Trade and Welfare*, New York: Oxford University Press, 1955.

Moggridge, D. E., "Policy in the Crises of 1920 and 1929," in C.P. Kindleberger and J.-P. Laffargue (eds), *Financial Crises: Theory, History and Policy*, Cambridge: Cambridge University Press, 1982.

Mundell, Robert A., "A Theory of Optimum Currency Areas," *American Economic Review*, September 1961, 51, pp. 657–65.

Nozick, Robert, *Anarchy, State and Utopia*, New York: Basic Books, 1974.

Ohlin, Bertil, *Interregional and International Trade*, Cambridge: Harvard University Press, 1933.

Okun, Arthur M., *Prices and Quantities*, Washington: Brookings Institution, 1981.

Olson, Mancur, *The Rise and Decline of Nations: Economic Growth, Stagflation and Social Rigidities*, New Haven: Yale University Press, 1982.

Pardee, Scott, "The Dollar," address before the Georgetown University Bankers Forum, Washington, DC, September 22, 1964.

Parliamentary Papers: Monetary Policy, Commercial Distress, Shannon: Irish University Press, 1957, 1969.

Patinkin, Don, "A 'Nationalist' Model," in Walter Adams (ed.), *The Brain Drain*, New York: Macmillan, 1968.

Robertson, Sir Dennis, "What Do Economists Economize?" in R. Leckachman (ed.), *National Policy for Economic Welfare at Home and Abroad*, New York: Doubleday, 1955.

Rohatyn, Felix G., *The Twenty-Year Century: Essays on Economics and Public Finance*, New York: Random House, 1984.

Rostow, Walt W., *The Stages of Economic Growth: A Non-Communist Manifesto*, Cambridge: Cambridge University Press 1960.

Sah, Raaj Kumar and Stiglitz, Joseph E., "Human Fallibility and Economic Organization," *American Economic Review Proceedings*, May 1985, 75, pp. 292–7.

Scitovsky, Tibor, "A Reconsideration of the Theory of Tariffs," reprinted in AEA *Readings in the Theory of International Trade*, Homewood: Richard D. Irwin, 1949.

Shonfield, Andrew, *International Economic Relations of the Western World*, vol. I, *Politics and Trade*, New York: Oxford University Press, 1976.

Singer, Peter, "Famine, Affluence and Morality," *Philosophy and Public Affairs*, Spring 1972, 1, pp. 229–43.

Smith, Adam, *The Theory of Moral Sentiments, or An Essay Toward an Analysis of the Principles by which Men Naturally Judge Concerning the Conduct and Character First of their Neighbours and then of Themselves*, 11th ed., Edinburgh: Bell and Bradfute, 1759; 1808.

————, *An Inquiry Into the Nature and Causes of the Wealth of Nations*, Canaan (ed.), New York: Modern Library, 1776; 1937.

Schmidt, Helmut, "Saving Western Europe," *New York Review of Books*, 31 May 1984, 31, pp. 25–7.

Stigler, George J., "Economics—The Imperial Science?" mimeo., 1984.

Stein, Herbert, *Presidential Economics: The Making of Economic Policy from Roosevelt to Reagan and Beyond*, New York: Simon and Schuster, 1984.

Van Dormael, Armand, *Bretton Woods: Birth of a Monetary System*, New York: Holmes and Meier, 1978.

Vaubel, Roland, "The Government's Money Monopoly: Externalities or Natural Monopoly?" *Kyklos*, 1984, 27, pp. 27–57.

Vernon, Raymond, *Sovereignty at Bay*, Cambridge: Harvard University Press, 1971.

————, *Storm over Multinationals*, Cambridge: Harvard University Press, 1977.

Walzer, Michael, "The Distribution of Membership," in Peter G. Brown and Henry Shue (eds), *Boundaries: National Autonomy and Its Limits*, Totowa: Rowman and Littlefield, 1981.

————, *Spheres of Justice*, New York: Basic Book, 1983.

21
Rules vs Men: Lessons from a Century of Monetary Policy

Introduction

The problem that Knut Borchardt tackled with his "Constraints and Room for Manoeuvre in the Great Depression of the Early Thirties"—to use the title in English[1]—is a pervasive one that permeates many aspects of economic, political, and personal life, and has a critical bearing on both efficiency and ethics. I choose to condense the issue as "rules vs. men," since it often appears in that guise. Most generally the question is when do circumstances of an extreme nature call for breaking rules and regulation, even the law, surely commitments made to others without force of law, when to depart from established principles or, to express it more pejoratively, ideologies to serve pragmatic ends. In bureaucratic organizations it is sometimes posed as when should an outranked official or a staff expert giving advice on what he or she is convinced is the right course to follow and is overruled resign, instead of subsiding quietly? The questions posing the issue are usually complex, intelligent and responsible persons can readily divide.

I offer two introductory examples: one close to a disaster, the other a success. With the integration of East with West Germany, no clear rule told how to handle the currency. The simple-minded political view, a mark is a mark, ran contrary to the advice of the Bundesbank and proved mistaken. In August 1982, on the other hand, as the Mexican debt crisis exploded, the Federal Reserve System, contrary to all rules and regulations of which I am aware, advanced $1 billion to the Mexican government as payment against future deliveries of oil to the Strategic Oil

Reprinted from Christoph Buchheim, Michael Hutter, and Harold James, eds., *Zerrissene Zwischenkriegszeit: Wirtschaftshistorische Beiträge* (Baden-Baden: Nomos Verlagsgesellschaft, 1994), 157–75.

Reserve of the United States, maintained in salt mines in Louisiana. After the second sharp rise in the price of oil engineered by OPEC in 1979, oil was clearly valuable collateral as well as a strategic commodity and wide understanding of this fact doubtless helped to quell any potential objection. There was no objection. Men had set aside the rules and met an emergency.

I come in due course to the question whether Heinrich Brüning, the German Chancellor in 1931 and 1932, was justified or not in pressing on with deflation and in putting the goal of bringing a halt to reparations ahead of tackling the issue of the rapid increases in unemployment in Germany in those years. Central to the issue is whether he had a choice or whether the commitments under the Dawes Plan, the Young Plan, the statutes of the Reichsbank and the like rendered any alternative course impossible. In the interest of full disclosure I should perhaps immediately confess that I am more or less on the side of Carl-Ludwig Holtfrerich's position that there were alternatives to deflation that promised better outcomes if Brüning had been forceful enough to break through the constraints upon him.[2] To regard the final end of reparations at the Lausanne Conference in the summer of 1932 as the successful culmination of Brüning's policy, even though he fell 100 meters from the goal by being voted out of office in May of that year, strikes me like Charles Lamb's recipe for roast pig which consisted in burning a house down around the animal.

To keep the discussion more general and to honor Knut Borchardt with whom I have collaborated and whom I greatly admire, I propose not an exercise dealing with an episode in economic history, but an essay in politico-economic behavior, using a number of historical examples.

I   English and French Examples from the 19th Century

Let me begin by citing a number of British authorities who have pronounced on the issue more or less concisely:

There are times when rules and precedents cannot be broken; others when they cannot be adhered to with safety.[3]

I am satisfied that laying down a "hard and fast rule"—on whether bankers' deposits at the Bank of England can be lent out—would be very dangerous; in very important and very changeable business, rigid rules are apt to be often dangerous ... no certain fixed proportion of its liabilities can in present times be laid down as that which the Bank ought to keep in reserve.... The forces of the enemy being variable, those of the defense cannot always be the same.

I admit this conclusion is very inconvenient ... unhappily, the rule which is the most simple is not always the rule which is most to be relied upon. The practical difficulties of life often cannot be met by very simple rules; those difficulties being complex and many, the rules of countering them cannot be single or simple. A uniform remedy for many diseases often ends by killing the patient.[4]

Bagehot does not dismiss the rule on bankers' balances entirely:

The idea that bankers' balances ought never to be lent is only a natural aggravation of the truth that these balances should be lent with extreme caution.[5]

Bagehot entered into this discussion in his first published paper which appeared in 1848, commenting on the controversy between the Banking and the Currency Schools of British monetary policy, over whether the money supply should be relatively fixed by being tied up to the Bank of England's bullion reserve, or elastic so as to move up and down with the expansion and contraction of commerce:

The currency argument is this: it is a great defect of a purely metallic circulation that the quantity of it cannot be readily suited to any sudden demand; it takes time to get new supplies of gold and silver, and, in the meantime, a temporary rise in the value of bullion takes place. Now as paper money can be supplied in unlimited quantities, however sudden the demand may be, it does not appear to us that there is an objection in principle to sudden issues of paper money to meet sudden and large extensions of demand. This power of issuing notes is one excessively liable to abuse. Such a power ought only to be lodged in the hands of government. It should only be used in rare and exceptional cases. But when the fact of an extensive and *sudden* [Bagehot's emphasis] demand is proved, we see no objections, but decided advantage, in introducing this new element into a metallic circulation.[6]

The distinction between the rule for normal times and that in a time of a sudden demand for money complicates the case for rules, especially as it carries the implication that men are needed to "prove" the existence of "an extensive sudden demand." The emphasis on suddenness brings up a qualification in the theory of rational expectations that unanticipated shocks may modify the rule that markets should be left alone to find their equilibria without government intervention. One emerges with two rules, one for ordinary times, say on trend, and another for financial crises when lender-of-last-resort action is needed. Historical revealed preference suggests that a normal rule, either let the market handle it, or supply money to the system at a regular rate of growth, is often set aside, at least briefly. Much depends on the nature of the shock—whether the bursting of a speculative bubble, or the outbreak of what promises to be a prolonged war.

One of the most powerful advocates of a fixed rule for supplying money, Milton Friedman, who would even go so far as to abolish central banks to get rid of their men who may be tempted to exercise judgment and adjust policy to circumstances, had considerable sympathy with the existence of two rules, when in his "Monetary History of the United States," written with Anna Jacobson Schwartz, he or they note that a financial crisis is like an avalanche, a slide of unstable earth previously held back by a rock that comes loose.[7] Quoting Bagehot's prescription that a financial crisis is like neuralgia, and one must not starve it carries the implication that the money supply at times must be elastic.[8]

Sir Robert Peel, the British prime minister in 1844, demonstrated a profound understanding of the dilemma posed by the choice between rules and men in commenting on the Bank Act in a letter of June 4, 1844:

My Confidence is unshaken that we have taken all the Precautions which legislation can prudently take against the Recurrence of a pecuniary Crisis [i.e. have drawn up a proper set of rules]. It may occur in spite of our Precautions; and if it be necessary to assume a grave responsibility, I dare say Men will be found willing to assume such a Responsibility.[9]

Before the passage of the Bank Act of 1844, the Bank of England had come to the rescue of financial markets on numerous occasions, and broken its internal rule on discounting which was to rediscount only two-months' commercial bills with two good London names. In various crises it loaned on out-of-town names, on mortgages, including some on unimproved land and one on a West Indian plantation, on the securities of a copper company through which it acquired in bankruptcy a copper works.[10] According to the testimony of Jeremiah Harman of the Bank of England it loaned in the panic of 1825 "by every possible means and in modes we have never adopted before in short, by every possible means consistent with the safety of the Bank, and we were not on some occasions over-nice."[11]

With the passage of the Bank Act of 1844, a Machiavellian device helped to regularize the handling of financial crises. As lender of last resort the Bank of England broke the rules limiting the issue of banknotes to the small (at that time) fiduciary issue against government bonds, plus gold in the Issue Department, but only after receiving a Letter of Indemnity from the Chancellor of the Exchequer stating that it would not be prosecuted for its violation of the law. This preserved the principle, but granted the exception. As is widely known, the Letter of Indemnity in 1848 and 1866 at times of crises so calmed the market that there was no need of an excess issue, and that in the crisis of 1857 the excess was very small.

The Letter of Indemnity was by no means the only device available for meeting a financial crisis. One might have returned to the issuance by the government of Exchequer bills, made available to merchants against the collateral of commodity inventories, and discountable at the Bank of England. This technique had calmed the roiled financial waters of the canal mania in 1793. It was not available in 1825, however, because when meeting with a deputation of merchants asking for Exchequer bills, Lord Liverpool, the Chancellor of the Exchequer, hoping to quell the agitated speculation, publicly refused, saying he would resign first. When panic ensued in 1825 in spite of his effort to forestall it, the Bank of England found a little breathing room to meet the run on its notes in a swap of silver against gold with the Bank of France, and a chance discovery of a box of one-pound notes that had been retired on its way to the resumption of the gold standard in 1821. More was needed, however, and the government ordered the Bank to lend £3 million to merchants against the collateral of commodity stocks, in effect, cutting out the intermediation of the Exchequer. The Court of Directors of the Bank seriously considered a motion to refuse to comply with the request, but ultimately went along, "the sullen answer of driven men" as Sir John Clapham put it.[12]

Lord Liverpool's refusal, of course, rested on his concern that repetition of a breach in standard practice would set a precedent, and constitute a change of rule. The same worry that continuous setting aside of rules would vitiate them led Lord Lidderdale, Governor of the Bank of England in 1890 at the time of the Baring crisis, to refuse to accept the offer of a Letter of Indemnity from the Chancellor, Viscount Goschen. He turned instead to another device, a guarantee of liabilities of the Baring bank. Similar guarantees had been used in 1857 in Hamburg, and twice in the 1880s in France, once half-heartedly in 1882 in the collapse of the *Union Générale*, to save the brokers in the bankruptcy but not the principal, and again, more seriously in 1888 when the *Comptoir d'Escompte* failed because of the collapse of the scheme of its president, Denfert-Rocherau, to corner the world copper market.[13] Both in 1857 in Hamburg, and in 1890 in London, but not in Paris in the 1880s, the guarantee of bank liabilities was combined with a foreign loan, in the earlier episode, the *Silberzug* (silver train) from Austria,[14] in the Baring crisis, two loans from the State Bank of Russia and the Bank of France.[15] One further alternative, which might be characterized as a policy, is to take no action, either because of procrastination, the fall of policy leaders into a catatonic state, or an ideological conviction that it is best to let the fire burn itself out and the victims take their medicine. Among the last group are persons who think that markets are always efficient. The number of those in the latter category tends to shrink when crisis actually arrives, and most governmental authorities and central bankers—occasionally also private bankers—feel a responsibility to take some action to correct or dampen a crisis.

While the Bank of England in the middle of the nineteenth century was settling into an orthodox routine, across the channel the Bank of France was confronted with a new political position following the Revolution of 1848 and the *coup d'état* of 1851. Both central banks had been established in wartime to assist government finance, the Bank of France in 1800 to promote Napoleon I's military adventures. The takeover by Napoleon III in December 1851 posed new problems for the Bank as the Emperor had been infected by Saint-Simonian doctrine that believed in vigorous promotion of economic activity by the state. The Bank was called upon to assist in a debt conversion to reduce interest rates from 5 to 4 percent, and to promote the lagging building of the French railway network by making advances on bonds issued by some railroads.[16] While these measures were carried through after an agreement between the Bank and the government on March 2, 1852, many of the Regents were worried and expressed the view that the Bank of England would not have made loans on the collateral of railroad bonds.[17] Starting on March 15, the Bank began to lend on the railroad bonds, many of them a new type, devised by Isaac Pereire, with a low rate of nominal interest, but sold at a deep discount so as to leave room for capital appreciation.[18] In signing the agreement a number of the regents asserted that it was their moral obligation to assist, but some felt they were directly feeding speculation. On March 25, the Bank went still further and agreed to make advances on the debt of the City of Paris, but absolutely refused to do so for Marseilles and Bordeaux.[19]

Intense speculation in railroad securities, spurred by the rivalry of the Rothschilds with the Pereires, with whom the Emperor had now fallen out, led him to decree an end to the formation of new railroad companies. The Bank of France continued to make advances for companies with unfinished construction products. Almost 600 million francs of advances were later made in the four years 1858–1861. Two directors were vigorously opposed, especially Lafond, who had quit the wine trade at age 45 "to join the upper classes."[20] Lafond asked whether the resumption of the advances to railway companies was legal, and received the reply from the Governor that it was legal in the spirit of the law if not the letter.[21] Much of the support for the railroad bond policy came from the iron and steel regents, especially Eugène Schneider of the Schneider-Creusot steel company. After 1861, the Bank halted its "exceptional aid" to companies.[22] Plessis goes on to discuss new advances to the government to assist Fould in a new bond conversion to bring the interest rate down from $4\frac{1}{2}$ to 3 percent. He remarks that aid to the Treasury was often dealt with discretely, was not discussed in the full Council of Regents but only in the Committee of Discounts. Little mention of the Bank's relations with the Treasury appears in the Minutes of the Bank as the question was left to the governor and the most influential regents.[23]

This somewhat cavalier disregard by men for law, principles of central banking, precepts and widely accepted practice opened up the possibilities for malfeasance and trouble, and there was of course some. Apart from the crisis of 1864 caused by the fall in the price of cotton at the end of the Civil War in the United States, however, the period of the Second Empire from 1851 to 1870, dominated by men rather than rules, and by men often locked in antagonistic battle with one another, were on the whole continuously prosperous, in considerable part because of the railroad boom financed by the Bank of France.

II   The Crisis of the Bank of France in 1924

I deal with one major incident of the 1920s before moving on to the Great Depression following 1929. At the end of the First World War, the French government had accumulated a substantial debt to the Bank of France for short-term advances—some 24 billion francs, which greatly enlarged the money supply and was regarded as highly inflationary. French experience with inflation, going back to the Mississippi bubble of John Law and the Assignats during the French Revolution had produced a hypersensitivity to that form of monetary pathology, and politicians of all stripes thought steps should be taken to head inflation off. In consequence, a convention was concluded between the Chamber of Deputies and the Treasury to reduce the debt by 2 billion francs a year, starting in 1921, with the goal of wiping it out entirely in twelve years. In addition, this so-called François-Marsal convention set a ceiling (*plafond*) on the Bank of France's note issue. The prospect at the time was that the Treasury's debt would ultimately be paid off through the receipt of reparations from Germany, and that the franc would be returned to prewar par.

The prospects of 1920 proved illusory, however. In 1921, the full two billion of Treasury debt was paid down but in 1922 only one billion, and in 1923 only 200 million.[24] Already a bright civil servant in the Treasury, Pierre de Mouÿ, began to agitate for change. In the first place, he pointed

out that the attempt to control the money supply through Bank of France
notes and its advances to the Treasury was futile because of the existence
of the large short-term Treasury debt in the form of *Bons de la Défense
Nationale*, billions of which matured every month, and which were equivalent to cash, since the Treasury had to pay off those that were not rolled
over. The skittishness of the public made any attempt to refund the Bons
at long term hopeless. Nor would political conditions permit a large increase in taxes, either a capital levy, as the Socialists wanted, or a tax on
income under conditions in which the existing income tax was widely
evaded. Proposals for taxes brought down the government, and called for
a new cabinet. De Mouÿ, in March 1923, the director of the *Mouvement
général des fonds* (public debt), wanted the government deficit—albeit a
decreasing one—financed by the Bank of France; there was no other way
to meet governmental expenditure—taxes, bond issues, or illegal borrowing from the major banks.[25] In his view the paranoia over inflation
was a chimera. A limited increase in Bank advances to the Treasury and
increase in the ceiling on the note issue, openly announced and explained,
was the safest course. Already the Bank and the Treasury were undertaking extraordinary measures to disguise the amount of money in circulation, which had to be reported weekly in the Bank's statement, moving
excess notes of a given branch to another branch as its day in the week to
report came up. De Mouÿ's recommendation found no response.

In early 1924 an opportunity to straighten out the position came with
an attack on the franc by financial interests in Holland, Austria and
Germany, against which after yielding some depreciation, a bear squeeze,
engineered by Lazard Frères with the help of a $100 million loan from J. P.
Morgan & Co., brought the franc back above the level at the start of the
attack. No advantage was taken of the respite, however, to take any fundamental steps through either increased taxes, reduced spending or debt
refunding. The franc struggled along but with the books of the Bank of
France heavily doctored. Advances to the government were made in contravention of the François-Marsal convention, but indirectly, by making
advances to the commercial banks which loaned to the government. It
was a time of lying.[26]

In mid-October 1924, one James LeClerc, an undergovernor of the
Bank of France, regarded by the governor, Georges Robineau, and his
secretary-general, Aupetit, as an outsider, discovered that the Bank's
statements had been falsified. He went to the Finance Minister, Etienne
Clémentel. There he was offered another job outside the Bank, but he
refused. Clémentel felt himself exposed as he had promised the Chamber

of Deputies that he would not "make inflation," i.e., evade the ceiling. He called Robineau and Aupetit to a meeting with the premier, Edouard Herriot, where possible alternative courses of action were discussed, not the recommendation of de Mouÿ for making a clean breast of it, citing the impossibility of the circumstances of 1924 of meeting the commitment of 1920, and openly borrowing on advances from the Bank, but what Jean-Noël Jeanneney calls various "silly ideas," reducing to minimum levels the balances from which the Treasury paid its bills, undertaking an intensive campaign to induce the public to make its payments by check instead of banknotes, issuing a new money in Madagascar and the Saar to replace Bank of France banknotes, which could then be cancelled.[27] Robineau told the Regents of the Bank of France on the eighteenth of December, and found them stupefied, fearful of being compromised. Herriot kept stalling for time, unable to decide among left-wing measures such as the capital levy or the right favoring cuts in spending, repeal of the 1918 ignored decree for the registration of exported capital. New ideas cropped up as the franc sank in the exchange market: a new Morgan loan and new squeeze, or the sale of 500 million francs worth of copper, stored in the Bourges arsenal. In March of 1925, François de Wendel, a right-wing Regent, told the government that unless an accurate balance sheet of the Bank was published by April 9 he would resign publicly. Herriot faced defeat either way: by announcing his deception or trying to levy new taxes. He hesitated further and then chose the taxes.[28] The political lives of the cabinet and the leadership at the Bank of France were numbered, and expired in mid-1926 after a long and agonizing struggle.

There is, of course, no assurance that if the policy of Pierre de Mouÿ offered in June 27, 1924 and repeated in October had been followed—announce that the government and the Bank were unilaterally to denounce the convention with the Chamber of Deputies, and the reasons why such a heroic measure was inescapable—matters would have worked out differently. It is virtually certain that the right wing—the so-called Wall of Money—would not have condoned it. Whether the public at large would have done is problematic. In any event, it is clear that the "men" involved—Herriot, Clémentel and Robineau—failed to rise to the occasion. The fate of the advocate of forthrightness followed classical lines: in the crisis month of December 1924, de Mouÿ was "kicked upstairs," to the position of director of customs, from which he retired six years later to join a bank at the age of 43.[29]

As an aside, I mention a postwar instance of a messenger with truth to convey who was not applauded for it. Emilio (Pete) G. Collado, director of the Office of Finance and Development in the Department of State in 1945, went to the meeting of heads of state at Potsdam in July and August with his superior, William L. Clayton, undersecretary of state for economic affairs, travelling by air. At Potsdam they caught up with the Secretary of State James F. Byrnes and President Harry S. Truman who had come by naval vessel, the U.S. cruiser *Augusta*. In a first meeting with Clayton and Collado, Secretary Byrnes mentioned that he and the President had decided to cancel immediately the Lend-Lease program of assistance to the Allies in the European theatre. Each had been a senator at the time of the passage of the Lend-Lease legislation in 1941, when the Roosevelt administration had promised that the program would not be continued beyond the end of the war. Collado, who was deeply informed about the details of lend-lease operations, protested to the Secretary, listing a series of problems of importance which would require lend-lease financing for an extended period. My memory is weak, but I recall one example, the need to lend-lease a hospital ship to Brazil to enable that country to return its wounded in Italy to their own country. The Secretary grew impatient and repeated: we have cancelled Lend-Lease. Collado returned to his list of problems. The Secretary grew irritated, and turning to Mr. Clayton, said, pointing to Collado, "I do not want to see that man again." In their postwar memoirs Truman and Byrnes acknowledge that the abrupt halt to Lend-Lease had been a mistake and each inferentially blamed the other.

III   Examples from the Great Depression

Matters are complicated in my first example as there were at least two sets of men, one in Washington and some of the regional Federal Reserve Banks outside of New York, members of the Federal Reserve Open-Market Committee Conference, recommending "rules" to the Federal Reserve Board which issued them to the Bank in New York, and the other carrying out operations in the financial capital in New York, face to face with financial conditions and in touch with foreign central banks. The balance between the two sets had been altered in October 1928 by the death of Governor Benjamin Strong, an experienced and authoritative central banker. His neophyte successor, George L. Harrison, was less well-placed to contest policy decisions he thought misguided. When the New York Stock Market crashed on October 24 and 29, 1929, Governor Harrison proceeded immediately to buy $160 million of U.S. government bonds in open-market operations to provide the money market with liquidity in

contravention, as widely thought, of the Open-Market Conference Committee instruction of August 1929 which authorized the New York Bank
to operate on its own initiative only within a limit of $25 million a week.
In addition, the New York Bank encouraged member banks to discount
freely. The Bank claimed that its open-market operations were not bound
by the Conference Committee limitation as it had a residual right to
operate on its own initiative as a matter of general credit policy. The
Board of Governors on the other hand took the view that the Bank's
action was close to insubordination. On November 12, the Open-Market
Committee Conference, with Governor Harrison presiding, recommended
abandonment of the $25 million a week limit, and fresh purchases of $200
million. The Board's response was that the position was too unclear to
formulate a long-run policy at the time, but in sudden emergency, when
consultation was difficult, it would not object to purchases by the New
York Bank.[30] With this less than whole-hearted support, the New York
Bank proceeded to buy $160 million of government securities during the
rest of November.

Tension between the Board and the Open-Market Committee on the
one hand and the New York Bank on the other was muddled by the fact
that the members of the Board of Governors were not unanimous and
that some governors of the other regional banks took strenuous opposition to the New York view. The episode runs in sharp contrast to the
stock market crash of October 19, 1987, when the Chairman of the Board
of Governors, Alan Greenspan, and the President of the New York Federal
Reserve Bank, Gerald Corrigan, moved instantly to flood the financial
market with reserves through open-market purchases, and offered to support any banks in temporary difficulty. Friedman and Schwartz on the
whole favor a fixed money supply or one growing at a regular rate, but
support the Harrison view of the October 1929 response to the crash on
lender-of-last-resort grounds, as noted earlier, making a distinction between an internal drain which must not be starved, and an external one
which calls for higher interest rates.[31]

After a series of bank failures in the Middle West and South-Central
part of the country in November 1930 came the important failure of the
Bank of the United States in December. The New York Fed kept advocating open-market operations but was resisted by the Board in Washington.
Because so many banks had run out of commercial bills eligible for rediscounting, the New York Bank urged the Board to allow it to discount
ineligible paper.[32] This was turned down. The Federal Reserve Bank of
New York with the support of the State Superintendent of Banks in the

state sought to put together a guarantee of the Bank of the United States liabilities through members of the New York Clearing House. At the last minute some of the leading banks refused to go along. The refusal is regarded by Friedman and Schwartz as based on discrimination against an outsider Jewish group.[33] A contrary view has been offered by Peter Temin that the Bank of the United States was too far gone with bad loans to speculators and its own offices to constitute a suitable candidate for rescue.[34]

The crisis then shifted to Europe. The failure of the Credit-Anstalt Bank in Vienna on May 11, 1931, which in some eyes, though not mine, marked the beginning of the international phase of the Great Depression, provided another example of rule breaking in the first instance, followed by second thoughts. The Credit-Anstalt was the largest of the Austrian banks with 53 percent of the deposits in the commercial banking system, a system that had been weakened by a banking crisis in 1924 when a number of Austrian banks had suffered heavy losses in speculation against the French franc, and again in 1929 when the second largest bank, at that time, the Bodencreditanstalt, failed, with many of its problem assets absorbed at overvalued levels into the Credit-Anstalt. The announcement of the failure was accompanied by a plan for reconstruction of the bank in which the Austrian government, the Rothschild interests in Austria and the Austrian National Bank would make up the bank's losses and contribute new capital. There was a heavy run on the Credit-Anstalt and the other leading banks in Vienna, which the Austrian National Bank met by discounting freely. In the absence of sufficient commercial bills called for by its regulators, R. Reisch, the Austrian National Bank president, liberally discounted finance bills, called by Aurel Schubert promissory notes. In four days, the panic run was brought to a halt.[35] To end the external drain the Austrian National Bank raised its discount rate and sought a loan from the Bank for International Settlements in Basle, which had opened the year before. The loan was provided but proved inadequate on several accounts: too small, too late, and carrying with it conditions that proved impossible for the Austrian government to meet and survive. After the initial successful spurt of domestic discounting, moreover, dissension developed within the Austrian National Bank, with the president wanting to continue discounting on terms which departed from the rules, but the vice-president and the director-general opposed. Inevitably the resulting hesitation was felt at home and abroad, the external drain continued, and the country was forced to impose control on foreign withdrawals.

As is well known the crisis spread to Germany and Britain. One could perhaps make a case that the Second Labour (MacDonald) government in Britain should have defiantly ignored the recommendations of the May Committee published in July 1931 that called for balancing the budget through cutting the dole (payments to the unemployed), but there were also the conditions to borrowing from official and private banks in the United States and France that the conservative policies of the May Committee be adhered to. A split developed in the Labour Party between those who called the May recommendations and the foreign conditions a "bankers' ramp" (in American English "racket"), and those who wanted to stay in power and operate within the constraints. The Labour government fell and was succeeded by a National government, with Ramsay Mac-Donald still as Prime Minister and Philip Snowden still Chancellor of the Exchequer. The government proceeded to reduce wages and the dole. A cut in Navy pay led to demonstrations by sailors in the naval base at Invergordon on September 16, regarded on the Continent of Europe as a mutiny, signifying a breakdown in one of the two traditional bulwarks of the British Empire, the Royal Navy and the Bank of England. Withdrawals of capital picked up speed. On September 21 the pound sterling gave up adherence to the gold standard. There was no real discussion of alternatives. A recent book on MacDonald characterized him as overworked and dispirited, abandoned by the Labour Party, welcoming the National government as a group of individuals with no set views rather than party politicians, and hence able to take hard decisions.[36] In the event, the movement from the formation of the National government to the forced depreciation of the pound which was not controlled in any way looked more like one of drift. The 30 percent depreciation of the pound (40 percent appreciation of the dollar, franc and Reichsmark) put sharp downward pressure on world commodity prices and accelerated deflation outside of the sterling area.

Depreciation of the world's key currency raised questions for all sorts of countries, questions which are still debated in those countries that did not follow the pound. Jürgen Schiemann has examined the controversy in Germany and concluded that such a course for the Reichsmark, assuming it had been possible, would have dampened the deflation somewhat but was unlikely to help the balance of payments.[37] Knut Borchardt thinks on the whole that public opinion would not have allowed Germany to abandon the parity achieved with difficulty in 1924. He further adduces technical reasons why such a course was undesirable, not all of which seem fully cogent. The international trade accounts were in surplus, but then sharp deflation reduces imports more than exports and leads to an export surplus; it would be unfair to German external creditors with claims in Reichsmarks, and would raise the Reichsmark equivalent of debts owed in foreign currencies (notably dollars), though these debts were not being serviced under the Standstill Agreement.[38] In the end he comes down to two powerful reasons, both of which, with the advantage of hindsight, seem to be based on faulty economic reasoning. Depreciation of the Reichsmark was regarded as inflationary, after the analogy of the early 1920s when inflation led to depreciation. But in severe depression some inflation, if it were true that depreciation would raise prices and incomes, was highly desirable. In addition the general public regarded depreciation as the policy of the extreme right, the National Socialist Party, so that adherence to gold was considered a bulwark against Hitler. Even Oberre-gierungsrat Wilhelm Lautenbach, whose Keynesian views well before the publication of *The General Theory of Employment, Interest and Money* (1936) were intensely debated in Germany in 1931 and 1932, was per-suaded that "in the matter of currency the utmost correctness is neces-sary."[39] But there was no discussion of the positive experiences of other countries like Sweden which followed the pound off gold. Their histories and constraints, to be sure, were different from those of Germany, but their experience raises questions about the economic arguments, espe-cially the fear of inflation, that seemed to count for so much.

Depreciation of the pound sterling called directly and indirectly for policy decisions in many countries. In one instance, the smaller countries of Europe which had lost part of their reserves held in sterling, immedi-ately turned and withdrew their dollar reserves in gold, followed at a more leisurely and dignified pace by the Bank of France. This posed a problem for the Federal Reserve System. The classic response to an exter-nal drain, according to Bagehot, as Friedman and Schwartz note, is to raise interest rates. On the other hand, the United States had responded to the gold inflow of the early 1920s by sterilizing it, selling off government bonds so as not to let commercial bank reserves rise. A symmetrical policy in response to the gold outflow would have been to leave in-terest rates (the rediscount rate) unchanged and offset the loss of gold reserves by buying government bonds.[40]

The New York Bank voted to follow the classic prescription and on October 6, 1931 voted to increase the discount rate from $1\frac{1}{2}$ to $2\frac{1}{2}$ percent. It informed vice-president W. Randolph Burgess, en route to Europe by ship, with an assistant, Emile Despres, of its decision. Despres urged Burgess to ask the Bank to delay long enough for them to send a message, and drafted one which Burgess sent, arguing strongly against the step. Friedman and Schwartz record that at the October 8 meeting in New York:

> The only discordant note was a cablegram from Burgess, who was in Europe on a mission from the Bank, recommending no action that would bring about higher money rates in the United States. The cablegram was read at the meeting, then disregarded.[41]

In the introduction to his collected papers, Despres writes: "Our sole accomplishment was to delay by all of one day what was perhaps the most disastrous policy decision of the Great Depression!"[42]

The Federal Reserve Bank of New York (and the Board which confirmed its recommendation) may have been, and in most judgments were wrong in raising the discount rate in October 1931, but the New York Bank continued to argue for expanding the money supply through open-market purchases of government bonds. Because of the gold losses, there was a problem, or at least what some officials of the system perceived as a problem, that of "free gold." With the stock-market collapse of 1929, a worldwide sharp decline in commodity prices occurred, as banks in the United States, loaded with illiquid brokers' loans, rationed credit to other borrowers, as recently explained by Ben Bernanke.[43] This affected especially commodity brokers in New York who needed credit to buy primary products shipped to that market on consignment to be sold on arrival. Without credit, commodities were dumped on the market and their prices plunged. The fall in price reduced the value of United States imports and the supply of eligible paper available for discount. The Federal Reserve Act of 1913 stipulated that the Federal Reserve liabilities, notes and deposits, had to be backed by gold up to a 40 percent minimum, with rediscounts for the remaining 60 percent, but that gold in excess of 40 percent, so-called free gold, could be substituted for rediscounts. The sharp decline in foreign and internal trade and the consequent fall in eligible paper made it necessary to use free gold as backing for the system's liabilities. If government bonds could have been substituted for commercial bills there would have been no problem. Without such authority, which was finally provided in the Glass-Steagall Act of February 27, 1932, open market operations which would have enlarged the liabilities of the Federal Reserve System might have run against a limitation because of a shortage of free gold. Friedman and Schwartz dismiss the problem with a long list of reasons: the Fed might have bought more bills if it had increased the interest rate it paid; commercial banks under the regulations could discount finance bills collateralized by government bonds; concern about free gold was by no means unanimous and came mostly from those who were advocating an enlarged program of open-market purchases; etc. Perhaps the most telling reason they give is that when the Glass-Steagall Act finally permitted the substitution of government paper for rediscounts, six weeks went by before the System began its massive buying program, not too little, as in so many instances, but too late.[44] Thirty-some years later it seems to this reader that Friedman and Schwartz push too hard. Free gold was, if not a solid obstacle to a determined policy of monetary expansion, at least perceived as such. Dynamic leadership, which President Hoover and his Board of Governors did not provide, would have gone to Congressional leaders and announced that the provisions of the Federal Reserve Act regarding the need for commercial bills, and the exclusion of governments as backing for the System's liabilities, were archaic, interfering with policy flexibility, and would be set aside. Legislation would be sought in due course but in the meantime it was necessary to act. But by this time President Hoover was committed to his particular panacea, the Reconstruction Finance Corporation, which came into being December 1931, and in addition was becoming catatonic.

Conclusion

It is, I hope, clear from the foregoing that I do not find Borchardt's conclusion that Brüning had no alternatives to this policy of deflation completely persuasive. To some degree his analysis resembles the form of argument that finds objections successively to paths A, B, C, D, and E, and having dismissed each in turn, concludes that that leaves F. Secondly I find him insufficiently critical of Brüning's strategy—to concentrate on reparations first and then on such other foreign-policy successes as the *Zollunion* and the *Panzerkreuzer* to each of which objection could be and was made, as opposed to domestic employment. Third, I was deeply impressed by the debate over the Lautenbach memorandum at the Reichsbank on September 16 and 17, 1931 (to the published transcript of which Borchardt contributed a lucid introduction and explanatory footnotes), which showed that the forces of a spending program, financed by Reichsbank credit, had important support not only in a few academic circles, but widely there and inside and outside government otherwise.[45] The record of the secret debate recently uncovered in the files of the Mt. Pelerin Society is highly moving, as in a Shakespearean drama, especially with the agonized interventions of Reichsbank president Hans Luther, fearful that his institution was to be molested. It is ironic that both in the free-gold case in the United States and the Lautenbach program, rejected proposals were adopted later and abundantly, if too late, with tragic economic consequences in the United States, and a benign economic but malign political outcome in Germany.

The dilemma posed by a choice between rules and men largely begs the question. There are, to be sure, times when rules, constraints, commitments, contract or treaty provisions stand in the way and should be transcended because of *force majeure*, acts of God, some *deus ex machina* that makes clear that all bets are off. The classic example, of course, is the outbreak of war. But many times the thrust of the rules is muddy, or there are two or more rules running in opposite directions, between which rational men may differ as to which should apply in particular circumstances. I have a strong propensity for citing the difficulty of choosing between "Look before you leap," and "He who hesitates is lost." The issue on whether or not to raise the rediscount rate of the Federal Reserve System in October 1931 after the gold drain to Europe stresses the ambiguity inherent in many economic conditions. The classic therapy may well call for meeting an external drain with a rise in interest rates, but when a number of small central banks panic, when world commodity prices have just been forced lower by the appreciation of the dollar, the French franc and the Reichsmark, and when there was little or no chance that the central banks in question would respond to a higher rate by reexchanging gold for dollars, the classic therapy might have been deemed to have no chance of working.

If one relies on men of responsibility to make the right choice in crisis among conflicting rules, or to follow an altogether different course for which no precedent exists, there is a danger of creating new precedents and new rules, which may be applied mistakenly under different circumstances. This is the inconvenience that Bagehot found in concluding that "the forces of the enemy being variable, those of the defense cannot always be the same." "Anything goes" as a slogan leaves room for authoritarian rule, such as Charles I's Stop of the Exchequer in 1672, or Philip II's unilateral conversion of short-term collateralized *asientos* into long-term *juros*, bonds denominated only in money in the late sixteenth century, or forced government loans to finance extravagances. British experience in financial crises in the nineteenth century seems to me to have combined the right mixture of an evidently temporary expedient— the Letters of Indemnity—with stern resistance to letting such action freeze into precedent on which markets could count.

The alternative to rules—men, which of course includes women—begs
another question. Men have different responsibilities, principles, under-
standings, interests. Like Justices of the Supreme Court in the United
States, highly trained successful men and women, deeply versed in the
law, they frequently differ in close decisions, five on one side, four on the
other. As widely noticed and sometimes derided, economic experts from
time to time offer diverging advices. One should also note the thought of
the American humorist, Mr. Dooley, that the Supreme Court follows the
election returns, so that public opinion is involved. With strong and cohesive leadership, near unanimity of experts and understanding or pliant
followership, men can be trusted in crisis to perform better than rules. I
judge the Marshall Plan to have been such a case, though a revisionist
view is not lacking.[46] In the ordinary crisis, however, if that is not an
oxymoron, the need may be not only to choose between rules in general
and more flexible decisions by men, but between the antithetical injunc-
tions, each right in its time and place: (this to the catatonic) "Don't just
stand there; do something," and (this to the hyperactivist) "Don't just do
something; stand there."

Notes

1. Borchardt, K., Constraints and Room for Manoeuvre in the Great Depression of the Early
Thirties: Toward a Revision of the Received Historical Picture, in: Borchardt, K.: *Perspectives
on Modern German Economic History and Policy*, translated by Peter Lambert, Cambridge
1991, pp. 143–60.

2. Holtfrerich, C.-L. Alternativen zu Brünings Wirtschaftspolitik in der Weltwirtschaftskrise?
Historische Zeitschrift 235, 1982, pp. 605–31.

3. Joplin, T.: Case for Parliamentary Inquiry into the Circumstances of the Panic, in: *A Letter
to Thomas Gisborne, Esq., M.P.*, London after 1832.

4. Bagehot, W.: Lombard Street (1873), in: St. John-Stevas, N. (ed.): *The Collected Works of
Walter Bagehot*, vol. IX, London 1978, pp. 207–8.

5. Bagehot, Lombard Street, p. 207.

6. Bagehot, W.: The Currency Monopoly (1848), in: *Collected Works*, vol. IX, p. 267.

7. Friedman, M./Jacobson Schwartz, A.: *A Monetary History of the United States, 1867–1960*,
Princeton 1963, p. 419.

8. Friedman and Schwartz, *Monetary History*, p. 395.

9. Great Britain, *Parliamentary Papers: Monetary Policy, Commercial Distress* (1857), Shannon
1969, vol. 9, p. xxix.

10. Clapham, J.: *The Bank of England. A History*, vol. 2, Cambridge 1945, pp. 206–7.

11. Bagehot, Lombard Street, p. 73.

12. Clapham, *Bank of England*, vol. 2, p. 108.

13. Bouvier, J.: *Le Krach de l'Union Générale, 1878–1885*, Paris 1960, chap. V.

14. Böhme, H.: *Frankfurt und Hamburg: Des Deutschen Silber- und Goldloch und die Aller-englischte Stadt des Kontinents*, Frankfurt 1968, pp. 255–68.

15. Clapham, *Bank of England*, vol. 2, pp. 329–30.

16. Plessis, A.: *La Politique de la Banque de France de 1851 à 1870*, Geneva 1985, chap. ii, esp. pp. 89–108.

17. Plessis, La Politique, p. 91.

18. Cameron, R.: *France and the Economic Development of Europe (1800–1914)*, Princeton 1961, p. 128.

19. Plessis, *La Politique*, pp. 105–6.

20. Plessis, A.: *Régents et gouverneurs de la Banque de France sous le Second Empire*, Geneva 1985, p. 144.

21. Plessis, *La Politique*, p. 287.

22. Plessis, *La Politique*, pp. 288–89.

23. Plessis, *La Politique*, p. 293.

24. Jeanneney, J.-N.: *Leçon d'histoire pour une gauche au pouvoir. La faillité du Cartel (1924–1926)*, Paris 1977, p. 33.

25. Schuker, S. A.: *The End of French Predominance in Europe: The Financial Crisis of 1924 and the Adoption of the Dawes Plan*, Chapel Hill 1976, p. 50.

26. Jeanneney, *Leçon d'histoire*, pp. 77–78.

27. Jeanneney, *Leçon d'histoire*, p. 83.

28. Jeanneney, *Leçon d'histoire*, pp. 90–110.

29. Schuker, *End of French Predominance*, note, p. 50.

30. Friedman and Schwartz, *Monetary History*, p. 363.

31. Friedman and Schwartz, *Monetary History*, p. 395.

32. Lucia, J. L.: The Failure of the Bank of the United States. A Reappraisal, in: *Explorations in Economic History* 22, 1985, p. 412.

33. Friedman and Schwartz, *Monetary History*, p. 309 note.

34. Temin, P.: *Did Monetary Forces Cause the Great Depression?* New York 1976, pp. 91–94.

35. Schubert, A.: *The Credit-Anstalt Crisis of 1931*, Cambridge 1985, chap. 2, esp. pp. 13, 147.

36. Williamson, P.: *National Crisis and National Government. British Politics, the Economy, and Empire, 1926–1932*. Cambridge 1992. I have not been able to see the book, but derive this account from a review by Daniel F. Calhoun in the Journal of Economic History 53, 1993, pp. 173–75.

37. Schiemann, J.: *Die deutsche Währung in der Wirtschaftskrise, 1929–1933. Währungspolitik und Abwertungskontroverse unter den Bedingungen der Reparationen*, Bern 1980.

38. Borchardt, K.: Could and Should Germany have Followed Great Britain in Leaving the Gold Standard? in: *Journal of European Economic History* 3, 1984, pp. 471–97. See also Borchardt, K.: Zur Frage der währungspolitischen Optionen Deutschlands in der Weltwirtschaftskrise, in: Borchardt, K./Holzheu, F. (eds.): *Theorie und Politik der internationalen Wirtschaftsbeziehungen*, Stuttgart 1980.

39. Borchardt, Should Germany have Followed Britain? p. 498.

40. Friedman and Schwartz, *Monetary History*, pp. 395–96.

41. Friedman and Schwartz, *Monetary History*, p. 381.

42. Meier, G. M. (ed.): International Economic Reform. *Collected Papers of Emile Despres*, New York 1973, p. xii.

43. Bernanke, B. S.: Nonmonetary Effects of the Financial Crisis in the Propagation of the Great Depression in: *American Economic Review* 73, 1983, pp. 257–76.

44. Friedman and Schwartz, *Monetary History*, p. 391.

45. Borchardt, K./Schötz, H. O. (eds.): *Wirtschaftspolitik in der Krise: Die (Geheim-) Konferenz der Friedrich List-Gesellschaft im September 1931 über Möglichkeiten und Folgen einer Kreditausweitung*, Baden-Baden 1991.

46. See, for example, Milward, A.: *The Reconstruction of Western Europe, 1945–51*, London 1984, esp. chap. I.

Sources

2. From *Harvard Business Review* 12, no. 4 (July 1934).

3. Originally published in the *International Adjustment Mechanism*, Conference Series no. 2, Proceedings of a Conference Held in October 1969, Boston, Mass., Federal Reserve Bank of Boston, March 1970, pp. 93–108.

4. Reprinted from the *Journal of Political Economy* 59 (1971): 20–55.

5. Originally published in *Journal of Economic History* 35 (1975): 20–44.

6. *Weltwirtschaftliches Archiv* III (1975): 253–281, 477–504.

7. A lecture given by the author when he was awarded the Bernhard Harms Prize at the Institut für Weltwirtschaft, Kiel, July 5, 1978, and originally published in *Weltwirtschaftliches Archiv*, 114, no. 3 (1978).

8. A seminar paper given to the Institute for International Economic Studies, University of Stockholm, 16 November 1982 and originally published in *Kyklos* 36, fasc. 3 (1983): 377–395.

9. Originally published in the *Economist* 218, no. 6389 (5 February 1966), with the addition of several sentences cut by that periodical for reasons of space. The italicized paragraphs at the beginning and end are by the *Economist*.

10. Originally published in the *Journal of Political Economy* 77, no. 6 (November/December 1969): 873–891. The writer is grateful for comments on an early draft by C. Fred Bergsten, Donald G. Heckerman, and Walter S. Salant.

11. Originally published in *Princeton Studies in International Finance* 36 (1974): 1–78.

12. Reprinted from *Manias, Panics, and Crashes: A History of Financial Crises*, 1st ed., 1989; 3d ed., 1996.

13. From *Economic Laws and Economic History*.

14. Originally published in Charles P. Kindleberger and Guido di Tella, eds., *Economics in the Long View; Essays in Honour of W. W. Rostow*, vol. 3: *Applications and Cases*, part 2 (London: Macmillan, 1982), 102–120.

15. Originally published in Steven Fazzari and Dimitry B. Papadimitrious, eds., *Financial Conditions and Macroeconomic Performance: Essays in honor of Hyman P. Minsky* (Armonk, N.Y.: M. E. Sharpe, 1992), 71–84.

16. Originally published in *Essays in International Finance*, no. 61 (Princeton, N.J.: Princeton University Press, August 1967).

17. A paper presented to the Economic History Society meeting at the University of Kent, Canterbury, England, 1972, and published in *Economic Notes* 1, nos. 2–3 Siena, 1972), 30–44. Reprinted with permission of Monte dei Paschi di Siena.

18. Reprinted from *The World in Depression, 1929–1939*, 2nd ed., 1986.

19. The Second Fred Hirsch Memorial Lecture, Warwick University, 6 March 1980, published in an abridged form in *Lloyds Bank Review*, October 1980, 1–11.

20. Presidential address delivered to the ninety-eighth annual meeting of the American Economic Association, 29 December 1985, New York, N.Y., and originally published in the *American Economic Review* 76, no. 1 (March 1986): 1–13.

21. Originally published in Christoph Buchheim, Michael Hutter, and Harold James, eds., *Zerrissene Zwischenkriegszeit Beiträge* (Baden-Baden: Nomos Verlagsgesellschaft, 1994), 157–175.

Index